Human Resource Management

Canadian Edition

Human Resource Management

PHILLIP C. WRIGHT, FIPD
University of New Brunswick

R. WAYNE MONDY, SPHR
McNeese State University

ROBERT M. NOE, SPHR
East Texas State University

In collaboration with
SHANE R. PREMEAUX, PHR
McNeese State University

Prentice Hall Canada Inc.
Scarborough, Ontario

Canadian Cataloguing in Publication Data

Wright, Phillip Charles
    Human resource management

1st Canadian ed.
Includes index.
ISBN 0-13-209214-X

1. Personnel management. 2. Personnel management –
Canada. I. Mondy, R. Wayne, 1940–   . II. Noe,
Robert M. III. Title.

HF5549.W75 1996   658.3   C95-933121-2

 ©1996 Prentice-Hall Canada Inc., Scarborough, Ontario
A Viacom Company

Prentice-Hall, Inc., Englewood Cliffs, New Jersey
Prentice-Hall International (UK) Limited, London
Prentice-Hall of Australia, Pty. Limited, Sydney
Prentice-Hall Hispanoamericana, S.A., Mexico City
Prentice-Hall of India Private Limited, New Delhi
Prentice-Hall of Japan, Inc., Tokyo
Simon & Schuster Asia Private Limited, Singapore
Editora Prentice-Hall do Brasil, Ltda., Rio de Janeiro

ISBN 0-13-209214-X

Acquisitions Editor: Patrick Ferrier
Developmental Editor: Maurice Esses
Copy Editor: Gilda Mekler
Production Editor: Mary Ann McCutcheon
Production Coordinator: Sharon Houston
Art Direction: Kyle Gell
Cover Design: Margot Boland
Cover Image: Paul Schulenberg
Page Layout: Debbie Fleming/Joan Morrison

Original edition published by Prentice-Hall, Inc.,
Englewood Cliffs, New Jersey. Copyright © 1996.

   3 4 5   CC   00 99

Printed and bound in United States

We welcome readers' comments, which can be sent by e-mail to
    collegeinfo_pubcanada@prenhall.com

To
Sara and Kenneth
PCW

To my daughters
Alyson Lynn and Marianne Elizabeth
RWM

To
Joanie
RMN

To my daughter
Paige Elizabeth
SRP

BRIEF CONTENTS

TABLE OF CONTENTS

CHAPTER 2 The Environment of Human Resource Management

CHAPTER 3 Job Analysis

PART TWO ■ HUMAN RESOURCES PLANNING, RECRUITMENT, AND SELECTION

CHAPTER 4   Human Resources Planning

CHAPTER 5 Recruitment

Chapter 6 Selection

PART THREE ■ HUMAN RESOURCE DEVELOPMENT

CHAPTER 7 Organizational Change and Human Resource Development

CHAPTER 8   Corporate Culture and Organization Development

CHAPTER 9   Career Planning and Development

CHAPTER **10**   Performance Appraisal

PART FOUR ■ COMPENSATION AND BENEFITS

CHAPTER 11   Financial Compensation

CHAPTER 12   BENEFITS AND OTHER COMPENSATION ISSUES

PART FIVE ■ SAFETY AND HEALTH

CHAPTER 13   A Safe and Healthy Work Environment

PART SIX ■ EMPLOYEE AND LABOUR RELATIONS

CHAPTER 14   THE LABOUR UNION

CHAPTER **15**   Collective Bargaining

CHAPTER **16**   INTERNAL EMPLOYEE RELATIONS

PART SEVEN ■ HUMAN RESOURCES RESEARCH

CHAPTER 17 Human Resources Research

PREFACE

This edition of *Human Resource Management* takes a pragmatic, applied approach to studying the human resource. Current concepts in human resource management (HRM) are supported by quotations from a wide variety of managers and consultants, many of whom contributed their comments specifically for this book. Thus, students will see that practising managers and professionals from both large and small organizations, in all parts of Canada, are concerned about the many facets of people management.

A common theme—the interrelationships among the many human resource management functions—runs throughout the book, as each function is described according to its relationship to the entire human resource management system. Each of these topics is written in a format suitable for students who are studying HRM for the first time. The book will expose these students to current practices and to problems encountered by practitioners through the use of numerous real-life illustrations and material from Canadian and international organizations.

Features of the Book

We have included many features to promote the readability and understanding of important human resource management concepts:

- A model (Figure 2-1) has been developed as a vehicle for interrelating the many facets of HRM. We believe this overview is a valuable teaching and study device.
- Key terms appear in boldface the first time they are defined or described in the chapter.
- Chapter objectives are listed at the beginning of every chapter to highlight the general purpose and the key concepts of the chapter.
- A case incident is provided at the beginning of each chapter to set the tone for a discussion of the major topics included within the chapter.
- A brief exercise, "HRM in Action," is included in the body of each chapter to permit students to make decisions concerning situations that could occur in the business world. A debriefing guide is provided in the *Instructor's Manual*.
- Each chapter concludes with a Summary, distilling the major points covered in the chapter.
- Questions for Review appear at the end of each chapter to test the student's understanding of the material presented in the chapter.
- A CBC video case appears at the end of each part of the textbook. Based on clips from the television programs *Venture* and *The Health Show*, these video cases allow students to tie information contained in the text to actual business situations.
- A running case about the hypothetical Parma Cycle Co. also appears at the end of each part of the textbook. Each segment takes the story line one step further, so that students become aware of day-to-day HRM problems as they are managed within a familiar business situation.

- HRM Incidents are provided at the end of each chapter, highlighting material of practical importance.
- A comprehensive exercise called "Developing HRM Skills: An Experiential Exercise" is provided at the end of each chapter from Chapter 2 onward. These exercises are designed to enhance class participation and group involvement. A comprehensive debriefing guide is included in the *Instructor's Manual*.
- A Glossary of all the key terms featured in the chapters appears at the back of the book.
- Because of the impact of the multinational environment on human resource management, new major multinational topics are highlighted in each chapter under the heading "A Global Perspective."

By exposing students to the latest HR practices, we aim not only to stimulate interest in our discipline but to illustrate how "textbook concepts" are used in well-managed organizations. Thus, we hope to make human resource management an essential part of every student's business education.

When preparing this Canadian edition, two major databases were consulted. ABI/INFORM™ (PROQUEST)* was found to be most useful for finding general HRM information, while CBCA** provided a wealth of Canadian examples.

Supplements

These supplements are available for use with this edition of *Human Resource Management:*

Instructor's Manual This manual outlines the basic structure of each chapter and contains suggestions on how to use the text more effectively. It also includes suggested lecture outlines and answers to end-of-chapter questions, end-of-part case studies, and video case study questions.

Test Item File   This item contains over 1000 multiple choice and true/false questions with relevant textbook pages listed for each question.

Prentice Hall Custom Test A computerized version of the Test Item File is also available for adopters.

CBC Video Cases Prentice Hall Canada and the CBC have worked together to bring you the best and most comprehensive video package available in the higher education market, containing clips from such CBC programs as *Venture* and *The Health Show*. Designed specifically to complement the textbook, this video library is an excellent tool for bringing students into contact with the world outside the classroom. These cassettes are available to instructors who adopt this textbook.

CBC 🍁

Electronic Colour Transparencies (available in Powerpoint files)

These overhead masters of selected graphic illustrations have been pulled from the text.

Acknowledgements

The assistance and the encouragement of many people is normally required in writing any book. Although it would be virtually impossible to list each person who assisted in this project, we feel that certain people must be credited for the magnitude of their contribution: in particular, Cathy McDonald, who provided steadfast support, despite bouts of illness; Gayle Day, who doubled her workload with patience and good humour; and Dianne Murphy, who helped with the final draft.

We also would like to thank Marthanne Lamansky and Tina Minter, both very competent and professional individuals, who were always available to ensure that our deadlines were met. As well, the support and encouragement of practising HRM professional and managers from many parts of Canada have made this book possible. Thanks go to Nick Lakoumentas, an MBA student from the University of New Brunswick, who prepared the seven video cases.

We would also like to thank the reviewers of this book:
Gini Sutherland, Sir Sandford Fleming College;
Kenneth Thornicroft, University of Victoria;
Deborah Hill-Smith, Conestoga College;
Nelson Lacroix, Niagara College; and
Daphne Gottlieb Taras, University of Calgary.

Finally, we would like to thank the people at Prentice Hall Canada Inc. who worked with us on this book: Patrick Ferrier, Maurice Esses, Mary Ann McCutcheon, and Gilda Mekler.

Phillip C. Wright
R. Wayne Mondy
Robert M. Noe
1996

* © Universal Microfilms
** © Micro Media

1

Human Resource Management: An Overview

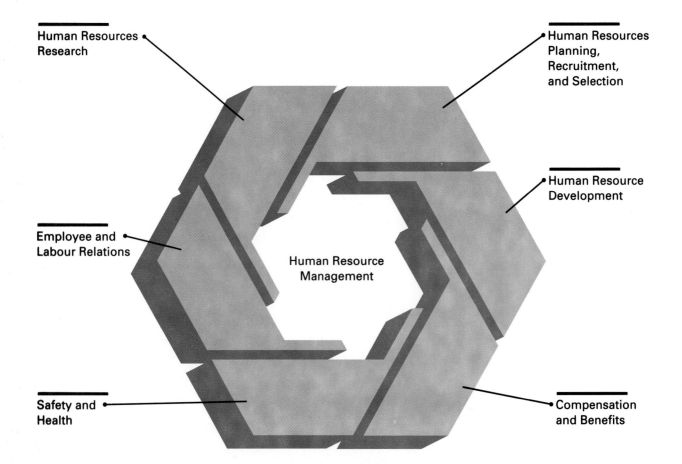

Human Resources Research

Human Resources Planning, Recruitment, and Selection

Employee and Labour Relations

Human Resource Development

Safety and Health

Human Resource Management

Compensation and Benefits

1. Distinguish between human resource management and the human resource manager. Describe the functions of human resource management.

2. Describe the changes that have taken place in the human resource field in recent years. Define human resource executive, generalist, and specialist. Describe the changes that occur in the human resource function as a firm grows larger and more complex.

3. Explain how human resources have become professionalized and the direction the profession has taken. Define ethics and relate ethics to human resource management.

A s Harry Jones, vice president of human resources for Handwell, headquartered in Calgary, rose to leave the executive meeting, he realized that his job would be even busier than usual during the next six months. Handwell Enterprises produces high-tech components for both government and private industry, and greater production capacity is needed to meet industry demands. A decision had been made at the meeting to open a new plant in Duncan, British Columbia. Harry and the company's managers had analyzed a number of sites and had determined that Duncan most closely met their needs. When the plant is completed in a year, 500 new employees must be available and trained. In addition, 75 employees at the Calgary facility will be transferred to Duncan. It is Harry's responsibility to ensure that qualified new workers are hired and trained, and that the transferred workers are effectively integrated into the work force.

Edward Tan is the supervisor of 10 Green Owl convenience stores in Southern Ontario. As the Green Owl chain is relatively small (only 40 stores), it has no human resource department. Supervisors are in charge of all employment activities for their own stores. Edward must ensure that only the best people are recruited for positions as store managers and then must properly train them. If one of the managers fails to report for an assigned shift and Edward cannot find a replacement, he is expected to work the shift. It is Friday afternoon and Edward is hurriedly attempting to locate a replacement because one store manager just quit without giving notice.

Judy Lynley is the industrial relations manager for Axton Pneumotives, a small manufacturer of pumps located in Sussex, New Brunswick. The sixty-five machine operators in the firm belong to the International Association of Machinists and Aerospace Workers. Judy has been negotiating with union leaders for five weeks with little success. The union members have threatened to walk off the job if the contract is not resolved by midnight. However, if Judy's firm agrees to all the union's monetary demands, it will no longer be competitive in the industry.

Harry, Edward, and Judy all have one thing in common: they are deeply involved with some of the challenges and problems related to human resource management. Managers of human resources must deal constantly with the often volatile and unpredictable human element that makes working in this field very challenging. Managing people in organizations is becoming more complex than ever because work environments are changing rapidly.

In the first part of this chapter, we distinguish between human resource management (HRM) and the human resource manager. Next, we review the human resource management functions. Then we present topics related to the evolution of human resource management, the globalization of HRM, and the changing world of the chief human resource executive. We make a distinction among human resource executives, generalists, and specialists, while discussing the human resource function in organizations of different sizes. Finally, we discuss professionalism and ethics, important issues to those who work in this dynamic discipline.

HUMAN RESOURCE MANAGEMENT AND THE HUMAN RESOURCE MANAGER

In recent years, the human resource management field has changed dramatically, creating a greatly expanded role for the human resource manager. As one leader in the field has suggested: "Yesterday, the company with access to the most capital or the latest technology had the best competitive advantage. Today, companies that offer products with the highest quality are the ones with a leg up on the competition. But, the only thing that will uphold a company's advantage tomorrow is the caliber of people in the organization."[1] Increasingly, human resources are seen as a key element in improving competitiveness.[2] In order to understand this evolution, we must make a distinction between human resource *management* and the human resource *manager*.

Human resource management (HRM) is the use of human resources to achieve organizational objectives. Managers at all levels must concern themselves with HRM, since they all meet their goals through the efforts of others, a process requiring the effective management of people. In a manufacturing firm, for example, the production manager meshes physical and human resources to produce goods in sufficient numbers and quality; the marketing manager works through sales representatives to sell the firm's products; and the finance manager obtains capital and manages investments to ensure sufficient operating funds. Although all three are involved in human resource management, they are not **human resource managers**. but *line* managers, people with formal authority and responsibility for achieving the firm's primary objectives. They are responsible primarily for specific functional areas of the business. Edward Tan, the convenience store supervisor for Southern Ontario, fully understands the challenges that a line manager faces with human resources, because he will have to work Friday night if he cannot find a replacement.

HRM, then, is moving away from being a transaction-based, paper-pushing, hiring/firing support activity toward becoming a decision-making function that deals with employees' performance and/or profitability.[3] This shift is illustrated by the words of a senior banking executive, who says: "I am now a strategic partner with line management and participate in business decisions which bring human resources perspectives to the general management of the company."[4]

"Strategic partner," a popular phrase these days, "means understanding the business direction of the company, including what the product is, what it's capable of doing, who the typical customers are and how the company is positioned competitively in the marketplace.[5]" In the words of David Crisp, vice-president of human resources at the Hudson's Bay Company in Toronto: "The critical success differentiator today is people. 'Best practices' and technology are available to anyone. Financing and customers will go to those companies whose people are fastest into the market with better ideas and better coordination. Our role is to make that possible."[6]

The human resource manager proposes human relations policies to be implemented by line managers. "The real human resource management game is played by the line manager. The human resource manager's role is to develop policies and programs—the rules of the game—and to function as a catalyst and energizer of the relationship between line management and employees."[7] There is a shared responsibility, then, between line managers and human resource professionals. The distinction between human resource management and the human resource manager is illustrated clearly by the following account:

> Bill Thieu, the production supervisor for Ajax Manufacturing, has just learned that one of his machine operators has quit. He calls Sandra Gianelli, the human resource manager, and says, "Sandra, I just had a Class A machine operator quit down here. Can you find some qualified people for me to interview?" "Sure Bill," Sandra replies. "I'll send two or three down to you within the week, and you can select the one that best fits your needs."

In this instance, both Bill and Sandra are concerned with accomplishing organizational goals, but from different perspectives. Sandra, as a human resource manager, identifies applicants who meet the criteria specified by Bill. Bill, who is responsible for the operator's performance, will make the final hiring decision. His primary responsibility is production. Hers is human resources. Sandra must deal constantly with the many problems related to human resources that Bill and the other managers face. Her job is to help them meet the human resource needs of the entire organization. In some firms her function is also referred to as personnel, employee relations, or industrial relations.

HUMAN RESOURCE MANAGEMENT FUNCTIONS

Today's human resource problems are enormous and appear to be ever evolving. Challenges for the human resource manager range from a constantly changing work force to the ever-present scores of government regulations. Because of the critical nature of human resource issues, they are receiving increased attention from upper management. Many HRM professionals report directly to the president or CEO. Others have progressed to the top management level.

Human resource managers develop and work through a human resource management system. As Figure 1-1 shows, six functional areas are associated with effective human resource management: human resource planning, recruitment, and selection; human resource development; compensation and benefits; safety and health; employee and labour relations; and human resources research. A major study conducted for the Society for Human Resource Management in the United States confirmed that these areas constitute the human resource management field.[8] A similar view is held by the Human Resources Professionals Association of Ontario and the Human Resources Institute of Alberta, Canada's two largest HRM associations, as they offer certification programs that closely parallel this classification.[9] Sound management practices are required for successful performance in each area. We discuss these functions next.

FIGURE 1-1
The Human Resource
Management System

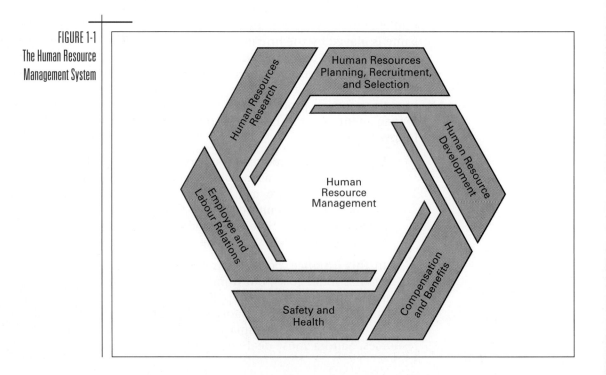

Human Resources Planning, Recruitment, and Selection

An organization must have qualified individuals in specific jobs at specific places and times in order to accomplish its goals. Obtaining such people involves human resource planning, recruitment, and selection.

Human resource planning (HRP) is the process of reviewing human resource requirements systematically to ensure that the required numbers of employees, with the required skills, are available when needed. Recruitment is the process of attracting these individuals in sufficient numbers and encouraging them to apply for jobs within the organization. Selection is the process through which the organization chooses, from a group of applicants, those individuals best suited both for the specific opening and for the company. Successful accomplishment of these three tasks is vital if the organization is to accomplish its mission effectively. Chapters 4, 5, and 6 are devoted to these topics.

Human Resource Development

Human resource development (HRD) helps individuals, groups, and the entire organization become more effective. Human resource development is needed because people, jobs, and organizations are always changing. Moreover, processes must continuously improve if the firm is to remain competitive. The development process should begin when individuals join the firm and continue throughout their careers.

Large-scale HRD programs are referred to as organization development (OD). The purpose of OD is to alter the environment within the firm so that employees perform more productively.

Other aspects of HRD include career planning and performance appraisal. Career planning is the process of setting human resource goals and establishing the means to achieve them. The career concerns of individuals and the needs of the organization cannot be considered in isolation from each other. Organizations should assist employees in career planning so that the needs of both can be satisfied.

Through performance appraisal, employees and teams are evaluated to determine how well they are performing their assigned tasks. Performance appraisal affords employees the opportunity to capitalize on their strengths and overcome identified deficiencies, thereby becoming more satisfied and productive.

Throughout this text, but especially in the HRD chapters (Chapters 7, 8, 9, and 10), we use the term operative employees. **Operative employees** are all the workers in an organization except managers, professionals (engineers and accountants, for example) and clerical staff, (such as secretaries). Steel workers, truck drivers, and waiters are examples of operative employees.

Compensation and Benefits

The question of what constitutes a fair day's pay has long plagued management, unions, and workers. A well-thought-out compensation system provides employees with adequate and equitable rewards for their contributions to meeting organizational goals. As used in this book, the term compensation includes all rewards that individuals receive from their employment. The reward may be one or a combination of the following.

- *Pay*: The money that a person receives for performing a job.
- *Benefits*: Additional financial rewards including paid vacations, sick leave, holidays and medical insurance.
- *Nonfinancial rewards*: Nonmonetary rewards, such as enjoyment of the work performed or a pleasant working environment.

Although compensation includes all rewards shown above, the increasing importance of benefits warrants separate treatment. We discuss many aspects of compensation in Chapter 11 and address benefits in Chapter 12.

Safety and Health

Safety involves protecting employees from injuries caused by work-related accidents. Health refers to employees' freedom from illness and their general physical and mental well-being. These aspects of the job are important because employees who work in a safe environment and enjoy good health are more likely to be productive and yield long-term benefits for the organization. For this reason, progressive managers have long advocated and implemented adequate safety and health programs. Today, because societal concerns about workplace health and safety are reflected in federal and provincial legislation, most organizations have become attentive to their employees' safety and health needs. Chapter 13 is devoted to the topic of safety and health.

Employee and Labour Relations

For the last fifteen years, the Canadian labour movement has managed to maintain union membership at slightly more than 37 percent of workers—excluding those in the agricultural sector. By contrast, in the United States, union membership has fallen 6 percent since 1983 to 15.8 percent of the work force.[10] In both Canada and the United States, however, a business is required by law to recognize a union and bargain with it in good faith if the employees want the union to represent them.

But the labour relations field is changing. Managers are becoming more professional in their approach. Worldwide competitive pressures are leading to a new employer militancy and more aggressive bargaining. In addition, technology is being used to reduce costs and to increase productivity, a trend that has reduced the number of jobs in blue-collar occupations, where unions have traditionally been well represented. In the public sector too, budget cutting has decreased the number of employees eligible to join unions. The future of Canadian unions then, is uncertain. Although membership has remained steady, there has been no growth, and economic trends, combined with the highly technical nature of many new jobs, may make it difficult for unions to maintain present membership levels. Furthermore, both unions and managers are under intense pressure to become more cooperative—a process that could undermine the traditional role of the union.[11] Chapters 14, 15 and 16 are devoted to the coverage of employee and labour relations issues.

Human Resources Research

Human resources research has been increasingly important and the trend is likely to continue. The human resources researcher's laboratory is the whole work environment. Studies may involve every HRM function. For instance, a study related to recruitment may suggest the type of workers most likely to succeed in a particular firm, or research on job safety may identify the causes of certain work-related accidents.

The reasons for problems such as excessive absenteeism, or too many grievances may not be readily apparent. When these problems occur, human resources research can shed light on their causes. In Sweden, for example, the labour force is highly educated and well trained. But the country's high income tax rates reduce the motivational power of pay, even incentive-type pay. Research at Sweden's Volvo factory revealed that the Swedes objected to the dirt and grime of the typical automobile factory. The close supervision and machine-paced work on the assembly lines were also unpopular. So Volvo built more pleasant and colourful factories, where teams of workers are, for the most part, allowed to manage themselves. Each team assembles a substantial portion of the car while it is moved from area to area. In the new Volvo plants, morale and productivity are better and absenteeism is lower than in the older factories.[12] Human resources research, then, is clearly key to developing the most productive and satisfied work force possible. As you will see in Chapter 17, a variety of quantitative methods are used in this research.

Interrelationships of HRM Functions

In fact, the functional areas outlined above are highly interrelated. Management must recognize that decisions in one area will affect other areas, and must be aware of potential effects. For example, managers who emphasize the recruitment and training of a sales force while neglecting to provide adequate compensation are wasting time, effort, and money. If managers truly care about the employees they have recruited, they must ensure a safe, healthy environment. An added benefit might be the development of a cooperative relationship with the union, one based on trust and mutual respect. The interrelationships among the six HRM functional areas will become more obvious as we address each topic in greater detail.

THE EVOLUTION OF HUMAN RESOURCE MANAGEMENT

One of the major changes in business in recent years has been the increased respect and responsibility afforded human resource professionals.[13] In 1990, for example, the job of human resource management was identified as one of fifteen fast-track careers in the United States.[14] Human resource managers are now expected to provide the direction necessary to meet the many human resource problems and challenges that continue to arise in modern businesses. Within the next decade, for example, the content of more than half of all existing jobs is likely to change, and 30 percent will be eliminated by technological advances.[15] When robots were introduced in the automobile industry, for instance, there was a major decrease in the demand for welders and painters, but a new demand for technicians who could program, install, and service automated equipment.[16] Human resource professionals have to respond positively to such trends within the context of their organizations' overall goals.

Not many decades ago, people in Canada (as well as those in the U.S.) who were engaged in human resource work had titles such as *welfare secretary* and *employment clerk*. Their duties were rather restrictive and often dealt only with such items as workers' wages, minor medical problems, recreation and housing.[17] Personnel, as human resources was most commonly called, was generally held in low esteem as a profession and reported to someone near the bottom of the organizational hierarchy. "In the past," says John L. Quigley, former vice-president administration for the Dr Pepper Company, a division of 7-Up Company, Inc., "the personnel executive was the 'glad hander' or 'back slapper' who kept morale up in a company by running the company picnic, handling the United Fund drive, and making sure the recreation program went off well." Those days are over in most organizations. The human resource manager's position is no longer a *retirement* position given to managers who cannot perform adequately anywhere else. Firms have learned that the human resource department can have a major effect on the organization's overall effectiveness and profitability.

Although there are no data for Canada, in the United States, the number of careers in the human resources area is projected to increase by 22 percent by the year 2000. Salaries are also improving.[18] As might be expected, salaries of corporate human resource executives depend largely on organizational size. In Canada, the average salary (1994) for top executive HRM managers at firms with yearly revenue of $10 million, was $73 418, including benefits and incentives. In firms with yearly revenues of $500 million, the average was $109 400 when benefits and incentives were added to the base salary. Location is an important determinant too. As might be expected, average top HRM salaries in Metro Toronto stood at $112 500, compared with $88 500 in Atlantic Canada.*

The type of work performed also has a major effect on the pay levels in large companies. Those specializing in labour relations and international HR enjoy the highest salaries, while development and employee relations are the lowest-paid areas.

A GLOBAL PERSPECTIVE

Canada is a trading nation. Although in 1992 almost 77 percent of our trade was with the United States (118.4 billion), Canadian companies are conducting business in many other countries.[19] Today, international corporations are becoming truly global, with business contacts in Hong Kong, Singapore, Japan, the United Kingdom, France, and Germany, to name only a few. Some multinationals are also showing interest in the developing economies of former *eastern bloc* countries. This interdependence of national economies has created a global marketplace, adding special challenges for human resource professionals.[20]

*The authors wish to thank William M. Mercer, Ltd. for providing these data.

For example, international firms will need to decide either to adapt recruiting and compensation practices, or to maintain common HRM policies across all locations. "While sometimes these decisions are partially answered by the strategy and structure decisions made by the organization, there still remains a great deal of latitude in the design of the final package of international human resource management practices."[21]

Among the most serious of the new challenges is the growing mismatch between emerging jobs that require higher-level skills and the skill levels of the people available to fill them. "Virtually any type of international problem, in the final analysis, is either created by people or must be solved by people. Hence, having the right people in the right place at the right time emerges as the key to a company's international growth. If we are successful in solving that problem, we can cope with all others."[22]

As firms broaden the scope of their activities, HRM practitioners will need additional skills to be able to advise on international taxation, develop international relocation and orientation programs, or arrange for translation. Even those who work only within their own country will need to acquire a broader perspective on their craft, along with the skills to administer more complex HR issues, as the task of helping various nationalities to work together has become one of the major challenges in the international HRM field.[23]

This global human resources role is a natural extension of the increased recognition of the strategic role that HRM must play. International expertise is a very real asset for human resources people because *every* company is challenged by the global marketplace. Some senior executives, however, are not sure that human resource managers are developing the necessary global focus, or are aware enough of international human resource issues.[24]

THE CHANGING WORLD OF THE HUMAN RESOURCE EXECUTIVE

The work of the human resource executive is greatly affected by top management's human resource priorities and by the major changes occurring in management responsibilities and organizational relationships. There is a growing recognition that people are an organization's greatest competitive asset: over the last decade, the only sustainable, competitive advantage has been the quality of people. This attitude is so dramatically changing the role of the human resource manager that the function of HR ten years from now will bear little resemblance to its function a decade ago.

All working individuals at every level are experiencing a dramatic pace of change in business. Change brings new terminology, techniques, and methods of organizing people that have a profound effect on the way we work. Mobility, empowerment, teams, virtual offices, telecommuting, downsizings, restructuring, increased global competition, technological advances, contingency, and reengineering, to name but a few of the new forces that affect people, have made the job of the human resource professional more complex than ever before. Consider Figure 1-2, which lists some of the trends in human resources, and you will have a brief insight as to why the HRM profession is in a state of flux.[25] The only certainty is continuous evolution. Yesterday's solutions may not be sufficient for today's challenges.

OUT:	Job titles and labels such as "employee," "manager," "staff," and "professional."
IN:	Everyone a business person, an 'owner' of a complete business process, president of his/her job.
OUT:	Chain-of-command, reporting relationships, department, function, turf, sign-off, work as imposed-from-above tasks.
IN:	Self-management, responsiveness, proactivity, initiative, collaboration, egalitarianism, self-reliance, standards of excellence, personal responsibility, work as collection of self-initiated projects and teams.
OUT:	Stability, order, predictability, structure, better-safe-than-sorry.
IN:	Flux, disorder, ambiguity, risk, better-sorry-than-safe.
OUT:	Good citizenship—show up, good soldier, 9-to-5 in cubicle, don't make waves, wait for someone else to decide your fate, work in same organization for thirty years, retire with gold watch.
IN:	Make a difference—add value, challenge the process, four hours or eighteen hours per day, job site wherever the action is, learn from mistakes, career mobility and fluidity, work your tail off and be intensely loyal to Company X for one year or ten years.

Source: Adapted from Oren Harari, "Back to the Future of Work," *Management Review* 82 (September 1993): 35.

HUMAN RESOURCE EXECUTIVES, GENERALISTS, AND SPECIALISTS

There are various classifications and levels within the human resource profession. An **executive** is a top-level manager who reports directly to the corporation's chief executive officer (CEO) or to the head of a major division. **A generalist** (often an executive) performs a variety of tasks and is involved in several, or all, of the six human resource management functions. **A specialist**, who may be a human resource executive, manager, or non-manager, is concerned with only one of the six functional areas of human resource management (see Figure 1-3).

The vice-president of industrial relations shown in Figure 1-3, for example, specializes primarily in union-related matters. This person is both an executive and a specialist. The human resource vice-president is both an executive and a generalist, with responsibility for a wide variety of functions. The manager of compensation and benefits is a specialist, as is the benefits analyst. Whereas an executive is identified by position level in the organization, generalists and specialists are distinguished by their breadth of responsibility.

The distinction between generalists and specialists should be even clearer after studying Figure 1-4. It lists the type of work assignments at various levels in the organization for both generalists and specialists. It is also interesting to note that career development can vary considerably from one corporation to another or even one department to another. For example, the lines between assignments for generalists and specialists blur at times and the career paths for both may not always be *up*, but may involve a series of transfers among the various HR specialties.

FIGURE 1-3
Human Resource Executives,
Generalists, and Specialists

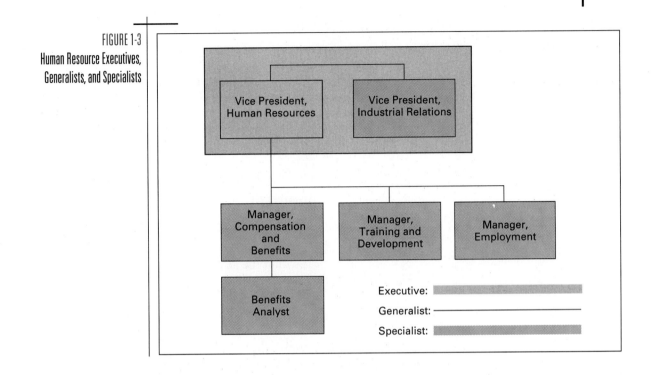

FIGURE 1-3
Human Resource Executives, Generalists, and Specialists

THE HUMAN RESOURCE FUNCTION IN ORGANIZATIONS OF VARIOUS SIZES

The human resource function tends to change as firms grow and become more complex—and as the function achieves greater importance. Although the purpose of human resource management remains the same, the approach followed in accomplishing its objectives often changes.

HRM IN ACTION

"Scotty, I know that you are the human resource manager, and I really appreciate your concern for my career, but the position you are offering me as assistant human resource director is, in my opinion, a dead-end job. Recruiters just find employees to fill vacant positions. They don't get involved in other areas of the company, so my achievements could go unnoticed and I'd be stuck there forever. Another thing, I have heard that top management really only cares about marketing, production, and finance—not human resources. I appreciate the thought, Scotty, but don't put me in a dead-end job."

How should Scotty respond?

STARTING ASSIGNMENT

Specialist

Work for a supervisor in an area like labor relations, employment, training, or benefits. This would be at a larger location, where the function is broken down into areas of specialty.

Generalist

Work for a supervisor or superintendent in several areas. You might be responsible for training, communications, employment, benefits, and safety. This would be at a smaller location with two or three HR professionals on the staff.

LATER ASSIGNMENTS

Specialist

Manage one or two areas of responsibility, such as labour relations, training, and development, a combination of employment and benefits. Again, this would be at a larger location.

Generalist

Manage the total human resource function:
- For a sub-unit within the location (such as for the maintenance department, or for a geographic area within the location),
- For a smaller Monsanto location, or
- For a larger location.

OPERATING COMPANY/STAFF DEPARTMENT

Specialist

Manage one or two functions, such as human resource planning, compensation, recruiting, or an entire company or staff department.

Generalist

Manage the total human resource function for a sub-unit within a company (e.g., a division) or for the entire company or staff department.

CORPORATE

Specialist

Work in or manage an entire area of expertise for the corporation, such as labour relations, employment equity, development, or benefits.

Generalist

Manage the total corporate human resource function.

Two bits of advice:

- Don't get hung up on whether you begin your career as a specialist or generalist. The lines between generalist and specialist are not as neat as the chart would indicate. For example, as an employment "specialist," you would become involved daily within questions of labor relations, compensation, human resource planning, employment equity policy, and much more! Or as a small-plant "generalist," you would have to learn the basics of several specialties. Also, the overwhelming odds are that you will get both types of exposure—specialist and generalist—in your career.

- Career development will not always be "up." It's to the professional's advantage to get as much experience and exposure as possible—and many times, this will mean lateral moves into different areas of specialty.

FIGURE 1-4   Career Development at Monsanto

Source: With the permission of the Monsanto Company.

FIGURE 1-5
The Human Resource Function
in a Small Business

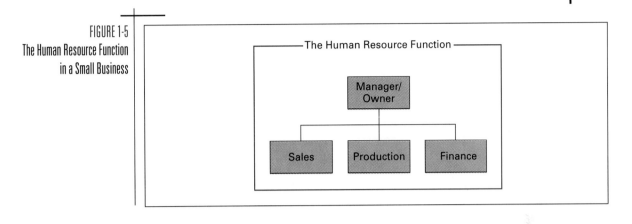

FIGURE 1-5
The Human Resource Function
in a Small Business

As Figure 1-5 suggests, small businesses seldom have a formal human resource unit or HRM specialist, as other managers handle human resource functions. The focus of their activities is generally on hiring and retaining capable employees.

This does not mean human resources are less important than in a large firm. In fact, mistakes may be more apparent in small firms. For example, if the owner of a small business hires her first and only full-time salesperson, who promptly alienates the firm's customers, the business might actually fail. In a larger firm, such an error would be much less devastating.

As a firm grows, a separate staff function may be required to coordinate human resource activities. In a fairly small firm, the person chosen to do so will be expected to handle most of the human resource activities; even in a medium-sized firm there is little specialization (see Figure 1-6). A secretary may be available to handle correspondence, but the entire department may consist of one human resource manager or professional.

When the organization's human resource function becomes too much for one person to handle, separate sections are often created and placed under a human resource manager: typically, human resource development, compensation and benefits, employment, safety and health, and labour relations (see Figure 1-7).

In still larger firms, the human resource function takes on even more responsibility, permitting even greater specialization. A typical organizational chart (Figure 1-8), illustrates such an organization. The unit responsible for compensation, for example, would likely include some specialists who

FIGURE 1-6
The Human Resource Function in a
Medium-Sized Firm

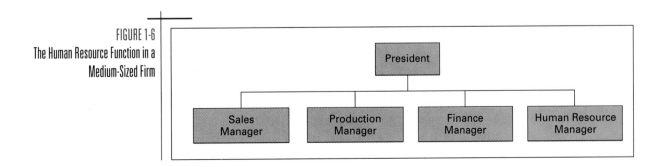

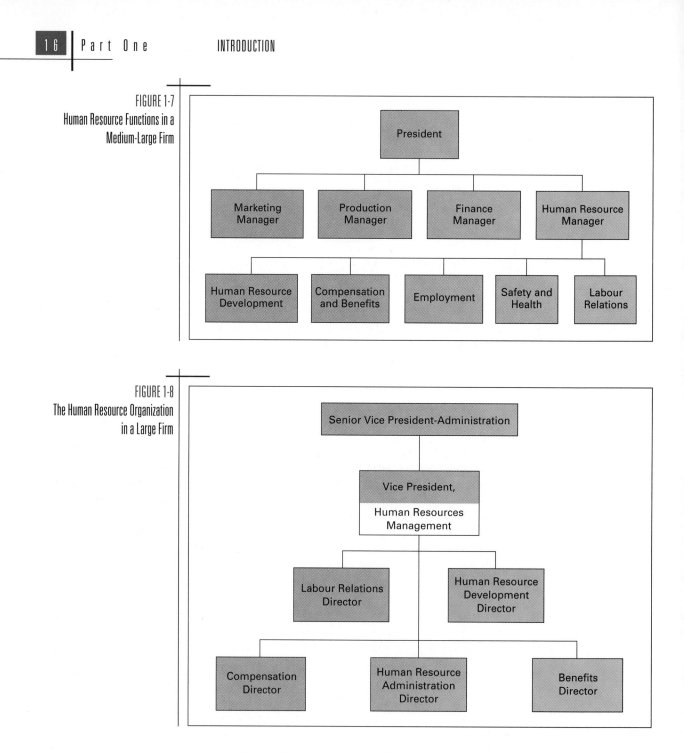

FIGURE 1-7
Human Resource Functions in a
Medium-Large Firm

FIGURE 1-8
The Human Resource Organization
in a Large Firm

concentrate on hourly wages and others who devote their time to salary administration. The vice-president of human resources works closely with top management in formulating corporate policy.

Figure 1-9 outlines the duties and the responsibilities of a chief human resources officer. The scope of this position is broad, ranging from the coordination, recommendation and implementation of plans to performance audits.

FIGURE 1-9
Functions of a Chief Human Resource
Officer

- Works as an integral member of the Organization Senior Management Team.
- Introduces concepts and strategies that allow for the development, design and continuous adjustment of HR programs, such as Staffing, Compensation, Benefits, Staff Development, Employee Relations, and Performance Management.
- Ensures HR programs and organization culture are compatible.
- Is aware of current and future internal and external issues and their potential effect on employees.
- Acts as a leader and a champion in executive boardroom for the most valuable resource;—the employees.
- Champions the human resource profession and its professionals.

Source: Published with the permission of Paul Thériault, V.P. Human Resources, N.B. Power.

THE PROFESSIONALIZATION OF HUMAN RESOURCE MANAGEMENT*

A **profession** is a vocation characterized by the existence of a common body of knowledge and a procedure for certifying members. Performance standards are established by members of the profession (self-regulation) rather than by outsiders. Most professions also have effective representative organizations that permit members to exchange ideas of mutual concern. These characteristics apply to the field of human resources; several well-known organizations serve the profession. Among the more prominent are the Canadian Compensation Association; the Canadian Payroll Association; the Human Resources Institute of Alberta; the Human Resources Professionals Association of Ontario; the International Foundation of Employee Benefit Plans; and the Ontario Society of Training and Development.

Canadian Compensation Association

The Canadian Compensation Association (CCA) is an integral part of the American Compensation Association, a nonprofit organization of more than 14 000 professionals based in Scottsdale, Arizona. The CCA is composed of more than 1000 professionals who design, implement, and manage compensation and benefits programs in their respective organizations. CCA/ACA provides seminars in the theoretical and practical aspects of the field.

The Certified Compensation Professional (CPP) program consists of a series of courses for compensation and benefits managers. The CCP designation is earned by passing seven examinations designed to measure mastery of the bodies of knowledge associated with the profession.

CCA courses are two-and-a-half days long, including an exam session on the third morning. They are conducted throughout Canada in most major

*Information concerning associations and institutes is adapted with the authors' permission from: Wright, Guidry and Blair (1994), pp. 108, 109, 133, 134, 179-182, 227, 228, 232, 233.

cities. Courses and exams offered by the ACA throughout the United States also qualify for CCP credit. Course catalogues and schedules are available from CCA Headquarters. Candidates must complete a battery of examinations, each consisting of 100 multiple-choice and true/false questions.

The CCP program is not restricted to CCA members; however, members receive reduced registration fees. CCPs seeking to retain the designation must accumulate twelve 'currency credits' every three years, earned through a variety of professional development activities.

Canadian Payroll Association

The Canadian Payroll Association is a not-for-profit trade association that currently has a membership of 2260 companies. The association experienced a 15 percent growth in membership between the years 1989 and 1994.

The CPA Payroll Management Certificate Program was established to make payroll training more accessible in Canada. It is open to anyone involved in the preparation of payroll. There are three levels of designation: Level I–Payroll Administrator (PA); Level II–Payroll Supervisor (PS); and Level III–Payroll Manager (PM). To obtain these designations, an individual must complete a series of required and elective professional courses offered through the program office at CPA National Office or by correspondence. Each course involves four assignments and a final exam.

Human Resources Institute of Alberta

The Human Resources Institute of Alberta (HRIA) was established to promote, encourage, and maintain professional standards in the human resource management field. The goals of the institute are to develop and maintain a level of knowledge and skills required of human resource practitioners; establish the standards and process for obtaining certification; and to attain recognition as a voice on human resource issues in the Province of Alberta.

The institute offers the Development Plan, by through which a members can further develop his or her knowledge in the human resource field through further education. It is the means by which members can acquire basic professional knowledge and the competence in Human Resource Management to meet the standard of practice required to achieve professional status. Certification is awarded based on a combination of experience, education, and training, and/or examination.

Human Resources Professionals Association of Ontario

The Human Resources Professionals Association of Ontario (HRPAO) offers the designation of Certified Human Resources Professional (CHRP) to professionals who 1) are full members in the Association; 2) have worked at least three years in the field at a professional level; and 3) have completed the Association's Certificate in Human Resources Management (CHRM) program (which requires completing eight CHRM courses and passing a Comprehensive Provincial Exam), or to seasoned members through a peer-review process. The exam follows completion of eight of eleven CHRM courses, of which four are mandatory: 1) Human Resource Administration, 2) Organizational Behaviour, 3) Finance and Accounting, and 4) Labour Economics. The rest of the courses are more specialized: Compensation; Training and Development; Industrial Relations; Occupational Health and Safety; Human Resource Planning; Human Resources Research and Information Systems; and a selection of designated elective courses. The courses may be taken at the Association's office in Toronto in the evenings, or credit may be obtained through HRPAO-approved university or college courses, or by application to the accreditation committee.

International Foundation of Employee Benefit Plans

The International Foundation of Employee Benefit Plans offers a certification program resulting in the designation Certified Employee Benefit Specialist (CEBS). The program consists of ten courses covering topics such as labour relations, group benefit and insurance plans, accounting, and investment analysis.

A candidate has the option of taking the courses through independent study or part-time classes in most major centres in Canada and the United States. Each course concludes with a two-hour examination consisting of 100 multiple-choice questions. Candidates must attain a minimum of 70 percent on each exam. In 1994, the Foundation had 7000, members, 60 percent of whom were women.

Ontario Society for Training and Development

Founded in 1946, the Ontario Society for Training and Development (OSTD) has established standards of professional competence and professional development programs that lead to certification. The *Human Resource Development (HRD) Certificate* is offered to students preparing for a career in the HRD field and to current practitioners and acknowledges the acquisition of basic theoretical knowledge.

The *Professional Development Accreditation Program (PDAP)* is designed to provide OSTD members with a framework for planning and organizing their personal development. It recognizes individuals' learning and professional achievements and accredits practitioners at a basic, intermediate, or advanced level. It requires self-assessment of competencies and continuing learning. The new *Certified Training and Development Professional (CTDP)* is the only professional designation in Canada specifically for T&D practitioners. All certificates require a written exam.

ETHICS AND HUMAN RESOURCE MANAGEMENT

The professionalization of human resource management has created the need for a uniform code of ethics. **Ethics** is the discipline dealing with what is good and bad, with right and wrong, with moral duty and obligation. More companies in North America are stressing ethical conduct in business. One major reason for this change is that employees are better educated and well versed in the realities of the workplace.[26] Apparently, the attitude has changed from "Should we be doing something in business ethics?" to "What should we be doing in business ethics?"[27]

Every day, people who work in human resources must make decisions that have ethical implications. Should a manager recommend against a woman applicant because she will be working exclusively with men? Should a very effective manager be fired because he violates certain company regulations? Can a manager share personal information about an employee gained accidentally? Such issues must be dealt with not from the standpoint of short-term benefit to the organization but on ethical grounds

There are many kinds of ethical codes. Most professions have their own. One example, from the Human Resources Institute of Alberta, is shown in Figure 1-10. In a growing number of companies as well, ethical codes have been established and communicated to all employees.[28]

Although few of the numerous codes that exist in our society conflict in principle, different codes may place greater or lesser emphasis on a particular aspect of ethics. And, of course, managers vary in the extent to which they apply their own codes under particular circumstances. It is vitally important that human resource managers isolate unacceptable practices and make serious attempts to themselves act ethically in dealing with others.

FIGURE 1-10
HRIA Code of Ethics*

As a member of the Human Resources Institute of Alberta, I will commit myself to the principles outlined in the Code of Ethics. I will support and foster society's code of ethical behaviour through a high standard of practice as a Human Resources Professional. As a Human Resources Professional I shall:

- Support, promote and apply the principles of human rights and dignity in the workplace, the profession and society;
- Treat information obtained in the course of business as confidential;
- Adhere to any statutory acts, regulations and by-laws, which relate to the field of Human Resources;
- Either avoid or disclose a potential conflict of interest which might influence personal actions or judgements;
- Refrain from using a position of trust to receive special benefits, financial or material gain for myself, employees, employers, associates, other parties, or the Human Resources Institute of Alberta;
- Strive for individual growth and thus advance professional standards as a Human Resources Practitioner;
- Acknowledge the original developers of material and concepts that I may use in my professional practice, and observe all laws and restrictions of copyright;
- Strive to balance organizational and individual needs and interests in the practice of the profession;
- Support other Human Resources Professionals in their adherence to this Code of Ethics.

*Unanimously approved by the Board of Directors, Human Resources Institute of Alberta, May 12, 1990, Calgary, Alberta. Reproduced with permission.

SCOPE OF THIS BOOK

Competence in human resource management is crucial to every organization's success. In order to be effective, HR managers must understand and be competent in a variety of HRM practices. Similarly, this text is designed to provide

- An insight into the role of human resource management in today's organizations.
- An understanding of human resource planning, recruitment, and selection.
- An awareness of the importance of human resource development.
- An appreciation of how compensation and benefits programs are formulated and administered.
- An understanding of safety and health factors as they affect a firm's profitability.
- An opportunity to view employee and labour relations from both unionized and nonunionized standpoints.
- An understanding of the role of research in human resource management.

Students often question whether the content of a book corresponds to the realities of the business world. In writing and revising this book, we have drawn heavily on the comments, observations, and experiences of human resource practitioners, as well as our own extensive research. We cite the human resource practices of leading business organizations to illustrate how theory can be applied in the real world. Our intent is to enable the student to experience human resource management in action.

This book is organized into seven parts. Combined, they provide a comprehensive view of human resource management.

Sections entitled HRM in Action, HRM Incidents, and Developing HRM Skills: An Experiential Exercise are included in all chapters. These sections permit you to make decisions about situations that could occur in the real world. They are designed to put you on the spot, to let you think through how you would react in typical human resource management situations. The Experiential Exercises, in particular, give you a chance to test your skill in dealing with the subject matter.

SUMMARY

Human resource management (HRM) is the utilization of the firm's human resources to achieve organizational goals. Human resource managers normally act in an advisory (staff) capacity, working with other managers regarding human resource matters. Human resource managers have primary responsibility of coordinating the firm's human resource actions through a well-conceived human resource management system that embraces the six functional areas of effective human resource management: human resource planning, recruitment, and selection; human resource development; compensation and benefits; safety and health; employee and labour relations; and human resource research.

An organization must have qualified individuals available at specific places and times to accomplish its goals. Among the tasks involved in accomplishing this objective are human resource planning, recruitment, and selection.

Human resource development (HRD) is designed to assist individuals, groups, and the entire organization in becoming more effective. These programs are needed because people, jobs, and organizations are always changing. Development should begin when individuals join a firm and continue throughout their careers. Large-scale HRD programs are referred to as organizational development (OD). Other aspects of HRD are career planning and development and performance appraisal.

An effective compensation and benefits system rewards employees adequately and equitably for their contributions to the organization. As used in this book, the term compensation includes all rewards that individuals receive as a result of their employment.

Safety involves protecting employees from injuries caused by work-related accidents. Health refers to employees' freedom from illness and their general physical and mental well-being. A business firm is required by law to recognize a union and bargain with it in good faith if the firm's employees want the union to represent them. However, union-free firms typically strive to satisfy their employees' work-related needs in order to make union representation unnecessary for individuals to achieve their personal goals.

Every human resource management function needs effective research. This need is particularly strong today because of the rapid changes taking place in the HRM field.

Within the human resource profession are executives, generalists, and specialists. Executives are top-level managers who report directly to the corporation's CEO or to the head of a major division. A generalist, who often is an executive, performs tasks in many human resource-related areas. A specialist may be an executive, a manager, or a nonmanager who is typically concerned with only one of the six functional areas of HRM.

As firms grow and become more complex, changes are required in the way human resource functions are implemented. The basic purpose of human resource management remains the same, but the approach followed in accomplishing its objectives often changes.

A profession is characterized by the existence of a common body of knowledge and a procedure for certifying members of the profession. Among the more prominent professional organizations in the field of human resources are the Society for Human Resource Management, the Human Resource Certification Institute, the American Society for Training and Development, the American Compensation Association, the National Human Resources Association, and the International Personnel Management Association.

Professionalization of human resource management created a need for a uniform code of ethics. Individuals working in human resources must constantly make decisions having ethical implications. Most professions, organizations, and individuals subscribe to ethical codes of one type or another.

TERMS FOR REVIEW

Human resource management (HRM)	Generalist
Human resource managers	Specialist
Operative employees	Profession
Executive	Ethics

QUESTIONS FOR REVIEW

1. Justify the statement "All managers are involved in human resource management."
2. Distinguish between human resource management and the human resource manager.
3. What human resource management functions must be performed regardless of the organization's size?
4. By definition and example distinguish among human resource executives, generalists, and specialists.
5. How does implementing human resource functions change as a firm grows? Briefly describe each stage of the development.
6. Define profession. Do you believe that the field of human resource management is a profession? Explain your answer.
7. Define ethics. Why is ethics important to the field of human resource management?

HRM INCIDENT 1

• A DAY TO REMEMBER

The day was one of the happiest in Ed Beaver's life. He had been told that he was being promoted to corporate vice-president for human resources from his present position as human resource manager for his firm's Agribusiness Group Head Office in Kitchener, Ontario. As he leaned back in his office chair, he felt a deep sense of accomplishment. He thought back to the day fifteen years earlier when, fresh out of university, he had joined Maple Leaf Foods, Shur-Gain Division in Truro, Nova Scotia as an assistant compensation specialist. He had always wanted to be in human resources, but he got his degree in business management because the university didn't have a human resource curriculum. Ed remembered how tense he was when he arrived at work that first day. University graduates were rarely given the opportunity to start work directly in human resources in those days, and he was the youngest employee in the department.

Ed learned his job well and the older workers quickly accepted him. Three years later he was promoted to compensation manager. Immediately after the promotion he was given the task of designing a new pay system for operative employees. As he remembers, "Designing the system wasn't difficult. Convincing the employees that the new system was better than the old one was the real chore." But he overcame that obstacle.

A few years later Ed moved up again. He was chosen to become the new human resource manager for a Maple Leaf poultry-processing facility in Walkerton, Ontario. The move re-quired a major adjustment for his family. At the time Ed's wife remarked, "I sure hated to move in the middle of the school year. And we'd just begun to enjoy our new house." Ed was able to find another house that the family came to like just as well, and the children adjusted quickly. The job was certainly no bed of roses. Six months after Ed arrived, he led negotiations for a new union contract. He worked night and day for months to develop a contract that would be acceptable to the company and the union. Successful signing of the new agreement was one of his most satisfying experiences.

Four years later, Ed was asked to become human resource manager for the Agribusiness Group. This part of the company was larger than the Walkerton facility and had many different types of problems. After a family discussion, the Beavers were off to the new location.

At that moment, Ed's reverie came to an end. He began to realize the challenge that the new job presented to him. As vice-president of human resources for Maple Leaf Foods, he would be responsible for human resource management activities in the company's many plants and warehouses, which employed 10 000 people! What an overwhelming responsibility he faced! Human resource management had changed greatly during the previous fifteen years, and the rate of change seemed to be accelerating. Ed wondered about these problems and the role he would play in solving them as the new vice-president for human resources.

QUESTIONS

1. Trace Ed's progression to vice-president of human resources. Do you believe that this progression qualifies him for the job?

2. What problems do you imagine Ed will face in his new role that he didn't have to deal with as plant human resource manager?

3. What future challenges do you think Ed will confront in the field of human resources?

HRM INCIDENT 2

• LEARN WHAT THEY REALLY WANT

Marie Trudel was exceptionally happy the day she received word of her appointment as assistant human resource director at Nelson Electronics in Edmonton, Alberta. Marie had joined the company as a recruiter three years earlier. Her background included a BBA degree from the University of New Brunswick with a concentration in human resource management and four years' experience as a human resource specialist with an import-export company.

As she walked to her office, she thought about how much she had learned while working as a recruiter. The first year with Nelson, she went on a recruiting trip to Mount Royal College, only to find that its placement director was extremely angry with her company. She was visibly upset when the placement director said, "If you expect to recruit any of our students, you people at Nelson had better get your act together." When she questioned the placement director, she learned that a previous recruiter had failed to show up for a full afternoon of scheduled interviews with Mount Royal students. Marie's trip ended amicably, though, and she eventually recruited a number of excellent employees from the college.

She learned another important lesson when the production manager asked for some help. "I need you to find an experienced quality control inspector," he said. "I want to make sure that the person has a degree in statistics. Beyond that, you decide on the qualifications." Marie advertised the position and checked through dozens of resumes in search of the right person. She sent each promising applicant to the production manager. This process went on for six months with the production manager giving various obscure reasons for not hiring any of the applicants. Finally, the production manager called Marie and said, "I just hired a QC person. He has a degree in history, but he seems eager. Besides, he was willing to work for only $1500 a month."

Marie learned more with each passing day. She felt that one of her greatest accomplishments was improving the firm's employment equity program. She was able to do so in part because one of her close friends in school had become a leader in the Mohawk Nation. With his advice, she was able to develop a recruiting program that attracted qualified aboriginal applicants to Nelson Electronics.

As Marie began to clean out her desk, she suddenly realized that the learning process was really just beginning. As assistant human resource director, she would be responsible not only for matters related to recruiting, but also for all aspects of human resource management. It was a little scary, but she felt ready.

QUESTIONS

1. What lessons can be learned from each of the three situations described?
2. How will the problems that Marie faces as an assistant human resource director differ from those she handled as a recruiter?

2

The Environment of Human Resource Management

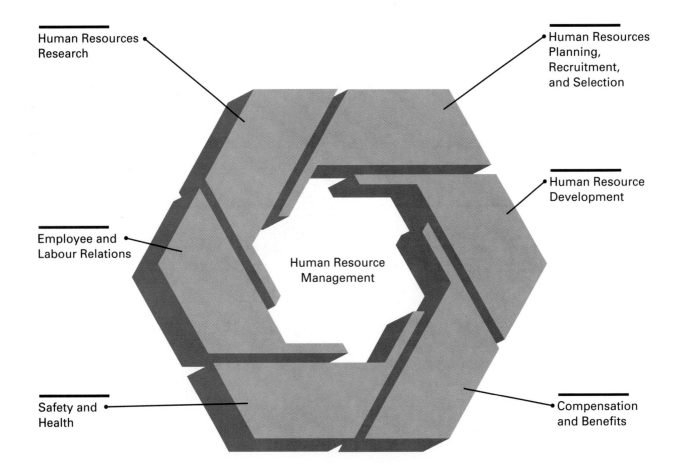

Human Resources Research

Human Resources Planning, Recruitment, and Selection

Human Resource Development

Employee and Labour Relations

Human Resource Management

Safety and Health

Compensation and Benefits

CHAPTER OBJECTIVES

1. Identify the environmental factors that affect human resource management.

2. State and describe the external environmental factors affecting human resource management. Distinguish between a proactive and a reactive response to the external environment.

3. Describe the diverse work force that management now faces.

4. Explain the importance of small business in today's work environment.

5. Identify and describe the internal environmental factors that affect human resource management.

As Wayne Simmons, vice-president of human resources for Ranger Manufacturing, returned to his office from the weekly executive staff meeting, he was visibly disturbed. Ranger, a producer of high-quality telecommunications equipment, is headquartered in Winnipeg, Manitoba and has manufacturing plants in Saskatchewan, Alberta, and British Columbia. Wayne had just heard a rumour that an overseas firm had developed a new manufacturing process—one with the potential to cut costs substantially. Should this report prove true, customers might well switch to the cheaper product. The three plants in the Longline Division that produce similar products would then be in serious trouble. The Longline Division had been expanding rapidly, but Wayne knew that demand for Ranger's product was far from automatic. He also knew that if the new technology was really superior, Ranger might have to cut back production severely or even close the three plants in the Longline Division. These plants are located in areas that are already experiencing high unemployment. Plant closings would have a devastating effect on the economies of their respective communities. A few workers could be transferred to other locations but most would have to be laid off. Thus Wayne is now keenly aware of ways in which the external environment can affect Ranger's manufacturing operations.

In this chapter, we identify significant external environmental factors and discuss how they can influence human resource management. Then we describe diversity in the work force and explain the importance of small business in today's work environment. Finally, we outline some of the major internal environmental factors that can affect human resource management.

ENVIRONMENTAL FACTORS AFFECTING HUMAN RESOURCE MANAGEMENT

Many interrelated environmental factors, both internal and external, affect human resource management (see Figure 2-1). Managers often have little if any control over the effects of the external environment: factors that impinge on the organization from the outside, such as competition, new technologies, interest rates and the like. They can, however, have some control over the important factors that arise from within the firm.

Certain interrelationships tend to complicate the management of human resources. For instance, human resource professionals constantly work with

FIGURE 2-1
The Environments of Human Resource Management

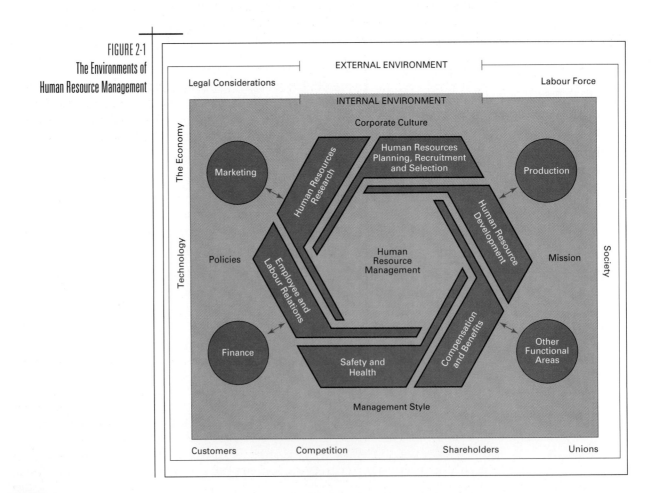

people who represent all organizational levels and functional areas. Therefore, they must recognize the different perspectives these individuals bring to HRM if they are to perform their own tasks properly. David Lozinski, General Manager of Human Resources at SaskTel in Regina is very much aware of this challenge. He sees the need to ". . . create a climate in which our people will be diverse, creative, flexible and highly skilled, accepting challenges and generating personal and corporate successes that will allow all of us to realize increased job satisfaction and security."[1]

Understanding the many interrelationships implied in Figure 2-1 is, therefore, essential for the human resource professional to help other managers resolve issues and problems. A production manager, for example, may want to give a substantial pay raise to a particular employee. The human resource manager may know that this employee does an exceptional job, but should also be aware that granting the raise may affect pay practices in the production department and set a precedent for the entire firm. The human resource manager may have to explain to the production manager that such an action isn't an isolated decision. Together the two managers may have to consider alternative means of rewarding the employee for superior performance, without upsetting the organization's reward system. Perhaps the human resource manager can point to a higher paying position that the employee is qualified to fill.

The implications of any individual act, then, must be considered in light of its potential effect on a department and on the entire organization. Human resource managers must realize the importance of taking an overall view, rather than concentrating on any narrow aspect of a company's operation. Although HRM tasks remain essentially the same in all settings, the manner in which they are accomplished may be influenced substantially by the external environment.

THE EXTERNAL ENVIRONMENT

External environment factors include the labour force, legal considerations, unions, shareholders, competition, customers, technology, the economy, and society as a whole (see Figure 2-1). Each one—either separately or in combination with others—can place constraints on the human resource manager's job. Thus, the HR manager must always try to identify and consider their effects.

The Labour Force

The labour force is the pool of individuals external to the firm from which the organization obtains its employees. The capabilities of a firm's employees determine to a large extent how well the organization can perform its mission. Since new employees are hired from outside the firm, the labour force is considered an external environmental factor. Labour force expectations, skills, and availability are always changing, inevitably affecting employee characteristics in every organization. In turn, changes in the people within an organization affect the way management must deal with its work force.

Thus, changes in the country's labour force create dynamic situations within organizations. This topic will be discussed later in this chapter under the heading "Managing the Diverse Work Force."

Legal Considerations

Another significant external force relates to federal and provincial legislation, including the many court and arbitration decisions interpreting it. These legal considerations affect virtually the entire spectrum of human resource management policy and practice. For example, any organization of more than 100 employees that is awarded a federal government contract over $200 000 must show that a viable employment equity program is in place.[2] How other legislation affects HRM will be described in the appropriate chapters, but an overview will prove useful at this point.

Two sets of legislation, federal and provincial, affect human resources management. Many of the industries engaged in interprovincial trade or business (e.g., banking, transportation) are regulated under the Federal Labour Code. The rest fall under provincial legislation. All labour legislation in Canada is similar, but the details vary. Some of these variations are illustrated in figures. In other areas, federal legislation has been used as a general example.

Another important part of our legislative framework is the Charter of Rights and Freedoms. Section 15, for example, outlines every citizen's rights before the law and provides the underpinnings for employment equity programs—legislation designed to promote equal employment opportunity for designated groups (women, minorities, aboriginal people, and the physically or mentally challenged). The charter also authorizes "affirmative action programs designed to improve the lot of other disadvantaged groups or individuals who may have suffered as a result of past discrimination."[3]

Society

Legislation is an institutional expression of the values of society. Society may also, however, exert pressure on human resource management in less formal ways. The public is no longer content to accept the actions of business without question. To remain acceptable to the general public, a firm must accomplish its purpose while complying with societal norms. Individuals and special interest groups have found that they can effect change through their voices, votes, and other actions. It is, in fact, largely through the influence of activists that so many new regulatory laws have been passed since the early 1960s.

The general public's attitudes and beliefs can also influence the firm's behaviour more directly. People's buying power, whether exerted through organized boycotts or simply through a series of individual decisions, affects a firm's profitability.

When a corporation behaves as if it has a conscience, it is said to be socially responsible. **Social responsibility** is the implied, enforced, or felt obligation of managers, acting in their official capacities, to serve or to protect the interests of groups other than themselves. Many companies develop patterns of concern for moral and social issues. They do so over time, through policy statements, practices, and the leadership of morally strong employees and managers. Open-door policies, grievance procedures, and employee benefit programs often stem as much from a desire to do what is right as from concern for productivity and the avoidance of strife.[4]

It may be asked, "Why should managers be concerned with the welfare of society? Their goal is to make a profit and grow." Obviously, a business must be profitable over the long term if it is to survive. But an important point also must be remembered: If a firm does not satisfy society's needs, ultimately it will cease to exist. A business operates by public consent, to satisfy society's requirements.

Although these issues relate to the organization as a whole, it can easily be seen how human resource managers might be expected to become involved. The organization is a member of the community in which it operates. Just as citizens work to improve the quality of life in their community, so too should managers respect and work with the other members of their community. For instance, a high unemployment rate may exist among a certain minority group within the firm's service area. A policy of hiring capable trainees in addition to qualified applicants may help to reduce unemployment for that group. In the long run, this philosophy will not only enhance the firm's image, but may also improve profitability.

In recent years, companies have been struggling with how they will compete in the new global environment. Managers are constantly looking for new ideas that will make their firms more efficient. Work forces are being trimmed. Even firms that are recovering are not rehiring. Rather, they are seeking other ways to get the job done.[5] In view of this new competitive environment, some are questioning whether efficiency and social responsibility can be married.[6] For example, IBM once had the reputation of never laying off employees. This reputation has been shattered recently by a series of massive layoffs. It would be reasonable therefore to question whether IBM can afford to continue the policies that earned it its reputation for being socially responsible.

Resource utilization, then, may need to be thoroughly analyzed to determine whether a particular *socially responsible* action really assists the firm in remaining competitive in this ever expanding global environment. Only time will tell whether the concept of social responsibility will survive.

Unions

Wage levels, benefits, and working conditions for millions of employees now reflect decisions made jointly by unions and management. A **union** is a group of employees who have joined together for the purpose of dealing with their employer. Unions are treated as an environmental factor because they become a third party in the relationship between the company and the employee. In a unionized organization, the union rather than the individual employee negotiates an agreement with management.

Indeed, unions exert a strong external influence even on nonunionized organizations. A management that does not want a union may take great care to provide satisfactory working conditions and competitive wages and benefits. Moreover, unions monitor broader trends in industry and in the economy, thus bringing broader demands and viewpoints into the firm.

Unions remain a powerful influence and union membership in Canada is holding steady at about 37 percent of the nonagricultural work force. However, as stated previously, union/management relations are in flux.[7] As new, more technical jobs require higher-level skills, the power and the influence of unions may decline. The emphasis will likely shift to human resource systems that deal directly with the individual worker and his or her needs.

Shareholders

The owners of a corporation are called **shareholders**. Because shareholders have invested money in the firm, at times they may challenge management initiatives. Managers may be forced to justify a particular program in economic terms. For example, a $50 000 management development program to make managers "more open and adaptive to the needs of employees" might meet opposition from shareholders unless management is prepared to explain how this expenditure will increase future revenues or decrease future costs.

Shareholders are wielding increasing influence. Indeed, there have been shareholder lawsuits against managers and directors, claiming they failed to look out for their interests. For example, when the surviving partner of a company called Kingpin cancelled an agreement to purchase shares from the deceased partner's widow because of severe cash flow problems, even though a number of interest-free loans had been made to the surviving partner and to other employees, the court ruled in the widow's favour. Although there was no evidence of dishonesty, the defence that the problem stemmed from hard economic times was not accepted.[8]

Competition

Unless an organization is in the unusual position of monopolizing the market it serves, other firms will be producing similar products or services. A firm must maintain a supply of competent employees if it is to succeed, grow, and prosper. But other organizations are also striving to meet those same objectives. A manager's major task is to ensure that the firm obtains and retains a sufficient number of employees in various career fields to allow it to compete effectively.

A bidding war often results when competitors attempt to fill certain critical positions. Because of the strategic nature of their needs, firms are sometimes forced to spend considerable amounts of money to recruit and retain highly skilled employees.

Customers

The people who use a firm's goods and services are also part of its external environment. Because sales are crucial to the firm's survival, management must ensure that its employment practices do not antagonize customers. The firm needs employees with the skills, qualification, and motivation to provide high-quality products and the after-purchase service that so often gains or loses future sales.

Technology

Few firms operate today as they did even a decade ago. And the rate of technological change continues to accelerate. Products not even envisioned a few years ago are now substantially changing the jobs of both workers and managers—including human resource managers. Within the next decade, more than half of all existing jobs are expected to change and another 30 percent will be eliminated altogether as a result of technological advances.[9] Furthermore, it has been estimated that by the year 2000, 75 percent of all jobs will involve the use of computers.[10] The traditional role of the secretary, for example, has changed substantially since the advent of word processing. Rather than writing or dictating a letter to give to the secretary, more and more managers are using word processors to enter and to print their own correspondence.

Typically, new skills are not in large supply; so recruiting qualified individuals in high technology areas is often difficult. On the other hand, once is valued skills are no longer required. Thus, during the next decade, one of the most challenging areas in human resource management will be training employees to keep up with rapidly changing technology.

Technological change has led the trend toward a service economy, which also affects the type and number of employees needed. While the number of jobs in the manufacturing (goods producing) sector has been decreasing by almost 100 000 yearly,[11] the number of service industry jobs has dramatically increased. By 1993, two-thirds of the jobs in Canada were in service-related industries.[12]

The Economy

The economy of the nation—as a whole and in its various segments—is a major environmental factor affecting human resource management. In general, when an economy is growing rapidly, it is more difficult to recruit qualified workers. Conversely, during a downturn, more applicants typically are available.

The situation is complicated further when one segment of the country is experiencing a downturn, another a slow recovery, and another an upswing. Such was the situation in the early 1990s: some of the western provinces were thriving, central Canada was gradually recovering, while Newfoundland was in the grip of a deep depression.

These internal situations are made worse by far-reaching changes in the way business is being conducted. According to F. H. Telmer, Chairman and CEO of Hamilton-based Stelco Inc., "in common with the rest of the manufacturing community, and indeed with business in general, . . . we have undergone and continue to undergo, change that is radical, profound and far reaching." He has also suggested that Canada has had to learn to cope with two forces at the same time: a recession and "a massive process of global economic restructuring." Thus, Canadian HRM professionals have had to work in an environment that, since 1990, has seen 3000 firms disappear in manufacturing alone.[13]

RESPONSES TO THE EXTERNAL ENVIRONMENT: PROACTIVE VERSUS REACTIVE

While external forces, by definition, are not within managers' control, their responses are. Managers may approach changes in the external environment proactively or reactively. A **proactive response** involves taking action in anticipation of environmental changes; responding to environmental changes after they occur is a **reactive response**. For example, while Ontario's pay equity legislation was weaving its way through the legislature, some companies were already designing programs to meet its anticipated provisions. Managers of these companies were being proactive. Those who waited until the law went into effect to plan for the required changes were being reactive.

Organizations exhibit varying degrees of proactive and reactive behaviour. In Ontario and elsewhere, some firms did only what the law required. Others went far beyond minimum compliance, allocating significant resources to create a more equitable work environment for employees, incidentally reducing the level of damaging law suits.[14]

A firm may be either reactive or proactive in any matter. Reactive managers, for example, may demonstrate concern for employee welfare only after a union organizing attempt begins. Proactive managers try to identify signs of discontent and deal with the causes before the situation becomes serious. Proactive managers *prevent* customer complaints rather than *handle* them. In the markets they serve, they tend to set the prices competitors must match. They install scrubbers on exhaust stacks *before* environmental groups begin picketing the plant and before provincial regulators take action.

In all matters, proactive managers initiate rather than react. And when an unanticipated environmental change occurs, they go beyond the minimum change forced on them. As Sonya Bata urged in her convocation address to Dalhousie University in Halifax (May 26, 1994), "let us try to concentrate more on our responsibilities as citizens. Let us realize that these problems are of our own making and we . . . have a responsibility to assist in finding a solution."[15]

MANAGING THE DIVERSE WORK FORCE

Canada has seen continued immigration from many lands during the last four decades. From McDonald's to Holiday Inn, Bell Canada to Levi Strauss, managers are learning not only to understand their kaleidoscopic work force, but also to manage in diverse work environments. At the same time as more businesses are expanding their operations overseas, many workers in Canada are working alongside individuals whose cultures differ substantially from their own, and more ethnic minorities are entering the work force.[16]

In Ontario, for example, native and minority groups, people with disabilities, and women make up approximately 60 percent of the work force. By the year 2003, more than 80 percent of all new employees will be members of one of these groups. However, because of barriers such as managerial attitudes, sexual harassment, poor communication, and lack of access for disabled people, there are still few professionals, managers and supervisors from these groups. More workers from these groups will need to be hired to fill the skills gap and if they cannot be encouraged to continue their education, there will be a smaller skills pool for the future. The setting of realistic and challenging goals for attracting, retaining and advancing members of these groups will become more important in the future.[17]

Attitude changes in the workplace will come only through a commitment by senior management and the development of policies on ethical behaviour and practice that are posted publicly and included in employee handbooks. According to Monica Armour, president of Transcultural Consultant Services of Toronto, unequal promotions, unequal access to jobs, combined with racial and sexual innuendo are the real causes of disharmony. Accurate, precise job descriptions are the best protection for management when disputes with workers arise. Job descriptions, complete with a checklist of specific skills and duties, ensure that jobs are filled according to ability.[18]

Diversity in the workplace must be accepted if a firm is to be globally competitive. Today, it would be socially irresponsible (and illegal in most jurisdictions) to proclaim in an advertising brochure that "none but white women and girls are employed," as did Levi Strauss & Company in 1908. Now, however, executives at Levi Strauss appear to be exceptionally committed to diversity management. Not only is the company currently recognized as one of the most ethnically and culturally diverse organizations in the world, but managers at Levi are doing their best to eliminate the "**glass ceiling**," the unwritten and sometimes unconscious reluctance to promote qualified minorities and women into a company's top ranks. Promoting diversity is not only socially responsible; it makes good business sense at Levi, allowing for the design and the development of merchandise for a diverse market—a factor decision makers may not have understood or appreciated in the past. The Dockers line of casual pants, for example, now worth more than $1 billion a year, has been credited to ideas obtained from Argentinian employees. Promoting diversity and social responsibility is often costly and time consuming, but Levi CEO Robert B. Haas believes that harnessing diversity will benefit the company well into the future. According to Levi executives, "Standing firm . . sends an important message to employees of all races and lifestyles."[19]

The challenge for managers in the coming decades will be to recognize that people with different characteristics often think differently, act differently, learn differently, and communicate differently. Because each culture, each business situation, and each person is unique, there are no simple rules; but experts in **managing diversity** suggest that both employees and employers need to develop patience, open-mindedness, acceptance, and cultural awareness.[20] Managers must have an acute awareness of characteristics common to a culture, race, gender, age, or sexual preference, while at the same time managing each employee as an individual.

Women in Business

In Canada, women have been joining the work force in ever increasing numbers. The first half of the 1980s saw an increase in employment rates of 74 percent for women between 25 and 44 years of age. However, men still held 77 percent of managerial positions, although women found it less difficult to obtain supervisory positions. A study published in 1994 reported that, "in a sample of 423 organizations, 30 percent of first-line supervisors [were] female, whereas only 17 percent of middle managers and eight percent of executives [were] women."[21] These data are similar to those in the United States, where 8.7 percent of those who hold titles similar to executive vice-president are women.[22]

Largely because of the number of women entering the work force, there are an increasing number of nontraditional households in Canada. These households include those headed by single parents and those in which both partners work full time. Women who formerly remained at home to care for the family today need and want to work outside the home. In fact, women are expected to account for 94 percent of labour force growth during the period from 1981 to 1998. If this valuable segment of the work force is to be effectively utilized, organizations must recognize fully the importance of addressing work/family issues.[23]

There has been a great deal of discussion about whether women are at a disadvantage in business because of their sex. Certainly the statistics on promotion into management positions are clear. Moreover, women as a group don't make as much money as men. Recent studies, however, have suggested that much of this income difference results from the demands of raising children and from career choices made by women.

When 1991 wage levels for single females were compared with salaries earned by single males, for example, wage discrepancies were negligible. Certainly during the first five years of their careers, male and female business school graduates experienced no differences, when measured against a "variety of work and career outcomes."[24] The big differences occur between married women and married men. As well, "women with children lag far behind their childless sisters."[25]

Regardless of whether women have been at a disadvantage in business in the past, however, it is apparent that businesses are having to adapt to employees' requirements for flexibility and innovation in child care services, benefit plans and work practices.

Child-care needs, for example, have traditionally been viewed as being outside the realm of the business world—a responsibility that employees had to bear and manage alone. This task is particularly difficult for single parents; even working couples generally cannot afford a full-time, live-in housekeeper. For many others, child care has had to be managed with the help of family or friends. Therefore, the need for alternative arrangements is evident.

Accordingly, some managers have begun to see that providing child-care services and workplace flexibility may influence workers' choice of employers. Some companies located in the same building or facility provide joint day-care service. Others, like IBM, provide day-care referral services. More and more employers are providing paid maternity leave (unpaid maternity leave is mandatory in Canada) and some offer paternity leave. Still other firms give time off for children's visits to doctors, charging the time against the parents' sick leave or personal time. Managers, then, need to be more sensitive and creative in accommodating the needs of working parents, one of the most valuable segments of the work force.[26]

The trend toward nontraditional and dual-career couples presents both challenges and opportunities for organizations. Firms must develop programs to accommodate employee needs. For example, when management wishes to transfer an employee, the employee's spouse may be unwilling to give up a good position or unable to find an equivalent position in the new location. Many companies, therefore, are offering placement assistance for such spouses.

People with Disabilities

According to one estimate, there are approximately 2.3 million disabled adults of working age in Canada, of whom 56 percent are in the work force.[27] A handicap, or disability, is a disadvantage that limits the amount or kind of work a person can do, or makes work performance unusually difficult. More common disabilities include limited hearing or sight, limited mobility, mental or emotional deficiencies, and various nerve disorders. Studies indicate that disabled workers perform as well as other employees in terms of productivity, attendance, and average tenure.[28] In fact, in certain high-turnover occupations, disabled workers had lower turnover rates. All human rights legislation in Canada prohibits discrimination against q*ualified individuals with disabilities.*

A serious barrier to effective employment of disabled people is bias, or prejudice. Managers need to examine their preconceived attitudes. Many people experience anxiety around workers with disabilities, especially if the disabilities are severe. Fellow workers may show pity or feel that a disabled worker is fragile. Some even show disgust. The manager can set the tone for proper treatment of workers with disabilities. If someone is unsure about how to act, or how much help to offer, the disabled person should be asked for guidance. Managers always must strive to treat employees with disabilities as they treat other employees, by holding them accountable for achievement.

Older Workers

The population is growing older, a trend that is expected to continue through the year 2000. Life expectancies continue to increase, and the baby boom generation (people born from the end of World War II through 1964) had only half as many children as their parents did.

HRM IN ACTION

Duane Roberts, a paraplegic, has just been assigned to your division as a radio dispatcher for your delivery trucks. The department has given you only limited information about Duane. But you know he is 32 years old and has held similar jobs before. You are in the dispatching office when you see a person you assume to be Duane coming up the sidewalk in his wheelchair. You think he might have a problem getting through the double glass doors in his path, which open against his direction of travel.

How would you handle the situation?

The *greying* of the work force has required some adjustments. As people grow older, their needs and interests may change.[29] Many become bored with their present careers and desire different challenges. Some favour less-demanding full-time jobs, others choose semiretirement, and still others prefer part-time work. Many require retraining as they move through the various stages of their careers.

Contingency Workers

In the late 1980s and early 1990s many companies drastically reduced their full-time work force. As the economy began to recover, these full-time employees often were not rehired. As companies continue to downsize and reorganize, many of them are employing contingency workers—employees hired by companies to cope with unexpected or temporary challenges. This work force consists of part-timers, freelancers, subcontractors, people hired through employment agencies, and independent professionals. These workers are usually paid less than full-time employees and almost never receive benefits. Some predictions suggest that contingency workers will make up approximately 50 percent of the work force by the year 2000. In the past, temporary employees were almost all clerical staff. Now, however, many are professionals, comprising about 20 percent of the total contingency work force.[30]

The use of contingency workers, however, is not without disadvantages. They tend to be less dependent on the firm and therefore less committed to it. Unless they are given extra training and closer supervision, they tend to exhibit high turnover and low productivity. If managed properly, however, contingency employees can provide a firm with a body of well-trained, long-term employees that can be expanded or contracted as business conditions dictate.[31]

The Small Business

During the 1980s and thus far in the 1990s, small and midsized companies created almost 87 percent of the jobs in Canada. In fact companies with sales of less than $2 million and fewer then 50 employees make up 97 percent of Canadian firms, employing 42 percent of the labour force.[32] Every year thousands of individuals, motivated by a desire to be their own boss, to contribute to the community,[33] or to earn a better income, launch new business ventures. These individuals, often referred to as entrepreneurs, have been essential to the growth and vitality of our economy. Entrepreneurs develop or recognize new products or business opportunities, secure the necessary capital, and organize and operate the business. Most people who start their own business get a great deal of satisfaction from owning and managing their own firm. Historically, it has been estimated that four out of five small businesses fail within five years. However, in a recent study it was found that survival had improved somewhat, although half still fail during their first three years.[34] Female entrepreneurs, however, seem to be performing somewhat better; the failure rate for these businesses is half that for those operated by men.[35]

Almost every large corporation began as a small business. For example, Steven Jobs and Steve Wozniak (the founders of Apple Computer Company) began making personal computers in Wozniak's garage. From this meagre beginning, Apple Computer evolved into a major personal computer maker.

There is no commonly agreed-on definition of what constitutes a small business. In HRM terms, however, a small business is one in which the owner-operator knows all the key personnel. In most small businesses, this key group would not exceed 12 to 15 people. The number of self-employed individuals is also growing rapidly. Between 1975 and 1990, the number of self-employed Canadians grew by 740 000; 44.6 percent of these individuals were women.[36]

The environment for managers in large and small businesses is often quite different. Managers in large firms may find it difficult to see how they fit into the overall organization. They may be separated from top decision makers by numerous managerial layers; they often know managers one or two layers above them, but seldom those higher up. In some large companies supervisors are restricted by written guidelines and rules. They may feel more loyalty to their workers than to upper management.

In contrast, managers in smaller businesses often identify more closely with the goals of the firm. They can readily see how their efforts affect the firm's profits. In many instances, lower-level managers know the company executives personally. These supervisors know that the organization's success is tied closely to their own effectiveness.

THE INTERNAL ENVIRONMENT

The firm's internal environment also has a considerable effect on human resource management. Here too, it is possible to be proactive or reactive. As indicated in Figure 2-1, the **internal environment** includes the firm's mission, policies, and corporate culture, the management style of upper managers, the number and type of employees, the informal organization, the structure of the organization, and perhaps unions. All these factors contribute to the interaction between HRM and other departments within an organization. Since these interactions play a large part in determining the overall productivity of the organization, it is vital that the relationships be positive, supporting the firm's mission.

Mission

Mission is the organization's continuing purpose or reason for being. Each management level should operate with a clear understanding of the firm's mission. In fact, those within each organizational unit (division, plant, department) should also have specific objectives that relate to the mission. Indeed, a key challenge involves positioning the company for the future.[37]

The company mission must be regarded as a major internal influence affecting all human resource management activities. Consider two companies, each having a broadly based mission, and envision how certain tasks might differ from one firm to the other. Company A's goal is to be an industry leader in technological advances. Its growth occurs through the pioneering of new products and processes. Company B's goal is one of conservative growth that involves little risk taking. Only after another company's product or process has proved itself in the marketplace will Company B commit itself.

Company A needs a creative environment to encourage new ideas. Highly skilled workers must be recruited to foster technological advancement. Proactive HR professionals pay constant attention to work force training and development. A compensation program designed to retain and motivate the most productive employees is especially important.

The basic human resource management tasks are the same at Company B, but the different mission alters how these tasks are carried out. First, a different kind of work force is needed. Highly creative individuals may not want to work for Company B and may, in fact, be a little disruptive. Because the mission encourages little risk taking, most of the major decisions are made at higher levels in the organization. Development of management and employees may receive less emphasis. The compensation program, too, may reflect the different requirements of this particular work force. As this comparison indicates, a human resource manager must clearly understand the company's mission.

Policies

A **policy** is a predetermined guide to thinking, established to provide direction in decision making. Policies should be considered as guides rather than as unchangeable rules; they need to be somewhat flexible, applied with interpretation and judgement. They can exert significant influence, however, on how managers accomplish their jobs. For example, many firms have an *open door* policy that permits an employee to take a problem to the next organizational level if it can't be solved by the immediate supervisor. Knowing that their subordinates can take problems to a higher echelon tends to encourage supervisors to try harder to resolve problems.

Many larger firms have policies related to every major operational area. Although policies are established for marketing, production and finance, the largest number often relate to human resource management. The following directives are examples of HRM policies.

- Provide employees with a safe place to work, by following and strongly supporting provincial safety regulations.
- Encourage all employees to achieve as much of their human potential as possible, by paying for part-time tuition at the local university or college.
- Provide compensation that will encourage a high level of productivity in both quality and quantity, by keeping wages 5 percent higher than the area average.
- Ensure that current employees are considered first for any vacant position for which they may be qualified.

Because policies are somewhat flexible, the manager is often guided as much by the *tone* of a policy as by the actual words. Consider, for example, a policy to ensure that "all members of the labour force have equal opportunity for employment." This policy implies more than merely adhering to certain laws and government regulations. To actively implement this policy, the manager will need to go beyond the minimum nondiscrimination required by law, perhaps by initiating a training program to permit hiring of minorities or women who are not immediately qualified to perform available jobs.

Corporate Culture

Corporate culture is a concept that refers to the characteristics of a firm's social and psychological climate. It can be defined as the system of shared values, beliefs, and habits within an organization that interacts with the formal structure to produce behavioural norms.[38] Managers can, and should, determine the kind of corporate culture they wish to create and then strive to make sure the desired culture develops. Dennis L. Nowlin, manager of executive development at 3M Corporation, has said that his company is challenged with "managing a large firm with the value system of a small business." Nowlin adds: "We work in a highly technical organization with many technical, research and development, and manufacturing specialists. . . My personal vision is to get every manager within 3M thinking from a general management perspective."[39]

Senior Management Style

Closely related to corporate culture is the way in which the attitudes and preferences of one's superiors affect how a job is done. This factor deserves special emphasis here because of the problems that can result if senior management's style differs from that of lower-level managers. In general, a lower-level manager must adapt to the superior's style. It is hard to be open and considerate, for example, when the boss believes in giving orders and having them followed. In this case, a lower-level manager's concerns about involving employees in decision making and giving them freedom may be seen as a lack of decisiveness. Even the company president must deal with the management style and attitudes of superiors, i.e., the board of directors.[40] The president may be a risk taker, for example, and want to be aggressive in the marketplace, but the board may prefer a more conservative approach.

Employees

Employees differ in capabilities, attitudes, personal goals, and personalities. As a result, behaviour that a manager finds effective with one worker may not be effective with another. In extreme cases, employees can be so different it is virtually impossible to manage them as a group. In order to be effective, the manager must consider both individual and group differences. A supervisor of experienced workers, for instance, may pay little attention to the technical details of the job and more to encouraging group cooperation, while a supervisor of inexperienced workers may focus mainly on the technical aspects of the task.

Informal Organization

New managers quickly learn that there are two organizations within the firm—one formal, the other informal. The formal organization is usually outlined on an organization chart and described in job descriptions. Thus, managers understand the official reporting relationships. But an informal organization exists alongside the formal one: a set of evolving relationships and patterns of human interaction that are not part of the official organization. These informal relationships are quite powerful. Assume, for example, that senior management has expressed total commitment to employment equity. An all-male work group may still resist the assignment of women to their group. The unwanted workers may be ostracized, or refused the usual friendly assistance in adapting to the new job. In extreme cases, derogatory jokes may be told within earshot. This kind of behaviour places the supervisor in a difficult position, caught between a formal policy and aggressive action arising from the informal organization.

Other Units

Managers must be keenly aware of interrelationships among divisions or departments, using these relationships to their best advantage (see Figure 2-2). The human resource department helps maintain a competent work force; the purchasing department buys material and parts. Because one department precedes another in the flow of work, the output of the first becomes the input of the second. Most managers soon discover that cooperation with other departments is necessary if the job is to be performed efficiently. Managers who fail to develop mutually supportive relationships with other managers may jeopardize the productivity of several departments.

FIGURE 2-2
Possible Relationships
with Other Departments

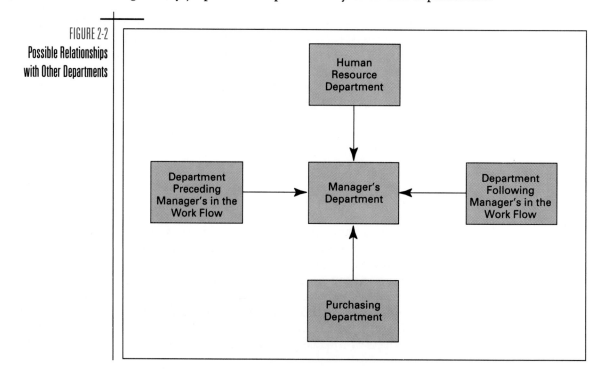

Many private-sector organizations do not have a union. Where a union does exist, it becomes an important factor in the firm's environment. While it is typically upper management that negotiates labour/management agreements, managers throughout the organization must implement the terms of the agreements. In most cases, agreements place restrictions on the manager's actions. For example, a manager who wants to shift a maintenance worker to an operator's job temporarily may be constrained from doing so by a labour/management agreement that specifies assignable tasks for each job. It must be remembered, however, that many jobs are now being defined more broadly, giving managers greater scope to assign tasks depending upon organizational needs.

While collective bargaining agreements can create impediments to change and prevent flexibility, they do offer the benefit of some predictability and stability to the labour-management relationship. For example, an agreement spanning two years allows management to calculate the exact labour cost of production for that period.

A GLOBAL PERSPECTIVE

Exports of Canadian goods and services now amount to more than $130 billion yearly. More than 30 percent of this country's wealth and the livelihood of approximately three million Canadians depend directly on trade.[41] Conducting business abroad has been made even more necessary and more feasible by global competition, air travel, satellite communication technology, and labour cost differentials. As a result, even smaller corporations have responded by establishing more operations overseas.[42]

Faced with increasing levels of export and overseas activity, human resources executives must acquire a global outlook and skills in international HRM.[43] Unfortunately, these skills are still not widespread. As Stephen van Houten, President of the Canadian Manufacturers' Association has stated: "Managers need greater awareness of global competitive developments, and they have to become comfortable doing business in new countries, often in foreign languages, and in innovative ways which will stretch all of their talents."[44] This challenge is often greater for small and midsized firms that must become more aggressive in the global marketplace.

Human resources professionals can be of direct help to senior managers, especially those in small and medium-size companies, where the CEO or top management team is likely to be personally involved in offshore commercial activity. In one study of 98 CEOs, for example, 42 percent felt they needed new knowledge and/or skills, and 52 percent indicated their job had changed.

Managing or motivating someone at a distance, and in another culture, could well require different skills and knowledge. Indeed, of the CEOs who indicated they exported to countries other than the United States, 60 percent suggested they needed new skills, such as learning about the foreign culture, adapting their negotiating style, and adapting their management technique

It would appear, therefore, that even the decision to export affects different levels of the organization. For instance, when the CEO needs retraining, there is a strong likelihood that employees will require new skills as well.[45]

Indeed, different types of people may need to be hired, a situation that becomes ever more complex as a company moves from an exporting mode to joint ventures or other types of more direct involvement in offshore commerce.[46] The HR professional, then, has an important role to play in helping a firm to succeed in the global marketplace.

Earlier in this chapter our discussion focused primarily on environmental factors that affected organizations located and conducting business only in Canada. The external environment in which multinational enterprises operate, however, is even more complex. A **multinational corporation (MNC)** conducts a large part of its business outside the country in which it is headquartered and has a significant percentage of its physical facilities and employees in other countries. Thus, as illustrated in Figure 2-3, multinational operations add another environmental layer to human resource management. To the basic human resources management tasks need to be added functions that relate to international taxation, relocation and international orientation, host government relations, translation, and repatriation.[47] A global perspective is presented in each chapter to emphasize the importance of the multinational environment for human resource management.

FIGURE 2-3
Human Resource Management in the
Multinational Environment

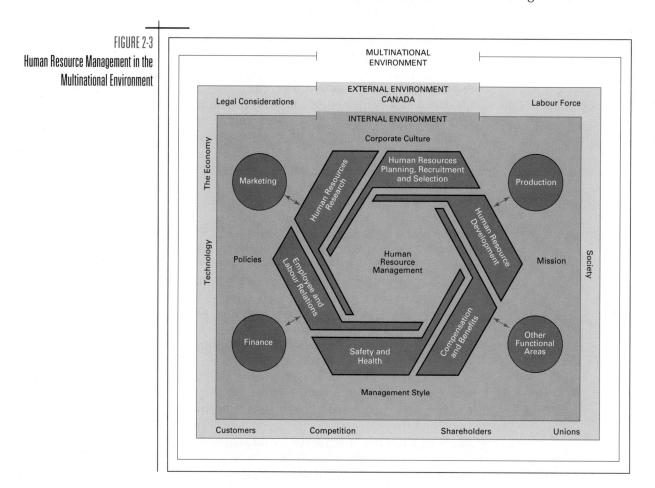

SUMMARY

Many interrelated factors, both external and internal, affect human resource management. Effective HRM requires careful consideration of all the environmental variables. External factors include legal considerations, society as a whole, shareholders, competition, customers, technological change, the labour force, and the overall economy.

An example of a law that affects how we work is the Canadian Charter of Rights and Freedoms, which outlines every citizen's legal rights and forms the legal background for all our employment equity legislation. Managers can either react to legislation or take a proactive approach, preparing their firms for social change before it occurs. In some companies, change is introduced that goes far beyond what the law requires.

Society influences how the human resource function is managed. Increasingly, firms must accomplish their purposes while meeting societal norms.

Technological change is occurring at an ever increasing rate, and few firms operate today as they did even a decade ago. Of major concern to those in HRM is the need for constant retraining.

The owners of a corporation are called shareholders. Because shareholders have invested in the firm, they may challenge programs considered by management to be beneficial to the organization.

Unless an organization is in the unusual position of monopolizing the market it serves, other firms will be producing similar goods or services. For a firm to succeed, grow, and prosper, it must be able to maintain a supply of competent employees.

Customers are those who use a firm's products. Because sales are crucial to the firm's survival, management must ensure those employment practices and the firm's employees do not antagonize customers.

The labour force is becoming increasingly diverse. The presence of employees from many ethnic and linguistic groups requires that managers be open-minded and develop cultural knowledge and sensitivity. Approaches to the structure of work must also adapt to the increasing proportion of the labour force made up of women, dual-career families, single parents, and older persons. Adaptations are also needed to allow full work force participation by people with disabilities. The nature of jobs themselves is also being redefined, as more companies hire contingent or part-time workers, often for shared jobs. In recent years small and midsized companies have created a large percentage of new jobs. Every year thousands of individuals, motivated by a desire to be their own boss or to earn a better income, launch new business ventures. Women seem to be especially skilled entrepreneurs, as the failure rate for female-owned small business is much lower than for those owned by men.

Unions are both an internal and an external factor. A union is a group of employees who have joined together for the purpose of dealing with their employer. Unions not only influence compensation and assignment of tasks within a company, but also exert a wider influence on industry as a whole, through pressure to match the gains they are able to achieve in a particular workplace.

Other major internal environmental factors include the company's mission (which will affect everything the company does and the manner in which it is done), the policies that grow out of the mission, the organization's corporate culture, the style of senior management, the characteristics of the work force, and the informal organization that develops among workers and managers.

Human resource managers must be guided by the company's mission. They must use good judgement in interpreting the intent rather than just the letter of policies. Usually they must adapt their own style to that of senior managers. They must always keep in mind the nature of the individuals they are managing and the needs and viewpoints of other units within the organization, since all must work together if the organization as a whole is to be effective.

The opening up of world markets and the growth in multinational corporations are forcing human resource managers, as well as CEOs, to develop a broader perspective and new adaptive skills.

TERMS FOR REVIEW

External environment

Social responsibility

Union

Shareholders

Proactive response

Reactive response

Managing diversity

Glass ceiling

Internal environment

Mission

Policy

Corporate culture

Informal organization

Multinational corporation (MNC)

QUESTIONS FOR REVIEW

1. What is meant by the statement, "The human resource manager's job is not accomplished in a vacuum?"
2. What factors make up the external environment of human resource management? Briefly describe each of these factors.
3. What internal environment considerations exert pressure on the human resource manager?
4. How could changes in an organizational policy affect the human resource professional's work? Give an example.
5. Define corporate culture. What effect could it have on human resource management?

HRM INCIDENT 1

• COMPLAINTS FROM MYTHANIA ABOUT THE WHINIANS

Throughout the last two decades, the trade deficit with Mythania has grown worse. The Mythanian share of Whinian markets has steadily increased, especially in automobiles and electronics, but very few products or services flow the other way. The steadily growing stock of Whinian dollars in Mythanian hands has been used to buy up an increasing number of Whinian companies. Everyone—labour unions, executives, and politicians—is whining about the loss of Whinian jobs. Citizens have expressed fear that the Mythanians would come to own too much of Whinian industry. Corporations are complaining that they are shut out of a potentially profitable foreign market.

The Whinians have accused the Mythanians of *dumping* products (that is, selling items in Whinia for less than the cost of production). Another complaint frequently heard is that the Mythanian government has erected every conceivable trade barrier to keep Whinian products out of Mythania, while Whinian markets are essentially open to Mythanian products.

But Herisial Mythgartner, senior vice-president of Hoopblader Electronics, says that the problems are Whinians'

own fault. Mythgartner describes what he sees as the *real* source of Whinian trade balance problems.

"In a nutshell, in Mythania we treat customers as God and you only say, 'The customer is king.' Let me explain. Hoopblader sells microwave ovens in Whinia. I have been trying for over a year to find a Whinian company to make some of the parts we need. We want to have the parts shipped to Mythania for installation in Whinia-bound ovens. That would improve your trade balance. It would also allow us to take advantage of present favourable exchange rates.

"But I cannot find anyone who will produce the quality we need to stay competitive. Whinian managers tell me, "This is as good as we can do. You will have to change your operation to make the parts work.' In Mythania, of course, suppliers value contracts like this and do all they can to meet our specifications. I am under a great deal of pressure to buy Whinian. But Whinian firms just do not seem to care about our needs.

"The same kind of attitude surfaces when I ask about shipping schedules. In our factories, we practise just-in-time inventory control. Mythanian suppliers deliver the parts we need just when we need them—and in small quantities. I know Whinian companies have to ship long distances. So we are willing to accept larger shipments and be somewhat flexible about delivery dates. But no Whinian firm I have talked to will guarantee even the week of delivery. They say there are too many variables involved—strikes, raw materials, shortages, shipping problems. In Mythania, a supplier would not ask me to worry about those things. I am the customer.

"The language also presents a problem. Whinian firms will not bother to use Mythanianese. They refuse to even print installation instructions and invoices in any language but Whinian. This is especially grating since we take the time to learn even local dialects of the Whinian language. Can any Whinian imagine buying a Hoopblader stereo

with the owner's manual written in Mythanian? We take care of those problems because Whinians are our valued customers."

Mr. Mythgartner went on to reemphasize that Whinian companies could sell as much in Mythania as Mythania sells in Whinia if they gave Mythanian customers proper regard.

QUESTIONS

1. Mr. Mythgartner's argument is similar to one being put forth in today's world. Who might make these statements about whom?
2. Discuss some of the external environmental factors faced by Canadian companies that wish to sell overseas.
3. If Mythania were a real country, how would a Canadian company approach that market; i.e., what is important to the Mythanians?

HRM INCIDENT 2

• GETTING BY?

As the human resource director for KBH Stores in Edmonton, Alberta, Virginia Simard knew that she had her work cut out for her. Company management was moving forward with a goal of opening 10 new stores in 12 months. KBH already employed 480 people in 35 stores, in addition to the headquarters staff of 31. Virginia knew that staffing the 10 new stores would require hiring and training about 150 people. She felt that her own small office was inadequately funded and staffed to handle this task. She sat at her desk, mulling over how to present a recommendation for her own staffing needs.

One of her concerns was broaching the subject with her boss because she had not officially been told of the expansion plans. Virginia had learned about them through the office grapevine. While she did not like being kept in the dark, she was not surprised that she hadn't been told. Glenn Sullivan, the president of KBH, was noted for his autocratic leadership style. Virginia had been warned early on that Glenn told subordinates only what he wanted them to know and that he expected everyone who worked for him to follow orders without question. He was not an unkind person, though, and Virginia had always gotten along with him well enough. She had never confronted Mr. Sullivan about anything, so it was with some concern that she approached him in his office later that day.

"Mr. Sullivan," she began, "I hear that we are going to be opening 10 new stores next year."

"That's right, Virginia," said Mr. Sullivan. "We've already arranged the credit lines and picked out several of the sites."

"What about staffing?" asked Virginia.

"Well, I assume you will take care of that, Virginia, when we get to that point."

"What about my own staff?" asked Virginia. "I think I am going to need at least three or four more people. And we are already crowded for space. So I hope you plan to expand the human resource office."

"Not really," said Mr. Sullivan. "The new demands on the human resource staff will be temporary. It wouldn't be cost effective to hire and train additions to your staff that will only be cut the next year. I am counting on you to plan the expansion staffing within our current proposed budget allowances for the human resource office. It may require some reallocation, but I am sure you can handle that."

QUESTIONS

1. What should Virginia do? Explain.
2. Describe the elements of the internal environment that the case highlights. How does each affect Virginia?

DEVELOPING HRM SKILLS: AN EXPERIENTIAL EXERCISE

This is an exercise involving Jesse Heard, the human resource manager at Parma Cycle Company; Gene Beairsto, the corporate planner; and Edmont Fitzgerald, the comptroller. Parma Cycle Company is one of only three companies in Canada that manufacture complete bicycles. Most of Parma's competitors import parts from other countries and assemble bicycles here. Parma Cycle currently employs about 800 workers at wages well above the average wage levels in the area. Most of these workers are machine operators and assemblers. Parma Cycle Company is experiencing severe difficulties competing with less expensive bicycles, and the time has come for Parma to lower its costs.

Jesse Heard, the human resource director is faced with a dilemma. Many of the current employees have been with the company for years. They are loyal and highly skilled. But yesterday, he received a call from Mr. Burgess, the President. He told Jesse to meet with the corporate planner and the comptroller to draft a plan that would move all but the most high-tech manufacturing to Mexico. Jesse realizes this move would remove 600 jobs.

Gene Beairsto has never had much power at Parma Cycle, although his title, corporate planner, sounds impressive enough. Primarily, he maintains a chart room and keeps track of various trends. He agrees that Parma Cycle Company is headed down-

hill because of depressed markets and an inability on the part of company managers to decrease unit costs. He agrees with Jesse that the most important asset that Parma Cycle has is a trained and loyal work force. While under the North American Free Trade Agreement it would be easy to shift production to Mexico, he is afraid that this would destroy the team spirit that now exists at Parma Cycle. He believes that workers are more likely than ever to respond to financial incentives, such as some kind of piecerate program or bonus system.

Edmont Fitzgerald, University of Western Ontario graduate in finance, believes that, above all, the corporation is an economic entity. He believes that market forces will take care of those workers who really wish to contribute to the economy. He believes in purchasing all resources, including labour, at the lowest possible price. He views the current situation as an opportunity to decrease costs radically and to increase profits.

Three students will serve as the Parma Cycle management: one as Jesse Heard, the human resource manager; one as Edmont Fitzgerald, the controller; and one as Gene Beairsto, the corporate planner. All students not playing roles in the exercise should carefully observe participants' behaviour. Instructors will provide participants with the necessary additional information.

3

Job Analysis

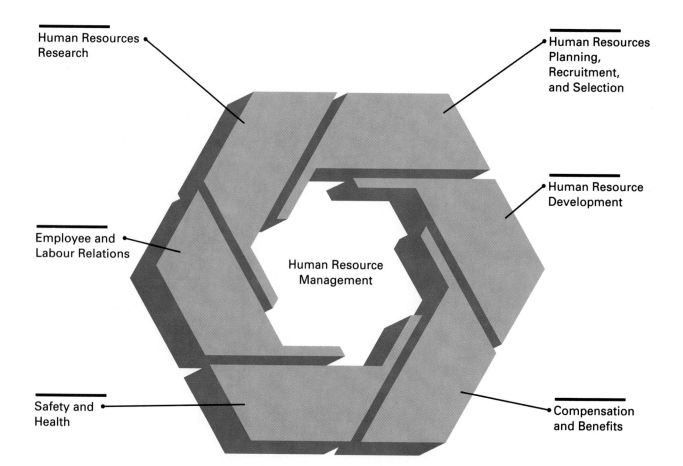

Human Resources
Research

Human Resources
Planning,
Recruitment,
and Selection

Human Resource
Development

Employee and
Labour Relations

Human Resource
Management

Safety and
Health

Compensation
and Benefits

1. Define job analysis, describe why it is the basic human resource tool, and explain the reasons for conducting job analysis.

2. List the types of information required for job analysis, name several job analysis methods, and explain how to conduct job analysis.

3. Explain how job analysis helps to satisfy various legal requirements.

4. Explain the components of a well-designed job description and job specification.

5. Explain reengineering and job design.

ary, I'm having trouble figuring out what kind of machine operators you need," said John Anderson, the human resource director at Gulf Machineries. "I've sent four people for you to interview who seemed to meet the requirements outlined in the job description. You rejected all of them."

"To heck with the job description," replied Mary. "What I'm concerned with is finding someone who can do the job. And the people you sent me couldn't do the job. Besides, I've never even seen the job description."

John took a copy of the job description to Mary and went over it point by point. They discovered that either the job description never fit the job, or the job had changed a great deal since it was written. For example, the job description specified experience on an older model drill press while the one in use is a new digital machine. Workers have to be more mathematically oriented to use the new machine effectively.

After Mary described the machine operators' duties and the skills they needed to perform them, John said, "I think that we can now write an accurate description of the job and use it to find the right kind of people. Let's work more closely so this kind of situation won't happen again."

The situation just described reflects a very common problem in human resource management: The job description did not adequately define the duties and skills needed to perform the job. Therefore, it became virtually impossible for the human resource director to locate people with the required skills. Job analysis was needed to resolve the problem. As we stress throughout the remainder of this book, job analysis is the most basic function of human resource management.

We begin the chapter by defining job analysis and explaining the reasons for conducting job analysis. Next, we review the types of information required for job analysis, discuss traditional job analysis methods, and illustrate new methods. Then we explain how job analysis data is used in preparing job descriptions and job specifications and how job analysis helps to satisfy various legal requirements. We end the chapter by examining reengineering and job design.

JOB ANALYSIS: A BASIC HUMAN RESOURCE TOOL

A **job** consists of a group of tasks that must be performed if an organization is to achieve its goals. A job may be held by only one person (e.g., the president) or by many people,(e.g., all data entry operators in a large firm.)

In a work group consisting of a supervisor, two senior clerks, and four word processing operators, there are three jobs and seven positions. A **position** is the collection of tasks and responsibilities performed by one person; there is a position for every individual in an organization. For instance, a small company might have 25 jobs for its 75 employees; in a large company 2000 jobs may exist for 50 000 employees. In some firms, as few as 10 jobs employ 90 percent of a work force.

Job analysis is the process of determining systematically the skills, duties, and knowledge required to perform jobs in an organization,[1] by obtaining answers to six important questions:

1. What physical and mental tasks does the worker accomplish?
2. When is the job to be completed?
3. Where is the job to be accomplished?
4. How does the worker do the job?
5. Why is the job done?
6. What qualifications are needed to perform the job?

Job analysis, then, provides a summary of a job's duties and responsibilities, its relationship to other jobs, the knowledge and skills required to perform it, and the working conditions under which it is performed. Job analysis is conducted after the job has been designed, the worker has been trained and the job is being performed. Facts are gathered, analyzed, and recorded about the job as it exists, not as it should exist. Determining what the job *should* be is a separate task, one most often assigned to industrial engineers or methods analysts.

Job analysis is performed on three occasions:

1. When the organization is founded and a job analysis program is initiated for the first time;
2. When new jobs are created;
3. When jobs are changed significantly as a result of new technology, methods, procedures, or systems.

The majority of job analyses are performed because of changes in the nature of jobs. Job analysis information is used to prepare both job descriptions and job specifications.

The **job description** is a document that provides information on the tasks, duties, and responsibilities of the job. The minimum acceptable qualifications that a person should possess in order to perform a particular job are contained in the **job specification.** We discuss both types of documents in greater detail later in the chapter.

REASONS FOR CONDUCTING JOB ANALYSIS

In this rapidly changing work environment, the need for a sound job analysis system is critical. New jobs are constantly being created and old jobs redesigned. Referring to a job analysis that was conducted only a few years ago may not provide accurate data. Job analysis, then, helps organizations recognize and cope with change.[2] As Figure 3-1 suggests, data derived from job analyses affect virtually every aspect of human resource management. A major use of job analysis data is in human resource planning. It is not enough, for example, to know that the firm will need 100 new employees to produce goods or services to satisfy sales demand; each job will likely require different knowledge, skills and ability levels. Obviously, effective human resource planning must take these differing job requirements into consideration. The knowledge to plan effectively, then, is derived from job analysis.[3]

Furthermore, employee recruitment and selection is haphazard if the recruiter does not know the qualifications needed to perform the job. Without up-to-date job descriptions and specifications, employees are recruited and selected for a job without clear guidelines, an approach that can have disastrous consequences. This practice is virtually unheard of when firms procure raw materials, supplies, or equipment. When ordering a photocopy machine, for example, the purchasing department develops precise specifications. The same logic, therefore, should apply when searching for a firm's most valuable asset—human resources.

Job specification information often proves beneficial in identifying human resource development needs. If the specification calls for particular knowledge, skills, or abilities that the person filling the position does not possess, training and/or development is probably in order. Training is designed to help workers perform duties specified in their present job descriptions, while development prepares them for promotion to higher level jobs or for the possibility of transfer within the organization.

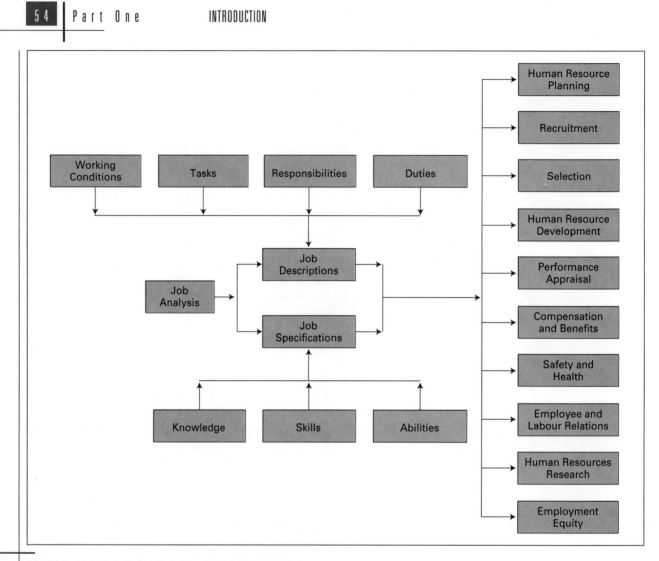

FIGURE 3-1 Job Analysis: The Most Basic Human Resource Management Tool

Employees should be evaluated (performance appraisal) in terms of how well they accomplish the duties specified in their job descriptions. A manager who evaluates an employee on factors not included in the job description might be accused of bias or even of discrimination.

Job analysis is also relevant to compensation. The relative value of a particular job to the company must be known before a dollar value can be placed on it. In relative terms, the more significant the duties and responsibilities, the more a job is worth. Jobs that require greater knowledge, skills and abilities are usually worth more to the firm. For example, the relative value of a job that calls for a master's degree normally would be higher than that of a job that requires only a high school diploma.

Information derived from job analysis is also valuable in identifying safety and health considerations. If an employee handles chemicals, for example, employers are required to state whether or not the job is hazardous. Workers in hazardous jobs also need specific information about these hazards to perform their jobs safely.

Job analysis information can also be used in employee and labour relations. When employees are considered for promotion, transfer or demotion, the job description provides a standard for comparison of performance. Whether or not the firm has a union, information obtained through job analysis can often lead to more objective human resource decisions.

When human resources research is undertaken, job analysis information provides the researcher with a starting point. If the human resource manager is trying to identify factors that distinguish successful employees from mediocre employees, for example, the researcher needs to study only those employees who have similar job descriptions/specifications.

Finally, job analysis is an important HRM tool for supporting the legality of employment practices. Data from job analyses may be needed to defend, for example, decisions involving promotion, transfers, and demotions.

Thus far, we have described job analysis as it pertains to specific HRM functions. In practice, however, these functions are interrelated, Job analysis provides the basis for tying the functional areas together and the foundation for developing a sound human resource program. In fact, according to Paul Thériault, vice-president, human resources for The New Brunswick Power Corporation: "job analysis is an integral component of any comprehensive human resource management strategy. In addition to determining and defining the specific job functions, we need to ensure that a link is established with other jobs within the unit, as well as the type of individual that would most likely be the best candidate for this position. We need to take the job analysis process far beyond the traditional narrow-focused approaches of the past."[4]

TYPES OF JOB ANALYSIS INFORMATION

Considerable information is needed to complete a job analysis. The job analyst identifies the job's duties and responsibilities and gathers the other types of data shown in Figure 3-2. Note that work activities, worker-oriented activities, and the types of machines, tools, equipment, and work aids used in the job are important. This information is used later to help determine the job skills needed. In addition, the job analyst looks at job-related tangibles and intangibles, such as the knowledge needed, the materials processed, and the goods made or services performed.

Some job analysis systems identify job standards. Work measurement studies, for example, may be needed to determine how long it takes to perform a task. In determining job context, the analyst studies the work schedule, financial and nonfinancial incentives, and physical working conditions. Since jobs are often performed in conjunction with other jobs, organizational and social contexts are also noted. And, finally, specific education, training, and work experience pertinent to the job are identified.

TRADITIONAL JOB ANALYSIS METHODS

Job analysis has traditionally been conducted in a number of different ways, because organizational needs and resources differ.[5] A specific method should be selected on the basis of the manner in which the information is to be

FIGURE 3-2
Types of Data Collected
in Job Analysis

1. Work activities
  a. Work activities and processes.
  b. Activity records (in film form, for example).
  c. Procedures used.
  d. Personal responsibility.

2. Worker-oriented activities
  a. Human behaviors, such as physical actions and communicating on the job.
  b. Elemental motions for methods analysis.
  c. Personal job demands, such as energy expenditure.

3. Machines, tools, equipment, and work aids used

4. Job-related tangibles and intangibles
  a. Knowledge dealt with or applied (as in accounting).
  b. Materials processed.
  c. Products made or services performed.

5. Work performance
  a. Error analysis.
  b. Work standards.
  c. Work measurements, such as time taken for a task.

6. Job context
  a. Work schedule.
  b. Financial and nonfinancial incentives.
  c. Physical working conditions.
  d. Organizational and social contexts.

7. Personal requirements for the job.
  a. Personal attributes such as personality and interests.
  b. Education and training required.
  c. Work experience.

Note: This information can be in the form of qualitative, verbal, narrative descriptions or quantitative measurements of each item, such as error rates per unit or noise level.

Source: Reprinted by permission of Marvin D. Dunnette.

used—e.g., job evaluation, pay increases or development—and of feasibility for a particular organization. We describe the most common methods of job analysis in the following sections.

Questionnaires

Questionnaires, in which employees are asked to identify their job tasks, are generally quick and economical to use. They do, however, have some limitations. Mailed questionnaires can elicit low return rates and incomplete responses. To overcome this drawback, the job analyst can administer a structured questionnaire to employees. The problem of inaccuracy remains, both because some employees may lack verbal skills, and because they may exaggerate the significance of tasks, suggesting that they have more responsibility than they actually have.

A portion of a job analysis questionnaire is presented in Figure 3-3. Although the entire questionnaire consists of 25 sections, only the first seven are shown here. These sections illustrate the depth of detail that can be collected by using questionnaires.

Observation

When using the observation method, the job analyst watches the worker perform job tasks and records his or her observations. This method is used primarily to gather information on jobs emphasizing manual skills, such as machine operator. Observation can also help the analyst identify interrelationships between physical and mental tasks. Observation alone, however, is usually insufficient, particularly when mental skills form a major part of the job. Observing a financial analyst at work, for example, would not reveal much about job requirements. Moreover, tasks that are performed only periodically might be missed.

Interviews

An understanding of the job may also be gained by interviewing both the employee and the supervisor. Usually the analyst interviews the employee first, helping him or her to describe the duties performed. Then the analyst contacts the supervisor for additional information, to check the accuracy of the information obtained from the worker, and to clarify certain points.

Employee Recording

Job analysis information can also be gathered by having employees describe their daily work activities in a diary or log. Again, the problem of employees exaggerating job importance may have to be overcome. This method allows a more complete understanding of highly specialized jobs, such as recreation therapist, but it is time consuming and costly.

FIGURE 3-3
Example of a Job-Analysis
Questionnaire

The information from this questionnaire will be used to write a job description as well as to define hiring qualifications and special job characteristics. Answer as best you can, and don't worry about anyone "grading" your answers; the basic information about the job is what is important.

Your job title _____ Date _____

Name of person to whom you report _____

Department _____ Shift _____

Your name _____ Phone ext. _____

How long have you been in this job? _____

1. Summarize in one or two sentences what your basic job function is. (What is the principal reason your job exists? What is your job designed to accomplish?)

   _____

2. Job responsibilities can be described in two ways:

What you do (the duties people can watch you do)	**Why you do it** (the effect or result you create)
A waiter/waitress, for example,	
Places silverware, plates, glassware (DUTIES)	*to present a ready and pleasing table* (RESULT)

List the major responsibilities of your job, including the approximate percentage of time spent on each. (It may be helpful to first list duties and then identify the results involved; or, if you prefer, list the major results expected of your job and then the duties required to accomplish each result.) Remember that sometimes two or three duties combine to produce the same result.

Duties	Results	% of time spent

(Add additional pages as necessary)

Rank in numerical order the responsibilities in order of importance to the organization:

Mark with a "D" the most difficult part of your job.

Mark with a "C" the responsibilities involving confidential data.

3. What formal course of instruction is required by law to perform this job?

   _____

   a) What formal courses of instruction might be helpful?

   _____

   b) What licensure or certification is required by law to perform this job?

   _____

4. What specific experiences or skills other than formal education do you feel a person must have in order to start this job today?

   _____

   a) Are there any jobs a person must have worked in before this job?

   _____

5. Given your answers to the above, how long do you feel it should take a qualified new person to perform this job competently?

   _____

6. The way you perform your job affects other people in terms of quality and quantity of service received, as well as time and money gained or lost.

People you affect	What would be the positive results of your good work on each type of person?	What typically might go wrong for each type of person if your job performance were poor? (Don't think of the rare catastrophe.)
Customers		
Suppliers		
Senior managers		
Employees in your own department		
Employees in other departments		

Example:

Suppliers	Suppliers can plan their own production to meet our needs on time and at the right price	Our customers do not receive orders on time, as our suppliers were delayed.

7. What part of your job entails the greatest chance for error?

_____

_____

   a. How often does this occur (daily, weekly, monthly)?

_____

_____

Source: Adapted from R.J. Plachy, *Building a Fair Pay Program.* New York: American Management Association, pp. 87, 89.

OTHER JOB ANALYSIS METHODS

Over the years, attempts have been made to provide more systematic methods of conducting job analysis. We describe several of these approaches next.

Functional Job Analysis

Functional job analysis (FJA) is a comprehensive job analysis approach that concentrates on the interactions among the work, the worker, and the organization. This method is worker-oriented, describing what a person actually does rather than his or her official responsibilities.[6] The following points are fundamental elements of FJA.

1. A major distinction is made between what gets done and what workers *do* to get things done. It is more important in job analysis to know the latter. For instance, a word processing operator doesn't keep the system running but performs a number of specific tasks to achieve this result.

2. Each job is defined by how individuals work with data, people, materials and/or equipment. *Only* those functions involved with data, people, materials and/or equipment are recorded.

3. These functions proceed from the simple to the complex. The least complex form of data use would be comparing and the most complex would be synthesizing. It is assumed that if an upper-level function is required, the related lower-level functions are also required.

4. This analysis provides two measures of the job. First, relative complexity is measured—that is, the complexity of the interrelationship among data, people, materials and/or equipment. Second, there is a measure of proportional involvement. For example, 50 percent of a person's time may be spent in analyzing, 30 percent in supervising and 20 percent in operating.[7]

One study determined that FJA was a useful technique for defining the work of heavy-equipment operators. Once the analysis was done, the knowledge, skills, and abilities required for that job could be communicated easily if needed for disciplinary matters, or for other purposes.[8]

HRM IN ACTION

"I can't figure out what kind of computer programmer you need, Alex," said Wiktor Nasierowski, the human resource director. "Every applicant I sent down was proficient in FORTRAN, just like it said in the job description". "Get real, Wiktor," replied Alex. "We haven't used FORTRAN in ten years. I need somebody who's up to date on the latest software. None of those people you sent me were qualified."

How would you respond?

Position Analysis Questionnaire

The **position analysis questionnaire (PAQ)** is a structured job analysis questionnaire that uses a checklist approach to identify job elements. Advocates of the PAQ believe that its ability to identify job elements, behaviours required of job incumbents, and other job characteristics makes this procedure suitable for analyzing virtually any type of job.

In one system, some 194 job descriptors relate to job-oriented elements. Each job descriptor is evaluated on a scale that measures extent of use, amount of time, importance of the job, possibility of occurrence, and applicability. With the aid of a computer program, each job is then scored relative to 32 job dimensions. The score derived represents a profile of the job, which can be compared with standard profiles to place the job into known job families; that is, jobs of a similar nature. The PAQ then identifies significant job behaviours and classifies jobs. Using the PAQ, job descriptions can be based on the relative importance and emphasis placed on various job elements.

The PAQ is completed by an employee or employees familiar with the job being studied—typically an experienced job incumbent or the immediate supervisor. The profiles and the job descriptions are then prepared by a job analyst.[9]

Management Position Description Questionnaire

The **management position description questionnaire (MPDQ)** is a checklist-based method designed to describe management positions. One example contains 208 items that are related to the concerns and responsibilities of managers.[10] These 208 items have been reduced to thirteen primary job factors:

1. Product, market, and financial planning
2. Coordination of other organizational units and workers
3. Internal business control
4. Products and service responsibility
5. Public and customer relations
6. Advanced consulting
7. Autonomy of action
8. Approval of financial commitment
9. Staff service
10. Supervision
11. Complexity and stress
12. Advanced financial responsibility
13. Broad human resources responsibility

The MPDQ has been used to determine the training needs of individuals who are about to move into managerial positions. MPDQ is also used to evaluate and to set compensation rates for managerial jobs and to assign the jobs to job families.

Occupational Measurement System[11]

Because of the many technological advances presently taking place, new and innovative job analysis methods are being developed.[12] The **occupational measurement system (OMS)** enables organizations to collect, store and analyze information pertinent to human resources by means of a computer database. The computer provides fast turnaround and more accurate job analysis, job descriptions, and evaluations. The computer also makes feasible the use of multiple regression statistical techniques that increase objectivity.

The OMS is designed to work with task-based information. Task-based job evaluation uses structured job analysis questionnaires as the basic input documents. These questionnaires are developed from a number of different sources, including a database of industry job tasks, the organization's job descriptions and job experts within the firm. The system includes a booklet with instructions and general information. The questionnaire contains items specifically tailored to the category of positions covered. Responses are given in data entry or optical scanning format. Sample items from a questionnaire are shown in Figure 3-4.

The OMS is an integrated computer software system specifically designed to process, to analyze, and to display task-based information. Typical reports generated by OMS are listed below.

1. A functional and a detailed task-level job description. The job descriptions include the functions performed by each employee, job, or job classification, the specific tasks covered by those functions and the amount of time spent on each function and task.

2. Skill and knowledge levels required to perform a function or a job as compared with those possessed by the incumbents and the differences between the two, if any, along with identified training needs.

3. Costs of production, both in terms of performance and supervision.

Combination of Methods

Usually, an analyst does not use one job analysis method exclusively. A combination of methods is often more appropriate. In analyzing clerical and administrative jobs, for example, mailed or directly administered questionnaires might be used, supported by interviews and limited observation. In studying production jobs, interviews supplemented by extensive work observation might provide the needed data. The analyst should employ any combination of techniques needed to conduct an effective job analysis.

CONDUCTING A JOB ANALYSIS

The job analyst is interested in gathering data on the duties involved in performing a particular job. The people who participate in job analysis should include at least the employee and the employee's immediate supervisor. Large organizations may have one or more job analysts, but in small organizations line supervisors may be responsible for job analysis. Organizations that lack this technical expertise often use outside consultants.

FIGURE 3-4
A Job Analysis Questionnaire

For Every Statement:

■ If task is part of your job, mark X in the first box.

■ If you PERFORM and/or SUPERVISE a task, rate it using the adjacent RELATIVE TIME SPENT scale:

1 = An extremely small amount of time.
2 = Between levels 1 and 3.
3 = A small amount of time.
4 = Between levels 3 and 5.
5 = A moderate amount of time.
6 = Between levels 5 and 7.
7 = A large amount of time.
8 = Between levels 7 and 9.
9 = A extremely large amount of time.

Relative time spent SUPERVISING ⎯⎯
Relative time spent PERFORMING ⎯⎯
Part of job ⎯⎯

CREDIT ADMINISTRATION

1. Works with officers on national accounts to solve credit problems.

2. Responds to inquiries from branches regarding consumer regulations.

3. Establishes goals for delinquency ratios, charge-offs and recoveries.

4. Maintains annual forecasts for nonaccrual loans and other nonperforming assets.

5. Develops loan policy and procedures.

6. Recommends loan policy and procedures.

7. Maintains annual forecasts of commercial, consumer and real estate loan losses.

8. Prepares reports on branch compliance with consumer regulations.

9. Recommends interest rates for loans.

10. Reviews periodicals for changes to consumer protection laws.

11. Reviews analysis reports and financial statement spreads.

12. Performs commercial credit investigations.

13. Prepares credit memos.

14. Prepares loan write-ups.

15. Assembles and interprets debtor credit information.

16. Surveys collateral status for credit extension on potential and current customers

17. Contacts credit agencies to secure credit reports and special services.

Source: Used with the permission of First Interstate Bancorp.

Before conducting a job analysis, the analyst learns as much as possible about the job by reviewing organizational charts and talking with individuals acquainted with the jobs to be studied. Then, the supervisor should introduce the analyst to the employees and explain the purpose of the job analysis. Although employee attitudes about the job are beyond the job analyst's control, the analyst must attempt to gain the trust and confidence of those whose jobs are being analyzed. Failure to do so may detract from an otherwise technically sound job analysis, as the employee may withhold information or provide inaccurate information. Upon completion of a job analysis, two basic human resource documents—job descriptions and job specifications—can be prepared.

THE JOB DESCRIPTION

Information obtained through job analysis is crucial to the development of job descriptions. Recall that previously we defined the job description as a document that outlines the tasks, duties, responsibilities and working conditions pertaining to a job.

Job descriptions, then, must be both relevant and accurate.[13] They should provide concise statements of what employees are expected to do on the job and indicate exactly what employees do, how they do it and the conditions under which the duties are performed.[14]

Among the items frequently included in a job description are

- Major duties performed;
- Percentage of time devoted to each duty;
- Performance standards to be achieved;
- Working conditions and possible hazards;
- Number of employees performing the job and reporting relationships;
- The machines and equipment used on the job.

As the contents of a job description may vary somewhat with the purpose for which it will be used, we now consider only those sections most commonly included.

Job Identification

The job identification section includes the job title, department, reporting relationship, and perhaps a job number or code. A good title will approximate closely the nature of the work content and will distinguish that job from others. Unfortunately, job titles are often misleading. *An executive secretary* in one organization may be little more than a highly paid clerk, whereas a person with the same title in another firm may have wide-ranging responsibilities. For example, one former student's first job after graduation was with a major tire and rubber company as an *assistant district service manager*. Because the primary duties of the job were to unload tires from trucks, check the tread wear and stack the tires in boxcars, a more appropriate title probably would have been *tire checker and stacker*.

One information source that assists in standardizing job titles is the *National Occupational Classification* (NOC).[15] The NOC includes standardized and comprehensive descriptions of job duties and related information for thousands of occupations. This standardization permits employers in different industries and different parts of the country to more accurately match job requirements with worker skills.

As an example, the NOC definition for a Specialist in Human Resources would be numbered 1121. The two digits "11" relate to Professional Occupations in Business and Finance, the digit "2" identifies Human Resources and Business Services Professionals, while the last "1" pinpoints Specialist in

Human Resources. This code, then, could identify any of the following major occupations:

- Business Agent, Labour Union
- Classification Officer
- Classification Specialist
- Compensation Research Analyst
- Conciliator
- Consultant, Human Resources
- Employee Relations Officer
- Employment Equity Officer
- Human Resources Research Officer
- Job Analyst
- Labour Relations Officer
- Mediator
- Union Representative
- Wage Analyst

All these jobs are filled by specialists in human resources who develop, implement, and evaluate human resource and labour relations policies, programs, and procedures, while advising managers and employees on personnel matters.

The NOC further defines Specialists in Human Resources as individuals who perform some or all of the following duties:

1. They develop, implement and evaluate personnel and labour relations policies, programs, and procedures.
2. They advise managers and employees on the interpretation of personnel policies, benefit programs, and collective agreements.
3. They negotiate collective agreements on behalf of employers or workers and mediate labour disputes and grievances.
4. They research and prepare occupational classifications, job descriptions, and salary scales.

They also administer benefit, employment equity, and affirmative action programs, and maintain related records systems, while coordinating employee performance and appraisal programs. Finally, they may research employee benefit and health and safety practices and recommend changes or modifications to existing policies.

To perform as a specialist in human resources one should have

1. a university degree or college diploma in a field related to personnel management, such as business administration, industrial relations, commerce or psychology

or

2. a professional development program in personnel administration; and
3. some experience in a clerical or administrative position related to personnel administration.

The National Occupation Classification also lists several other occupations in the HRM field:

- Human Resources Managers—code 0112,
- Personnel and Recruitment Officers—code 1223,
- Personnel Clerks—code 1442,
- Professional Occupations in Business Services to Management—code 1122,
- Training officers and instructors—code 4131.

Date of the Job Analysis

The job analysis date is placed on the job description to aid in identifying job changes that would make the description obsolete. Some firms have found it useful to place an expiration date on the document. This practice ensures periodic review of job content and minimizes the number of obsolete job descriptions.

Job Summary

The job summary provides a concise overview of the job. It is generally a short paragraph that states job content.

Duties Performed

The body of the job description delineates the major duties to be performed, usually in sentences beginning with an action verb such as *receives, performs, establishes*, or *assembles* that explain each duty. Machines operated and working conditions also are included.

Job Specification

Recall that we defined the job specification as a document containing the minimum acceptable qualifications that a person should possess in order to perform a particular job. Items typically included in the job specification are educational requirements, experience, personality traits and physical abilities. In practice, job specifications are often included as a major section in a job description.

Figure 3-5 is an actual job description provided by General Mills, Inc. As you can see, the qualifications needed for the job of *Secretary II* include keyboarding at least sixty words per minute and demonstrated proficiency in English grammar, punctuation, spelling, and proper word usage. This type of information is extremely valuable in the recruiting and selection process.

There are many different job description formats in use. In Ontario (as of 1995) job descriptions must contain sections on skill, effort, including mental and physical demands, and working conditions. Other jurisdictions may have other requirements, and legislation can change.

After jobs have been analyzed and the descriptions written, the results should be reviewed with the supervisor and the employee to ensure that they are accurate, clear, and comprehensible. The courtesy of reviewing results with employees also helps to gain their acceptance. Because the job description and the job specification are often combined into one form, we use the term *job description* to include both documents.

FIGURE 3-5
A Job Description

POSITION TITLE				POSITION NUMBER 217
				APPROVAL RHS

DIVISION OR STAFF DEPARTMENT All	LOCATION All	REPORTS TO		EFFECTIVE DATE May 1992
DEPARTMENT OR ACTIVITY	SECTION	POINTS 165	GRADE 6	REVISED

JOB SUMMARY
Performs clerical and administrative duties for a manager and often one or more staff members of a major function.

NATURE OF WORK
Performs a wide variety of office duties including most of the following:
a. Data entry of correspondence, reports, manuscripts, graphs, charts, etc., from notes, dictating machine, and/or hand written drafts proficiently and with minimum direction and instructions.
b. Receiving telephone calls and visitors skillfully and handling incoming mail efficiently.
c. Originating routine correspondence and handling inquiries, and routing non-routine inquiries and correspondence to proper persons.
d. Establishing and maintaining department files and records.
e. Assuming responsibility for arranging appointments and meetings, screening calls, and handling personal and confidential matters for superior.
f. Assembling, organizing, processing, and evaluating data and reports; operating office machines needed for accomplishing this.
g. Performing administrative duties and special projects as directed, such as collecting and compiling general reference materials and information pertaining to company, division, or department practices and procedures.

Works independently, receiving a minimum of supervision and guidance on established office procedures. Relieves supervisor of minor administrative details. May have some light work direction over others in department. Structure is light and most work is not checked.

QUALIFICATIONS
High school education or its equivalent plus three years of clerical experience, including one year with the Company, and a word processing skill of at least 60 WPM. Demonstrated proficiency in English grammar, punctuation, spelling, and proper word usage. Must be able to anticipate problems and use sound judgment and tact in handling confidential matters, screening telephone calls and visitors, and scheduling superior's time. Must have the ability to acquire a thorough knowledge of the organization's policies, procedures, and personnel in order to relieve superior of specified administrative duties. A basic figure aptitude and/or a working knowledge of certain word processing packages may be necessary depending on the specific job.

Source: Used with the permission of General Mills, Inc.

Job Analysis and the Law

Although job analysis is essential to many aspects of human resource management, including recruitment, selection, promotion, and training, the process can also play a major role in legal compliance. Documentation from the Ontario Pay Equity Commission in 1989 and 1990 set the standards for such data collection. Government documents pertaining to pay equity suggest that the questionnaire and/or the interview methods can be used, but that any information collected must be gender-neutral. In Ontario objections or complaints are settled by Review Officers employed by the Pay Equity Commission, although unions, employees or employers might request a further hearing concerning a Review Officer's decision. The job analysis process, therefore, has become an important part of the legal framework, especially in the areas of human rights and employment/pay equity.

Although pay equity legislation tends to change, depending upon the political party in power, in some jurisdictions attempts are likely to continue to eliminate that portion of the wage gap between men and women created by the undervaluation of the work that women do.[16] Employment equity, in one form or another, will continue to be an important part of Canadian business practice. One of the steps in this process is the collection of bias-free information through job analysis.[17]

REENGINEERING

When business problems occur, workers are often blamed, even though the real cause may lie in process design. Unfortunately, many managers do not think of changing processes and systems, or the way work is accomplished. Rather than looking for process problems, managers often focus on worker deficiencies. If processes and/or systems are inefficient, substantial improvements in productivity can often be made through reengineering.

Reengineering involves managers in rethinking and redesigning their business systems to become more competitive. For example, at U.S.-based international giant Procter & Gamble (P&G), a decade of acquisition and foreign expansion had resulted in an unwieldy organization, with out-of-control costs (overhead had risen 2 percent in only three years). P&G's solution to the problem is to "bottom-up reengineer" to cut costs in sales, research and administration. Ten teams are determining how to streamline the company. The company has "people checking people," to determine who to cut, how many to cut, and how to improve the basic areas of sales, research, and administration. P&G has gone far beyond superficial strategy change; management is now involved in a far-ranging self-appraisal aimed at streamlining the entire organization.

The key to this reengineering effort is that real contributors will remain at P&G. According to the Chairman of the Board: "Real contributors don't have to worry [about the cuts]." One place where cuts are necessary, however, is in the United States, where overlapping staffing is prevalent. Managers at P&G have been trying to boost performance in marketing sales and logistics for years, but with limited success. Top management now believes, however, that reengineering is the answer.[18]

Reengineering is "the fundamental rethinking and radical redesign of business processes to achieve dramatic improvements in critical, contemporary measures of performance, such as cost, quality, service, and speed."[19] In fact, according to George Harvey, President and CEO of Unitel Communications Inc., their new organizational structure "will be designed around serving the empowered customer. Research and development, marketing, sales, human resources—EACH and every department's design may have to be turned upside down; some departments may be eliminated for good."[20] Reengineering, then, emphasizes the complete redesign of work, forcing companies to organize around processes instead of functional departments. It is not incremental changes that are desired, but rather radical change that revamps entire operations.

Ideally, managers must rethink and redesign entire business systems, as reengineering focuses on the overall aspects of job design, organizational structure, and management systems. The process stresses that work should be organized around outcomes, as opposed to tasks or functions. But reengineering should never be confused with restructuring (discussed in Chapter 4), even though workforce reduction may result.[21]

The reengineering approach has impressed some experts so much that they believe it will displace Total Quality Management at many companies.[22] In a recent survey, senior executives suggested that reengineering would play a major role in most corporate plans.[23] Some firms, such as Eastman Kodak Company and American Express, have gone so far as to appoint senior officers for reengineering.

Process manager is a term that is often used in the language of reengineering. As opposed to managing a function (e.g., production, marketing, finance), a process manager is responsible for accomplishing all operations associated with a specific process, such as cost control or customer relations. Some organizations are experimenting with video technology as part of the reengineering process. A pilot program at Ford Motor Co. of Canada Ltd.'s Windsor plant, for example, involves a computer program that uses digitized video to catalogue the steps involved in every job description at the Essex engine plant and at the Windsor engine plant No. 1. This program will point to ways of reengineering work processes to avoid accidents and repetitive motion injuries. After the jobs are analyzed, they will be given a priority according to risk and engineers will attempt to correct any safety problems, issues, or concerns. Workers can also get a copy of the job analysis to better understand the risk elements involved. This program was designed with help from Digital Renaissance Inc. of Toronto.[24]

JOB DESIGN

The previous section focused on processes, systems, and the concept of reengineering, which requires a certain degree of job design or redesign. In fact, in many organizations the complete reengineering described in the previous section is not necessary, as goals can be accomplished through changes in job design. **Job design** is the process of determining the specific tasks to be performed, the methods used in performing these tasks, and the relationship of the job to other work in the organization. Several concepts related to job design (job enrichment, job enlargement, and employee-centred work re-design) will be discussed next.

Job Enrichment

In the past two decades, there has been considerable interest in application of job enrichment techniques in a wide variety of organizations. Strongly advocated by Frederick Herzberg, job enrichment is a process of changing the content of a job so as to provide greater challenge to the worker. **Job enrichment**, then, is not concerned with promotion, but rather with the expansion of responsibilities within a job that usually remains at the same level within the company. The employee has the opportunity to derive a feeling of achievement, recognition, responsibility, and personal growth. Although job enrichment programs are not always successful they have often brought about improvements in job performance and in the level of employee satisfaction.

According to Herzberg, five principles should be followed when implementing job enrichment:

1. *Increasing job demands*: The job should be changed in such a way as to increase the level of difficulty and responsibility.
2. *Increasing the worker's accountability*: More individual control and authority over the work should be allowed, while the manager retains ultimate accountability.
3. *Providing work scheduling freedom*: Within limits, individuals should be allowed to schedule their own work.
4. *Providing feedback*: Timely periodic reports on performance should be made directly to employees rather than to their supervisors.
5. *Providing new learning experiences*: Work situations should include opportunities for new experiences and for personal growth.[25]

Job Enlargement

Many people have attempted to differentiate between job enrichment and job enlargement. The job enrichment process, sometimes called a vertical expansion, adds responsibilities over work, including decision making and the exercise of self-control. Conversely, **job enlargement** involves changing the scope of a job by expanding duties horizontally—that is, assigning a wider variety of duties at a similar level of responsibility. For example, job enlargement might entail teaching a machine operator to run two or three different machines instead of only one. Job enrichment could require the operator to be responsible for scheduling machine use or suggesting set-up improvements. What the two processes have in common is that they add variety and interest to the job duties.

Employee-Centred Work Redesign[26]

A concept designed to link the mission of the company with the job satisfaction needs of employees is **employee-centred work redesign**. Employees are encouraged to become involved in redesigning their work to benefit both the organization and themselves. Workers can propose changes in job design to make their jobs more satisfying, but they must also show how these changes better accomplish the goals of the entire unit. With this approach, the contribution of each employee is recognized, while at the same time, the focus remains on accomplishing the organizational mission.

A GLOBAL PERSPECTIVE

In international organizations, job redesign can involve international cooperation. A striking example of the latter, aimed at redesigning the way jobs are done to increase global quality and productivity, occurred at a plant in Fremont, California, where General Motors and Toyota have established a joint venture called NUMMI to weld and assemble Geo Prisms and Toyota Corollas. Before the NUMMI joint venture, the General Motors Fremont plant had had one of the worst records in the company for poor labour relations and defective production. The plant was a typical assembly-line operation, in which workers and supervisors tried to produce as much as possible, while letting quality control inspectors discover the defects.[27]

Four years after General Motors entered into a joint venture with Toyota, the plant's productivity and quality levels rivalled Japan's best and exceeded anything in the U.S. automobile industry. What caused these changes? It can't be the workers, since they are still members of the United Auto Workers (UAW), and they are paid union-scale wages and benefits. Nor did the change spring from the introduction of advanced robotics. It occurred because of a revolutionary team-production system run by the workers themselves. Each worker is responsible for quality control and for ensuring that no car moves on to the next station unless every job already done on it is perfect. The system was worked out between the plant's Japanese and U.S. managers and the UAW members on the assembly line.[28] The key to this success did not lie in technology, work force composition, specific management practices, or absence of collective bargaining. Rather the key came in the higher expectations the Japanese managers held for their workers. High expectations lead to delegation, participation and a sense of trust, all reciprocated with high performance.[29]

Conflict is common in international alliances, especially when they involve high-technology companies and human egos. NUMMI's lessons for these alliances are simple ones: 1) Involve all parties in the effort to redesign jobs; 2) be willing to listen and be receptive to new ideas; and 3) learn from each other's strengths and weaknesses.[30]

At NUMMI, production processes are dynamic, based largely on teamwork and the Toyota Production System. In addition, there are only three job classifications at NUMMI: production workers, general maintenance, and tool and die workers. This is highly unusual for a U.S. automobile assembly plant and even rarer for a unionized plant. There are no artificial lines drawn around functions. This flexibility enables teamwork to excel. There is frequent job rotation, which eliminates mind-dulling repetition and redundancy, but requires a great deal of training and cross-training. All of the NUMMI work force receive training and all associates (they're not called workers) effect process change, both internal and external. Even vendor-related processes are open for review. As staffing and sourcing decisions are made by teams, human resource managers are always trying to reinvent the job to match the performance goals of the organization.[31]

$\mathcal{S}$UMMARY

A job consists of a group of tasks that must be performed for an organization to achieve its goals. The systematic process of determining the duties and skills required for performing the organization's jobs is referred to as job analysis. Job analysis has become a focus of HRM because selection methods need to be job related.

Job analysis information is used to prepare both job descriptions and job specifications. A job description specifies the tasks, duties, responsibilities, and working conditions associated with a job. A job specification states the knowledge, skills, and abilities a person must possess in order to perform the job. In practice, the two are often combined in one document.

Job analyses may be conducted in several different ways: questionnaires, which may be mailed or administered in person, direct observation of the employee at work, interviews of the employee and supervisor, and recording in a diary or log. In recent years, attempts have been made to provide more systematic methods for conducting job analysis. These newer approaches include 1) functional job analysis (FJA), 2) the position analysis questionnaire (PAQ), 3) the management position description questionnaire (MPDQ), and 4) the occupational measurement system (OMS). Finally, the analyst may use a combination of any of these methods.

The sections most commonly used in a job description are 1) job identification, 2) date of the job analysis, 3) job summary, 4) duties performed, and 5) working conditions. In some provinces, pay equity regulations require that job descriptions contain at least four elements: knowledge and skill, effort, responsibility, and working conditions. Some of the items often included in the job specification section include requirements for education, experience, personality traits, and physical abilities.

Information gathered in job analysis may be used as the starting point for changes of various types. Reengineering involves managers in a process of rethinking and redesigning their business systems to become more competitive. Reengineering is the fundamental rethinking and radical redesign of business processes to achieve dramatic improvements in critical, contemporary measures of performance, such as cost, quality, service, and speed.

Job design is the process of determining the specific tasks to be performed, the methods used in performing these tasks, and the relationship of the job to other work in the organization. Job enrichment refers to basic changes in the content and level of responsibility of a job to provide a greater challenge for the worker. Job enlargement involves changes in the scope of a job to provide greater variety for the worker.

TERMS FOR REVIEW

Job	Management position description questionnaire (MPDQ)
Position	Occupational measurement system (OMS)
Job analysis	Reengineering
Job description	Job design
Job specification	Job enrichment
Functional job analysis (FJA)	Job enlargement
Position analysis questionnaire (PAQ)	Employee-centred work redesign

QUESTIONS FOR REVIEW

1. What is the distinction between a job and a position? Define job analysis.
2. Discuss what is meant by the statement, "Job analysis is the most basic human resource management tool."
3. Describe the traditional methods used to conduct job analysis.
4. List and briefly describe the types of data that are typically gathered when conducting job analysis.
5. What are the basic components of a job description? Briefly describe each.
6. What are the items typically included in a job specification?
7. Briefly describe a) a position analysis questionnaire (PAQ); and (b) a management position description questionnaire (MPDQ).
8. Distinguish among reengineering, job design, job enrichment, and job enlargement.

HRM INCIDENT 1

• WHO NEEDS JOB DESCRIPTIONS?

John Iannides, accounting supervisor, was clearly annoyed as he approached his boss, Gerald Jones. He began, "Gerald, this note you sent me says I have to update descriptions for all ten of the jobs in my department within the next two weeks."

"Well, what's the problem with that?" asked Gerald.

John explained, "This is a waste of time, especially since I have other deadlines. It will take at least 30 hours. We still have two weeks of work left on the internal audit reviews. You want me to push that back and work on job descriptions? No way. We haven't looked at these job descriptions in years. They'll need a great deal of revision. And as soon as they get into the hands of the employees, I'll get all kinds of flak."

"Why would you get flak for getting the job descriptions in order?" asked Gerald.

John answered, "This whole thing is a can of worms. Just calling attention to the existence of job descriptions will give some people the idea that they don't have to do things that aren't in the description. And if we write what the people in my division really do, some jobs will have to be upgraded and others downgraded, I'll bet. I just can't afford the morale problem and the confusion right now."

Gerald replied, "What do you suggest, John? I have been told just to get it done, and within two weeks."

"I don't want to do it at all," said John, "But certainly not during the audit period. Can't you just go back up the line and get it put off until next month?"

QUESTIONS

1. What have John and Gerald forgotten to do prior to the creation of job descriptions? Why is that step important?
2. Evaluate John's statement, "Just calling attention to the existence of job descriptions will give some people the idea that they don't have to do things that aren't in the description."

HRM INCIDENT 2

• A JOB WELL DONE

As Professor Allard toured the Mountjoy Tube Company plant in Magog, Quebec, he became more and more impressed with his young guide, Jim Murdoch. Jim was the assistant human resource director at Mountjoy Tube and was primarily responsible for job analysis. An industrial engineer was assigned full time to the human resource department to assist Jim in job design. Professor Allard had been retained by the human resource director to study Mountjoy Tube's job analysis system and to make recommendations for improvements. He had gone through the files of job descriptions in the human resource office with Jim and found them, in general, to be complete and directly related to the jobs performed.

One of the first stops on the tour was the office of the weld mill supervisor, a 3m by 3m room out on the factory floor with glass windows on all sides. As Jim approached, the supervisor, Roger Duchesne, was outside his office.

"Hi, Jim," he said.

"Hello, Roger," said Jim. "This is Professor Allard. Could we look at your job descriptions and chat with you for a moment?"

"Sure, Jim," said Roger, opening the door. "Come on in and have a seat and I'll get them out." From their vantage point, the men in the office could see the workers in the weld mill area. As they reviewed each job description they observed every worker actually performing the work described. Roger Duchesne was familiar with each of the jobs. He was very knowledgeable about the job descriptions themselves, having contributed to the preparation or the revisions of each one.

"How are the job descriptions related to the performance evaluations here?" asked Professor Allard.

"Well," answered Roger, "I only evaluate the workers on the items in the job descriptions, which we came up with through careful job analysis. That way, I know I have to correct the job descriptions when something changes and they get too far out of whack with the job the guys are really doing. Jim's held training sessions for all us supervisors so that we understand how all this stuff ties in together: job analysis, job descriptions, and performance evaluations. I think it's a pretty good system."

Jim and Professor Allard went on to several other areas of the plant and found similar situations. Jim seemed to have a good relationship with each of the supervisors, as well as with the plant manager and the three midlevel managers they visited. As they headed back to the front office, Professor Allard was considering the comments he would soon make to the plant manager.

QUESTIONS

1. What desirable attributes of job analysis are evident at Mountjoy Tube Company?
2. What kind of report do you think Professor Allard should present to the plant manager?
3. Describe the relationship that might exist between the industrial engineer and the assistant human resource director regarding job analysis.

DEVELOPING HRM SKILLS: AN EXPERIENTIAL EXERCISE

Developing and updating job descriptions is an integral part of the job of any human resource professional. Without properly designed job descriptions, performing some human resource management activities is extremely difficult. This exercise will permit you to gain a better appreciation of what is involved in preparing job descriptions, as job descriptions may vary even when the job analysis information is similar.

As the lone human resource specialist at Ottawa-based Shore Machine Works Ltd., you have been involved in job analysis planning for a new facility in Cambridge, Ontario. Most of the job analysis data have been gathered, and now it is time to prepare specific job descriptions. You have been given a stack of job analysis information sheets and assigned the task of writing job descriptions based on this information. When the production manager, Ed Kabadi, handed you the data sheet, he said, "I'd like you to do the first one, and then bring it to me and we'll go over it together".

The initial job description will be for the position of Spot Welder. Work Activities primarily involve welding parts together. All parts consist of thin steel pieces weighing less than two pounds. The preformed pieces to be welded together are taken from numbered bins surrounding the spot welder, placed in position on the machine, and welded. Relationship With Other Workers is fairly standard for a factory floor worker. Other machine operators running similar machines are within view, 5 to 12 m away. The crane operator moves the parts bins to this work station and away as required, placing them wherever specified by the operator. There is little time for social interaction on the job. Degree of Supervision involved is fairly standard in this industry. The spot welder supervisor supervises twelve operators, all doing essentially the same job. Operators are expected to do their jobs with very little supervision, consulting the supervisor infrequently. Records and Reports are not generated as part of this job. Skill and Dexterity Requirements are marginal. In order to meet the standard times, the worker must be able to take two parts from separate bins, place them together in the correct position and complete the part within 3.2 seconds. Working Conditions are not ideal; the work station is relatively crowded, the operator is required to wear safety goggles, ambient temperature varies from 10º C to 28º C in summer. The noise level is about 60 decibels, safe but distracting, and the lighting is excellent.

Each participant will use the Job Description Form and develop an appropriate job description. Several class members can participate. Instructors will provide the participants with any additional information necessary to complete the exercise.

PART ONE:

CASE 1 Parma Cycle Company: An Overview

Parma Cycle Company of Delta, British Columbia, is the only company that manufactures complete bicycles in Canada. Most of Parma's competitors import parts from other countries and assemble bicycles here. Even Parma finally began to import many parts, mainly from Italy, Japan, and, more recently, Korea. By the late 1980s, Parma Cycle employed about 800 workers, most of them machine operators and assemblers. The area around Delta, like most regions of Canada, suffered from layoffs in the late 1980s. But conditions steadily improved during the mid-1990s, with unemployment falling below the national average of about 9.5 percent. Per capita income in Delta was above the national average in 1995, making the region a high-cost place to produce. Although there had been temptations to move the facility to Mexico, the President had decided to stay in Canada for at least the next five years.

Bicycles are classified into eight types, including one-speed, low-priced multispeed, sport, touring and all-terrain. Parma Cycle makes only one-speed and low-priced multispeed bicycles, leaving the premium types to Schwinn, Panasonic, Peugeot, and a host of other competitors. Parma distributes bicycles under its own name through distributors to small retailers. However, most of the bicycles Parma manufactures are purchased by large national retailers and marketed under those retailers' house names. A few bicycles are exported to Europe and South America, but Parma finds it difficult to compete in the international market with Japanese and Italian manufacturers.

Parma Cycle Company, Inc., is a publicly held corporation, although 30 percent of its shares are controlled by a major recreational conglomerate corporation. There have been rumours of a takeover from time to time, but none ever materialized. Because of depressed earnings in the late 1980s, Parma's stock declined from $27 per share to $13 per share. Although interest rates fell after 1992, they increased again following the 1995 federal budget. The company found it costly, therefore, to raise funds to purchase new computerized milling machines that had been developed for bicycle manufacture. A high-performance racing cycle was planned for introduction in the late 1990s. But a research and development program aimed at cutting the cost of producing that bicycle was cancelled because of the high cost of financing.

Jesse Heard is the human resource director. He went to work at Parma Cycle in 1966. His first job was as a painter, when painting was done with a hand-held spray gun. He was later promoted to supervisor and worked in several departments at the plant. Parma encourages its supervisors to advance their education. Because the company paid for tuition fees, as well as books, Jesse had gone on to Simon Fraser University, receiving his bachelor's degree in personnel administration in 1976. Jesse was immediately promoted to a job in the human resource department and three years later became the human resource director.

In May 1994, the B.C. Human Rights Commission received a complaint about employment practices at Parma. It was alleged that while the proportion of women in the plant approached 75 percent, only eight percent of the Parma Cycle managers were female. There were only two female managers above the level of supervisor. Jesse Heard was advised of the complaint. He felt that the company was doing everything it should with regard to equal opportunity.

The company had an affirmative action program that encouraged managers to employ minority group members and women. In fact, Jesse's efforts to encourage the employment of women and minorities had provoked some managers to complain to the company president, his immediate superior.

In general, the working environment at Parma Cycle is a good one. The company has a relatively flat organizational structure with few managerial levels, as shown in Figure I-1.

Most of Parma's workers are of European descent and are accustomed to working in a factory environment. Beginning in 1988, the company conducted periodic

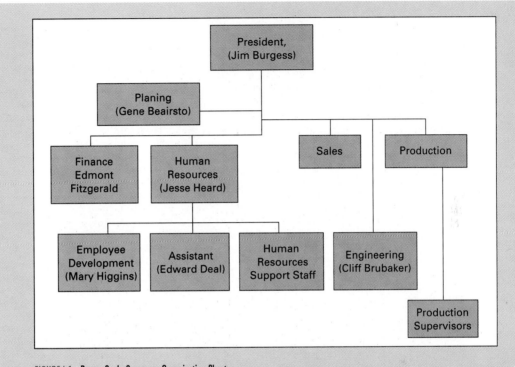

FIGURE 1-1   Parma Cycle Company: Organization Chart

management training seminars in which managers were taught to be sensitive to workers and to cooperate with one another. The management philosophy was always one of decentralized authority. Managers, like Jesse Heard, were almost completely responsible for their own operations.

As a result of an aggressive safety program, there have been no fatal accidents at Parma during the last ten years. Work-related injuries remain well below the industry average. In 1990 the ventilation system in the factory was modernized. The lighting is good and the health and safety officer once remarked that the air was cleaner inside the factory than outside.

Gene Beairsto, the corporate planner, has said that he believes the company spends too much money on employee safety and working conditions and that this is a reason for Parma's declining profits. The company's mission has not changed since 1960, when it was stated as: "To enhance the wealth of the common shareholder through efficient production and aggressive marketing of bicycles while contributing to the well-being of our workers and to the stability of the Delta-area economy."

Parma's work force is represented by the International Association of Machinists and Aerospace Workers. Employee recruitment is done primarily through referrals from current workers. Selection is based on personal interviews, evaluation of job-related application forms, and, for certain jobs, a basic skills test conducted by the supervisor. The supervisor makes the final hiring decision. Workers must join the union before the end of a three-month probationary period. Over the years, the union has negotiated a wages and benefit package that is above average for the Delta area.

The Delta factory is laid out, coincidentally, like a bicycle wheel, with component manufacturing departments representing the tire and spoke areas, and assembly being done in the centre of the factory, representing the hub. The factory work is neither especially difficult nor complicated. Technology for the bicycles Parma makes has changed very little over the years, and most of the jobs have become standardized.

Growing foreign competition, however, has necessitated an increased emphasis on productivity and a heightened concern for quality. Consequently, workers are encouraged to put forth additional effort, and production standards have been raised to the point where many employees complain of the faster work pace. The productivity improvement program was carried forward with the union's assistance. The union justified its participation on the basis of saving jobs. The last strike at Parma occurred in 1976.

QUESTIONS

1. Discuss the external environment of Parma Cycle Company and its effect on human resource management.
2. Is the internal environment at Parma Cycle a good one? Explain.

PART ONE:

CBC ☬ VIDEO CASE Revamping Workplace Communication

For some time, women have campaigned to be treated equally in the job market. Although women have made tremendous gains, mostly resulting from permanent changes in the labour market over the past 20 years, equality has never been achieved.

Consider that over a generation ago the "typical" Canadian family was comprised of a male breadwinner and a female homemaker. In 1961, almost three-quarters (70 percent) of families could be described in this manner. By 1991, however, fewer than one in five households fit the traditional model. Today, the female participation rate in the Canadian economy is almost 70 percent, up from 49 percent in 1973. In the past two decades, every country in the OECD (Organization for Economic Cooperation and Development) has seen the female participation rate in the workforce increase by an average of 2 percent per year. At the same time, the proportion of men entering the workforce has fallen, partly because younger men have stayed in school longer, whereas their older counterparts have opted for early retirement.

While women have applauded the openness with which certain companies have recruited and promoted them, other employees, chiefly men, have felt threatened by the inclusion of women within their working environment. This fear has little to do with overt discrimination, but rather with a corporate culture that for decades fostered and protected a standard hiring practice code that favoured white males who looked and dressed alike. Over decades, then, many managers fell into the psychological trap of hiring the image and the likeness of themselves, a habit that once established is difficult to break. Many managers have felt more comfortable with men, especially during tough economic times, when it is more comforting to entrust critical decisions to a known quantity: i.e., a man.

Although most men claim not to feel threatened by the influx of women into the working environment, some disturbing trends show up. Men who do not consider themselves bigots still show certain traits and characteristics that make it difficult for them to function efficiently with working women. For example, research shows that when men and women are together, women are less likely to talk. Catherine Krupnick, a Harvard University researcher conducted a 1989 study of Wheaton College two years after it became co-ed. She noticed that although men made up only 10 percent of the student body, they did 25 percent of the talking. Men, it seems, are not generally shy about promoting themselves, either, but women are. Women are also more likely than their male counterparts to reject a job transfer, ask for fair compensation, cultivate relationships, join a management club, work out deficiencies, and even take time off from the tasks at hand. Generally speaking, a woman will not go out of her way to promote herself, whereas a man will go out of his way to make himself known to the boss. These fundamental differences tend to create situations in which men are seen to discriminate against women.

By the end of the decade, there will be more women in the workforce than ever before, as low 1970s birth rates make it almost a certainty there will not be enough males to fill all the positions the economy will generate. Managers will be forced to realize that hiring women and visible minorities to fill responsible positions will be to their competitive advantage. Management will have to become more flexible, less insistent, for example, that a valued employee choose between having a child or accepting a promotion.

Change already is occurring, as more and more resources are devoted to developing female middle managers. CIBC, Ontario Hydro, Northern, Telecom and Nova Corp are but a few Canadian companies in which management is trying not only to create better working environments for their female employees, but also to foster a culture designed to appreciate and keep them. At Monsanto Chemical, keeping talented female employees became a priority after exit interviews with departing women revealed a glass ceiling that limited promotions. The culture was changed by implementing a formal diversity program and evaluating managers partly on the basis of how well they train and promote women.

The consulting firm Arthur Andersen recently hired a University of Illinois psychology professor to help implement a diversity program designed to foster a more progressive culture. The program aimed to help female employees acquire broad-based skills that would further their advancement within the company. As well, senior management needed to be convinced that both men and women were willing to accept new assignments in different departments.

Most managers are trying to build a more flexible corporate culture that will make it easier for both groups to communicate with each other, while allowing women to break through the glass ceiling. At CIBC, one of Canada's largest banks, although only

14 percent of top executives are women, more than 50 percent of middle managers are female. To protect its investment in talented women, the bank decided to change its traditional male culture.

With the help of an expert on gender issues, male CIBC employees were shown how their behaviour could leave their female counterparts out of the informal loop where some of the most important business decisions are made. For example, women complained that these decisions were often made after work when "the boys" got together for a drink. The goal at CIBC is to bridge the communication gap between male and female employees in the hope that a healthier working environment will result.

Managers who adopt equal employment practices are realizing that hiring the best and the brightest makes good business sense. In the future, no company will be competitive if serious efforts are not made to change the way managers regard their hiring practices and their employees. In organizations where there is no change, valuable brainpower will leave, perhaps sounding the death knell for the entire

work group. In many organizations the change to a more equality-based culture will not be made easily. The focus, therefore, should be to show how equality enhances profitability, as diversity programs will succeed not out of some noble belief in altruism, but rather out of corporate competitiveness. Only then can gender diversity programs succeed.

QUESTIONS

1. How would you respond to a working environment poisoned by gender incompatibilities?
2. What long-term policies would you institute to solve the problem?
3. After confronting a negative situation and correcting it, what tools would you use to make sure the new policy was actually working?
4. Do you believe that a solution to gender inequality can be found?

Video Resource: "Men/Women," *Venture* 480 (March 20, 1994).

4

Human Resources Planning

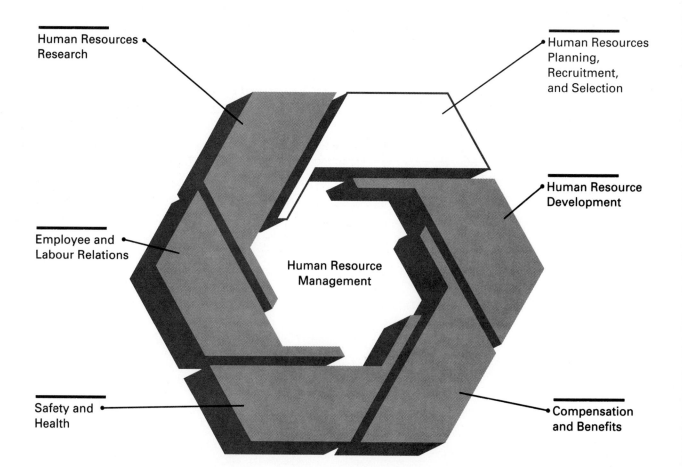

Human Resources
Research

Human Resources
Planning,
Recruitment,
and Selection

Human Resource
Development

Employee and
Labour Relations

Human Resource
Management

Safety and
Health

Compensation
and Benefits

CHAPTER OBJECTIVES

1. Explain the human resources planning process and define the basic terms used in forecasting.

2. Describe some human resource forecasting techniques and explain how human resource requirements are forecast.

3. Explain how human resource availability is forecast and state what a firm can do when a surplus of workers exists.

4. Describe the concept of downsizing.

5. Describe the importance of a human resources information system.

ark Swann, the marketing director for Sharpco Manufacturing, commented at the weekly executive directors' meeting, "I have good news. We can get the large contract with Medord Corporation. All we have to do is complete the project in one year instead of two. I told them we could do it."

Linda Crane, the vice-president of human resources, brought everyone back to reality by asserting, "As I understand it, our present work force does not have the expertise required to produce the quality that Medord's particular specifications require. Under the two-year project timetable, we planned to retrain our people gradually. With this new time schedule, we will have to go into the job market and recruit workers who are already experienced in this process. We may need to analyze this proposal further to see if that is really what we want to do. Human resource costs will rise considerably if we attempt to complete the project in one year instead of two. Sure, Mark, we can do it, but with these constraints, will the project be cost effective?"

ark has failed to take into account the importance of human resources
planning. In today's fast-paced, competitive environment, failure to
recognize the importance of human resources planning will often destroy an otherwise well designed plan.

Our overall purpose in this chapter is to explain the current role and
the nature of human resources planning. First, we define human resources
planning and describe the planning process. Then we review forecasting terminology and examine some human resource forecasting techniques. Next,
we discuss forecasting human resource requirements and availability and
examine a firm's options when it has a surplus of workers. Next, we describe
the concept of downsizing, followed by an example of effective human resources planning. We devote the final sections of the chapter to a discussion
of human resources information systems.

THE HUMAN RESOURCES PLANNING PROCESS

Human resources planning (HRP) is the process of reviewing human resource requirements systematically to ensure that the required number of
employees, with the required skills, are available when they are needed.[1]
Human resources planning is vitally important to all companies, especially
to those with overseas operations, where human resource issues present the
greatest challenge.[2]

HRP involves matching the internal and the external supply of people
with anticipated job openings over a specified period of time. There is a
growing mismatch, however, between emerging jobs and qualified people
available to fill them. The labour pool is changing as Canadian companies
try to cope with rapid technological change and with increasing economic
globalization. The quality of the labour pool is vital to the success of any
global organization. To properly develop global employees, it is imperative
that human resource managers provide individual technological training
and cross-cultural training, and help broaden employee perspectives and relationships so they can deal effectively with organizational change.[3]

As illustrated in Figure 4-1, traditionally, strategic planning—which requires consideration of both the external and the internal environments—
precedes human resources planning. **Strategic planning** is the process by
which senior management (often with input from other key employees) determines both overall purposes and objectives and how they are to be
achieved.[4] There is a growing realization among professional managers, however, that human resource managers should take part in the strategic planning process. Strategic human resources planning, then, should influence
organizational strategy.[5]

According to a recent American survey of top-level executives, the best
methods of improving quality and overall productivity are directly related to
human resource issues. As suggested in Figure 4-2, motivation, culture, and
education were rated as the best methods for increasing productivity. Employees must be adequately motivated, they must be prepared to deal with
the existing corporate culture (or the culture must be modified) and they
must be appropriately educated to cope with the challenges of their jobs.

FIGURE 4-1
The Human Resources Planning Process

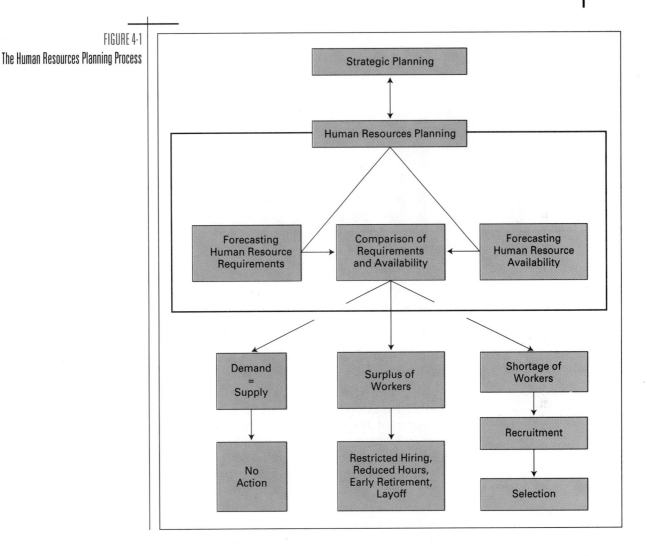

Thus, human resource issues are the key to improving quality and productivity.[6] These data further support the argument for integrating HR considerations into a firm's strategic plans.

After the organization's strategic plan has been formulated, more detailed human resources planning can begin. Strategic plans are reduced to specific quantitative and qualitative human resource plans. For example, note in Figure 4-1 that human resources planning has two components: requirements and availability. Forecasting human resource requirements involves determining the number and type of employees needed, by skill level and by location. These projections will reflect factors such as production plans and changes in productivity. To forecast availability, the human resource manager looks to both internal sources (presently employed employees) and external sources (the labour market). When employee requirements and availability have been analyzed, it can be determined whether a firm will have a surplus or a shortage of employees. Ways must be found to reduce the

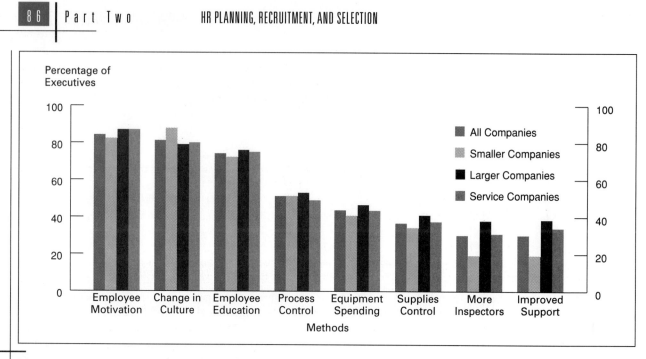

FIGURE 4-2   Effective Methods for Improving Quality and Productivity

number of employees if a surplus is projected. Some of these methods include restricted hiring, reduced hours, early retirements, and layoffs. If a shortage is forecast, the proper number and quality of workers must be recruited from outside the organization.

Because conditions in the external and the internal environments can change quickly, the human resources planning process must be continuous. Changing conditions can affect the entire organization, requiring extensive modification of forecasts. In general, planning enables managers to anticipate and to prepare for changing conditions. HRP, in particular, allows for

HRM IN ACTION

"Cynthia, what do you mean by saying that I'm going to have to justify my need for the typesetter's position? One of my 10 employees in this job just quit, and I want a replacement now. There have been 10 typesetters in my department for the 13 years that I've been here, and probably a long time before that. If we've needed them in the past, certainly we will need them in the future." This is the beginning of a conversation between Josée Guidry, a first-line supervisor with Allen Industries, and Cynthia Lee, the human resource manager.

How should Cynthia respond?

flexibility in the area of human resources management, a quality that has been much needed over the past ten years as economic factors have led to work force reductions in many organizations.

TERMINOLOGY OF FORECASTING

Four main terms are used in forecasting. First, the **long-term trend** is a projection of demand for a firm's products, typically five years or more into the future. For the hypothetical company illustrated in Figure 4-3, the long-term trend is for increased sales: Sales are expected to double during the period shown. Early recognition of such trends is crucial. A firm may not be able to fill the positions necessary to support increased sales quickly if considerable training is required. Some employees may need extensive training before they are capable of taking on new or added responsibilities. Proper estimation of long-term trends, therefore, is essential for organizational success.

Second, **cyclical variations** are reasonably predictable movements about the trend line that occur over a period of more than a year. Cyclical variations may be caused by war, elections, changes in economic conditions, consumer demand, or societal pressures. Typically, these variations last between one and five years. Anticipating cyclical demand is important because of the potential for severe peaks and valleys. Extra people may be required to meet high cyclical demand, even though a stable long-term demand has been forecast. Conversely, although the long-term forecast may be upward, conditions such as a short-term recession may require a temporary work force reduction.

Third, **seasonal variations** are reasonably predictable changes that occur over a period of a year. Seasonal variations do follow a cycle, and they may fluctuate drastically (see Figure 4-3). Most electric shavers, for example, are sold during the Christmas holiday season, whereas motor boats are bought primarily in the spring. These variations, occurring within a twelve-month period, are of most immediate concern in many firms. Planning is

FIGURE 4-3
Forecasting Terminology Example

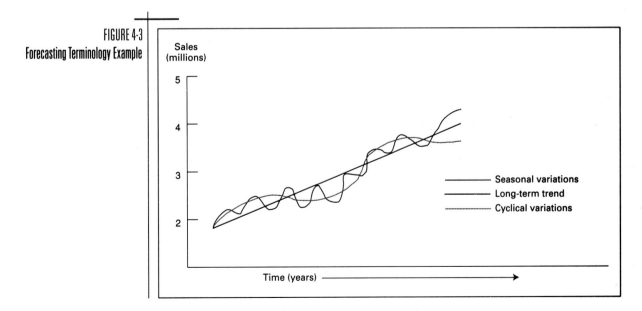

needed to maintain a stable work force, while meeting variable production and inventory requirements.

Finally, **random variations** are changes without pattern; the addition of a new tax would be an example. Even the most sophisticated forecasting techniques cannot anticipate these changes. Management, therefore, must anticipate and plan for long-term trends and cyclical and seasonal variations, and be prepared to deal with random occurrences.

HUMAN RESOURCES FORECASTING TECHNIQUES

Several techniques are currently in use for forecasting human resource requirements and availability (both qualitative and quantitative). Several of the better known methods are described in this chapter.

Zero-Base Forecasting

The **zero-base forecasting** approach uses the organization's current level of employment as the starting point for determining future staffing needs. Roughly the same procedure is used for human resources planning as for zero-base budgeting: each budget must be rejustified each year. If an employee retires, is fired, or leaves the firm for any other reason, the position is not automatically filled. Instead, an analysis is made to determine whether or not the firm can justify filling it. Equal concern is shown for creating new positions when they appear to be needed. The key to zero-base forecasting is a thorough analysis of human resource needs.

Bottom-Up Approach

The bottom-up approach to employment forecasting is based on the rationale that each unit manager is knowledgeable about employment requirements. Using the **bottom-up approach**, each successive level in the organization—starting with the lowest—forecasts its requirements, ultimately providing an aggregate HR forecast. Human resource forecasting is often most effective when managers project their human resource needs at regular intervals, comparing their current and anticipated staffing levels, so that human resource professionals have adequate lead time to explore internal and external sources.

Use of Predictor Variables

Another means of forecasting human resource requirements is to use past employment levels to predict future requirements. **Predictor variables** are factors known to have had an impact on employment levels. One of the most useful predictors of employment levels is sales volume. Often there is a direct relationship between demand and the number of employees needed. In Figure 4-4, a firm's sales volume is depicted on the horizontal axis and the number of employees required is shown on the vertical axis. In this illustration, as sales increase, so does the number of employees. Using this method, managers can approximate the number of employees required at different demand levels.

FIGURE 4-4
The Relationship of Sales Volume to
Number of Employees

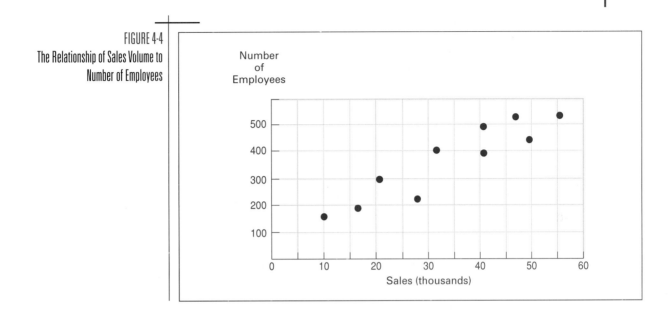

With the increased use of computers and statistical software packages, human resource managers can use **regression analysis** to predict one item (known as the dependent variable) through knowledge of other items (known as the independent variables). When there is one dependent variable and one independent variable, the process is called simple linear regression. When there is more than one independent variable, the technique is called multiple regression.

Regression is often used because of the direct relationship between demand for a firm's goods and/or services and employment levels. However, multiple regression generally produces results superior to those obtained from simple linear regression because the technique recognizes that a variety of factors may influence future employment levels. Along with sales, an analyst might also use other variables like work force productivity.

Simulation

Simulation is a technique for experimenting with a real-world situation through a mathematical model—an abstraction that represents the situation. Thus, a simulation model is an attempt to re-create a real-world situation through mathematical logic in order to predict the future. Simulation allows the human resource manager to ask many *what if* questions without having to make a decision that would have real-world consequences.

A simulation model might be developed to represent the interrelationships among employment level and many other variables. The manager could then ask *what if* questions such as:

- What would happen if we put 10 percent of the present work force on overtime?
- What would happen if the plant used two shifts? Three shifts?

This sort of exploration may permit the human resource manager to gain insight into a problem before making an actual decision.

FORECASTING HUMAN RESOURCE REQUIREMENTS

A **requirements forecast** is an estimate of the number and the kinds of employees the organization will need at various times in the future. Before human resource requirements can be projected, demand for the firm's goods or services must be forecast. This forecast is then used to calculate the number of people required to meet planned demand. For a firm that manufactures personal computers, for example, the number of units to be produced, sales calls to be made, vouchers to be processed, or a variety of other activities needs to be forecast. Manufacturing 1000 personal computers each week might require 10 000 hours of work by assemblers during a 40-hour week. Dividing the 10 000 hours by the 40 hours in the work week gives 250 assembly workers needed. Similar calculations are performed for the other jobs needed to produce and to market the product.

FORECASTING HUMAN RESOURCE AVAILABILITY

Forecasting requirements provides managers with the means of estimating how many and what types of employees will be required. But there is another side to the issue:

> A large manufacturing firm on the West Coast was preparing to begin operations in a new plant. Analysts had already determined that there was a high long-term demand for the new product. Financing was available and equipment was in place. But production did not begin for two years! Management had made a critical mistake: They had studied the demand side of human resources but not the supply side. There weren't enough qualified employees in the local labour market to operate the new plant. New workers had to receive extensive training before they could move into the newly created jobs.

Determining whether the firm will be able to secure employees with the necessary skills, and from what sources, is called an **availability forecast.** This calculation helps the human resource manager to determine whether the needed employees may be obtained from within the company, from outside the organization, or from a combination of the two sources.

Internal Sources of Supply

Many of the workers needed for future positions may already work for the firm. If the firm is small, management may know all the workers well enough to match their skills and aspirations with company needs. If, for instance, the firm is creating a new sales position, it may be common knowledge that Mary Fallego, a five-year employee with the company, has both the skills and the desire to take over the new job. This unplanned process of matching people and positions may be sufficient for smaller firms. As organizations grow, however, the matching process becomes increasingly difficult, often requiring the development of management and skills inventories.

MANAGEMENT INVENTORIES

Managerial talent is an essential resource in every organization. Thus, some firms maintain better data on managers than they do on nonmanagerial employees—although this priority is changing with the realization that everyone in the organization is important. A **management inventory** contains detailed information about each manager. It is used to identify individuals who have the potential to move into higher-level positions. As this type of inventory provides information for both replacement and promotion decisions, it would likely include data such as:

- Work history and experience
- Educational background
- Assessment of strengths and weaknesses
- Developmental needs
- Promotion potential at present and with further development
- Current job performance
- Field of specialization
- Job preferences
- Geographic preferences
- Career goals and aspirations
- Anticipated retirement date
- Personal history, including psychological assessments.

SUCCESSION PLANNING

Because of the tremendous changes confronting management in the 1990s, succession planning has become more important than ever before, as a profile must be developed that describes individuals who can lead the organization effectively, both now and in the future.[7] In a 1990 survey of over 400 boards of large North American companies, nearly three-quarters of the firms questioned had a succession plan.[8]

Figure 4-5, for example, depicts a manager in the top box with immediate subordinates in the lower boxes. The list below explains the key elements and symbols in the diagram.

1. *Position Box:* The position title and incumbent's name appear in each box. The symbol* preceding the name identifies incumbents who will retire between 1996 and 2000, indicating that short-range planning is required.

2. The symbol ** preceding the name identifies incumbents who will retire between 2001 and 2007, indicating that long-range planning is required.

3. If the word *Open* appears in the box, the position is unfilled.

4. If the word *Future* appears, the position is anticipated but does not yet exist.

5. *dev pgm:* identifies the particular development program in which the employee participates.

FIGURE 4-5
Career Planning Inventory
Organization Review Chart

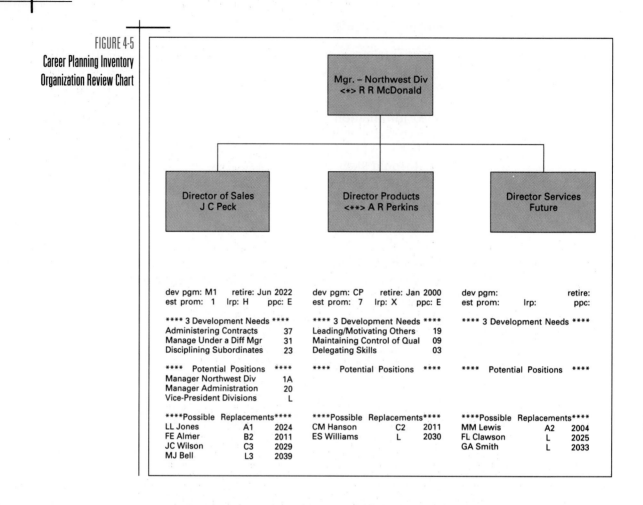

6. *retire*: the month and year of the employee's planned retirement.

7. *est prom*: indicates the employee's estimated potential for promotion.

8. *lrp*: indicates the employee's long-range career potential with the company.

9. *ppc*: indicates the incumbent's current organizational level.

10. *3 Development Needs*: describes three priority development needs that have been identified.

11. *Potential Positions*: the title of each position to which the incumbent is potentially promotable, along with codes that indicate an estimate of when the employee would be ready.

12. *Possible Replacements*: the names of up to ten possible replacements for the incumbent, with codes indicating when the replacements would be ready for promotion to this position.

An example of effective succession planning occurred recently at a company where a senior vice-president of finance retired. Following his departure, nine people moved up in the organization. At the end of the chain reaction, a young college student was hired as a financial analyst.[9]

Succession planning is important in both large and small businesses. One of the largest food processing companies in Canada—New Brunswick-based McCain Foods—was almost torn apart when two brothers (who had acted as co-presidents for many years) could not agree on who should succeed them.

Smaller businesses, too, are often family run. The difficulty of succession is "too much for many businesses: statistics show that 70 percent of family-owned companies [in Canada] never make it to the second generation, and a staggering 90 percent never see a third." With proper succession planning, however, many of these business failures might be prevented.[10]

SKILLS INVENTORIES

A skills inventory includes information on the availability and the preparedness of nonmanagerial employees to move either into higher-level positions, or laterally within the organization. Although the process and the intent of a skills inventory are similar to the management inventory, the information differs. A skills inventory contains

- background and biographical data
- work experience
- specific skills and knowledge
- licences or certifications held
- in-house training programs completed
- previous performance appraisal evaluations
- career goals.

A properly designed and updated skills inventory system permits management to identify employees with particular skills and match them to the changing needs of the company.

External Supply

Unless a firm is experiencing declining demand, some employees will have to be recruited from outside the organization. Finding and hiring new employees capable of performing immediately, however, is usually quite difficult. The best source of supply varies by industry, firm, and geographic locality. Some organizations find their best sources of potential employees are colleges and universities. Others get excellent results from vocational schools, competitors, or even unsolicited applications.

If the company has information revealing where present employees were recruited, HR professionals can develop statistics that identify the best sources. For example, a firm may discover that graduates from a particular college or university adapt well to the firm's environment and culture. Similarly, one large farm-equipment manufacturer has achieved excellent success in recruiting from regional schools located in rural areas. Managers in this firm believe that since many students come from a farming environment, they can adapt more quickly to the firm's operational methods.

Other firms may discover from past records that the majority of their more successful employees live no more than 20 miles from their place of work. This information may suggest recruiting efforts be concentrated within that particular geographic area.

Forecasting can assist not only in identifying where potential employees may be found, but also in predicting the type of individuals likely to succeed in the organization. A regional medical centre—located far from any large metropolitan area—reviewed its employment files for registered nurses. It discovered that RNs born and raised in smaller towns adapted better to the medical centre's small-town environment than those from large metropolitan areas. After studying these statistics, management modified its recruiting efforts.[11]

Similarly, managers in one large convenience store chain were disturbed by their unusually high employee turnover rate. When they analyzed their recruiting practices, they discovered that the large majority of short-term employees were "walk-ins", attracted by a sign in a store window announcing that a position was available. These individuals, often unemployed at the time, were highly transient. This source of supply virtually guaranteed a high turnover rate. Management then found new sources of supply, significantly reducing turnover.

RESPONDING TO A SURPLUS OF EMPLOYEES

When a comparison of requirements and availability indicates a worker surplus, restricted hiring, reduced hours, early retirements and layoffs may be required to correct the situation. Downsizing, one common reaction to labour surpluses, will be discussed as a separate topic.

Restricted Hiring

When a firm implements a restricted hiring policy, the work force is reduced by not replacing employees who leave. New workers are hired only when overall organizational performance might be affected. For instance, if a quality control department that consisted of four inspectors lost one to a competitor, this individual probably would not be replaced. If the firm lost all its inspectors, at least some hiring would take place to ensure continued operation.

Reduced Hours

Reaction to declining demand may also involve reducing the total number of hours worked. Instead of continuing a 40-hour week, management may decide to cut each employee's time to thirty hours. This cutback normally applies only to hourly employees because management and other professionals are usually paid a salary, not an hourly wage.

Early Retirement

The early retirement of some present employees is another way to reduce numbers. Some employees will be delighted to retire, but others will be somewhat reluctant. The latter may be willing to accept early retirement if the total retirement package is made attractive enough.

Layoffs

At times, a firm has no choice but to lay off part of its work force. A layoff is not the same as being fired, but it has the same basic effect—the worker is no longer employed. If the firm has a union, layoff procedures are usually stated clearly in the labour-management agreement. Typically, workers with the least seniority are laid off first. If the employees are not represented by a union, management may base layoffs on a combination of factors, including seniority and productivity level. When managers and other professionals are laid off, the decision is likely to be based on ability, although internal politics may also be a factor.

Downsizing

Tied very closely to layoffs is **downsizing**, also known as restructuring and rightsizing, a one-time change in the number of people employed by a firm. The trend among many companies in the 1980s and early 1990s was to cut staff and downsize.

In Canada, General Motors will have eliminated 8000 jobs by 1995; Petro-Canada and Shell Canada are closing service stations; Canadian National is eliminating 11 000 jobs; Sears Canada is reducing staff from 54 000 to 43 000; Air Canada cut 2200 jobs during 1992 and another 1200 in 1993; Moore Corporation is closing three manufacturing plants in North America as part of a 23 000-person cut in its worldwide work force.[12] These are but a few of the many Canadian firms that have downsized in recent years. The CEOs of these corporate giants and those who manage smaller corporations "are engaged in the biggest, most complex challenges of their careers. For many of them, it's an incredibly demanding juggling act; simultaneously cutting debt, boosting productivity, redefining markets and meeting fierce new competition. Almost overnight, entire product lines and sales strategies can become obsolete."[13] The common thread that runs through all this restructuring is that personnel cuts are inevitable.

Thus, one result of downsizing is that many layers are often pulled out of an organization, making it more difficult for individuals to get promoted. In addition, when one firm downsizes, sometimes others feel compelled follow if they are to be competitive. Thus, more and more individuals are finding themselves plateaued in the same job until they retire. To reinvigorate demoralized workers, some managers are providing additional training, lateral moves, short sabbaticals, and compensation based on a person's contribution rather than title.[14] In some firms, employee enthusiasm is rekindled by providing raises based on additional skill acquisition and use.

Historically, firms have downsized in difficult times and rehired when business conditions improved. Today, with firms competing globally, managers are rethinking their automatic rehiring strategies. Arvin Industries, for instance, a manufacturer of automotive components, had cut its work force by 10 percent since 1990 to just under 16 000. By 1993 the company had rebounded, with profits estimated to grow at an annual rate of 20 percent through 1995. Even with this success, though, Arvin is not rehiring but trying to trim staff still further. According to Arvin's human resources director, "To remain globally competitive, we must continue to streamline operations and keep a tight rein on labour costs."[15]

Although there have been undoubted successes, Canadian experiences with downsizing appear to be mixed. A 1994 survey by Wyatt Co. of Montreal, which included 148 companies from across Canada, reported that after downsizing and restructuring:, only 1.61 percent reached their cost reduction goal; only 2.37 percent reported increased profitability, 3.17 percent increased competitive advantage, and 4.27 percent improved customer satisfaction. At the same time, 45 percent of companies did not eliminate any of the work that would have to be done by the remaining employees, and 52 percent did not increase automation. As a result, 70 percent of the respondents felt restructuring had an adverse effect on workloads and 59 percent reported morale problems. (It probably did not help that in 81 percent of the cases, employees were told about the restructuring through a letter from upper management, rather than through direct and ongoing communication.) In 5.51 percent of cases, the companies had to refill some of the vacant positions.

The survey also showed that it takes at least six months for the remaining staff to recover.[16] The survivors of downsizing, then, need help too. The *survivor syndrome* is characterized by "decreased motivation, morale and loyalty to the organization, and increased stress levels and scepticism among remaining employees."[17] Indeed, managers will still face high personnel costs if they ignore the needs of survivors. HRM professionals, therefore, need to establish employee assistance programs, while working to change the culture to help regain lost trust.[18]

HUMAN RESOURCES PLANNING: AN EXAMPLE

The human resources planning model presented in Figure 4-1 is a generalized one. Each firm must tailor human resources planning to fit specific needs. Figure 4-6 shows the human resources planning process for Honeywell, Inc. We discuss each element of the plan in the following sections.

Organizational Goals

To be relevant, a human resources planning process should be closely tied to the organization's strategic goals. The plan must be based on information from sales forecasts, market trend analyses, predictions about technological advances, and planned changes in processes and productivity. Considerable effort should be devoted to securing reliable forecasts of business trends and needs—especially in terms of quantity and quality of labour—as these data are the basic inputs into human resources planning.

Human Resources Needs Forecast

The second element in the planning process is forecasting human resource needs based on business strategies, production plans, and the various indicators of change in technology and operating methods. Forecasting is usually done by using historical data and ratios (such as indirect:direct labour) and adjusting them for productivity trends. The result is a spreadsheet containing the desired number, mix, cost, new skills, and job categories of employees, as

FIGURE 4-6
Elements of a Human Resource Plan

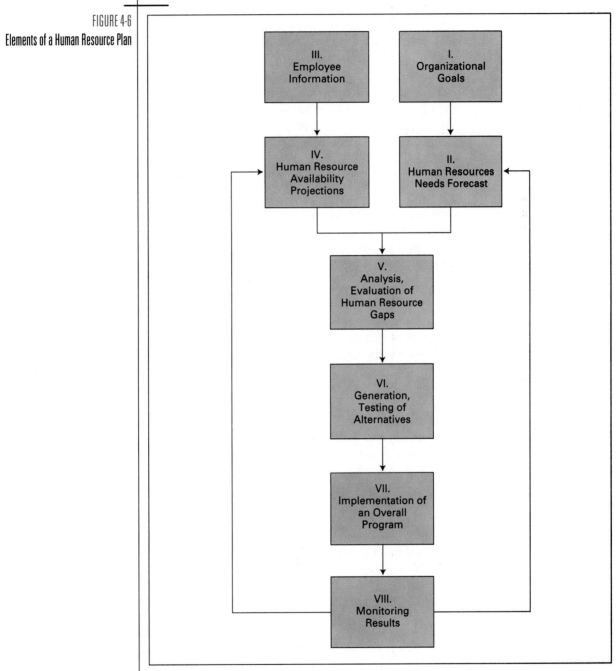

Source: Used with the permission of Honeywell, Inc.

well as the number and levels of managers needed to accomplish the organization's goals. Experience has shown that producing this forecast is the most challenging part of the planning process because it requires creative and highly participative approaches to dealing with business and technical uncertainties projecting several years into the future.

Employee Information

A third element is the maintenance of accurate information on the composition, assignments, and capabilities of the current work force. This information includes job classifications, age, sex, organization level, rate of pay, and job functions. Employee information may also include résumé data, such as skills, education, training received, and career interests. Much of the needed data can be found in existing data systems (such as payroll, performance review, or professional development).

Human Resource Availability Projections

The fourth part of the planning process is estimating which current employees might be available in the future. By projecting past data about the size, organization, and composition of the work force and about turnover, aging, and hiring, employee availability at a specific future date can be estimated. The result is a picture of the organization's current human resource pool and how it can be expected to evolve over time.

Analyzing and Evaluating Human Resource Gaps

The fifth task in planning is comparing what is needed with what is available in terms of numbers, mix, skills, and technologies. This comparison permits the human resource manager to isolate gaps and surpluses, while evaluating where the most serious mismatches are likely to be. This type of analysis should help management answer key questions such as the following.

- Are imbalances developing between projected human resource requirements and availability?
- What is the effect of current productivity trends and pay rates on work force levels and costs?
- Do turnover problems exist in certain jobs or age levels?
- Are there problems of career blockage and obsolescence?
- Are there sufficient high-potential managers to fulfil future needs?
- Is there a shortage of any critical skills?

This analysis permits the development of long-range plans for recruiting, hiring, training, transferring, and retraining appropriate numbers and types of employees.

Generating and Testing Alternatives

The analysis of human resources should reveal the strengths and the weaknesses in the organization's policies and practices, including staffing plans, promotion practices and policies, organization design, training and development programs, salary planning, and career management. This phase of the planning process explores the implications of the analysis and generates alternatives to current practices and policies. Some of the more comprehensive human resources planning systems use modelling to simulate potential skill profiles and organization structures that would result from specific changes in employment strategies or policies. Computer modelling is usually used to project the consequences of complex alternatives. Manual systems, however, can be equally useful in many circumstances.

Implementing an Overall Human Resource Program

After considering alternatives, management decides on an overall plan to meet the organization's human resource needs. This plan must then be translated into practical programs with specific plans, target dates, schedules, and resource commitments. The overall human resources plan should shape an organization's staffing plan, human resource development activities, mobility plans, productivity programs, bargaining strategies, and compensation programs.

Monitoring Results

The final element in any human resources planning process is to provide a means for management to monitor the overall program. This step should address questions such as the following:

- How well is the plan working?
- Is it cost effective?
- What is the actual effect of the plan on the work force (as compared to the predicted plan)?
- Where are the plan's weaknesses?
- What changes will be needed during the next planning cycle?

HUMAN RESOURCES INFORMATION SYSTEMS

A **human resources information system (HRIS)** is any organized approach to obtaining relevant and timely information on which to base decisions concerning the human resource. An effective HRIS is crucial to sound human resource decision making.

Typically, HR professionals use computers and other sophisticated technologies to process data that reflect the day-to-day operations of a company, organized in a format that facilitates decision making. An HRIS should be designed to provide information that is

- *Timely*—A manager needs up-to-date information;
- Accurate—A manager must be able to rely on the information;
- *Concise*—A manager can absorb only so much information at a time;
- *Relevant*—A manager should receive only the information needed in a particular situation; and
- Complete.

The absence of even one of these characteristics makes the decision-making process less effective. An HRIS generates several important types of data.

ROUTINE REPORTS

Business data that are summarized regularly are referred to as routine reports. Weekly and monthly employment status reports may be sent to supervisors and middle managers, whereas quarterly reports may be forwarded only to senior management.

EXCEPTION REPORTS

Exception reports highlight variations in operations serious enough to require management's attention. One type is the quality-exception report, completed when the number of product defects exceeds a predetermined maximum. The human resource manager may use this information to identify training needs.

ON-DEMAND REPORTS

An on-demand report, as the name suggests, provides information in response to a specific request. For example, a human resource manager might want to know the number of engineers with five years' work experience who speak fluent French.[19]

FORECASTS

As discussed previously, forecasting applies predictive models to specific situations. Managers need forecasts of the number and types of employees required to satisfy projected demand for the firm's product or service.

Creating the HRIS

No HRIS will lead to a smoothly functioning system unless it is backed up by a major commitment from senior executives. That said, there are four steps in system design that will provide the types of report needed while being timely, accurate, concise, relevant, and complete. These steps may overlap considerably.

STEP 1: STUDY THE PRESENT SYSTEM

In assessing the existing information system, three questions need to be answered:

1. What is the present flow of information?
2. How is the information used?
3. How valuable is this information to decision making?[20]

A prime example of a flawed system was encountered by a consultant appointed to develop a human resources information system for a national forest products firm. In studying the firm's existing system, he was amazed to discover a large amount of duplication and wasted effort. Some weekly reports were inappropriate for decision making; to prepare another, two employees had to work a total of eight hours. If this report was late, the vice-president's secretary would send a strongly worded reprimand to the delinquent division chief. When the information arrived at headquarters, however, it was neatly filed and never used. When the consultant questioned this practice, it was finally revealed that this information had been asked for about five years ago—as a one-time report. Preparation of the report had continued through the administrations of three vice-presidents, because no one thought to stop it.

STEP 2: DEVELOP A PRIORITY FOR INFORMATION AND A CONCEPTUAL DESIGN

Once the current system is thoroughly understood, it is used to develop a prioritized information listing. Which data are critical to the manager's decision making and which are merely nice to have? The HRIS design must ensure provision of high-priority information; data lower on the priority list should be generated only if their benefits exceed the cost of producing them. For example, the weekly report just described should not have had the priority it was accorded.

Individual managers should first develop their own priority lists, which should then be integrated into a single list for the entire organization. Some departments may find that their "top priority" information comes far down on the list; the needs of the organization as a whole must come first.

STEP 3: DEVELOP THE NEW INFORMATION SYSTEM

Once the information needs are determined, a conceptual design of the human resources information system is developed. Information judged not worth the cost of collection should be excluded. Then, a system of high priority reports should be developed and diagrammed. At this stage the entire organization is treated as a unit to eliminate duplication of information.

STEP 4: IMPLEMENT THE HRIS

Once the formal model is finalized, the new human resources information system must become operational. Space is allocated, computer equipment is selected, and all the structural details are worked out. This process usually involves purchasing or developing software; the choice of human resource software is almost always the responsibility of the human resource department.[21] Training in the software and in the system as a whole must be planned and implemented. Then the organization's data can be entered into the system.

Once all these steps are completed and the final checks are made, the human resources information system can begin to function. The HRIS must be maintained continuously and enhanced as needed to keep the system effective.[22]

AN ILLUSTRATIVE HRIS

Historically, the accounting information system was the first to be established in a firm, and the human resource information system was often the last. Managers now realize that a properly developed HRIS can provide tremendous benefits to the organization.

Figure 4-7 presents an overview of a human resources information system designed for one organization. Tying together data from many sources, the system makes available many types of output data that have far-reaching human resources planning and operational value.

When a system is properly designed, information needed in the firm's human resource decision-making process is readily available. For example, many firms are now studying historical trends to determine the best means of securing qualified applicants. In addition, complying with statutes and government regulations would be extremely difficult were it not for the modern HRIS. As the human component of the firm gains greater importance, use of the HRIS is likely to expand.

Companies are now developing decision support systems that allow users to interact directly with a computer to get information. A decision support system lets managers call up a menu of sophisticated database systems capable of retrieving, displaying, and processing information. Graphics, simulation, modelling and quantitative analysis are typically available.[23]

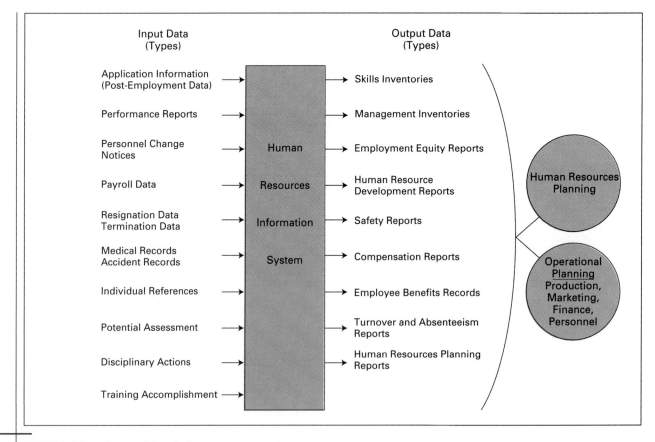

FIGURE 4-7   A Human Resources Information System

One firm that has pioneered the development of human resources information systems is Information Science Incorporated (INSci). Founded in 1965, InSci was the first company to engage in the commercial development of computer-based human resource information systems. InSci's comprehensive concept of human resource management consists of human resource, payroll, pension, health claim, flexible compensation, and decision support systems. All this information is provided in a format that can be used for planning.

A GLOBAL PERSPECTIVE

Because of the complexity of managing a global labour force, developing an effective human resources information system is crucial to organizations with global ambitions. Effective information is one of the factors that determine how well a human resource professional can globalize his or her function.

Human resource professionals in each overseas location must be experts on local laws, customs, and salary structures. It is essential, therefore, that they have high quality information. At present, few companies with global operations have the essential information they need when they need it. The sophisticated new interactive decision support systems may help overcome this gap. For example, Dow's chemical group has established a goal of linking human resource managers at locations around the world electronically through a PC-based network, thereby providing greater access to international personnel records and other data. Presently, however, local laws and restrictions make establishing an effective international HRIS very complicated.[24]

Another company that values information highly is 7-Eleven Japan. According to Richard Rawlinson, managing director of the Tokyo office of Consultant Monitor Company. "No other retailer in the world has defined its business so tightly around information. At the heart of the information system is a custom made NEC personal computer in each store. The system tracks the buying habits of customers by sex and approximate age. The system is extremely easy to use with easy to follow graphics and coded keys. By adding a very powerful Hewlett-Packard system, 7-Eleven Japan can effectively staff stores, help manufacturers develop new products, and allow headquarters to monitor individual store and aggregate sales. The system is a model for what a global information system should be; it is timely, accurate, useful, and easy to use.[25]

Sharing information from a centralized database, then, is essential for maximizing the effectiveness of human resource professionals who must find good employees. As Frank Hasenfratz (CEO of Guelph, Ontario's Linamar Corporation) has suggested, one key to success in international business is to pick the right senior executives, and to treat them well. "Honest, hardworking managers will surround themselves with the same type of people."[26] Centralized databases make it feasible to keep track of individuals with cross-cultural management skills and to use them more efficiently.

Summary

Human resources planning (HRP) is the process of systematically reviewing human resource requirements to ensure that the required number of employees, with the required skills, are available when they are needed. Strategic planning is the determination of overall organizational purposes and goals and how they are to be achieved. Strategic plans affect every major department and activity, including human resources management.

Human resources planning has two components: requirements and availability. Forecasting human resource requirements involves determining the number and the type of employees needed, by skill level and location. In forecasting the availability of human resources, managers look to both internal sources (the present employees) and external sources (the labour market).

After requirements and availability have been analyzed, management can forecast whether there will likely be a surplus or shortage of employees in the future. If a surplus of workers is projected, ways must be found to reduce the number of employees. These methods include restricted hiring, reduced hours, early retirements, and layoffs. If layoffs are unavoidable, the company should try to support the remaining workers to alleviate the diminished morale that commonly occurs. If a shortage is forecast, the firm must look outside the organization to recruit and to select the proper quantity and quality of workers. Downsizing, also known as restructuring or "rightsizing," describes a one-time change in the organization and the number of people who are employed.

Four basic terms are used in forecasting. First, the long-term trend represents the expected demand for a firm's goods or services, typically five years or more into the future. Second, cyclical variation is a reasonably predictable movement about the trend line that occurs over a period of more than a year. Third, seasonal variations are reasonably predictable changes that occur over a period of a year. Finally, random variations are changes for which there are no patterns.

Several techniques of forecasting human resource requirements and availability are currently used by human resource professionals. The zero-base forecasting approach uses the organization's current level of employment as the starting point for determining future staffing needs. The bottom-up approach is a forecasting method that progresses upward from lower organizational units to provide an aggregate forecast of employment needs for the organization. Another method is to use past employment levels as a predictor of future requirements. Regression analysis is used to predict one item (the dependent variable) through knowledge of other items (the independent variables). Simulation is a technique for testing alternatives that uses a mathematical model to represent a real-world situation.

A management inventory contains information about each manager for use in identifying individuals with the potential to move into higher level positions or to be transferred. A skills inventory is information maintained on the availability and readiness of non-managerial employees to move into higher level or lateral positions.

A human resources information system (HRIS) is any organized approach to obtaining relevant and timely information on which to base human resource management decisions. An HRIS produces reports and other data to facilitate the decision making process.

TERMS FOR REVIEW

Human resources planning (HRP)
Strategic planning
Long-term trend
Cyclical variations
Seasonal variations
Random variations
Zero-base forecasting
Bottom-up approach
Predictor variables

Regression analysis
Simulation
Requirements forecast
Availability forecast
Management inventory
Skills inventory
Downsizing
Human resources information system (HRIS)

QUESTIONS FOR REVIEW

1. Describe the human resources planning process.
2. Identify and define the basic terms used in demand forecasting.
3. Identify and briefly describe the methods used to forecast human resource needs.
4. Distinguish between forecasting human resource requirements and availability. Use definitions and examples.
5. What actions could a firm take if it had a worker surplus?
6. Distinguish between a management inventory and a skills inventory. What are the essential components of each?
7. Define and describe the purpose of downsizing.
8. What is the purpose of a human resources information system? What are the basic steps to developing an HRIS?

HRM INCIDENT 1

• A DEGREE FOR METER READERS?

Judy Feinstein was the HR recruiter for SaskGas Electric Company, a small supplier of natural gas and electricity for Moose Jaw, Saskatchewan, and the surrounding area. The company had grown rapidly during the first half of the 1980s, and this growth was expected to continue into the 1990s. In January 1989, SaskGas purchased the utilities system serving neighbouring Mitchell County. The expansion concerned Judy. The company workforce had increased by 30 percent the previous year and Judy had found it a struggle to recruit enough qualified job applicants. She knew that new expansion would intensify the problem.

Meter readers were of particular concern. The tasks required in meter reading are relatively simple. A person drives to homes served by the company, finds the gas or electric meter, and records its current reading. If the meter has been tampered with, it is reported. Otherwise no decision making of any consequence is associated with the job. The reader performs no calculations.

The pay was $8.00 per hour, high for unskilled work in the area. Even so, Judy had been having considerable difficulty keeping the 37 meter reader positions filled.

Judy was thinking about how to attract more job applicants when she received a call from the human resource director, Sam McCord. "Judy," Sam said, "I'm unhappy with the job specification calling for only a high school education for meter readers. In planning for the future we need better educated people in the company. I've decided to change the education requirement for the meter reader job from a high school diploma to a university degree."

"But, Mr. McCord," protested Judy, "the company is growing rapidly. If we are to have enough people to fill those jobs we just can't insist on finding university applicants to perform such basic tasks. I don't see how we can meet our future needs for this job with such an unrealistic job qualification."

Sam terminated the conversation abruptly by saying, "No, I don't agree.

We need to upgrade all the people in our organization. This is just part of a general effort to do that. Anyway, I cleared this with the president before I decided to do it."

QUESTIONS

1. Should there be a minimum education requirement for the meter reader job? Discuss.
2. What is your opinion of Sam's effort to upgrade the people in the organization?
3. What legal ramifications, if any, should Sam have considered? Does the company have the right to change this hiring policy?

HRM INCIDENT 2

• A BUSY DAY

Dave Johnson, human resource manager for Eagle Aircraft, had just returned from a brief vacation in Cozumel, Mexico. Eagle produces small commercial aircraft and its work force in 1995 totaled 236. Dave's friend Carl Edwards, vice-president for marketing, stopped by to ask Dave to lunch, as he often did. In the course of their conversation Carl asked Dave's opinion on the president's announcement concerning expansion.

"What announcement?" was Dave's response.

Carl explained that there had been a special meeting of the executive council to announce a major expansion, involving a new plant to be built nearby. He continued, "Everyone at the meeting seemed to be completely behind the president. Joe diNardo, the controller, stressed our independent financial position; the production manager had written a complete report on the equipment we are going to need, including avail-

ability and cost information. And I have been pushing for this expansion for some time. So I was ready. I think it will be good for you too, Dave. The president said he expects employment to double in the next year."

As Carl left, Rex Schearer, a production supervisor, arrived. "Dave," said Rex, "the production manager jumped on me Friday because maintenance doesn't have anybody qualified to work on the new digital lathe they are installing."

"He's right," Dave replied. "Maintenance sent me a requisition last week. We'd better get moving and see if we can find someone." Dave knew that it was going to be another busy Monday.

QUESTIONS

1. What, if anything, should Dave do about the expansion? Explain.
2. Discuss any additional problems uncovered by the case and discuss what should be done to solve them.

DEVELOPING HRM SKILLS: AN EXPERIENTIAL EXERCISE

This exercise is designed to give participants experience in dealing with some aspects of planning that a typical human resource manager faces. Students will also be exposed to some of the activities that human resource managers confront on a daily basis. The old axiom, *plan your work and work your plan*, will probably have new meaning after this exercise.

You are the human resource manager at a large canning plant. Your plant produces several lines of canned food products that are shipped to wholesale distributors nationwide. You are responsible for the human resource activities at the plant.

It is Monday morning, August 30. You have just returned from a week-long corporate executives' meeting at the home office. The meeting was attended by all human resource managers from every one of the company's plants. You returned with notes from the meeting and other materials you were given concerning the company's goals and plans for the next six months. When you arrive at your office (an hour early), you find your *in basket* full of notes, messages, and other correspondence.

The material provided to participants represents your notes and information from the meeting,

plus what was in your *in basket*. You must go through these and be prepared for the meeting the plant manager has scheduled for 8:00 a.m. It is now 7:30 a.m. Remember, you need to deal with some items immediately, some later today, and some tomorrow or later in the week. You will need to sort, prioritize, and set up your plan of activities. Participants will sort the material and information according to some priority in order to sequence handling issues properly. After sorting, participants can address each item concerning the action they plan to take. The participants will do the following on each item:

1. Note when it is to be handled.
2. Note who is to handle it, if not themselves.
3. Note what is to be done or who is to be informed.
4. If a meeting is to be called, set up an agenda.
5. If a memo or notice is to be sent out, write it.

Instructors will provide the participants with additional information necessary to participate.

CHAPTER 5

Recruitment

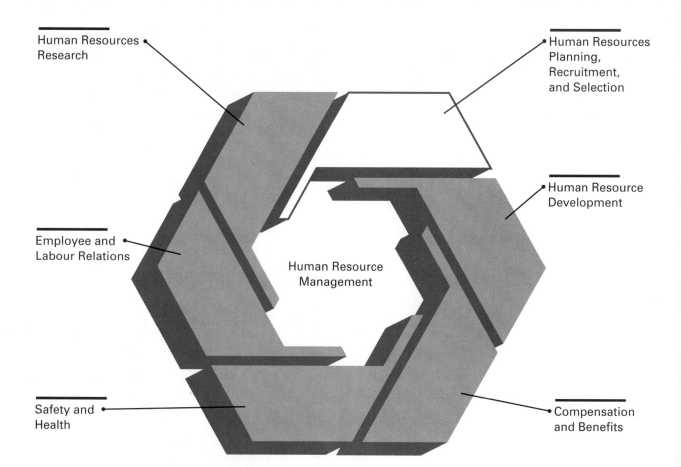

Human Resources
Research

Human Resources
Planning,
Recruitment,
and Selection

Human Resource
Development

Employee and
Labour Relations

Human Resource
Management

Safety and
Health

Compensation
and Benefits

1. Describe the recruitment process and identify actions that might be considered before resorting to outside recruitment.

2. Describe the external and the internal factors that can influence the recruitment process and explain internal recruitment methods.

3. Identify the various sources and methods available for external recruiting.

4. State what should be done to ensure that recruitment efforts meet legal requirements.

orothy Bryant, the owner of a small company involved in the development of multimedia training systems, had obtained a large contract that necessitated the recruitment of two software design engineers. After considering various recruitment alternatives, Dorothy placed the following ad in a local newspaper with a circulation in excess of 100 000:

EMPLOYMENT OPPORTUNITY
FOR SOFTWARE DESIGN ENGINEERS

2 positions available for software design engineers desiring career in growth industry.

Prefer recent university graduates with good appearance.

Apply Today! Send your résumé, in confidence, to: D.A. Bryant
X-Sell Software Development Ltd.,
P.O. Box 1515
Fredericton, N.B. E3B 5X6

More than 300 applications were received in the first week, and Dorothy was elated. However, when she reviewed the applicants, it appeared that few people possessed the desired qualifications for the job. To make matters worse, she received a call from the Human Rights Commission. It appeared that several potential applicants had complained about the way the ad was written.

orothy learned, the hard way, the importance of proper recruiting practices. Obviously she had failed to include specific job requirements in her newspaper advertisement and the wording was suspect. As a result, an excessive number of unqualified people applied. Also, there was a potential legal problem because Dorothy used a subjective criterion, *good appearance*, which was not job related. In addition, stating a preference for a *recent university graduate* may also have been ill-advised because of the age implication. Adding further to Dorothy's problem is the potential liability her advertisement created for the firm by implying a *career* for employees. Her corporate attorney will probably advise her to avoid any semblance of creating an implied contract for a candidate who is hired. The individual may later be discharged and then sue the company for wrongful dismissal. Dorothy found that preparing an effective, legally sound, recruitment advertisement isn't as simple as it once was.

Tapping appropriate sources of applicants and using suitable recruitment methods are essential to maximize recruiting efficiency and effectiveness. We begin this chapter by describing the recruitment process and the alternatives to recruitment. Next, we describe the external and the internal environments for recruitment. Then we present methods used in external and internal recruitment and how they should be tailored to the sources. The final portion of the chapter explains the effects of legislation on recruiting efforts.

THE RECRUITMENT PROCESS

Recruitment is the process of "informing, searching for and attracting applicants with the necessary abilities, attitudes and motivation, in order to offset shortages identified in human resource planning."[1] The applicants with qualifications most closely related to job specifications may then be selected.

How many times have we heard chief executive officers state, "Our most important assets are human?" While this statement has probably always been true, an increasing number of managers are beginning to believe it. Hiring the best people available has never been more critical than today. And hiring decisions can be no better than the alternatives generated through professionally-managed recruitment activities.

In most medium-sized and large organizations, the human resource department is responsible for the recruitment process. In small firms like Dorothy's, recruitment is usually handled by individual managers. Regardless of who is responsible, bringing people into the organization is an essential function in every firm.

As illustrated in Figure 5-1, when human resources planning indicates a need for employees,[2] alternative ways to meet this demand may be evaluated. Frequently, recruitment begins when a manager initiates an **employee requisition**, a document that specifies job title, department, the date the employee is needed for work, and other details (see Figure 5-2). With this information, the human resource manager can refer to the appropriate job description to determine what qualifications are needed. At times, firms continue to recruit even when they have no vacancies. This practice permits them to maintain recruitment contacts and to identify exceptional candidates for future employment.

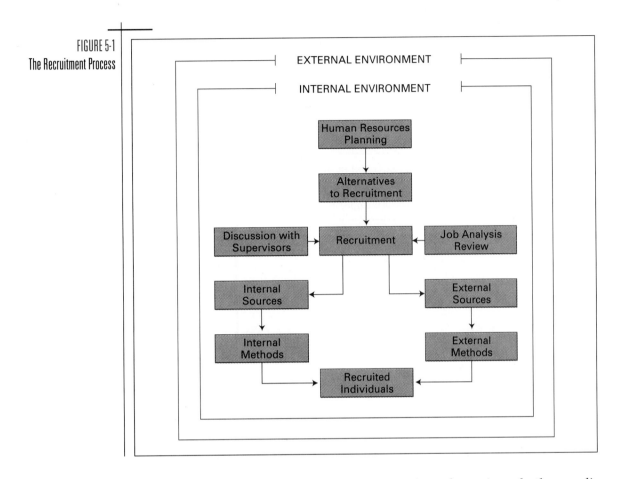

FIGURE 5-1
The Recruitment Process

The next step in the recruitment process is to determine whether qualified employees are available within the firm (the internal source) or whether they must be recruited from external sources, like colleges, universities, or other organizations.

Since recruiting is expensive, both in domestic and in international business, it is important to use effective sources and methods: that is, those that will find the best qualified employees at the lowest cost. Progressive human resource managers keep records of recruitment, selection, development, deployment, and retention costs so they can judge which types of HR activities are most cost effective in relation to results.[3]

Recruitment sources are where qualified individuals can be found. **Recruitment methods** are the specific means by which potential employees can be attracted to the firm. When the sources have been identified, appropriate methods for either internal or external recruitment are used to accomplish recruitment objectives.

Companies may discover that some recruitment sources and methods are superior to others for locating and attracting potential executive talent. One large equipment manufacturer determined that medium-sized universities located in rural areas were good sources of potential. Other firms may arrive at different conclusions; it is vital that sources and methods be tailored to the organization's needs.

FIGURE 5-2
An Employee Requisition

JOB NUMBER	JOB TITLE	DATE OF JOB VACANCY	DATE REPLACEMENT NEEDED
PLEASE CHECK	☐ Permanent	☐ Temporary	☐ Part-Time
	☐ Salary	☐ Hourly Wage	Job Class

REASON FOR REQUEST: What management or employee action(s) caused the opening?	
BRIEF DESCRIPTION OF MINIMUM QUALIFICATIONS FOR THE JOB CANDIDATES:	
BRIEF DESCRIPTION OF JOB DUTIES	

LOCATION NAME	
DATE	MANAGER'S SIGNATURE

ALTERNATIVES TO RECRUITMENT

Even when human resources planning indicates a need for additional or replacement employees, management may decide against immediate recruitment. Recruitment and selection costs are still high, although they have declined somewhat because of Canada's high unemployment rates. Often included in the calculation are costs of the search process, interviewing, agency fee payment, relocation, and administration or processing. Although selection decisions are not irreversible, once employees are hired, they may be difficult to remove, even if their performance is marginal. Therefore, a firm should consider its alternatives carefully before recruiting. Alternatives to recruitment commonly include overtime, subcontracting, and contingent workers.

Overtime

Perhaps the most commonly used method of meeting short-term fluctuations in work volume is through overtime. Overtime may help both the employer and the employee. The employer benefits by avoiding recruitment, selection, and training costs, while the employee makes additional money.

Along with these advantage, there are potential problems. Many managers believe that when they work employees for unusually long periods of time, the company pays more and receives less in return. Employees may become fatigued, lacking the energy to perform at a normal rate, especially when excessive overtime is required. As well, employees may, consciously or unconsciously, pace themselves so that overtime will be necessary. They may also become accustomed to the added income, increasing their standard of living to the level permitted by this additional money. Then, if overtime is no longer required and their paycheque shrinks, they become disgruntled.

Overtime practices vary greatly across Canada. Statistics Canada has reported that more than 11 million hours of overtime were worked in 1993, some of it paid and some unpaid. As of February 1993, 10 percent of workers covered by major collective agreements of 500 workers or more had the absolute right to refuse overtime, and another 24 percent had the right to decline in certain circumstances. Much of the overtime is done without pay by white-collar workers who are trying to compensate for staff cutbacks in service industries, with some even involving workers who are technically eligible for overtime payment, but are discouraged from claiming it for budgetary reasons.[4] HR managers need to study overtime patterns and the reasons employees are working overtime. Although in some cases, overtime is welcomed (the Canadian Auto Workers Union has found that workers want all the overtime they can get), in other situations excessive work hours should be curtailed.[5]

Subcontracting

Even when a long-term increase in demand for a firm's goods or services is anticipated, management may still decide against further hiring. Rather, the firm may choose to subcontract the work to another organization, an approach with special appeal when the subcontractor has greater expertise in producing certain goods or services. This arrangement often benefits both parties and takes advantage of the many skills available among the self-employed, the fastest growing employment sector in Canada.[6]

Contingent Workers

As described in Chapter 2, contingent workers, also known as part-timers, temporaries, and independent contractors, make up a fast-growing segment of our economy. Many of these contingent workers are women. Nearly 60 percent of the total growth in employment in 1993 consisted of part-time work and almost three-quarters of the 85 000 workers involved were adults rather than youths). In fact, female part-time employment increased steadily during 1993 to slightly over 1 million. Unfortunately, the proportion of these women who were working part time involuntarily (because of lack of full-time work) rose from 33 to 37 percent.[7]

What accounts for the rapid growth in part-time jobs? The total cost of a permanent employee is generally estimated at 30 to 40 percent above gross pay. This amount does not include, among other things, the costs of recruitment. To avoid some of these costs and to maintain flexibility as workloads vary, many organizations use part-time or temporary employees.

RECRUITMENT AND THE EXTERNAL ENVIRONMENT

As with the other human resource functions, factors external to the organization can significantly affect the firm's recruitment activities. Of particular importance is the demand and supply of specific skills. If demand for a particular skill is high relative to supply, for example, an extraordinary recruiting effort may be required.

When the unemployment rate in an organization's labour market is high, the firm's recruitment process may be simplified, as the number of unsolicited applicants is usually greater and the increased size of the labour pool provides a better opportunity for attracting qualified applicants. Conversely, as the unemployment rate drops, recruitment efforts must be increased and new sources explored.

Local labour market conditions are of primary importance in recruitment for most nonmanagerial, many supervisory, and even some middle-management positions. Filling top executive and professional positions however, often involves national or even international recruiting. For example, when the board of McCain Foods the New Brunswick frozen-food processing giant wished to appoint a new chief executive officer, they chose an experienced executive from Britain.[8] That a foreigner was chosen is not surprising, as McCain's products are sold around the globe. The CEO of Air Canada is an American, chosen after an extensive search failed to find any high profile Canadian who wanted the job.[9]

Although the recruiter's day-to-day activities provide a feel for the labour market, accurate employment data—found in professional journals and Statistics Canada reports—is essential. Legal considerations also play a significant role in recruitment practices. Nondiscriminatory practices at this stage of first contact are essential. We discuss this topic in more detail later in this chapter.

The firm's corporate image can be a valuable recruiting tool. If present employees believe their employer deals with them fairly, the word-of-mouth support they pass on is of great value in establishing credibility with prospective employees. A reputation as a good place to work can result in more and better qualified applicants, who are more enthusiastic about job offers.

THE INTERNAL ENVIRONMENT OF RECRUITMENT

Although the labour market and the government exert powerful external influences, the organization's own practices and policies also affect recruitment. Increasingly, managers who want to recruit and retain talented employees will have to create supportive internal environments, in which people can feel committed to their work, and can contribute to their full potential. Many managers believe that a good working environment is the best route to long-term global success.[10]

Human Resources Planning

Human resource planning is usually necessary to attract enough qualified prospective employees. Only after examining alternative sources of recruits and determining the most productive methods to approach them can the human resource manager make appropriate recruitment plans.

Promotion Policies

An organization's promotion policy can also affect recruitment. An organization can develop either a policy of promotion from within or a policy of filling positions from outside the organization. Depending on the circumstances, both approaches may have merit.

Promotion from within (PFW) is the policy of filling vacancies above entry-level positions with current employees. When promotion from within is emphasized, workers have an incentive to strive for advancement. Seeing co-workers being promoted makes employees more aware of their own opportunities and often improves morale.

Another advantage of internal recruitment is that managers are usually aware of their employees' capabilities. Although job performance alone may not be a reliable criterion for promotion, most employees' personal and job-related qualities will be known. Employees have a reputation, as opposed to being an *unknown quantity*.

Other benefits include a higher return on past investment in the individual, and a senior employee who starts off with knowledge of the firm, its policies, and its people.

Yet is unlikely that management could or would adhere rigidly to a practice of promotion from within. The vice-president of human resources for a major automobile manufacturer offers this advice: "A strictly applied 'PFW' policy eventually leads to inbreeding, a lack of cross-fertilization, and a lack of creativity. A good goal, in my opinion, is to fill 80 percent of openings above entry-level positions from within." From time to time, new blood is needed to provide the new ideas and innovation that must take place if firms are to remain competitive.

Hiring Relatives

Regulations related to the employment of relatives also may affect recruitment. While in some firms employees are encouraged to refer relatives and friends, in others this practice is discouraged. As well, certain working relationships among relatives are avoided. In many chartered accounting firms, for example, there has been a long-standing agreement that spouses should not work together if one needs to check the work of the other, a seemingly practical policy. As these firms cannot legally discriminate on the basis of "marital status", (see Figure 5-3) however, these long-standing antinepotism practices may have to be reviewed. Indeed, in some provinces (Alberta, New Brunswick, PEI, and Newfoundland) it is legal to refuse employment to all near relatives except the spouse. Human resources professionals are well advised, therefore, to check carefully with the appropriate human rights commission before implementing antinepotism policies. Figure 5-3 combines data from all the human rights codes in Canada to show how jurisdictions vary in terms of prohibited grounds for discrimination.

METHODS USED IN INTERNAL RECRUITMENT

To identify current employees capable of filling vacant positions, managers can use management and skills inventories, job posting, and bidding procedures.

Prohibited Grounds	Federal	British Columbia	Alberta	Saskatchewan	Manitoba	Ontario	Quebec	New Brunswick	Prince Edward Island	Nova Scotia	Newfoundland	Northwest Territories	Yukon
Race or colour	●	●	●	●	●	●	●	●	●	●	●	●	●
Religion or creed	●	●	●	●	●	●	●	●	●	●	●	●	●
Age	●	● (19-65)	● (18+)	● (18-64)	●	● (18-65)	●	●	●	●	● (19-65)	●	●
Sex (incl. pregnancy or childbirth)	●	●[1]	●	●	●[2]	●	●	●	●[1]	●	●[1]	●[1]	●
Marital Status	●	●	●	●	●	●	●[3]	●	●	●	●	●	●
Physical/Mental handicap or disability	●	●	●	●	●	●	●	●	●	●	●	●	●
Sexual orientation	●[4]	●		●	●	●	●	●	●[1]	●	●[1]	●	●
National or ethnic origin (incl. linguistic background)	●			●[5]	●	●[6]	●	●	●	●	●	●[5]	●
Family status	●	●		●	●	●	●[3]			●		●	●
Dependence on alcohol or drug	●	●[1]	●[1]	●[1]	●[1]	●[1]		●[1,7]	●[1]	●[7]			
Ancestry or place of origin		●	●	●	●	●	●	●				●[5]	●
Political belief		●			●		●	●	●	●			●
Based on association					●	●			●	●			●
Pardoned conviction	●	●					●	●			●		
Record of criminal conviction		●						●					●
Source of income				●[8]	●						●		
Place of residence												●	
Assignment, attachment or seizure of pay											●		
Social condition/origin							●				●		
Language							●						

Harassment on any of the prohibited grounds is considered a form of discrimination.

* Any limitation, exclusion, denial or preference may be permitted if a bona fide occupational requirement can be demonstrated.
1) complaints accepted based on policy
2) includes gender-determined characteristics
3) Quebec uses the term "civil status"
4) pursuant to a 1992 Ontario Court of Appeal decision, the Canadian Human Rights Commission now accepts complaints on the ground of sexual orientation
5) defined as nationality
6) Ontario's Code includes only "citizenship"
7) previous dependence only
8) defined as "receipt of public assistance"

This document is also available on computer diskette and as a sound recording to ensure it is accessible to people who are blind or vision impaired.

Threatening, intimidating or discriminating against someone who has filed a complaint, or hampering a complaint investigation, is a violation of provincial human rights codes, and at the federal level is a criminal offence.

This chart is for quick reference only. For interpretation or further details, call the appropriate commission.

FIGURE 5-3 Employment: Prohibited Grounds of Discrimination

Source: Canadian Human Rights Commission. "Employment: Prohibited Grounds of Discrimination." Reproduced with permission of the Ministry of Supply and Services Canada, 1993.

As suggested in Chapter 4, management and skills inventories permit organizations to assess whether current employees possess the qualifications for open positions. As a recruitment device that supports promotion from within, these inventories have proved to be extremely useful—provided they are kept up to date.

Job posting is a procedure for informing employees that job openings exist. **Job bidding** is a technique that permits employees who believe they possess the required qualifications to apply for a posted job. Figure 5-4 illustrates the procedure a medium-sized firm might use. Larger firms often provide employees with a weekly list of job openings, encouraging all qualified employees to apply.

The bidding procedure minimizes the complaint, commonly heard in many companies, that insiders never hear of a job opening until it has been filled. The process reflects an openness that most employees value highly. A firm that offers freedom of choice and encourages career growth has a distinct advantage.

Conversely, when internal bidders are unsuccessful, the reason must be explained to them. Indeed, unless managers take care to ensure that the most qualified applicant is chosen, the system will lack credibility. It must be remembered, too, that even a well designed job posting and bidding system won't eliminate complaints completely.

EXTERNAL SOURCES OF RECRUITMENT

At times, HR managers must look outside to find employees, particularly when 1) expanding the workforce; 2) looking for specific skills; 3) filling

FIGURE 5-4
Job Posting and Bidding Procedure

Responsibility	Action Required
Human resource assistant	1. Upon receiving a Human Resource Requisition, write a memo to each appropriate supervisor stating that a job vacancy exists. The memo should include a job title, job number, pay grade, salary range, a summary of the basic duties performed, and the qualifications required for the job (data to be taken from job description/specification).
	2. Ensure that a copy of this memo is posted on all company bulletin boards.
Supervisors	3. Make certain that every employee who might qualify for the position is made aware of the job opening.
Interested employees	4. Contact the human resource department.

entry-level jobs; or 4) seeking employees with different backgrounds to provide new ideas. As Figure 5-5 suggests, even when promotions are made internally, entry-level jobs must be filled from the outside. In this example, the president's retirement leads to a series of internal promotions. Ultimately, however, the firm has to recruit externally to fill the entry-level salary analyst's position. If the president's position had been filled from the outside, the chain-reaction of promotions from within would not have occurred.

Depending on the type and the level of qualifications desired, employees may be attracted from a number of outside sources.

High Schools and Vocational Schools

Organizations concerned with recruiting clerical and other entry-level operative employees often depend heavily on high schools and vocational schools. Many schools have outstanding training programs for specific occupational skills such as home-appliance repair and small-engine mechanics. Some companies work with schools to ensure a constant supply of trained individuals with specific job skills. In some areas, companies even loan employees to schools to assist in the training programs.

Community Colleges

Many community colleges are sensitive to the specific employment needs in their local labour markets, graduating highly sought-after students with

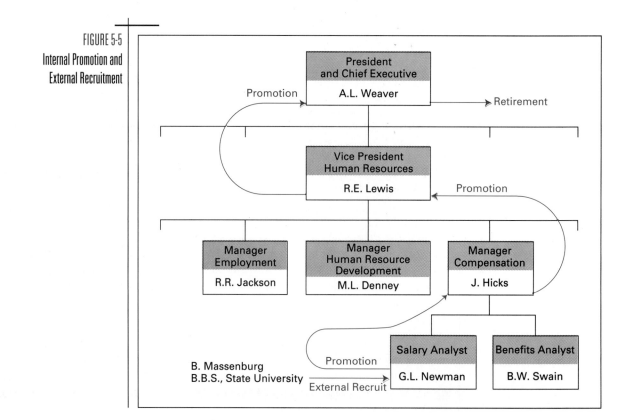

FIGURE 5-5
Internal Promotion and
External Recruitment

marketable skills. In Canada, there is no "typical" community college. In some provinces they offer two-year (or shorter) programs designed specifically for the job market. In others, they offer vocational training plus preparation toward four-year university degree programs. Many community colleges also have excellent middle-management programs combined with training for specific occupations. In addition, college career centers often facilitate the recruitment process by providing a place for employers to contact students.

Colleges and Universities

Universities represent a major source of potential professional, technical, and management employees for many organizations. Firms commonly send recruiters to campuses to interview prospective employees, although cost-reduction programs and labour market conditions have reduced this practice in recent years. Because on-campus recruitment is mutually beneficial, employers and university staff should develop and maintain close relationships. It is important that HR managers know the curricula and the quality of all learning institutions in their recruitment area.

Competitors and Other Firms

When recent experience is desired, competitors and other firms in the industry or geographic area may be the most important source of recruits. In the past, one of every three people—especially managers and professionals—changed jobs every five years. The present economic uncertainty may have reduced job mobility, but many people are still willing to move for the right job. At any given time, approximately 5 percent of the working population is either actively seeking a new job or at least receptive to change.

Although some consider the practice ethically debatable, many managers tend to eye their competitors' best people when they need to fill key positions, an approach called corporate raiding. Volkswagen recently drew the ire of General Motors when Jose Ignacio Lopez de Arriortua, head of GM's huge purchasing operation, was lured away. Not only was GM's management fearful of Lopez divulging company trade secrets; it was also alleged that Volkswagen stepped up its efforts to raid other key GM executives. The chairman of Opel claimed that VW had targeted more than 40 managers at Opel and General Motors.[11]

Smaller firms, in particular, look for employees who have been trained in larger organizations with greater resources for human resource development. For example, if the managers of an optical firm believed their operation was not large enough to provide extensive training and development, a person recruited by this firm into any significant management position likely would have held at least two previous positions with competitors.

The Unemployed

The unemployed often provide a valuable source of recruits. Companies may go out of business, cut back, or be merged with other firms, leaving qualified workers without jobs. With Canada's continually high unemployment rates, many qualified individuals with good work records are looking for work. This source should not be ignored.

Older People

Older workers, including those who are retired, may also be a valuable source of employees. Despite the stereotypes, the facts show that older people can perform some jobs extremely well. For example, when Kentucky Fried Chicken Corporation had difficulty recruiting younger workers, it turned to older individuals and those with disabilities. The results were dramatically reduced vacancy and turnover rates within six months.

Unfortunately, in Canada, this valuable resource is often wasted. by discrimination against older workers. According to a report by Blossom Wigdor, chair of the National Advisory Council on Aging, some organizations have unwritten rules prohibiting the hiring of older workers, particularly when the job entails meeting the public.[12] Although the Canadian Human Rights Commission thus far has failed to include older workers on the list of groups protected by fair-hiring laws, HR professionals need to ensure that *ageism*, the conscious or unconscious discrimination against older people, is not tolerated. Indeed, in some companies—Kenworth of Canada, for example—management has found that retraining older blue-collar workers is a good investment.[13]

Self-Employed Workers

Finally, the self-employed worker may also be a good potential recruit. As suggested previously, the self-employed make up the fastest growing employment category in Canada. All manner of skill and experience—technical, professional, administrative, or entrepreneurial—can be found among these individuals. Human resources managers will need to persuade these talented people to leave the freedom that self-employment affords, however, as many operate their own businesses in preference to working for someone else.[14]

There is the danger too, that working for a wage will become less attractive when the new employee is faced with the realities of corporate life. To cite but one example, when Ken Jensen, President of JCS Consulting Services Inc. of Maryhill, Ontario went to work for his major client after almost 15 years as a self-employed consultant, the arrangement lasted only three months. Mr. Jensen found corporate life too restrictive. He is now self-employed again and still works for his client (among others), but both parties have learned a valuable lesson about the psychology of the self-employed.[15]

EXTERNAL METHODS OF RECRUITMENT

Once the best source for applicants has been determined, the human resource manager seeks to attract them through targeted recruitment methods. The method depends on the source and the type of person sought. While advertising, employment agencies, and employee referrals may be effective in attracting working individuals with virtually every type of skill,, recruiters, special events, and internships are used to attract students, especially those attending colleges and universities. Executive search firms and professional organizations are particularly helpful in recruiting managerial and professional employees.

Advertising

Advertising communicates the firm's employment needs to the public through media such as radio, newspaper, television, and industry publications. Advertisements should be written carefully. Obviously, HR professionals should give prospective employees an accurate picture of the job, while at the same time appealing to the self-interest of prospective employees by emphasizing the job's unique or interesting qualities. The message also must indicate how an applicant is to respond: in person, by telephone or by submitting a résumé. The advertisement, however, is conveying more than this specific job information. It is representing the organization to applicants and to the public. Human resource managers must decide on the corporate image they want to project.

Experience with various media will suggest the most appropriate advertising medium for specific types of jobs. The medium that provides the broadest coverage for the least expense is the newspaper advertisement. The drawback to help-wanted ads is that they invariably attract a large number of unqualified individuals, increasing the likelihood of making poor selection decisions.

On the other hand, the broad coverage makes a newspaper an ideal medium for creating awareness and for generating interest in the company as a whole, thus encouraging prospective candidates to seek information about the firm and other possible job opportunities. Examination of the Saturday edition of any major newspaper reveals the extensive use of advertising in recruiting practically every type of employee.

Certain media attract audiences that are more homogeneous in terms of employment skills, education, and orientation. Advertisements placed in publications like The *Financial Post* relate primarily to managerial, professional, and technical positions. The readership is generally mobile and qualified for many of the positions advertised. By contrast, an advertisement placed in the *Vancouver Sun* would reach a more local market with a more varied skill base. Focusing on a specific labour pool, then, minimizes the likelihood of receiving unqualified applicants.

Virtually every professional group publishes a journal and there are many other widely read specialist publications. Advertising for a human resource executive position in *Canadian HR Reporter*, for example, would hit the target market because it is read almost exclusively by human resource professionals. Professional journals, like The *Canadian Manager*, also are widely used. Using journals, however, presents some problems. For one thing, they lack scheduling flexibility. Their deadlines may be weeks prior to the issue date, an obvious limitation when immediate staffing needs arise.

Recruitment advertisers assume that qualified prospects who read job advertisements in newspapers or professional and trade journals are dissatisfied enough with their present jobs to pursue the opportunities advertised. This assumption is not always true, especially for those who are not actively considering a job change. In high-demand situations, therefore, the firm needs to consider all available media resources.

Other media might include radio, billboards, and television. These media are likely to be more expensive than newspapers or journals, but they have been used with success in specific situations. One regional medical center, for example, used billboards to attract registered nurses. A large manufacturing firm achieved considerable success in advertising for production trainees by means of spot advertisements on the radio. An electronics firm used television to attract experienced engineers when it opened a new facility and needed more engineers immediately.

When hiring needs are urgent, television and radio may provide good results; but they may not be sufficient on their own. Broadcast messages can alert people to an opportunity but are too brief to convey much more than the general type of job available and an address and phone number. For this reason, broadcasting and print media are often used together.

Employment Agencies

An **employment agency** is an organization that helps firms recruit employees and individuals find jobs. These agencies have proven quite useful to many employers because they perform many of the recruitment and selection functions.

Private employment agencies are used by firms for virtually every type of position. They are best known, however, for recruiting white-collar employees. Occasional difficulties stem from a lack of industry standards, giving parts of the industry a bad reputation. However, a number of highly reputable, professionally managed employment agencies have operated successfully for decades. These agencies offer an important service by bringing qualified applicants together with potential employers.

Individuals should look for agencies where the fee is paid by the employer. One survey found employment agency fee schedules (charged to the employer) ranged from 25 to 35 percent of gross annual salary of the position to be filled.[16]

Employment agencies can be found in many countries, so that global companies can obtain temporary employees in numerous locations. The scope of the industry can be seen from the following list of the number of countries of operation and the cities of origin of the world's biggest temporary services providers:

- Drake Personnel (22 countries), Winnipeg
- Manpower (36 countries), Milwaukee, Wisconsin
- ADIA (27 countries), Lausanne, Switzerland
- ECCO (28 countries), Paris, France
- Olsten (4 countries), New York
- Kelly (15 countries), Troy, Michigan
- Robert Half/Accountemps/Office Team (7 countries), New York.[17]

Human Resources Development Canada

Human Resources Development Canada operates a large number of Canada Employment Centres (CEC) in every province and territory. Employers with jobs to fill can call in "job orders" describing the nature of the job, basic duties, pay, location and any other relevant information. These orders are entered in an automated job bank.

Job seekers can access this job bank either at CEC offices or through terminals placed in shopping malls and other public places. Applicants can be instructed to submit résumés, call, or visit the employer depending upon location and/or employer preference. The employer is responsible for screening and contacting the applicants for interviews. CECs also offer other services to both employees and employers. Job seekers who require additional information, counselling, or training, for example, can be helped, depending upon the results of a "service needs determination" performed by CEC staff. Then they may be eligible for counselling, retraining, or other assistance.

Company Recruiters

The most common use of recruiters is to work with technical and vocational schools, community colleges, and universities. The key contact for recruiters on college and university campuses is often the director of student placement, who identifies qualified candidates, schedules interviews, and provides suitable interview rooms. This assistance enables organizations to use their own recruiters efficiently. Furthermore, the administrator is in an excellent position to find appropriately qualified students

Résumé databases, discussed later in this chapter, have already begun to alter the way university recruitment is approached. The database system allows recruiters to receive copies of students' résumés before they visit the campus. University and college recruitment becomes much more effective; recruiters can identify the most promising schools as well as specific students.[18]

Considering the importance of the occasion, the interview itself is often short—about thirty minutes on average. Recruiters' main purpose is to determine which individuals possess the best qualifications and/or attitudes. Recruiters may spend over half the time discussing the student's college or university education, eliciting information about knowledge and skills required by the job. As demonstrated by the following list, answers to apparently straightforward questions may reveal more than the information requested.[19]

Information Sought	Topics
Intelligence and aptitudes	Grades
	Amount of effort to achieve grades GMAT, GRE or other test
Motivation	Effort spent on academic work Employment while attending school
Judgement and maturity	Decisions involving choice of college and major field
Analytical power	Reasons for subject preferences
Leadership and ability to get along with people	Participation in extracurricular activities

Responding to criticism from the business community, the curricula at many business schools have been revised in recent years to emphasize topics such as communication, values, negotiation, international competitiveness, quality management, leadership, creativity, ethics, team building, and cross-cultural understanding. Questions focusing on these areas may be asked in campus interviews.[20]

An applicant should prepare carefully for the recruitment interview. In order to make a good impression, the prospect must do some research on the company. The school's placement service often has literature on the organization and its operations. In addition, a library search may yield information about the company's sales, number of employees, products and other data. With these facts, prospects can engage the recruiter in conversation and ask relevant questions. Against other applicants with similar backgrounds and skills, an informed prospect always has a competitive advantage over those who are poorly prepared.

Recruiters should remember that the interview is two-way communication; as well as questioning the prospect, the recruiter is conveying information about the company, its products, general organizational structure, policies, compensation and benefits programs and the position to be filled.

The interviewee, too, is looking for more than facts; the manner and approach of the company recruiter plays a vital role in attracting applicants. The interviewee often perceives the recruiter's actions as a reflection of the character of the firm. Recruiters thus must always be aware of the image they present at the screening interview, because this short encounter makes a lasting impression. If the recruiter is dull, the interviewee may think the company dull; if the recruiter is abrupt or discourteous the interviewee may well attribute these characteristics to the firm.

Special Events

Holding **special events** is a recruiting method that involves an effort on the part of a single employer or a group of employers to attract a large number of applicants for interviews. Job fairs, for example, are designed to bring together applicants and representatives of various companies.[21] From an employer's viewpoint, a primary advantage of job fairs is the opportunity to meet a large number of candidates in a short time—usually one or two days. Business alliances frequently sponsor job fairs, as they provide a recruitment method that offers the potential for a much lower cost per hire than traditional approaches. Student organizations also sponsor recruiting events, such as the one advertised in Figure 5-6.

Internships

An **internship** is a special form of recruiting that involves placing a student in a temporary job. In this arrangement, there is no obligation by the company to hire the student permanently or by the student to accept a permanent position with the firm following graduation. Typically, an internship involves a temporary job for the summer months or a part-time job during the school year. In many instances, students alternate their schedules by working full time one semester and studying full time the next. During the internship, the student gets to view business practices firsthand, while contributing to the firm by performing needed work.

FIGURE 5-6
Announcement of a Student-Sponsored
Recruiting Event

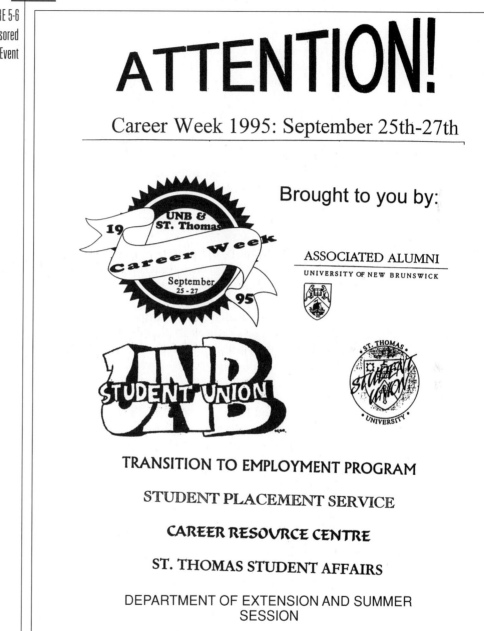

FIGURE 5-6
Announcement of a Student-Sponsored
Recruiting Event

Through this relationship, a student can determine whether or not a company would be a desirable employer. Similarly, by having a longer period of time to observe the student's job performance, management can make a better judgement regarding the person's qualifications and potential. In addition to other benefits, internships provide opportunities for students to bridge the gap from business theory to practice.

For example, Allstate Insurance Company has carried the concept of internships one step further, suggesting that internships can also serve as a strategic HR retention tool. A goal has been set of hiring 60 percent of the company's 1995 entry-level staff from its internship program, called "the ten-week interview." This firm's employment director prefers to have turnover occur at the beginning, by eliminating the mismatches, rather than two years later.[22]

Internships also serve as an effective public relations tool, providing visibility for the company name and its products or service. Local communities have a favourable view of firms that offer internships.

Executive Search Firms

Executive search firms may be used to locate experienced professionals and executives when other sources prove inadequate. **Executive search firms** are organizations that search out the most qualified executive available for a specific position. They are generally retained by the companies needing specific types of individuals.

Throughout North America, executive search is a rapidly growing industry with estimated revenue reaching $2.5 billion annually. More than 4 million potential candidates are contacted in order to place 80 000 executives.[23] The executive search industry has evolved from a basic recruitment service to a highly sophisticated profession serving a greatly expanded role. Search firms now assist organizations in determining their human resource needs, establishing compensation packages, and revising organizational structures.

Many well known executives have been recruited by executive search firms. For example, Gary Betman, Commissioner of the NHL was placed by Andrew MacDougall of Spencer and Stuart and Associates (Canada) Ltd., a Toronto-based firm that specializes in recruiting top management.[24]

Most executive search firms differ from employment agencies and job advisory consultants in that they do not work for individuals. Search firms that work for corporations and governmental agencies are paid a retainer fee for each search, regardless of whether or not a suitable candidate is recruited. These firms often develop a close relationship with their clients. They acquire an intimate knowledge of the organization, its culture, goals, structure, and the position to be filled. Retainer firms typically recruit executives for middle and upper level management positions or senior technical positions calling for salaries of over $60 000.

Contingency search firms, which grew out of the employment agency industry, focus on lower to mid-management and some technical positions, with salaries from $30 000 to $70 000. Unlike retainer search firms, these organizations are paid only when a candidate is accepted.[25]

An executive search firm's representatives often visit the client's offices to interview management, in order to gain a clear understanding of the company's goals and the job qualifications required. After obtaining this information, they contact and interview potential candidates, check references, and refer the best qualified person or persons to the client for the selection decision. Information sources include networking contacts, files from previous searches, specialized directories, personal calls, previous clients, colleagues, and unsolicited résumés.[26] The search firm's fee is generally a percentage of the individual's compensation for the first year. Expenses are paid by the client.

The relationship between a client company and a search firm should be based on mutual trust and understanding. Both parties gain most from their relationship when they interact often and maintain good communication.[27] In order to be successful, the search firm must understand in detail the nature of the client's operations, the responsibilities of the position being filled, and the client's corporate culture. Similarly, the client must understand the search process, work with the consultant and provide continuous, honest feedback.

Professional Associations

Finance, marketing, accounting, and human resource professional associations provide recruitment and placement services for their members. The Canadian Institute of Management, for example, operates a job referral service for members seeking new positions and for employers with positions to fill.

Employee Referrals

Many organizations have found that employees can assist in the recruitment process by actively soliciting applications from their friends and associates. In some organizations, especially where certain skills are scarce, this approach has proven quite effective. For example, at one high tech company, hires from employee referrals have risen from 15 percent to 52 percent in the past few years. This firm has found that as referrals have become their primary recruitment and retention approach, the costs of advertising and placement agencies have been significantly reduced. With a goal of not only attracting employees but also retaining them, management has found that this recruitment method results in effective employee/employer bonding.[28]

Unsolicited Walk-In Applicants

If an organization has the reputation for being a good place to work, qualified prospects may be attracted without extensive recruitment efforts. Acting on their own, well-qualified workers may seek out the company to apply for a job. Unsolicited applicants who apply because they are favourably impressed with the firm's reputation often prove to be valuable employees.

Recruitment Databases/Automated Applicant Tracking Systems

Computers have greatly influenced many HRM functions, a trend likely to accelerate. The size of databases operated by several independent networks continues to grow as some firms downsize and others become more aware of what computers can do. Some firms, for example, permit employers to advertise job listings to on-line subscribers or to access a résumé database. Others offer résumé banks of individuals at all career levels in a wide variety of fields.[29] Three central databases can be accessed by corporate clients using their own PCs. When a candidate's background matches an open position, the client may obtain a copy of the résumé. This process of matching candidates with positions dramatically reduces paperwork costs. For example, it typically costs $1000 to conduct a job search through one national database firm. An executive search firm, on the other hand, may charge as much as $30 000 to hire a $90 000-a-year executive. The cost and time saved by using databases may make some recruiting methods obsolete, although databases won't completely replace currently used systems. Searches for CEOs, for example, will always be politically sensitive and require special handling.[30]

Internal databases make automated applicant tracking systems possible. Using an automated system, information can be drawn from a database to produce fast and accurate requisitions. Next, applicant information can be accessed. In seconds, the few individuals who meet specific selection criteria can be identified out of a group of many applicants. The selection procedure, discussed in the next chapter, can also be facilitated, as managers can quickly and easily get a detailed profile of each candidate.

An automated tracking system streamlines the recruitment process and permits managers to spend more time finding high quality candidates. HR professionals gain access to a sophisticated means of handling all steps of the recruiting process, from generating routine correspondence to tracking requisitions and scheduling interviews. As well, because databases provide detailed documentation about hiring practices, they can be a tremendous help in meeting employment equity guidelines.[31]

TAILORING RECRUITMENT METHODS TO SOURCES

Because each organization is unique in many ways, the types and the qualifications of workers needed to fill positions vary greatly. Successful recruitment must be tailored to the needs of both the firm and the type of position being filled.

A human resource professional must first identify the source (*where* prospective employees are) before choosing the methods (*how* to get them). Suppose, for example, that a large firm has an immediate need for an accounting manager with a minimum of five years' experience and no one within the firm has these qualifications. Qualified people can most likely be found working at another firm, very possibly a competitor. The recruiter might find a pool of qualified applicants by advertising in *The Financial Post* or in *CA Magazine*, through an executive search firm, by attending meetings of professional accounting associations, or through a combination of these methods.

In contrast, suppose a firm needs 20 entry-level machine operators, whom the firm is willing to train. High schools and vocational schools would probably be good recruitment sources. Other methods of recruitment might include newspaper advertisements, sending recruiters to vocational schools, and employee referrals. Figure 5-7 shows a matrix that depicts methods and sources of recruitment for a data processing manager.

Decisions on recruiting methods will also be affected by external environmental factors, including market supply and job requirements. Each organization should maintain employment records and conduct its own research to determine which sources and methods are most appropriate under various circumstances. For the most prevalent recruiting source and method by various job categories (in the United States), see Figure 5-8.

FIGURE 5-7
Methods and Sources of Recruitment for a Data Processing Manager

SOURCES	METHODS OF RECRUITING										
	Advertising	Private employment agencies	Public employment agencies	Recruiters	Special events	Internships	Executive search firms	Unsolicited applications	Professional associations	Employee referrals	Unsolicited applicants
High schools											
Vocational schools											
Community colleges											
Colleges and universities											
Competitors and other firms	×	×					×		×		
Unemployed											
Self-employed											

ELIMINATING DISCRIMINATION

In spite of human rights legislation,[32] human resource practices that have an unequal effect on women, persons with disabilities, aboriginals, and minorities are deeply embedded in some organizations. A traditional recruitment method, such as employee referrals, for example, may perpetuate the effects of past discrimination, even after other discriminatory practices have been discontinued. The result, though not necessarily conscious, is a continuation of what has been labelled systemic discrimination.[33] Similarly, it may be discriminatory for a firm located near a First Nations reserve to insist on high school graduation for entry-level positions. Relatively few potential aboriginal applicants may have completed high school, although they could be quite capable of doing the job.[34] Or recruiters may overlook certain sources in the belief, based on entrenched stereotypes, that members of one sex would not be interested in, or competent at, certain jobs.

It must be remembered that the ethnic composition of society has changed radically. According to Michelle Falardeau-Ramsay, Deputy Chief Commissioner of the Canadian Human Rights Commission, in "1967, only 3.2% of the Canadian population cited ethnic origins other than Europeans. Today, the census figure for visible minorities alone is nearly triple that percentage."[35] Our society,

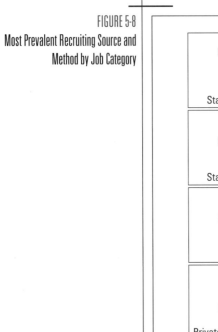

FIGURE 5-8
Most Prevalent Recruiting Source and Method by Job Category

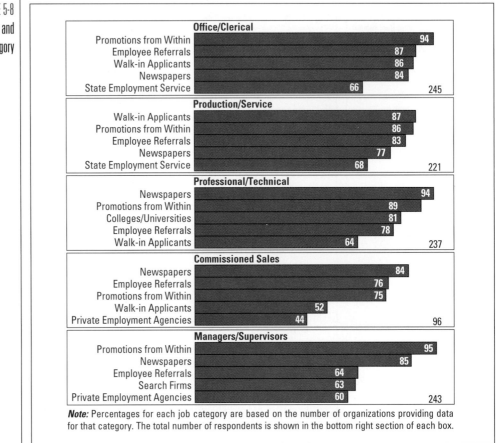

Office/Clerical
- Promotions from Within — 94
- Employee Referrals — 87
- Walk-in Applicants — 86
- Newspapers — 84
- State Employment Service — 66
- 245

Production/Service
- Walk-in Applicants — 87
- Promotions from Within — 86
- Employee Referrals — 83
- Newspapers — 77
- State Employment Service — 68
- 221

Professional/Technical
- Newspapers — 94
- Promotions from Within — 89
- Colleges/Universities — 81
- Employee Referrals — 78
- Walk-in Applicants — 64
- 237

Commissioned Sales
- Newspapers — 84
- Employee Referrals — 76
- Promotions from Within — 75
- Walk-in Applicants — 52
- Private Employment Agencies — 44
- 96

Managers/Supervisors
- Promotions from Within — 95
- Newspapers — 85
- Employee Referrals — 64
- Search Firms — 63
- Private Employment Agencies — 60
- 243

Note: Percentages for each job category are based on the number of organizations providing data for that category. The total number of respondents is shown in the bottom right section of each box.

Source: K. Michele Kacmar, "Look at Who's Talking," *HR Magazine* 38 (February 1993): 57.

then, is becoming increasingly diverse and complex. HRM professionals must be sure that all HR systems (recruitment, promotion, discipline, etc.), fall within the law.

As we discussed earlier in this chapter, the law varies depending upon where a firm operates. Everywhere in Canada it is illegal to consider race, religion, gender, disability, or marital status in making employment decisions such as hiring, firing and promoting. On the other hand, one may, for example, discriminate on the basis of sexual orientation in Alberta or the Northwest Territories, but not in the rest of Canada (see Figure 5-3).[36]

Some groups are opposed to **employment equity** and charge that it results in so-called reverse discrimination. There is another side to the story, however. Because of past unequal opportunity, women, minority group members, aboriginals, and people with disabilities may not respond to traditional recruitment methods until specific action is taken to attract them. Unless special efforts are made, it is questionable whether they will ever be proportionally represented in the work force. Therefore, any organization that adopts employment equity (either voluntarily or by mandate) should implement recruitment

HRM IN ACTION

Juan Gonzales and Debra Coffee, two executives from competing firms, met at their annual professional conference. They were discussing the effect of recent human rights commission rulings on their firms. Juan said, "I don't think we will have any difficulty at our company. We don't employ any persons with disabilities but then all our production jobs require able-bodied men."

"Have you considered making reasonable accommodations for applicants with disabilities?" Debra asked. After thinking a moment, Juan replied, "I don't believe so, Debra. You see, our executive group is very pleased with the productivity in our plant. I really don't think they want to fix something that isn't broken."

As a human resource professional, how would you respond?

and other employment programs that make sure women, minorities, aboriginals and those with disabilities will be included in decision making. These programs should be carefully monitored to ensure their effectiveness.

The Government of Canada has published specific guidelines to help employers achieve equality in the workplace. The guidelines cover grounds of discrimination such as sex, ancestry, colour, disability, marital status, or other non-bona-fide occupational requirements. Implementing equity and reporting the results is mandatory for organizations that fall under the Canada Labour Code (federal crown corporations, interprovincial transportation companies, communication agencies, and banks).[37] Other companies, too, may be well advised to follow the guidelines voluntarily. All organizations of 100 people or more that wish to sell goods or services worth more than $200 000 to the Federal Government must, as spelled out in the Employment Equity Act:

> . . . in consultation with such persons as have been designated by the employees to act as their representative or, where a bargaining agent represents the employees, in consultation with the bargaining agent, implement employment equity by:
> (a) identifying and eliminating each of the employer's employment practices, not otherwise authorized by a law, that results in employment barriers against persons in designated groups; and
> (b) instituting such positive policies and practices and making such reasonable accommodation as will ensure that persons in designated groups achieve a degree of representation in the various positions of employment with the employer that is at least proportionate to their representation:
> > i) in the work force or
> > ii) in those segments of the work force that are identifiable by qualifications, eligibility or geography and from which the employer may reasonably be expected to draw or promote employees.[38]

Employers must submit certain reports to demonstrate that they are complying with these regulations. To help HR managers initiate employment equity, the following framework has been developed, so that personnel systems can be reviewed and adjusted.[39]

PHASE I: ORGANIZATIONAL READINESS

STEP 1: PREPARATION

- Establish senior level commitment.
- Define mechanisms for consultation with employee representatives (e.g., bargaining agents).
- Identify communications resources.
- Assign senior staff and resources.
- Identify organizational values and attitudes, and sources of support for or resistance to employment equity.

STEP 2: ANALYSIS

- Collect personnel information.
- Evaluate current work force information.
- Review formal and informal personnel policies and practices.
- Identify barriers to employment equity in policies and practices.

PHASE II: MANAGEMENT OF CHANGE

STEP 3: PLANNING

- Establish goals and timetables.
- Design new or modified personnel systems and procedures.
- Develop special measures and reasonable accommodations.
- Determine monitoring and accountability mechanisms.

STEP 4: IMPLEMENTATION

- Assign line management responsibility and accountability.
- Implement Employment Equity Plan of Action.
- Support plans with a communications strategy.

PHASE III: MAINTENANCE OF CHANGE

STEP 5: MONITORING

- Establish feedback and problem-solving mechanisms.
- Carry out regular orientation and training programs for supervisors.
- Follow through in management performance evaluation.
- Reward achievements.
- Maintain and update personnel information.
- Make adjustments to program as required.

Designing an Employment Equity Program: Implications for Managers[40]

Employment equity programs, whether legislated or voluntary, are a reality of our present day human resources environment. Despite the recent swing to right-wing governments in provinces like Alberta and Ontario, there does still seem to be a general desire on the part of society to provide more equitable opportunities for everyone. Some strategies can help managers develop and implement employment equity programs.

ANALYSIS

A critical prelude to any such program is an environmental scan to consider both internal and external influences. As illustrated in Figure 5-9, factors that must be considered include education/skills, demographics, and political, legal, social/cultural, economic, and technological implications. An examination of these elements will help to determine what needs to be done, the potential effects on the organization, the most effective way to communicate the plan to workers and to ensure acceptance, and the potential benefits and disadvantages to the organization.

An important component of the environmental scan is work force analysis, since the employment equity plan will be based on the data obtained. The analysis must, therefore, reflect as closely as possible the representation of designated groups within the current employee mix. Such a study is not a simple task, because many employees feel uncomfortable about disclosing personal information, particularly if they feel that it may be used against them in any way. It is imperative, therefore, to design the survey and to conduct the analysis in such a way as to secure the trust of employees.

FIGURE 5-9
An Environmental Analysis

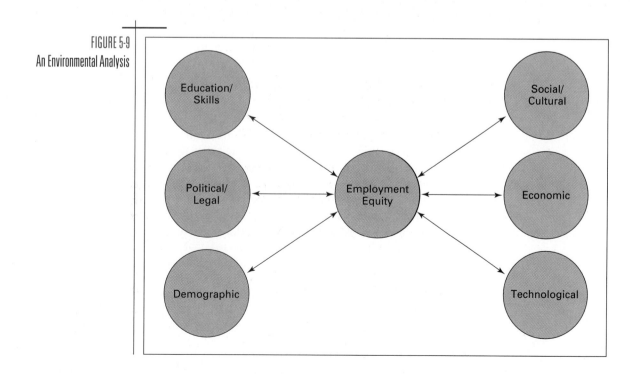

IMPLEMENTATION

Employment equity programs will have a better chance in an atmosphere that encourages flexibility, openness, and tolerance of differences. An open-minded approach is especially critical if it becomes necessary to modify job requirements or responsibilities to accommodate the special needs of a particular employee. Conflicts may arise from perceptions of reduced productivity or a backlash by workers from more traditional backgrounds.

There is, however, a spin-off benefit for the company. The creativity and problem-solving skills that workers and managers must use to successfully adapt the workplace for employment equity are precisely the qualities that can make them more effective in fulfilling their job responsibilities.

The development of partnerships with other community resources will also be helpful. It is neither possible nor practical for human resources managers (nor other managers for that matter) to acquire the knowledge and expertise required to modify jobs for individuals with varying needs and abilities. Community organizations and special interest groups can suggest ways to adapt jobs with technical aids or simple realignment of duties. They are also a valuable source of information about funding programs for wage and/or equipment subsidies, and can assist with staff training and sensitization.

ANALYSIS OF RECRUITMENT PROCEDURES

HR managers should analyze their recruitment procedures to make sure they are not discriminatory. For example, is overreliance on employee referral and unsolicited applicants perpetuating the composition of the organization's work force?

It is helpful to develop a record of applicant flow, which includes personal and job-related data on each applicant. It indicates whether or not a job offer was extended and an explanation of the decision. Such records enable the HR professional or manager to analyze recruitment and selection practices and to take corrective action when necessary. This record will also be extremely useful if the firm's hiring practices are ever questioned. As well, recruiters should be trained to use objective, job-related standards.

MINORITY MEMBERS AS RECRUITERS

Recruiters occupy a unique position in terms of encouraging or discouraging minority groups, women, and people with disabilities to apply for jobs. Hiring qualified members of these groups as recruiters can be an effective way to broaden the range of applicants. If this is not feasible, another strategy is to have an operative employee or manager who is a member of a minority group accompany recruiters on visits to schools and colleges or participate in career days. Such employees should also be asked for input into recruitment planning and can serve effectively as referral sources.

The image of the company shown in help-wanted advertisements and brochures should be kept in mind as well. Pictures of ethnic minority members, women, and disabled employees—not in a section on employment equity, but used casually to illustrate other aspects of the company—give credibility to the message that a firm offers equal opportunity to everyone.

ADVERTISING

With few exceptions, jobs must be open to all individuals. Therefore, sex-segregated advertisements must not be used unless the applicant's sex is a bona fide occupational qualification. The burden of proof is on the employer to establish that the requirement is essential to successful performance of the job.

In one instance, for example, a public service agency needed orderlies to work with elderly male patients in their homes, where they would help the client with washing, toileting, etc. But the elderly men refused to allow women (mostly young women), to help them. The agency was in a dilemma. On the one hand, the human rights code prohibited gender discrimination; on the other, the clients were refusing the agency's services. The human rights commission was approached and permission was granted to advertise for male orderlies. Females could still appeal, however, if they thought the practice was discriminatory.

WORKING TOGETHER

To achieve long-term success, employment equity will need to become a more collaborative effort between all the parties involved. Government needs to streamline its administrative requirements and reduce bureaucracy. Educators should examine their programs to ensure they are appropriate for designated groups. The designated groups themselves must become proactive in helping to design programs that will aid their members and in researching ways to effectively accommodate them in employment without sacrificing company productivity. Finally, employers need to become more flexible and creative in integrating designated group members into their workplace.

If all interested parties work in partnership and demonstrate a collective will to make employment equity work, the ultimate success will some day be achieved: the program will no longer be needed because all citizens are treated as equals.

A GLOBAL PERSPECTIVE

Internationally, recruitment is no less vital than in Canada. No firm anywhere on the planet is able to avoid the pressures of increasing competition. Competition in the labour market is just as intense as it is in the product market.

Obtaining employees from competitors has long been a practice within our own borders. Because of the scarcity of top talent, similar practices likely will occur on a global scale. Recall McCain's recruitment of a top British executive.

Many of the recruitment methods used in Canada are also common practice in other countries. Even some alternatives to recruitment are identical. The use of temporary help, for example, is not foreign to Europe.[41] In fact, in Western Europe, the temporary help industry is larger than in North America. While language is not a major problem, cultures and employment laws vary from country to country. For example, although recruiting in the United Kingdom is much the same as in Canada, it is legal to discriminate on the basis of age.[42]

In other parts of Europe, however, hiring temporary help is much more highly regulated. In France, for example, the law requires that temporary employees be paid the same rate as full-time employees, plus a premium. Germany also is highly regulated, as temporary workers are considered to be permanent employees of the employment agency that employs them. Since younger workers in Japan are not as loyal to their employers as their parents, a temporary employment sector is starting to develop. Japanese laws, however, are new and relatively inflexible. For example, they specify the kinds of work a temporary worker can perform and permission must be granted for any changes.[43]

A formidable task facing many multinational firms is the recruitment and development of a cadre of managers and executives who understand and can operate effectively in the global market environment. Many companies are attempting to provide suitable international experience for high-potential managers early in their careers, and are highlighting these international opportunities in recruiting university graduates. There is also an increase in external recruitment to fill management positions abroad.

Unfortunately, some firms seem to be unwilling to recruit and develop women as international managers. This reluctance is of particular concern because recent research suggests that women are more sensitive to cultural differences and, therefore, more able to work effectively with managers from other countries. To recruit effectively in the global marketplace, it is essential that human resource managers not ignore any portion of the labour pool.[44]

SUMMARY

Recruitment is the process of attracting individuals on a timely basis, in sufficient numbers and with appropriate qualifications, while encouraging them to apply for jobs with an organization. When human resource planning indicates a need for employees, a firm should first evaluate alternatives to hiring additional workers. Common alternatives to recruitment include assigning overtime, subcontracting, and hiring contingent workers.

When these other alternatives won't meet the demand, the recruitment process starts. Frequently, recruitment begins when a manager initiates an employee requisition. The next step is to determine whether or not qualified employees are available within the firm (the internal source), or must be recruited externally from sources such as colleges, universities, or other organizations. Recruitment sources are places where qualified individuals can be found. Recruitment methods are the specific means by which potential employees are attracted to the firm. After identifying sources of potential employees, the human resource manager chooses the appropriate methods for internal and/or external recruitment.

External factors can significantly affect a firm's recruitment activities. Of particular importance is the demand and supply of specific skills in the labour market. If demand for a particular skill is high relative to supply, an extraordinary recruitment effort may be required. When the unemployment rate in the firm's labour market is high, its recruitment process may be simplified. Legal considerations and the firm's corporate image also play significant roles in recruitment practices.

An organization's promotion policy can also have a significant effect on recruitment. An organization can use one of two promotion approaches: a policy of promotion from within or a policy of filling positions from outside the organization. Depending on the circumstances, either approach (or a combination) may have merit.

Tools used for internal recruitment include management and skill inventories, as well as job posting and bidding procedures. Management and skills inventories indicate whether current employees possess the qualifications needed for promotion or reassignment. Job posting informs employees of job openings. Job bidding permits employees who believe they possess the required qualifications to apply for a posted job.

Job candidates may be attracted from various outside sources. Firms often depend heavily on high schools and vocational schools when recruiting clerical and other entry-level operative employees. Many community colleges are sensitive to specific employment needs in local labour markets. They graduate highly sought-after students. Colleges and universities represent a major source of recruitment for many organizations. Competitors and other firms in the same geographic area or industry may be the most important source of recruits for positions in which recent experience is desired. The unemployed, the self-employed, and older individuals may also be good sources of recruits.

Recruitment methods such as advertising, employment agencies, and employee referrals may be effective in attracting individuals with virtually every type of skill. Recruiters, special events, and internships are used primarily to attract college and university students. Executive search firms and professional organizations are particularly useful in the recruitment of managerial and professional employees.

Discrimination in employment is prohibited on a number of grounds, including race, religion, gender, disability, marital status, and age. In line with society's general desire to provide more equitable opportunities for everyone, the government of Canada and most provincial governments have published specific guidelines to help employees achieve equality in the workplace. In spite of human rights legislation, certain human resource management practices that have a discriminatory effect on women, minority groups, and handicapped individuals are deeply embedded in some organizations. To ensure that recruitment programs are nondiscriminatory, HR managers must analyze their recruitment procedures.

Globally, recruitment tends to be more difficult than recruiting at home, as often different laws and regulations apply. Unfortunately, in many firms there is an unwillingness to recruit women for overseas assignments, even though research suggests they tend to be more sensitive to cultural differences.

TERMS FOR REVIEW

Recruitment
Employee requisition
Recruitment sources
Recruitment methods
Promotion from within (PFW)
Job posting

Job bidding
Employment agency
Special events
Internship
Executive search firms
Employment equity

QUESTIONS FOR REVIEW

1. Describe the basic components of the recruitment process.
2. What are some alternatives to recruitment?
3. List and discuss the various external and internal factors that may affect recruitment.
4. What is meant by the term *internal recruitment*? Describe the advantages and disadvantages of internal recruitment.
5. Describe the methods commonly used in internal recruitment.
6. Discuss the reasons for an external recruitment program.
7. Distinguish between sources and methods of external recruitment. Identify various sources and methods of external recruitment.
8. Explain the difference between an executive search firm and an employment agency.
9. How can a firm improve its recruiting efforts under the law?
10. How can recruiters ensure that provincial/federal employment equity guidelines are followed?

HRM INCIDENT 1

• RIGHT IDEA, WRONG SONG

Robert was human resource manager at Epler Manufacturing Company in Edmonton, Alberta. He was considering the need to recruit qualified women for Epler when Betty Quan walked into his office.

"Got a minute?" asked Betty. "I need to talk to you about next week's job fair at Fairview College."

"Sure," Robert replied, "but, first I need your advice about something. How can we get more women to apply for work here? We're running ads on the Community Service Channel along with the classified ads in The Edmonton Journal. I think you and John have made recruiting trips to every community college within 200 miles. We've encouraged employee referral, too, and I still think that's our most reliable source of new workers. But we just aren't getting any female applicants."

From the president on down, the management at Epler claimed commitment to employment equity. According to Robert, the commitment went much deeper than posting the usual placards and filing an *employment equity plan* to qualify for the federal government contracts. Still, the percentage of female employees at Epler remained at only 30 percent. Epler paid competitive wages and had a good training program.

One need was for machine operator trainees. The machines were not difficult to operate and there was no educational requirement for the job. There were also several clerical and management trainee positions open.

QUESTION

1. Evaluate the current recruitment effort. How could Robert attain the firm's employment equity goal?

HRM INCIDENT 2

• TIME TO DO SOMETHING

Five years ago when Bobby Bret joined Crystal Productions as a junior accountant, he felt that he was on his way up. He had just graduated with a B+ average from university, where he was well liked by his peers and the faculty and had been an officer in several student organizations. Bobby had shown a natural ability to get along with people, as well as to get things done. He remembered what Roger Friedman, the comptroller at Crystal, had told him when he was

hired, "I think you will do well here, Bobby. You've come highly recommended. You are the kind of guy that can expect to move right up the ladder."

Bobby felt that he had done a good job at Crystal, and everybody seemed to like him. In addition, his performance appraisals had been excellent. However, after five years he was still a junior accountant. He had applied for two senior accountant positions, but they were both filled by people hired from outside the firm. When the accounting supervisor's job came open two years ago, Bobby had not applied. He was surprised when his new boss turned out to be a hotshot graduate from the University of Windsor, whose only experience was three years with a large chartered accounting firm. Bobby had hoped that Ron Hrynciuk, a senior accountant he particularly respected, would get the job.

On the fifth anniversary of his employment at Crystal, Bobby decided it was time to do something. He made an appointment with the comptroller. At that meeting Bobby explained to Mr. Friedman that he had worked hard to obtain a promotion and shared his frustration about having been in the same job for so long. "Well", said Mr. Friedman, "you don't think that you were all that much better qualified than the people that we've hired, do you?"

"No", said Bobby, "but I think I could have handled the senior accountant job. Of course, the people you have hired are doing a great job too."

The controller responded, "We just look at the qualifications of all the applicants for each job and, considering everything, try to make a reasonable decision."

QUESTIONS

1. Explain the effect of a promotion-from-within policy on outside recruitment.
2. Do you believe that Bobby has a legitimate complaint? Explain.

DEVELOPING HRM SKILLS: AN EXPERIENTIAL EXERCISE

Human resources managers are responsible for preparing job descriptions. From these job descriptions, profiles of the types of individuals needed can be developed and recruitment activities can be designed. The human resource manager must determine where the best applicants are located (recruitment sources) and how to entice them to join the organization (recruitment methods). This exercise is designed to provide an understanding of the relationship between recruitment sources and methods. Each participant will identify both recruitment sources and methods for the job description.

The job opening is for a human resources assistant who will report to the manager of employee relations and recruitment. The accountability objective for the position is fairly standard. This position is accountable for performing employment activities for the off-site claims division in order to staff the organization with proficient, suitable personnel and to provide effective administration of human resource policies and procedures. The successful applicant will have a university degree, preferably in business administration, but needs little or no experience because he or she will be placed in a six-month training program before assuming these duties. Span of control (that is, the workers reporting to the person in this position) is limited to one clerk and one secretary. Primary duties include recruitment and interviewing of applicants for employment (clerical, technical and professional), devising recruiting advertisements, screening, performing reference checks, and administering standard skills tests where applicable.

The incumbent will function independently as a counselling source and choose appropriate methods of communicating information to personnel while creating an atmosphere of impartiality and equality. The incumbent may also assess training needs for on-site personnel. In order to make personnel recommendations, the incumbent must maintain an updated database that includes all areas of human resources, be knowledgeable about the external environment and be aware of the internal climate. Knowledge of the employment marketplace, as well as hiring practices and legal considerations is required. Excellent interpersonal skills and the ability to establish rapport are mandatory.

Using this job description, participants will attempt to determine the most appropriate recruitment sources and methods. Any additional information necessary to complete the exercise can be obtained from the instructor.

CHAPTER

6 Selection

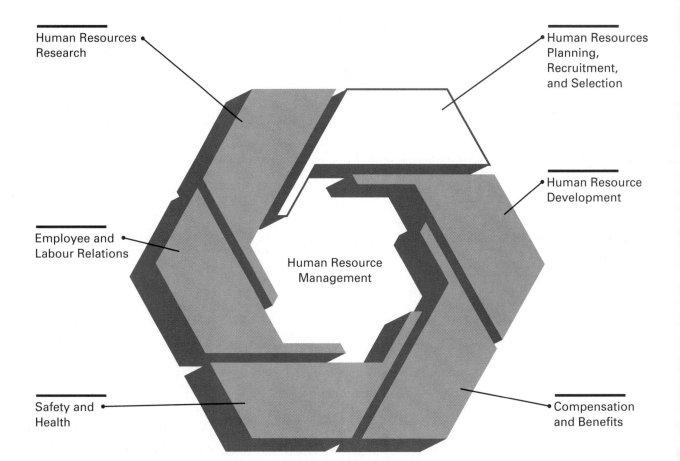

Human Resources
Research

Human Resources
Planning,
Recruitment,
and Selection

Human Resource
Development

Employee and
Labour Relations

Human Resource
Management

Safety and
Health

Compensation
and Benefits

CHAPTER OBJECTIVES

1. Define selection, explain how environmental factors affect the selection process, and describe the selection process.
2. Describe the importance of the preliminary interview and the review of the application for employment in the selection process.
3. State the role of tests and the importance of interviewing in the selection process.
4. State why reference checks and background investigations are conducted and explain the considerations related to acceptance or rejection of job applicants.
5. Describe staffing in the multinational environment.

*J*anisha Patel is the owner/manager of Quality Printing Company. Because of an increase in business, shop employees have been working overtime for almost a month. Last week, Janisha put an advertisement in the newspaper to hire a printer. Three people applied for the job. Janisha considered Mark Ketchell the only one to be qualified. She called Mark's previous employer in Saskatoon, who responded, "Mark is a diligent, hardworking person. He is as honest as the day is long. He knows his trade, too." Janisha also found that Mark had left Saskatoon after he was divorced a few months ago and that his work had deteriorated slightly prior to the divorce. The next day, Janisha asked Mark to operate one of the printing presses. Mark did so competently, so she decided immediately to hire him.

Mary Howard is the shipping supervisor for Oshawa Warehousing, a major food distributor. One of Mary's truck drivers just quit. She spoke to the human resource manager, Purvi Ragani, who said that she would begin the search right away. The next day an advertisement appeared in the local paper for the position. Purvi considered three of the 15 applicants to be qualified and called them in for an initial interview. The next morning Purvi called Mary and said, "I have three drivers who look like they can do the job. When do you want me to set up an interview for you with them? I guess you'll want to give them a driving test at that time." Mary interviewed the three drivers and gave them each a driving test and then called Purvi to state her choice. The next day the new driver reported to Mary for work.

These incidents provide a glimpse into the selection process. In the first instance, Janisha Patel, as owner/manager of a small printing shop, administered the entire selection process herself. In the second case, Purvi, the human resource manager, was involved heavily in the selection process, but Mary, the shipping supervisor, made the decision. Knowledge of the selection process, however, was important in both situations.

We begin the chapter with a discussion of the selection process and the environmental factors that affect it. Then, we describe the preliminary interview and review of the employment application employment and the résumé. Next, we discuss the administration of selection tests, validity studies, cutoff scores, and types of employment tests. In the ensuing sections, we present the employment interview and methods of interviewing. We follow those topics with a discussion of reference checks, background investigation, retention, and polygraph tests. Then we describe factors related to the selection decision, physical examination, and acceptance or rejection of job applicants. The final section relates to staffing in the multinational environment.

THE SIGNIFICANCE OF EMPLOYEE SELECTION

Whereas recruitment encourages individuals to seek employment with a firm, the purpose of the **selection** process is to choose from a group of applicants the individual best suited for a particular position. As might be expected, recruitment procedures affect the quality of the selection decision, as managers may be forced to employ marginally acceptable people if recruitment efforts identify only a few qualified applicants.

Most managers admit that employee selection is one of their most difficult, and most important business decisions.[1] As Peter Drucker has stated, "No other decisions are so long lasting in their consequences or so difficult to unmake. And yet, by and large, executives make poor promotion and staffing decisions. By all accounts, their batting average is no better than .333: At most, one-third of such decisions turn out right; one-third are minimally effective, and one-third are outright failures."[2] If too many mediocre or poor performers are hired, a firm cannot be successful long. Even if management has done everything else right—made realistic plans, designed a sound organizational structure, and implemented sound control systems—business goals cannot be attained without competent people.

When hidden costs, such as loss of productivity and overtime for the remaining staff, are added, the cost of replacing a key employee approaches twice his or her annual salary.[3] Another estimate has valued replacement as high as $500 000 per hire. While these figures may appear to be excessive, it is important to consider the productivity difference between high and low performers—a differential estimated to be as high as three to one.[4] A firm that selects qualified employees, therefore, reaps substantial benefits, which are repeated every year the employee is on the payroll.

The selection process affects other human resource functions, and is in turn influenced by them. If the selection process provides only marginally qualified employees, for example, management will have to intensify training efforts. Conversely, should the firm's compensation package be inferior to the competition's, attracting the best qualified applicants may be difficult.

The goal of the selection process is to match people with jobs. If individuals are overqualified, underqualified, or for any reason do not *fit* into the job or into the organizational culture, they will be more likely to leave the firm. In global terms, the Canadian labour market is extremely mobile;[5] the percentage of those who leave their jobs can approach 20 percent in any given year. It appears that much of the movement is among the 16-24 age group, as "younger groups engage in more job-shopping with fewer constraints such as loss of significant pension credits . . ."[6]

While some turnover may be desired, it is expensive—not only because of the visible costs of recruitment, relocation, and training, but, more importantly, because of the effects on performance. For example, product research and development can be delayed, manufacturing might become inefficient, and even market penetration could be slowed. Two studies conducted almost a decade apart indicate these expenses, although rarely measured, account for 80 percent or more of turnover costs.[7]

As emphasized in Chapter 3, job analysis provides data for preparing job descriptions and specifications, which in turn are essential for making good selection decisions. When selection criteria don't match the real needs of the job, the selection process is flawed from the start. Therefore, human resource managers must update job descriptions and specifications continually.

ENVIRONMENTAL FACTORS AFFECTING THE SELECTION PROCESS

A standardized screening process could greatly simplify the selection procedure. Development of a general process, however—even if it were possible—would not eliminate the necessity to depart from normal practice to meet the unique needs of particular situations. As one human resource manager suggested, "The only thing certain is that exceptions will be made."

Legal Considerations

As we outlined in Chapter 5, legislation and Human Rights Commission decisions have had a major effect on human resource management. It is imperative that human resource managers have extensive knowledge of the legal aspects of selection, including awareness of what selection criteria to avoid. Figure 6-1 identifies criteria that should be carefully avoided because of their discriminatory potential.

FIGURE 6-1   A Guide to Screening and Selection in Employment

Subject	Avoid Asking	Preferred	Comment
Name	about name change whether it was changed by court order, marriage, or other reason maiden name Christian name		if needed for a reference, to check on previously held jobs or on educational credentials
Address	for addresses outside Canada	ask place and duration of current or recent addresses	
Age	for birth certificates, baptismal records, or about age in general age or birthdate	ask applicants if they have reached age (minimum or maximum) for work as defined by law	if precise age required for benefits plans or other legitimate purposes it can be determined after selection
Sex	Mr/Mrs/Miss/Ms males or females to fill in different or coded applications if male or female on applications about pregnancy, childbirth or childcare arrangements; includes asking if birth control is used or child bearing plans	can ask applicant if the attendance requirements or minimum service commitment can be met	any applicants can be addressed during interviews or in correspondence without using courtesy titles such as Mr/Mrs/Miss
Marital Status	whether applicant is single, married, divorced, engaged, separated, widowed or living common-law whether an applicant's spouse is subject to transfer about spouse's employment	ask whether there are any known circumstances that might prevent completion of a minimum service commitment, for example	if transfer or travel is part of the job, the applicant can be asked if this would cause a problem information on dependents for benefits can be determined after selection
Disability	for listing of all disabilities, limitations or health problems whether applicant drinks or uses drugs	ask if applicant has any condition that could affect ability to do the job	a disability is only relevant to job ability if it: – threatens the safety of property of others

Subject	Avoid Asking	Preferred	Comment
Disability *(continued)*	whether applicant has ever received psychiatric care or been hospitalized for emotional problems	ask if the applicant has any condition which should be considered in selection	– prevents the applicant from safe and adequate job performance even if reasonable efforts were made to accommodate the disability
Medical Information	if currently under physician's care

name of family doctor

if receiving counselling or therapy | | medical exams should be preferably conducted after selection and only if an employee's condition is related to the job duties. Offers of employment can be made conditional on successful completion of a medical |
| **Affiliations** | for list of club or organizational memberships | membership in professional associations or occupational groups can be asked if a job requirement | applicants can decline to list any affiliation that might indicate a prohibited ground |
| **Pardoned Conviction** | whether an applicant has ever been convicted

if an applicant has ever been arrested

does applicant have a criminal record | if bonding is a job requirement ask if applicant is eligible | inquiries about criminal record/convictions— even those which have been pardoned—are discouraged unless related to job duties |
| **References** | | | the same restrictions that apply to questions asked of applicants apply when asking for employment references |
| **Family Status** | number of children or dependents

about arrangements for child care | if the employer has a policy against the hiring of close relatives, an applicant can be asked about kinship to other employees | contacts for emergencies and/or details on dependents can be determined after selection |
| **National or Ethnic Origin** | about birthplace, nationality of ancestors, spouse or other relatives

whether born in Canada

if naturalized or landed immigrants

for proof of citizenship | since those who are entitled to work in Canada must be citizens, landed immigrants or holders of valid work permits, applicants can be asked if they are legally entitled to work in Canada | documentation of eligibility to work (ie. papers, visas, etc.) can be requested after selection |

Subject	Avoid Asking	Preferred	Comment
Military Service	about military service in other countries	inquiry about Canadian military service where employment preference is given to veterans, by law	
Language	mother tongue where language skills obtained	ask if applicant understands, writes or speaks languages which are required for job	testing or scoring applicants for language proficiency is not permitted unless fluency is job-related
Race or Colour	any inquiry which indicates race or colour, including colour of eyes, skin or hair colour		information required for security clearances or similar purposes can be obtained after selection
Photographs	for photo to be attached to applicants or sent to interviewer before interview		photos for security passes or company files can be taken after selection
Religion	about religious affiliation, church membership, frequency of church attendance if applicant will work a specific religious holiday for references from clergy or religious leader		employers are to reasonably accommodate religious needs of workers
Height and Weight			no inquiry unless there is evidence that they are bona fide occupational requirements

FIGURE 6-1   A Guide to Screening and Selection in Employment (continued)

Source: Reproduced with permission from the Canadian Human Rights Commission and the Minister of Supply and Services Canada, 1993.

Speed of Decision Making

The time available to make the selection decision can also have a major effect on the process. Suppose, for example, the production manager comes to the HR office and says, "My only process control operators were just killed in a car accident! I can't operate until those positions are filled." In this instance, speed is crucial. A few phone calls, two interviews, and a prayer may constitute the entire selection procedure. Conversely, selecting a chief executive officer may take an entire year, with considerable attention to the careful study of résumés, intensive reference checking, and hours of interviews. At times, business pressures will dictate exceptions to the company's closely followed selection policies and procedures.

Organizational Hierarchy

Even under normal circumstances, different approaches to selection are followed when filling positions at various levels. Consider the differences in hiring a senior executive and a clerical worker. Extensive background checks and interviewing (perhaps two or three interviews) would be conducted to verify the experience and the capabilities of applicants for the executive position. On the other hand, an applicant for a clerical job most likely would take a word processing test followed by a short employment interview, and a reference from the last or present employer would be obtained. It is not the procedure that differs so much, then, but the amount of time, effort, and expense involved.

This concept is important, because poor selection can lead to high severance/termination costs. As with hiring, the cost of getting rid of poor performers varies with the level at which they are working. Dismissing a CEO, for example, can cost millions, while severance for a machine operator (although still costly), is normally limited to a few weeks' pay, plus recruitment costs, retraining, and lost productivity expenses.

Applicant Pool

As the selection process can be effective only if there are several qualified individuals for each position, a number of applicants should be interviewed for every job. At times, only a few applicants with the required specialized skills may be available. The selection process then becomes a matter of choosing whoever is at hand. Expansion and contraction of the labour market also exert considerable influence on availability and thus on the selection process.

The number of people hired for a particular job compared to the individuals in the applicant pool is often expressed as a **selection ratio**.

$$\text{Selection ratio} = \frac{\text{Number of persons hired to fill a particular job}}{\text{Number of available applicants}}$$

A selection ratio of 1.00 indicates that there is only one applicant for each position. Maintaining an effective selection process is difficult in this situation. People who might otherwise be rejected are often hired. The further the ratio falls below 1.00, the more alternatives the manager has in making a selection decision. For example, a selection ratio of 0.10 indicates that there are ten applicants for each position.

Except for specialized and skilled technical positions, many employers, especially those who advertise, receive more inquiries than they want. With a country-wide unemployment rate of more than nine percent, there is no shortage of applicants for most jobs. Yet in some job categories, such as computer software engineers and skilled craftspeople, there are chronic shortages.

Type of Organization

The economic sector, of the organization—private, government or not-for-profit—can also affect the selection process. A private-sector business is profit oriented, thus prospective employees are screened according to how well they might help achieve profit goals. When selecting employees for the private sector, the total individual is considered, including job-related personality factors.

Conversely, in the federal public service system, the hiring department must establish a "statement of qualifications" for the job to be filled. The interview process must measure each of the factors or characteristics outlined in the statement. Managers are discouraged from asking questions about other topics or issues.

Individuals being considered for positions in not-for-profit organizations (such as Scouts Canada, YMCA, or a women's shelter) confront still a different situation. The salary level may not be competitive with private and governmental organizations. Therefore, a person who fills one of these positions must be not only qualified, but also dedicated to this type of work.

Probationary Period

Many firms use a probationary period to evaluate new employees' performance and suitability. This procedure may be either a substitute for certain phases of the selection process, or a check on its validity. The rationale is that if individuals can perform successfully on the job during the probationary period, similar behaviour is likely to continue over the long term. Newly hired employees should be monitored to determine whether or not the hiring decision was a good one. Joan Milne, President of Taylor Enterprises, a large Toronto-based association management firm, has stressed the importance of probation: ". . . at Taylor Enterprises we find that the probationary period is the best way to find out what a person is really like. Probationary periods are an essential part of the hiring process."[8]

Even in unionized firms, a new employee typically is not protected by the union-management agreement until after a certain probationary period of from 60 to 90 days. During that time, an employee may be terminated with little or no justification, although terminations at the very end of the probation period have been challenged. When the probationary period is over, however, firing a marginal employee may prove to be quite difficult. Firms with collective agreements must be especially careful to select the most productive workers. Once they come under the union-management agreement, its terms must be followed in changing the status of a worker.

Employees who leave voluntarily or who are terminated for nonperformance should be given an exit interview to determine possible deficiencies in the selection process.[9] The results of this interview should be shared with all managers who are involved in selecting employees.

THE SELECTION PROCESS

Figure 6-2 outlines the selection process in general. If résumés have been submitted, they will be screened or examined to reject any obviously unqualified candidates. A short list then will be created, containing those candidates to

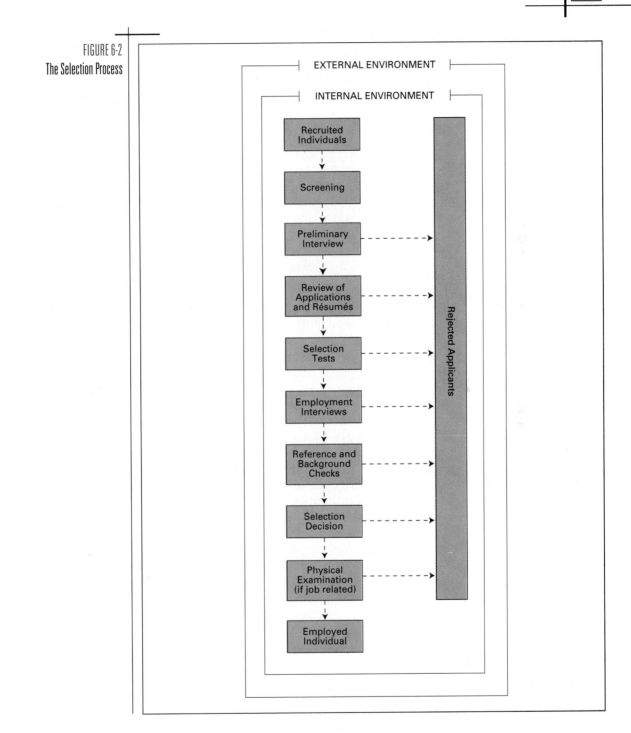

FIGURE 6-2
The Selection Process

be called for a preliminary interview, after which obviously unqualified candidates are rejected. Next, applicants complete the firm's application for employment. They then progress through a series of selection tests, the employment interview, and reference and background checks. The successful applicant sometimes is required to undergo a physical examination, but only after receiving an offer of employment and only if physical condition is related to job performance.

There are variations on this procedure. Some firms do not use preliminary interviews or testing. For some jobs, résumés are not required; instead the HR professional uses the application to conduct the initial screening.

Preliminary Interview

After the screening process, selection can begin with a preliminary interview to eliminate those who obviously do not meet position requirements. A preliminary interview may have other benefits. It is possible, for example, that other positions are available, and a skilled interviewer may be able to redirect a potentially valuable applicant. For instance, a person may be unqualified to fill a vacant electrician's position but be well suited to work as a maintenance technician. This type of interviewing thus not only builds goodwill for the firm, but can maximize recruitment and selection effectiveness.

Review of Application for Employment

Another early step in the selection process may involve completion of an employment application. (The form may be completed before or after the preliminary interview or, if preliminary interviews are not used, before or after the employment interview, depending upon whether or not a résumé has been submitted.)

A well-designed and properly used application form can save time. Because essential information is included and presented in a standardized format, it can be more effective than résumés in reducing dozens of applicants to a few bona fide candidates. The specific type of information requested on an application for employment may vary from firm to firm, but sections are usually provided for name, address, telephone number, education, and work history. Two more items should be standard: a statement asking the applicant to certify that everything on the form is true and an authorization to check references.[10]

An employment application form must meet not only the firm's information needs but also Human Rights requirements. An example of a properly designed application form is provided in Figure 6-3. Potentially discriminatory questions about such factors as gender, race, age, and number of children living at home do not appear on the form.

The information contained in a completed employment application is compared to the job description to determine whether or not a potential match exists between the firm's requirements and the applicant's qualifications. This comparison is often difficult, as applicants frequently attempt to present themselves in an exaggerated, somewhat unrealistic light. Comparing past duties and responsibilities with those needed for the present job opening isn't always easy.

In some companies terminals have been installed on which applicants can complete a job application form. A few human resource departments are setting up optical scanning programs that can handle the first-level application screening. These programs may also scan applications for other jobs the applicant may be qualified to fill. This comprehensive approach is not only more objective, but also less expensive than conventional screening systems.[11]

FIGURE 6-3
An Application for Employment

POSITION VACANCY APPLICATION

Position Vacancy Number _____   Position Title _____

Department/Faculty _____
Résumé attached   ☐ Yes   ☐ No
Are you currently working for The XYZ Corporation?   ☐ Yes   ☐ No
Have you previously worked for The XYZ Corporation?   ☐ Yes   ☐ No

PERSONAL DATA

Name _____
                        Family Name   Given Names

Address _____
                   Number and Street   City   Province   Postal Code

Telephone Number _____
                              Home   Business
Are you legally entitled to work in Canada?   ☐ Yes   ☐ No

EDUCATION

Institution Attended	Grade, Degree, Diploma or Certificate Completed	Course or Area of Study
Elementary School		
Secondary School		
Community School		
University		
Post Graduate		

List any other special training or educational experience completed, for instance, certificates, apprenticeships, seminars, conferences:
_____
_____
_____

EMPLOYMENT HISTORY

List previous employment in order, beginning with present or last employer. Your present employer will not be contacted without your approval.
_____

Employer _____   Started: Month/Year _____   Left: Month/Year _____

Address _____   Reason for Leaving _____

_____   Main Duties _____

Position _____   Salary _____
Department _____
Supervisor's Name and Title _____
Supervisor's Business Telephone Number _____
May we contact the employer?   ☐ Yes   ☐ No   *(Note: at least three similar sections would be included)*

GENERAL

Please detail any other relevant qualifications you have, for example, volunteer work experience, supervisory experience, promotions received, computer hardware and software knowledge, languages, equipment operated:
_____
_____
_____
_____

Why have you applied for this position? Discuss some of your key reasons such as qualifications, experience, special interests, or opportunities. Are there any additional comments you wish to make to support your application?
_____
_____
_____
_____

At what salary or rate of pay would you expect to start? $_____

DECLARATION

I certify that the information provided in this application form is accurate and complete. I am aware that misrepresentation or falsification may result in rejection of my application or dismissal from employment.

Date _____   Signature _____

Review of Résumés

A **résumé** is a common method applicants use to present background information. Even when résumés are not required by prospective employers, they are frequently submitted by job seekers. While there are no standard rules for designing résumés, there are some general guidelines to follow, depending upon the type and level of position sought. Figure 6-4 shows an example of a résumé submitted by a recent university graduate for a position in a public accounting firm. As illustrated in this example, there is significant *white space*, which makes it more easily read. The current and permanent addresses and telephone numbers of the applicant are prominently located. An *objective*

FIGURE 6-4
Example of Resumé
for an Entry Level Position

HENRY DUPONT

Current Address: Permanent Address:
15 Ridgewood Court   561 Springer Ave.
London, Ont.   Vancouver, BC
N6H 4N1   V5B 3R8
705-594-3869   604-876-5468

OBJECTIVE: To obtain an entry-level position in a Public Accounting firm.

EDUCATION: **Master of Business Administration**, December 1994
                      University of Western Ontario
                 Bachelor of Science in Business Administration, May 1992
                      University of New Brunswick
                 Concentration: Individual and Corporate Tax with emphasis on
                                  Management Information Systems
                 Cumulative GPA: 3.7

HONOURS: Dean's List in Accounting and Finance
                 Full Academic Scholarship
                 President of Summer Conference Program

ACCOMPLISHMENTS: Conducted TQM seminars
                       Successfully completed ISO-9000 courses
                       Graduate-Assistant to the Associate Dean

EXPERIENCE: **ASSISTANT ADMINISTRATOR**

3/95 – Present   Touch of Class Foods Corporation
(full time)   Accounting Department
                 • responsible for maintaining A/P and A/R ledgers
                 • originated a responsive invoice program
                 • prepared corporate tax returns and all schedules
                 • oversaw intern program
                 • initiated ISO-9000 Certifications in all areas of plant production

Summer 1993   **PERSONAL ASSISTANT**
Spring 1994   Mr. Charles Brandon
                 Park Board of Trustees
                 • Research and Development with City Sewer District
                 • Assisted with general accounting procedures
                 • Assisted with customer related issues
                 • Assisted with the allocation of public funds

COMPUTER SKILLS: Microsoft Word, AmiPro, WordPerfect 5.1 - 6.1, Lotus 1 2 3,
                       Microsoft Excel, Quattropro, Windows and Window
                       Applications

AFFILIATIONS: ISO-9000 Certified Consultant
                    TQM National Association

REFERENCES: Available upon request

statement is written to describe the type of opportunity desired. Since most recent graduates are being hired for their potential value to a firm, education, listed next, is a vital factor at this stage. Work experience, especially internships where students have worked in their field, then should be shown in reverse chronological order.

Prospective employers spend little time reading résumés. It is imperative, therefore, that the document be concise. A typical college or university graduate's résumé should be only one page. The résumé should be neat, and grammatical errors must be avoided. A single error here can mean immediate rejection.

If the résumé is targeted to a specific job opening, it should reflect the skills and abilities of the applicant as they apply to the open position. Use of personal computers makes it feasible to tailor résumés for specific purposes. In the few seconds recruiters spend scanning a résumé, they have to determine the extent to which the applicant's qualifications meet the requirements of the job.

The experienced professional's résumé differs somewhat from that of a new graduate. For example, in lieu of an objective statement, a summary of several skills related to requirements of the open position would be more appropriate. Although education may still be an important factor, the candidate's experience should take priority and appear next. Rather than focusing on responsibilities in each previously-held position, the applicant should emphasize accomplishments. Self-improvement activities, rather than hobbies, should be included. This résumé may be longer than one page, while still being concise.[12]

Applicants must be careful that all the information is accurate. Résumé fraud is "being done regularly," according to Allen Beech, President of Drake Beam Morin of Canada Ltd., who reports that about 15 percent of the résumés he reviews are "in some way fraudulent".[13] But "one silly, stupid mistake can cost you the job. It is grounds for being fired . . . because you've intentionally lied," says David Sanderson-Kirby, vice-president of Sanderson Kirby and Associates, an executive career counselling firm).[14]

ADMINISTRATION OF SELECTION TESTS

Selection tests are often used to assist in assessing an applicant's qualifications and potential for success. In Canada, few laws or regulations govern testing. In all jurisdictions, however, complaints can be made to the relevant Human Rights Commission if an applicant feels that a preemployment test is written in such a way as to discriminate against job seekers because of country of origin, disability, or any of the other criteria listed in human rights legislation. In fact, "a major argument used successfully in the courts against testing was that the questions were biased in favour of white, middle-class Canadian-born candidates and discriminated against minorities and new immigrants."[15]

Evidence suggests that the use of tests is widespread, more so in the public sector than in the private sector and in medium-sized and large companies than in small companies. Large organizations are likely to have trained specialists to run their testing programs.[16]

Advantages of Selection Tests

Testing has remained an important selection tool because it is one of the most reliable and accurate means of choosing candidates from a pool of applicants.[17] As with all selection procedures, it is important to identify the essential functions of each job and to determine the skills needed to perform them. Thus, the most widely-used tests evaluate specific skills like keyboarding speed and accuracy. In fact, abilities testing can even help to select workers with the capability to perform safely a variety of physically demanding tasks.[18] Fortunately there is a wide range of tests available, allowing some companies to conduct a battery of skill, aptitude, and personality tests.[19]

Disadvantages of Selection Tests

Job performance is related primarily to an individual's ability and motivation to do the job. Selection tests may predict an applicant's ability to do the job but they are less successful in indicating how much the applicant will want to perform it. For one reason or another, many employees never seem to reach their full potential. The factors related to success on the job are so numerous and complex that selection may always be more of an art than a science.

Another potential problem, related primarily to personality tests and interest inventories, has to do with applicants' honesty. An applicant may be strongly motivated to respond to questions untruthfully or to provide answers that he or she believes the interviewer expects. To prevent such behaviour, some tests have built-in lie detection scales, but intelligent individuals often detect them.

Another common problem is test anxiety. Applicants often become quite fearful when confronting yet another hurdle that might eliminate them from consideration. The test administrator's reassuring manner and a well-organized testing operation should serve to reduce this threat.

The dual problems of hiring the unqualified or less than qualified while rejecting qualified candidates will still exist regardless of the procedures followed. Managers can minimize such errors only through the use of well-developed tests administered by competent professionals. Even the best tests, however, are not perfect predictors. For these reasons, tests alone should never be used as the entire selection process; rather, test results should be considered in conjunction with other selection tools.

Characteristics of Properly Designed Selection Tests

Properly designed selection tests are standardized, objective, based on sound norms, reliable and—of utmost importance—valid. We discuss the application of these concepts next.

STANDARDIZATION

Standardization refers to the uniformity of the procedures and conditions related to administering tests. A comparison of the performance of several applicants on the same test is meaningful only if all have taken the test under conditions as close to identical as possible. For example, the instructions and the time allowed must be the same, and the physical environment should be similar. If one person takes a test in a noisy room and another takes it in a quiet environment, differences in test results are likely. Even when test administration procedures are specified by a test's developers, test administrators are responsible for providing standardized conditions.

OBJECTIVITY

Objectivity in testing is achieved when everyone scoring a test obtains the same results. Multiple-choice and true-false tests are said to be objective. The person taking the test either chooses the correct answer or does not. Scoring these tests is a mechanical process that lends itself to machine grading.

NORMS

A **norm** provides a frame of reference for comparing an applicant's performance with that of others. Specifically, a norm reflects the distribution of many scores obtained by people similar to the applicant being tested. The scores will tend to be distributed according to the normal probability curve presented in Figure 6-5. Standard deviations measure the amount of dispersion of the data. A normalized test will have approximately 68.3 percent of the scores within +1 standard deviation from the mean. Individuals scoring in this range would be considered average. Individuals achieving scores outside the range of +2 standard deviations would probably be highly unsuccessful or highly successful, depending on the particular criteria used.

FIGURE 6-5
A Normal Probability Curve

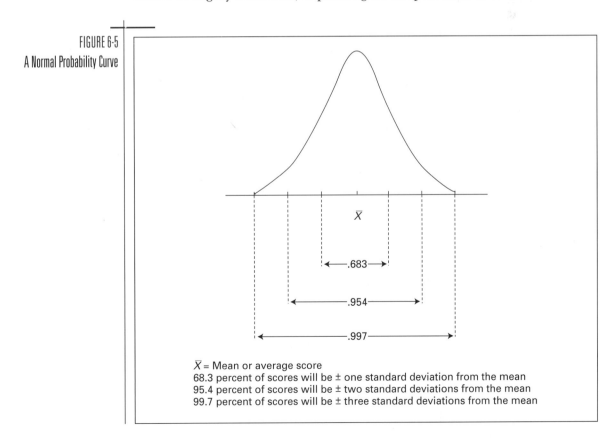

$\bar{X}$ = Mean or average score
68.3 percent of scores will be ± one standard deviation from the mean
95.4 percent of scores will be ± two standard deviations from the mean
99.7 percent of scores will be ± three standard deviations from the mean

When a sufficient number of employees are performing the same or similar work, employers can standardize their own tests, but most rely on a national or large-sample norm provided by the test's authors. A prospective employee takes the test, the score obtained is compared to the norm, and the significance of the test score is determined.

RELIABILITY

Reliability is the extent to which a test provides consistent results. Reliability data reveal the degree of confidence that can be placed in a test. If a test has low reliability, its validity as a predictor will also be low. However, the existence of reliability does not in itself guarantee validity.

To ensure its usefulness, the test's reliability must be verified. The **test-retest method** is a technique for determining reliability by giving the test twice to the same group of individuals and correlating the two sets of scores. A perfect positive correlation is +1.00. The closer the reliability coefficient is to perfection, the more consistent the results and, therefore, the more reliable the test. Problems with this method include the cost of administering the test twice, the possibility that testees will recall test questions, and the learning that may take place between tests.

A similar method is the **equivalent forms method**, which checks reliability by correlating the results of tests that are similar, but not identical. This approach overcomes some of the difficulties encountered with the test-retest method, but developing two forms of a test can be expensive. To overcome this weakness somewhat, the **split-halves method** may be used. This method tests reliability by dividing the results of a test into two parts and then correlating the results of the two parts. The one-time administration of the test has the obvious advantage of minimizing costs. Also, there is no opportunity for learning or recall that might distort the second score.

VALIDITY

The basic requirement for a selection test is that it be valid.[20] **Validity** is the extent to which a test measures what it purports to measure. If a test cannot indicate ability to perform on the job, it has no value as a predictor. Validity has always been a major concern in testing; concerns about equal employment opportunity have made it even more important to be able to demonstrate the validity of a selection test.

Validity is commonly reported as a correlation coefficient, which summarizes the relationship between two variables. For example, these variables may be the score on a selection test and some measure of employee performance. A coefficient of 0 shows no relationship, while a coefficient of either +1.0 or -1.0 indicates a perfect relationship, one positive and the other negative. Naturally, no test will be 100 percent accurate, yet HR managers strive for the highest feasible coefficient. The cumulative body of research indicates that tests yield correlation coefficients of from .30 to .60, depending upon the test and the position.[21] If a test is designed to predict job performance and validity studies of the test indicate a high correlation coefficient, most prospective employees who score high on the test will probably prove to be high performers.

In Canada, employers are not yet legally required to validate their selection tests. Generally speaking, validation is required only when the selection process as a whole results in an adverse effect on women, people with disabilities, or minorities. Validation of selection tests is expensive. However, management cannot know whether or not the test is actually measuring the qualities and abilities being sought without validation.

CUTOFF SCORES

After a test has been shown to be valid, an appropriate cutoff score must be established. A **cutoff score** is the score below which an applicant will not be selected. Cutoff scores will vary over time because they are directly related to the selection ratio. The more individuals apply for a job, the more selective the firm can be and, therefore, the higher the cutoff scores. Cutoff scores should normally be set to reflect a reasonable expectation of acceptable proficiency.

An example of what would likely occur if a validated test were administered to prospective employees is shown in Figure 6-6. In this firm experience indicates that individuals who score 40 and above on the test will be successful, while those who score below 40 will be less successful. Note that test results do not predict performance with precision. A small number of individuals who scored below the cutoff score of 40 proved to be good workers; some applicants scoring above 40 proved to be less successful. The test nevertheless appears to be a reasonably good predictor of success; but because is it not a totally accurate predictor, test results should serve as only one of several criteria in the selection decision.

Types of Employment Tests

Individuals differ tremendously in the characteristics they can bring to bear on job performance. These differences, many of which are measurable, relate to cognitive abilities, psychomotor abilities, job knowledge, work samples,

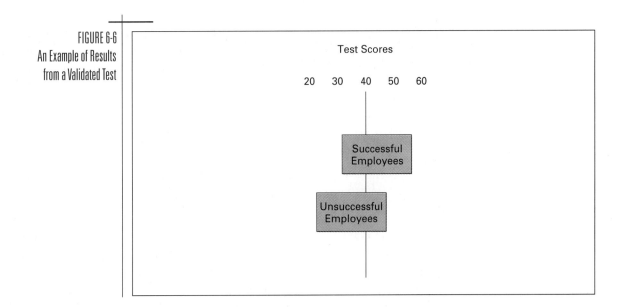

FIGURE 6-6
An Example of Results from a Validated Test

vocational interests, and personality. Some employers have also tested applicants for illegal drugs and for AIDS.

COGNITIVE APTITUDE TESTS

Cognitive aptitude tests measure an individual's ability to learn, as well as to perform a job. This type of test is particularly appropriate for making a selection from a group of inexperienced candidates. Job-related abilities may be classified as verbal, numerical, perceptual speed, spatial, and reasoning.

PSYCHOMOTOR ABILITIES TESTS

Psychomotor abilities tests measure strength, coordination, and dexterity. The development of tests to determine these abilities has been accelerated by miniaturization in assembly operations. Much of this work is so delicate that magnifying lenses must be used; thus the psychomotor abilities required to perform the tasks are critical. While standardized tests are not available to cover all these abilities, it is feasible to measure those necessary for many routine production jobs and some office jobs.

JOB KNOWLEDGE TESTS

Job knowledge tests are designed to measure a candidate's knowledge of job duties. These tests are available commercially, but job analysis results may also be used to design a test specifically for any job. While such tests frequently involve written responses, they may be administered orally. Regardless of the format, they contain key questions that serve to distinguish experienced, skilled workers from the rest.

WORK-SAMPLE TESTS

Work-sample tests require an applicant to perform a task or set of tasks representative of the job. Recent evidence suggests they are extremely valid, reduce test anxiety and are acceptable to applicants.

VOCATIONAL INTEREST TESTS

Vocational interest tests indicate the occupation in which a person is most interested and is most likely to be satisfied. These tests compare the individual's interests with those of successful employees in a specific job.

Interests appear to be stable over time and have been related to success in some fields, but they must not be confused with aptitudes or abilities. Tests for these characteristics should be used along with interest tests. Moreover, answers to interest test questions can be faked easily. Although interest tests may have some application in employee selection, their primary use has been in counselling and vocational guidance.

PERSONALITY TESTS

As selection tools, personality tests have not been as useful as other types, as they often have low reliability and validity. Because some personality tests emphasize subjective interpretation, they should be administered by a qualified psychologist.

DRUG TESTING

Few issues generate more controversy today than drug testing. Proponents of drug testing programs contend that they are necessary to ensure workplace safety, security, and productivity. They are also viewed as an accurate measure of drug use and as a means to deter it. Critics of drug testing argue just as vigorously that drug testing is an unjustifiable intrusion into an employee's private life.[22]

In the winter of 1993, two prominent Canadian lawyers, Robert Solomon and Sydney Usprich, published a paper in *Business Quarterly* in which they tried to sort out the complicated legal and moral arguments surrounding employment drug testing (EDT). Even these experts were forced to admit that

> the question of EDT does not permit simplistic answers. Compounding the difficulty is the overriding problem of striking the proper balance between a worker's legitimate privacy rights and an employer's valid concerns for safety and efficiency in the workplace. Given the various legal issues and the lack of definitive precedents, it is difficult to formulate a policy that will not be challengeable on some level.[23]

In other words, the entire issue is a legal and ethical tangle that will take some time to sort out. HR professionals, then, should approach drug testing with caution, checking with legal counsel and with the appropriate Human Rights Commission on a case-by-case basis.

So important is this issue that several senior executives have commented publicly. Maurice Strong, then chairman of Ontario Hydro, said that ". . . Ontario Hydro does not engage in drug testing. Rather, we have in place, policies and procedures which address this issue, such as those governing hiring practices and probationary periods."[24] Bob Peterson, chairman and CEO of Imperial Oil Ltd., described how a drug testing program was instituted, with employee involvement, after a number of accidents in which drug abuse was thought to have been associated. He went on to explain:

> with regard to testing, all job applicants are subject to pre-employment drug testing as a condition of employment. . . . All employees are subject to alcohol and drug testing following a significant accident or near miss at work and where there is reasonable cause to do so. Employees in safety-sensitive or specified executive positions are subject to random alcohol and drug testing.[25]

These two different companies may have two quite different approaches, but each is trying to cope with this issue in as fair a manner as possible. To illustrate further the complexity of this issue, the Imperial Oil drug and alcohol policy will be challenged at an Ontario Human Rights Board of Inquiry, to determine whether or not it contravenes the Ontario Human Rights Code.[26]

Finally, James Stanford, president and CEO of Petro-Canada seems to have taken a middle ground:

> In Petro-Canada we will drug test in limited circumstances. If the law demands drug testing, Petro-Canada will comply. We may use drug testing in conjunction with a medical rehabilitation program. Finally, if commercial

arrangements with partners in business ventures ask for drug testing for legitimate safety concerns, we will consider it.[27]

This policy appears to require that HR professionals assess and make a decision in unique situations.

TESTING FOR ACQUIRED IMMUNE DEFICIENCY SYNDROME (AIDS)

In Canada, individuals with AIDS and those who test positive for the HIV virus cannot be denied employment as a result of this medical condition. Only in certain circumstances can the condition be taken into account, such as in some health care settings or in work requiring international travel where a foreign government might deny entry to HIV-positive employees. HIV testing, then, cannot be used as a selection tool except in these rare circumstances. HR professionals should obtain advice before attempting any such test.

THE EMPLOYMENT INTERVIEW

The **employment interview** is a goal-oriented conversation in which the interviewer and applicant exchange information. Historically, interviews have not been valid predictors of success on the job. Most interviews have correlation coefficients in the 0.00 to .30 range.[28] Nevertheless, they continue to be the primary method used to evaluate applicants, used by virtually every company in Canada. As illustrated later in this chapter, some managers have made progress in improving interview validity.

The employment interview is especially important because the applicants who reach this stage are considered to be the most promising candidates. They may have survived a preliminary interview and scored satisfactorily on selection tests. At this point, the candidates appear to be qualified. Every seasoned manager knows, however, that appearances can be misleading. Additional information is needed to determine whether or not the individual is willing to work and can adapt to the organization.

Legal Implications of Interviewing

Since the interview is a form of test, it should be subject to the same validity requirements as any other step in the selection process. Few managers, however, are willing to pay the cost of validating interviews. They can be validated only through extensive follow-up: a method that requires collecting data over a long period of time. There is significant evidence to suggest, however, that if two managers in a firm interview the same applicant at different times, the outcomes may differ.

In fact, the interview is perhaps more vulnerable to charges of discrimination than any other tool used in the selection process. In most cases, there is little or no documentation of the questions asked or of the answers received. The interviewer may tend to ask irrelevant questions that would never appear on an application form. Some interviewers are inclined to ask questions that are not job related or that reflect their personal biases.[29] Because there is no record of the interview, the dubious questions go unchallenged.

Nevertheless, interviewing in this manner is risky and can lead to charges of discrimination. Since an interview is a test, all questions should be job related.

Interviewer Objectives

The goal of the employment interview is to obtain information on which decisions can be made about the candidate's suitability for the job. To do so, interviewers should strive to accomplish the following objectives.

CREATE AN APPROPRIATE ENVIRONMENT

The interviewer should try to establish rapport with the applicant. It is essential that the interviewer obtain accurate information from the candidate and honest communication is more likely to take place in a climate of mutual trust and confidence.

OBTAIN BEHAVIOURAL, JOB RELATED INFORMATION FROM THE APPLICANT

The interview should complement other selection tools by obtaining additional job-related information about the applicant. As well, certain points might require clarification, uncovering details that are needed to make a sound selection decision.

PROVIDE INFORMATION ABOUT THE JOB AND THE COMPANY

General information about the job, company policies, products, and services should be communicated to the applicant in a realistic manner. The job should neither be oversold nor made to appear more difficult than it actually is.

DETERMINING THE NEXT STEP

After the interview is concluded, the interviewer must determine whether or not the candidate is suitable for the open position. If the conclusion is positive, the process continues. If there appears to be no match, the candidate is eliminated from consideration.

A note of warning comes from Clare Copeland, CEO of Peoples Jewellers:

> Sounds crazy but many organizations fail by hiring good people. We meet, interview people we are impressed with and hire them and wonder why they don't work out. Don't hire good people —hire the *right* people . . . measure constantly and hire against the ability to do the job . . your hirings will determine your success or failure, so you better get good at it and treat it as the vital job it is.[30]

Interviewee Objectives

It is important to remember that interviewees also have expectations:[31]

- to be listened to and understood;
- to have ample opportunity to present their qualifications;

- to be treated fairly and with respect;
- to be allowed access to information about the job and the company;
- to be given enough information to make an informed decision concerning the desirability of the job.

Interview Content

The specific content of employment interviews varies greatly by organization and job level. The following general topics, however, appear fairly consistently: technical competence (often revealed through academic achievement and occupational experience); personal qualities (such as interpersonal skills); and potential, which includes the candidate's career orientation. A general guideline is that " . . . seventy percent of job and interview should be devoted to determining the expected behaviour of the candidate in the actual job situation."[32] Any question, therefore, should relate specifically to some aspect of the vacant job or to the candidate's potential future with the firm.

ACADEMIC ACHIEVEMENT

In the absence of significant work experience, a person's academic background takes on greater importance. Records should not be accepted at face value, however, as more than one recruiter has fallen victim to misrepresentation of academic credentials.[33]

As well, the interviewer should try to discover any underlying factors related to academic performance. For example, a student who earned only a 2.28/4.0 GPA may turn out to be a very bright person who, because of financial difficulties, worked virtually full time while still participating in a variety of activities. On the other hand, a student in different circumstances who received a 3.8/4.0 GPA may not be a strong candidate for the position.

WORK EXPERIENCE

In exploring an individual's work experience , the interviewer is trying to determine the applicant's skills, abilities, and willingness to handle responsibility. While successful performance in one job does not guarantee success in another, past performance does provide an indication of the employee's ability and willingness to work. Note that job titles do not represent the same job content in all organizations. It is important to find out what actual tasks and responsibilities the applicant had in a position.

PERSONAL QUALITIES

Personal qualities usually observed during the interview include physical appearance, speaking ability, vocabulary, poise, adaptability, and assertiveness. Even though he or she may have personal preferences, the interviewer must make every effort to keep personal biases not related to the job out of the selection process.

Because of the legal ramifications, it is unwise to permit the applicant's personal characteristics to influence the selection decision. Physical appearance, for example, would likely be an occupational qualification only in rare cases, such as if the vacant job required an actress to portray the early career of Julia Roberts. Similarly, speaking ability, vocabulary, poise, and type of voice may be job-related qualifications for a sportscaster and assertiveness may be required for a credit collector's job.

INTERPERSONAL SKILLS

To a degree, the interview may permit the observation of an applicant's interpersonal skills. The interviewee may be playing a role, however, that portrays a personality far different from his or her normal self. Studies have indicated that candidates are often hired on the basis of their interviewing skills, rather than their ability to perform the job. For this reason, the interviewer may need to ask questions regarding the applicant's interpersonal relationships with people in other social and civic situations.

Most jobs are not performed in isolation and the need to interact is often essential. In fact, most failures in the workplace are due not to lack of technical ability but rather to poor interpersonal skills. An individual may be a competent worker, but if he or she cannot work well with other employees, chances for success are greatly diminished. This concept is especially important in a business world where increasing emphasis is being placed on the use of teams.[34]

CAREER ORIENTATION

Questions about a candidate's career objectives may help the interviewer determine whether or not the applicant's aspirations are realistic. The odds are high, for example, that a recent college graduate who expects to become a senior vice-president within six months will become dissatisfied quickly.

The interviewer should present an honest and accurate description of career prospects within the organization. Deception may well prove counterproductive if the applicant is hired and later becomes dissatisfied as the truth unfolds. The firm may lose a substantial investment in the form of recruitment, selection, and training if a promising new employee leaves after only a few months on the job.

Types of Interviews

Interviews can range from highly structured to free flowing. Since the interview is a test, structured interviews have become popular, as they are more legally defensible. Aside from the legal ramifications, however, the HR professional needs to use the best method of making selection decisions. Historically, interviews have had very poor validity, but it is possible, using a structured format that focuses on job-related questions, to obtain acceptable validity coefficients.

THE UNSTRUCTURED (NONDIRECTIVE) INTERVIEW

In the **unstructured interview**, the interviewer asks probing, open-ended questions. This type of interview is comprehensive, as the interviewer encourages the applicant to do much of the talking. This nondirective technique is often more time-consuming than the structured interview. The result is that different information can be obtained from each candidate, making comparison difficult. Compounding this problem is the likelihood of ill-advised, potentially discriminatory information being discussed. The applicant, who is being encouraged to speak candidly, may volunteer information that the interviewer doesn't need or want to know. Unsuccessful applicants who are subjected to this interviewing approach could claim later that failure to get the job was based on the employer's use of this information.

THE STRUCTURED (DIRECTIVE OR PATTERNED) INTERVIEW

The **structured interview** consists of a series of job-related questions that are consistently asked of each applicant for a particular job. Use of structured interviews increases reliability and accuracy by reducing subjectivity and inconsistency. Recent research suggests that the reliability and the validity of a structured interview is twice that of the unstructured variety.[35]

Interviewers should follow a structured, systematic interview procedure, therefore, in order to obtain the information necessary to evaluate each candidate fairly and objectively. The advantages of structure are diminished, however, if the interviewer is biased or "forms a quick first impression based on an obvious or outstanding characteristic of an applicant and may compound the problem by making inappropriate inferences from these features."[36] An idea (even held unconsciously) that blonds are dumb or fat people are lazy, for example, can result in the rejection of some excellent candidates.

A structured job interview may contain any of four types of questions:

1. **Situational questions** pose a hypothetical job situation and ask what the applicant would do in that situation.
2. **Job knowledge questions** probe the applicant's job-related knowledge. These questions may relate to basic educational skills or to complex scientific or managerial techniques.
3. **Job-sample simulation questions** or activities involve situations in which an applicant may be required to perform a sample job-related task. When this procedure isn't feasible, a job simulation may be used. Answering these types of questions or proving task mastery may require physical activity.
4. **Worker requirements questions** seek to determine the applicant's willingness to conform to the requirements of the job. For example, the interviewer may ask whether or not the applicant is willing to perform repetitive work, or to move to another city. The nature of these questions serves as a realistic job preview that may aid in self-selection.

A properly designed structured interview, then, will contain only job-related questions. Each question should be asked for a specific purpose. An illustration of a patterned interview guide for discussing work experience is provided in Figure 6-7.

FIGURE 6-7
Portion of a Patterned Interview Guide

1. Job Related Skills
- Please describe a typical day on your last job
- Describe your most noteworthy achievement for me (either present or former job)
- Can you tell me how you would install (any procedure that relates to the vacant job)

2. Intelligence, Aptitude and Personality
- How do you make important decisions?
- Discuss how your present employer might or could be more successful or efficient.
- Describe our company; what do you know about it?

3. Attitude/Personality
- What interests you about this job?
- Why do you want to leave your current employer?
- Describe your weaknesses/strengths
- Are you a risk-taker? Tell me about the risks you took during your last three jobs: what happened?

Source: Adapted from R. Half, "The art and science of hiring." *CGA Magazine*, 28(7) (1994), 45–48.

BEHAVIOUR DESCRIPTION INTERVIEWING

The **behaviour description interview** is a type of structured interview in which questions are designed to probe the candidate's past behaviour in specific situations. Judgements about the applicant's personality are avoided, as are hypothetical and self-evaluative questions.[37] The situational behaviours are selected carefully for their relevance to job success. Questions are formed from these behaviours and applicants are asked how they performed in the described situation. For example, a candidate for an engineering position might be asked, "Tell me about a time when you had to make an important decision without having all the information you needed." Benchmark answers derived from behaviours of successful employees are prepared for use in rating applicant responses.

Behaviour description interviewing is more accurate than traditional interviewing in predicting whether or not applicants will be successful on the job; validity coefficients have been shown to be several times higher.[38] One caveat, however, is that the *correct* answer for evaluating responses may reflect behaviour that is representative of the white, male employee. Women and minorities may not have the life experiences that provide similar responses. Individuals from other cultures may experience similar problems. For example, the Japanese culture emphasizes conformity, not individuality. Being asked to describe how they best demonstrated their management skills in a certain situation could be embarrassing to someone from any group-oriented culture.[39]

Methods of Interviewing

Interviews may be conducted in several ways. In a typical employment interview, the applicant meets one-on-one with an interviewer. As the interview may be a highly emotional occasion for the applicant, meeting alone with the interviewer is often less threatening than facing more than one person.

In a **group interview**, several applicants interact in the presence of one or more company representatives. This approach may provide useful insights into the candidates' interpersonal competence as they must engage in group discussion. Another advantage of this technique is that it saves time for busy professionals and executives.

In a **board interview**, one candidate is interviewed by several representatives of the firm. Although a thorough examination of the applicant is likely, the interviewee's anxiety level is often high. A vice-president of industrial relations for an aircraft firm stated, "We use a three-person board to screen each applicant, asking a series of questions designed to ferret out the individual's attitudes toward former employers, jobs, etc." Naturally, the amount of time devoted to a board interview will differ depending on the type and level of job. Indeed, there are doubts about the board interview, as one author has suggested:

> If possible, it is a good idea to introduce leading job candidates to several levels of management. But, don't hire by committee! Committees often end up hiring a "compromise candidate" who neither completely pleases nor offends anyone on the committee. This choice is seldom the best person for the job.[40]

Most interview sessions are designed to minimize the candidate's stress level. The **stress interview**, however, intentionally creates anxiety to determine how an applicant will react to stress on the job. The interviewer deliberately makes the candidate uncomfortable by asking blunt and sometimes discourteous questions. The purpose is to determine the applicant's tolerance for stress. This knowledge may be important if the job requires the ability to deal with a high stress levels. In one stress interview situation, for example, candidates were required to add nine to another number that appeared on a screen as they were being interviewed aggressively by a board. Needless to say, many people do not fare well in this sort of atmosphere.

Thus, many human resource professionals believe the stress interview to be not only inconsiderate, but ineffective. They feel that information exchange in a stressful environment often is distorted and misinterpreted, that the data obtained are not the type upon which to base a selection decision. It seems clear, then, that stress interviews are not appropriate for the majority of work situations.

Interview Planning

Interview planning is essential to effective employment interviews. The physical location of the interview should be both pleasant and private, providing for a minimum of interruptions. The interviewer should become familiar with the applicant's record by reviewing the data collected from other selection tools. In preparing for the interview, a job profile should be developed, based on the job description. After job requirements have been listed, it is helpful to have an interview checklist that includes these hints:

- Compare applicant's application and résumé with job requirements.
- Develop questions related to qualities sought.
- Prepare a step-by-step scenario of how to present the position, company, division, and department.
- Determine how to ask for examples of past applicant behaviour, not what future behaviour might be.[41]

The Interviewer and the Interview Process

The interviewer should possess a pleasant personality, empathy, and the ability to listen and to communicate effectively. He or she should have a through knowledge of job requirements and the applicant's qualifications as they relate to the vacant job. In order to elicit needed information, the interviewer must create a climate that encourages the applicant to speak freely. Conversation should not become too casual, however, as engaging in friendly chitchat with candidates wastes time and might bring to light irrelevant information that affects the interviewer's judgement.

When one office manager made friendly enquiries about a job applicant's children, he thought he was merely breaking the ice and setting the tone for an effective dialogue. A year later, however, he was the target of a lawsuit filed by the unsuccessful applicant. The applicant claimed to have been the victim of sexual discrimination, because she had told the manager she needed day care when she went to work. She claimed that a man would not have been asked questions about his children.

To minimize these incidents, employers should use structured interviews and ask the same questions of all applicants. It is also critical to record the applicant's responses. If a candidate begins volunteering personal information that is not job related, the interviewer should steer the conversation back on course. It might do well to begin the interview by tactfully stating, "This selection decision will be based strictly on qualifications. Let's not discuss topics such as religion, social activities, national origin, sex, or family situations. We are definitely interested in you personally. However, these factors are not job related and will not be considered in our decision."[42] Figure 6-8 illustrates some potential problems that can be circumvented by a competent interviewer using a properly planned, structured interview format.

When the interviewer has obtained the necessary information and answered the applicant's questions, the interview should be concluded. At this point, the interviewer should tell the applicant when he or she will receive notification of the selection decision. If this promise is broken, the relationship between the applicant and the organization will be antagonistic. No manager wants a large number of rejected applicants to tell their friends and relatives about unfair treatment.

FIGURE 6-8
Potential Interviewing Problems

Inappropriate Questions
Many questions are inappropriate. If asked, the responses create a legal liability for the employer. The most basic interviewing rule is: "Ask only job-related questions!"

Premature Judgements
Research suggests that interviewers often make judgements about candidates in the first few minutes of the interview, ignoring a great deal of potentially valuable information.

Interviewer Domination
In successful interviews, information flows both ways. Therefore, interviewers must learn to be good listeners as well as suppliers of information.

Inconsistent Questions
If interviewers ask all applicants essentially the same questions and in the same sequence, the applicants are judged on the same basis. This technique enables better decisions to be made.

Central Tendency
When interviewers rate virtually all candidates as average, they fail to differentiate between strong and weak candidates.

Halo Error
When interviewers permit a single personal characteristic or a cluster of characteristics to influence their overall impression of candidates, the best applicant may not be selected.

Contrast Effects
An error in judgement may occur when an interviewer meets with several poorly qualified applicants and then confronts a mediocre candidate. By comparison, the last applicant may appear to be better qualified than he or she actually is.

Interviewer Bias
Interviewers must understand and acknowledge their own prejudices and learn to deal with them. The only valid bias for an interviewer is to favour the best qualified candidate for the open position.

Lack of Training
When the cost of making poor selection decisions is considered, the expense of training employees in interviewing skills can easily be justified.

Behaviour Sample
Even if an interviewer spent a week with an applicant, the behaviour sample might be too small to judge the candidate's qualifications properly. In addition, candidates seldom behave typically or naturally during an interview as they are trying to impress.

Nonverbal Communication
Interviewers should make a conscious effort to view themselves as applicants do in order to avoid sending inappropriate or unintended nonverbal signals.

Realistic Job Previews[43]

Many applicants have unrealistic expectations about the prospective job and the employer. These inaccurate perceptions sometimes result when interviewers try too hard to create an attractive corporate image. Too many interviewers are overly enthusiastic about the job and the company, leading to mismatches of people and positions. The problem is compounded when candidates exaggerate their qualifications.[44] To correct this situation from the employer's viewpoint, a realistic job preview should be given to all applicants either early in the selection process, or before a job offer is made.

A **realistic job preview (RJP)** conveys information in an unbiased manner about tasks the person would perform, about expected behaviour, and about company policies and procedures. This approach helps applicants develop a more accurate perception of the job and the firm. Considerable research confirms the effectiveness of RJPs. Although applicants who take part in an RJP tend to accept job offers less often than those who do not, their productivity is virtually the same as candidates selected without one. The important results are that employees experiencing RJPs exhibit lower turnover and greater job satisfaction.[45]

Whether or not RJPs are the cause of this satisfaction, however, is open to debate. One recent study has suggested that companies using RJPs for selection should be aware that people appear to react differently to them. Only a portion of applicants exposed to an RJP will refuse a position because of a partly unfavourable preview. The remaining applicants may choose to accept a position because of the "air of honesty" engendered by the RJP. This is, in a sense, the opposite of the intended effect of using an RJP. Proponents suggest RJPs are to be used to convey realistic job expectations, not to influence acceptance rates.

Whatever the reason, RJPs do seem to accomplish the main purpose of reducing turnover. RJPs have been found to increase commitment to a job choice, in part because of this air of honesty, which is valued highly by job applicants.[46]

PERSONAL REFERENCES

Reference checks may provide additional insight into the information furnished by the applicant and allow for verification of its accuracy. In fact, applicants are often required to submit the names of several **referees**, people who can provide additional information about them. The flaw with this step in the selection process is that virtually everyone can name three or four people who are willing to make favourable statements about him or her. Furthermore, personal references are likely to focus on the candidate's personal characteristics. Objective, job-related data are seldom gathered from these sources. For this reason, most organizations place more emphasis on investigations of previous employment.

EMPLOYMENT REFERENCES

Employment references seek data from work-related **referees** (including previous employers), usually supplied by the applicant. The intensity of these background investigations depends on the level of responsibility inherent in the position to be filled.

As with the personal reference, the main problem faced by an interviewer is obtaining an objective account of the applicant's work history. The reference check is best done only after a tentative hiring decision has been made, or after a short list of two or three candidates have been interviewed. Today, most references are checked by phone. Except in parts of Europe, written opinions have fallen into disfavour, perhaps because of the perceived opportunity for legal action (although in fact, one is as responsible for untruthful spoken references as for written ones).

Before checking references, the employer should ask the applicant for permission in writing, along with a signed statement not to hold referees liable for their opinions (note, though, that this latter requirement has not been tested extensively in Canadian courts). Then, the check should be made by two people, using an extension phone.

The first task is not only to verify the dates of employment but to determine the referee's relationship with the applicant so that the validity of the information can be judged. In fact, some authors suggest that peers and subordinates should be included, although what little research we have indicates that former supervisors are the best source.

Questions, determined by the key characteristics of the job, should be agreed upon in advance and shared between the two interviewers. Each interviewer should make notes, outlining both answers received and impressions. Similar questions should be asked about each potential recruit. Anything that can be asked legally in an interview can be included during the reference check, including schools and universities attended, the validity of qualifications, dates of employment work habits, and whether or not the former or present employer would rehire the applicant. Likewise, the interviewers should not ask about topics that should be avoided in an interview, including marital status, child care arrangements, age, disability, religion, race, or national origin.

Once the process is complete, extreme care must be taken to maintain confidentiality. Perceived problem areas, however, should always be investigated further.

The two-person check, while not infallible, tends to eliminate untruthful interviews. In addition, the recruiter is protected, in that two sets of collaborative notes (dated and signed) provide a record that is hard to contest.[47] As fear of defamation liability is a major concern when conducting reference checks in Canada,[48] this dual interviewer technique should be used whenever possible.

BACKGROUND INVESTIGATIONS

As well as a work-related reference, a background investigation should be completed because credential fraud has increased in recent years. Remember the previous section on résumé fraud, which suggested that some job applicants are not what they present themselves to be. Some applicants are not even *who* they say they are. Others may exaggerate their skills, education, and experience if given the chance. For example, one firm gave applicants a list of equipment and asked them to identify the items they were qualified to operate. A high percentage of the candidates indicated they could operate equipment that doesn't exist![49]

Consider the following true story:

Accountants are hard to come by in northern mining towns. That's why Mike Black was so delighted when he received a résumé in the mail from Conrad Stevenson. Conrad (so his letter said) had been working at a mine in South America. Because of continuing political unrest, he felt it was wise to move his wife and two small children back to safer political climes.

Mike was pleased, too, with Conrad's qualifications. A degree in accounting and membership of two financial associations were supported by five years of practical experience. He immediately sent off an enthusiastic fax, asking Conrad to write to the mine as soon as he returned home.

About six weeks later, Conrad arrived. An affable, easygoing sort of chap with a ready smile and a quick wit, Mike hired him on the spot! And he proved to be a good worker, as well as a welcome addition to the somewhat meagre social life at the mine.

In the spring, mine managers have their annual convention. Although serious papers are presented and there are seminars to attend, the gathering tends to be one long party. Mike and his wife attended, as they always did, and did a lot of partying, as they always did. At one such cultural gathering, Mike was holding forth at some length about his "good luck" in acquiring Conrad Stevenson—"before the rest of you guys could get your hands on him!"

In the corner sat a quiet little man from a mine in South America. After a while, he beckoned Mike over to join him.

"Tell me," he said, "is this fellow Stevenson a friendly sort of guy, blond, quick with his tongue—great man at a party?"

Mike replied, "Yeah, that would be him—you know Conrad?"

The little man looked sad. "I hate to tell you this, but if 'Conrad' is who I think he is, his real name is Ralph Fox. We fired him last year for stealing. And you can forget about all those fancy qualifications of his. They're phony! I'm afraid you've fallen victim—as we did—to an accomplished con artist."[50]

All the cost of firing Conrad and auditing the accounts to be sure he hadn't stolen anything could have been avoided if Mike Black had made one long-distance telephone call to Conrad's previous employer.

Virtually every qualification an applicant lists can be verified.[51] Small firms may not possess the staff to screen thoroughly the backgrounds of prospective employees, and even large organizations may prefer to use the specialized services of professional screening firms. Some background checks may be performed within 24 hours for a few dollars per search.[52] For example, U.S.-based Pinkerton Security and Investigation Services screens more than one million job applicants each year for its own operations and for its clients.[53] Regardless of how they are accomplished, background investigations have become increasingly important in making sound selection decisions.

POLYGRAPH (LIE DETECTOR) TESTS

The polygraph is used only rarely in Canada. Information obtained in this manner cannot be used as evidence in Canadian courts. Use of this method can signal a lack of trust that is difficult to overcome. Furthermore, polygraphs are legally prohibited as a selection tool in some jurisdictions. It is unwise even to consider this method of verifying information.

THE SELECTION DECISION

After obtaining and evaluating information about the finalists, the manager must take the most critical step of all: making the hiring decision. The other stages in the selection process have been used to narrow the number of candidates. The final choice will be made from among those still being considered—after reference checks, selection tests, background investigations, and interview information have been evaluated.

It is not always the person with the best overall qualifications who is hired. Rather, the person whose qualifications most closely conform to the requirements of the open position should be selected. If management is to invest thousands of dollars to recruit, select, and train an employee, it is important to hire the most qualified available candidate for the position.

Human resource professionals are involved in all phases leading up to the final employment decision. The final selection, however, should be made by the manager responsible for the new employee's performance—the person who will have to supervise and work with the successful applicant. In making this decision, the operating manager may or may not ask for advice from the human resource manager. The role of the HRM professional is to provide service and counsel.

PHYSICAL EXAMINATION

After the decision has been made to extend a job offer, the next phase of the selection process can involve a physical examination. Physical examinations are performed only if the job requires a clearly determined level of physical effort, or if there is some physical attribute crucial to job performance, like the ability to climb telephone poles. If the examination reveals a condition prohibiting the performance of required tasks, the individual can only be rejected if reasonable accommodations can not be made to allow the employee to perform the work. When women were first hired as telephone installers, for example, one phone company imposed a height restriction, as shorter women could not get ladders down off the trucks. An arbitration board ruled that the practice was discriminatory, as all the firm had to do was to provide stools for workers to stand on while removing the ladders. Rejections based on physical inability then, must be studied carefully to ensure that "reasonable accommodation" cannot be made.

ACCEPTANCE OF THE JOB APPLICANT

Assuming that the physical examination (if appropriate) fails to uncover any disqualifying medical problems, the applicant can be employed. The starting date is normally based on the wishes of both the firm and the individual. If currently employed by another firm, the individual customarily gives between two and four weeks' notice. Even after this notice, the individual may need some personal time to prepare for the new job. This transition time is particularly important if the new job requires a move to another city. Thus the amount of time before the individual can join the firm is often considerable—but it is necessary to make these accommodations.

Management may also want the individual to delay the date of employment. If, for example, the new employee's first assignment upon joining the firm is to attend a training school, the individual may be requested to delay joining the firm until the school begins. Delays for the benefit of the employer should not be extended too long, especially if an undue hardship would be placed on the employee.

REJECTION OF JOB APPLICANTS

Applicants may be rejected during any phase of the selection process. When someone applies for a position, that person is signifying: "I think I am qualified for the job. Why don't you hire me?" Tension builds as the applicant progresses through the selection process. If the preliminary interview suggests the applicant is not qualified, the ego damage is likely to be slight. The HR professional may even be able to steer the individual to other jobs in the firm that better match his or her qualifications.

Most people do not enjoy the employment interview. Taking a test that could affect one's career, for example, can be extremely stressful, Indeed to be told, "There does not appear to be a proper match between your qualifications and our needs" can be a painful experience. Most HR managers recognize this fact and attempt to let the individual know as quickly and as kindly as possible. But it is often difficult to tell people they will not be hired. The best HR professionals can do is to make selection decisions objectively. Most individuals can, with time, accept the fact they were not chosen.

It is imperative that all unsuccessful applicants be informed. Applicants who are left hanging will eventually figure out that they didn't get the job, but will be antagonized by the lack of courtesy. It is foolish to alienate people who may be potential future employees, or potential customers. The way the information is conveyed will affect the applicant's reaction. When considerable time has been spent going through the selection process, a company representative may contact the applicant and explain why another person was offered the job. But increasingly, time constraints force the employer to write a rejection letter. Such a letter, however, can still be personalized. While an impersonal letter of rejection often angers the recipient, a personal touch will often ease the stigma and avoid hostile feelings toward the company.

STAFFING IN THE MULTINATIONAL ENVIRONMENT

When hiring for international operations, employers have a number of decisions to make. For example, should they use an **expatriate** work force (i.e., people from the parent company) or rely on local talent? What qualities will make individuals successful? In short, what does global talent look like? While there may be no single answer to this question, a profile of Mary Beth Robles may provide a clue:

HRM IN ACTION

Julie Thompson, the production manager for Ampex Manufacturing, called her friend Will Danowicz in human resources to ask a favour. "Bill, I have a friend I'd like you to consider for the new sales manager's position. I really like the fellow and would appreciate anything you could do."

"Tell me about the person," said Will.

"He just graduated from Brock University with a degree in history, I believe. He has no real work experience, but I am sure he could learn quickly. His parents are really good friends of mine, and I sure would like to help him out."

How would you respond?

Mary Beth Robles has an office suite not unlike other executives. The plaques on her wall, however, are written in Portuguese, her coffee cup is filled with black espresso, and the speed dial on her phone lists numbers in Manila and Mexico City in addition to her headquarters in New York. As director of marketing for Colgate-Palmolive Co. in Brazil, the New York native is fluent in English, Spanish and Portuguese. She also speaks a little French. She's lived in Madrid and Washington, D.C. and her assignments with the company include Mexico, Uruguay and Atlanta.[54]

Regardless of the nature of their business, organizations need to locate people with "a good fit" for global operations. Global workers also will become increasingly mobile. They will be recruited, selected, and moved with less regard to national boundaries. At some point in the future, human resources will cross national borders as easily as computer chips and cars.[55]

Global staffing has been called the Achilles' heel of international business. Inappropriate selections are often made that hamper the multinational operation. Although specific failure rates vary by country and company, as many as 40 percent of all expatriate assignments fail due to poor performance or the inability of the expatriate to adjust to the foreign environment. Worse, it has been estimated that as many as 50 percent of those who do *not* return early function ineffectively. Less than one-third of expatriate failures are considered to be job related. The primary reasons for failure include family situations that disrupt the adaptation of the employee and the expatriate's lack of interpersonal skills. The two most important causes are the inability of the spouse and the inability of the employee to adjust to an unfamiliar foreign culture.[56]

The high failure rate is perhaps not surprising. After being carefully selected for the assignment and briefed on the new job and locale, employees based in Canada conduct business in familiar surroundings. In contrast, the multinational environment is often unfamiliar, and conducting business as it has always been done may be ineffective. Everyday living tasks also may be very different and unnerving. Poor selection, coupled with the stress of living and working overseas, are documented contributors to mental breakdown, alcoholism, and divorce.

There are three primary reasons why North Americans who are sent overseas fail: 1) their families are misjudged, or are not even considered at the time of selection; 2) they are selected because of their domestic reputation; or 3) they lack adequate cross-cultural training.[57] To overcome these obstacles, human resource managers should plan carefully to ensure that people chosen possess certain characteristics. Obviously, they must be technically qualified to do the job, but managers seem to pay too little attention to other criteria. For example, few firms administer tests to determine the relational/cross-cultural/interpersonal skills of their selectees. Other qualities are also needed:

- a genuine desire to work in a foreign country;
- spouses and families who have actively encouraged the person to work overseas;
- cultural sensitivity and flexibility;
- a sense for politics.

Several surveys of overseas managers have revealed that the spouse's opinion and attitude should be considered the most important screening factor. Cultural sensitivity is also essential to avoid unnecessarily antagonizing host country nationals.

The process of selecting a current employee for a foreign posting should involve broad measurement and evaluation of the candidate's expertise. Psychological tests, stress tests, evaluations by the candidate's superiors, subordinates, peers, and acquaintances, and professional evaluations from licensed psychologists can all aid in ascertaining the candidate's current level of interpersonal and cross-cultural skills. The candidate's spouse and children should undergo modified versions of the selection process, since family members confront slightly different challenges than do employees.

In selecting individuals for overseas assignments, management must recognize that no one style of leadership will be equally effective in all countries. People in various countries have widely divergent backgrounds, education, cultures, and religions. They live within a wide variety of social conditions, economic, and political systems. Employers must consider all these factors because they can have a dramatic effect on the working environment of the person selected.

It seems reasonable that a successful international manager should possess the following qualities:

- a knowledge of history, particularly in countries of old and homogeneous cultures;
- an understanding of the economic and sociological structures of various countries;
- an interest in the host country and a willingness to learn and use the language;
- a respect for differing philosophical and ethical approaches to living and to business practice.

In addition to choosing the most suitable employees, managers also must assemble a cost-effective workforce. The costs of hiring depend on the norms for salaries and benefits in the emplloyee's country. Many countries in Europe and elsewhere have employment costs lower than Canada's (although the weakness of the Canadian dollar has narrowed the gap somewhat.)

Using a cost-benefit strategy, employers should hire local nationals whenever possible, or concentrate on obtaining foreign service employees from low-allowance and lower-cost locations such as the United Kingdom. To minimize relocation cost, employers should, whenever possible, reassign employees who are already overseas. Some companies try to cut costs overseas by hiring only single employees. Discriminating on the grounds of marital status is contrary to most Canadian employment standards and human rights legislation. There is nothing illegal, however, in making no provisions for family. For example, internal or external job advertising can make it clear that the successful applicant will have to bear the expenses of relocating and housing family. This type of offer will likely attract only single people or childless couples, but it is not considered discriminatory under existing legislation.

The methods for selecting a cost-effective international staff will continue to evolve. Employers must search constantly for innovative methods of recruiting and selecting a qualified work force. They must not, however, focus on cost to the detriment of hiring appropriate candidates.

Failures are even more costly than the initial selection expense. One human resource professional estimates that the cost of a failed expatriate employee is three times the individual's salary, not including the price of lost productivity.[58]

A GLOBAL PERSPECTIVE

In the global job market, human resource managers are facing a growing mismatch between new jobs requiring higher level skills and the people available to fill them. The global labour pool is reduced when employers overlook female managers. There are three perceived reasons for not offering global assignments to women: that women do not want to be international managers; that other companies refuse to send women abroad; and that foreigners are prejudiced against female managers. According to a survey conducted by McGill University professor, Nancy J. Adler, women do want overseas assignments as much as their male counterparts, but four times as many North American firms are reluctant to select women for international assignments. It should be noted, too, that although few overseas management assignments are currently given to women, 97 percent of the women who have had overseas assignments were successful. As for the perception that women will face prejudice overseas, this belief may be exaggerated. Even in traditionally male-dominated Japan, Adler reports that female managers are viewed as professionals.[59]

Coping with human resource problems in the global environment is very complex. Canadian human resource managers must find a way to educate, or reeducate, much of the Canadian labour force to give us a competitive advantage; they must review carefully the human resource situation in host countries; and they must plan to cope with the limitations of the labour situation and take advantage of strengths in host country labour forces.

S UMMARY

Selection is the process of choosing, from a group of applicants, those individuals best suited for a particular position. The process often begins with an initial screening to eliminate applicants who obviously do not meet position requirements. The next step may involve having the prospective employee complete an employment application.

Selection tests are often used to help assess an applicant's qualifications and potential for success. Properly designed selection tests are standardized, objective, based on sound norms, reliable, and—most importantly—valid. After a test has been validated, an appropriate cutoff score must be established. An applicant scoring less than the cutoff score will be disqualified. Measurable characteristics related to job performance include cognitive aptitudes, psychomotor abilities, job knowledge, work samples, vocational interests, and personality. Some firms also test applicants for drug use.

The employment interview is a goal-oriented conversation in which the interviewer and the applicant exchange information. Interviews may be conducted in several ways. In a group interview, several applicants interact with one or more company representatives. In a board interview, one candidate is interviewed by several company representatives. The stress interview intentionally creates anxiety to determine how an applicant will react in certain types of situations. A realistic job preview (RJP) conveys unbiased job information to the applicant.

Reference checks provide additional information about the applicant. They are used to verify the accuracy of the data he or she provides. Often a background investigation into the applicant's credentials and employment history is necessary.

The hiring decision is based on all the information obtained from various sources. The final decision should be made by the manager who will be responsible for the new employee. After the decision has been made to extend a job offer, the successful candidate may, if the job requires physical activity, take a physical examination. In these cases, a job offer is contingent on the candidate's passing of the physical examination. Rejections should be handled courteously to maintain goodwill toward the company.

It should be noted, too, that selecting individuals for international assignments poses special problems. Not only is it important to select the right manager or professional, but the expatriate's family must be able to cope with the foreign environment. The selection process, then, should be conducted with extreme care, as poor performance abroad can be costly for both the employee and the firm.

TERMS FOR REVIEW

Selection	Vocational interest tests
Selection ratio	Employment interview
Résumé	Unstructured interview
Standardization	Structured interview
Objectivity	Situational questions
Norm	Job knowledge questions
Reliability	Job-sample simulation questions
Test-retest method	Worker requirements questions
Equivalent forms method	Behaviour description interview
Split-halves method	Group interview
Validity	Board interview
Cutoff score	Stress interview
Cognitive aptitude tests	Realistic job preview (RJP)
Psychomotor abilities tests	Reference checks
Job knowledge tests	Referees
Work-sample tests	Expatriate

QUESTIONS FOR REVIEW

1. What basic steps normally are followed in the selection process?

2. Identify and describe the various factors outside the control of the human resource manager that could affect the selection process.

3. What would be the selection ratio if there were 15 applicants to choose from and only one position to fill? Interpret the meaning of this selection ratio.

4. How should a firm use selection tests to avoid discriminatory practices?

5. What is the general purpose of the preliminary interview?

6. What types of questions should be asked on an application form?

7. What basic conditions should be met if selection tests are to be used in the screening process? Briefly describe each.

8. Briefly describe the objectives of the employment interview.

9. Define each of the following terms: a) nondirective interview; b) structured interview; c) group interview; d) board interview; e) stress interview.

10. What purpose do reference checks and background investigations serve?

11. What are the reasons for administering a physical examination?

HRM INCIDENT 1

• BUSINESS FIRST

As production manager for Thompson Manufacturing, Jack Tozer has the final authority to approve the hiring of any new supervisors who work for him. The human resource manager performs the initial screening of all prospective supervisors and then sends the most likely candidates to Jack for interviews.

One day recently, Jack received a call from Pete Peterson, the human resource manager: "Jack, I've just spoken to a young woman who may be just who you're looking for to fill that final line supervisor position. She has some good work experience and it appears as if her head is screwed on straight. She's here right now and available if you could possibly see her." Jack hesitated a moment before answering, "Gee, Pete,"

he said, "I'm certainly busy today but I'll try to squeeze her in. Send her on down."

A moment later Daisey Wong, the new applicant, arrived at Jack's office and introduced herself. "Come on in, Daisey," said Jack. "I'll be right with you after I make a few phone calls."

Fifteen minutes later Jack finished the calls and began talking with Daisey. Jack was quite impressed. After a few minutes Jack's door opened and a supervisor yelled, "We have a problem on line number 1 and need your help."

Jack stood up and said, "Excuse me a minute, Daisey." Ten minutes later Jack returned, and the conversation continued for ten more minutes before a series of phone calls again interrupted them.

The same pattern of interruptions continued for the next hour. Finally Daisey looked at her watch and said, "I'm sorry, Mr. Tozer, but I have to pick up my husband." "Sure thing, Daisey," Jack said as the phone rang again. "Call me later today."

QUESTIONS

1. What specific policies should a company follow to avoid interviews like this one?
2. Explain why Jack, not Pete, should make the selection decision.

HRM INCIDENT 2

• SHOULD WE INVESTIGATE?

Patsy Swain, district sales manager for Avco Electronics, was preparing to interview her first applicant, Ray Wyscup, for a sales representative position. She had advertised for an individual with detailed knowledge of computers and spreadsheet software in addition to at least five years' sales experience.

"Hello, Ray, I'm Pat Swain. I've looked at your résumé and am anxious to talk to you about this job. You have a very impressive sales record."

"It's nice to meet you, Pat. Your ad in the *Journal* certainly caught my attention. I would like to catch on with a firm offering such a promising career."

"Glad you saw it Ray. We like to believe that our firm is unique and truly has something to offer top calibre people such as you. Why don't you begin this session by telling me all about yourself? We are a very close-knit group here and I would like to learn about you and your family."

Ray appeared to be very relaxed and comfortable in Pat's presence. He began, "Well, you see, I'm a single parent with two preschool children. Since I'm only 41 years old, I'm pretty well able to keep up with their various activities. Of course you understand that one gets sick occasionally and this causes me to take a few personal days off. But, I've always been able to handle it. This circumstance wouldn't affect my job performance."

"Well, I'm sure it wouldn't. I also have some youngsters at home," Pat replied. "Would you now tell me about your last job with IBX?" Ray, feeling more confident than ever, began, "Well, Pat, I had a brief, but very successful stint with them. But I had rather you not contact them about me. You see, my regional manager and I had a personality conflict and I'm afraid he might not tell a straight story."

"I see," Pat said. "What about your position before that, your job with Uniserv?"

"I did well there too," Ray stated. "But that outfit went bankrupt. I have no idea where any of those people are now."

After the interview had continued for about an hour, Pat said, "Well, I guess that about wraps it up, Ray, unless you have questions for me?"

"No," Ray responded, "I believe I understand the nature of the position and I can assure you that I will do a great job for you." Pat smiled and nodded and the two shook hands as Ray departed.

QUESTIONS

1. Do you agree with the interview format provided by Patsy Swain? Explain.
2. How will Patsy handle a background investigation of Ray Wyscup?

DEVELOPING HRM SKILLS: AN EXPERIENTIAL EXERCISE

As all managers recognize, many factors must be considered in selecting employees. In this exercise, George Nakash has just been promoted, but before he starts his new job, he must choose his replacement. George's firm has an employment equity program, but presently there are few women in management. George has some excellent employees to choose from, but there are many factors to consider before a decision can be made.

Senior managers have made it clear that they expect George to select an individual who can perform as well as he has over the last six years. The majority of the people he worked with on the line have made it clear that they want Sam. The women on the line have indicated, to everyone who will listen that it is time for a female supervisor in at least one division. But it is George's decision and he must select the best person, regardless of any criticism he may receive.

Sam Craik, employed by the company for 11 years, is one possible candidate. He wants this promotion, needs the higher pay, wants the respect and influence to be gained, and admires the nice office that George has now. Sam is recognized as one of the most technically capable individuals in the division. He is from the old school of thought: We get things done through discipline, and we don't put up with people allowing their personal problems to interfere with work.

Frieda Lott, an employee for seven years, is another candidate for promotion. She wants the job primarily because she can do good work and represent the women on the line. She believes she can deal effectively with the personal problems of others. She is recognized as technically capable and has an undergraduate degree in management.

Fred Rogov, an employee of the company for six years, is the final candidate. He believes he should get the promotion primarily because he can do the best job. Fred is very capable, but not quite as familiar with all the technical aspects of the job as Frieda or Sam. He has a degree in liberal arts, but he is taking business classes at night. Fred is also actively involved in the community and has held various civic offices.

Four individuals will have roles in this exercise: one as George Nakash, the current supervisor, and three as the candidates for promotion. Instructors will provide the participants with additional information necessary to complete the exercise.

PART TWO:

CASE II Parma Cycle Company: Workers for the New Plant

Gene Beairsto, the corporate planner at Parma Cycle Company, was ecstatic as he talked with the human resource director, Jesse Heard, that Tuesday morning in early 1996. He had just received word that the board of directors had approved the plan for Parma's new eastern plant, to be located in Digby, Nova Scotia.

"I really appreciate your help on this, Jesse," Gene said. "Without the research you did on the human resource needs for the new plant, I don't think that it would have been approved."

"We still have a long way to go," said Jesse. "There's no doubt that we can construct the building and install the machinery, but getting skilled workers in Digby, may not be so easy."

"Well," said Gene, "the results of the labour survey that you did in the area last year indicate that we'll be able to get by. Anyway, some of the people here at Parma surely will agree to transfer."

"When is the new plant scheduled to open?" asked Jesse.

Gene replied, "The building will be finished in June, the machinery will be in by July, and the goal is to be in production by September." "Gosh," said Jesse, "I'd better get to work."

A few minutes later, back in his office, Jesse considered what the future held at Parma Cycle. The company had been located in Delta, British Columbia since its founding. It had grown over the years to become the nation's third largest bicycle manufacturer. The decision to open the eastern plant had been made in hopes of cutting production costs, through lower wages and improving quality. Although no one ever came right out and said it, it was assumed that the eastern plant would be nonunion. The elimination of union work rules was expected to be a benefit.

The Town of Digby had offered a 10-year exemption from all property taxes. This was a significant advantage because tax rates in the Delta area were extremely high. As well, there were generous financial incentives to be had from the government of Nova Scotia.

Jesse was pleased that he had been involved in the discussions from the time that the new plant had been first suggested. Even with all the advanced preparation he had done, he knew that the coming months would be extremely difficult for him and his staff.

As Jesse was thinking about all this, his assistant, Ed Deal, walked in with a bundle of papers. "Hi, Ed," said Jesse, "I'm glad you're here. The Digby plant is definitely on the way and you and I need to get our act together."

"That's great," said Ed. "It's quite a coincidence, too, because I was just going over this stack of job descriptions, identifying which ones might be eliminated as we scale back at this plant."

Jesse said, "Remember, Ed, we are not going to cut back very much here. Some jobs will be deleted and others added. But out of the 800 positions here, I'll bet that not more than 40 will actually be cut."

"So, what you are saying is that we basically have to staff the plant with people we hire from the Digby area?" Ed asked.

Jesse replied, "No, Ed, we will have some people here who are willing to transfer even though their jobs are not being eliminated. We will then replace them with others we hire in the Delta area. Most of the workers at Digby, though, will be recruited from that area."

"What about the management team?" asked Ed. "Well," said Jesse, "I think the boss already knows who the main people will be over there. They are managers we currently have on board plus a fellow we located at a defunct three-wheeler plant in Quebec."

"Who will be the human resource director down there?" asked Ed. "Well," replied Jesse, "I don't think I'm talking out of school by telling you that I plan to recommend you for the job."

After letting that soak in for a minute, Ed said, "It's no secret I was hoping for that. When will we know for sure?"

"There's really not much doubt," said Jesse, "I'm so sure that I've decided to put you in charge of human resources for the whole project. During the next two weeks

I'd like you to put together a comprehensive plan. I want a detailed report of the people we will need, including their qualifications. Secondly, we need more information about the labour supply around Digby. Finally, I'd like for you to come up with a general idea of who might be willing to transfer from this plant. They are really going to be the backbone of our work force at Digby."

"Okay, Jesse, but I'll need a lot of help," said Ed as he gathered his papers and left. As Jesse watched Ed leave he thought he noticed a certain snappiness about Ed's movements that had not been there before.

QUESTIONS

1. What procedures should be followed in determining the human resource needs at the new plant?

2. How might Jesse and Ed go about recruiting workers in Digby? What about managers?

PART TWO:

CBC VIDEO CASE Downsizing

A healthy work environment is one where employees can grow both professionally and personally. With the advent of recession in the early 90s, managers began to downsize, reengineer, and reinvent their organizations in order to make their firms leaner and meaner. However, few companies that have undergone restructuring have reported increases in profits and even fewer have seen enhanced productivity. To make matters worse, the first wave of downsizing was not the last but the first of many.

The net result has been a demoralized, disloyal and dysfunctional work force, which worries more about the future than company profitability. This mood among employees leads to absenteeism, stress-related injuries and a justifiable fear that loyalty does not mean much anymore, because anyone might soon be terminated. Yet these are the very employees that management needs to revitalize the company and to bring it back to prosperity.

Managers once believed that terminating people was necessary for organizational survival. At the time, it was not evident that dysfunctional corporate cultures caused employees to behave inappropriately and to be unproductive. Therefore, managers downsized without changing their work methods, believing (wrongly) that the survivors would become more competitive. Indeed, they expected people to empower themselves when, in fact, they could not, given their constricted environment.

Managers have now come to the realization that the demise of job security has poisoned the working atmosphere at all levels of corporate Canada. If stable employment cannot be guaranteed, then management has an obligation to help employees become more employable, both within the organization and elsewhere. Thus, we see increased spending on training and more emphasis on transferring employees to profitable areas. As well, corporate-sponsored career development centres are being opened. These facilities not only help displaced workers, but also help those who are still within the company. Staff offer tips on résumé writing, interviewing techniques, educational opportunities and internal career openings.

Since the old way of managing was ineffective, new ideas about employment security have surfaced, including one that the CEO of General Electric, Jack Welch, has dubbed "employability". The challenge for HRM departments is not to replace traditional job security with something similar, but rather to avoid dependent relationships both from the employer and the employee perspective. Continual training is the key. HR professionals are trying to encourage employees to train themselves rather than to wait for company representatives to tell them what kind of training they need.

The high-technology sector is the area where this idea was first implemented, due to the constant evolution of products as well as the continual movement of employees between computer companies. Hewlett-Packard and Intel Corp., for example, both boast career centres where employees can search for new jobs with the help of human resources professionals or on their own using on-line services or computer programs that list information about Internet opportunities. In these companies, it is believed that employees have a responsibility not only to work but also "to shop" for other job opportunities where their skills might be used.

In-placement, as the process has come to be known, is a commitment by management to finding as many internal jobs as possible for those about to be displaced. Intel is in the vanguard of this movement. If a worker's job is to be eliminated, that individual has four months to do research and to find a new position. During this period, the employee can undergo training to customize his or her skills for an upcoming position within the company. If an internal placement is not found, the employee goes on a "standby" list and is contacted when an appropriate job becomes available.

Self-training is another idea that is becoming popular. Computer companies, for example, generally have an 18-month timespan between a new product release and the evolution of the next generation. In this rapidly changing environment, technicians must upgrade their skills constantly because their knowledge becomes obsolete within two years. In many firms, including Hewlett-Packard, employees are encouraged to train themselves through continuous learning. This policy has been part of Hewlett-Packard's corporate culture for over 30 years. In the preamble of H-P's corporate objectives, cofounder David Packard stated that "...in an era of increasing change, continuous learning must be undertaken by all from top to bottom in the organization." One would think that equipping workers with such portable skills would only hasten their departure from the company. Not so. Hewlett-Packard's commitment to retraining has fostered a healthy yet competitive working environment. As a result H-P has one of the lowest turnover rates in the electronics industry.

Another company that has adopted similar tactics, albeit under different circumstances, is IBM. Since 1992, IBM has laid off over 200,000 people worldwide. Borrowing ideas from such successful companies as Intel and Hewlett-Packard, IBM managers in Canada offer employees the opportunity to gain portable, marketable skills as a means of boosting their morale and confidence.

The aim of IBM, H-P, Intel and other high-tech companies is to encourage individuals to initiate the training process themselves, which has the added benefit of giving them a level of confidence that enhances their job performance. When an employee takes charges of his/her employability through continual training, the result is personal skills security. Conversely, management values highly skilled and educated employees. Moreover, by providing them with an environment in which they can continually upgrade their skills, management reduces the turnover rate.

Since ongoing training does not fit into the plans of every organization, some Canadian companies have opted for different incentives to reestablish a trusting employee/employer relationship. The management of Starbucks, a Vancouver coffee chain, for example, run a program called Beanstock, which allows employees to buy company stock at a discount. They also give employees who work only 20 hours per week all the benefits a full-time employee receives. At MDS, a medical testing company, management now asks for employee input, and in most cases heeds the advice it receives from workers. Although the days of high staffing levels are past and few jobs are permanent today, managers should review all the options before terminating employees. The maintenance of a healthy organization should be a high-profile management objective.

QUESTIONS

1. What first step should managers take if they want to foster a trusting relationship with their employees?

2. What, if any, are the benefits to the employee?

Video Resource: "Morale Crisis," Venture 411 (November 22, 1992).

CHAPTER 7

Organizational Change and HR Development

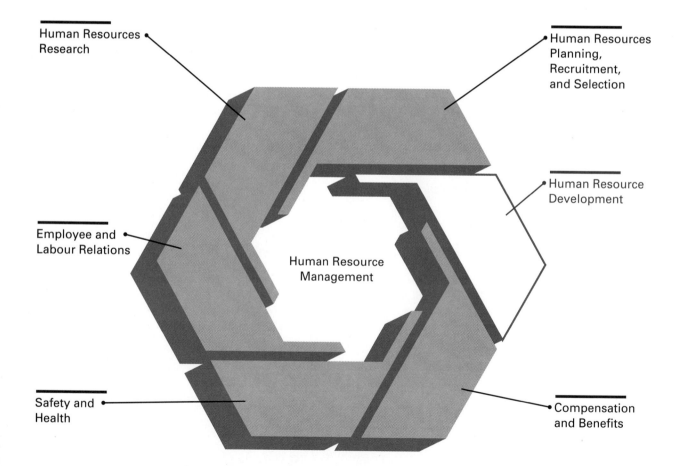

Human Resources Research

Human Resources Planning, Recruitment, and Selection

Human Resource Development

Employee and Labour Relations

Human Resource Management

Safety and Health

Compensation and Benefits

1. Describe organizational change; define and explain the scope of human resource development (HRD).

2. Describe the HRD process and identify the factors that influence HRD.

3. Explain how HRD needs are determined and HRD objectives are established.

4. Describe the significance and methods of employee orientation.

5. Describe management development and explain training methods for entry-level professional and operative employees.

6. Identify several HRD media and explain how they would be used; explain how HRD programs are implemented and evaluated.

Marian Lillie, an experienced accountant, had handled the administrative tasks for an automobile dealership for over ten years. She was familiar with all aspects of the business. Two months ago, the dealership was sold to a young man who had graduated from a prominent university in British Columbia. Soon after he assumed control of the firm, he automated every conceivable administrative function. Marian was not consulted at any point in the process. She was, however, presented with a procedures manual when the project was completed. Later she was overheard telling a co-worker, "I know this new system is not going to work."

Howard Folz, a young university graduate with a major in Management Information Systems, was elated over a job offer from the region's largest employer. When he arrived for his first day of work, his supervisor, Peggy Rodman, took him on a tour of the office and factory. He was shown all the facilities, the firm's cafeteria, and finally his own work station. Peggy's final remarks to him were, "We are delighted to have you with us, Howard. I will let you have your first assignment right after lunch. It's a simple system that involves two of our electronics groups utilizing fibreoptics. I'll check with you in a few days to see how you're doing." As Peggy left his work area, Howard was aghast. He wondered if he had just received all the initial training he would get.

It isn't difficult to imagine Marian Lillie's opposition to a system she doesn't understand. Her statement suggests she isn't likely to support the changes made without consulting her. Howard has a different, but equally serious problem. The university training he received in MIS was excellent, but he had learned very little about electronics, fibreoptics, or his new employer's organization.

We devote the first portion of this chapter to a discussion of organizational change, to defining human resource development (HRD) and to describing the HRD process. Then we describe factors that influence HRD. Next, we address elements of the HRD process: determining HRD needs, establishing objectives, orientation, and selecting HRD methods. This section is followed by a discussion of management development and other training methods. In the final portion of the chapter we consider uses of various HRD methods and media and discuss how HRD programs are implemented and evaluated.

ORGANIZATIONAL CHANGE

Change involves moving from one condition to another, a process that may affect individuals, groups, and entire organizations. Today, change seems to be the only constant in modern business, whether it is the radical restructuring of a firm that trims a 4000-person headquarters down to 200 people[1] or the subtler changes to systems that occur at an ever accelerating pace.

The most prominent current changes to organizations include changes

- in organizational structure caused by mergers, acquisitions, rapid growth, and downsizing;
- in the way people work, resulting largely from computerization;
- in human resources in response to a diverse work force.

In the words of Keith Gilbert, vice-president of industrial relations (Ontario), for Molson Breweries: "a fundamental shift in the structure of organizations . . . that's what will sustain change."[2]

Everyone is affected by these changes. As change agents, human resource professionals must understand the change sequence, the accompanying difficulties, and the ways to reduce resistance to change.

THE CHANGE SEQUENCE

Because of the impact of any change on the organization and its employees, a change should be undertaken only when a real need exists. Of course, circumstances in the internal or external environments may make change desirable or even necessary (see Figure 7-1). Some managers tend to feel that "we have always done it this way, so why argue with success?" A firm's past success, however, does not guarantee future prosperity, or even survival. As Gordon Simpson, managing partner of The Mansis Development Corporation has suggested: "The workplace is changing dramatically and demands for the highest quality of product and service are increasing. To remain competitive in the face of these pressures, employee commitment is crucial. This reality is applicable to all organizations but of particular importance to small business."[3]

The impetus for change usually comes from a belief that the organization and its human resources can be more productive and successful after change occurs. But if change is to be implemented successfully, the process must be approached systematically. The change sequence begins with preparation and continues after change is implemented. A new, flexible position must be developed capable of dealing with present requirements while adapting to further change.

Finally, part of any effective change is evaluating the effectiveness of the change. A primary measure of effectiveness is how the new program affects a firm's *profitability* or *ability to meet objectives*. Human resource development aimed at supporting change is an ongoing process, because both the organization's internal and external environments are dynamic, always impinging on the status quo.

FIGURE 7-1
The Organizational Change Sequence

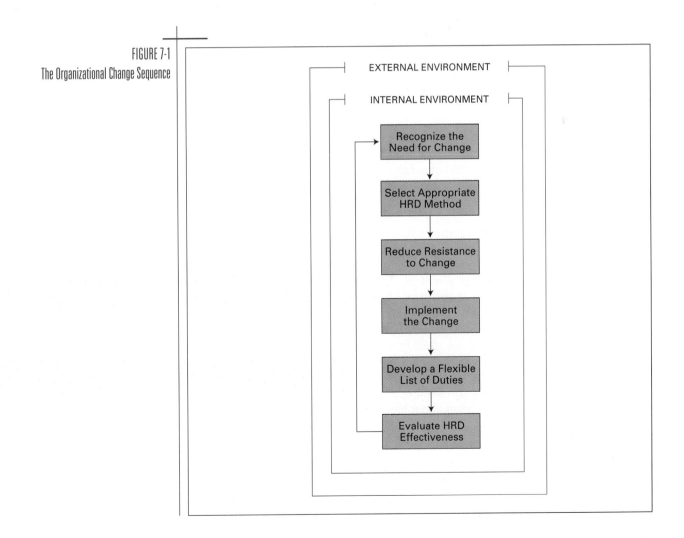

Resistance to Change

Any change will be accomplished more satisfactorily if the person involved desires the change and/or believes it is necessary. At times, accepting something new may be extremely difficult because a shift in attitude is required. Although Marian Lillie may not risk her job by overtly resisting change, her grudging compliance may, in fact, mean that the new system won't work. It needn't have been that way. If the new owner had prepared her for change by working with her at all stages of the project, she would probably have accepted it far more willingly. Reducing resistance to change is crucial to success.

Reasons for Resisting Change

Employees' so called "*natural resistance*" to change has been discussed widely. Although change is often resisted, sometimes quite vigorously, this opposition is not innate. Rather, the resistance may be explained in terms of employee expectations and past experiences. Individuals often resist change when they feel their basic needs will not be met. For example, one of the most frightening prospects for many people is the threat of unemployment. At times, changes in methods and systems do downgrade and eliminate jobs. However, change can also generate the need for higher-level skills. Yet many employees believe they lack the flexibility to adjust. Because most adults derive their primary income from their work and are unable to obtain the basic necessities of life if unemployed, it is easy to understand the threatening nature of change.

Along with the threat of unemployment, many changes in organizations are perceived to disrupt established social groups and friendships. Because many social needs are satisfied on the job, any threat to these relationships may be resisted.

A perceived threat to a person's status in the organization may also be a powerful reason for resisting change. Many workers invest their lives in their jobs. They are likely to resist any change if they fear it will upset their standing in the organization or their sense of importance. The master machinist faced with automation, for example, may fear that his high-level skill will no longer be needed and that his prestige will be lowered.

Regardless of the reasons individuals resist, management must take action to minimize the potential loss of productivity associated with change. Productivity and accuracy generally decline during periods of change, for instead of thinking about their work, employees are worrying about their survival, or their loss of status. They may also be absent more, either because of stress-induced illness or because they are looking for another job.

In summary, the prospect of change can threaten every level of human need. This threatening feeling often encourages employees to resist. This resistance is not *natural*, but based on reasons perceived (by the employee) to be logical.

Reducing Resistance to Change

In order for a firm to gain general acceptance for a needed change, management must be aware of ways to lessen resistance. Acceptance may take time. As Wayne Hanna, a member of the Coopers & Lybrand Consulting Group has suggested, management may "recruit individuals who are open to new ideas but . . . [shouldn't] try to avoid conflict by whitewashing differences."[4] There are more constructive approaches.

BUILDING TRUST AND CONFIDENCE

Bringing about a change in attitude requires trust and respect between the person attempting to implement the change and the individual(s) affected. The degree of employee trust and confidence in management is related directly to past experiences. If employees have suffered in the past as a result of change, they may attempt to avoid change in the future. When management has misrepresented the effects of change, resistance tends to be even greater. For example, when faced with the prospect of having to reduce the work force, management may assure employees that layoffs will be based on individual performance. But if previous layoffs appeared to be determined by seniority or favouritism, employees will be sceptical.

Conversely, management builds trust by dealing with employees in an open and straightforward manner. Workers who are told that they need additional training, for example, will accept the idea much more readily if they have confidence in management. The desired level of trust cannot be achieved quickly; trust stems from a long period of fair dealing.

DEVELOPING OPEN COMMUNICATION

In some organizations, a great deal of information is treated as confidential that need not be. Information may be withheld from employees for a variety of reasons, including management's unwillingness to share. Regardless of the reason, secrecy creates a climate of mistrust and fear, as inaccurate rumours of planned change may circulate. By sharing information with employees, managers show their respect for employees' need for information.

EMPLOYEE PARTICIPATION

People such as Marian Lillie are more inclined to accept change if they are given the opportunity to participate in the planning. If management determines that a department's operating budget must be cut by 25 percent, for example, the unit manager may accept this change more readily if he or she is permitted to help determine where the cuts should be made. Participation is more effective when permitted in the early planning stages. Caution is in order, though. Consider the effect of the change on the individuals involved. Management should not, for example, expect employees to participate in their own layoffs.[5]

When Shaw Cable of Edmonton purchased Trillium Communications of Barrie, Ontario, for example, an estimated 40 of 100 employees were laid off as part of a company restructuring. It is rumoured that even Trillium's human resources manager was unaware of the cutback. Obviously these employees could not be asked to participate in "such a severe and deep cut."[6]

In general, though, encouraging participation helps to overcome resistance In some cases, it may even be possible to create a climate in which employees aggressively seek change. Sylvia Lee, President of Lee Communications in Grand Centre, Alberta, has suggested that

Involving people creates synergy, and synergy creates excitement. That's the productivity part. Not only do you get far better ideas from the group than you would from one person alone, but you also get the added bonus of "buy in." Here's the morale part—people who are part of the solution are part of the resolution. An employee who buys in to the decision because she helped reach it is going to get involved in implementing it. Synergy and buy in—here's nothing to beat the raw power of that combination.[7]

To achieve such an atmosphere, managers must work to assuage employees' fears of being unable to satisfy personal needs. Managers must be convinced that it is, usually, their own actions—not the employees' inherent nature—that lead to hostility. Arthur Church, president and CEO of Goderich, Ontario-based Champion Road Machinery Ltd., summarizes this concept bluntly: "If anything goes wrong, 85 percent of the time it's management's fault."[8] Only when this philosophy is accepted can the effectiveness of human resource development programs be maximized.

HUMAN RESOURCE DEVELOPMENT: DEFINITION AND SCOPE

Human resource development (HRD) is planned, continuous effort by management to improve employee competency levels and organizational performance through training and development programs. In practice, HRD may be referred to as training and development (T&D) or simply training, but a distinction sometimes is made between these two terms.

Training is designed to permit learners to acquire knowledge and skills needed for their present jobs.[9] Showing a worker how to operate a lathe, or a supervisor how to schedule daily production, is an example of training. The recent growth in training activity stems from the need to adapt to rapid environmental changes, to improve the quality of products and services, and to increase productivity. **Development** involves a longer-term focus that looks beyond today and today's job[10] by preparing employees to keep pace with the organization as it changes and grows. With rapid advances in technology, developing human resources has become crucial.

As jobs grow more and more complex, the need for improved human relations within a firm also becomes increasingly significant, adding another dimension to the HRD process. Because of the rapidity of technical change and the effect of this change on employees, training and development need to be conducted continuously.

The connection between economic survival and productivity is obvious. Increasing productivity, a primary purpose of HRD, is a strategic goal for many firms. Recently, Canadians were warned that unless we invest more in training our human resource, the entire country will experience decreased living standards.[11] In 1990, four billion dollars was spent on training in Canada. The average expenditure of $849 per employee was 50 percent lower than the comparable figure in the U.S. The gap may be narrowing, as training budgets in Canada are increasing rapidly.[12]

We still spend much less on T&D, however, than other countries. Despite some impressive expenditures by governments ($6 billion in Ontario alone), Canada lags far behind many industrialized countries in the amount spent on training and in training time. Compared to the seven hours of yearly training given to the average Canadian employee, the average Swedish employee gets 170 hours and the average Japanese employee gets 200 hours! As of 1992, only 11 percent of Canadian employees had been given training on computers.[13]

Canadian managers are still not according training the importance it deserves. Indeed, in one Conference Board of Canada survey, training was not even included on the list of most pressing personnel management issues[14] (see Figure 7-2). There are some indications of attitude change, however, as managers are becoming more aware of the profit-generating potential of a trained work force. Increasingly, employees are being viewed "as the root of competitive advantage."[15] As well, training resources are being distributed more equally across all employment categories, whereas in the past, expenditures were directed heavily toward professionals, managers and executives.[16]

Another major goal of HRD is to prevent skill obsolescence at all levels. Not only can effective HRD programs play a vital role in achieving this goal, they can upgrade employees' skills to qualify them for promotion. Thus, in addition to meeting company needs, management is responsible for helping employees upgrade their skills, based primarily on employee aptitudes and interests. Human resource development costs, then, should be accepted as an investment in human resources; returns of investment in HRD should be compared against investing in alternate forms of productivity improvement, such as new equipment and/or systems.[17]

THE HUMAN RESOURCE DEVELOPMENT PROCESS

Major adjustments in the external and the internal environments necessitate corporate change. The general human resource development process that helps facilitate this change is shown in Figure 7-3. Once the need for change is recognized, the process of determining training and development needs begins with two questions:

1. What are our training needs?

2. What do we want to accomplish through HRD activity?

FIGURE 7-2
Most Pressing Personnel Management Issues (in rank order)

1. Personnel reshuffling due to restructuring or downsizing
2. Compensation or cost of labour
3. Industrial relations
4. Health care and other benefits
5. Pay and employment equity

Source: Reproduced with permission from The Conference Board of Canada.

FIGURE 7-3
The Human Resource Development
Process

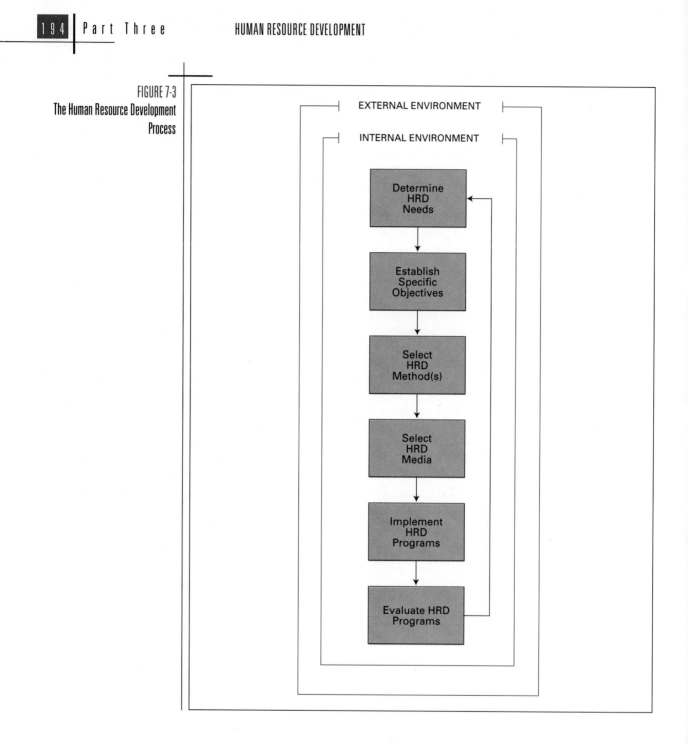

T&D objectives might be as narrow as improving the supervisory ability of one manager, or as broad as honing the management skills of all first-line supervisors. After stating the objectives, management can determine appropriate methods and media for accomplishing them. HRD must be evaluated continuously to ensure that all activities are designed to further organizational objectives.

In some companies, training departments are being considered as profit centres rather than as overhead. A training department that is evaluated on results must function like a miniature business, charging internal departments as if they were outside clients.[18]

FACTORS INFLUENCING HUMAN RESOURCE DEVELOPMENT

Several of the most important influences on training and development are shown in Figure 7-4. How these factors are addressed often determines whether or not HRD objectives are achieved.

Management Support

First and most important, training and development programs must have top management's full support. This support must be real—not merely lip service—and must be communicated to the entire organization. Employees will be convinced that HRD is an important part of the job when senior executives provide the resources needed and when they themselves take part in training activities.

In addition, other managers, both generalists and HRD specialists, should be committed to the HRD process. The views of several practitioners concerning the HRD manager's role are presented in Figure 7-5. The consensus is that the HRD manager operates in a staff, or advisory, capacity. According to one prominent director of corporate management development, "The primary responsibility for training and development lies with line managers, from the president and chair of the board on down. HRD management merely provides the technical expertise, plus blood, sweat and tears." All managers, then, must be convinced there will be a tangible payoff if resources

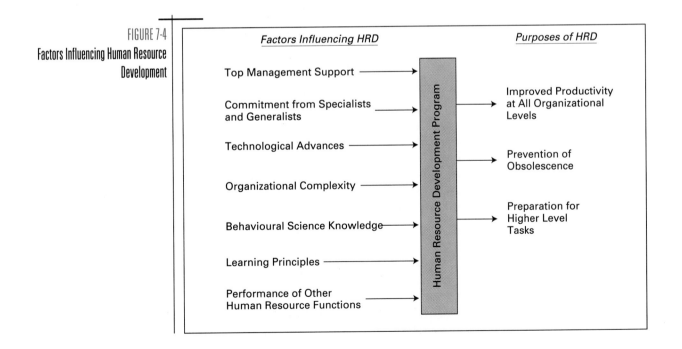

FIGURE 7-4
Factors Influencing Human Resource Development

FIGURE 7-5
The Role of the Human Resources
Development Manager

EXECUTIVE	COMMENTS
Senior Adviser, Personnel Development, major oil company	Principal role is to be a consultant to managers to help identify 1) operating problems or potential problems; 2) scenarios or alternative courses of action to solve these problems or prevent them from occurring; and 3) feedback processes to see that on-job results are consistent with stated management goals.
Director of Personnel, Photography processing company	The role varies greatly, depending on the industry and the individual in the job. My perception is that the role is becoming more important and is expanding into nontraditional training and development functions.
District Manager, Training, Major telephone company	The role of the training/development manager is a staff function that must prove to the line organization and users that the services provided are job relevant, and will improve productivity, lower costs, and increase profits.
Development and Planning, Major pharmaceutical company	Plan, develop, and administer programs that meet the needs of line managers in assisting their people to obtain the knowledge and skills they need to perform their present jobs satisfactorily; prepare employees for future jobs in the company; and assist them in achieving their personal goals.

are committed to training. The best way to ensure that HRD activities meet corporate needs is to involve line personnel in all phases of the planning and delivery process.[19]

Some form of cost-benefit analysis should be made prior to implementing any HRD activity. Ideally, the training or development program should be job-related and should improve productivity, lower costs and/or increase profits. This step is too often omitted; according to a Conference Board of Canada study, only 5 percent of all training courses seem to be "subjected to a return on investment evaluation."[20]

Learning and the Individual Employee

So far, we have been discussing training from the point of view of the organization's goals. Learning, however, is accomplished by individual workers, and training is a benefit to the individual learners. All learning is to some degree a self-determined activity and leads to self-development. Moreover, people learn best when they are interested. Thus an important role of the HRD manager is to help people set and reach their personal goals and to obtain the knowledge and the skills they need for present and future jobs. The HRD manager explains the type of training available, shows how to take advantage of various learning opportunities, and encourages learners to meet their goals.

The self-development concept leads to the philosophy that learning should be a life-long activity. Indeed, life-long learning is considered to be an important factor in an organization's ability to compete internationally.[21]

In recent years, increasingly rapid changes in products, systems, and methods have had a significant impact on job requirements. Thus, employees need to upgrade their skills constantly and to develop an attitude that permits them not only to adapt to change, but also to accept and even to seek change.

Many organizations have changed dramatically as a result of downsizing, technological innovations, and customer demands for new and better products and services. The result often is that more work must be accomplished by fewer people at a more complex level. Supervisors and operative employees working in self-directed teams are performing duties that were once assigned to middle managers. All these changes result in a greater need for training and development.

Human resource managers themselves must work to stay abreast of the vast body of new knowledge relating to their field that has emerged from the behavioural sciences in the last few decades. Today's managers must be aware of this knowledge and capable of using it. Some of this knowledge relates to how people, especially adults, learn. Effective trainers must know more than the subject matter. They must have an understanding of the learning process. Although much remains to be learned about this process, some general principles are accepted. Figure 7-6 lists fundamental learning concepts.

Most of these concepts are familiar from other areas of human resource management. Behaviour that is reinforced (rewarded), for example, is more likely to recur; thus, management should strive to ensure that desired behaviour—whether productivity on the job or the acquisition of a new skill—is rewarded. Not all rewards are tangible (see Chapter 12). Praise for accomplishments can be an effective reinforcer; the learner's own satisfaction at accomplishment is a potent reward, and recognition can help to intensify this satisfaction.

Other Human Resource Functions

From the human resource manager's viewpoint, the relative success of other human resource functions affects HRD. If recruitment and selection attract only marginally qualified employees, for example, a more extensive HRD program may be needed to train entry-level workers. Conversely, a firm that pays competitive salaries may find it easier to attract qualified workers, reducing the need for basic skills training while motivating them to participate in further skills upgrading. A competitive compensation plan may also help lower the turnover rate, thereby minimizing the need to train new workers continually.

Employee relations can also influence the HRD program. Workers want to feel their employer cares for them. One way to express this philosophy is through management's support of HRD. Conversely, good employee relations

FIGURE 7-6
General Learning Concepts

- Behaviour that is reinforced (rewarded) is more likely to recur.
- This reinforcement is most effective when it immediately follows the desired behaviour and is clearly connected with it.
- Mere repetition, without reinforcement, is an ineffective approach to learning.
- Threats and punishment have variable and uncertain effects on learning. Punishment may disturb the learning process.
- The reinforcement that transfers best to other situations is the sense of satisfaction that stems from achievement.
- The value of an external reward depends on who dispenses it. If the reward giver is highly respected, the recipient values it more.
- Learners progress in an area of learning only as far as they need to to achieve their purposes.
- Individuals are more likely to be enthusiastic about a learning situation if they have participated in planning it.
- Group members can sometimes learn as much from each other as from the leader.
- Autocratic leadership makes group members more dependent on the leader and generate resentment in the group.
- Overstrict discipline is associated with greater conformity, anxiety, shyness, and acquiescence; greater permissiveness is associated with initiative and creativity.
- Excessive criticism and discouragement damage people's self-confidence and sense of worth and reduce their level of aspiration.
- When people experience too much frustration, their behaviour ceases to be integrated, purposeful, and rational.
- People who have met with little success and continual failure are not apt to be in the mood to learn.
- Individuals tend to think best when they encounter an obstacle or intellectual challenge that is of interest to them.
- The best way to help people form a general concept is to present an idea in numerous and varied situations.
- Learning from reading is consolidated better by time spent recalling what has been read than by rereading. Group discussion, writing about the text, and applying the information all aid in recall.
- People remember new information better if it confirms their previous attitudes.
- What is learned is more likely to be available for use if it is learned in a situation much like that in which it is to be used.
- The best time to learn is when the learning can be useful. Motivation then is at its strongest peak.
- People learn best when they can start with their own experience.
- People learn best when their own knowledge is valued. Every learner has something to teach and every teacher has something to learn.
- People learn by doing.

will help training programs run more smoothly and successfully. The HRD process can also train managers to deal more effectively with employees and their problems, as managers can be taught to treat employees as individuals.

The value placed on employee health and safety also affects the HRD process. A strong emphasis on this area can pave the way for extensive training programs throughout the organization. Providing a healthy and a safe work environment has substantial benefits, because the firm gains a reputation as a rewarding place in which to work.

DETERMINING HUMAN RESOURCE DEVELOPMENT NEEDS

The first step in the HRD process is to determine specific training, education, and development needs. In today's highly competitive business environment, it is a waste of resources to plunge into training programs because "other firms are doing it" or with a vague idea that some sort of training will solve all performance problems.[22] Training costs time and money. It should be undertaken only after a thorough performance analysis has identified real needs and only after exploring other interventions.[23]

A 1993 survey conducted by The Conference Board of Canada documented what executives considered the major training and development challenges for all types of employees (see Figure 7-7).[24]

Three types of analyses are required in order to determine HRD needs: organization analysis, task analysis, and person analysis.[25]

FIGURE 7-7
Critical Training and Development Challenges for Major Employee Groups (in rank order)

EXECUTIVE	CLERICAL & OFFICE
1 Leadership	1 Technical skills
2 Strategic planning	2 Quality & customer service
3 Managing change	3 Teamwork & team building
MANAGEMENT	**PRODUCTION**
1 Leadership	1 Technical skills
2 Managing change	2 Quality & continuous improvement
3 Management & supervisory skills	3 Teamwork & team building
PROFESSIONAL & TECHNICAL	**SERVICE**
1 Technical knowledge & skills	1 Quality & customer service
2 Interpersonal skills	2 Technical skills
3 Quality & customer service	3 Quality & continuous improvement
SALES & MARKETING	**TRADES**
1 Sales & negotiation skills	1 Technical skills
2 Quality & customer service	2 Trades upgrade
3 Technical knowledge & skills	3 Quality & continuous improvement

Organization analysis examines the entire firm to determine where training and development should be conducted, studying structures, strategic goals, and plans. HRD should not be considered in isolation but as part of overall human resource planning. In fact, Keith Gilbert, vice-president of industrial relations (Ontario) for Molson Breweries has suggested that "a fundamental shift in the structure of organizations . . . [is often necessary to] sustain change."[26]

In conducting a task analysis, two primary factors should be determined: importance and proficiency. *Importance* relates to the relevance of specific tasks and behaviours in a particular job and the frequency with which they are performed. *Proficiency* is the employees' competence in performing these tasks. The appropriate data can be gleaned from job descriptions, performance appraisals, and interviews or surveys of supervisors and job incumbents.[27]

Person analysis focuses on the individual employee, dealing with two questions: *Who needs to be trained?* and *What kind of training is needed?* The first step in a person analysis is to compare employee performance with established standards. If the person's work is acceptable, training may not be needed. If the employee's performance is below standard, further investigation will be needed to identify the specific knowledge and skills required for satisfactory job performance.[28] Tests, role playing, and assessment centres may be helpful in conducting person analyses. The results from career planning programs also may be useful.

ESTABLISHING HRD OBJECTIVES

Clear, concise, and measurable HRD objectives must be formulated. Without them, it is impossible to design meaningful HRD programs and difficult to evaluate them. The following example of an objectives and knowledge requirements statement has been adapted from an Ontario government publication:

EXAMPLES OF PERFORMANCE OBJECTIVES AND KNOWLEDGE REQUIREMENTS

By spending $XXX on training employees to use the new computer system, The XYZ Corporation will meet the following objectives:

- 50 percent reduction in order processing time from receipt of order to shipping the product
- elimination of late penalties on accounts payable
- 100 percent of customer invoices mailed within 24 hours after shipment of product
- 50 percent reduction of accounts receivable
- 30 percent reduction in inventory
- elimination of back orders

Knowledge Required

- terminology
- system configuration
- interaction of hardware and software

- system start-up and shut-down procedures
- software packages (e.g. DOS, inventory, etc.)
        capabilities
        uses within The XYZ Corporation
- file set up
- file accessing
- file updating
- report generation

Skills Required

- keyboarding
- basic care of the system
- accessing appropriate software
- inputting and changing data
- report generation
- basic troubleshooting[29]

The statement above clearly establishes the purpose or *utility* of the proposed training activity. Managers would have little difficulty in determining whether this is the type of training a subordinate needs. The specific learning objectives leave little doubt of what should be learned from the training. Action words such as reduction and elimination, along with appropriate percentages, are used to forecast the specific results of the program. Using these objectives, the HRD specialist will be able to determine whether or not the trainees have obtained the necessary skills. For example, measurements of pre-training and post-training order-processing time determine whether there has been a 50 percent reduction.

ORIENTATION

After hiring, the initial HRD focus is on orientation. **Orientation**, a common type of formal training in Canadian organizations, consists of activities that help new employees fit into the company, the job, and the work group. A well-planned orientation makes many of the other human resource management tasks easier. Companies recognize the benefits of orientation; according to a 1993 study conducted by the Canadian Labour Market and Productivity Centre, new employee orientation is the most widespread form of training in Canada, accounting for 20 percent of all training hours.[30]

A typical orientation program explains requirements for promotion and work rules. The mechanics of promotion, demotion, transfer, resignation, discharge, layoff, and retirement should be detailed in policy handbooks and given to each new employee. A summary of employee benefits is often provided.

While many HRD methods are not aimed at new employees, some firms have developed sophisticated approaches to orientation. For example, at Federal Express, computer-based training is used for orienting new employees. Laser disks (discussed later in this chapter) provide a two-hour program offering detailed information on corporate culture, benefits, policies, and procedures. The program also outlines the company's organizational structure and features a video message from the chief executive officer.[31]

Disney's orientation begins in the selection interview with a realistic job preview, as discussed in the previous chapter, aimed at ensuring employees understand that a Disney job is not all glamour, but also hard work. At Disney University, all new *cast members*, as employees are called, attend a two-day seminar focusing on corporate traditions and values, while obtaining the necessary generic skills: information giving and customer relations. Disney's approach to orientation is so impressive that people from other well-known North American businesses attend seminars, learning to apply Disney's orientation techniques in their own firms.[32]

Orientation is often the joint responsibility of the training staff and the line supervisor. As the new employee is concerned primarily with the job and with his or her supervisor, line involvement reduces anxiety about these factors, allowing the corporate message to be communicated more effectively. Successful orientation activities also tend to have a high degree of senior management involvement in program development and delivery.

Peers are also excellent information agents as they are accessible to the newcomers, often more accessible than the boss. Peers also tend to have empathy for new people, experience within the organization, and the technical expertise to which new employees need access. Furthermore, close contact with peers helps new employees understand their co-workers' behavioural patterns, an important factor in effective job performance. There are, however, drawbacks to the peer orientation approach, sometimes called "following Nellie," or the "buddy system." Care must be taken to choose the right guide; otherwise the trainee might be exposed to bad work habits, safety procedures, and/or attitudes.

Purposes of Orientation

A new employee's first few days on the job may be spent in orientation, but in some firms it is felt that learning is more effective if spread over a period of time. For example, Web Industries' program is delivered in 20 one-hour sessions over four weeks.[33] Similarly, at Micron Technology, a computer chip manufacturing firm, the multicultural environment is emphasized in two-and-a-half hour sessions for 30 participants who meet once a week for six weeks. Topics covered include

- joining the company team;
- participating in groups;
- gaining responsibility;
- planning employee development;
- resolving workplace issues;
- dealing with change.

Micron's program is called *Reaching High Performance*. Company executives believe it guides new employees through the corporate culture and trains them to become valued members of the company team.[34]

EASING ADJUSTMENT TO THE ORGANIZATION

Orientation helps the new employee to adjust to both the formal and the informal organization. Management wants the employee to become productive as rapidly as possible. To do so, the employee needs to know specifically what the job involves. Explanations from the supervisor concerning the job can do much to speed this process.

Many of the benefits of orientation, however, relate to the informal organization. New employees are not automatically greeted enthusiastically. There may even be hazing and kidding. To reduce new employee anxiety, attempts should be made to integrate the person into the informal organization as quickly as possible.

Texas Instruments conducted research many years ago that clearly revealed the importance of the informal group. New employees were assigned randomly to one of two training groups: one took a traditional orientation program, the other an experimental *socialization program*. The latter group covered such subjects as career management, the importance of politics, picking the right boss, and the importance of being at the right place at the right time. At the end of two years, the learning rates of the two groups were compared. Employees in the socialization program proved to be significantly superior on all measures to those in the traditional group. The most dramatic finding was that turnover among professionals such as engineers and computer specialists was 40 percent lower than for those in the traditional group.[35]

Characteristically, new employees start with enthusiasm, creativity, and commitment. These qualities will gradually fade if an inept orientation program fails to integrate new hires. Conversely, an effective program enhances the employment relationship and provides the foundation for employee motivation, commitment, and productivity.

GIVING INFORMATION ON TASKS AND EXPECTATIONS

Employees need to know precisely what their job consists of and what is expected of them. Orientation should also cover standards to qualify for pay raises, criteria for promotion, and rules of the company and the work unit.

REINFORCING A FAVOURABLE IMPRESSION

The final purpose of orientation is to create and maintain a favourable impression of the organization and its work. The orientation process can do much to allay new employees' doubts about whether they have made a sound employment decision.

Stages in Effective Orientation

There are three stages to an effective orientation program: a company overview, an introduction to the department, and follow-up.[36]

First, the HR department presents general information on matters that relate to all employees, such as a company overview, review of company policies and procedures, and salary levels. A checklist is often used to ensure that certain information is included (see Figure 7-8). It is also helpful for the new employee to know how his or her department fits into overall company operations. As well, orientation programs should provide information about how company products or services benefit society as a whole.

FIGURE 7-8
Checklist for New Employees

NEW EMPLOYEE CHECKLIST

Name _____ Employment Date _____

Position Title _____ Department _____

Pay Grade _____ Appointment Type: PT ____ FT ____ Supervisor _____

Probationary Period Ends _____

Five Month Performance Appraisal Due _____

Information Provided:

Orientation packet	By: _____	Date _____
I.D. card	By: _____	Date _____
Staff handbook	By: _____	Date _____
Grievance guide	By: _____	Date _____
Retirement information	By: _____	Date _____
Life insurance	By: _____	Date _____
Disability insurance	By: _____	Date _____
Supplementary health insurance	By: _____	Date _____

I understand that an exit interview with a Human Resource Department representative is required of all terminating employees receiving benefits.

I have received the information checked above, understand my employment status, and have been fully informed about my insurance options and benefits.

I have chosen not to enrol in Supplementary health, Life, Disability insurance. (Circle those you are not enrolling in.)

_____
Employee Signature   Date

_____
Human Resource Representative   Date

Effective Date _____

The employee's immediate supervisor is usually responsible for the second stage of orientation, although in some instances, the supervisor may delegate this task to a senior employee. Topics and events to be covered include an overview of the department, a review of job requirements, a tour, a question and answer session and introductions to other employees. In addition, safety needs to be stressed from the very first day on the job.[37] At this point, then, it is crucial that the supervisor clearly explain performance expectations and specific work rules. As well, the supervisor should try to ease the new hire into the informal work group as quickly as possible.

The third stage involves an evaluation and follow-up conducted by the human resource department in conjunction with the immediate supervisor. The new employee does not go through the orientation program only to be forgotten. During the first week or so, the supervisor works with the new employee to clarify information and make sure that integration into the work group takes place. Human resource professionals assist supervisors to ensure that this vital third step is accomplished.

Training the Supervisor

One of the most important aspects of an orientation program is training supervisors to conduct orientation properly. Human resource professionals can provide the new employee with general information, but it is the supervisor who must integrate the employee into the work setting.

The supervisor should first express confidence that new employees are going to do well. People often begin work not fully convinced that they are capable of doing the job. Supervisors need to reassure nervous beginners that they would not have been hired if management didn't believe they would be successful. Second, supervisors need to explain both the good and the bad points of the job. During the orientation period, managers often spend most of their time emphasizing the enjoyable aspects, leaving the new employees to discover the less appealing features on their own. Studies have verified that in-depth employee understanding of job requirements lowers turnover rates. Ideally, new employees will have received a realistic job preview, so they will not encounter unpleasant surprises. Third, the new employee should be informed of supervisor likes and dislikes in terms of job performance. Every supervisor has particular preferences—usually small things that they react to favourably or unfavourably. Knowing these preferences, employees can more easily adapt to a particular work situation. For example, a supervisor who is concerned about neatness should let new employees know. Fourth, both company standards and any unique customs of the employee's particular work group should be explained. All company rules, especially those pertaining to the new hire's section, should also be covered. Finally, the supervisor should introduce the new employee to members of the work group, identifying any informal group leaders. Here again, an attempt should be made to minimize the number of surprises. Starting off badly with informal group leaders can hurt the new employee's chances for quick acceptance. In jobs that require considerable interaction among group members, group acceptance is especially important.

Reorientation

While orientation programs typically are conducted for new employees, programs may sometimes be needed for long-term employees As organizations change, different management styles may develop, communication methods may be altered, and the structure of the organization itself may—and typically does—take on a new form. Even the corporate culture may evolve into something different over time. Any of these changes may warrant reorientation, or employees may find themselves working in organizations that are vastly different from what they have come to recognize and expect.

SELECTING HRD METHODS

When a person is working on a car, some tools are more helpful in doing certain tasks than others. The same logic applies when considering the diverse HRD methods shown in Figure 7-9. Some apply only to managers and entry-level professionals, some to operative employees, and some to both. Some HRD takes place on the job; some takes place in classrooms and other sites.

MANAGEMENT DEVELOPMENT

A firm's future lies primarily in the hands of its management. Thus, it is imperative that managers keep up with the latest developments in their respective

FIGURE 7-9
Human Resource Development Methods

METHOD	UTILIZED FOR			CONDUCTED	
	Managers and entry-level professionals	Operative employees	Both	On the job	Off the job
Coaching/mentoring			X	X	
Business games	X				X
Case study	X				X
Conference method	X				X
Behaviour modelling	X				X
In-basket training	X				X
Internships	X			X	
Role playing	X				X
Job rotation			X	X	
Programmed instruction			X		X
Computer-based training			X		X
Classroom lecture			X		X
On-the-job training		X		X	
Apprenticeship training		X		X	X
Simulators		X			X
Vestibule training		X			X

fields and—at the same time—manage an ever changing work force operating in a dynamic environment. Many organizations, therefore, place a strong emphasis on training and development programs for managers.

Management development consists of all learning experiences that result in an upgrading of skills and knowledge required for current and future managerial positions. While critical knowledge and skills are provided by organizations in development programs, the process also requires individual commitment. In fact, taking responsibility for one's own development may be the most important aspect of management development.[38] As one director of staffing and development for a western grain distributor suggested: "In my company, executives won't go to courses. Instead, I am being increasingly called on to help executives find tools they can use to do their jobs better."[39]

First-line supervisors, middle managers and executives may all be expected to participate in management development programs. These programs are offered in-house, by professional organizations, and by colleges and universities. In-house programs are planned and presented by a firm's HRD specialists. Line managers often conduct segments of a program.

Professional organizations, colleges, and universities are additional sources of management training. Organizations such as the Canadian Institute of Management provide courses and conduct conferences and seminars in a number of specialties. Numerous universities also provide management training and development programs. At times, colleges and universities possess expertise not available within business organizations. In some cases, academicians and management practitioners present HRD programs jointly. A recent survey revealed the most frequently mentioned reasons for conducting management training outside the company:

- an outside perspective
- new viewpoints
- possibility of taking executives out of the work environment
- exposure to faculty experts and research
- broader vision.

Contrast these ideas with the most frequently mentioned reasons for keeping management training inside the company:

- training is more specific to needs
- lower costs
- less time
- consistent, relevant material
- more control of content and faculty
- helps develop organizational culture and teamwork.[40]

According to a 1993 survey of all American companies with 100 or more employers, management skills development was the most nearly universal form of training, provided in 91 percent of firms. The majority of firms used a combination of in-house and outside training (see Figure 7-10.) [41]

An impressive array of training methods is available.

FIGURE 7-10
General Types of Training

Types of Training	% Providing[1]	In-House Only (%)[2]	Outside Only (%)[3]	Both (%)[4]
Management Skills/Development	91	12	18	61
Basic Computer Skills	90	21	14	55
Communication Skills	87	21	12	53
Supervisory Skills	86	18	12	56
Technical Skills/Knowledge	82	22	6	54
New Methods/Procedures	80	38	5	37
Executive Development	77	8	26	44
Customer Relations/Services	76	25	9	41
Personal Growth	73	14	15	45
Clerical/Secretarial Skills	73	23	18	32
Employee/Labor Relations	67	23	12	31
Customer Education	65	28	5	31
Wellness	63	21	15	28
Sales Skills	56	15	11	30
Remedial/Basic Education	48	11	21	15

Of all organizations with 100 or more employees...
[1]Percent that provide each type of training
[2]Percent that say all training of this type is designed and delivered by in-house staff
[3]Percent that say all training of this type is designed and delivered by outside consultants or suppliers
[4]Percent that say training of this type is designed and delivered by a combination of in-house staff and outside suppliers.

Source: Paul Froiland, "Who's Getting Trained," *Training* (October 1993), p. 60.

Coaching and Mentoring

Coaching is an on-the-job approach to management development in which the coach (usually a senior manager) and the trainee (usually a less experienced manager) jointly identify changes required in particular areas of performance and then develop a plan to try out new behaviours.[42] The plan will outline on-the-job assignments, special projects, or even transfers that might help the junior manager gain the required skills and knowledge. The approach is to use opportunities available in the workplace as management development tools. Outside activities such as speaking engagements, conference attendance, and professional publishing also can be part of the plan. The key elements, however, are that development is planned, uses (mostly) workplace opportunities and becomes part of a continual transfer of skills.[43] Thus, for this approach to be effective, the relationship between the supervisor and subordinate must be based on mutual trust and confidence.

Mentoring is a management development technique, similar to coaching, in which the trainee is given the opportunity to learn on a one-to-one basis from a more senior person. The mentor is usually an older, more experienced executive located anywhere in the organization who serves as a host, friend, confidant, and advisor to a new firm member. The relationship may be formally planned or it may develop informally, but informal relationships are less effective. Some research suggests there is a positive relationship between career prospects, higher incomes, and intensive mentoring.[44] Mentoring, then, is an important technique for improving the career prospects of all individuals within an organization.[45]

Business Games

Simulations that represent actual business situations are referred to as **business games.** These simulations attempt to duplicate selected factors in a particular situation, which are then manipulated by the participants. Business games involve two or more hypothetical organizations competing in a given product market. The participants are assigned roles such as president, comptroller, or marketing vice-president. They make decisions affecting price levels, production volumes, and inventory levels. Their decisions are manipulated by a computer program, so that the results simulate those of an actual business situation. Participants are able to see how their decisions affect other groups and vice versa. When a management trainee makes a bad decision that loses a million dollars (on screen), that trainee remembers the lesson learned—with no loss to a real company.

Case Study

The **case study** is a training method that asks trainees to solve real or simulated business problems. The trainee is expected to make decisions based on study of the information given in the case and, if an actual company is involved, on independent research of the company's environment. Typically, the case study method is used in the classroom with an instructor who serves as a facilitator.[46]

Conference Method

The **conference** (or discussion) **method** is a widely used instructional approach that brings together individuals with common interests to discuss and attempt to solve problems. Often the leader of the group is the supervisor. The group leader's role is to keep the discussion on course. As problems are discussed, the leader listens and permits group members to solve their own problems. Individuals engaged in the conference method, although in training, work to solve problems they may face in their everyday activities.

Behaviour Modelling

Behaviour modelling uses live demonstrations or videotapes to illustrate effective interpersonal skills or managerial functions. For example, a supervisor might act out how he or she would discipline an employee who has been consistently late in reporting to work. Since the situations presented are typical of the firm's problems, the participants are able to relate the behaviour to their own jobs. Behaviour modelling has been used successfully to train supervisors in such tasks as conducting performance appraisal reviews, correcting unacceptable performance, delegating work, improving safety habits, handling discrimination complaints, overcoming resistance to change, orienting new employees, and mediating between conflicting individuals or groups.[47]

In-Basket Training

In-basket training is a simulation in which the participant is given a number of typical memoranda, reports, and telephone messages. These papers, presented in no particular order, call for actions ranging from urgent to routine handling. The participant is required to act on the information, assigning a priority to each situation and making decisions.

Internships

As illustrated in Chapter 5, an internship program is a recruitment method whereby college or university students divide their time between attending classes and working for an organization. Internships can also serve as an effective training method.

From the employer's viewpoint, an internship provides an excellent means of viewing a potential permanent employee at work. Internships also provide advantages for students. The experience they obtain through working enables them to integrate theory learned in the classroom with the practice of management. At the same time, the interns' experience will help them determine whether or not the type of firm and the job appeals to them.

The Canadian Council for Aboriginal Business, for example, placed approximately 500 native students in internships over seven years. This program is part of a move toward developing an entrepreneurial spirit among aboriginal peoples.[48] Other Canadian examples include Bell Northern research, where up to 800 university students per year are training during four-month cooperative education work terms and Gandalf Technological Inc., where about 20 students are hired on 16-month internships.[49]

Role Playing

During a **role playing** exercise, participants are required to respond to specific problems they may encounter in their jobs. They learn by doing. Role playing is often used in management development. The technique is effective for teaching skills such as interviewing, grievance handling, performance appraisal, conference leadership, team problem solving, effective communication, or analysis of leadership styles. The Developing HRM Skills exercises in this book are an example of role playing.

Job Rotation

Job rotation involves moving employees from one job to another to broaden their experience, providing the breadth of knowledge often needed for performing higher level tasks. Rotational training programs help new employees understand a variety of jobs within their fields. There are, however, potential problems with this technique. New hires may be given such short assignments they feel more like visitors in a department than a part of the work force. Since they often do not develop a high level of proficiency, they can lower the overall productivity of the work group. In addition, other employees may resent a *fast-track* employee rotating through their department who may in time become their boss.

Programmed Instruction

A teaching method that provides instruction without the intervention of an instructor is called **programmed instruction (PI).** Information is broken down into small portions, or frames. The learner reads each frame in sequence and responds to questions, receiving immediate feedback on response accuracy. If the answers are correct, the learner proceeds to the next frame. If incorrect, the learner repeats the frame. Primary features of this approach are immediate reinforcement and the ability of learners to proceed at their own pace. Programmed instruction material may be presented in a book or by more sophisticated, usually computerized, media.

Computer-Based Training

Computer-based training takes advantage of the speed, memory, and data manipulation capabilities of the computer. Increased speed of presentation and lessened dependence on an instructor are advantages, as instruction can be provided either in a central location or in a satellite office. Some students, however, object to the absence of a human facilitator. As well, hardware and software are costly, though the cost per student may be acceptable for a large number of trainees.

In using computers for training, the world of interactive technology is fast becoming a reality. Canadian firms are investing billions of dollars a year in this training approach. Laser disks, CD-ROM, interactive-voice systems and other devices (see Figure 7-11) are revolutionizing the way training and development programs are delivered. An HR department can now provide up-to-date information on demand and distribute it nationally or globally.[50] A good example is Speedy Muffler King, a company with almost 900 shops in Canada, the United States, France, Belgium and Germany, where continuous training for employees includes lessons on in-shop computers covering customer service procedures and technical updates on repairs.[51]

Computer-based training is clearly more than a fad. In fact, over 80 percent of large organizations use computers in training.[52] One market research firm has predicted that in the United States, businesses will increase their investment in multimedia training almost tenfold during the mid-1990s and similar trends are likely in Canada. Much of that investment is expected to be in CD-ROM, which has the ability to deliver information in an interactive form. For example, Holiday Inn Worldwide is investing $60 million in a system that will put multimedia training stations in the chain's 1600 hotels in Canada, Latin America, and the United States.[53] Programs such as this may provide increased retention rates at lower cost. Studies have suggested that laser disk instruction takes 30 percent less time to achieve learning objectives than traditional classroom training. A 1988 study conducted at General Motors indicated that students trained using interactive learning programs scored an average of 83 percent on a final exam compared with 63 percent for classroom-trained students. Still other studies have suggested that cost savings of 50 percent or more can be achieved.[54]

FIGURE 7-11

Interactive Technology at a Glance

	Technology	Cost	Advantages	Disadvantages	Comments
CD-ROM	Uses a laser to read up to 600 megabytes of text, graphics, audio and video off a 4 1/2 inch aluminum disc. Works in conjunction with either a PC (DOS or Windows) or a Macintosh.	$300-$700 per unit; approximately $4,500 for a complete station. Off-the-shelf software generally runs $75-$1,500 per program; custom programs can cost $2,000-$10,000 to produce	Excellent for combining text and graphics on the same screen. Can be modified internally to save space; thousands off of the shelf programs and applications available, including many reference guides.	Video quality not up to par with laser discs. Not capable of displaying video full screen.	Useful for most programs.
Satellite Instruction	Uses a satellite to link various locations into a single classroom.	Highly variable, depending on the set-up. Conventional classroom training generally ranges from $150-$300 per day per student; other programs can cost $8,000-$10,000 per location for a single day.	Provides an efficient way to train large numbers of people in a consistent way without investing large sums to fly them into a corporate training center. For incentive-based programs (see sidebar), can make learning entertaining and fun.	Requires a relatively large investment that may be suitable only for large companies. Individuals sometimes think that systems are unwieldy and inflexible.	Becoming more popular. New wrinkles offering intriguing possibilities.
CD-1	Stand-alone unit uses a laser to read up to 72 minutes of video and data from a 4 1/2 inch disc to a monitor.	$500-$600 per unit; $400-$1,200 for an accompanying monitor. Kiosk configuration can run $200-$10,000.	Interactive video without a computer. Portability makes it ideal for remote training and recruiting.	Can't store data on how system is being used; can't administer tests or track scores.	More sophisticated than a VCR; less sophisticated than CD-ROM or laser disc.
Interactive-Voice Technology	Uses a program installed on a conventional PC to create an automated phone-response system.	$10,000-$75,000	Can be produced internally or purchased from outside firm. System can be updated, and new recordings added with relative ease. Frees HR staff to handle other projects; can slash spending costs for producing benefits booklets and job-opening notices.	Poorly designed or overly complicated system can create headaches for those trying to use it. System must be thoroughly tested so as not to provide inaccurate information.	Quickly growing in popularity as a way to provide information on benefits and accounts; and as a way to post job openings electronically.
Laser Disc	Uses a laser to read one hour of video (two hours at a lower resolution) from a 10-inch disc. Picture can be displayed on a TV monitor or computer.	$300-$1,000 per unit; approximately $4,500-$5,000 for a complete station. Off-the-shelf software runs $1,000-$15,000; custom software can run as high as $300,000.	Highest-quality video of any disc-based medium; also capable of producing digital audio. Can be used as a basic video data base with a bar-code reader or controller; or as part of a sophisticated computing system when interfaced to a PC or Macintosh.	Bulky discs; can't be used for as many applications as CD-ROM; requires a special video card (DVI) inside the computer.	Has become the media of preference for interactive training because of high-quality video and sound.

Source: Reprinted from Samuel Greengard, "How Technology Is Advancing HR," *Personnel Journal* (September 1993), pp. 82–83.

Distance Learning and Videoconferencing

For the past decade, a number of firms in Canada have used **videoconferencing** and satellite classrooms for training. This approach to training is now interactive, offering much of the flexibility and spontaneity of a traditional classroom. At one IBM subsidiary, for example, highly sophisticated programs are offered over a satellite-based network. At each of the 44 sites on the system, a 25-inch monitor is used on a desk equipped with a student response unit connected to other classrooms and to the instructor. The student response unit has a voice-activated microphone, question and question-cancel buttons, and keypads that allow students to answer questions from the instructor. This technology can ensure consistent instruction, broaden access to training, and make it possible to train more people at lower costs per person.[55] It has proved its worth for remote locations with small numbers of learners, and offers particular benefits for multinational operations with far-flung operations, in which travel expenses can take an unacceptably large percentage of total training budgets.

While the main users to date have been universities, it will not be long before the private sector becomes heavily involved. The international electronics giant, Philips, has created a new Canadian subsidiary (Philips Media) to market interactive training software. As an estimated 57 percent of training courses bought by Canadian businesses in 1993 included the use of video.[56] It is but a small step to the adoption of videoconference training. Indeed, in the United States, about 10 percent of organizations with more than 100 employees used videoconferencing for some type of training in 1991.[57]

Classroom Lecture

The traditional **classroom lecture** continues to be effective for certain types of employee training, as the lecturer may present a great deal of information in a relatively short time. Lectures are more effective when groups are small enough to permit discussion, when the lecturer is able to capture the imagination of the class, and when audiovisual equipment is used appropriately.

MANAGEMENT DEVELOPMENT PROGRAMS AT IBM

At IBM in the United States, formal management development programs are conducted for three groups :

- *new managers*—those who have been appointed to their first level of management responsibility;
- *middle managers*—those who are responsible for managing managers;
- *executives*—those who have reached top-management positions as well as those who are considered to have potential for such responsibility.

IBM emphasizes regular and continuous development, with at least one week a year of formal training for every manager. As job demands increase, more and more organizations are expected to implement management development programs.

At IBM Canada Ltd., a new division, Skill Dynamics Canada, has been created to market continuing education to managers from companies across Canada. Skill Dynamics offers courses in mental fitness, creative problem-solving strategies, communications, risk-taking, and project management, taught by in-house professionals and experts from all over the world. These skills are needed, argues company literature, because corporations must change from top-down, hierarchy-based structures to fast-moving, multi-faceted, multiskilled organizations in which all levels cooperate. Employees can no longer see themselves as having the right to a job but must earn that right through continuous learning and skill upgrading.[58]

SUPERVISORY MANAGEMENT TRAINING PROGRAMS: AN ILLUSTRATION

Many firms also conduct supervisory training programs to help line managers perform to their maximum potential. Figure 7-12 shows an overview of a training program designed to give new supervisors the skills and knowledge they need to manage people effectively. The training program is also available to supervisors with long-term service who wish to update their knowledge. A five-day live-in session is supported by pre- and postsession activities.

Several weeks before the session participants are asked to prepare by

■ identifying productive and nonproductive activities;
■ discussing the basic elements of their jobs with their bosses;

FIGURE 7-12
An Overview of a Large Corporation's
Supervisory Training Program

Presession Activities	Five-Day, Live-In Session Activities		Postsession Activities	
	Support subjects	Key course subjects	Program evaluation	
Time Analysis	Why We Are Here	Performance Planning and Review	Formulate an Action Plan Project	Approval and Implementation of an Action Plan Project
Work Analysis	Analyzing Performance Problem	Documentation Skills		
Performance Planning Discussion	Training	Employee Ranking	Rank Session's Topics	Possible Performance Planning and Review Discussions
Selecting an Action Questionnaire Plan Project	Special Health Services	Salary Administration	Evaluate Program	Follow-up
				to Participant and Boss
Writing a Performance Evaluation	Time Management Employment Compliance	Employee Development		
Interview with a Coordinator				
Time: Completed Prior to Start of Program	*Time:* 1 1/2 days	*Time:* 2 1/2 days	*Time:* 1 day	2-4 months after session

Source: Used with the permission of the Chevron Corporation.

- selecting a major opportunity or problem that both the participant and the boss are committed to deal with (this becomes an action plan); and

- sending a sample of an employee evaluation to the training program coordinator.

The live-in session begins on a Sunday night with a social gathering, dinner, and a business meeting. Participants are asked to describe their jobs and to discuss their action plans. A senior manager meets with the group to discuss the role of the supervisor, the purpose of the program, and the expected on-the-job results.

A number of support and key course subjects are presented, as well as information on laws, company policies, and practices. Action plan projects are worked on during the program evaluation phase.

These plans are implemented in the post-session phase. Unsatisfied training needs are emphasized in this phase, and appropriate changes are made to ensure that the training program continues to have practical value to both the employee and the company.

Training supervisors to manage their people in a supportive fashion can have both measurable and intangible benefits. A large (4700 responses) 1994 study completed at BC Telecom, for example, found that employees who worked for supervisors they regarded as supportive missed less work, were less tense, felt more secure, and were confident about their ability to get ahead in the company.[59]

TRAINING METHODS FOR ENTRY-LEVEL PROFESSIONAL EMPLOYEES

Firms have a special interest in college- and university-trained employees hired for entry-level professional positions, including management trainees. General Electric, for example, conducts a number of new employee programs, including the internationally known information systems manufacturing program (ISMP). This two-year program combines rotational work assignments with graduate-level seminars to prepare employees to design, program, and implement integrated computerized and manual information systems.

The ISMP emphasizes challenging work assignments of varying lengths in such areas as programming, systems analysis and design, computer centre operation, project management, and functional work. Individual progress is determined by employee performance and demonstrated potential. A candidate for ISMP must have taken at least two computer science courses in university and have a bachelor's degree in a related field. Selection for the program is based on a careful review of the employee's course curriculum, academic records, leadership in extracurricular activities, and work experience. Other training programs for college and university graduates may be more or less structured than GE's ISMP but *practical* experience, alone or in combination with other methods, appears to be an essential common element.[60]

TRAINING METHODS FOR OPERATIVE EMPLOYEES

High priority should also be given to training and development for operative employees: the people actually producing goods and services. Every position in an organization is necessary or it would not (or should not) exist; organizations rely heavily on their clerical staff, systems analysts, manufacturing associates, and other operative employees.

Training needs for these employees have changed with the redefinition of many jobs. In firms using self-directed work teams, operative employees make many decisions previously reserved for management. In the food industry, for example, industry leaders like Kraft General Foods, Heinz, Campbell, Weston Foods, and Coca-Cola Bottlers have switched to Total Quality Management (TQM). Employees are trained to function as a group, replacing the traditional hierarchy of worker–supervisor–manager. At Ault Foods, for example, eight levels of administration have been reduced to four, as now work groups make many decisions that were once the responsibility of managers. To prepare workers for such responsibility, the emphasis in employee training has shifted from how to use machinery to a wide range of personal and technical improvement skills aimed at problem solving. Similarly, at McCormick Canada Inc. in London, Ontario, basic communication training for all production workers is emphasized and job applicants at Campbell Soup Company are interviewed to determine their suitability for teamwork.[61]

In this section, we present an overview of the HRD methods most commonly used in training operative employees. In addition, recall that some methods listed in Figure 7-9 are applicable to both management and operative employees.

On-the-Job Training

On-the-job-training (OJT) permits an employee to learn job tasks by actually performing them, thus avoiding the problem of transferring what has been learned to the job. Another benefit may be increased motivation, because it is clear to learners that they are acquiring the knowledge needed to perform their jobs. As the vice-president of HR for a major Canadian retail company indicated, people "have a very low tolerance for sitting in classrooms learning out-dated theories. They want something useful, right now!"[62] However, the emphasis on production may detract from the learning process if trainees feel too much pressure to perform.

Both the manager and the trainee must recognize that OJT is a joint effort. To make OJT effective, the manager must create a climate of trust and open communication. The technique was successful for Recton Machine Works Ltd. in Sault Ste. Marie, Ontario, where an in-house job training strategy resulted in a 15 percent increase in production, allowing this 60-year-old company to expand.[63]

Apprenticeship Training

All training must "fit" into a culture or it will not be effective, used, or accepted. Unfortunately, **apprenticeship training** never captured the imagination of the Canadian public, politicians, or educators.[64] Except in the construction industry (there are a few other exceptions), apprenticeships have never fit into the mainstream North American culture.

Industry has generally been unwilling to invest in apprenticeships, as skilled labour shortages could be made up through immigration. As our standard of living fell relative to other countries throughout the 1980s and 1990s, however, fewer trained individuals migrated to this country. The result is that in both Canada and the United States there is a critical shortage of skilled labour.[65] In addition, only 30 percent of our high school graduates are expected to earn college diplomas or university degrees. If Canada is to remain competitive, politicians and educators must refocus their attention on the other 70 percent, who will most likely constitute the pool from which future skilled employees and technicians must be drawn.[66]

To make apprenticeships more acceptable as an alternative to college or university, the prestige of technical studies has to be raised and hands-on (cooperative) components made more meaningful. Students and parents must become convinced that apprenticeship leads to interesting careers and an acceptable standard of living. Advocates of apprenticeship can point to the successful example of Germany, where 65 percent of graduating engineers have previous apprenticeship training.[67]

Apprenticeship can be described as an integrated HRD technique that combines on-the-job training with classroom instruction. Any training for skills occupations must teach a body of skills and supporting theory.[68] The job instruction component of apprenticeship is used to teach the requisite skills of a particular trade or occupation. Classroom instruction, which constitutes a relatively minor portion of the program (usually about 10 percent), teaches related theory and design concepts. For example, the four-year plumber program includes only three eight-week in-school sessions. In the classroom, plumber apprentices learn about such things as the physical properties of

HRM IN ACTION

Lon Williams, the training and development manager, was studying the weekly training schedule when he heard a tap at his door. "Got a minute, Lon?" asked Oscar Ribeiro, production manager.

"Sure, come on in," said Lon. "What've you got?"

"You may know that I recently hired John Bryan, a retired infantry officer who wanted to begin his second career with us. John's military record was excellent, but I was shocked when I heard through the grapevine about his high-handed methods. Apparently he still thinks he's in the army the way he bosses people around. When I spoke to John, he said, 'I've been successful for 20 years managing people and using these exact methods.' Lon, something has to be done. Do you have any ideas?"

How would you respond?

piping and other plumbing materials, industry codes, safety rules and operating procedures, trade tools and equipment, soldering techniques and the characteristics of various fittings and piping systems. On the job the trainees become familiar with relevant codes, regulations, and specifications and learn to install, service, and test systems and equipment.

The Canadian apprenticeship system presently covers more than 65 traditionally regulated occupations in four occupational sectors: construction (e.g., stonemason, electrician, carpenter, plumber), motive power (motor vehicle mechanic, machinist), industrial (industrial mechanic, millwright) and service (baker, cook, hairstylist). In some of these regulated occupations, apprentices must earn a "Certificate of Qualification" by passing a provincial government examination. Apprentices who pass an interprovincial examination with a minimum grade of 70 percent are awarded a "Red Seal", indicating their qualifications are acceptable across the country.

This apprenticeship training differs from other job instruction techniques in that it is regulated through a partnership of government, labour, and industry. The Canadian federal government pays for in-school training and income support, provincial governments administer the programs and pay for classroom facilities and instructors, employers absorb the costs of workplace training, and apprentices initiate the process by finding employers willing to sponsor them.

This partnership can provide an effective and powerful mechanism to match human resources with opportunities in industry, given social and economic constraints. Consensus among the partners and cooperation among program participants are, however, critical. If the partners have conflicting goals, both the quality of training and the ability of the system to solve shortages of skilled labour will suffer.[69]

Unlike corporate-sponsored training programs which address the specific needs of an organization, apprenticeships are focused on the collective training needs of specific occupations within broad industrial categories.[70] Consequently, the skills learned through apprenticeship training are transferable within an occupation, across provincial or state boundaries. For example, in the construction industry, carpenters, electricians, plumbers, and masons are trained to meet standards recognized throughout the trade. This flexibility provides advantages to the worker and the industry when regional fluctuations occur in the supply and demand of skilled labour. The system is highly dependent on employers, however, for they must accept the responsibility for establishing and maintaining adequate standards of job performance.

In determining acceptable qualifications and performance standards for the future, industry and government must address the special needs of new labour groups like women and minorities, eliminating standards or test criteria which might unjustly limit opportunities. For example, criteria pertaining to physical strength might be relaxed or eliminated by making simple changes in job design. More flexible work schedules may also be required to respond to the special needs of working mothers or employees with different religious or cultural backgrounds.[71]

Simulators

Simulators are training devices of varying degrees of complexity that model the real world. They range from simple paper mock-ups of mechanical devices to computerized simulations of total environments. Human resource development specialists may use simulated sales counters, automobiles, or airplanes.

Although simulator training lacks the immediacy and realism of on-the-job training, simulation is a useful way to give trainees preliminary experience of large, expensive equipment or dangerous environments. A prime example is in the training of airline pilots, but at the Centre for Marine Simulation in Atlantic Canada, marine simulators help to train those who work at sea.[72] Similarly, a Brampton, Ontario company (Atlantic Aerospace Corp), supplies aircraft maintenance simulator systems, both civilian and military, in Canada, Australia, the United States, and Saudi Arabia.[73] Space simulators allow astronauts to practise moving in an environment as close as possible to weightlessness. Sophisticated computer simulations let firefighters test strategy without burning real forests.

Vestibule Training

Vestibule training takes place away from the production area on equipment that closely resembles equipment used on the job. For example, a group of lathes may be located in a training centre, where the trainees will be instructed in their use. This approach allows trainees to focus on learning the required skills without the stress of actual job performance, and also avoids disrupting production or customer service.

CHOOSING AN HRD METHOD

A study of organizations with 100 or more employees suggested that the two methods used by almost all firms are videotapes and lectures (see Figure 7-13). While a slightly higher number of firms use videotapes than lectures, the figures do not imply that employees spend more time watching videos. The question on the survey was "Do you use it?" not "How much do you use it?" Other methods used by more than half of responding organizations include one-on-one instruction, slides, role plays, and audiotapes.[74]

MEDIA

Training programs may be enhanced with the use of various **media**: special methods of communicating ideas and concepts. Multimedia presentations, using the computer in conjunction with video and/or other media, appear to offer tremendous potential. More conventional media include videotapes, films, closed-circuit television, slide projectors, overhead and opaque projectors, flip charts, and chalkboards.

FIGURE 7-13
Frequency of Use of Human Resource
Development Methods

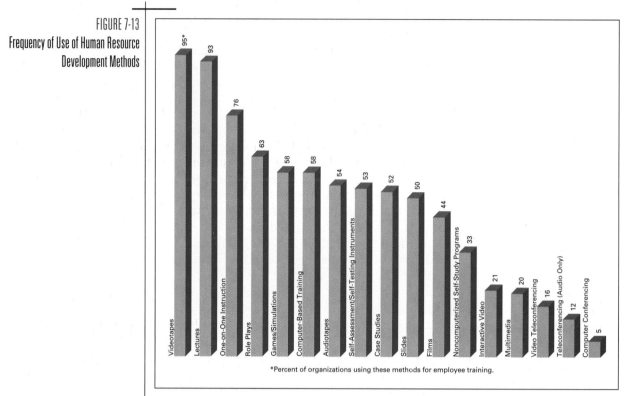

*Percent of organizations using these methods for employee training.

Source: Reprinted from Paul Froiland, "Who's Getting Trained?" *Training* (October 1993), p. 57

Visual aids can greatly facilitate learning. It has been estimated that almost 75 percent of what we learn is learned by sight, while approximately 75 percent of what we hear is forgotten within two days.[75] Thus a lecture may be more interesting and effective when complemented by overhead transparencies or a video.

IMPLEMENTING HRD PROGRAMS

A well-conceived training program may fail if management can't convince the participants of its merits. Participants must believe the program will help them achieve their personal and professional goals. The credibility of HRD specialists, in turn, may depend on a series of successful programs.

Implementing HRD programs is often difficult because managers, typically action-oriented, feel they are too busy. According to one management development executive, "Most busy executives are too involved chopping down the proverbial tree to stop for the purpose of sharpening their axes." Another difficulty is finding qualified trainers. In addition to possessing communication skills, the trainers must know the company's philosophy, objectives, and formal and informal organization and the training program's goals. Human resource development requires more creativity than perhaps any other human resource specialty.

A new program must be monitored carefully, especially during its initial phases. Training implies change, which some employees may resist vigorously. Others may simply wait, perhaps hoping that the program will fail. Participant feedback is vital so that the problems inevitable to any new program can be resolved before they undermine the program. Scheduling training for present employees may be particularly difficult because they already have specific full-time duties. Although it is the line manager's job to have positions covered while an employee is in training, the HRD manager must help with arrangements.

Records should be maintained on each employee's training program and performance both during training and on the job. This information is important not only in charting the individual employee's progress but also in measuring program effectiveness.[76] It can also be necessary to prove that supervisors have been trained properly—for example, when accidents are investigated.

EVALUATING HUMAN RESOURCE DEVELOPMENT

Although billions of dollars a year are spent on employee training, there is no clear consensus within the training community on how to determine its value. Obviously, the credibility of HRD can be greatly enhanced by showing how the organization benefits from training programs. Thus, the HRD department must document its results in the form of memoranda to management and written reports.[77]

HRD professionals have taken several approaches to determining the worth of specific programs. These involve evaluations of 1) the participants' opinions of the program, 2) the extent to which participants have learned the material, 3) the participants' ability to apply the new knowledge, and 4) whether or not training goals have been achieved.[78]

Participants' Opinions

Asking participants' opinions is an inexpensive approach that provides both immediate response and suggestions for improvements. Opinions, however, must be interpreted cautiously because they are subjective: they measure perceived learning rather than actual learning. For example, questionnaires filled out by recent participants in a three-day executive seminar in Bermuda are unlikely to be very critical. Even a seminar in a less exotic location can provide a welcome break from a hectic job, and this relief may lead to glowing evaluations. As well, participants may not want to spoil the chances of others who might be chosen for future courses.

Extent of Learning

Tests of skill and knowledge may be used to determine what the participants have learned. The same test (or a similar one, using the split-halves technique described in chapter 6) is administered before and after training. The testing method is strengthened by randomly assigning employees to an experimental group, which receives a particular training program, and a control group, which does not. Differences between the two groups on post-test results are attributed to the training.

Behavioural Change

While tests may indicate accurately what has been learned, they give little insight into whether the desired behavioural changes will take place. For example, a manager may learn about motivational techniques, but have difficulty applying the new knowledge. Consider the following scenario.

> Pat Sittel sat in the front row at a company-sponsored supervisory training seminar on empowering employees. As the lecturer made each point, Pat would nod her head in agreement. At the end of the two-day seminar, Pat demonstrated her understanding by writing an excellent essay on empowerment. Returning to her department, Pat tossed the essay onto her secretary's desk. "Ruth, stop working on those letters and get this typed up right away," she barked. "And then tell Bob I want to see him. He didn't make out that last report the way I told him to." Although she had understood the material presented in the seminar, Pat's failure to apply what she had learned didn't benefit the organization.

Behavioural change needs to be evaluated by the employee's supervisor. For example, Pat's manager might have been alerted to her overly intervening management style by the excessive overtime she put in. Measuring her overtime hours after training would give a partial objective measure of behavioural change; the supervisor might also get a more subjective impression of her management style by observing that morale in Pat's department was still low.

Accomplishment of HRD Objectives

Another approach to evaluating HRD programs involves determining the extent to which stated objectives have been achieved. If the objective of an accident prevention program is to reduce the number and severity of accidents by 15 percent, for example, comparing accident rates before and after training provides a useful measurement of success. The problem is that many programs dealing with broader topics are more difficult to evaluate.

For example, suppose a group of executives were sent to a university for a one-week course in management and leadership development, and their performance actually improved after the course. This benefit might or might not be reflected in the overall performance level of the group, because other variables might distort the picture. Perhaps a mild recession has forced the layoff of several key employees; a competing firm has lured away one of the department's top engineers; or the company president has pressured the employment director to hire an incompetent relative. In any of these cases, the managers' new skills would not show up in an objective measure of department performance.

Thus, problems associated with evaluation make it difficult to establish clear proof of the effect of training on performance. Nevertheless, it is important for human resource managers to continue to obtain evidence of HRD's contributions to achieving organizational goals.[79]

A GLOBAL PERSPECTIVE

Because of the cost of global staffing and the staggering cost of failed expatriate assignments, employee orientation takes on increased importance in global operations.[80] Orientation for global assignments must incorporate cultural elements. Indeed, David Wheatley, director of DFW Consulting, a British firm, has suggested that "in order to be effective internationally, you have to not only be aware of different cultures, you must respect them and reconcile them."[81] The introduction should also include an overview of the history, traditions, and corporate values of partners. Then, a description of the new venture, its organization, and management structure should be presented, followed by an introduction to the manager, department, and coworkers.[82]

International orientation should be a thoroughly planned, in-depth process that takes a long-term approach including provisions for follow-up and evaluation. The benefits of these programs are now just beginning to become evident. Two years after developing an orientation system, for example, Corning, Inc., showed a 69 percent reduction in voluntary turnover among new hires, a 8:1 benefit/cost ratio in the first year, and a 14:1 ratio annually thereafter.[83]

Training in Canada differs markedly from that provided in other countries. In the past, Canadian employers have tended to focus training efforts primarily on highly educated employees, although there is some evidence that this trend is changing.[84] In contrast, German firms usually control training by providing financial support for technical schools, apprenticeship programs, and on-the-job training. Approximately 70 percent of German workers who do not attend university receive these types of training. Companies in Sweden and other industrial nations also supply more training than do North American firms.[85] In 1980, the Japanese spent an average of only $200 U.S. per employee, but by 1990, this expenditure had doubled. In fact, some large firms spend as much as $1200 U.S. per person. In contemporary Japan,

- over 90 percent of new employees receive orientation training;
- 85 percent of firms have employee-development plans;
- 80 percent supply follow-up training within one year;
- 80 percent of newly assigned managers receive primary management training;
- 80 percent of middle managers obtain management development training;
- 70 percent of firms offer new-employee training within two to three weeks of employment; and
- 60 percent of firms assign orientation homework between hiring and reporting to work.

Both the General Motors-Toyota NUMMI joint venture and the Chrysler-Mitsubishi Diamond Star alliance have made new employee orientation and training high priorities. Each joint venture spent millions of dollars on orientation and training long before it started manufacturing operations.

The success of these companies suggests that international alliances should expend as much effort preparing new employees to deal with the social context of their jobs (and to cope with the insecurities and frustrations of a new learning situation) as they do developing the technical skills that employees need to perform effectively.[86]

SUMMARY

Change involves moving from one condition to another, a process that affects individuals, groups, and entire organizations. The impetus for change comes from a belief that the organization and its human resources can be more productive and successful after change occurs. Reducing resistance to change is crucial to success. The change sequence does not end when a change is implemented. A new and flexible position capable of dealing with present requirements and adapting to further change must be developed. The final phase of the change sequence involves evaluating the effectiveness of the specific HRD method chosen.

Human resource development (HRD) is planned, continuous effort by management to improve employee competency levels and organizational performance through training and development. Training is designed to permit learners to acquire the knowledge and the skills needed for their present jobs. Development has a more long-term focus, involving learning that looks beyond today's job. The general human resource development process that helps to facilitate change involves a series of steps: 1) determine HRD needs, 2) establish specific objectives, 3) select HRD methods, 4) select HRD media, 5) implement the program, and 6) evaluate program effectiveness.

Orientation is the guided adjustment of new employees into the company, the job, and the work group. There are three different stages in an effective orientation program: 1) general information about the organization, usually provided by the human resource department; 2) specific job training conducted by the employee's immediate supervisor; and 3) evaluation and follow-up conducted by the human resource department in conjunction with the immediate supervisor.

Management development consists of all learning experiences that result in an upgrading of skills and knowledge required for current and future managerial positions. Coaching is an on-the-job approach to management development in which opportunities available in the workplace are used as developmental tools. Similarly, mentoring provides the opportunity to learn on a one-to-one basis from a more experienced manager or senior professional.

Simulations that represent actual business situations are referred to as business games. The case study is a training method that uses real or simulated business situations.

The conference, or discussion method, is a widely used instructional approach that brings together individuals with common interests to discuss and to attempt to solve problems. Behaviour modelling uses live demonstrations or videotapes to illustrate effective interpersonal skills and managerial functions. In-basket training is a simulation in which the participant is given a number of typical business papers such as memoranda, reports, and telephone messages. An internship program is a recruitment method whereby college or university students divide their time between attending classes and working for an organization. During a role playing exercise, participants are required to respond to specific problems they may encounter in their jobs. Job rotation involves moving employees from one job to another to broaden their experience. A teaching method that provides instruction without the intervention of an instructor is called programmed instruction (PI). Computer-based training takes advantage of the speed, memory, and data manipulation capabilities of the computer for greater flexibility. Videoconferencing and satellite classrooms also are used for training. Although lacking the glamour of newer approaches, the classroom lecture continues to be effective in some situations.

In firms using self-directed work teams, operative employees may need training, as they make many decisions previously reserved for management. On-the-job training (OJT) is a less formal approach to training that permits an employee to learn job tasks by performing them. Apprenticeship training combines classroom instruction with on-the-job training. Simulators are training devices of varying degrees of complexity that model the real world. Vestibule training takes place away from the production area on equipment that closely resembles equipment used on the job.

HR professionals have taken several approaches to determining the worth of specific programs. These involve evaluations of 1) the participants' opinions of the program, 2) the extent to which participants have learned the material, 3) the participants' ability to apply the new knowledge, and 4) whether or not stated training goals have been achieved.

In the international arena, training, especially orientation, has become an important part of international HRM. As global staffing is expensive and the cost of expatriate failure staggering, HR professionals must conduct in-depth orientation programs that are thoroughly planned, take a long-term approach, and include provisions for follow-up and evaluation.

TERMS FOR REVIEW

Human resource development (HRD)	Role playing
Training	Job rotation
Development	Programmed instruction (PI)
Orientation	Computer-based training
Management development	Videoconferencing
Coaching	Classroom lecture
Mentoring	On-the-job training (OJT)
Business games	Apprenticeship training
Case study	Simulators
Conference method	Vestibule training
Behaviour modelling	Media
In-basket training	

QUESTIONS FOR REVIEW

1. What are the steps involved in the organization change sequence?
2. What can the manager do to reduce resistance to change?
3. Define and explain the scope of human resource development.
4. What are the general purposes of HRD?
5. Describe the HRD process.
6. Define orientation and explain the importance of employee orientation to a firm.
7. Define management development. Why is it important?
8. List and describe the primary methods used in management development.
9. What methods are used primarily to train operative employees?
10. What are some of the means of evaluating HRD programs? Discuss the strengths and limitations of each method.

HRM INCIDENT 1

• WHAT TO DO?

"I'm a little discouraged," said Susan Matthews to the training officer. "I keep making mistakes running the new printing press. It's a lot more complicated than the one I operated before, and I just can't seem to get the hang of it."

"Well, Susan," responded Mahmoud Askar, "maybe you're just not cut out for the job. You know that we sent you to the two-week refresher course in Montreal to get you more familiar with the new equipment."

"Yes," said Susan, "they had modern equipment at the school, but it wasn't anything like this machine."

"What about the factory rep?" asked Mahmoud. "Didn't he spend some time with you?"

"No, I was on vacation at that time," said Susan.

Mahmoud responded, "Have you asked your boss to get him back for a day or two?"

"I asked him," said Susan, "but he said training was your responsibility. That's why I'm here." After she was gone, Mahmoud began composing an urgent e-mail message to the printing press manufacturer.

QUESTIONS

1. What steps in the HRD process has the company neglected?
2. Is Mahmoud taking the proper action? What would you do?

HRM INCIDENT 2

• MANAGEMENT SUPPORT OF HRD?

As the initial training session began, John Robertson, the hospital administrator, spoke of the tremendous benefits he expected from the management development program the hospital was starting. He also complimented Mariko Ohi, the human resource director, for her efforts in arranging the program. As he finished his five-minute talk, he said, "I'm not sure what Mariko has in store for you, but I know that management development is important, and I'll expect each of you to put forth your best efforts to make it work." Mr. Robertson then excused himself from the meeting and turned the program over to Mariko.

For several years Mariko had been trying to convince Mr. Robertson that the supervisors could benefit from a management development program. She believed that many problems within the hospital were management related. Reluctantly, Mr. Robertson had agreed to authorize funds to employ a consultant. Through employee interviews and self-administered questionnaires completed by the supervisors, the consultant attempted to identify development needs. The consultant recommended twelve four-hour sessions emphasizing communication, leadership, and motivation. Each session was to be repeated once so that supervisors who missed it the first time could attend the second offering.

Mr. Robertson had signed the memo that Mariko had prepared, directing all supervisors to support the management development program. There was considerable grumbling, but all the supervisors agreed to attend. As Mariko replaced Mr. Robertson at the podium, she could sense the lack of interest in the room.

QUESTIONS

1. Have any serious errors been made so far in the management development program? What would you have done differently?
2. What advice do you have for Mariko at this point to help make the program effective?

DEVELOPING HRM SKILLS: AN EXPERIENTIAL EXERCISE

Effective training cannot occur unless both content and methodology fit into the organization's culture.

Today will be a training day, with the training specialist from the main office attempting to train an unwilling supervisor. The specialist has almost completed this very difficult task and is looking forward to the last training session. All of the supervisors in this training session have risen through the ranks and have a definite dislike for university graduates. In addition, they all believe that they are experts on training in their areas. The training specialist wants to just get through this last briefing. As with the other supervisors, he'll show this supervisor the basics, and then go back to the main office where people are more receptive. As with the others, if no in-depth questions are asked, he'll provide no additional details. He really doubts if the main office expects much improvement anyway. This operation seems to be going okay as it is.

The supervisor involved in this training session is opposed to the training specialist trying to tell the supervisors how to train and resents being told that all supervisors must operate according to the methods of the company's new owner. This supervisor is scheduled to meet with the training specialist to learn how to train. It is rumoured that the specialist is some 24-year-old university graduate. According to the supervisor, "I was training my people before this hotshot was born. All of a sudden, we can't do anything right. I look forward to my private session. I'm going to reeducate the kid on training."

Two students will play roles in this exercise: one as the training specialist and the other as the supervisor. All students not playing roles should carefully observe the behaviour of both participants. The instructor will provide the participants with additional information necessary to complete the exercise.

8

Corporate Culture and Organizational Development

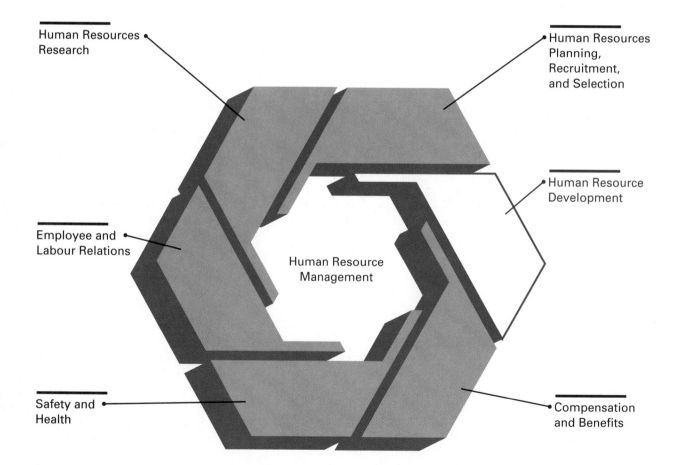

Human Resources Research

Human Resources Planning, Recruitment, and Selection

Human Resource Development

Employee and Labour Relations

Human Resource Management

Compensation and Benefits

Safety and Health

1. Define corporate culture and describe the factors that affect it.

2. Explain the various types of cultures. Describe the participative culture and the importance of changing corporate culture.

3. Define organization development and describe traditional organization development methods.

4. Outline newer organization development methods that enhance total quality management and team building.

5. Explain the use of consultants in organization development and describe the ways managers can evaluate OD programs.

*D*uring the past four years, the profits of International Corporation have declined sharply. Teddy McCoy, International's CEO, is especially concerned about the results of an attitude survey, which revealed that 60 percent of International's employees were dissatisfied with their jobs. Teddy felt certain this condition was related directly to an excessive number of product recalls and employee turnover. In a recent board meeting he asserted, "With competition from both domestic and foreign corporations increasing, broad changes are needed throughout the firm if International is to survive and prosper. If we maintain the status quo, we may go under."

In all likelihood, International Motor Corporation requires an organization development program. In this chapter, we define *corporate culture* and then present factors that create a culture. Next, we describe types of cultures, focusing on participation. The discussion then turns to organization development (OD) methods, including total quality management and team building. Finally, we cover the use of consultants and organization development evaluation.

CORPORATE CULTURE DEFINED

When beginning a new job, an employee may hear, "This is the way we do things around here." This bit of informal communication refers to something more formally known as corporate culture.[1] **Corporate culture** is the system of shared values, beliefs, and habits that interact with the formal organization structure to produce behavioural norms. These patterns of standards, assumptions, values, and norms are shared by organizational members,[2] providing guidelines for employee behaviour.

Culture governs what the company stands for, what overall direction it takes, and how problems and opportunities are defined. It determines resource allocation, organizational structure, the systems in use, the people hired, the fit between jobs and people, and the required results and rewards.[3] Corporate culture is similar in concept to climate. Just as the weather is described by variables such as temperature, humidity, and precipitation, so corporate culture reflects characteristics such as friendliness, supportiveness, and risk taking. Each individual forms perceptions of the job and the organization over a period of time, as he or she works under the general guidance of a superior and a set of organizational policies. Thus, a firm's culture affects job satisfaction as well as job performance. Each employee may assess the nature of an organization's culture differently, however, depending on his or her own personality and preferences. Dissatisfied employees may even leave an organization in the hope of finding a more compatible culture.

In all modern businesses, but especially in creative sectors (like advertising, for example), the firm's most important asset is people. "They are the repositories of creativity, reputations and contacts, and if they are antagonised, they can walk out the door and take the business with them."[4]

According to Anthony Jay, an eminent researcher, "It has been known for some time that corporations are social institutions with customs and taboos, status groups and pecking orders. But they are also political institutions, autocratic and democratic, peaceful and warlike, liberal and paternalistic."[5] What Jay was writing about, although the term had not then achieved broad usage, was *corporate culture*. Businesses are being forced to make many changes to stay competitive. Managers must find ways to improve quality, to increase speed of operations, and to adopt a customer orientation. These changes are so fundamental, they must take root in a company's very essence—in its culture.[6] Corporate culture plays an integral role in accomplishing an organization's mission and objectives; therefore, the factors that determine corporate culture are also crucial to success.

FACTORS THAT INFLUENCE CORPORATE CULTURE

The culture of an organization originates from senior management, stemming largely from what these executives do, rather than what they say. Other factors can also interact to shape the culture of a firm, including work group relationships, managers' and supervisors' leadership styles, organizational characteristics, and administrative processes (see Figure 8-1). The external environment also influences corporate culture.

It must be remembered, too, that the business world has changed. Robert Rogers, chief operating officer at Development Dimensions International, has described how his father worked in the same firm for 42 years, exchanging loyalty, dedication, and hard work for "a job he could count on to support his family." This "psychological contract of trust" was broken in the 1970s, '80s and '90s, so that today there is growing employee cynicism in the workplace: "employees are loyal to themselves and their profession, not to a particular organization or position."[7] This trend has occurred in an era in which managers need to harness the talents of every employee if a firm is to succeed.

Hence the vital importance of creating an effective culture. Global competition has also changed priorities for many firms. One international oil company, for example, had always "overprized vision and undervalued hands-on, day-to-day management" until global pressures started to mount. Management then discovered that profits, more than any one single factor, are essential for global success.[8]

FIGURE 8-1
Factors That Influence Corporate Culture

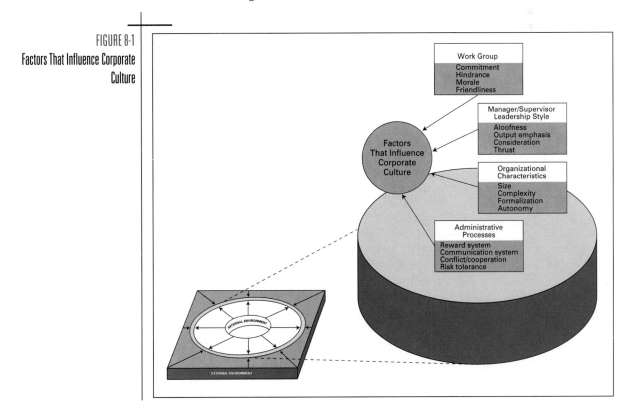

The Work Group

The characteristics of the immediate work group will affect one's perception of corporate culture. For example, commitment to the mission of the work group directly influences cultural perceptions. *Commitment* refers to whether or not a group is really working. At Boulangeries Weston Québec, for example, one of the most important factors in getting people to work effectively together was getting across the reasons for performance standards. Now "they understand that the profit lost due to the rejection of one loaf of bread can only be recovered by producing five additional loaves."[9] It is the culture that determines (in large part) whether individual employees place their firm's best interests over short-term individual considerations, or whether they think, "I'm tired today, who cares if the damn bread is a little burned."

If the work group as a whole is not committed to performing good work, it is difficult for individual members to obtain high levels of output and satisfaction. Morale and friendliness within the group also affect the environment of the work group and the perceived nature of the corporate culture.

Manager/Supervisor Leadership Style

The leadership style of the immediate supervisor will have a considerable effect on culture: whether the manager is aloof and distant, for example, or always pushing for output. Group effectiveness is enhanced by a supervisor who is considerate and hard working and who sets a good example. In fact, it has been claimed that a leader's personality is correlated directly with a firm's strategic direction and level of success. Vision as measured on a "Personality Index" also seems to be correlated with sales growth and profitability.[10]

The management role must change dramatically. Instead of fostering a controlled environment, in which every employee is expected to act (and dress) in roughly the same manner, "for today's best managers, the job is to encourage idiosyncrasies and harness them to corporate ends."[11]

Organizational Characteristics

Organizations vary in size and complexity. Large organizations tend to be more specialized and impersonal. Labour unions often find that large firms are easier to organize than smaller ones, because smaller firms tend to have a more closely knit social structure and to foster more informal relationships among employees and management. Complex organizations sometimes employ a greater number of professionals and specialists, which alters the general approach to problem solving.

Organizations also vary in the degree to which policies are written and in attempts to program behaviour through rules, procedures, and regulations. They can be distinguished, too, by the degree of decentralization of decision-making authority, which, in turn, affects management autonomy and employee freedom.

Toronto-based steel processor FedMet Inc., for example, had experienced a series of poor years between 1988 and 1991, as sales fell by 30 percent. The turnaround is attributed to a change to a more decentralized, cooperative management style that led to lower product rejection rates, higher production volume, and an increase in the on-time delivery rate from 58 to 90 percent. Employers have stated they now look on their boss as a customer rather than as an employer.[12]

Although smaller businesses have been held up as examples of what organizations should be like (they're more flexible), large multinationals are not about to disappear. In fact, some authors suggest that increasing globalization is likely to play to the multinationals' strengths, as they can manufacture and distribute wherever they can discover or create demand. Despite the problems associated with size, then, (work overload, worker alienation, lack of creativity) those larger firms that have adopted modern management techniques may fare very well. For example: "Percy Barnevik, who heads Asea Brown Boveri (ABB), a Swiss-Swedish engineering giant, applies a 30 percent rule to businesses he acquires, allocating 30 percent of central staff to independent profit centres, 30 percent to operating companies and getting rid of 30 percent entirely; only 10 percent are left in head office. His corporate headquarters in Zurich has a staff of about 170."[13] Similarly, at PanCanadian Petroleum Ltd, increased focus on employee input and teamwork, which moved decision making down to the field operator level, has resulted in $5 million in cost savings. Indeed, suggestions from operators have doubled gas output and identified bottlenecks in production.[14] These policies, only some of many creative ideas for managing the human resource, illustrate how organizational characteristics can be changed to develop a different culture designed to make large firms more efficient.

Administrative Processes

Managers who can develop direct links between performance and rewards tend to create cultures conducive to achievement. Communication systems that are open and free-flowing tend to promote participation and creative environments. The general attitudes toward tolerance of conflict and risk handling also have considerable influence on teamwork, innovation, and creativity. From these and other factors, organization members develop a subjective impression of the organization and whether or not it is a good place to work. These impressions enhance or detract from performance, satisfaction, creativity, and commitment.

TYPES OF CULTURES

At times an organization must alter its culture in order to survive. This was the situation faced by IBM when the computer industry changed drastically in the 1980s and early 1990s. Alterations must be made carefully, though; organizations that "fail to address the human factor . . . are likely to poison the well [of employee goodwill] they will need to tap for subsequent renewal."[15]

Management must be aware of the various types of corporate culture and why one particular culture may prove superior to another. Most behaviouralists advocate the adoption of an open and participative culture, even contending that such a culture is best for all situations. This type of culture is characterized by

- trust in subordinates;
- open communication;
- considerate and supportive leadership;
- team problem solving;
- worker autonomy;
- information sharing; and
- high output goals.

Some Canadian businesses are culturally permissive, guided by the philosophy that organization members who are free to choose among alternatives make the soundest decisions. Managers who adopt this philosophy feel

HRM IN ACTION

Wayne, Yusuf, and Robert were supervisors with a small chain of fifteen convenience stores in North Vancouver. Each had responsibility for five stores and reported directly to the company president, but they all worked as a team. Wayne coordinated the scheduling of clerks at all fifteen stores, Yusuf took care of inventory control and purchasing, while Robert took responsibility for recruiting and hiring. Otherwise, they each did whatever needed to be done.

The situation changed markedly within a year, however, when the president, wishing to relieve himself of daily details, promoted Robert to vice-president. Another supervisor, Phillip, was hired to manage Robert's five stores. At first, everything went well, but soon Robert, who was much more involved in store management than the president had been, told the three supervisors he wanted each of them to take care of their own five stores.

Wayne, Yusuf, and Phillip initially resisted Robert's frequent orders and demands. After a few reprimands, though, the men decided to do as Robert wanted. They rarely saw one another, and each took care of all aspects of store operations, as well as filling in for clerks who were late or sick. There were frequent problems, however, as Robert accused the three supervisors of working against him and threatened them with dismissal if operations did not improve. Wayne, Yusuf, and Phillip saved him the trouble; they quit within days of one another. The president fired Robert a few days later.

Explain the corporate culture that existed before and after Robert's promotion to vice-president.

that when employees are asked to give up some of their individuality for the common good, the end result is often reinforcement of the status quo. In this era of rapid change, the results can be stagnation and lack of creativity.

The opposite of the open and participative culture is the closed, autocratic environment. It, too, may be characterized by high output goals. But such goals are more likely to be imposed on the organization by dictatorial or even threatening leaders. The greater rigidity in this culture results from strict adherence to a formal chain of command, narrower spans of management, and stricter individual accountability. The emphasis is on the individual rather than on teamwork. The result is that employees often do only what they are told to do.

A GLOBAL PERSPECTIVE

When a Canadian corporation expands operations to another country, an alliance is often formed with a company in the host country. Alliances are useful for all partners because collaboration makes it possible to share the costs and the risks of conducting business, enabling companies to share financial resources, technology, production facilities, marketing expertise, and of course, human resources.

Once the firms begin working together, it is essential that the corporate cultures and management styles of the partners blend together as quickly as possible,[16] since long-term success requires a corporate culture that supports the goals of the organization and deals effectively with the business environment. It is not easy, however, to create such a culture within a global operation, especially one that involves partners with different cultural backgrounds. As Ricky Chan, Deputy Chairman of the Hong Kong-based Logic International Holdings Ltd., (an office furniture manufacturing and distribution group) suggests:

> We have to remember that joint ventures have more than one parent. Constant attention is needed, therefore, as unlike shareholders, the joint venture partners are visible, powerful and capable of disagreeing about anything and everything. At the Board level, for example, there may be differences in priorities, direction and perhaps even in basic business values and ethics. At the functional management level, divided loyalty can be a problem, as staff assigned by the various partners look for signals from their parent company, rather than from the venture's general manager.

Despite all the disadvantages, the risk reduction, economies of scale, and the ability to meet or even block larger competition has lead to the formation of joint ventures by the tens of thousands. Some operate relatively smoothly, others obviously fail, but ignoring these cultural aspects of the business can lead to failure.[17] The likelihood of success for a joint venture seems to be directly proportional to the willingness of the major partners to assume active managerial responsibility, to share in key decisions, and to pay constant attention to maintaining a workable culture.[18]

THE PARTICIPATIVE CULTURE

Many organizations still have a highly structured approach to management. Consequently, most attempts to alter organizational culture have been directed toward increasing participation in both planning and decision making.

Values of Participation

The value of involving more people in the decision-making process relates primarily to productivity and morale. Increased productivity can result from the generation of ideas that encourage a more cooperative work effort. Employees who are involved in areas that matter to them will often respond to shared problems with innovative suggestions and unusually productive effort. Thus a participative work culture can lead to

- increased acceptance of management's ideas;
- increased cooperation between management and staff;
- reduced turnover;
- reduced absenteeism;
- reduced complaints and grievances;
- greater acceptance of changes; and
- improved attitudes toward the job and the organization.

Greater employee participation seems to have a direct and immediate effect on employee morale. Employees take more interest in the job and in the organization. They tend to accept—and sometimes initiate—change, not only because they understand why change must occur, but also because they are more secure as a result of knowing more about organizational plans and requirements. But while most experience and research suggests there is a positive relationship between employee participation and measures of morale, turnover, and absenteeism, there appears to be little correlation between job satisfaction levels and productivity.

Limitations of Participation

Despite its benefits, therefore, the participative approach to decision making has certain prerequisites:

1. Sufficient time must be allowed for employees to become accustomed to participating, as in the past, silence was rewarded, not speaking out.
2. Potential participants must have both the ability and a reason to participate; and
3. The present structure and work organization must be adapted to reward those who participate.

Group participation is not feasible when immediate decisions are required; the manager may be forced to make a decision and issue directives. Thus, in some environments it must be understood that the usual participative structures will have to be set aside from time to time.

Participation calls for some measure of self-discipline instead of relying on others. Subordinates must learn to handle freedom; supervisors must learn to trust subordinates. Thus, whether greater involvement in decision making can be developed depends largely on the abilities and the interests of both subordinates and managers. There is little point in consulting someone who knows or cares nothing about the subject of consultations. As organizations and technology become increasingly complex and as management becomes more professional, employee participation will involve more cooperation-seeking and information sharing. Not all employees, however, *want* to participate in decisions about their work; some people resent added job responsibility and will resist increased involvement.

CHANGING THE CORPORATE CULTURE

Environmental factors such as governmental action, work force diversity, and global competition often necessitate a change in culture. In extreme cases, management may be required to make a complete break with the past. This process, called re-engineering, is an attempt to build the business, or parts of the business, as if nothing had existed before. In other words, management starts from the beginning to create entire new structures, work organizations, systems, and sometimes even a new work force. This drastic action can destroy the existing organization, but often attempts are made to salvage the best parts of what existed before.[19]

To take advantage of the diversity of the Canadian work force, many managers are attempting to create cultures in which all employees can contribute and advance in the organization on the basis of ability. HR professionals know that critical factors such as retention, motivation, and advancement are highly dependent upon how employees react to their work culture.

A recent American survey of a group of managers with high representations of women and minority groups, for example, identified several problem areas inherent in counterproductive cultures:[20]

- *Fighting stereotypes*: The most serious problem faced by women and minority managers related to frustrations in coping with gender and race stereotypes;
- *Discrimination and harassment*: Whether experiencing discrimination personally or witnessing it, managers reported that such incidents made them question whether or not they fit in with the firm;
- *Exclusion and isolation*: Women and minority managers indicate they are often excluded from social activities and left out of informal communication networks;
- *Work-family balance*: Women managers expressed the view that *playing the game* often requires compromising personal values and conforming to the expectations of others;
- *Career development*: In some organizations, opportunities for career progression still seem to be limited for women and minority managers.

These problem areas illustrate legitimate concerns that managers must consider in revamping their corporate cultures. Taken together, women and minorities represent a significant percentage of employees entering the work force. If their talents are to be used to the fullest, corporate cultures of the future must reflect their needs.

Management in many firms has also felt a need to change the corporate culture to improve quality, service, and cost effectiveness in order to survive in the face of global competition.

In changing a firm's culture, as much of the organization should be involved as possible, from the chief executive officer to the operative employees. The need to change, along with the outcomes being sought, should be communicated clearly to all members of the organization.

Change of this magnitude often is called organization development. As Philip Hughes, manager of HR systems at Union Gas in Chatham, Ontario has indicated: "The reality is as soon as you do something to change your business, there are human resources repercussions."[21] While the heading of the following section, Organization Development, suggests that it is the organization that will be changed, in reality we are interested in people and how people can work together more effectively.

ORGANIZATION DEVELOPMENT

To survive and prosper in the highly competitive global environment of the next decade, organizations must be transformed into market-driven, innovative, and adaptive systems. In many firms, this urgent need is met through organization development, an HRD approach that involves everyone and everything in the organization. **Organization development (OD)** is an organization-wide application of behavioural science knowledge to the planned development and reinforcement of a firm's strategies, structures, and processes in order to improve effectiveness.[22]

While early OD applications focused on employee satisfaction, employee and organizational performance are now being emphasized as well. Although OD interventions don't produce a detailed plan, they do provide an adaptive strategy for planning and implementing change. In addition, OD ensures the long-term reinforcement of change.

Organization development may involve changes in the firm's strategy, structure, and processes. In dealing with structure, the focus is on how people are grouped within the organization. The firm's processes include methods of communication and problem solving.[23] "Organizations must develop the capacity to learn effectively from past successes and failures and to apply the lessons to renewal."[24] As one Canadian author has suggested, businesses need to move toward "system learning," which "takes place when the organization develops the systematic processes to acquire, use and communicate organizational knowledge."[25]

We will first discuss traditional OD approaches, including survey feedback, quality circles, management by objectives, job enrichment, transactional analysis, quality of work life, and sensitivity training. These techniques may be combined to provide a strategic approach to changing an organization. We will then look at two more recent methods: total quality management and team building.

Survey Feedback

Survey feedback is a process of collecting data from an organizational unit through the use of a questionnaire or survey. A developing trend has been to combine survey feedback with other OD interventions, although it is a powerful intervention in its own right.[26] Survey feedback involves a number of steps:

- Members of the organization, including top management, are involved in planning the survey.
- The survey instrument is administered to all members of the organizational unit.
- An OD consultant analyzes the data, tabulates results, suggests approaches to diagnosis, and trains participants in the feedback process.
- Data feedback begins at the top level of the organization and flows downward to groups reporting at successively lower levels.
- Feedback meetings provide an opportunity to discuss and to interpret data, to diagnose problem areas, and to develop action plans.[27]

An example of a management survey feedback instrument is provided in Figure 8-2. This instrument is used to analyze management performance in leadership, motivation, communication, decision making, goals, control, and other critical areas. Using a continuum, employees are asked to check the point that best describes their organization currently and the point that represents the most desirable state. Averaging the responses and charting them creates an organizational profile. Figure 8-2 represents a company with dissatisfied employees. On average, these employees perceive their company's leadership as *condescending*, for example, but believe leaders *should* show *substantial* confidence in subordinates.

Quality Circles

Quality circles are volunteer employee groups that meet regularly with their supervisors to identify production problems and to recommend solutions. These recommendations are then presented to higher-level management for review. Approved solutions are implemented with employee participation.

In Japan, millions of workers participate in quality circles, resulting in billion-dollar savings annually. Even though the corporate culture in Canada is different, an increasing number of firms are adapting the quality circle concept to their operations. In fact, some larger firms may have several hundred quality circles. In a survey of 585 industrial companies in Vancouver, Edmonton, and Toronto, 90 percent of the respondents claimed to encouraged ongoing skill development, and slightly over half (52 percent) had installed quality circles.[28]

In spite of numerous successful applications, however, the quality circle concept does not work well in many North American organizations. To implement a successful quality circle program, the firm must set clear goals and communicate both goals and results widely. Top management must support the program and create a climate conducive to participative management. A

FIGURE 8-2

An Example of a Survey Feedback Questionnaire

		Present State		Desired State	
LEADERSHIP	How much confidence is shown in subordinates?	None	Condescending	Substantial	Complete
	How free do they feel to talk to superiors about job?	Not at All	Not Very	Rather	Fully
	Are subordinates' ideas sought and used, if worthy?	Seldom	Sometimes	Usually	Always
MOTIVATION	Is predominant use made of (1) fear, (2) threats, (3) punishment, (4) rewards, (5) involvement?	1, 2, 3 Occasionally 4	4, Some 3	4, Some 3 and 5	5, 4, based on group-set goals
	Where is responsibility felt for achieving organization's goals?	Mostly at Top	Top and Middle	Fairly General	All Levels
COMMUNICATION	How much communication is aimed at achieving organization's objectives?	Very Little	Little	Quite a Bit	A Great Deal
	What is the direction of information flow?	Downward	Mostly Downward	Down and Up	Down, Up, and Sideways
	How is downward communication accepted?	With Suspicion	Possibly with Suspicion	With Caution	With an Open Mind
	How accurate is upward communication?	Often Wrong	Censored for the Boss	Limited Accuracy	Accurate
	How well do superiors know problems faced by subordinates?	Know Little	Some Knowledge	Quite Well	Very Well
DECISIONS	At what level are decisions formally made?	Mostly at Top	Policy at Top, Some Delegation	Broad Policy at Top, More Delegation	Throughout but Well Integrated
	What is the origin of technical and professional knowledge used in decision making?	Top Management	Upper and Middle	To a Certain Extent Throughout	To a Great Extent Throughout
	Are subordinates involved in decisions related to their work?	Not at all	Occasionally Consulted	Generally Consulted	Fully Involved
	What does the decision making process contribute to motivation?	Nothing, Often Weakens It	Relatively Little	Some Contribution	Substantial Contribution
GOALS	How are organizational goals established?	Orders Issued	Orders, Some Comment Invited	After Discussion, by Orders	By Group Action (Except in Crisis)
	How much covert resistance to goals is present?	Strong Resistance	Moderate Resistance	Some Resistance at Times	Little or None
CONTROL	How concentrated are review and control reactions?	Highly at Top	Relatively Highly at Top	Moderate Delegation to Lower Levels	Quite Widely Shared
	Is there an informal organization resisting the formal one?	Yes	Usually	Sometimes	No—Same Goals as Formal
	What are cost, productivity, and other control data used for?	Policing, Punishment	Reward and Punishment	Reward, Some Self-Guidance	Self-Guidance Problem Solving

Source: Adapted by permission of the publisher, from Michael E. McGill, *Organizational Development for Operating Managers*, p. 232. Copyright 1977, by AMACOM, a division of American Management Association, New York. All rights reserved.

qualified manager must be selected to administer the program, and individual participants must receive quality circle training.

Management by Objectives

Management by objectives (MBO) is a management philosophy that emphasizes the setting of objectives by agreement of superior and subordinate.

These objectives are then used as the primary basis for motivation, evaluation, and self-management. Objectives may be very specific operational targets, such as "a 30 percent increase in sales" or "production of 800 units per month," or may relate to personal growth or career development. As a management approach that encourages employers to anticipate and to plan, MBO directs efforts toward attainable goals, and discourages guessing, or making decisions based on hunches.

MBO can be used at all organizational levels. Investors' Group Inc. of Winnipeg attributes its success partly to an insistence that sales representatives set income goals using a management by objectives technique.[29]

Since MBO emphasizes participative management, the approach becomes an important method of organization development that focuses on the achievement of individual and organizational goals. Individual participation in goal setting and the emphasis on self-control promote not only personal growth but also organizational success.

Management by objectives is a dynamic process that must be continually reviewed, modified, and updated. Senior management must initiate the MBO process by establishing long-range goals (see Figure 8-3) and must support the process. The president and vice-president of human resources (superior and subordinate), for example, might jointly establish the firm's long-range goals in the HR area, along with intermediate- and short-term objectives. At this point, president and vice-president agree on the subordinate's performance objectives and action plans, which outline how the objectives will be achieved. The subordinate proceeds to work toward his or her goals. At the end of the appraisal period, both parties review the subordinate's performance and determine what can be done to overcome any problems or to enhance the employee's strengths. Goals then are established for the next period and the process is repeated. During this process, too, the Vice-President would be setting goals with the HR professionals and even support staff, so that MBO reaches throughout the organization.

From an organization development standpoint, MBO

- provides an opportunity for development of managers and employees;
- increases the firm's ability to change;
- provides a more objective and tangible basis for performance appraisal and salary decisions;
- results in better overall management and higher performance levels;
- provides an effective overall planning system;
- forces managers to establish priorities and measurable targets or standards of performance;
- clarifies specific roles, responsibilities, and authority;
- encourages joint participation in establishing objectives;
- promotes accountability;
- lets individuals know clearly what is expected of them,
- improves internal communication;
- helps identify promotable managers and employees; and

FIGURE 8-3
The MBO Process

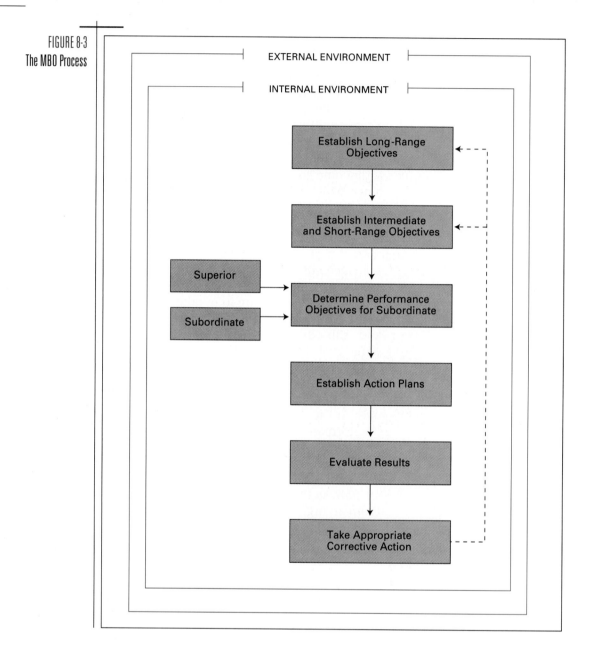

■ increases employee motivation and commitment.

There are, however, potential problems in implementing MBO. Without the full support of senior management, the process is likely to fail. This commitment may be difficult to obtain, because implementing an MBO system often takes from three to five years. The long-term objectives on which MBO is based may be difficult to establish, as in many businesses there is a tendency to concentrate on short-term plans. The MBO system can create a seemingly insurmountable amount of paperwork if it isn't closely monitored. Finally, some managers believe that MBO is excessively time consuming. The process forces them to think ahead and to determine how their goals and actions fit into the corporate strategy, not an easy task for many managers.

Job Enrichment

As defined in Chapter 3, job enrichment is the deliberate restructuring of a job to make it more challenging, meaningful, and interesting. This process emphasizes the accomplishment of significant tasks, so the employee gains a sense of achievement. Job enrichment takes an optimistic view of employee capabilities, presuming that individuals have the ability to perform more difficult and responsible tasks than they are currently performing. Furthermore, there is an assumption that most employees will respond favourably if challenged and that as a result, motivation and productivity will improve.

Job enrichment applied on a broad scale, therefore, becomes an important OD method, as the increased responsibility and challenge promotes continuous employee development. Thus, the nature of enriched jobs requires that employees keep their skills up to date.

Transactional Analysis[30]

Although not currently a popular OD intervention, transactional analysis was used for a number of years as a technique for teaching behavioural principles. **Transactional analysis (TA)** is a method that considers each individual's three ego states—the Parent, the Adult, and the Child—in helping people understand interpersonal relations. TA provides a system for forming a mental image of the emotions and the thought processes used during interactions, either in a social or in a business setting. Thus, employees begin to understand the emotions and needs of customers or fellow employees, while learning to respond appropriately to a wide variety of work-related situations.[31]

Quality of Work Life

Quality of work life (QWL) is the degree to which members of a work organization are able to satisfy their most important personal needs through organizational experiences. QWL programs include job redesign, the creation of autonomous work groups, and employee participation in decision making. A fundamental assumption is that QWL programs will increase job satisfaction and motivation, which in turn will lead to increased productivity.[32]

QWL programs are not short-term, quick-fix solutions. A successful program requires careful planning, The goals of a QWL program should be the joint responsibility of management and workers. Certain guidelines, however, may be helpful:

- Managers need to redefine *how we work in this organization*.
- The willing participation of people at all levels of the organization must be solicited.
- A commitment from formal and informal leaders that goes beyond the rhetoric of endorsement and support must be demonstrated daily.

- Management must communicate and integrate strategic goals into the day-to-day business operations.
- New approaches and processes must be developed in most work situations, as business processes are never static, requiring constant adjustment or reengineering in response to changing internal and external environments.[33]

Research conducted on QWL programs has found mixed results. Although many successes have been reported, it is often difficult to determine the variable responsible for production increases. HR managers need to recognize that a QWL program is an experiment and that there is no conclusive formula to ensure success.[34]

Sensitivity Training

Sensitivity training is an OD technique designed to make individuals more aware of themselves and of their effect on others. Different from traditional forms of training (which tends to stress the learning of a predetermined set of concepts),[35] sensitivity training features a group—often called a training group or T-group—in which there is no preestablished agenda or focus. The trainer's role is to serve as a facilitator in an unstructured environment where participants are encouraged to learn about themselves and others in the group. The objectives of sensitivity training are to enhance self-awareness, gain insight into one's own and others' behaviour, acquire the ability to analyze interpersonal behaviour, and improve group functioning.[36]

Ideally, when sensitivity training begins there is no agenda and no leader. Through dialogue people begin to learn about themselves and others. Participants are encouraged to look at themselves as others see them. Then, if they want to change, they can attempt to do so. Although the purpose of sensitivity training (to assist individuals to learn more about how they relate to other people) cannot be questioned, the technique has been criticized. It is clear that sensitivity training often involves anxiety-provoking situations as stimulants for learning, and participants often undergo severe emotional stress during training. In addition, some critics believe that it is one matter for participants to express true feelings in the psychological safety of the laboratory, but quite another to face their co-workers.[37] Information learned in a sensitivity group may prove to be irrelevant or even damaging, unless the participant returns to an organizational environment that supports the use of that knowledge. Individuals may be encouraged to be open and supportive in the T-group, but when they return to their jobs, they often revert to past behaviour patterns. Sensitivity training flourished in the 1970s, but is rarely used now.

Total Quality Management

Total quality management (TQM) is defined as a commitment on the part of everyone in an organization to excellence, with an emphasis on constant improvement achieved through teamwork and continuous upgrading. Many companies have 'total quality' programs that integrate all departments. Implied in the concept is a commitment to be the best and to provide the highest quality products and services, meeting or exceeding customer expectations. Managers make massive changes to stay competitive, constantly seeking ways to improve quality and to increase speed of operations, while adopting a customer orientation. These changes are so fundamental they must take root in a company's very essence, which means in its *culture*.

Thus, TQM often involves major cultural changes that require new ways of thinking and strong leadership at all levels. Individuals throughout the organization must be inspired to do their jobs differently. They must understand what needs to be done and why. Typically employees are made responsible for their own quality. This added responsibility requires reorganizing their jobs to give employees the authority to reject or rework products as they see fit.

Unfortunately, most TQM programs fail, despite the considerable amount of money spent, because the changes do not go deep enough. In such incomplete programs the principles of TQM may be used in peripheral departments rather than integrated into the core business. Senior executives do not get involved and there is no commitment to continued training. Old management structures are retained and the focus is on operations rather than thinking. This failure of imagination is easy to understand, since most managers are trained to look for simple solutions to immediate problems rather than dealing with complex, system-oriented concerns that take a major effort over time to produce results. TQM theory is often difficult to insert into long-standing corporate cultures, partly because it does not take into consideration managers' needs for high security and belonging. As well, in many companies, TQM results are not measured, and reward structures and not rearranged to encourage and to promote new behaviour, as employees often are excluded from the decision and power structures.[38]

Despite such difficulties in implementation, TQM remains a valid technique to keep and to improve market share by improving customer satisfaction. Instead of accepting the status quo, employees at all levels continually seek alternative methods or technologies that will improve existing processes. TQM provides a strategy for reducing the causes of poor quality, thereby increasing productivity.

TQM, then, is a process of continual quality improvement. In the short term, once every internal process is operating at or above a desired quality level, reliance on costly inspection practices can be reduced or eliminated. Attention can then be turned to monitoring the entire business to determine what sources of variation are still present. If variation can be eliminated, then production processes can be more precise, leading to fewer defects or errors, and quality will exceed customer expectations.

TQM increases employee participation, creating new roles for all organizational members. Senior management, middle managers, first-level supervisors, and all other employees must embrace the TQM philosophy and work to ensure its acceptance. For example, as all employees assist in determining and analyzing sources of process variation, they are expected to develop joint proposals for reducing or eliminating variance.

Thus, cultural change must precede or accompany the introduction of total quality management. TQM is not a body of regulations that can be forced upon employees. Unfortunately, the organizational culture required to support TQM concepts is not likely to be installed quickly. Five to ten years are generally needed for such massive changes to permeate the organization. Since a company's culture is largely a product of positively (or negatively) reinforced behaviour, the route to change is almost always through education and training.[39] In addition, employee selection practices will be a central component in implementing the TQM philosophy. "The ultimate goal is to so ingrain basic cultural change that the slogan TQM will fade, leaving the principles and practices of TQM as a permanent, normal way of conducting business."[40]

Team Building and Self-Directed Teams

The assembly lines at Volvo's two innovative factories look strange to anyone used to the American conveyor belt system. Here, "work teams build cars much like doctors operate on a patient. Each car frame sits on its individual rotating holder while the assembly crew attach the pieces. Instead of supervisors and engineers, workers manage the shop floor." This radical change was initiated because Sweden's highly educated and well-trained labour force does not like to work in conventional factories; close supervision and machine-paced assembly line work were major causes of employee dissatisfaction.

Thus, this factory environment is conducive to self-management. Work teams assemble entire cars and assist in certain management activities. To prepare new workers for such responsibility, Volvo gives them 16 weeks' training before they are allowed to assemble cars, and 16 months more of on-the-job orientation.

In Sweden, as in many other countries, the move toward *functional work teams i*s increasing, as traditional manufacturing methods have become outmoded. This approach to automobile manufacturing, is not, however, without disadvantages. Disagreements among team members lead to problems in some teams. Still, few employees wish to return to the old way where supervisors make all the decisions. Moreover, the teams are more productive than individuals working on traditional assembly lines.

Many work situations make it imperative to subordinate individual autonomy in favour of cooperation within a group. Building effective teams has, therefore, become a business necessity. At the Alberta-Pacific Forest Industries Inc. mill near Boyle, Alberta, for example, maintenance workers have been divided into self-directed work teams. Each team consists of a planner, an area maintenance engineer, a team leader, and the required tradespeople. A production team consists of a leader and a production specialist, plus appropriate trades. Together, the maintenance and the production teams form a core that runs the wood room as a business unit. Eventually, each core team will run its area as a profit centre, taking full responsibility for operations. A member of a core team is part of a shift team council that discusses strategy for the day. Then one or two council members meet with the management team to discuss long- or medium-term solutions to problems that have occurred over the past 24 hours.[41]

Team building is the conscious effort to develop effective self-directed teams, each composed of a small group of employees responsible for an entire work process or segment. Team members work together to improve their operation or product, plan and control their work, and handle day-to-day problems. They may even become involved in broader, company-wide issues, such as vendor quality, safety, and business planning.[42]

A recent survey conducted by a human resources consulting firm found that 27 percent of the respondents currently use self-directed teams. Half the respondents predicted that the majority of their work force will be organized in teams within the next five years.[43]

The reason? Teams are more productive, sometimes bringing gains of as much as 30 percent. Effective work teams focus on solving their own work problems. The team-building process begins when the team leader defines a problem that requires organizational change (see Figure 8-4). The team then diagnoses the problem to determine the underlying causes, usually related to breakdowns in communication, inappropriate leadership styles, or deficiencies in organizational structure. Next team members consider alternative solutions and select the most appropriate. From their discussions, a commitment to the proposed course of action is likely to emerge. The interpersonal relations developed by team members also improve chances for implementing change. Team building, therefore, is a process by which participants and facilitators experience increasing levels of trust, openness, and willingness to explore core issues that affect the ability to work productively.[44]

Self-directed work teams are difficult to build in a traditional factory work environment and there will always be resistance from those workers who are not able to adapt. Psychological barriers that keep workers and managers in separate roles must be broken down, a process that can lead to conflict and fear on both sides. Teams bypass the usual routes of command and communication by drawing members from various parts of the company. Supervisors become coaches or facilitators. Teams need their own structure and tend to work best within well-entrenched quality programs such as continuous improvement, under which members look for ways to cut costs, save time, or improve the product. The company organization is flattened by streamlining layers of management, placing supervisors and functional team leaders on a management steering committee, and allowing workers to assume day-to-day decision-making responsibility. When teams do not work, it is often because of lack of management support. Note too, that old hierarchies can return once initial enthusiasm for the new order wears away.[45]

An example of effective teamwork can be found at the Shell Canada lubricants factory in Brockville, Ontario. Employing approximately 75 workers, this facility has about the same output as the two factories it replaced. Five integrated computer systems are used to pull together operations along with three self-managed teams called job families. Each operator must know all the jobs within the team and at least one skill in each of the other two groups. Jobs are rotated about every 18 months. Each worker is expected to understand the entire business. As the hierarchical structures and the old command-and-control mentality have been discarded, staff absenteeism has fallen to about one-third the normal rate in manufacturing. While the Montreal and Toronto factories it replaced did almost no exporting, the Brockville plant is able to export to 44 countries.[46]

FIGURE 8-4
The Team-Building Process

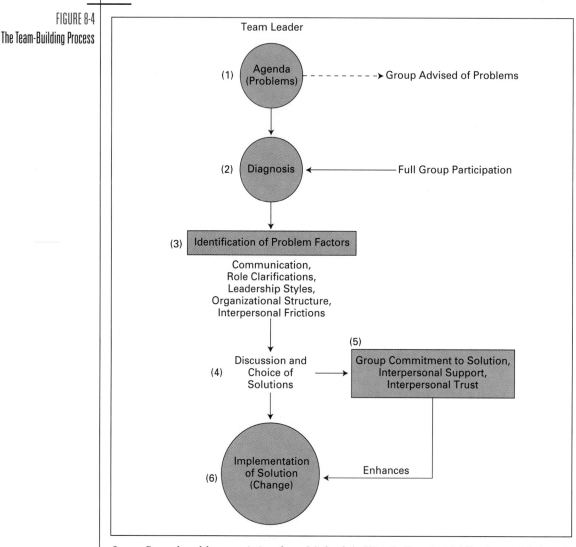

USE OF CONSULTANTS

Organization development efforts rely heavily on the use of qualified consultants who work with teams. The consultant, a facilitator, helps both management and work teams identify goals and overcome obstacles. The consultant also guides implementation of planned change.

Consultants use their specialized knowledge to propose interventions in the organization's activities and help managers bring about change in areas such as communication, leadership styles, and motivational techniques.

A consultant may come from within the organization, or from the outside. Management frequently believes that an outside expert brings objectivity to a situation and gains acceptance and trust from employees more easily. Conversely, many believe that an internal consultant, who knows both the formal and informal nature of the organization, often produces desired results at a lower cost.

EVALUATING ORGANIZATION DEVELOPMENT

When an OD intervention has been implemented, the question must be asked: "Did anything happen as a result of this experience?" All too often the answer is: "We don't know." Evaluating organizational development programs is more difficult than determining whether or not an employee has learned to operate a particular piece of equipment. Nevertheless, managers need to know whether tangible benefits have resulted from an OD program (which probably cost considerable time and money) in order to plan for future changes or interventions,

One means of measuring program effectiveness is to assess changes in meeting performance criteria. Some of the factors to be measured might include 1) productivity, 2) absenteeism, 3) turnover, 4) accident rate, 5) overtime costs, or 6) scrap levels. A lower turnover rate, for example, might mean that employees are more satisfied with their work and have chosen to remain with the firm. Lower production costs per unit suggests that workers may be paying more attention to their work. Although these data are useful, they probably will not provide the entire answer, as a variety of factors, both inside and outside the firm, can influence the work force.

Managers should not wait for the program's completion to begin measuring effectiveness. Rather, evaluation should be a continuous process using performance criteria to measure the effect of the change effort. Questionnaires should be administered periodically over an extended period of time.

SUMMARY

Corporate culture is the system of shared values, beliefs, and habits within an organization that interacts with the formal structure to produce behavioural norms. Thus, the organization's reward system identifies the types of behaviour and attitudes that are important for success.

Corporate culture develops from examples set by senior management, stemming largely from what they do, not what they say. Other factors also interact to shape the culture of a firm: organizational characteristics, administrative processes, organizational structure, and management style.

Most behaviouralists advocate an open and a participative culture, which some contend to be best for all situations. The opposite of the open and participative culture is a closed and autocratic one. This culture's greater rigidity results from strict adherence to a formal chain of command, a narrower span of control, and stricter individual accountability.

The prevailing managerial approach in many organizations is highly structured. Consequently, most attempts to alter organizational culture have been directed at creating a more open and participative culture, which often improves employee morale and satisfaction.

Greater employee participation in decision making involves certain prerequisites: 1) the will to expend sufficient time, 2) adequate ability and interest on the part of the participants, and 3) willingness to change structures and systems.

Organization development (OD) applies behavioural science knowledge to an organization-wide effort aimed at improving effectiveness. Some traditional OD techniques include survey feedback, quality circles, management by objectives, job enrichment, transactional analysis, quality of work life, and sensitivity training. Total quality management and team building are newer methods. Some of these techniques may be combined to provide a strategic approach to organization development.

Organization development efforts rely heavily on the use of qualified consultants who work with groups of managers and workers throughout the organization. The consultant is a facilitator who helps the groups to identify goals and to solve problems that interfere with goal achievement. The consultant also may be responsible for helping to guide implementation of planned change.

One method of measuring program effectiveness is to assess changes in meeting performance criteria such as: productivity, absenteeism rate, turnover accident rates, overtime costs, and scrap levels. However, other environmental factors may also influence these measures

TERMS FOR REVIEW

Corporate culture
Organization development (OD)
Survey feedback
Quality circles
Management by objectives (MBO)

Transactional analysis (TA)
Quality of work life (QWL)
Sensitivity training
Total quality management (TQM)
Team building

QUESTIONS FOR REVIEW

1. Define corporate culture. What factors determine corporate culture?
2. Does a participative culture improve productivity? Defend your answer.
3. What are the values of an open and a participative culture?
4. What are the limitations of participation?
5. Define each of the following terms:
    a. Organization development
    b. Survey feedback
    c. Quality circles

d. Job enrichment
e. Quality of work life
f. Transactional analysis
g. Sensitivity training
h. Total quality management
i. Team building
6. How can organization development programs be evaluated?
7. Explain how consultants are used in organization development initiatives.

HRM INCIDENT 1

• IMPLEMENTING TEAM BUILDING

When Bruce McDaniel retired because of ill health in 1991, he appointed his 26-year-old son, Jim, as president of the family firm. The company, McDaniel Corporation of Regina, Saskatchewan, markets a line of hospital beds. The company manufactures the metal frames for the beds and purchases hydraulic items, springs, and certain other parts. The company also sells hospital furniture items and maintains a crew to repair the McDaniel beds. Employment at the firm totals about 500.

Jim was eager to take over. With an MBA from the University of Saskatchewan and two years of experience with the company, he believed that he was well prepared. One of the first things Jim wanted to do was to give decision-making authority to the managers. He remarked, "I felt this would let me pay attention to the big picture while the day-to-day problems were solved lower in the organization." He felt that one effective tool for helping him shift more authority downward in the organization would be the use of work teams.Bruce McDaniel had been president and owner of McDaniel Corporation for 30 years. During that time the firm had grown from a small hospital supply company with three employees to its present size. Bruce had been a hard worker, often putting in 15 hours a day. Jim described his dad as a "pleasant autocrat" because he insisted on making every important decision, but Bruce had such an affable personality that no one objected.

For a while, Jim tried to behave pretty much as his father had, giving managers firm decisions on matters they brought to him. But about a month after his father's retirement, Jim called a meeting to tell the managers that the firm was going to implement work teams throughout the organization. He made a brief presentation to them about how the teams would be set up. He emphasized that they would have to give more responsibility to the work teams and that he expected all supervisors to assist in team building.

QUESTIONS

1. Did the proper environment exist for developing work teams? Explain.
2. Discuss any likely pitfalls to the development of work teams.

HRM INCIDENT 2

• CLOSE TO THE VEST

Over the past few years, sales at Glenco Manufacturing had fallen, reflecting an industry-wide decline. During this time, Glenco had even been able to increase its share of the market slightly. Although forecasts indicated that demand for its products would improve in the future, Cecil Leung, the company president, believed that something needed to be done immediately to help the firm survive this temporary slump. As a first step, he employed a consulting firm to determine whether or not reorganization might be helpful.

A team of five consultants arrived at the firm. They told Mr. Leung that they first had to gain a thorough understanding of the current situation before they could make any recommendations. Mr. Leung assured them that the company was open to them. They could ask any questions that they thought were necessary.

The grapevine was full of rumours virtually from the day the consulting group arrived. One employee was heard to say, "If they shut down the company, I don't know if I could take care of my family." Another worker said, "If they move me away from my friends, I'm going to quit."

When workers questioned their supervisors, they received no explanations. No one had told the supervisors what was going on, either. The climate began to change to one of fear. Rather than being concerned about their daily work, employees worried about what was going to happen to the company and their jobs. As a result, productivity dropped drastically.

A month after the consultants departed, an informational memorandum was circulated throughout the company. It stated that the consultants had recommended a slight modification in the top levels of the organization to achieve greater efficiency. No one would be terminated. Any reductions would be the result of normal attrition. By this time, however, some of the most productive had already found other jobs and company operations were severely disrupted for several months.

QUESTIONS

1. Why did the employees assume the worst?
2. How could this difficulty have been avoided?

DEVELOPING HRM SKILLS: AN EXPERIENTIAL EXERCISE

In every organization, human resource professionals work with many individuals and groups. Cooperation is necessary if the tasks involved in human resource management are to be accomplished effectively. The Blue-Green exercise provides the opportunity to experience some of the interrelationships that occur in a structured setting, such as an organization or work group, and to examine the effect of teams on the work culture.

The Blue-Green exercise works best with groups of 12 to 40, and works equally well with people who have been working together for some time and with heterogeneous groups whose members barely know one another. Its impact, however, is probably greater for people required to work together.

The language used by the person conducting the exercise is extremely important, so participants should listen carefully to the rules. Participants usually find the experience enlightening.

The group will be divided into four subgroups of as nearly equal size as possible. These subgroups will be designated as Teams A-1, A-2, B-1, and B-2. Instructors will provide participants with the additional necessary information.

9

Career Planning and Development

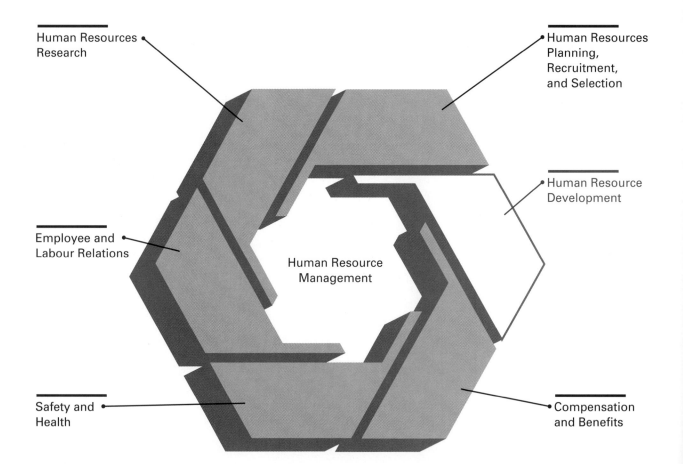

Human Resources
Research

Human Resources
Planning,
Recruitment,
and Selection

Human Resource
Development

Employee and
Labour Relations

Human Resource
Management

Safety and
Health

Compensation
and Benefits

1. Define career planning and career development and describe factors affecting career planning.

2. Explain the importance of individual career planning and how a thorough self-assessment is crucial to career planning.

3. Explain the nature of career planning, discuss career paths, and describe plateauing.

4. Describe career development and the avenues available for beginning a career in human resources management.

B ob Allen and Thelma Gowen, both supervisors at Canadian Electronics of Hamilton, were in the employee lounge having a cup of coffee and discussing a point of mutual concern. Bob said, "I'm beginning to get frustrated. When I joined Canadian four years ago, I really felt that I could make a career here. Now I'm not so sure. I spoke with the boss last week about where I might be in the next few years and all she kept saying was, 'There are all kinds of possibilities.' I need more than that. I'd like to know what specific opportunities might be available if I continue to do a good job. I'm not sure if I want to spend my whole career here. I know we have cut out several management levels in the last couple of years. But there may be better chances for advancing my knowledge in other areas. This is a big company."

Thelma replied, "I'm having the same trouble. She told me, 'You are doing a great job and we want you to stay at Canadian.' I'd also like to know what other jobs are available if I get the proper training."

Obviously, Canadian Electronics has no career planning and development program. Bob is frustrated, and Thelma wants to know what career avenues are available to her. Lacking this knowledge, they may decide not to remain with the company. Career planning and development are also important to the employer, because management must ensure that people with the necessary skills and experience will be available when needed.

In this chapter, we discuss the concept of career planning and development and identify several factors that affect the planning process. Then we discuss the nature of career planning in terms of individual career planning, career paths, and plateauing. An employer's perspective on career development is then described. We follow that with a section on methods used in career planning and development. We devote the last part of the chapter to the process of beginning a career in human resources management.

CAREER PLANNING AND DEVELOPMENT DEFINED

A **career** comprises the general types of jobs one chooses to pursue throughout one's working life; one may, for example, seek a career in broadcasting, or a career in the military. **Career planning** is an ongoing process whereby an individual sets career goals and identifies the means to achieve them. The major focus of career planning should be the matching of personal goals with realistic work opportunities.

Career planning should not concentrate only on advancement opportunities. Many traditional middle management positions have disappeared. Indeed, from a practical standpoint, there never were enough high-level positions to make upward mobility a reality for everyone. At some point, therefore, career planning needs to focus on achieving personal successes that do not necessarily involve promotion.

Individual career plans and organizational human resource requirements cannot be considered in isolation from each other. A person whose individual career plan cannot be followed within an organization will probably leave the firm sooner or later—or, if forced to stay by lack of opportunities elsewhere, may become demoralized and less productive. Helping employees with career planning, therefore, meets the organization's needs as well as the individual's.

A **career path** is the job sequence one is likely to follow: for example, copy editor, production editor, managing editor or vice-president. **Career development** is a formal human resource planning program designed to ensure that people with the proper qualifications and experience are available when needed. Career planning and development benefit both the individual and the organization.

Rather than paying close attention to this important HRM function, however, Dr. Gordon Cassidy, Director of the Queen's University National Executive MBA program, has found that, "too often, organizations respond to human resource issues, particularly succession, in a crisis management mode. Career development is a critical element in ensuring the organization is mentoring and preparing people for more senior positions when they become vacant in the organization. Care and attention must be given not only to satisfying the current human resource requirements, but those that are likely to occur in the future. Only in so doing can the organization remain competitive and successful."[1]

FACTORS AFFECTING CAREER PLANNING

Life Stages

As people change constantly, they view their careers differently at various stages of their lives. Some of these changes result from the aging process, while others stem from opportunities for personal growth and increased status (see Figure 9-1).

The first stage, establishing identity, is typically reached between the ages of 10 and 20, when the individual explores career alternatives and begins to move into the adult world. Stage two (somewhere between the ages of 20 to 40) involves professional growth and becoming established in a career, including choosing an occupation and defining a career path. Self-maintenance and self-adjustment, characteristics of the third stage, generally last to age 50 and beyond. At this point, a person either accepts life as it is or attempts to make adjustments. Often career change and even divorce occur during this phase, because individuals seriously question the quality of their lives. The final stage (decline) is sometimes seen as a time of diminishing physical and mental capabilities, during which a person may have lower aspirations and less motivation.

In reality, although the older worker may be less able to perform intense physical work, most of the perceived problems associated with this

FIGURE 9-1
Life Stages

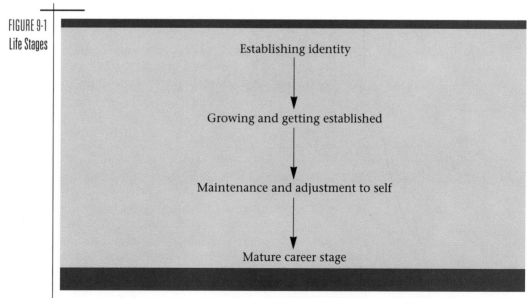

Source: Adapted from James W. Walker, *Human Resource Planning*. (New York: McGraw-Hill Book Company, 1980). Used with permission of the McGraw-Hill Book Company.

final career stage are erroneous.[2] This is a fortunate discovery, as it is likely that in the future, many Canadians will be required to work into their 70s.[3] HR managers, then, will need to change entrenched attitudes that discriminate against older workers.

Even though most individuals develop skills and gain experience throughout their working lives, the majority of developmental activities are directed at new or younger workers. Yet employees need career development as much in the later years as they do in the early career stages, especially since downsizing and the elimination of layers of management requires all employees to accomplish a wider variety of tasks.

Career Anchors

All of us have different aspirations, backgrounds, and experiences. Our personalities are moulded, to a certain extent, by the results of our interactions with our environments. Edgar Schein's research identified five different motives that account for the way people select and prepare for a career. He called them **career anchors**.[4]

1. *Managerial Competence*. The career goal of managers is to develop qualities of interpersonal, analytical, and emotional competence. People using this anchor want to manage people.
2. *Technical/Functional Competence*. The anchor for technicians is the continuous development of technical talent. Many of these individuals do not seek managerial positions.
3. *Security*. The anchor for security-conscious individuals is to stabilize their career situations, often by tying themselves to a particular organization or geographical location.
4. *Creativity*. Creative individuals tend to be entrepreneurial. They want to create or build something that is entirely their own.
5. *Autonomy and Independence*. The career anchor for independent people is a desire to be free from organizational constraints. They value autonomy. They want to be their own boss and work at their own pace.

One of the implications of the career anchor concept is that managers need to be flexible enough to provide their employees with alternative paths to satisfy varying needs.

The Environment

The work environment in which career planning takes place has changed rapidly in recent years. For example, across the country and around the world, downsizing has displaced workers and managers alike in massive numbers. As Charles W. Sweet, president of A. T. Kearney, an executive recruiting firm, has suggested, "The way people approached their careers in the past is history. It will never, never, never return."[5]

For many workers, in this drastically changing work environment, career planning involves finding ways to retain their present jobs. (Career-minded individuals must heed the Red Queen's admonition to Alice: "It takes all the running you can do, to keep in the same place.")[6] This environmental change was dramatically emphasized by William Bridges, author of *JobShift*, "We used to read predictions that by 2000 everyone would work 30-hour weeks, and the rest would be leisure. But as we approach 2000 it seems more likely that half of us will be working 60-hour weeks and the rest of us will be unemployed."[7]

Similarly, many formally promotable professionals are frustrated because their careers are stalled, in a phenomenon Cec Brown of the firm Brown Wallace Bond calls underpromotion. In these circumstances, Dugald Smith of Price Waterhouse suggests there are three choices: "stick it out where you are [and] try to rise above the blockage; pull out and find another job; or turn inward for self-fulfillment from non-work activities".[8] Any course of action, however, should be planned carefully; otherwise, potential opportunities are likely to be missed.

CAREER PLANNING

Everyone who wishes to be among the employed half of the work force (including HRM professionals) needs to engage in career planning. Through career planning, a person evaluates his or her own abilities and interests, considers alternative career opportunities, establishes career goals, and plans practical development activities.

According to one Canadian study, four characteristics help professionals survive in a competitive work world. They know what they do well and stick to it; they work fast; they improve constantly; and they collaborate with others to get a job done. A fifth characteristic might be added: an egalitarian outlook that sees every person as important. The story is told of five managers all trying to compete for a promotion that required extensive use of computers. The three who did not succeed were reluctant to take instruction from their secretaries, who turned out to be the best computer teachers in the company.[9]

The following guidelines are useful throughout a career, but especially when preparing to embark upon a new career path.

FOURTEEN STEPS ON A NEW CAREER PATH

1. *Accept the new values of the workplace by showing how you can help the company meet profitability objectives* through increasing profits, cutting costs, increasing productivity and efficiency, improving public relations, even getting new clients.

2. *Continually look for newer and better ways to be of more value* to your employer. Too many who did a good job 15 or 20 years ago are today doing the same thing and thinking that they are still doing a good job. Your company has changed; you need to change with it.

3. *Don't keep yourself stuck in an 'information vacuum.'* Today you can no longer afford to be unaware of what is happening to your company, industry, community, country, or for that matter, the world.

4. *Don't be reactive.* Those who are successful today are those who prepare ahead of time, anticipate problems and opportunities, and get ready.

5. *Continually seek out a new education.* Expanded knowledge, increased information, and new skills are appearing at record pace. Those who are successful are those who find out what new skills and knowledge they need and take the extra time and trouble to learn them. The others will not be competitive.

6. *Develop significant career and financial goals and detailed plans* to reach them. Otherwise, you are vulnerable.

7. *Avoid a state of denial.* When a person is in denial, he or she will ignore signs that something is wrong. Denial is one of the major reasons why people become immobilized, unable to deal with problems or change.

8. *Prepare for survival in your present career and for taking the next job or career step.* Have you explored alternatives? Are your job search skills those of today, or are you using antiquated job search methods?

9. *Become motivated by your goals, not by anger, fear, or hopelessness.* In difficult and uncertain career situations, it is human nature to have strong feelings. The problem is that too many of us let those feelings guide our actions and our words.

10. *Market yourself aggressively.* Whether or not you have a job, in order to survive and be successful, you must learn to market yourself: network with others, let others know about the good work you do, and don't make unnecessary enemies. In particular, learn to market yourself within your present organization.

11. *Improve your motivation and commitment.* Employers are no longer looking for those who are good enough, they are looking for those who are the most highly motivated. Demand and get the best out of yourself. Go to seminars. Get counselling if there is a motivational block. Rejuvenate your enthusiasm and demonstrate it at work.

12. *Place your weaknesses and inadequacies in perspective;* do not allow them to loom so large in your mind that all you can think about is failure. Remember that no one is without weaknesses and inadequacies.

13. *Realize that to survive and prosper in today's world, your primary job is to change yourself.* You are the one who has to keep up with your training and education. You are the one who has to learn new skills in networking. You are the one who has to develop a different perspective on your career.

14. *There's no reason HR professionals can't take advantage of the same professional counselling and guidance available to others.* Give yourself this advantage and you can move forward confidently to define the career path you want.[10]

Career planning often begins with an entry level job and initial orientation. Management then starts to compare the employee's performance with job standards, noting strengths and weaknesses. This assessment assists the employee in making a tentative career decision, usually one that can be altered later as the process continues. This initial career decision is based on a number of factors, as personal needs, abilities, and aspirations are matched with organizational needs. Management can then schedule human resource development programs that relate to the employee's specific needs. A person who wants a career in human resources management, for example, may require some training in benefits and compensation.

Career planning, however, is an ongoing process that takes into consideration the changes that occur in people, in organizations and in the environment. Maintaining flexibility is necessary in today's dynamic organizational environment, as the firm's requirements change, and people revise their career expectations. Some employees still might prefer a career path characterized by promotion—climbing the corporate ladder. But in today's less vertical corporate world, workers may have to consider other options that may or may not lead to higher salaries and/or status. For example, they might move sideways to a more dynamic department; with no change in salary or title; leave the organization for a more rewarding career elsewhere; remain in the same position and try to enhance their skills and explore new horizons; or move down to a less prestigious job that promises more growth.[11]

Promotions, then, are not always the most desirable career alternative; especially if a firm is inflexible, a promotion may sometimes lead to a dead-end position. To refuse a new job, however, takes careful planning. One's immediate supervisor should be contacted and an alternate career direction discussed. For example, suppose that Carol performs so well as a technician that her manager wants to "promote" her to a management position, but Carol feels her talents and interests are technical, not managerial. She might propose becoming a master technician instead. To make this suggestion acceptable, she must be convince management that she is more valuable where she is.

One should be wary of suggestions that one will "grow into the job," especially if the proposed work does not seem to fit either interests or talents. The new job must challenge existing skills and build new ones. Accepting a promotion for the sake of change can be a mistake.[12]

Individual Career Planning

Career planning begins with understanding oneself. One is then in a position to establish realistic career goals and to determine how to achieve these goals. Learning about oneself is referred to as **self-assessment**. Any characteristic that could affect one's future job performance should be considered. Realistic self-assessment may help a person avoid mistakes that could affect his or her entire career progression. Often (especially in this era of high unemployment) an individual accepts a job without considering whether or not it matches his or her interests and abilities, an approach that can result in failure. (Ideally, one should wait for a more suitable job, even if it carries a lower salary. If there is no choice but to accept a really unsuitable job, one should continue to look about for other options.) A thorough self-assessment helps to match an individual's specific qualities and goals with the right job or profession. Some useful tools include the strength/weakness balance sheet and the likes and dislikes survey.

STRENGTH/WEAKNESS BALANCE SHEET

A self-evaluation procedure that assists individuals in becoming aware of their strengths and weaknesses is called a strength/weakness balance sheet. Employees who understand their strengths can use them to maximum advantage, while avoiding work situations emphasizing areas of weakness. Furthermore, by recognizing weaknesses, they are in a better position to overcome them.

To use a strength/weakness balance sheet, the individual lists strengths and weaknesses *as he or she perceives them*. This last phrase is important because of the importance of self-image to behaviour. Thus, a person who believes that he or she will make a poor first impression when meeting someone probably will make a poor impression. The perception of a weakness (or strength) often becomes a self-fulfilling prophecy.

The balance sheet is prepared by drawing a line down the middle of a sheet of paper and labelling the left side *strengths* and the right side *weaknesses*. Then, all perceived strengths and weaknesses are recorded. No one else need see the results. The primary consideration is complete honesty.

Figure 9-2 shows an example of a strength/weakness balance sheet. Obviously Wayne (the person who wrote the sheet) did a lot of soul-searching in making these evaluations. Typically, a person's weaknesses will outnumber strengths in the first few drafts. As the person repeats the process, however, some apparent weaknesses may eventually be recognized as strengths. Obtaining a clear understanding of one's strengths and weaknesses takes time; typically, the process should take a minimum of one week. The balance sheet will not provide all the answers, but many people have gained a better understanding of themselves by completing one.

Other self-assessment methods are also available. One author has devised a personal analysis called DATA (for *desires, abilities, temperament,* and *assets*) which he suggests can be used to make realistic career choices. In his review of four books about career management, Ray Brillinger found that the writers agree on six essential points:

1. The era of the single-employer (life long) career is past for almost everyone.
2. Virtually everyone must learn to practice self management—teams and networking have replaced the traditional boss.
3. Career planning must be proactive (attempting to forecast future events), not passive (waiting for an event to happen before acting).
4. Flexibility, adaptability, and life-long learning are keys to career success,
5. All jobs must be refined and redefined constantly.
6. Success is possible, but the methods have changed.

The general idea, then, is that "conventional wisdom doesn't work anymore." New methods of both planning and defining careers are essential.[13]

FIGURE 9-2
Strength/Weakness Balance Sheet

STRENGTHS	WEAKNESSES
Work well with people.	Do not like constant supervision.
Like to be given a task and get it done in my own way.	Don't make friends very easily with individuals classified as my superiors.
Good manager of people.	Am extremely high-strung.
Hard worker.	Often say things without realizing consequences.
Lead by example.	Cannot stand to look busy when there is no work to be done.
People respect me as being fair and impartial.	Cannot stand to be inactive. Must be on the go constantly.
Tremendous amount of energy.	Cannot stand to sit at a desk all the time.
Function well in an active environment.	Basically a rebel at heart but have portrayed myself as just the opposite. My conservatism has gotten me jobs that I emotionally do not want.
Relatively open-minded.	
Feel comfortable in dealing with high-level businesspersons.	Am sometimes nervous in an unfamiliar environment.
Like to play politics. (This may be a weakness.)	Make very few true friends.
Get the job done when it is defined.	Not a conformist but appear to be.
Excellent at organizing other people's time.	Interest level hits peaks and valleys.
Can get the most out of people who are working for me.	Many people look on me as being unstable. Perhaps I am. Believe not.
Have an outgoing personality—not shy.	Divorced.
Take care of those who take care of me. (This could be a weakness.)	Not a tremendous planner for short range. Long-range planning is better.
Have a great amount of empathy.	Impatient—want to have things happen fast.
Work extremely well through other people. Get very close to few people.	Do not like details.
	Do not work well in an environment where I am the only party involved.

Source: Wayne Sanders

LIKES AND DISLIKES SURVEY

An individual should also consider likes and dislikes as part of the self-assessment. A **likes and dislikes survey** helps people recognize restrictions they place on themselves. Some employees, for example, aren't willing to live in certain parts of the country; some aren't willing to travel more than a certain number of days per year. Such feelings limit the jobs that would be suitable for the person. Recognizing such self-imposed restrictions before the issue arises may reduce future career problems.

Some people would rather work within major organizations that sell well-known products. Others prefer smaller organizations, believing that the opportunities for advancement may be greater or that the work environment is more congenial. All such preferences that could influence job choice and performance should be listed in the likes and dislikes survey (see Figure 9-3).

Such self-assessment tools can also lead to an understanding of personal career motives, setting the stage for pursuing a management career, seeking further technical competence, or perhaps planning towards one's own business. A person with little desire for the responsibilities of management, for example, should not enter management training.

People who know themselves can more easily plan their careers successfully. Many people, however, choose their careers unwisely, on the basis of the opportunities of the moment, the wishes of others', or notions of success they have not really examined in light of their own feelings.

Getting to know oneself is not a singular event. As people progress through life, their priorities change. People may think that they know themselves quite well at one stage of life and later begin to see themselves quite differently. Self-assessment, therefore, should be viewed as a continuous process.

THE CANADIAN ENVIRONMENT

One career preference being expressed by some Canadians is a move out of the country entirely. According to a 1992 article in *Canadian Business*, an increasing number of executives, professionals, and postgraduate students are choosing to work and live abroad, particularly in the United States, and to remain there for their working lives. The problems in Canada are not only the high tax rate and the high cost of living, but the lack of opportunities to manage large operations, or to be sufficiently challenged. These same factors make it difficult to recruit the best candidates for Canadian companies.

While changes in tax structure and the repositioning of social programs can make companies more competitive, there must be changes in attitude to make it more attractive for executives to return to Canada.[14]

FIGURE 9-3
Likes and Dislikes Survey

LIKES	DISLIKES
Like to travel.	Do not want to work for a large firm.
Would like to live in the East.	Will not work in a large city.
Enjoy being my own boss.	Do not like to work behind a desk all day.
Would like to live in a medium-size city.	Do not like to wear suits all the time.
Enjoy watching football and baseball.	
Enjoy playing racquetball.	

Source: Wayne Sanders

Organizational Career Planning

While the primary responsibility for career planning rests with the individual,[15] managers should assist actively in the process. From the organization's viewpoint, career planning is a formal program that attempts to maximize each employee's potential contributions.

The identification and establishment of career paths within a firm is referred to as **organizational career planning**, a process aimed at harnessing the human resource to better achieve organizational goals. Career planning programs are vital in today's environment, in which traditional vertical mobility has all but disappeared. In most organizations, career planning programs are expected to achieve one or more of the following objectives:

- *More effective development of available talent.* Individuals are more likely to be committed to development that is part of a specific career plan.

- *Self-appraisal opportunities for employees considering new or nontraditional career paths.* Some excellent employers do not view traditional upward mobility as a career option since fewer and fewer promotion options are available. Many HR professionals agree with Dolf Balkema, Vice-President of U.S.-based A. T. Kearney's Amsterdam office, who regards flatter organizations as preferable, in part because there are fewer power games to play: "They're no longer up the ladder because the ladder has been taken away."[16]

- *More efficient development of human resources within and among divisions and/or geographic locations.* Career paths should be developed that cut across divisions and geographic locations.

- *A demonstration of a tangible commitment to equity in employment.* It is often difficult to find qualified women and minorities to fill vacant positions. One means of overcoming this problem is to establish an effective career planning and development program.

- *Satisfaction of employees' personal development needs.* Individuals who see their personal development needs being met tend to be more satisfied with their jobs and with the organization.

- *Improvement of performance through on-the-job training experiences provided by horizontal and vertical career moves.* The job itself is the most important influence on career development. Each job can provide different challenges and experiences.

- *Increased employee loyalty and motivation, leading to decreased turnover.* Individuals who believe that management is interested in their careers will be more likely to remain with the organization.

- *A method of determining training and development needs.* If a person desires a certain career path and does not presently have the proper qualifications, a career plan will identify a training and development need.[17]

While all these objectives may be desirable, a successful career planning program depends on management's ability to meet those objectives considered most crucial to employee development and to the achievement of organizational goals.

CAREER PATHS

Recall that a career path is a flexible line of progression along which an employee moves during employment with a company. Historically, career paths have focused on upward mobility within a particular occupation. Now, however, any one of four career paths may be developed: traditional, network, lateral skill, and dual.

Traditional Career Path

The **traditional career path** is one wherein an employee progresses upward in the organization from one specific job to the next. The assumption is that each preceding job is essential preparation for the next, higher-level job. Therefore, an employee must move, step by step, from one job to the next to gain needed experience and preparation.

One of the biggest advantages of the traditional career path is that it is straightforward. The path is clearly laid out, and the employee knows the specific sequence of jobs through which he or she must progress.

Today, however, the traditional approach has become harder to follow because of changes in the workplace: 1) a massive reduction in management positions and levels, due to mergers, downsizing, stagnation, and reengineering; and 2) a decrease in paternalistic feelings toward employees, resulting in

HRM IN ACTION

"Fred, since you work in human resources, maybe you can explain why we hired Mary Moore," Sam Hakala asked of the human resource manager, Fred McCord.

"What's the problem with Mary, Sam?"

"Well, I went in to see Mary and asked her to develop a career plan for me. I wanted to know how long it will take me to advance up the corporate ladder. She obviously doesn't know much about career planning."

"What did she do, Sam?" Fred asked.

"Well, instead of outlining a career plan, she said that I would need to first gain some self-insight. I've been here five years, and now she says I don't have enough self-insight, can you believe that? She wants me to do her job for her. In my opinion, someone should clean house in that department."

How would you respond?

less job security and an erosion of employee loyalty. In addition, the work environment is changing so rapidly that new skills must be learned constantly. The certainties that characterized yesterday's business methods, then, have vanished in many industries. A predictable, secure career path will be open to only a very few employees.

Network Career Path

The network career path contains both a vertical sequence of jobs and a series of horizontal opportunities. This approach recognizes the interchangeability of experience at certain levels and the need to broaden experience at one level before promotion to a higher level. The vertical and horizontal options lessen the probability of career blockage. One disadvantage of this type of career path is that it is more difficult to explain to employees the specific route their careers may take for a given line of work.

Lateral Skill Paths

Traditionally, a career path was viewed as moving upward to higher levels of management in the organization. The previous two career path methods include this possibility. But even when modern corporate structures mean no promotion is available, it does not follow that an individual has to remain in the same job for life. Lateral moves within a firm can be taken to revitalize and to find new challenges. No pay raise or promotion is involved, but individuals can increase their value to the organization by gaining a broad range of experience.

Dual Career Path

The dual career path was originally developed to deal with the problem of technically trained employees who had no desire to move into management. The **dual career path** recognizes that technical specialists should be allowed to contribute their expertise to a company without having to become managers. In organizations such as National Semiconductor, for example, a technologically advanced firm with worldwide markets, a dual career approach was set up to encourage and to motivate individual contributors in engineering, sales, marketing, finance, human resources, and other areas.[18] Individuals in these fields can increase their specialized knowledge, make increased contributions to the firm and be rewarded without entering management. Compensation is comparable for technical and management jobs considered to be at a similar level.

The dual career path is becoming increasingly popular. In our highly technical world, specialized knowledge is often as important as managerial skill. Rather than creating poor managers out of competent technical specialists, the dual career path permits an organization to retain both highly skilled managers and highly skilled technical people.[19]

Managers at Dow Corning have created what is described as multiple ladders. Here, individuals can progress upward in research, technical service and development, or process engineering without being forced into a management role (see Figure 9-4).

FIGURE 9-4
Multiple Ladders at Dow Corning

Managerial	Research	Technical Service and Development	Process Engineering
Vice-President, R&D			
Director			
Manager	Senior Research Scientist	Senior Development Scientist	Senior Process Engineering
Manager	Research Scientist	Development Scientist	Process Engineering Scientist
Section Manager	Associate Research Scientist	Associate Development Scientist	Associate Process Engineering Scientist
Group Leader	Senior Research Specialist	Senior TS&D Specialist	Senior Engineering Specialist
	Research Specialist	TS&D Specialist	Senior Project Engineering
	Project Chemist	TS&D Representative	Project Engineer
	Asociate Project Chemist	TS&D Engineer	Development Engineer
	Chemist	Engineer	Engineer

Source: Charles W. Lentz, "Dual Ladders Become Multiple Ladders at Dow Corning," *Research Technology Management* 33 (May–June 1990), p. 28.

Adding Value to Retain Present Job

In the present work environment, employees need to be viewed as continually *adding value* to the organization. William J. Morin, chairman of the outplacement firm, Drake Beam Morin, has suggested that "Employees will have to anticipate where they can add value to their companies and take charge of their own destiny."[20] If they cannot add value, their employer may not need them.

Workers must anticipate what tools will be needed for success in the future and obtain these skills as part of a career management plan. According to Pat Milligan, a partner at Towers Perrin, a human resources consulting firm, the new attitude among managers is: "There will never be job security. You will be employed by us as long as you add value to the organization, and you are continuously responsible for finding ways to add value. In return, you have the right to demand interesting and important work, the freedom and resources to perform it well, pay that reflects your contribution, and the experience and training needed to be employable here or elsewhere."[21]

As an employee increases his or her value to an organization, the employee's value in the overall job market also increases. In today's work environment, job security can be defined as the ability to find another job, a concept that might be called enlightened self-interest. A person must discover what employers need and then develop the necessary skills to meet these needs. As one Avon executive stated, "Always be doing something that contributes significant, positive change to the organization. That's the ultimate job security."[22] For many workers, the only tie that binds a worker to the company is a common commitment to success and growth.

As a result, both employers and employees are assessing success and opportunity in terms of lateral movement, not formal promotions. Dr. Malcolm Weinstein, an industrial psychologist with Wilson Bonwell, a Vancouver-based international firm of industrial psychologists, says that "today's workers must envision their career not as a continuum, but as a series of projects in which they constantly learn new skills, grow as individuals and, hopefully, improve their salary."[23]

Job Revitalization and Career Enhancement

Many organizations are not able to reward employees with raises and promotions while still remaining competitive in the global marketplace. This climate has created productivity and absenteeism problems. Organizations, then, need to reinvigorate demoralized employees. As one senior HR executive has noted: "We're working to help people revitalize their jobs in a way that will benefit them and the company."[24] Managers must try to spur productivity by offering their people additional training, lateral moves, short sabbaticals, and compensation based on contribution rather than title.[25]

Compensation, then, is one way flattened organizations can spur enthusiasm. Skills-based pay rewards people with raises unaccompanied by promotions. The more skills one acquires and puts to use, the more one can earn.[26]

As reduced levels of management and downsizing increase the pressure on those who remain, lateral moves have become the most common way to reenergize the work force. In one major oil company 6500 employees have been laid off and over 1000 people deployed to different areas of the company during the past two years. As the CEO indicated, however, "That's not as easy as it sounds. Relocation and retraining expenses can run around $75,000 a person." Similarly, General Motors, which by 1995 had cut its vast white-collar work force nearly in half to about 70 000, is paying some $10 million a year for 6100 employees to be retrained in a variety of skills, ranging from carpentry to the basics of automotive design.[27]

Career Path Information

Information concerning career opportunities must be available before individuals can begin to set realistic objectives. One way to provide this information is to develop career path data for each job, based on job descriptions, on historical trends, or on similarities to other jobs in the same job family. Career path information is particularly useful because it

- outlines how each job relates to other jobs;
- presents career alternatives;
- describes educational and experience requirements for a career change; and
- points out the orientations of other jobs.[28]

Another way to obtain information is through outside organizations. The Women's Advertising Club of Toronto, for example, was founded in 1933 to provide a forum for women in advertising to exchange ideas, further their knowledge of the business, and help advance their careers. At present, the club focuses on networking and career development.[29]

Similarly, the Data Processing Management Association (DPMA) has introduced industry-wide standards for information systems career paths. The DPMA's Professional Development Program (PDP) establishes more than 200 job definitions and outlines the requirements for each. The DPMA has also instituted an Individual Training Plan designed to meet the performance requirements of the PDP.[30]

Plateauing

People who aspire to move upward within their present organization may often be frustrated by **plateauing**. Plateauing, the state in which an employee's job functions and work content remain the same because of a lack of promotional opportunities with the firm, occurs at some point to almost everyone pursuing a career.[31] Plateauing has become more common because many organizations are downsizing and hierarchies are flattening, just as the baby-boom generation (those born between 1944 and 1954) is reaching its prime. In addition, women and minorities are now competing for positions that once were not available to them.

In our society, promotion has always been an important measure of success. Thus, plateauing will present new challenges for those involved with career planning and development, if employees are to be kept productive and interested in their work. This problem can be approached in several ways. As mentioned previously, individuals can be moved laterally within the organization. Although status or pay may remain unchanged, the employee is given the opportunity to develop new skills. Managers who want to encourage lateral movement may also choose to use a skill-based pay system. Another approach is job enrichment. Here, the challenges associated with the job are increased (without promotion), giving the work more meaning, leading to a greater sense of accomplishment. Approximately one in 10 mid-sized to large companies offers such enrichment opportunities.

Exploratory career development, usually comprising short-term assignments in an area of potential interest, is yet another way of dealing with plateauing. These temporary transfers give an employee the opportunity to test ideas in another field without being committed to an actual move.

In North America, demotions have usually been associated with failure, but limited promotional opportunities may make them more legitimate career options. If the stigma of demotion can be removed, more employees—especially older workers—might choose to make such a move. In certain instances this approach might open up a blocked promotional path, while at the same time permitting a senior employee to escape unwanted stress without being thought a failure.

Career Development

Career development is the formal approach taken by management to ensure that people with the proper qualifications and experience are available when needed. Thus, career development includes any activity (formal or informal) that enables a person to add value continuously, in order to satisfy organizational needs, both now and in the future. This process should involve everyone in the company.[32] Career development programs may be conducted in-house or by outside sources, such as professional organizations, colleges or universities.

In-house programs are usually planned and implemented by a training and development unit within the firm's human resource department. Line managers often conduct program segments. Outside the company, organizations such as the Canadian Institute of Management and the Human Resources Professional Association of Ontario are active in conducting conferences, seminars and other types of career development programs.

Certain principles should be observed when planning career development programs. First, the job itself has the greatest influence on career development. When each day presents a different challenge, what is learned on the job may be far more important than formally planned development activities. Second, the type of developmental skills needed should be determined by specific job demands. The skills necessary to become a first-line supervisor, for example, will likely differ from those needed for a promotion to middle management. Third, development will occur only when a person has not yet obtained all the skills demanded by his or her current job. Transferring an employee to a new job he or she is already fully capable of doing will produce little or no learning. Finally, the time required to develop the skills necessary for a planned goal can be reduced by identifying a rational sequence of job assignments.

Responsibility for Career Development

Many key individuals must work together if an organization is to have an effective career development program. Management first must make a commitment to support the program through policy decisions and by allocating sufficient resources. Human resource professionals are responsible for implementation, as they provide the necessary information, tools, guidance, and liaison with top management. The employee's immediate supervisor is responsible for providing support, advice, and feedback. The supervisor's attitude indicates to the employee the level of support for career development within the organization. (According to a 1991 survey, Canadian employees do not feel supported. A survey of 2400 employees in British Columbia, found that 70 percent thought that their managers did not promote the most deserving people, 59 percent were dissatisfied with career development opportunities, and 60 percent thought their employers did not show a genuine interest in their well-being.[33]) Ultimately, however, the individual is responsible for developing his or her own career.[34]

Methods of Organization Career Planning and Development

Managers can assist individuals in career planning and development in numerous ways. Some current methods, most of which are used in various combinations, are listed here.

SUPERIOR/SUBORDINATE DISCUSSIONS

The superior and subordinate jointly agree on career planning and development activities. The resources made available to achieve these objectives may support formal or informal development programs. Human resource professionals are often called on for assistance, as are psychologists and guidance counsellors.

COMPANY MATERIAL

Some firms provide material specifically developed to assist their employees in career planning and development. This material can be tailored to the firm's special needs.

PERFORMANCE APPRAISAL SYSTEM

The firm's performance appraisal system can also be a valuable tool in career planning. Noting and discussing an employee's weaknesses and strengths can uncover development needs and suggest possible opportunities. If overcoming a particular weakness seems difficult or impossible, an alternate career path may be the solution.

WORKSHOPS

Some organizations conduct workshops to help employees develop career paths. Employees define and match their specific career objectives with the needs of the organization.

A GLOBAL PERSPECTIVE

It is estimated that 20 percent of the personnel sent abroad return prematurely; many others endure global assignments but are ineffective in their jobs, while their social lives can suffer to the point of marriage break-up. As a result, some consultants are advising their clients to hire a professional relocation services firm to help ease the problems of managers working abroad.[35]

The main reason for expatriate failure is culture shock, the feelings of anxiety regarding customs and security that can appear when an individual deals with a foreign society. Culture shock is often accompanied by medical and personal problems that can continue even after the employee returns home. In fact, one study found that many returned expatriates faulted their companies for not doing more 1) to prepare them for the shock of living in another culture; 2) to help their spouse find a job; or 3) to plan how the overseas assignment would fit into their career path.[36]

Returning employees are nearly always placed in positions with less decision-making ability and autonomy, lower pay, and fewer benefits. Worse, approximately one-quarter of all expatriates do not have a position to return to. Others leave the company immediately, take demotions, or relocate.[37] Many of these setbacks result from inadequate career planning, in that the overseas assignment is not regarded as part of an agreed-upon career path.

BEGINNING A CAREER IN HUMAN RESOURCES MANAGEMENT

Individuals who want a career in human resources management may either work in another field and transfer later, or they may obtain an entry-level position in human resources management. To ascertain the most appropriate career path, a number of human resource practitioners with large American firms were asked a series of questions:

1. Which entry-level position in your firm would be most helpful to a person who wants a career in human resources management?

2. What types of education or experience are most desirable for these entry-level positions?

3. Which human resource entry-level position would best assist a person's career progression in your firm?

As suggested in Figure 9-5, the responses varied considerably. Some managers stress work in other functional areas before an employee moves into human resources management, while others believe in direct entry into the human resource area.

Practitioners, then, do not agree on the most appropriate entry-level position. The nature of the firm's business or senior management's human resource philosophy may account for these differences. In some organizations, managers stress the need to obtain operating experience before entering human resource management. In others direct entry is seen as the more suitable beginning.

It is no longer sufficient for organizations to employ human resource people who want a career in human resources mainly because they like people and enjoy helping others. In fact, people who regard the helping aspect of the job as their primary role are usually unsuccessful as human resource managers, as the profession has become more and more oriented toward making a measurable contribution to profitability, or to organizational effectiveness.

Company	Entry-Level Position	Education/Experience
A.B. Dick Company	*Assistant Hourly Employment Manager Shop Foreman Assistant Salary Administrator	Bachelor's degree for all positions
Bristol-Myers Products	Human Resource Assistant	Bachelor's degree with two or three years' experience in general human resource work
Conoco, Inc.	*Human Resource Trainee Any position with Conoco	Bachelor's or master's degree in human resource administration, industrial relations, organizational development, business, or engineering
Denny's, Inc.	*Interviewer	Bachelor's degree in business or two years in human resource interviewing
	Wage and Salary Analyst	Bachelor's degree and one year of experience in human resources, preferably with compensation experience
	Human Resource Administrator	Bachelor's degree and/or two years' experience in human resources
GAF Corporation	*Production Supervisor Industrial Engineer Wage and Salary Analyst Safety Specialist	B.S.I.E., B.S.M.E., B.B.A. B.A. with relevant course work B.Sc. with relevant course work
General Cable Technologies	Assistant Plant Industrial Relations Manager Compensation Analyst	B.Sc. in industrial relations B.Sc. in industrial relations
Gerber Products Company	*Supervisor Trainee *Administrative Trainee	Four years of university Four years of university
Grumman Corporation	*Salary Analyst Employment Interviewer Career Development Analyst	Bachelor's degree in any of a variety of concentrations including psychology, business, and data processing
Hartmarx	Human Resource Assistant Compensation Assistant Employee Relations Assistant Human Resource Director (small plant or store)	Bachelor's or master's degree in business, human resources, or employee relations

*Indicates best entry-level position.

FIGURE 9-5   Careers in Human Resource Management

Company	Entry-Level Position	Education/Experience
International Paper Company	*Supervisor—Employee Relations	B.Sc. or B.A. in human resource or industrial management
	Administrator—Industrial Relations	B.Sc. or B.A. in industrial labour relations, or B.S. in industrial management
	Entry-level specialist assigned to the Corporate Human Resources Department	
Manville Corporation	*Employee Relations Supervisor	Bachelor's degree and some plant experience desirable
	*Plant Supervisor *Benefits Clerk	
Motorola, Inc.	*Employment Interviewer	B.Sc. or B.A.; no experience
Nabisco Brands, Inc.	*Human Resource Assistant (Field)	Bachelor's degree in such fields as business or psychology
Rockwell International Corporation	Supervisory Trainee (Field) Industrial Relations Trainee	M.B.A. in human resources or industrial relations
Shell Oil Company	Employee Relations Analyst	Bachelor's or master's degree in human resources or industrial relations preferred
Squibb Corporation	Human Resource Assistant (nonexempt recruiting)	Two or three years' experience in human-resource-related activities preferred
Stokely-Van Camp Inc.	Employee Relations — Management Trainee	Master's degree (preferably in human resources)
Teledyne, Inc.	*Wage and Salary Representative	B.A. or human resource or financial administrative experience
	Labour Relations Representative	B.A. or general plant or human resource administrative experience
Trans World Airlines	Reservation Sales Agent	High school diploma, customer contact, and sales experience
USX	Labour Relations Trainee Employee Relations Trainee	Law degree
	Line Operations Management Trainee	Master's degree, certification, experience Technical degree plus leadership
Walt Disney Productions	Human Resource Interviewer	People skills; B.A. and/or equivalent
	Human Resource Assistant Wage and Salary Analyst	Salaried experience and statistical orientation

SUMMARY

A career is a general course a person chooses to pursue throughout his or her working life. Career planning is an ongoing process whereby the individual sets career objectives and identifies the means to achieve them. Career paths outline a series of jobs through which an employee may move during employment with a company. Career development is an organization's formal approach to ensuring that people with the proper qualifications and experience are available when needed.

Individuals change constantly, thus they view careers differently at various life stages. Edgar Schein's research identified five different motives that account for the way people select and prepare for a career. He called them career anchors: managerial competence, technical/functional competence, security, creativity, and autonomy and independence. The work environment in which career planning takes place is changing rapidly, as downsizing has displaced workers and managers alike in massive numbers.

Learning about oneself is referred to as self-assessment. Two useful tools in this endeavour are a strength/weakness balance sheet and a likes/dislikes survey.

The process of establishing career paths within a firm is referred to as organizational career planning. Depending on the organization and the nature of the jobs involved, one of four types of career paths may be used: traditional, network, lateral skill, and dual.

Plateauing occurs when job functions and work content remain the same because of a lack of promotional opportunities within the firm. Plateauing has become more common recently because many organizations are downsizing, hierarchies are flattening, and the baby-boom generation is just reaching its prime.

Managers can assist their employees with their career planning and development in many ways. Some currently used methods (most of which are used in various combinations), are superior/subordinate discussion, company materials, performance appraisal systems, and workshops.

As 20 percent of personnel sent abroad return prematurely and others are ineffective, in some firms consultants are hired to help relocate employees. Many returning expatriates blame their employers for not preparing them properly and for poor career planning.

For individuals desiring a career in human resources management, there are two ways of entering the field: from another work area, or directly into an entry-level position in human resources. Practitioners don't agree on the best entry point.

TERMS FOR REVIEW

Career
Career planning
Career path
Career development
Career anchors
Self-assessment
Strength/weakness balance sheet

Likes and dislikes survey
Organizational career planning
Traditional career path
Network career path
Dual career path
Plateauing

QUESTIONS FOR REVIEW

1. Define the following terms: a) Career; b) Career planning; c) Career path; d) Career development.
2. Identify and discuss life stages as they affect one's career.
3. List and briefly define the five types of career anchors.
4. How should a strength/weakness balance sheet and a likes/dislikes survey be prepared?
5. What kind of questions should a person involved in career planning attempt to answer?
6. What objectives are career planning programs expected to achieve?
7. What are the types of career paths? Briefly describe each.
8. Define plateauing. How does plateauing affect human resource management?
9. Identify and describe some of the methods of organizational career planning and development.
10. What are the two ways to enter the field of human resources? Why might a firm favour one means over the other?

HRM INCIDENT 1

• IN THE DARK

"Could you come to my office for a minute, Tony?" asked Terry Geech, the plant manager. "Sure, be right there," said Tony Ricci. Tony was the plant's quality control director. He had been with the company for four years. After completing his degree in mechanical engineering, he had worked as a production supervisor and then as a maintenance supervisor, prior to moving to his present job. Tony thought he knew what the call was about.

"Your letter of resignation catches me by surprise," began Terry. "I know that Wilson Products will be getting a good person, but we sure need you here, too."

"I thought about it a lot," said Tony, "but there just doesn't seem to be a future for me here." "Why do you say that?" asked Terry.

"Well," replied Tony, "the next position above mine is yours. With you being only 39, I don't think it's likely that you'll be leaving soon."

"The fact is that I am leaving soon," said Terry. "That's why it's even more of a shock to learn that you're resigning. I think I'll be moving to the corporate office in June of next year. Besides, the company has several plants that are larger than this one, and we need good people in those plants from time to time, both in quality control and in general management."

"Well, I heard about an opening in the Hamilton plant last year," said Tony, "but by the time I checked, the job had already been filled. We never know about opportunities in the other plants until we read about the incumbent in the company paper."

"All this is beside the point now. What would it take to get you to change your mind?" asked Terry. "I don't think I will change my mind now," replied Tony, "because I've given my word that I am going to join them."

QUESTIONS

1. Evaluate the career planning and development program at this company.
2. What actions might have prevented Tony's resignation?

HRM INCIDENT 2

• DECISIONS, DECISIONS

A nervous Jerry Crow was ushered into the Levitt Corporation president's office by the secretary. In the office he encountered Allen Anderson, the human resource manager, and Mr. Gorman, the vice-president. Jerry was flattered when Mr. Gorman stood to shake his hand.

"I'll make this short and sweet," Mr. Gorman said. "You probably have heard that Allen plans to retire at the end of next year. In preparing for the staff changes, we would like to move you in as his assistant to get some cross-training experience."

Jerry responded, "Why me, Mr. Gorman? I'm a purchasing coordinator; I've never even worked in the human resource area."

"Well," replied Mr. Gorman, "we've been watching you carefully. I have personally reviewed your qualifications. From the company's standpoint, we know you can do the job. We need people who have been out in the company and can bring fresh perspectives to the human resource area." Mr. Gorman instructed Jerry to discuss the idea with Allen. Then he said he had to leave for another meeting. As he shook Jerry's hand, he said, "We would like to coordinate your transition from the purchasing department to make it as smooth as possible for everyone, and I know you're involved in some priority projects over there. Allen will get back with me on a time frame after you and he talk."

Jerry was 32 and he had been with Levitt for seven years. His business administration degree, from the University of Victoria, had included a heavy concentration in the behavioural sciences. He thought this background probably was a factor in his selection. But Jerry had worked only in purchasing. After three successful years as a buyer, he had been promoted to purchasing coordinator, with responsibility for supervising eight buyers and a small clerical staff.

He knew he was respected throughout the company. This was especially true in the production department, which had a great deal of interaction with purchasing. The production manager made no secret of his high regard for Jerry. Jerry also had taken time to get to know members of the finance and research department. His purpose in pursuing all of these relationships, though, was to help him do his purchasing job better. He had no idea at all that he would be considered for a job in the human resource department.

QUESTIONS

1. How should Jerry respond to the new assignment? Discuss.
2. What are the main qualifications for a senior human resource manager? Discuss Jerry's apparent qualifications for such a job.

DEVELOPING HRM SKILLS: AN EXPERIENTIAL EXERCISE

Career planning and development is extremely important to many people. Workers want to know how they fit into the future of the organization. Employees who believe that they have a future with the company are often more productive than those who don't. This exercise is designed to assist in understanding what it takes for a human resource professional to progress through an organizational hierarchy. This progression depends partly on the individual's self-perceptions and perceptions of past experiences with the company. The exercise provides one method of individual career planning for the human resource manager described in the following scenario.

The individual being evaluated is 35 years old today and is put in a reflective mood by the birthday. At a career crossroads, this person looks back on 10 years of moderate success but realizes that few others in the organization of comparable age have more education or work experience. In fact, the company has several middle-and upper-level managers who are much older, often less intelligent, and who seem to spend an inordinate amount of time at the country club.

Assume that you are this person and have set your sights on an important human resource middle-management position in the next five to seven years, and a top management position with your organization in the next 10 to 15 years. You have figured out there are 20 factors that determine upward movement in your organization. You are now trying to decide which are most important for survival and success, and which are least important. This decision will determine whether you take the career path to organizational survival and success, or the path to career failure and stagnation.

Each student will be given a list of 20 factors. You will rank the importance of each factor for your survival and success in the organization. Write the number 1 beside the most important factor, the number 2 beside the second most important factor, and so on.

Everyone in the class can participate in this exercise. Instructors will provide the participants with additional information necessary to complete the exercise.

10 Performance Appraisal

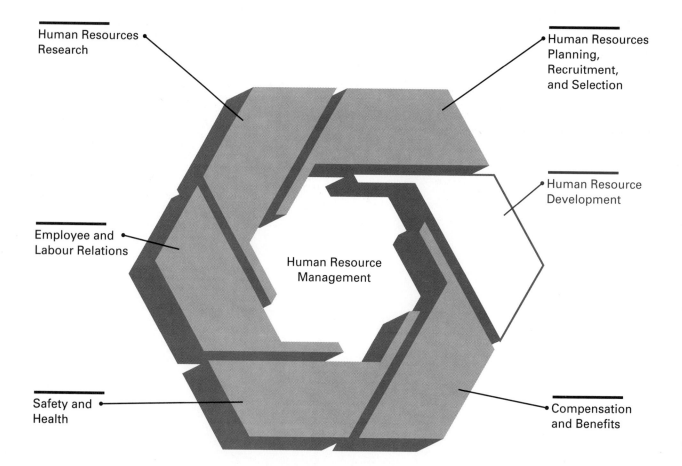

Human Resources Research

Human Resources Planning, Recruitment, and Selection

Human Resource Development

Employee and Labour Relations

Human Resource Management

Safety and Health

Compensation and Benefits

M arco Ghignoni, vice-president of production for Black and Decker, was concerned. "Doug, he exclaimed, "we must increase our productivity. If we don't, the foreign competition is going to eat our lunch. Worker productivity hasn't declined much, but our people seem to have little incentive to work together to improve it."

"I agree with you, Marco," said Doug Overbeck, vice-president of human resources. "We really don't have a good system for evaluating team results, while at the same time recognizing differences in individual performance. I'm convinced that our team approach in manufacturing is sound. But, it does bring us new problems with performance appraisal and our reward system. We need to take some action in these areas—and fast!"

arco and Doug had begun to realize a need for identifying both team and individual performance. When a performance appraisal system is focused solely on individual results, it isn't surprising that employees show little interest in working in teams.[1] On the other hand, individual contributions must also be taken into account.

We begin this chapter by defining performance appraisal and describing its uses. Then we outline the performance appraisal process and discuss responsibility for appraisal. Next we discuss the performance appraisal period, appraisal methods, and associated problems. We describe the characteristics of an effective appraisal system, the legal implications, the appraisal interview, and assessment centres. The purpose of this chapter is to emphasize the importance of performance appraisal as it relates to organizational effectiveness, and especially to developing the firm's human resources.

According to Gary Graham, President of Westinghouse Canada, it takes "the average manufacturing company in Canada a full seven hours and forty-five minutes out of every eight hour production shift simply to cover operating costs. It will take another $5^{1/2}$ minutes to pay corporate and capital taxes. Slightly less than ten minutes will be left over to make money . . ."[2] Faced with these statistics, managers need to develop the most efficient work force possible. Performance appraisal is one of the chief means of providing feedback to employees concerning the calibre of their contribution to company success.

THE NEED FOR PERFORMANCE APPRAISAL

Nothing is more discouraging for a top producer than to receive the same pay increase as a marginal employee. Even though the late W. Edwards Deming once said bluntly, "pay is not a motivator,"[3] a traditional and widely used individual incentive to do superior work has been destroyed if payment systems are not appropriate. At the same time, if work is organized around groups, team performance must also be considered. **Performance appraisal (PA)**, then, is a formal system of periodic review and evaluation of an individual's or team's job performance.[4]

Conducting performance appraisals is probably the most frustrating task in the field of human resource management. It has been suggested that in over 80 percent of firms, there is dissatisfaction with the appraisal system.[5] General disenchantment with appraisal systems was expressed by one HR executive who described the process as a *search for the impossible*.[6] A report in *The Financial Post* has suggested that Canadian managers average 4.2 hours completing each employee appraisal. As well, according to David Whitney, President of Austin Hayne: "informal research told us it [appraisals] was something they [managers] liked least about their job."[7]

PA, then, often is perceived as a negative, frustrating, difficult-to-master activity. If managers didn't have to make decisions about developmental needs, promotions, pay raises, terminations, transfers, the legal ramifications of HR, and admission to training programs, fewer employees would receive this much needed feedback. If managers could be guaranteed that they would never be required to defend themselves in court against wrongful termination suits or charges of discrimination, perhaps PA would not be such a critical management task. The multiple uses of PA data, however, lead most managers to conclude that although PA is a difficult process to devise and to administer, key organizational and employee needs are met through performance appraisal.

Even though developing an effective performance appraisal system will continue to be a high priority for human resource managers, it must be remembered that performance appraisal is not an end in itself, but rather a means to enhance performance. Concurrently, appraisers must take into account factors beyond the employees' control. Performance appraisal, however, is one of the many human resource management activities that must be owned by line managers. While human resource professionals may play a critical role in developing and coordinating PA systems, for the process to be successful, line personnel must be heavily involved in the appraisal procedure. Approached in this manner, PA has the best chance for successful implementation.

USES OF PERFORMANCE APPRAISAL

In many organizations, the primary goal of an appraisal system is to improve performance. A potential problem, however, and possibly a primary cause of the dissatisfaction with PA, is that managers expect too much from one appraisal plan. In developing a new appraisal system to fit a changed corporate culture at one large chemical company, for example, it was found that three separate assessments were needed; one to address development and coaching, another specifically for compensation, and a third for selection.[8]

Despite widespread scepticism, a properly designed system, combined with intense communication, can help achieve organizational objectives and enhance employee performance.[9] In fact, PA data are potentially valuable for use in numerous human resource management functions.

Human Resource Planning

Data must be available that describe the promotability and the potential of all employees, as succession planning is a key concern for many firms. A well-designed appraisal system provides a profile of the organization's human resource strengths and weaknesses.

Recruitment and Selection

Performance evaluation ratings may be helpful in predicting the future achievement levels of job applicants. For example, it may be determined that the most successful managers in a firm (identified through PA) exhibit certain behaviours when performing key tasks. These data may provide benchmarks for evaluating applicant responses obtained through behaviour description interviews (discussed in Chapter 6). Also, when validating selection tests, employee ratings may be used as the variable against which test scores are compared. In this instance, correct determination of the selection test's validity would depend on the accuracy of appraisal results.

Human Resource Development

A performance appraisal should point out individual needs for training, education, and development. If Mary Jones' job requires skill in technical writing, for example, and she receives a marginal evaluation on this factor, additional training in written communication may be indicated. If the human resource manager finds that a number of first-line supervisors are having difficulty in administering discipline, training sessions addressing this problem may be suggested. By identifying deficiencies that adversely affect performance, human resource and line managers are able to develop HRD programs that permit individuals to build on their strengths and minimize their deficiencies. An appraisal system does not guarantee that employees will be properly trained and developed, but it does make the task of determining training and development needs easier.

Career Planning and Development

Career planning and development may be viewed from either an individual or an organizational viewpoint. In either case, PA data are essential in considering an employee's potential. Managers may use this information to counsel subordinates and to assist them in developing and implementing their career plans.

Compensation Programs

Performance appraisal provides a basis for rational decisions regarding pay increases. Most managers believe that outstanding job performance should be rewarded tangibly with raises. To encourage good performance, therefore, a firm should design and implement a fair performance appraisal system and then reward the most productive workers and teams accordingly.[10]

Internal Employee Relations

Performance appraisal data are also used frequently for decisions concerning promotion, demotion, termination, layoff, and transfer. An employee's performance in one job, for example, may be useful in determining his or her ability to transfer to another job on the same level. Similarly, when performance is unacceptable, the PA is necessary if management is to justify demotion, termination, or retraining. When employees are working under a labour agreement, layoffs are typically based on seniority. When management has more flexibility, however, an employee's performance record may be a more significant criterion.

Assessment of Employee Potential

Some managers attempt to assess employee potential as they appraise job performance. It has been said that the best predictors of future behaviour is past behaviour. An employee's past performance in a job, however, may not accurately indicate future performance in a higher level or in a different position. The best salesperson in the company may fail as district sales manager. The best computer programmer may make an incompetent data processing manager. Overemphasizing technical skills and ignoring other equally important human resources management skills is a common error when promoting employees into management jobs. Recognition of this problem has led some managers to separate performance appraisal, which focuses on past behaviour, from the assessment of potential, which is future oriented. These firms have established *assessment centres*, which we discuss later.

THE PERFORMANCE APPRAISAL PROCESS

While there are few established rules, three key concepts govern performance appraisals: they should be written, systematic, and regular.[11]

Remember that a performance appraisal is a legal document. Often a manager will give a favourable appraisal to a below-average employee in order to avoid conflict. If that employee is ever fired for poor performance, however, the favourable report can be used in court as part of a wrongful dismissal claim. Conversely, an HR policy requiring that managers be completely honest when appraising their staff, supported by proper documentation and counselling, will strengthen the employer's claim that any employee has been dismissed for just cause.[12] This external factor has increased in importance as job security has diminished and the number of wrongful dismissal claims has risen.

The labour union is another possible external influence. Unions have traditionally stressed seniority as the basis for promotions and pay increases and opposed the use of management-designed performance appraisal systems. However, many union executives have now accepted the need for change. (Chapters 14 and 15 will describe the evolving nature of labour relations in North America.)

The internal environment can also affect the performance appraisal process. With production teams, for example, overall team results as well as individual contributions must be recognized. Measuring actual contribution in such an environment may be quite difficult. Setting specific goals is the starting point for any PA process (see Figure 10-1). The purpose of PA should be clearly defined and communicated. Dr. Peter Allan of Pace University in New York has listed nine reasons employers usually advance for conducting appraisals:

1. to enable management to pay more careful attention to employee behaviour, in order to improve the coaching process,

2. to enhance employee motivation by providing job-related feedback,

3. to gather data for enhancing work performance,

4. to create a database to support HR decisions concerning compensation, work assignments, employee development, succession planning, etc.,

5. to single out employees with promotion potential,

6. to obtain feedback from employees concerning likes/dislikes, expectations and career plans,

7. to obtain the necessary documentation to withstand potential law suits for wrongful dismissal or other legal challenges,

8. to assist the HR planning process,

9. to develop information for HR research such as test validation or training evaluation.[13]

FIGURE 10-1
The Performance Appraisal Process

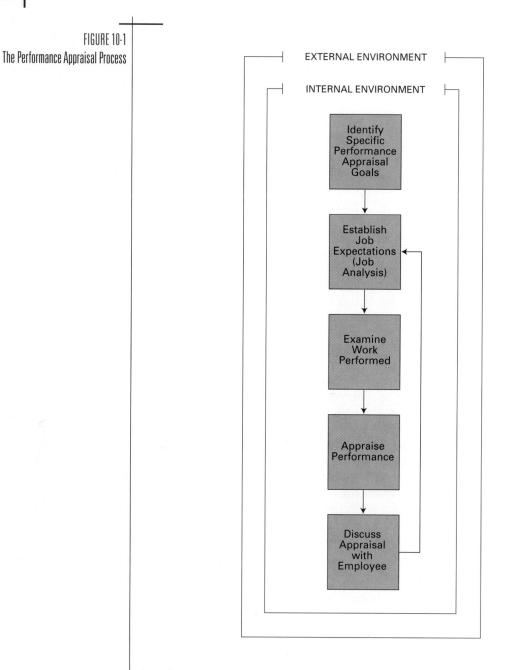

Source: Adapted from Oren Harari, "Back to the Future of Work," *Management Review* 82 (September 1993): 35.

Few PA systems will serve all of these functions. Managers should study their needs and then design the PA process to benefit both the organization and the individual or team.

The goals set should be supported by a thorough job analysis, so that employees are measured on essential job duties and work behaviour. Too often, appraisal systems focus on personality traits (e.g., attitude, cooperation, initiative), rather than on job performance. After specific appraisal goals have been established, the PA format has been chosen (see following pages), and the job analyses completed, individuals and teams must be made aware of job standards. Informing employees of what is expected of them is a most important employee relations task.

Although work performance is observed continuously and feedback (both negative and positive) should be immediate, it is at the end of the appraisal period (usually a year, but in some firms six months) that the appraiser evaluates work behaviour against established performance standards. The evaluation results are then communicated to the employee.[14] The performance evaluation discussion with the supervisor serves to reestablish job requirements.

RESPONSIBILITY FOR APPRAISAL

In most organizations, the human resource department is responsible for coordinating the design and implementation of performance appraisal programs. It is essential, however, that line managers participate directly in program design, since it is they who will likely conduct the appraisal interviews.

There are several ways to manage the appraisal process. While the supervisor has traditionally held sole responsibility for PA, several other models are now in use.

Immediate Supervisor

There are several reasons for relying on the first-line supervisor: The supervisor 1) is usually in the best position to observe the employee's job performance; 2) is responsible for managing a particular unit; and 3) is responsible for subordinate training and development.

Conversely, the immediate supervisor may emphasize certain aspects of employee performance and neglect others. As well, supervisors have been known to manipulate evaluations to justify pay increases and promotion decisions. In project or matrix organizations, the functional supervisor may not have the opportunity to observe performance often enough to form a valid judgement. Nevertheless, immediate supervisors will likely continue to be involved in evaluating performance.

Subordinates

Some senior executives have consented to evaluation of managers by their subordinates. They reason that subordinates are in an excellent position to judge their superior's managerial effectiveness. Advocates of this approach believe that supervisors will become especially conscious of the work group's needs and will do a better job of managing. Critics are concerned that the manager will be caught up in a popularity contest, or that employees will fear reprisal. If this approach is to succeed, evaluator anonymity must be guaranteed, a particularly difficult task, especially in a small department or if demographic data are included in the evaluation.

Peers

Peer appraisal has long had proponents who believed the approach is reliable if a work group is stable over a reasonable time and performs tasks that require considerable interaction. Encouraged by TQM concepts, managers are increasingly using teams, both traditionally managed and self-directed. It is likely, therefore, that peer rating within groups will grow in popularity. Team evaluation has several advantages.[15]

- Team members know each other's performance better than anyone else.
- Peer pressure is a powerful motivator.
- Knowing that teammates will be evaluating their work may increase team members' commitment and productivity.
- Because it involves many opinions, peer review is not dependent on one person's idiosyncrasies.

Problems with peer evaluations include the time required and the difficulty in distinguishing between individual and team contributions. In addition, some team members may feel uncomfortable appraising their co-workers.

Peer evaluation works best in a participative culture but results vary. At one Quaker Oats plant, for example, a peer review plan was used for ten years before it was abandoned; however "there was no incentive for people to be strict about it." A success story comes from W.L. Gore, where Gore associates (not called employees) are organized in work teams that handle performance problems. They also perform other traditional human resource functions such as hiring and firing.[16]

Group Appraisal

Group appraisal involves a team of two or more managers who are familiar with the employee's performance. If a person works regularly with both the data processing manager and the financial manager, for example, these two individuals might make the evaluation jointly. An advantage of this approach is increased objectivity. A disadvantage is that the role of the immediate supervisor is diminished. Also, it may be difficult to get managers together for a group appraisal because of other demands on their time.

Self-Appraisal

In one small firm, 300 wage earners evaluate themselves using a rating scale with 17 specific factors. Each employee's tutor also evaluates the employee. The two are then required to reconcile any significant differences.[17] If employees understand the objectives they are expected to achieve and the standards by which they are to be evaluated, they are—to a great extent—in the best position to appraise their own performance. Many people know what they do well on the job and what they need to improve. If they are given the opportunity, they will criticize their own performance objectively and be prepared to take remedial action.[18] In addition, because employee development is self-development, employees who appraise their own performance may become more highly motivated. Self-appraisal has great appeal to managers who are concerned primarily with employee participation and development.

Combinations

The approaches just described are not mutually exclusive. In fact, many managers are beginning to involve multiple sources that include both external and internal customers, a process known as 360-degree feedback. In one insurance firm, for example, a combination of supervisor, self, and peer assessment has been developed. This approach, called the *consensus review process*, produces more meaningful appraisals.[19]

An appraisal system that involves multiple evaluators will take more time and be more costly. A high degree of trust among participants and substantial training in appraisal techniques are needed regardless of how the process is conducted. These factors may take on increased importance when a combination of raters is involved. Nevertheless, the manner in which firms are now being organized may require innovative alternatives to traditional top-down appraisals.

THE APPRAISAL PERIOD

Performance evaluations are usually conducted at specific intervals. typically either annually or semiannually. As well, many new employees are evaluated just before the end of their probationary period. Evaluating new employees several times during their first year of employment is also a common practice. The appraisal period may begin on each employee's date of hire, or all employees may be evaluated at the same time. Although both practices have advantages, in large organizations there may not be sufficient time to evaluate each employee adequately if appraisals are conducted all at the same time.

PERFORMANCE APPRAISAL METHODS

Managers may choose from among several appraisal methods or use combinations of methods. As the main purpose of PA is to provide feedback and to help employees become more effective, however, collaborative methods are usually more appropriate.

Rating Scales

Perhaps the most widely used appraisal method, which rates employees according to defined factors, is called the **rating scales method.** Using this approach, judgements about performance are recorded on a scale. The scale is divided into categories, described either by number (e.g., 1 to 5) or, more often, by adjectives: for example, poor, fair, competent, and superior (see Figure 10-2a). In addition, descriptions can be added (see Figure 10-2b). While an overall rating may be provided, the method generally allows for the use of more than one performance criterion. One reason for the popularity of the rating scales method is its simplicity and speed.

FIGURE 10-2A
The Rating Scales Method: Sample 1

PERFORMANCE FACTORS:	POOR	FAIR	COMPETENT	SUPERIOR	EXAMPLES & EXPLANATIONS: DESCRIBE SITUATIONS PORTRAYING PERFORMANCE LEVEL
1. **Efficiency:** productivity, quantity, time utilization, organization					
2. **Understanding:** comprehension, learning ability, retention					
3. **Detail attention:** attentiveness, persistence, accuracy, thoroughness					
4. **Cooperation:** consideration of others, ability to work with others, willingness to carry own weight					

The factors chosen for evaluation are typically of two types: job-related behaviour and personal attributes. Job-related factors usually include quantity and quality of work; personal attributes may include dependability, initiative, adaptability, and cooperation.[20] The rater (evaluator) completes the form by indicating what degree of each factor is most descriptive of the employee's performance.

In some firms, space is provided for the rater to comment on the evaluation given for each factor. This practice may be especially encouraged, or even required, when the rater gives either the highest or lowest rating. For instance, if an employee is rated *unsatisfactory* on initiative, the rater provides written justification for this low evaluation. The purpose of this type of requirement is to avoid arbitrary or hasty judgements.

As shown in the example in Figure 10-3, each factor and each degree should be defined. In order to receive an *exceptional* rating for the factor quality of *work*, a person must consistently exceed the prescribed work requirements. The more precisely the various factors and degrees are defined, the better the rater can evaluate performance. Evaluation agreement throughout the organization is achieved when each rater interprets the factors and the degrees in the same way.

Many rating scale performance appraisal forms also provide for an assessment of the employee's growth potential. The form shown in Figure 10-3 contains four categories ranging from *now at or near maximum performance in present job* to *no apparent limitations*. Although there are drawbacks in at-

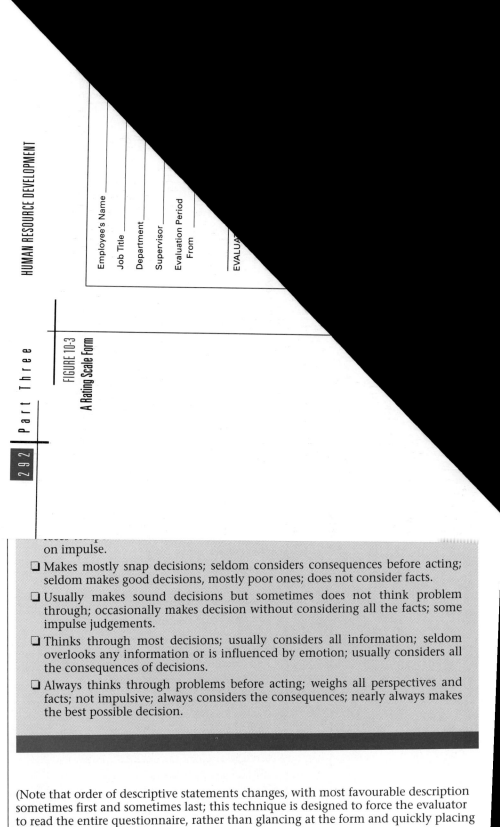

FIGURE 10-3
A Rating Scale Form

HUMAN RESOURCE DEVELOPMENT

Employee's Name

Job Title

Department

Supervisor

Evaluation Period
From

EVALUA

on impulse.

❑ Makes mostly snap decisions; seldom considers consequences before acting; seldom makes good decisions, mostly poor ones; does not consider facts.

❑ Usually makes sound decisions but sometimes does not think problem through; occasionally makes decision without considering all the facts; some impulse judgements.

❑ Thinks through most decisions; usually considers all information; seldom overlooks any information or is influenced by emotion; usually considers all the consequences of decisions.

❑ Always thinks through problems before acting; weighs all perspectives and facts; not impulsive; always considers the consequences; nearly always makes the best possible decision.

(Note that order of descriptive statements changes, with most favourable description sometimes first and sometimes last; this technique is designed to force the evaluator to read the entire questionnaire, rather than glancing at the form and quickly placing check marks.)

_____ to _____

Instructions for Evaluation:

1. Consider only one factor at a time. Do not permit rating given for one factor to affect decision for others.

2. Consider performance for entire evaluation period. Avoid concentration on recent events or isolated incidents.

3. Remember that the average employee performs duties in a satisfactory manner. An above average or exceptional rating indicates that the employee has clearly distinguished himself or herself from the average employee.

...TION FACTORS

	Unsatisfactory. Does not meet requirements.	Below average. Needs improvement. Requirements occasionally not met.	Average. Consistently meets requirements.	Good. Frequently exceeds requirements.	Exceptional. Consistently exceeds requirements.
QUANTITY OF WORK: Consider the volume of work achieved. Is productivity at an acceptable level?					
QUALITY OF WORK: Consider accuracy, precision, neatness, and completeness in handling assigned duties.					
DEPENDABILITY: Consider degree to which employee can be relied on to meet work requirements.					
INITIATIVE: Consider self-reliance, resourcefulness, and willingness to accept responsibility.					
ADAPTABILITY: Consider ability to respond to changing requirements and conditions.					
COOPERATION: Consider ability to work for and with others. Are assignments, including overtime, willingly accepted?					

POTENTIAL FOR FUTURE GROWTH AND DEVELOPMENT:

☐ Now at or near maximum performance in present job.

☐ Now at or near maximum performance in this job, but has potential for improvement in another job, such as:

_____

☐ Capable of progressing after further training and experience.

☐ No apparent limitations.

EMPLOYEE STATEMENT: I agree ☐ Disagree ☐ with this evaluation

Comments:

_____

_____

Employee	Date
Supervisor	Date
Reviewing Manager	Date

tempting to evaluate both past performance and future potential at the same time, this practice is often followed.

Despite their convenience and comprehensiveness, rating systems are obsolete, as the criteria used are not measurable. For example, it is impossible to measure accurately the difference between "fair" and "competent" in the form in Figure 10-2a. Even the attempts to add description (Figure 10-2b), fail to make the system precise. Figure 10-3 illustrates a much more sophisticated attempt, but the difference between a *2* and a *4* is left to the supervisor's judgement, rather than to some objective measure. Despite their popularity, then, rating scales should be avoided wherever possible.

Critical Incidents

The **critical incident method** requires that written records be kept of highly favourable and highly unfavourable work behaviours. When such a behaviour or behaviour pattern affects the department's effectiveness significantly—either positively or negatively—the manager writes a note, called a critical incident, in the employee's file. At the end of the appraisal period, the rater uses these records, along with other data, to evaluate employee performance. Using this method, the appraisal is more likely to cover the entire evaluation period and not, for example, to focus on the last few weeks or months. If a supervisor has many employees to rate, however, the time required for recording behaviours may become excessive.

Essay

Using the **essay method**, the rater writes a brief narrative describing the employee's performance. This method tends to focus on extreme work behaviour, rather than routine day-to-day performance. Ratings of this type depend heavily on the evaluator's writing ability. Some supervisors, because of their excellent writing skills, can make even a marginal worker appear to be a superior performer. Comparing essay evaluations might be difficult because there is no common criteria. Some managers believe, however, that the essay method is not only the simplest but also the best approach to employee evaluation.

Work Standards

The **work standards method** compares each employee's performance to a predetermined standard, or expected level of output. Standards reflect the normal output of an average worker operating at a normal pace. Work standards may be applied to virtually all types of jobs, but they are used most frequently for production jobs. Several methods may be used to determine work standards, including time study and work sampling.

An obvious advantage of using standards as appraisal criteria is objectivity. In order for employees to perceive that the standards are objective, however, they should understand clearly how they were set. It follows that the rationale for any changes to standards also must be carefully explained.

Ranking

In using the **ranking method,** the rater places all employees from a group in rank order of overall performance. For example, the best employee in the department is ranked highest and the poorest is ranked lowest. A major difficulty occurs when a number of employees perform at similar levels.

Paired comparison is a variation of the ranking method in which the performance of each employee is compared with every other employee in the group. The comparison is often based on a single criterion, such as overall performance. The employee who receives the greatest number of favourable comparisons is ranked highest.

Forced Distribution

Under a **forced distribution method,** the rater is required to assign individuals to a limited number of categories similar to a normal frequency distribution. As an example, employees in the top 10 percent are placed in the highest group, the next 20 percent in the next group, the following 40 percent in the middle group, the next 20 percent in the second lowest group and the remaining 10 percent in the lowest category. This approach is based on the rather questionable assumption that all groups of employees will have the same distribution of excellent, average, and poor performers. In a department where everyone is rated as outstanding, for example, the supervisor would be hard pressed to decide who should be placed in the lower categories.

Forced-Choice and Weighted Checklist Performance Reports

The **forced-choice performance report** requires the appraiser to choose from a series of statements that are most or least descriptive of the employee. One difficulty with this method is that the descriptive statements may be virtually identical, so that it may be difficult for the appraiser to decide which to choose.

Using the **weighted checklist performance report,** the rater completes a form similar to the forced-choice performance report. The form includes questions related to the employee's behaviour, which are answered either positively or negatively. In compiling a total score, different weights are assigned to the various responses; the rater is not aware of each question's weight.

These methods strive for objectivity by relying on the rater's observations rather than overall judgements. A limitation to this approach, however, is that since the evaluator does not know which items contribute most to successful performance, the information compiled cannot be used in employee development. Furthermore, both these forms are expensive to design.

Behaviourally Anchored Rating Scales

The **behaviourally anchored rating scale (BARS) method** combines elements of the traditional rating scales and critical incident methods. Using BARS, job behaviours derived from critical incidents, (i.e., effective and ineffective behaviour) are described more objectively. Individuals familiar with a particular job can identify its major components. They then rank and validate specific behaviours for each of the components. Because BARS typically requires considerable employee participation, the method may be accepted more readily by both supervisors and subordinates.

Using BARS, various performance levels are shown along a scale and described in terms of an employee's specific job behaviour. For example, when evaluating the factor "Ability to Absorb and Interpret Policies," the *very positive* end factor might be: "This interviewer could be expected to serve as an information source concerning new and changed policies for others in the organization." Conversely, the *very negative* end might read: "Even after repeated explanations, this interviewer could be unable to learn new procedures." There might be several levels in between the very negative and the very positive level (see Figure 10-4). Instead of using adjectives at each scale point, BARS uses behavioural anchors related to the criterion being measured. This modification clarifies the meaning of each point on the scale. Instead of providing a box to be checked for a category such as *Very Positive* performance, the BARS method provides examples of such behaviour. This approach facilitates discussion of the rating because specific behaviours can be addressed.[21] Although this approach was developed to overcome weaknesses in other evaluation methods, reports on the effectiveness of BARS are mixed, as BARS does not seem to be superior to other methods in overcoming rater errors, or in achieving psychometric soundness.[22] A specific deficiency is that the behaviours are activity-oriented rather than results-oriented, thus posing a potential problem for supervisors, because they must rate employees who are performing the activity, but not necessarily accomplishing desired goals.

Management by Objectives

As previously discussed, employee input is central to using the MBO concept, potentially the most effective method of evaluating an employee's performance. When administering traditional approaches to performance appraisal, personal traits (e.g., cooperation, dependability) are often the major criteria for evaluating performance. In addition, the role of the evaluating supervisor is similar to that of a judge. Management by objectives, however, shifts the appraisal focus from the worker's personal attributes to job performance, while the supervisor's role is transformed from umpire to counsellor and facilitator. Also, the employee changes from passive bystander to active participant.

Individuals jointly establish measurable objectives with their superiors, who then give them latitude in how to achieve these objectives. Jointly established goals allow the employee to be actively involved in the PA process. This ownership of objectives increases the likelihood they will be met.[23]

When MBO is used, the supervisor tends to keep communication channels open throughout the appraisal period. Then the employee and the supervisor meet for an appraisal interview, during which they formally review the extent to which objectives have been achieved and discuss the actions needed to solve remaining problems. This problem-solving discussion is likely to be the last in a series of conversations designed to assist the employee in progressing according to plan. Finally, objectives are established for the next evaluation period and the process is repeated. (See Figure 10-5.)

Interviewers and claims deputies must keep abreast of current changes and interpret and apply new information. Some can absorb and interpret new policy guides and procedures quickly with a minimum of explanation. Others seem unable to learn even after repeated explanations and practice. They have difficulty learning and following new policies. When making this rating, disregard job knowledge and experience and evaluate ability to learn on the job.

Very Positive	9	This interviewer could be expected to serve as an information source concerning new and changed policies for others in the office.
	8	Could be expected to be aware quickly of program changes and explain these changes to employers.
	7	Could be expected to reconcile conflicting policies and procedures correctly to meet immediate job needs.
	6	Could be expected to recognize the need for additional information to gain better understanding of policy changes.
Neutral	5	After receiving instruction on completing ESAR forms, this interviewer could be expected to complete the forms correctly.
	4	Could be expected to require some help and practice in mastering new policies and procedures.
	3	Could be expected to know that there is a problem, but might go down many blind alleys before realizing they are wrong.
	2	Could be expected to incorrectly interpret program guidelines, thereby referring an unqualified person.
Very Negative	1	Even after repeated explanations, this interviewer could be expected to be unable to learn new procedures.

Source: Adapted from Cheedle W. Millard, Fred Luthans, and Robert L. Ottemann, "A New Breakthrough for Performance Appraisal," *Business Horizons,* 19 (August 1976), p. 69. Copyright © 1976 by the Foundation for the School of Business at Indiana University. Reprinted by permission.

Name:		Position Title: Production Manager	Department: Manufacturing
Functions	**Objectives**	**Results**	**Problems and Solutions**
1. Select and train employees	A. All new employees prescreened and approved by HR Department B. Training plan written for all new employees by 10/12/XX	A. Hired one (1) person without aid of Personnel; released before 90-day probation ended. B. Training plan written by 10/12/XX	A. Follow the rules. B. None.
2. Supervise and coordinate work of employees	A. No more than three (3) grievances per month. B. Employee productivity rate at 98 percent of standard.	A. Averaged 4 per month. B. Productivity at 96 percent	A. Ask Labour Relations Manager to help analyze grievance pattern – eliminate problem areas by 6/1/XX. B. Work with Industrial Engineering to fine-tune systems.
3. Schedule Production	A. No down time except for breakdown of major line. B. No more than one (1) delay per week in shipping orders.	A. No breakdowns. B. No delays.	A. None. B. None.
4. Maintain Safe Work Practices	A. Discuss all accidents with Safety Director. B. No lost time accidents.	A. Discussed all but three (3) cases. B. Three (3) lost time accidents.	A. Reevaluate this objective and see if another approach would be more satisfactory by 3/1. B. Investigate each accident and tie in with (a) above by 3/1/XX.

FIGURE 10-5   An Example of Performance Appraisal Using MBO

In private-sector organizations, profit is the major performance indicator. Hence, all activities should be measured against this criteria. At the individual level, Paul Sharmon, president of Focused Management Information Inc., a firm that helps managers develop innovative cost management techniques, has developed a system called "integrated performance management". Writing in *CMA Magazine*,[24] he describes a process that, while not easily summarized, provides an example of current thinking:

   1. Identify with high-level goals through needs analysis and break them down into key (measurable) variables such as, time, quality, and cost.

2. Develop costing and budgeting systems that isolate human activity, so that the "people" contribution to profitability of each product or service is understood.

3. After developing these high-level measures, break them down into "sub-processes": for example, a high-level measure might be to have 99.8 percent of customers completely satisfied with the organization. One part (sub-process) of this activity might be "dispatch" which 1) processes 3000 inquiries yearly, dispatches 1500 service calls within 18 minutes of customer service request; 2) answers phone on first ring with 95 percent frequency; 3) customer questionnaire response "satisfied or fully satisfied" with service 98 percent of the time; 4) keeps within $175 000 budget. It is now possible to see how measurable individual performance outputs can fit into the main process.

4. A compensation and reward system now can be developed, as the performance standards are well known and measurable.

While only a sketchy summary can be provided here, the main point is that managers need to develop systems that appraise people on measurable criteria that relate closely to profitability or some other measure of efficiency. Many of the PA methods described previously are in widespread use. In order to remain competitive, however, employers must move away from traditional PA systems to more sophisticated concepts that link individual and team performance to both strategy and profitability.

PROBLEMS IN PERFORMANCE APPRAISAL

Many performance appraisal methods have been criticized severely. The rating scales method, however, seems to have received the greatest negative attention.

Lack of Objectivity

A potential weakness in traditional performance appraisal methods is lack of objectivity. As mentioned previously, commonly used rating scale factors such as attitude, loyalty, and personality are difficult to measure. In addition, these factors may have little to do with an employee's job performance. Employee appraisal based primarily on personal characteristics may place the employer in an untenable position if legal action is taken, as management would be hard pressed to show these factors to be job related. Some subjectivity will always exist in appraisal methods. The use of job-related factors, however, increases objectivity.

Halo Error

Halo error occurs when the evaluator places too much importance on a factor, giving a good or a bad overall rating based on this one factor. For example if a supervisor placed a high value on *neatness* (only one of several factors used in a company's performance appraisal system) and gave a sloppy employee a low ranking based primarily on this factor, the appraisal would suffer from the "halo effect". Whether the action is conscious or unconscious, allowing the low ranking on neatness to carry over to other factors results in an inaccurate and possibly unfair PA. Of course, if the individual were very neat, the opposite could have occurred.

Leniency/Strictness

Giving undeserved high ratings is referred to as **leniency** and is often motivated by a desire to avoid controversy. The practice is most prevalent when highly subjective (and difficult to defend) performance criteria are used and the rater is required to discuss evaluation results with employees. Leniency may contribute to several problems. For example, when deficiencies are not discussed with employees, they may not understand the need to improve their performance. Other employees, especially superior performers, may resent lenient evaluations, especially if promotions and pay increases are involved. Finally, it will be difficult to terminate poorly performing employees if they have been given satisfactory evaluations.[25]

Being unduly critical of an employee's work performance is referred to as **strictness.** Although leniency is usually more prevalent than strictness, some managers evaluate their employees more rigorously than the company standard. When one manager is overly strict on an entire unit, workers in that unit may be awarded smaller pay raises and be overlooked for promotion. As well, strictness applied to a particular individual may lead to charges of discrimination.

One study revealed that over 70 percent of responding managers believe that inflated and lowered ratings are given intentionally to subordinates. Figure 10-6 outlines these managers' rationale. The results suggest that the validity of many performance appraisal systems is flawed. Evaluator training, then, should be provided to emphasize the harm done by rater errors.

Central Tendency

Central tendency is a common error that occurs when employees are incorrectly rated near the average or middle of a scale. Some rating scale systems require the evaluator to justify in writing extremely high or extremely low ratings. In these instances, the rater may avoid possible controversy or criticism by giving only average ratings.

Recent Behaviour Bias

Every employee should know when he or she is scheduled for a performance review. Consciously or not, employees often improve their performance in the days or weeks before the scheduled evaluation and raters remember recent behaviour more clearly than past actions. Performance appraisals generally cover a specified period of time, however, and an individual's performance should be considered for the entire period.

FIGURE 10-6
Reasons for Intentionally Inflating or
Lowering Ratings

INFLATED RATINGS

- The belief that accurate ratings would have a damaging effect on the subordinate's motivation and performance
- The desire to improve an employee's eligibility for merit raises
- The desire to avoid airing the department's dirty laundry
- The wish to avoid creating a negative permanent record of poor performance that might hound the employee in the future
- The need to protect good performers displaying great effort even when results are relatively low
- The wish to reward employees displaying great effort even when results are relatively low
- The need to avoid confrontation with certain hard-to-manage employees
- The desire to promote a poor or disliked employee up and out of the department

LOWERED RATINGS

- To scare better performance out of an employee
- To punish a difficult or rebellious employee
- To encourage a problem employee to quit
- To create a strong record to justify a planned firing
- To minimize the amount of the merit increase a subordinate receives
- To comply with an organizational edict that discourages managers from giving high ratings

Source: Clinton Longenecker and Dean Ludwig, "Ethical Dilemmas in Performance Appraisal Revisited," *Journal of Business Ethics* 9 (December 1990), p. 963. Reprinted by permission of Kluwer Academic Publishers.

Personal Bias

Supervisors who conduct performance appraisals may have personal biases related to employee characteristics: e.g., race, religion, gender, disability, or age. Policies prohibiting discrimination should be in place, therefore, and supervisors need to be trained in appraisal techniques. As well, records should be kept that track appraisal results by various categories, so that patterns of discrimination can be spotted. Discrimination in appraisal can be based on many other factors. For example, mild-mannered people may be appraised more harshly because they are not likely to contest the results while aggressive people are often given better appraisals to avoid strife.

HRM IN ACTION

"Carmen, you're the human resource manager and I have a human resource problem that I need your advice on," said Gopalan Srinivasan, production supervisor for Service International. "Tom has worked for me for four years. He is likable and never misses a day of work. However, he is mediocre at his job, despite numerous retraining attempts, conferences, and even incentives. I hear too that the company is preparing for a work force reduction. As I was working on Tom's appraisal this morning, he stuck his head in the door, handed me three cigars, and said that his wife had just had triplets. That sure puts pressure on me."

If you were Carmen, how would you respond?

CHARACTERISTICS OF AN EFFECTIVE APPRAISAL SYSTEM[26]

Appraisal system validation may be the most certain approach of determining whether or not the system is obtaining accurate results. Validation studies, however, can be costly and time consuming. Also, many smaller firms may not have enough positions to meet technical validation requirements. It is unlikely that any appraisal system will be immune to legal challenge. Systems that possess certain characteristics, however, may be more legally defensible. But legality is not enough. The organization needs a system that is ethical: that provides an honest assessment of work behaviour that permits the mutual development of a plan to improve individual and/or group performance.[27] The following factors assist in accomplishing this purpose.

Job-Related Criteria

The criteria used for appraising employee performance must be job related. More specifically, job information should be determined through job analysis. Although subjective factors, such as initiative, enthusiasm, loyalty, and cooperation are important, they defy definition and measurement. Unless these factors can be clearly shown to be job related, they should not be used in formal evaluations.

Performance Expectations

Managers must explain performance expectations to their subordinates in advance of the appraisal period; it is not fair to evaluate employees using criteria they know nothing about. As Deanna Porter, manager of marketing and business development for Markham, Ontario-based Municipal Leasing suggests,

> There are three important things to remember when conducting an appraisal interview. Firstly, be accurate, and be able to support your appraisal

with objective information and reliable examples. Secondly, focus on behaviours and results, not attitudes. Finally, be fair and assess the whole review period rather than the most recent performance. Assess the pattern of behaviour rather than the exceptions to the pattern. The appraisal should not be a surprise to the employee.

Discussing performance expectations builds mutual respect between the supervisor and the employee. People tend to work better in a work setting where expectations have been set through a process of discussion and agreement."[28]

The establishment of highly objective work standards is relatively simple in areas such as manufacturing, assembly, and sales. In many other types of jobs, however, this task is more difficult. Still, evaluation must take place, and performance expectations, however elusive, should be defined in understandable terms.

Standardization

Employees in the same job category under the same supervisor should be appraised using the same evaluation instrument. It is also important that appraisals be conducted regularly over similar periods of time: typically one year, but more frequently in many forward-thinking firms.

Another aspect of standardization is formal documentation. Employees should sign their evaluations. If the employee refuses, the manager should document this behaviour. Records should also include a description of employee responsibilities, expected performance results, and the way these data will be viewed in making appraisal decisions. Traditionally, in many smaller firms performance appraisal systems were informal; with advances in computer software, however, there are many HR systems on the market designed specifically for small business.

Qualified Appraisers

Responsibility for evaluating employee performance should be assigned to the person, or people, who directly observe at least a representative sample of job performance. Usually, this person is the employee's immediate supervisor, but, as previously discussed, other approaches are gaining in popularity.

The immediate supervisor may have difficulty appraising performance objectively in matrix organizations, where employees may be formally assigned to a supervisor but work under various project managers. Also, a new supervisor may initially have insufficient knowledge of employee performance. In these situations, multiple raters may be used. To ensure consistency, appraisers must be well trained. Training should emphasize that performance appraisal is a significant component of every manager's job, as is ensuring that subordinates understand what is expected of them. Training should be ongoing to respond both to changes in the appraisal system and to the possibility that over time, supervisors may deviate from established procedures.

Open Communication

Most employees want to know how well they are performing. A good appraisal system provides highly desired, continuing feedback, aimed at avoiding surprises during the appraisal interview. Even though the interview presents an excellent opportunity for both parties to exchange ideas, it should not serve as a substitute for day-to-day communication. On the other hand, a performance appraisal system should allow immediate access to information on all employees. The PA also alerts managers to individuals who need to improve their performance. Finally, the system permits HR professionals to take proactive measures (e.g., counselling, training, or transfer), to salvage those who are not performing satisfactorily.

Employee Access to Results

As appraisal systems are designed to improve performance, withholding appraisal results is counterproductive. Employees often do not perform well without having access to this information. Also, permitting employees to review appraisal results allows them to detect any errors that may have been made, to disagree with the evaluation and/or to formally challenge the results.

All employees should be given access to their personal employment files, including performance appraisal data. Employees will not trust a system that withholds information. Secrecy invariably breed suspicion, thwarting efforts to increase employee involvement and motivation. Supervisors must make an effort to salvage marginal employees, but those in this category should be told specifically what will happen if their performance does not improve.

Due Process

As in any industrial relations function, ensuring due process is vital. A formal procedure should be in place that permits employees to appeal appraisal results they consider to be inaccurate or unfair.

Legal Implications

Wrongful termination suits have increased greatly during the past decade. In Canada, firings must be made for "just cause". Poor performance is an example of just cause, but the employer must document the misconduct or shortcoming, describe what conduct is expected, provide a reasonable time for the employee to meet expectations, and issue a statement that failure to comply will result in termination. Hence, an appraisal system is essential to avoid what Malany Franklin, an employment law specialist with Borden and Elliot, describes as every employer's nightmare: the newly-terminated employee who spends "hours visiting the employment standards office, the unemployment insurance commission, the human rights commission and a lawyer."[29]

The Appraisal Interview

The weak point in most evaluation processes is the appraisal interview, usually conducted at the end of the appraisal period. This interview is essential for employee development. Effective performance appraisal systems, however, generally require more than a single interview. Instead, supervisors should maintain a continuous dialogue with employees emphasizing 1) their own responsibility for development and 2) management's supportive role in the appraisal function.

A successful appraisal interview should be structured so that both the supervisor and the subordinate view the process as a problem-solving opportunity, rather than as a fault-finding session. The supervisor should consider three areas when planning an appraisal interview: 1) discussing the employee's performance; 2) assisting the employee in setting objectives; and 3) suggesting means for meeting them. For example, should an employee fail to meet certain objectives, both parties should agree on the specific improvement needed during the next appraisal period. In suggesting ways to meet objectives, the supervisor should recommend specific actions.

The interview should be scheduled soon after the end of the appraisal period, as employees usually know when their interview should take place and their anxiety tends to increase when it is delayed. Interviews with top performers are often pleasant experiences, but supervisors may be reluctant to meet face-to-face with poor performers, tending to postpone these anxiety-provoking sessions.

At one Canadian community college, newly-hired teachers are placed on a year's probation, transferring to permanent status only on completion of their first academic year. Hence, they expect to be appraised and formally notified of their status by June of their first year of employment. In one instance, June came and went, and nothing was communicated. One instructor began to have stress problems and even postponed buying a house. It was only when the next year's teaching schedule was published (with his name on it!) that he knew his job was secure. By not respecting the appraisal period, this employer created unnecessary stress and tension that affected both the instructor and his family. When questioned later about the incident, the department chair replied: "Surely it was obvious, the man had done an excellent job." Employers should not leave employees to guess how well they have performed; timely, formal communication is essential.

The amount of time devoted to an appraisal interview varies considerably, depending on company policy and job level. Many managers have learned that as soon as pay is mentioned in an interview, the topic tends to dominate the conversation. For this reason, a common practice is to defer pay discussions for one to several weeks after the appraisal interview. At American Express's Financial Services unit, for example, most employees receive formal evaluations at the end of each year; the salary review is conducted one day to three weeks later.[30]

Conducting an appraisal interview requires tact, patience, and considerable skill. Praise should be provided when warranted, but praise has only limited value if not clearly deserved. Criticism is especially difficult to give, as even "constructive criticism" often distresses and angers employees. Yet it is difficult for a manager at any level to avoid criticism when conducting appraisal interviews. The supervisor should realize, however, that all individuals have some deficiencies that may not be changed easily. Continued criticism may lead to frustration and damage employee development. Again, this possibility should not allow undesirable employee behaviour to go unnoticed. Discussions of sensitive issues, however, should focus on the deficiency, not on the person. Threats to the employee's self-esteem should be minimized whenever possible.

A serious error is to surprise the subordinate by mentioning some past mistake or problem. For example, if the incident had not been previously discussed, it would be most inappropriate for the supervisor to state: "Two months ago, you failed to properly coordinate your plans for implementing the new automated resume review procedure." Good management practice dictates that such situations be dealt with when they occur and not be saved for the appraisal interview.

The performance appraisal process should be a good experience for the employee. Ideally, employees will leave the interview feeling friendly toward the supervisor and the company and optimistic about the job and themselves. Too often, they leave feeling discouraged or hostile. The prospects for improved performance will be bleak if the employee's ego is deflated. Past behaviour can't be changed, but future performance can. Specific plans for the employee's development should be outlined clearly and mutually agreed upon. Cessna Aircraft Company has developed several helpful hints for supervisors who must conduct appraisal interviews (see Figure 10-7).

A GLOBAL PERSPECTIVE

A general management survey on perceptions of national management style was given to 707 managers representing diverse industries from the U.S., Indonesia, Malaysia, and Thailand. Results on survey items related to the design of performance appraisal systems revealed significant variances in management style. These differences suggesting that North American performance appraisal principles may not transfer well across cultures.[31]

Yet an effective international system is essential for credible employee evaluations.[32] Valid performance appraisal is hard to achieve in Canada; evaluating overseas employees makes a normally complex problem extremely difficult.[33]

A strength in one culture might be considered a weakness in another. For example, the amount of time spent in personal conversation with a customer relates to cultural norms. What might be seen as wasting time on idle chatter in one country might be ordinary professional courtesy in another—and offensive curiosity in a third. In some cultures, managers are expected to make decisions, while employees expect to follow orders; in others, employees want to participate in decision making and authoritarian managers are seen as obsolete. The issue of appropriate performance standards also comes into question. An inflexible performance appraisal system can create a great deal of misunderstanding and even personal offence,[34] especially among foreign nationals working for a Canadian employer.

FIGURE 10-7
Suggestions for Conducting Appraisal
Interviews

1. Give the employee a few days' notice of the discussion and its purpose. Encourage the employee to give preparatory thought to his or her job performance and development plans. In some cases, have employees read their written performance appraisal prior to the meeting.

2. Prepare notes and use the completed performance appraisal form as a discussion guide so that each important topic will be covered. Be ready to answer questions employees may ask about why you appraised them as you did. Encourage your employees to ask questions.

3. Be ready to suggest specific developmental activities suitable to each employee's needs. When there are specific performance problems, remember to "attack the problem, not the person".

4. Establish a friendly, helpful, and purposeful tone at the outset of the discussion. Recognize that it is not unusual for you and your employee to be nervous about the discussion, and use suitable techniques to put you both more at ease.

5. Assure your employee that everyone on Cessna's management team is being evaluated so that opportunities for improvement and development will not be overlooked and each person's performance will be fully recognized.

6. Make sure that the session is truly a discussion. Encourage employees to talk about how they feel they are doing on the job, how they might improve, and what developmental activities they might undertake. Often an employee's viewpoints on these matters will be quite close to your own.

7. When your appraisal differs from the employee's discuss these differences. Sometimes employees have hidden reasons for performing in a certain manner or using certain methods. This is an opportunity to find out if such reasons exist.

8. These discussions should contain both constructive compliments and constructive criticism. Be sure to discuss the employee's strengths as well as weaknesses. Your employees should have clear pictures of how you view their performance when the discussions are concluded.

9. Occasionally the appraisal interview will uncover strong emotions. This is one of the values of regular appraisals; they can bring out bothersome feelings so they can be dealt with honestly. The emotional dimension of managing is very important. Ignoring it can lead to poor performance. Deal with emotional issues when they arise because they block a person's ability to concentrate on other issues. Consult Personnel for help when especially strong emotions are uncovered.

10. Make certain that your employees fully understand your appraisal of their performance. Sometimes it helps to have an employee orally summarize the appraisal as he or she understands it. If there are any misunderstandings, they can be cleared up on the spot. Ask questions to make sure you have been fully understood.

11. Discuss the future as well as the past. Plan with the employee specific changes in performance or specific developmental activities that will allow fuller use of potential. Ask what you can do to help.

12. End the discussion on a positive, future-improvement-oriented note. You and your employee are a team, working toward the development of every-one involved.

Source: Used with the permission of Cessna Aircraft Company.

These problems may be avoided if HR professionals help managers to develop appraisal systems that enhance administrative decision making, as well as personal development. In addition, performance objectives for job assignments or tasks should be developed whenever possible. Third, managers must allow more time to achieve results in an overseas assignment. Finally, the objectives of the appraisal system should be flexible and responsive to potential markets and environmental contingencies.[35]

Assessment Centres

As previously suggested, many employee performance appraisal systems evaluate past performance and potential for advancement at the same time. In other organizations, however, assessment centres are used for assessing potential. At an **assessment centre**, employees are required to perform simulated, job-analysis-based activities similar to those they might encounter on the job. Usually the assessors observe the employees in an environment removed from the normal workplace. Typically the assessors are experienced managers who both participate in the exercises and evaluate performance. As many as half a dozen assessors may evaluate each participant. Assessment centres are used to 1) identify employees who have higher-level management potential, 2) select first-line supervisors, and 3) determine employee development needs.[36] The assessment centre approach provides greater data reliability and validity than promotion systems based on seniority or work history and appears to be a more accurate predictor than aptitude tests.[37]

SUMMARY

Performance appraisal is a system that provides a periodic evaluation of individual or group job performance. The fundamental purpose of performance appraisal, however, is to improve organizational effectiveness. Identification of specific objectives provides the starting point for the performance appraisal process. Next, supervisors should discuss with employees the major duties contained in their job descriptions, as they must understand what is expected of them. Observed work behaviour is then evaluated periodically against previously established job performance standards, and the evaluation results are discussed with the employee. This performance evaluation interview serves to reestablish job requirements in the employee's mind.

The human resource department is responsible for designing and coordinating the performance appraisal process. Line managers, however, must play a central role if the process is to be successful. Employee evaluation is usually performed by the immediate supervisor. Some systems, however, use subordinates, peers, a group, or the employee (self-appraisal), either singly or in combination.

Performance appraisal methods include 1) rating scales, 2) critical incidents, 3) essay, 4) work standards, 5) ranking, 6) forced distribution, 7) forced-choice and weighted checklist performance reports, 8) behaviourally anchored rating scales, and 9) management by objectives. Rating scales are the traditional method, but are always somewhat inaccurate because the rating attributes are not measurable and some subjectivity is unavoidable. MBO-based systems go furthest to focus on job-related factors and on measurable results. Problems associated with performance appraisal may include lack of objectivity, halo error, leniency, strictness, central tendency, recent behaviour bias, and personal bias.

At the end of the appraisal period, the evaluator conducts a formal appraisal interview with the employee. The key to a successful interview is to structure it so that both the manager and the subordinate approach the session as an opportunity for problem solving rather than fault finding. While this interview is an essential employee development opportunity, it does not replace continuous dialogue between employee and manager.

Because improperly constituted systems can result in costly legal action against a firm, appraisal systems must be based on job content.

In a global context, other nationalities often have management philosophies and styles that differ from North American practice. Canadian performance appraisal methods, therefore, may not be appropriate for use in overseas operations. HR professionals need to develop appropriate systems acceptable to those who work in other cultures.

An assessment centre requires employees to perform activities similar to those that they might confront in an actual job. Assessment centres are being used increasingly for 1) identifying employees who have management potential, 2) selecting first-line supervisors, and 3) determining employees' development needs.

TERMS FOR REVIEW

Performance appraisal (PA)
Group appraisal
Rating scales method
Critical incident method
Essay method
Work standards method
Ranking method
Paired comparison
Forced distribution method

Forced-choice performance report
Weighted checklist performance report
Behaviourally anchored rating scale (BARS) method
Halo error
Leniency
Strictness
Central tendency
Assessment centre

QUESTIONS FOR REVIEW

1. Define performance appraisal and briefly discuss the basic purposes of appraisals.

2. What are the steps in the performance appraisal process?

3. Many different people can conduct performance appraisals. Briefly describe the various alternatives.

4. Briefly describe each of the following methods of performance appraisal: a) rating scales; b) critical incidents; c) essay; d) work standards; e) ranking; f) forced distribution g) forced-choice and weighted checklist performance reports; h) behaviourally anchored rating scales; and i) management by objectives.

5. What are the various problems associated with performance appraisal? Briefly describe each.

6. Why should employee performance and development be discussed separately from pay increases?

7. What are the characteristics of an effective appraisal system?

8. What are the legal implications of performance appraisal?

9. Describe how an assessment centre could be used as a means of performance appraisal.

HRM INCIDENT 1

• LET'S GET IT OVER WITH

"There, at last it's finished," thought Roy Baker, as he laid aside the last of 12 performance appraisal forms. It had been a busy week for Roy, who supervises a road maintenance crew for the Nova Scotia Department of Highways.

The Premier, in passing through Roy's district a few days earlier, had complained to the area superintendent that repairs were needed on several of the highways. Because of this criticism, the superintendent had assigned Roy's crew an unusually heavy workload. In addition, Roy received a call from the personnel office that week telling him that the performance appraisals were late. Roy explained his predicament, but the personnel specialist insisted that the forms be completed right away.

Looking over the appraisals again, Roy thought about several of his staff. The performance appraisal form had places for marking quantity of work, quality of work, and cooperativeness. For each characteristic, the employee could be graded outstanding, good, average, below average, or unsatisfactory. Since Roy's crew had completed all of the extra work assigned for that week, he marked every worker outstanding in quantity of work. He marked Josh Blum average in cooperativeness because Josh had questioned one of his decisions that week. Roy had decided to patch a pothole in one of the roads, and Josh thought the small section of road surface ought to be broken out and replaced. Roy didn't include this incident in the remarks section of the form, though. As a matter of fact, he wrote no remarks on any of the forms.

Roy felt a twinge of guilt as he thought about Roger Brokopp. He knew that Roger had been slacking off and the other workers had been carrying him for quite some time. He also knew that Roger would be upset if he found that he had been marked lower than the other workers. So he marked Roger the same to avoid a confrontation. "Anyway," Roy thought, "these things are a pain in the neck, and I really shouldn't have to bother with them."

As Roy folded up the performance appraisals and put them in the envelope for mailing, he smiled. He was glad he would not have to think about performance appraisals for another six months.

QUESTIONS

1. What weaknesses do you see in Roy's performance appraisals?

HRM INCIDENT 2

• PERFORMANCE APPRAISAL?

As the production supervisor for Sweeny Electronics, Mike Mahoney was generally well regarded by most of his subordinates. Mike was an easygoing man who tried to help his employees any way he could. If a worker needed a small loan until payday, he would dig into his pocket with no questions asked. Should an employee need some time off to attend to a personal problem, he would not dock the individual's pay; rather, he would take up the slack himself until the worker returned.

Everything had been going smoothly, at least until the last performance appraisal period. One of Mike's employees, Bill Overstreet, had been experiencing personal problems for the past year. Bill's wife had been sick much of the time; she was expected to live no more than six months. Bill's son had a speech impediment and the doctors had recommended a special clinic that would require him to live in a residence in another town. As well, Bill's wife really wanted to see her mother in England before she died, a trip that Bill would be hard pressed to afford, but under the circumstances, he couldn't refuse.

When it was time for Bill's annual performance appraisal, Mike decided he was going to do as much as possible to help him. Although Bill could not be considered more than an average worker, Mike rated him outstanding in virtually every category. Because the firm's compensation system was tied heavily to the performance appraisal, Bill would be eligible for a merit increase of 10 percent in addition to a regular cost of living raise.

Mike explained to Bill why he was giving him such high ratings, and Bill acknowledged that his performance had really been no better than average. Bill was very grateful and expressed this to Mike. As Bill left the office he was excitedly looking forward to telling his friends about what a wonderful boss he had. Seeing Bill smile as he left gave Mike a warm feeling.

QUESTIONS

1. From the standpoint of Sweeny Electronics', what difficulties might Mike Mahoney's performance appraisal practices create?
2. What can Mike do now to mitigate the damage done by his evaluation of Bill?

DEVELOPING HRM SKILLS: AN EXPERIENTIAL EXERCISE

Some managers do not take PA as seriously as they should. This attitude is counterproductive, frequently lowering individual and group productivity.

Larry Cheechoo, supervisor of the electrical department, has a busy day scheduled, but he needs to squeeze in the last of his performance appraisals. They are due today, and he has only one more signature to get. Upon arriving for work he thinks, "I hate doing performance appraisals. It's the worst part of a supervisor's job. But, it does give me the chance to let my people know where they have to pull up their socks. The guy I'm appraising today has always exceeded his quotas, he is very helpful to those he likes, and he is excellent on the new computerized production setup; but if he wants to advance, he will need to change his behaviour. He seems to have problems working with the females on the line, and he doesn't seem to be very openminded. Also, on September 23 he failed to secure his work area. This guy really has problems. Maybe our talk will do some good; either way I need to get this done. On the bright side, this is the last performance appraisal until next year."

Today is the day that Alex Martin gets his performance appraisal, and he is excited about it. Before the meeting with Larry, his supervisor, he thinks, "I've been very good on the new computerized setup, and very helpful to my friends on the line; this will help me get my promotion. I expect that the boss saved my performance appraisal for last to praise my performance and recommend me for that promotion that I've been deserving for some time. I've been passed over for promotion far too long, this has been a great year for me, and this will cap off a year of excellent performance."

When these two get together there will be a meeting of two quite different minds. In all likelihood, the meeting will be filled with disagreement, dissatisfaction, and maybe even hard feelings. This exercise will require one person to play the supervisor and another to be the evaluated employee. As only two can play, the rest should observe carefully. Instructors will provide the participants with additional information necessary to complete the exercise.

PART THREE:

CASE 3 Parma Cycle Company: Training the Work Force

As the September 1996 date for the new plant opening drew near, Mary Higgins, director of employee development at Parma Cycle Company in Delta, B.C., grew increasingly nervous. With only six months to train the work force of the new Nova Scotia plant, Mary knew that there was little room for error.

Mary had already arranged to lease a building near the Digby factory site, and some of the machinery for the new plant was being installed in that building for training purposes. Most of the machinery was similar to that already being used at Parma, and Mary had selected trainers from among the supervisory staff at the Parma plant. One machine, however, a robotized frame assembler, was entirely new. The assembler was being purchased from a Japanese firm. Mary had sent two operators to train in the Japanese factory. They were both back.

Mary had made two trips to Digby. She had also retained a training consultant, a management professor from the University of New Brunswick. The training consultant had agreed to help Mary plan the training program and to evaluate the program as it went along. It was at the consultant's suggestion that Mary decided to use a combination of vestibule training and classroom lectures in developing a trained work force prior to factory start-up time. In the past, Parma Cycle had used on-the-job training almost exclusively, but she felt this approach wasn't feasible at the new plant.

As Mary was thinking about how short the time was, the phone rang. It was the human resource director, Jesse Heard, telling her that he was ready for their meeting. When she got to his office, she found him studying a training report she had prepared a few days earlier.

"Mary," said Jesse, "It looks like you have things well under control for the Digby plant. But I don't see anything here about training the employees who are going to be transferred over from this plant."

"Well," said Mary, "they have all been working in bicycle manufacture for quite a while. I thought it might not be necessary to have any formal training for them."

"That's true," said Jesse, "but most of them will be taking different jobs when they move to Digby."

"I'll get on it right away," said Mary.

"What are we going to do about supervisory training at the Digby plant?" asked Jesse.

Mary replied, "I think we'll use the same system we use here for the long haul. We'll bring our supervisors up through the ranks and have quarterly off-site seminars. To start, the supervisors who move from Delta can help train the others."

Jesse asked, "What do you think about bringing the supervisors hired in Digby up here for a few days to help them learn how we do things?" "That's a good idea," said Mary. "We can pair them off with some of our better people."

"That won't help us with performance evaluations, Mary," said Jesse. "You know we're going to use a different system down there. We've decided to use management by objectives down to the supervisory level and a new three-item rating scale for the workers."

"I know that," answered Mary. "I had planned classroom training on that beginning the month after start-up at the Digby plant. I'm going to conduct those sessions myself. Because the performance scores will be used to allocate incentive bonuses, I want to make sure they are consistently assigned."

"Mary," said Jesse, "I'm really impressed with the way you are taking charge of this training effort. Just keep up the good work." "Thank you, Jesse," said Mary. "I'll get back to you next week on the training I recommend for the workers who will transfer from Delta."

QUESTIONS

1. Describe how an untrained person hired in Digby could become a competent machine operator by the time the new plant opens.

2. Do you think Mary needed the training consultant? Why or why not?

3. What do you think of Mary's idea to have the supervisors for the new plant trained by those transferred from B.C.? Explain

PART THREE:

CBC ❀ VIDEO CASE Performance Appraisal and Termination

The two areas in HRM that create the most difficulty for managers are performance appraisal and the general issue of evaluation. Employees frequently criticize performance appraisals as misleading and inadequate, while HR professionals often have difficulty persuading managers to carry out proper performance appraisals. The problem usually stems from poor appraisal design and a lack of adequate training for managers on how to assess and discuss performance constructively. Improving these feedback mechanisms can enhance employee performance, and clarifying performance standards can help focus the appraisal process on measurable criteria, thus avoiding personality issues.

When designing an employee appraisal system, the first step is to involve both managers and employees. The problem with many appraisal programs is that they have been copied from other companies. Often different elements are pieced together from several sources. The result is a grab bag of questions and approaches that have little to do with the employee's work situation. Including managers and employees in the design process ensures the resulting performance appraisal system will have credibility. As well, the tendency will be to avoid techniques that lead to confrontation.

Too many managers implement performance appraisal systems from the top down, causing resentment among employees, who feel they are being disciplined like little children. By inviting input into performance appraisal design, both management and employees can create systems that measure goals while creating healthy working environments.

A second important issue is to design a plan that measures improvement or decline in performance in some quantifiable way. It is important, as well, to focus only on job-related activities. Feedback must be job-specific, not personal. When necessary, criticism should be directed at job behaviour instead of personal attributes. A good appraisal system evaluates groups and sub-groups of specific job responsibilities. The results are then discussed with the employee and a plan is developed to enhance strengths and, if necessary, to improve on weaknesses.

A third consideration in any face-to-face meeting is to stress the positive aspects of performance. Each employee will have strengths and weaknesses. The key is to start with strengths and to build positive, two-way communication. Another helpful method is to ask employees to list their strengths and weaknesses and to provide ideas as to how they could improve on weaknesses. The employee can then discuss the issues that hinder performance.

While evaluation is a complex issue, undoubtedly the most traumatic event in a manager's professional life is the act of firing an employee, as the process is emotionally disturbing and extremely stressful for all participants. There are many tactless and insensitive ways to terminate an employee. It is important that it be done professionally. A professional approach is necessary 1) to protect the organization's name; 2) to make sure the terminated worker understands the reason why he or she is being dismissed and his/her options in the job market; 3) to minimize the effect on other employees.

When terminating an employee, the first step is planning. The meeting should be scheduled as early as possible in the week. The location is important, as well. A private location such as a boardroom, where the manager has a psychological advantage, is usually best. In many cases, it is advisable to have a third party present, perhaps a HRM professional, who will be able to answer any questions related to severance or benefits. Management should know what legal obligations the firm has to the employee with regard to severance and benefits. The manager also should inform the former employee of his/her right to seek independent counsel on the question of whether or not the severance package is fair.

The reasons for termination should be explained in a clear, concise and calm manner. The reasons should not be addressed in detail, but rather left to a letter of termination. Therefore, the meeting should not take more than 15 minutes,

The employee's full range of emotions should be anticipated: anger, disappointment and denial. Management should be supportive of a worker's plight, yet stand firm, stating that the firing is irreversible. Mentioning the terminated worker's accomplishments and talents, without giving false hope, is also important. Individuals who may require professional counselling can be helped by the HR professional.

Terminating an employee and giving employee performance appraisals are difficult processes to manage. Nevertheless, workplace change and increased competition require that both be used. Through planning, participation and feedback, the HR professional can help to create a more humane and progressive environment which has a positive effect on profitability.

QUESTIONS

1. Your boss asks you, as head of Human Resources, what techniques she should use to terminate an employee. What advice would you give her?
2. If you were to design a performance appraisal program what elements would you incorporate? Whose advice would you ask?

Video Resource: "Fireproofing," *Venture* 509 (October 9, 1994).

C H A P T E R

11

Financial Compensation

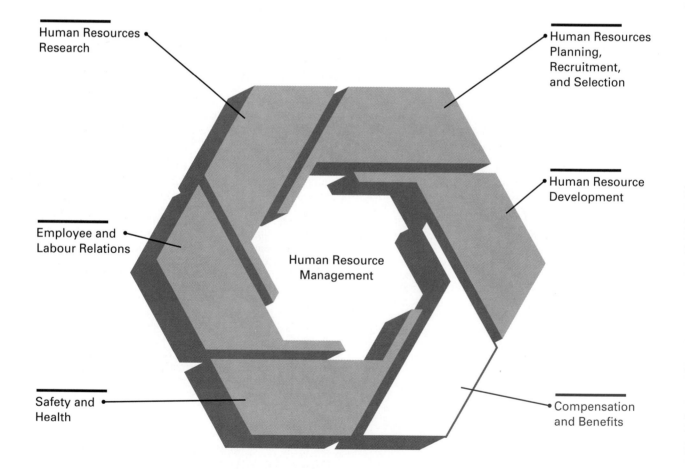

Human Resources Research

Human Resources Planning, Recruitment, and Selection

Human Resource Development

Employee and Labour Relations

Human Resource Management

Safety and Health

Compensation and Benefits

E arl Lewis and his wife are excited as they leave their home for a shopping trip. Earl has just learned that his firm is implementing a new variable pay system and that his long record of high performance will finally pay off. He looks forward to the opportunity to increase his income so he can purchase some needed items for a new home.

Inez Scoggin's anxiety over scheduled chemotherapy for cancer has been somewhat relieved. Her supervisor has assured her that a large portion of her drug costs will be covered by the firm's supplementary health insurance plan.

Trig Ekeland, executive director of the local YM/YWCA, returns home tired from his job each evening no earlier than six o'clock. His salary is small compared to the salaries of many other local managers who have similar responsibilities. Yet, Trig is an exceptionally happy person who believes that his work with youth, civic leaders, and other members of the community is extremely important and worthwhile.

Joanne Abrahamson has been employed by a large manufacturing firm for eight years. Although her pay is not what she would like it to be, her job in the accounts payable department enables her to have contact with some of her best friends. She likes her supervisor and considers the overall working environment to be great. Joanne would not trade jobs with anyone she knows.

ompensation and benefits obviously are important to Earl Lewis and Inez Scoggin, as they are to most employees. However, for Trig and Joanne, other factors in a total compensation package also assume great importance. These components include a pleasant work environment and job satisfaction. Because the concept has many elements, compensation administration is one of the most difficult and challenging human resource areas to manage.

We begin this chapter with an overview of compensation and a discussion of compensation equity. Next, we outline determinants of individual financial compensation, including the influence of the organization and the labour market. We then discuss the job and the role of job evaluation. The employee as a determinant of compensation is then presented, followed by job pricing and other compensation issues.

COMPENSATION: AN OVERVIEW

Compensation refers to all rewards that individuals receive in return for their labour (see Figure 11-1). **Direct financial compensation** consists of pay received in the form of wages, salaries, bonuses, and commissions (Earl Lewis's new paycheque, for example). **Indirect financial compensation** (benefits) includes all financial rewards that are not included in direct compensation. Inez Scoggin's drug plan is an example. As illustrated in Figure 11-1, this form of compensation includes a wide variety of benefits.

Nonfinancial compensation includes the satisfaction a person receives from the job or from the psychological and/or physical environment of the job. Trig Ekeland and Joanne Abrahamson, for example, are receiving important forms of nonfinancial compensation. Trig receives satisfaction from the work itself. Joanne receives nonfinancial compensation from the environment of her job, particularly the contact it provides with friends.

To remain competitive, compensation systems must be developed to reward performance that relates directly to key business goals.[1] In determining effective rewards, however, the uniqueness of each employee must be considered. People have different needs or reasons for working. The most appropriate compensation package will meet these needs. When people are having difficulty providing food, shelter, and clothing for their families, for example, money may be the most important reward. Yet, some people work long hours, receive little pay and still love their work. To a large degree, then, adequate compensation is in the mind of the employee.

COMPENSATION EQUITY

Management must create work environments that attract, motivate, and retain competent employees. As achieving these goals is accomplished largely through a firm's compensation system, managers must strive for compensation equity. **Equity** refers to the perception that one is being treated fairly. When chief executives are paid millions of dollars in one year and receive huge bonuses along with other benefits, for example, serious questions arise within organizations as to what constitutes fairness.[2]

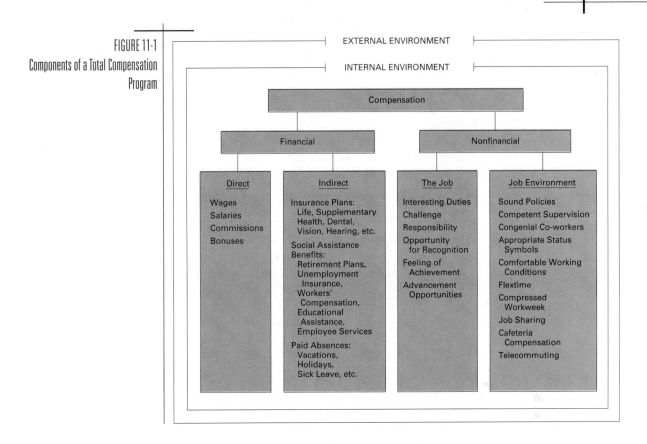

FIGURE 11-1
Components of a Total Compensation Program

A condition of **external equity** exists when a firm's employees are paid comparably to those who perform similar jobs in other firms. Compensation surveys enable organizations to determine the level of external equity. **Internal equity** exists when employees are paid according to the relative value of their jobs within an organization. Job evaluation is a primary means for determining internal equity. **Employee equity** can be defined as a process of ensuring that individuals performing similar jobs for the same firm are rewarded according to factors unique to the employee, such as performance level or seniority. Equity concerns might include salary equity, promotion equity, recognition equity, and raise equity.[3] **Team equity** is achieved when more productive teams receive greater rewards than less productive groups. Performance levels are generally determined through appraisal systems.

Inequity in any category can result in severe morale problems. If employees feel they are being compensated unfairly, they may restrict their efforts or leave the firm, damaging the organization's overall performance. If two accountants in the same firm are performing similar jobs and one is acknowledged to be superior to the other, while both receive equal pay increases, employee equity is denied and the more productive employee is likely to be unhappy.

Most workers are concerned with pay equity, both internal and external. From an employee relations perspective, internal equity is probably more important. Employees, who are likely to have more information about pay issues within their own organization, use these data to form perceptions of equity.[4] On the other hand, to remain viable, an organization must be competitive in the labour market. External equity, therefore, must always be a prominent consideration. The difficulty in maintaining equity on all fronts has long been an organizational dilemma.

Don MacLeod, a principal in D.G.M. Consulting Services of Cambridge, Ontario speaks of the universal perception: "I know for certain that I deserve more." McLeod adds that "compensation negotiations are an arduous process for both sides in the discussion and have proven to be a source of vast animosity throughout history."[5]

DETERMINANTS OF INDIVIDUAL FINANCIAL COMPENSATION

Compensation theory has never been able to provide a completely satisfactory answer to the question of how to determine what an individual is worth on the job market. While no scientific approach is available, a number of relevant factors are typically used to determine individual pay (see Figure 11-2), including the organization, the labour market, the job, and the employee.[6]

There are national trends, too. Although Canadians have borrowed heavily from the United States when designing pay systems, for example, long-term incentive plans now represent approximately 35 percent of basic pay for Canadian executives, far below the 75 percent common in U.S. firms.[7]

THE ORGANIZATION AS A DETERMINANT OF FINANCIAL COMPENSATION

Managers tend to view financial compensation as both an expense and an asset. Compensation is an expense, in the sense that it reflects the cost of labour. In service industries, for example, labour costs account for more than 50 percent of all expenses. Financial compensation is an asset, however, when the system induces employees to put forth their best efforts and to remain in their jobs. Compensation programs can influence employee work attitudes and behaviour, encouraging workers to be more productive.[8]

Corporate culture has a major influence on an individual's financial compensation. Management often—formally or informally—establishes compensation policies that determine whether the organization will be a pay leader or a pay follower, or will strive for an average position in the labour market. **Pay leaders** pay higher wages and salaries than competing firms. They feel able to choose high-quality, productive employees from a larger pool of better qualified applicants than is available to companies paying lower salaries. The **going rate** is the average pay that most employers provide for the same job in a particular area or industry. In many organizations, there is a policy that calls for paying the going rate. Managers at these organizations believe that they can employ qualified people while still remaining competitive by keeping labour costs down. Managers who choose to pay below the going rate because of poor finances or because they believe that they do not require highly capable employees are **pay followers.** This policy often leads to difficulties. Consider the case of Melvin Denney.

FIGURE 11-2
Primary Determinants of Individual
Financial Compensation

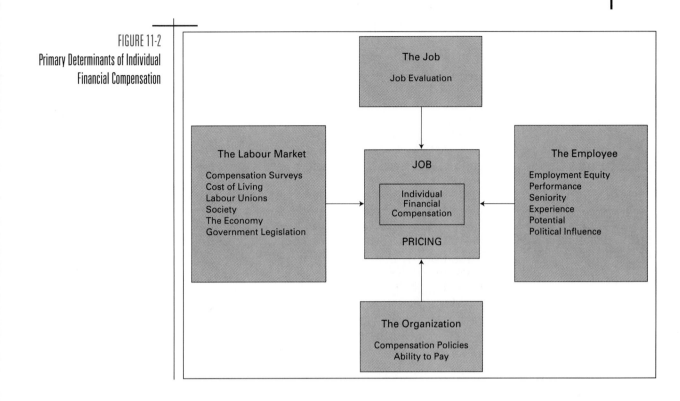

Melvin Denney managed a large, but financially strapped farming operation in Saskatchewan. Although no formal policies had been established,
Melvin had a practice of paying the lowest wage possible. For example, one
of his farmhands, George McMillan, was paid minimum wage. During a
period of three weeks, George wrecked a tractor, severely damaged a combine, and stripped the gears in a new pickup truck. Melvin grumbled,
"George is the most expensive darned employee I've ever had."

As Melvin discovered, paying the lowest possible wage didn't save
money; the practice was extremely expensive. In addition to relatively unproductive workers, pay followers may have a high turnover rate, as their
most qualified employees often leave to join better paying organizations. Incompetent or disgruntled employees can have particularly disastrous consequences for the firm if they are in positions that involve customer contact.
No firm can tolerate continued poor customer service in today's competitive
global environment.

The organizational level at which compensation decisions are made can
also affect pay. To ensure consistency, these decisions are often made by senior managers. There are advantages, however, to making pay decisions at
lower levels, where there is better information about employee performance,
as top-level executives can err when they make decisions in isolation from
lower-level managers.

An assessment of ability to pay is also an important factor in determining
pay levels. Financially successful firms tend to provide higher than average
compensation.[9] An organization's financial strength, however, establishes only

the upper pay ranges. To arrive at a specific pay level, other factors must be considered. Indeed, poorly-designed compensation systems can harm an entire organization. Managers in many Canadian firms are no longer content with long-standing compensation practices. As one has survey suggested, there is a dramatic increase in the number of companies in which compensation schemes linked to "quality performance" are planned.[10]

THE LABOUR MARKET AS A DETERMINANT OF FINANCIAL COMPENSATION

Many employees judge the fairness of their compensation against the standard of the going rate within the labour market. The **labour market** comprises all potential employees located within a geographical recruitment area. For managers or specialized professionals, this recruitment area may extend nationally or even internationally, Markets for operative employees are usually more localized, and the going rate can vary considerably from one labour market to another within the same country. Secretarial jobs, for example, may carry an average salary of $29 000 per year in a large, urban community but only $18 000 or less in a small town. Compensation managers must be aware of these differences in order to compete successfully for employees.

Compensation Surveys

Large organizations routinely conduct compensation surveys to determine prevailing pay rates and benefits within labour markets. These surveys not only determine the low, high, and average salaries for a given position, but provide a sense of what competitors are paying.[11]

Prior to conducting a compensation survey, decisions are made to determine 1) the geographic area of the survey, 2) the specific firms to be contacted, and 3) the jobs to include. The geographic area is often defined from employment records, which indicate the maximum distance employees are willing to travel to work. The firms to be contacted are often from the same industry, but may also include others that compete for the same skills. Because obtaining data on all jobs may not be feasible, the human resource department often surveys only benchmark jobs. A **benchmark job** is one that is well known in the company and industry, one that represents the entire job structure, and one in which a large percentage of the workforce is employed.

A primary difficulty in conducting a compensation survey involves the determination of comparable jobs. Job titles have little value in compensation surveys; different approaches to job design and organizational structure may mean that a job in one company resembles only roughly a job with a similar title in another. Instead, the analyst must use job descriptions when requesting compensation data.

There are other ways to obtain compensation data. Periodically, some professional organizations conduct surveys. The Society of Management Accountants, for example, publishes a yearly survey organized by province. As well, Statistics Canada issues a number of reports that detail salaries and wages. Labour Force Annual Averages and Employment Earnings and Hours are but two of many sources managers can use, especially when looking for data segmented by province, industry, age groupings, or sex. They may supplement these data with commercially available survey information supplied by other organizations like Hay Management Consultants Ltd. and William M. Mercer Ltd.

Cost of Living

The logic for using cost of living as a partial pay determinant is that if prices rise over a period of time and pay does not, *real pay* actually decreases. A pay increase must be roughly equivalent to the increased cost of living to maintain the level of real wages. For example, if an individual earns $24 000 during a year in which the average rate of inflation is five percent, a $100-per-month pay increase will be necessary merely to maintain that person's standard of living.

People living on fixed incomes (primarily the elderly and the poor) are most affected by inflation, but many employees also suffer financially. In some firms, therefore, pay increases are indexed to the inflation rate, even to the point of sacrificing *merit money* to provide across-the-board increases.

Labour Unions

The collective bargaining process between management and unions obviously has great potential impact on compensation decisions. The union affects company compensation policies in three important areas: 1) the standards used in making compensation decisions, 2) wage differentials, and 3) payment methods.[12]

When a union uses comparable pay as a standard in making compensation demands, the employer must obtain accurate labour market data. When cost of living is emphasized, management may be pressured to include a **cost-of-living allowance (COLA)** as part of the payment package. This clause in a labour agreement means that wages automatically increase as the Statistics Canada cost-of-living index rises.

Management may want to use incentive schemes to encourage greater productivity. Implementation of these plans, however, may be impossible if the union strongly opposes this approach. Employee acceptance is essential, and union opposition may make the plan unworkable. It should be noted, however, that many unions are forging new alliances based on mutual gains for both labour and management. Linda McKenna, vice-president, personnel and industrial relations, Western Canada, for Molson Breweries, for example, has described attempts to create a different, more cooperative approach to labour relations, in order to improve "the operation's ability to perform in an increasingly competitive market, thus generating tangible benefits for all stakeholders."[13] As these relationships become more common, it may be possible to craft more mutually advantageous payment systems. Chapter 15 describes both traditional and changing labour relations in Canada.

Society

Compensation paid to employees affects a firm's prices for its goods or services. For this reason, consumers may also be interested in compensation decisions. Attempts to increase Canadian telephone rates have generally met with consumer resistance, for example,[14] as have increased insurance premiums.[15]

Businesses in a given labour market are also concerned with the pay practices of new firms locating in their area. In one instance, when the management of a large electronics firm announced plans to locate a branch plant in a relatively small community, it was confronted by local civic leaders. Their questions largely concerned the firm's wage and salary rates. Subtle pressure was applied to keep the company's salaries comparable to other wages in the community. The electronics firm agreed to begin operations with initial compensation at a lower level than it usually paid. But the firm's management made it clear that a series of pay increases would be given over a period of two years to maintain its own pay leader policy.

The Economy

The economy also affects financial compensation decisions. A depressed economy generally increases the labour supply, serving to lower the average wage rate. Labour unions, government, and society are all less likely to press for pay increases in a depressed economy. Conversely, in most cases, the cost of living will rise in an expanding economy, exerting upward pressure on pay levels. As Western economies swing through their "boom-to-recession" cycles, demands for increased wages tend to fluctuate as well.

Legislation[16]

Federal and provincial laws also affect compensation. Employment standards legislation sets out minimum compensation. In Canada, both the federal parliament and the provinces have the power to enact labour laws that regulate compensation. Federal powers are limited to those industries outlined in Figure 13-1 and to the Yukon and Northwest Territories (although, in practice, territorial governments have the same powers over labour standards as the provinces). With minor exceptions, provincial legislatures regulate most other aspects of commerce within their boundaries.

HOURS OF WORK AND OVERTIME PAY

By 1900, Factory and Mining Acts, the forerunners of modern employment standards legislation, had been passed in most provinces. From these beginnings can be traced our present-day concern with the conditions under which individuals work. These laws, however, reflect Canada's diversity.

> There is little consistency across the country in legislation on hours of work and overtime. In some jurisdictions there is real regulation of the permitted hours of work and in others there is none; in some there is an elaborate mechanism for creating exceptions and in others bureaucracy is seldom involved; in some the overtime pay provisions are apparently intended to protect all employees, in others only those working at the minimum wage level.[17]

Nonetheless, there are two common concepts: the standard and the maximum hours that can be worked per week. Within this context, there are ranges. Similarly, provisions for overtime vary across jurisdictions (Figure 11-3).

MINIMUM WAGES

Attempts to regulate the minimum wage date from 1900 with the passage of the federal Fair Wages Policy. It was not until 1920, however, that legislation (six provinces) was in place to protect the most vulnerable and exploited groups: women and child labourers. Minimum Wage Orders covering males began to be passed during the late 1930s, but did not become widespread until the 1950s. Incredibly, as recently as 1974 there were differences in minimum wage levels payable to men and women. As well, many provinces enacted "geographical differentials" whereby employers could pay lower wages in rural areas, and youth differentials were common until they were repealed under the Charter of Rights and Freedoms (1982).

Even today, there are a variety of systems too detailed to outline here. Most Canadians, however, are covered by the rates listed in Figure 11-4.

EQUAL PAY FOR EQUAL WORK

Equal-pay-for-equal-work legislation is almost universal in Canada. Typically, these laws prohibit employers from paying less to women who perform the same jobs as men. This concept allows for differences based on seniority, merit, or quantity of output. Most legislation (again, there are exceptions) allows individuals to initiate legal action or to complain before a tribunal or Employment Standards Officer.

EQUAL PAY FOR WORK OF EQUAL VALUE

This topic has generated intense debate within Canadian society.[18] Since legislation varies widely, individual Acts must be consulted, but the general intent is to end discriminatory compensation practices, whereby there are differences in wages between males and females employed within the same organization and performing work of equal value.

The Canadian Human Rights Act (federal) and The Quebec Charter of Rights and Freedoms apply concepts to all organizations under their jurisdiction, in the private as well as the public sector. Federally, Labour Canada enforces a three-step process—education, monitoring, inspection—to ensure compliance in federally-regulated workplaces. All other jurisdictions have some form of legislation or regulations designed to protect women from wage discrimination.

PAY EQUITY

Similar to equal pay for work of equal value, pay equity legislation seeks "to redress systemic gender discrimination in compensation performed by employees in female-dominated job classes, usually in the public and parapublic

Jurisdiction	Standard	Maximum	Overtime Paid After:	Exclusions[*]
Federal	8 hrs/day 40 hrs/wk	48 hrs/wk	8 hrs/day; 40 hrs/wk $1^{1/2}$ times pay	averaging allowed
Alberta	8 hrs/day 44 hrs/wk	within a 12-hr period/day	8 hrs/day; 44 hrs/wk $1^{1/2}$ times pay	overtime agreements allowable
British Columbia	8 hrs/day 40 hrs/wk	— —	8 hrs/day; 40 hrs/wk $1^{1/2}$ times pay 11 hrs/day; 48 hrs/wk 2 times pay	
Manitoba	8 hrs/day 40 hrs/wk	8 hrs/day 40 hrs/wk	8 hrs/day; 40 hrs/wk $1^{1/2}$ times pay	professionals and some others
New Brunswick	—	—	44 hrs/wk $1^{1/2}$ times pay	—
Newfoundland	40 hrs/wk	—	40 hrs/wk $1^{1/2}$ times pay	professionals; students
Nova Scotia	48 hrs/wk	—	48 hrs/wk $1^{1/2}$ times pay	managerial and some others
Ontario	44 hrs/wk	8 hrs/day 48 hrs/wk	44 hrs/wk $1^{1/2}$ times pay	managerial and some others
PEI	48 hrs/wk	—	48 hrs/wk $1^{1/2}$ times pay	salespersons on commission and others
Quebec	44 hrs/wk	—	44 hrs/wk $1^{1/2}$ times pay	many: see Act
Saskatchewan	8 hrs/day 40 hrs/wk	44 hrs/wk	8 hrs/day 40 hrs/wk $1^{1/2}$ times pay	managerial, professionals and others

FIGURE 11-3 **Hours of Work and Overtime Pay**

*Note: Exceptions tend to be extensive; the appropriate legislation should be consulted.

Source: Data obtained from Human Resources Development Canada, Employment Standards Legislation in Canada (1995-96). (Ottawa: Canada Communications Group, Minister of Supply and Services. DSS Cat. #631-781/1996 E.)

FIGURE 11-4
Minimum Wage Rates

Jurisdiction	Rate	Effective Date
Federal	$4.00	May 26, 1986
Alberta	$5.00	April 1, 1992
British Columbia	$7.00	October 1, 1995
Manitoba	$5.00	
	$5.25	
	$5.40	January 1, 1996
New Brunswick	$5.00	October 1, 1991
Newfoundland*	$4.75	April 1, 1991
Northwest Territories*	$6.50 or	
	$7.00†	April 1, 1991
Nova Scotia	$5.15	January 1, 1993
Ontario	$6.85	January 1, 1995
Prince Edward Island	$4.75	April 1, 1991
Quebec	$6.00	October 1, 1994
Saskatchewan	$5.35	December 1, 1992
Yukon Territory	$6.72	October 1, 1994

*Sixteen years of age and over.
†For areas distant from the NWT highway system.
Source: Adapted from *Employment Standards Legislation in Canada* (Ottawa: Minister of Supply and Services), p. 34.

sectors."[19] The purpose, then, is to change past practice, so that female-dominated jobs (e.g., librarian) are not paid less than male-dominated jobs (e.g., electrician) found to be of equal value.

In much of Canada, pay equity programs apply only to the public sector. The status of pay equity may depend upon the political climate, or the social philosophy of the party in power, as successive governments amend the legislation.[20]

THE JOB AS A DETERMINANT OF FINANCIAL COMPENSATION

Individual jobs are a major determinant of financial compensation levels, as employees are paid for the value attached to duties, responsibilities, and other job-related factors like working conditions. Techniques for determining a job's relative worth include job analysis, job descriptions, and job evaluation.

Job Analysis and Job Descriptions

Before the relative difficulty or value of jobs can be determined, their content must be defined through the job analysis process. As explained in Chapter 3, job analysis is a systematic method of determining the skills and the knowledge required for performing jobs. The job description is the primary product of job analysis, consisting of a written document that describes job duties and responsibilities. Job descriptions are an essential part of all job evaluation systems, the success of which depends largely on the accuracy and clarity of the job description.

Job Evaluation

Job evaluation is a technique or a process used to determine the relative value of one job in relation to every other job. The purpose of job evaluation is to eliminate internal inequities stemming from illogical pay structures. For example, a pay inequity exists if the mailroom supervisor earns more money than the accounting supervisor. More specifically, job evaluation has the potential to

- describe the organization's job structure;
- bring equity and order to the relationships among jobs;
- develop a hierarchy of job value that can be used to create a pay structure; and
- achieve a consensus among managers and employees regarding jobs and pay within the firm.[21]

The purposes of job evaluation relate closely to the concept of internal pay equity. Although individuals may be concerned with external equity, most accept that their pay should be determined by 1) their contribution to the organization and 2) the pay and the contributions of fellow employees performing comparable work. Employees quickly become unhappy when they perceive that someone in the organization receives more pay for performing work at the same or a lower level.

The human resource department is usually responsible for administering job evaluation programs. The job evaluation process, however, is typically conducted by a committee consisting of managers from different functional areas. A typical committee might include the human resource director as chairperson and the vice-presidents for finance, production, and marketing. Committee composition, however, often depends on the type and the level of jobs being evaluated. Including employee representatives is also wise, since results are more likely to be accepted.

It is important for the committee to always keep personalities out of the evaluation process. Maeve Quaid, in her book, *Job Evaluation: The Myth of Equitable Assessment,*[22] argues strongly that it is impossible to be completely objective when assigning relative worth to jobs. Further, she suggests that senior managers sometimes manipulate job evaluation systems, reintroducing biases to conform to organizational politics. While hers is a minority view, Quaid's work should alert both managers and employees to the possibility that job evaluation systems can be subverted, either for personal gain or for the advantage of favourite employees.

Care must be taken, then, when implementing job evaluation programs. In small and medium-sized organizations, job evaluation expertise is often lacking and management may elect to use an outside consultant to enhance objectivity. Four job evaluation techniques are in general use: ranking, classification, factor comparison, and points rating, but there are innumerable variations of these methods.[23] A method is often modified to fit a particular work environment.

RANKING METHOD

The simplest of the four job evaluation methods is the **ranking method**. The raters examine each job description and arrange the jobs in order according to their perceived value to the company. This non-quantitative procedure is almost the same as that discussed in Chapter 10, when rankings are used for performance appraisals. The only difference is that jobs, not people, are being evaluated. As with all the methods, the first step in ranking jobs is conducting job analysis and writing job descriptions.

CLASSIFICATION METHOD

The **classification method** involves defining a number of classes or grades to describe a group of jobs. Using this method, the raters compare the job description with the class description. The class description that most closely agrees with the job description determines the job's classification. For example, in evaluating a word processing clerk, the description might include: 1) data enter letters from prepared drafts; 2) address envelopes; 3) deliver completed correspondence to unit supervisor.

Assuming that the remainder of the job description includes similar routine work, this job would most likely be placed in the classification called "clerk," rather than "administrative assistant," which might be the next highest classification. Clearly, defining grade descriptions for many diverse jobs is difficult. For this reason, some organizations have developed systems that combine classification with other methods of job evaluation.[24]

FACTOR COMPARISON METHOD

Factor comparison is more complex than the two previously discussed qualitative methods. When using the **factor comparison method**, raters need not consider the entire job. Instead they make decisions on separate aspects, or factors, of the job, assuming there are five universal job factors:

- mental requirements, which reflect mental traits such as intelligence, reasoning, and imagination;
- skill, which pertains to facility in muscular coordination and training in the interpretation of sensory impressions;
- physical requirements, which involve sitting, standing, walking, lifting, etc.;
- responsibilities, which cover areas such as raw materials, money, records, and supervision; and
- working conditions, which reflect the environmental influences of noise, illumination, ventilation, hazards, and hours worked.[25]

A committee first ranks each of the selected benchmark jobs as to relative degree of difficulty for each of the five factors. The committee then allocates total pay rates for each job to each factor, on the basis of the importance of the respective factor to the job. This step is the most difficult to explain satisfactorily to employees, because the decision is highly subjective.

A job comparison scale, reflecting rankings and money allocations, is developed next (see Figure 11-5). All jobs shown, except for *Programmer Analyst*, are original benchmark jobs. The scale is then used to rate other jobs in the group being evaluated. The raters compare each job, factor by factor, with those appearing on the job comparison scale. Then they place them on the chart in an appropriate position. For example, suppose the committee is evaluating the programmer analyst job. The committee determines that this position should rank lower on "mental requirements" than a systems analyst but higher than a programmer. The job would then be placed on the chart between these two jobs, at a point agreed upon by the committee. In this example, the committee evaluated the mental requirements factor at $3.80 (a point between the $4.00 and $3.40 values that had been allocated to the benchmark jobs, systems analyst and programmer). The committee repeats this procedure for the remaining four factors and then for all jobs to be evaluated. Adding the values of the five factors for each job yields the total monetary value (wage) for the job.

The factor comparison method provides a systematic approach to job evaluation. At least two problems, however, should be noted. The assumption that the five factors are universal has been questioned, because certain factors may be more appropriate to some job groups than others. Also, while the steps are not overly complicated, they are somewhat detailed and may be difficult to explain.

	Mental	Skill	Physical	Responsibility	Working Conditions
$4.00 3.80	Systems Analyst (Programmer Analyst)			Systems Analyst	
3.50	Programmer			Programmer	
		Data Entry Clerk Console Operator Programmer			
2.50	Console Operator	Systems Analyst			
2.00				Console Operator	
1.50	Data Entry Clerk			Data Entry Clerk	Data Entry Clerk Console Operator Systems Analyst Programmer
1.00			Data Entry Clerk Systems Analyst Programmer Console Operator		

FIGURE 11-5 Job Comparison Scale

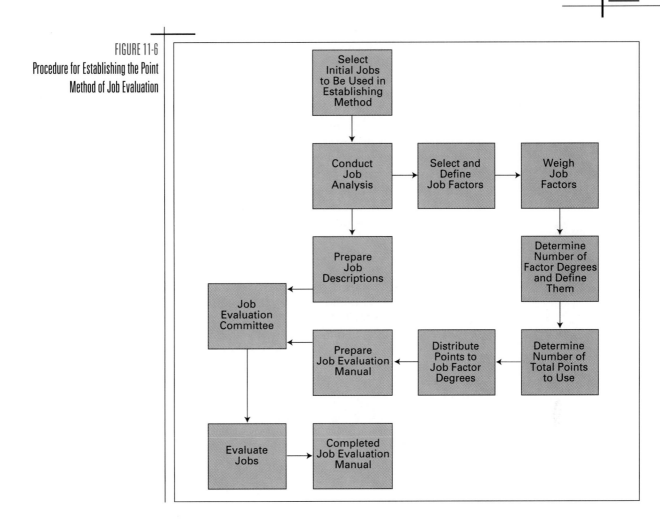

POINT METHOD

When using the **point**, or **points rating**, **method**, raters assign numerical values to specific job components or factors. The sum of these values provides a quantitative assessment of a job's relative worth.[26] Many job evaluation plans in use today stem from some variation of the point method.

The point method requires selection of job factors according to the nature of the specific group of jobs being evaluated. Normally, a separate plan is developed for each group of similar jobs (job clusters) in the organization. Production jobs, clerical jobs, and sales jobs are examples of job clusters. The procedure for establishing a point method is illustrated in Figure 11-6. After determining the group of jobs to be studied, analysts conduct job analyses and write job descriptions. A job evaluation committee will later use these descriptions as the basis for making evaluation decisions.

It should be noted that some consultants are moving away from job descriptions toward position analysis questionnaires (PAQ), as the formal job description takes too much time to write. The PAQ can be completed independently by both the employee and the manager; the results are then compared, discrepancies are discussed, and a final list of job duties, responsibilities, and authorities is compiled.

Next, the analysts select and define the factors to be used in measuring job value. These factors become the standards used for job evaluation. They can best be identified by individuals who are thoroughly familiar with the content of the jobs under consideration. Education, experience, job knowledge, mental effort, physical effort, responsibility, and working conditions are examples of factors typically used. Each factor should be significant in helping to differentiate jobs. Factors that exist in equal amounts in all jobs obviously would not serve this purpose. As an example, in evaluating a company's clerical jobs, the working conditions factor would be of little value in differentiating jobs if all jobs in the cluster were located in the same building. The number of factors used varies with the nature of the job cluster, according to the subjective judgement of the committee.

The committee must establish factor weights according to their relative importance in the jobs to be evaluated. For example, if experience is considered quite important for a particular job cluster, this factor might be weighted as much as 35 percent. In an office cluster, physical effort (if used at all) would be assigned a low weight—perhaps less than 10 percent.

The next step is to determine the number of degrees for each job factor and to define each degree. Degrees represent distinct levels associated with a particular factor. The number of degrees needed for each factor depends on job requirements. If all jobs in a particular cluster required virtually the same level of formal education (a high school diploma, for example), fewer degrees would be appropriate than if some jobs in the cluster required advanced degrees.

The committee then determines the total number of points to be used in the plan. The number may vary, but 500 or 1000 points may work well. The use of a smaller number of points (for example, 50) would not provide the proper distinctions among jobs, whereas a larger number (such as 50 000) would be unnecessarily cumbersome. The total number of points in a plan indicates the maximum points that any job could receive.

The next step is to distribute point values to job factor degrees, as shown in Figure 11-7.

FIGURE 11-7
An Example of the Point System (Using a Total of 500 Points)

Job Factor	Weight	Degree of Factor 1	2	3	4	5
1. Education	50%	50	100	150	200	250
2. Responsibility	30%	30	70	110	150	
3. Physical Effort	12%	12	24	36	48	60
4. Working Conditions	8%	8	24	40		

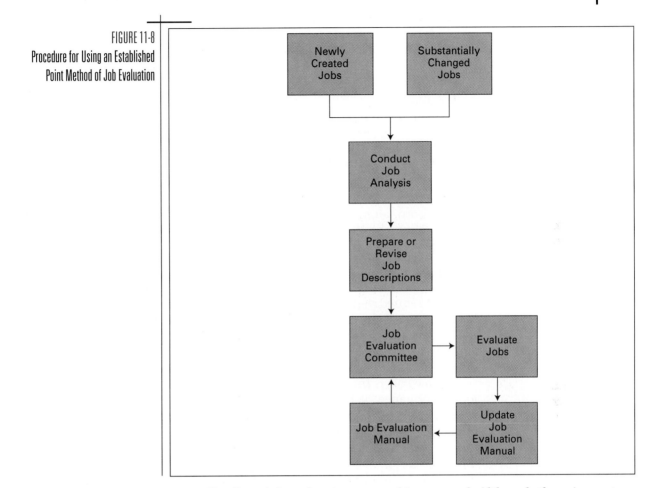

FIGURE 11-8
Procedure for Using an Established Point Method of Job Evaluation

Finally, a job evaluation manual is prepared. Although there is no standard format, the manual often contains an introductory section, factor and degree definitions, and job descriptions.

The job evaluation committee then evaluates jobs in each cluster by comparing each job description with the factors in the job evaluation manual. Point plans have been criticized for the amount of time and effort required to design them and for supporting traditional bureaucratic management.[27] A redeeming feature of the method, however, is that once developed, the plan may be used over a long period of time.

The procedure for using an established point method is presented in Figure 11-8. As new jobs are created and the contents of old jobs changed substantially, job analysis must be conducted and job descriptions rewritten. The job evaluation committee evaluates the jobs and updates the manual. Only when job factors change, or for some reason the weights assigned become inappropriate, does the plan become obsolete.

It should be noted that not all organizations create their own job evaluation system. There are many validated programs for sale. Typically, a consulting firm would be contacted. One such firm is KPMG, with offices across Canada. KPMG representatives market a job evaluation plan called the Aiken Plan consisting of nine factors:

- complexity judgement
- education
- experience
- initiative
- result of errors
- contacts
- supervision—character
                —scope
- physical demands
- working conditions

This plan, already validated, is sold to clients (e.g., The Toronto Transit Commission), along with appropriate support from company job-evaluation experts. Thus, the long process of setting up a unique job evaluation system is avoided.

THE HAY GUIDE CHART-PROFILE METHOD (HAY PLAN)[28]

A highly refined version of the point method is marketed in Canada by Hay Management Consultants. The **Hay guide chart-profile method** contains only a few factors: know-how, problem solving, accountability, and, where appropriate, working conditions. Point values are assigned to these factors to determine the final point profile for any job.

Know-how is the total of all knowledge and skills needed for satisfactory job performance. It has three dimensions: the amount of practical, specialized, or scientific knowledge required; the ability to coordinate functions or units; and the ability to deal effectively with people. *Problem solving* is the degree of original thinking required by the job in analyzing, evaluating, creating, reasoning, and making conclusions. Problem solving has two dimensions: the thinking environment in which problems are solved (from strict routine to abstractly defined); and the thinking challenge presented by the problems (from repetitive to uncharted). Problem solving is expressed as a percentage of know-how, since people use what they know to think and make decisions. *Accountability* is the responsibility for action and accompanying consequences. The three dimensions of accountability are the degree of freedom the job incumbent has to act, the job impact on end results, and the job's financial impact.

The Hay Plan is an extremely popular approach to determining compensation. It is used by some 5000 employers worldwide. In Canada over 600 organizations use the system, including the majority of those in the Financial Post Top 500 listing.[29] The popularity of the Hay Plan gives it an important advantage: It facilitates job comparison between firms. Thus, the method serves to determine both internal and external equity.

A NOTE OF DISAGREEMENT

Despite their worldwide use, there have been questions about the fairness of points-based evaluation systems. One expert has protested:

In reality, the use of numbers creates an illusion of objectivity, measurement and "science". However, enumeration of subjective assessments does not render these measurements any more objective than they were in the first place. . . . The factors considered in most job evaluation systems are not only subjective. They are artifacts of our past."[30]

To replace points-based systems, he has suggested a method that uses "Time Span of Discretion" (TSOD), defined as "the target (not actual) time to complete the longest task (elapsed time, from start to finish) for which the incumbent is held responsible. The longer the TSOD the more complex the task. It has been claimed that TSOD works better than job evaluation point factors.[31]

Given the immense number of organizations that use points-based systems, it is unlikely that an alternative will become accepted in the near future. It should be noted, however, that HR professionals are searching constantly for better methods, so that no matter how widespread a practice becomes, it is not immune to criticism and, ultimately, to change.

Questions have been asked for decades as to which is the best plan. In a sample of 16 organizations, one early study found that jobs were rated very much alike regardless of which job evaluation plan was used.[32] But other authors have disagreed, concluding that choice of job evaluation method does influence relative value and thus, compensation levels.[33]

Most recently, Professor J. B. Cunningham from the School of Public Administration, University of Victoria and Stephen Graham from B.C.'s Ministry of Health completed a study based on government jobs. They found that "the job classification and point rating plans offer the most assistance in rating individual jobs. Raters had a higher level of agreement using the job classification plan than in the factor comparison and ranking plans."[34] In addition, "evaluators using the point rating plan were more consistently reliable for rating different types of jobs."[35] It must be remembered that this study was conducted in a government setting. Still, the results suggest that if applied objectively (see previous comments by Quaid) by well-trained evaluators, job evaluation can be an effective tool on which to base a compensation system, although the more sophisticated techniques are likely to yield more accurate results.

JOB PRICING

The primary considerations in pricing jobs are organizational policies, the labour market, and the job itself. If allowances are to be made for individual factors, they too must be considered. Recall that the process of job evaluation results in a job hierarchy. It might be shown, for example, that a senior accountant is more valuable to the organization than a computer operator, who, in turn, is more valuable than a senior invoice clerk. At this point, the relative value of these jobs to the company is known, but their absolute value isn't. Placing a dollar value on the worth of a job is called **job pricing**, a procedure that takes place after the job has been evaluated and the relative value of each job has been determined. As shown in Figure 11-2, however, additional factors should be considered in determining the job's absolute value. Firms often use pay grades and pay ranges in the job pricing process.

Pay Grades

A **pay grade** is a grouping of similar jobs, designed to simplify the job pricing process, in that it is much more convenient to price 15 pay grades than 200 separate jobs. The rationale behind this approach is similar to the common academic practice of grouping grades of 90 to 100 into an *A* category, grades of 80 to 89 into a *B*, etc. A false implication of preciseness is also avoided. (While job evaluation plans may be systematic, none is scientific.)

Plotting jobs on a scatter diagram is often useful in determining the appropriate number of pay grades. In Figure 11-9, for example, each dot on the scatter diagram represents one job. The vertical position of the dot represents pay, and the horizontal position evaluated points, which reflect relative worth. By following this procedure, it is likely that a certain point spread will work satisfactorily. In this diagram, for example, a 100-point spread in evaluated points (with a total of 500 points) constitutes a pay grade. Although each dot represents one job, there may be dozens of individuals who fill that one job. The large dot at the lower left represents data entry clerk, evaluated at 75 points. That job's hourly rate ($7.90) represents either the average wage currently being paid for the job, or its market rate, depending on how management wants to price jobs.

A **wage curve** (or pay curve) is fitted to the plotted points in order to create a smooth progression between pay grades. The line is drawn to minimize the distance between all dots. This line—a line of *best fit*—may be straight or curved. When the point system is used, however, a straight line usually results (see Figure 11-9). Two approaches used in drawing this wage line are the least squares line (a statistical version) and the less sophisticated *eyeball* approach. Some compensation specialists use the latter because it's simpler and because the value given to each point was derived by consensus among committee members, not by statistical analysis. It makes little sense to take qualitatively determined inputs and to analyze them statistically.

Pay Ranges

The next step is to decide whether all individuals performing the same job will receive equal pay or whether pay ranges will be used. A **pay range** includes a minimum and a maximum pay rate with enough variance between the two to allow for significant pay differences. Pay ranges are generally preferred because they allow employees to be paid according to length of service and quality of performance. When pay ranges are used, a method must be developed to advance individuals through the range. Although in many organizations pay increases are based on seniority, in others only outstanding performers are allowed to advance to the top of their pay ranges.

Referring again to Figure 11-9, note that anyone can readily determine the minimum, midpoint, and maximum pay rates per hour for each of the five pay grades. For example, for pay grade 5, the minimum rate is $12.20, the midpoint is $13.50, and the maximum is $14.80. The minimum rate is normally the rate a person receives when joining the firm. The maximum pay rate represents the maximum an employee can receive for that job, regardless of how well or how long the job is performed. A person at the top of a pay grade would have to be promoted into a job in a higher pay grade in

FIGURE 11-9
Scatter Diagram of Evaluated Jobs
Illustrating the Wage Curve, Pay
Grades, and Rating Ranges

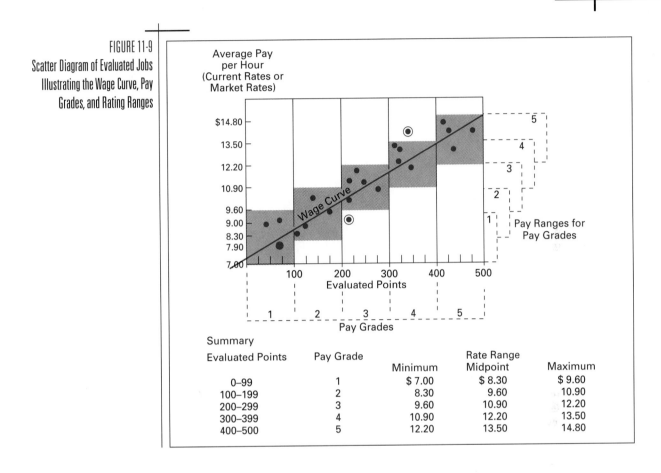

Summary

Evaluated Points	Pay Grade	Rate Range		
		Minimum	Midpoint	Maximum
0–99	1	$ 7.00	$ 8.30	$ 9.60
100–199	2	8.30	9.60	10.90
200–299	3	9.60	10.90	12.20
300–399	4	10.90	12.20	13.50
400–500	5	12.20	13.50	14.80

order to receive pay increases unless 1) an across-the-board adjustment is made, or 2) the job is reevaluated and placed in a higher pay grade.

Numerous managers have agonized over trying to justify a pay system to an employee who is doing a tremendous job but is at the top of a pay grade. Consider this situation:

Everyone in the department realized that Marta Vazquez was the best secretary in the company. At times she appeared to do the job of three secretaries. Colin Merideth, Marta's supervisor, was especially impressed. Recently he had a discussion with the human resource manager to see what could be done to get a raise for Martha. After Colin described the situation, the human resource manager's only reply was, "Sorry, Colin. Marta is already at the top of her pay grade. There is nothing you can do except have her job upgraded or promote her to another position."

Situations such as Marta's present managers with a perplexing problem. Many would be inclined to make an exception to the system and give Marta a salary increase. However, this action would violate the basic principle that every job in the organization has a maximum value, regardless of how well it is performed. In addition, making exceptions to the compensation plan could soon result in widespread pay inequities, as other employees would demand special treatment as well.

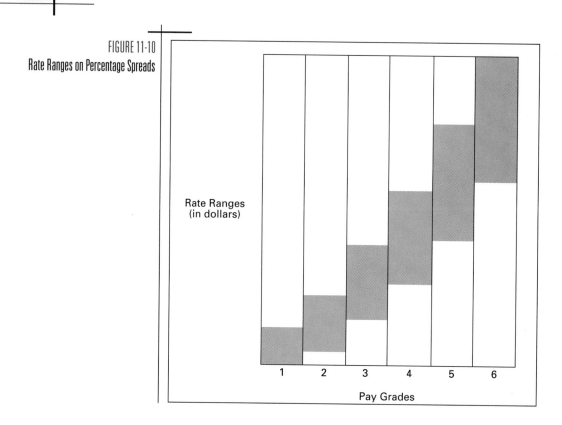

FIGURE 11-10
Rate Ranges on Percentage Spreads

The rate ranges, therefore, should be large enough to provide incentives to do a better job. At times, only very large pay differentials are meaningful, especially at higher job levels. This is the logic for having the rate range become increasingly wide at each consecutive level (see Figure 11-10). Consider, for example, what a $100 per month salary increase would mean to a file clerk earning $1800 per month (a 5.5 percent increase) compared with a senior cost accountant earning $4000 per month (a 2.5 percent increase). Assuming an inflation rate of 3 percent, the file clerk's real pay would increase somewhat while the cost accountant would fall behind.

Some workplace conditions do not favour pay ranges. In a situation in which all or most jobs are routine, for example, with little opportunity for employees to vary their productivity, a single, or fixed, rate system may be more appropriate. When single rates are used, everyone working the same job receives the same pay, regardless of seniority or productivity.

Adjusting Pay Rates

When pay ranges have been determined and jobs assigned to pay grades, it may become obvious that some jobs are overpaid and others underpaid. Underpaid jobs are normally brought up to the minimum of the appropriate pay range as soon as possible. Referring again to Figure 11-9, the lower circled dot represents a job evaluated at about 225 points, enough to fall in pay grade 3 (200-299 points). Employees working in this job, however, are being paid $9.00 per hour, 60 cents per hour less than the minimum for the pay grade ($9.60 per hour). Some jobs in pay grade 2 and even in pay grade 1 are paid more. Good management practice would be to correct this inequity as rapidly as possible, by placing the job in the proper pay grade and increasing the pay of those who work in that job.

A word of caution: Suppose there were a large number of employees in the job just described; immediately increasing the rate by 60 cents per hour might place a considerable strain on the organization. Assuming a 40-hour week, for every 100 employees in the job, payroll costs would rise $2400 weekly or $124 800 per year. Although management may want to increase pay immediately, the raise may have to be phased in over a period of months or even years.

Overpaid jobs present more of a problem. In Figure 11-9, the circled dot near the top represents a job overpaid for pay grade 4. Employees in this job earn $14.00 per hour, or 50 cents more than the maximum for the pay grade. This type of overpayment is referred to as a "red circle" rate.

An ideal solution to the overpayment problem is to promote the employee—but only if the employee is qualified for a higher rated job and a job is available. Another possibility would be to bring the job rate and employee pay into line through a pay cut—perhaps a logical approach, but a harsh one; management should not punish employees for a situation they did not create. Between these two extremes is a third: to freeze the rate until across-the-board pay increases bring the job into line, i.e., to "red circle" the job. If the past few decades are an indication of the future, rising pay levels will eventually solve the problem.

Obviously the people who hold red circled jobs will be unhappy; considerable morale problems can result. Where red circling is the only option, then, the rationale must be explained carefully and productivity levels should be monitored closely.

A GLOBAL PERSPECTIVE

Designing compensation programs for expatriates and local nationals is especially difficult. In Canada, most firms have a single policy that covers all employees. Firms that operate overseas, however, may have numerous standards, depending on the employee's situation. Allowances may be given for the number of children in a household, or an allowance may be provided for transportation if the employee lives a certain distance from the workplace, but not if accommodation is close by. Base pay may appear to be low at first glance, but the benefits package is often much better, when allowances for social conditions are considered.[36]

For example, HR Education Development Ltd., a private sector training company with business interests in Hong Kong, the Philippines and Guangzhou, China, has employed a number of young Canadian business graduates as trainers and consultants. While the base pay is only $800 Cdn. per month, trainers receive free lodging, maid service, a generous food allowance, medical insurance, and free return transportation. This package has an estimated value of $23 000 Cdn. When the opportunity of gaining international experience and making foreign contacts is added, this compensation arrangement can be attractive.[37]

Several questions arise, therefore, when considering compensation levels for global employees. In the case of alliances, should the partners' compensation systems be linked, or will they be synthesized into a common system? Will compensation rates be adjusted for local markets, or tied to similar jobs in the partner's home country? Often each partner in a venture has an established pay policy and those policies differ. At the very least, partners in these ventures need to reach an agreement on the broad objectives of a compensation program for employees.[38]

Global compensation programs should be designed to establish and to maintain a consistent relationship between the compensation of employees in all international alliances. The programs should also maintain compensation levels that are reasonable in relation to the practices of leading competitors. Failure to establish a uniform compensation policy can result in predictably adverse results, especially for employees doing the same jobs. Poorly designed compensation systems will inevitably lead to low morale, motivational problems, and less productive employees.[39] Despite these problems, the financial compensation provided to most expatriate managers appears to be satisfactory. According to a survey by Richard A. Guzzo, 80 percent of the respondents were satisfied with their financial rewards. The same respondents, however, were not pleased with their *nonfinancial* support, including proper preparation for overseas assignments and appropriate career path development.[40]

THE EMPLOYEE AS A DETERMINANT OF FINANCIAL COMPENSATION

In addition to the organization, the labour market, and the job, compensation factors related to the employee also are essential in determining pay equity.

Pay for Performance

Rewarded behaviour tends to be repeated. The greatest obstacle to organizational success is that many managers are not rewarding the behaviour they need to make their enterprise a world-class competitor.[41] With increasing domestic and international competition, a high level of performance from each employee is essential. For this reason, the pay-for-performance concept is being adopted widely in the United States. In Canada, however, a survey conducted for Chris Schrik, Director of Research for the Ontario Federation of Labour, has suggested that if managers want employees to be concerned with the pay/performance linkage (e.g., increasing economic value), they need to give workers "a greater stake in the work environment". But he expressed doubt that this stake would be forthcoming, despite all the talk to the contrary. "In the short term, most companies see it [allowing greater participation] as threatening."[42]

A *Financial Times* survey indicated that the Canadian business community as a whole is not enthusiastic about pay-for-performance concepts, a realization that some experts find "shocking." David Rainville, a principal with Toronto-based William M. Mercer Ltd., has reiterated: "relating pay to performance is a powerful tool in setting clear corporate objectives. Compensation should support management's overall strategy, and we don't see that here."[43]

Indeed, this lack of attention to pay-for-performance has been linked with Canada's poor competitiveness rankings (about 11th in the world).[44] (No research, however, has been found to support these speculations.)

Certainly Canadian labour unions have remained unconvinced of the merits of tying pay to profitability. Union executives argue that factors beyond an employee's control could result in poor profits, thus wiping out negotiated pay gains.[45] The *Financial Times of Canada* found that only 39 percent of the 504 companies in the sample had a formal, performance-based compensation plan. Large companies, however, were more likely to use such systems; 61 percent of firms with annual sales of more than $10 million linked pay to productivity, compared to 30 percent of firms with sales of less than $5 million. (No data were given for medium-sized firms.)

Worldwide as well, pay-for-performance seems to be a large-company phenomenon. For example, Bob Turner, vice-president of the consulting firm Towers, Perrin, has suggested that 90 percent of companies with more than $1 billion in sales use annual bonuses as incentives and 80 percent have long-term incentive plans in place.[46]

Competitive pressures are bringing about changes even in Japan, where, historically, people worked as a group and the achievers often carried the laggards. A 1992 survey of 500 companies found that 14.6 percent had installed merit pay systems, up from 10.4 percent a year earlier. Currently, most of these firms are limiting the system to managers as a means of saving on labour costs while promoting individual accountability. Managers in firms such as Honda, Fujitsu, and Fujisawa Pharmaceutical are now writing specific goals and holding employees accountable for meeting them.[47]

The most common type of pay for performance is the annual bonus tied to 1) a firm's overall results, 2) the performance of a business unit, 3) the manager's individual performance, or 4) a combination of all three. Bonuses, in addition to eliciting better performance, provide an advantage in that they are not added to base pay and they must be earned each year, allowing management to restrict fixed costs while providing an incentive for improved performance.[48] It is difficult to justify merit pay increases based on a previous employment period but added perpetually to base pay.

Advantages cited for performance-based pay include[49]

- increased job satisfaction;
- increased productivity;
- reduced avoidable absenteeism;
- decreased voluntary turnover;
- improved quality of the employee mix.

Top performers are attracted to firms that base pay on performance. In particular, pay-for-performance appears to attract people with a strong work ethic[50] and people with a more entrepreneurial outlook.[51]

Bonuses based on organizational performance work best when a firm is profitable. When profits declined and paycheques shrank during the last recession, managers in some firms were pressured by employees to revert to previous pay systems. Another problem encountered with pay for performance involves the manner in which rewards are allocated. When mediocre performance is rewarded with a 3 percent increase, while superior performance earns 5 percent, there is little incentive to be superior. The failure to differentiate adequately among performance levels may explain why some managers are unhappy with the results of their pay for performance plans.

A prerequisite for any pay system tied to performance is a sound performance appraisal program, as there must be a valid means of determining performance level. Difficulties associated with this requirement may also explain why in some firms, there are problems with pay for performance programs.

Incentive Compensation

A significant Canadian economic dilemma in recent years has been our productivity growth rate relative to other nations. This problem has given even greater importance to human resource management, as productivity growth stems not only from capital investment but from the proper utilization of human resources.

While compensation is most often determined by how much time an employee spends at work, compensation programs that relate pay to individual productivity are referred to as **incentive compensation.** The purpose of all incentive plans is to improve individual employee productivity in order to gain a competitive advantage. Therefore, management must use various rewards and focus on the needs of employees as well as the firm's business goals.[52]

Money can serve as an important motivator for those who value it—and many people do. A clear relationship, however, must exist between performance and pay if money is to serve as an effective motivator.

Output standards must be established before any type of incentive system can be introduced. These standards are a measure of work that an average, well-trained employee, working at a normal pace, should be able to accomplish in a given period of time. For example, management may determine that employees in a particular department should be able to produce five finished parts per hour. The standard then becomes five. Historically, time study specialists in industrial engineering or methods departments have been responsible for establishing work standards. Increasingly, however, teams comprising individuals who *own* various processes are playing a major role in standards determination. Regardless of how standards are determined, incentive compensation offers a direct approach to balancing pay and performance. This type of compensation can be offered on an individual or group basis.

Individual Incentive Plans

A predetermined amount of money paid for each unit produced is called a straight **piecework** plan. The piece rate is calculated by dividing the standard hourly output into the job's pay rate: if the standard output is 0.04 hour per unit, or 25 units per hour, and the job's pay rate is $8 per hour, the piece rate would be $0.32. Thus, an employee who produced at the rate of 280 units per day would earn $89.60 in an eight-hour day. Most incentive plans in use today have a guaranteed base. In this example, it would be the $8 per hour rate.

When using a **standard hour plan**, time allowances are calculated for each unit of output. Again, assume that 25 units per hour, or 0.04 hour per unit, is the standard output, $8 the hourly job rate, and eight hours the time worked per day. Under these assumptions, an employee would have an allowance of 0.04 hour per unit of output. An employee producing at the rate of 280 units per day would receive an allowance of 0.04 hour per unit for all units produced in a day. Therefore, in an eight-hour day, this employee would earn 11.2 standard hours (280 units × 0.04 hour per unit). The pay for the day would be 11.2 standard hours × $8 per hour, or $89.60. The standard hour plan has the characteristics of the straight piecework plan; however, its advantage is that piece rates need not be recalculated for every pay rate change.

One potential problem with both plans is related to the output standard. Often, workers distrust the standards established by industrial engineers. They may also view with considerable scepticism any change to a standard, although change may be justified in the eyes of management.

When individual output cannot be easily distinguished, group- and company-wide plans offer alternatives to individual incentive plans.

Profit Sharing

Profit sharing is a compensation plan that distributes a predetermined percentage of the firm's profits to employees. Many managers view this type of plan as a chance to integrate employee interests with those of the company. Profit-sharing plans can aid in recruitment, motivation, and employee retention, factors that relate directly to productivity.

Profit sharing tends to tie employees to the economic success of the firm, resulting in increased efficiency and lower costs. In recent years, however, variations in profitability have undermined some such schemes. Poor profits may be a serious problem, especially when employees have become accustomed to receiving added compensation, or when the plan itself represents a major portion of the firm's benefits program. In the past, employee profit-sharing schemes have been regarded by the small business sector as expensive goodwill gestures. They are now becoming more popular as a way to improve corporate performance and earnings. According to a report prepared by Coopers & Lybrand's owner-management services practice, about 20 percent of small firms have implemented profit-sharing plans compared to only 5 percent five years ago. These plans generally are introduced at the same time as pay reductions either for managers or for all employees. Profit-sharing plans are likely to be more important and used more frequently in the future, because they benefit both the employer and the employee.[53]

Seniority

The length of time an employee has been associated with the company, division, department, or job is referred to as seniority. While management generally prefers performance as the primary basis for compensation changes, labour agreements tend to favour seniority. Many union members believe that seniority provides a fair, objective basis for pay increases. There is also a widespread feeling that performance evaluation systems are too subjective, allowing management to reward favourite employees arbitrarily.

An acceptable compromise between performance and seniority might be to permit employees to receive pay increases to the midpoints of their pay grades on the basis of seniority. The rationale is that workers performing at an acceptable level should eventually receive the average wage or salary of their pay grades. Progression beyond the midpoint, however, should be based on performance. This practice would permit only outstanding performers to reach the maximum rate for the grade, reflecting the initial rationale for rate ranges.

Skill-Based Pay

Most compensation systems focus on the relative worth of jobs to the organization. In contrast, skill-based pay, or pay for knowledge, compensates employees on the basis of job-related skills and knowledge. The purpose of this approach is to encourage employees to acquire additional skills/knowledge that will not only increase their value to the organization, but also improve its competitive position. Today's downsizing and the elimination of many middle management jobs have left fewer promotional opportunities. There needs to be room for growth within jobs so that employees can be motivated by factors other than promotions and titles.

At one high-tech company, management determined that the automatic wage progression system was not working well. In developing an alternative—a pay for skills program—it was decided the program should be developed by teams rather than by individuals. A multidisciplinary implementation team was formed that included a compensation specialist, an organizational development expert, a trainer, a systems analyst, and an employee relations professional. The team's objective was to provide leadership, create guidelines, facilitate the development process, and coordinate plan approvals. A majority of employees and managers like the new program and productivity improvements have been greater than anticipated.[54]

Acquiring additional skills also allows employees the opportunity to increase their earnings without moving permanently to a higher level job, an important consideration in a highly competitive environment with limited promotional opportunities. Skill-based pay is often used in combination with autonomous work groups or other job enrichment techniques.

A strong commitment to human resource development is needed to implement these programs. In addition, research has revealed that it takes an average of only three years to reach a maximum level in a skill-based pay system. Another problem is that payroll costs tend to escalate. It is conceivable that a firm could have, in addition to high training and development costs, a very expensive work force possessing more skills than are really useful to the firm.[55]

A survey conducted by Towers Perrin, however, indicated that more than 70 percent of the employers surveyed reported lower operating costs and other significant benefits from their pay-for-skills programs.[56]

Experience

Regardless of the nature of the task, on-the-job experience may greatly enhance a person's ability to perform, especially if progressively more sophisticated skills have been acquired in a successful work environment. Individuals who express pride in their long tenure may be justified, but only if their experience has been of the right kind. A manager who has become more and more autocratic over a 20-year career, for example, would not be valued in a progressively managed firm. Nevertheless, experience is often indispensable for gaining the insights necessary for performing many tasks.

Membership in the Organization

Some components of individual financial compensation are given to employees without regard to the particular job they perform or their level of productivity. These rewards are provided to all employees because they are members of the organization. For example, an average performer occupying a job in pay grade 1 may receive the same number of vacation days, the same amount of group life insurance, and the same reimbursement for educational expenses as a superior employee working in a job classified in pay grade 10. In fact, the worker in pay grade 1 may get more vacation time if he or she has been with the firm longer. Rewards based on organizational membership are intended to maintain a high degree of stability in the work force (e.g., reduce turnover) and to recognize loyalty.

Potential

An individual's potential is useless if never realized. Yet some employees are paid on the basis of their potential. To attract talented young people to the firm, the overall compensation program must appeal to those with no experience or immediate ability to perform difficult tasks. Many young employees are paid well because they have the potential to advance to more challenging positions.

Traditionally, recent college and university graduates do not have enough business experience for HR managers to judge their true worth to the organization. In the absence of a significant work record, employers must look elsewhere for factors that might predict a graduate's success at work. Grades may be considered if they can be shown to be job relevant. Student employment of virtually any type is preferred by many employers because of the opportunity it provides for displaying job-related behaviours. Information may also be sought about leadership in student professional or social organizations.

OTHER COMPENSATION ISSUES

Several issues that affect compensation deserve special mention. They include pay secrecy, pay compression, supplementary hourly rates, team-based and executive compensation, compensation for professionals, and sales compensation.

Pay Secrecy

In some organizations, pay rates are kept secret. If a firm's compensation plan is illogical, secrecy may indeed be appropriate, because only a well-

HRM IN ACTION

Lynn Marlow, the data processing manager for National Insurance Company, was perplexed as she spoke to Graham Johnston, the human resource manager. Lynn said, "I'm having real trouble recruiting programmers and systems analysts. As you know, I have 10 programmers and four systems analysts in my area. Do you realize that just in the last six months, I've had seven programmers and three systems analysts quit? All good people, too, experienced and competent. I asked them why; mostly they said they were leaving for more money or better prospects. And who am I getting to replace them? Mostly kids fresh out of college or people who've done a lot of something else and precious little programming. They seem to be the best we can find. Is it any wonder the data processing centre is always behind schedule?"

How should Graham respond?

designed system can stand careful scrutiny. An open system would almost certainly require managers to explain to subordinates the rationale for pay decisions. But secrecy can be damaging. If compensation data are not freely communicated, rumours can breed misinformation and misunderstanding.[57]

According to Jeffrey Pratt, a Director of Operations for Beaver Foods, "the free and accurate communication of pay ranges within an organization is a key factor in enhancing the trust levels of employees. As the rate of change in the workplace increases daily, and as employees' perception of their relative job security becomes tarnished, secrecy surrounding pay rates is often the catalyst for significant workplace disharmony."[58] In addition, managers who are unaware of their colleagues' pay rates tend to overestimate the pay of managers around them. These perceptions sap motivation and contribute to turnover.[59]

Ideally, managers should strive to develop a logical pay system that reflects both internal and external equity. Employees should participate in the design process as much as feasible. HR managers should take the lead in ensuring that employees understand how their pay is calculated. Obviously, not every employee will be satisfied either with the pay policy or with the numbers. The dissatisfaction and the low morale associated with a secret pay system, however, make openness a much more defensible practice.

Pay Compression

Pay compression refers to a situation in which the pay differential between one pay level and the jobs above or below is too small. Pay compression may arise in several ways, including 1) hiring new employees at higher or comparable pay rates to longer-service employees; 2) making pay adjustments at the lower end of the job hierarchy without commensurate adjustments at the top; 3) granting pay increases on a cents-per-hour basis over a long period. Percentage increases, on the other hand, maintain relative differences in pay rates. Compression usually results in dissatisfied higher-level employees, as a flattened pay curve provides little financial incentive to strive for promotion or to accept more responsibility.

Supplementary Pay for Special Working Conditions

Sometimes the working conditions in a particular job may vary from time to time. When an employee is given an assignment that constitutes a hardship, there may be additional pay on top of the normal wage.

HAZARD PAY

Additional pay provided to employees who work under extremely dangerous conditions is called **hazard pay.** A window washer working on skyscrapers might be given extra compensation because of dangerous working conditions. Similarly, military pilots receive extra money in the form of flight pay.

SHIFT DIFFERENTIALS

A shift differential is paid to employees for the inconvenience of working undesirable hours. For example, employees who work the second shift (afternoon shift) from 4:00 P.M. until midnight might receive $0.50 per hour above the base rate for that job. The third shift (graveyard shift) often warrants an even greater differential, perhaps an extra $0.70 per hour. Shift differentials are sometimes based on a percentage of the employee's base rate.

Team-Based Compensation

One survey has suggested that the use of team-based compensation has risen significantly. In 1993, up to 70 percent of respondents reported using team-based incentives, up from 59 percent in 1990. In most firms, however, the number of employees affected is small, ranging from 1 percent to 20 percent of the work force.[60] Still, firms organized around teams appear to be growing in number, encouraging HR professionals to develop team-oriented compensation systems.

These pay plans must not only promote internal equity, but also encourage participation among team members in meeting predetermined objectives. Four design features should be considered:

1. a direct and obvious link with the firm's strategic plan;

2. clearly defined, measurable team goals;

3. a system for allocating team-based incentives, either equally to all team members, or differentially in proportion to base pay; and

4. a method of separating team-based payment or incentives from base or regular salary.[61]

The goal is a work environment in which compensation is used as one element in developing the attitude, "We're all in this together."

Executive Compensation

All over the world, executive compensation has come under increased public and shareholder scrutiny.[62] The size of compensation packages, the rationale for levels of payment, and issues of disclosure have all been debated fiercely. The arguments about executive pay appear to originate in the United States where some CEOs are making millions of dollars. A 1992 report in *Canadian Business*, however, suggests that in Canada the situation is somewhat different. Canadian CEOs in firms with sales in the $250 million range made an average of $407 600 in salaries, bonuses, and benefits; American CEOs in similar companies averaged $747 500.[63]

This difference may explain why many of this country's "best and brightest managers have left Canada for better opportunities in the United States and elsewhere. Without world-class compensation and other career challenges, combined with our high taxes, Canada risks becoming marginalized in a global economy that requires managers with world-class talent."[64] Thus, Canadian employers need to look seriously at external equity, not only within Canada, but in a global sense as well.

In determining executive compensation, salary growth for the highest-level managers is related to overall corporate performance. Compensation levels for the next management tier are determined by overall corporate performance integrated with market rates and internal considerations. For lower-level managers, salaries are often determined on the basis of market rates, internal pay relationships, and individual performance.

In general, the higher the managerial position, the greater the flexibility managers have in designing their jobs. Management jobs are often difficult to define because of their diversity. And when they are defined, they are described in terms of anticipated results rather than tasks, or how the work is accomplished. Thus, market pricing may be the best approach to use in determining executive pay, as these jobs are critically important to the organization and the people involved are highly skilled and difficult to replace.

Executive compensation is comprised of five elements: 1) base salary, 2) short-term incentives or bonuses, 3) long-term incentives and capital appreciation plans, 4) executive benefits, and 5) perquisites.[65] In addition, design of executive compensation must take into account ever-changing tax legislation.

Compensation for Professionals[66]

Professionals are paid for the knowledge they bring to the organization. Compensation programs for professionals are often administered differently from those for managers. Although many professional employees eventually become managers, a dual compensation track can be developed for those who are unable or unwilling to pursue a management career. This approach provides a separate pay structure for professionals that overlaps the managerial pay structure. Under a dual compensation system, then, high-performing professionals do not need to become managers in order to obtain higher pay. This concept is important, as in some firms there have been serious organizational problems when highly competent professionals felt compelled to become a managers, but were unable to perform well in the management role.

In one instance, the best salesperson in a firm was promoted to sales manager. As managerial skills are quite different from selling skills, he was performing so poorly in the new job that the president was considering dismissal. Not only had the firm lost a top sales representative, one member of the management team was incompetent and sales everywhere were declining. The problem was solved, however, by offering the sales manager a demotion back to sales representative, a move that was accepted gladly. If this company had established a dual compensation track, the considerable losses incurred from losing a top seller while gaining an incompetent manager might have been avoided.

The career curves, shown in Figure 11-11, have been developed for determining professional compensation. They are based on the assumption that the more experience an individual has, the higher his or her earnings should be. As Figure 11-11 indicates, however, varying performance levels are also considered. For example, an individual with eight years' experience (see the boxed area) may earn from less than $3300 per month to more than $5925, depending on his or her performance appraisal rating (employee rating *E* being the highest and rating *A* the lowest). Career curves are similar to the pay grades shown in Figure 11-9.

FIGURE 11-11
Professional Career Curves

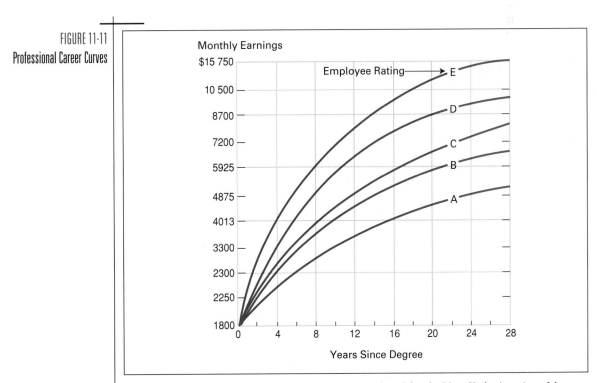

Sales Compensation

Because compensation program design for sales employees involves unique considerations, some executives assign this task to the sales staff rather than to the HRM unit. Still, many general compensation concepts, such as job content, and job market value, apply to sales jobs.

The straight salary approach is one extreme in sales compensation. Sales managers may adopt straight salary systems if they stress after-sale service. At the other extreme is straight commission, in which pay is a percentage of sales; a salesperson on straight commission receives no pay if there are no sales.

Between these extremes are an endless variety of part-salary, part-commission combinations. The possibilities increase when various types of bonuses are added to the basic compensation package. The emphasis given to either commission or salary depends on several factors, including management's philosophy toward service, the nature of the product, and the amount of time required to close a sale. In addition to salary, commissions and bonuses, salespeople often receive other forms of incentive, as sales contests that offer prizes or expense-paid vacations are common.

This emphasis on incentives sets sales compensation apart from other compensation programs, as the nature of sales work can simplify the problem of determining individual output. As well, years of experience in sales compensation has supported the concept that rewards are directly related to performance.

SUMMARY

Compensation refers to the rewards that individuals receive in return for their labour. Direct financial compensation consists of the pay that a person receives in the form of wages, salary, bonuses and/or commissions. Indirect financial compensation (benefits) includes all financial rewards that are not included in direct compensation. Nonfinancial compensation consists of the satisfaction a person receives directly from the job or from the psychological and/or physical job environment. All these types of compensation make up a total compensation program.

Equity refers to the individual's perception of being treated fairly. External equity exists when employees performing jobs within a firm are paid at levels comparable to those paid for similar jobs in other firms. A variety of surveys are conducted to determine external equity. Internal equity occurs when employees are paid according to the relative value of their jobs within the organization. Job evaluation is a primary means for determining internal equity. Employee equity exists when individuals performing similar jobs in a firm are paid differently according to nondiscriminatory factors unique to the employee, like productivity.

Organizational characteristics, the labour market, the job, and the employee all affect the individual's financial compensation.

Job evaluation is the process used to determine the relative values of jobs within a firm. The purpose of job evaluation is to eliminate internal pay inequities resulting from illogical pay structures. There are four job evaluation methods in common use: ranking, classification, factor comparison, and point rating. The ranking and classification methods are qualitative, whereas the factor comparison and point methods are numerically based.

Placing a dollar value on a job is called job pricing. Jobs are priced after they have been evaluated and the relative value of each job in the organization has been determined. A pay grade is a grouping of similar jobs used to simplify the job pricing process. A pay range includes a minimum and maximum pay rate, with enough variance between the two to allow for significant pay differences. Pay ranges allow employees to be paid according to length of service and performance levels. When pay ranges are used, a method must be developed to advance individuals through the range.

In the case of international alliances, global compensation programs must consider how the pay systems of the various partners are to be related. In these situations, an agreement should be reached concerning the broad objectives of the compensation system.

The employee is also a determinant of compensation. Pay for performance is less common in Canada than in the United States, but a range of systems are used, including annual bonuses, piecework and profit-sharing schemes. An individual's compensation may also recognize seniority, levels of skill or knowledge, experience, and potential.

Organizations in which pay rates are kept a secret often experience morale problems. Pay compression occurs when workers perceive that the differential between their pay and that of employees in jobs above or below them is too small.

As more and more individuals are working in teams, team-based compensation has become a major concern.

Despite widespread public and shareholder indignation at high executive salaries, executive compensation for top Canadian executives has in fact not kept pace with global trends. Many highly qualified managers have left Canada to take jobs elsewhere.

Professionals are initially compensated primarily for the knowledge they bring to the organization. Many professional employees eventually become managers. For those who don't want to move into management, some organizations have created a dual compensation track.

Compensation programs for sales employees involve unique considerations; systems may range from straight salary to straight commission, with many variations in between. Strong financial incentives are typical.

TERMS FOR REVIEW

Compensation	Ranking method
Direct financial compensation	Classification method
Indirect financial compensation	Factor comparison method
Nonfinancial compensation	Point method
Equity	Hay guide chart-profile method
External equity	Job pricing
Internal equity	Pay grade
Employee equity	Wage curve
Team equity	Pay range
Pay leaders	Incentive compensation
Going rate	Piecework
Pay followers	Standard hour plan
Labour market	Profit sharing
Benchmark job	Pay compression
Cost-of-living allowance (COLA)	Hazard pay
Job evaluation	Shift differential

QUESTIONS FOR REVIEW

1. Define each of the following terms: a) compensation; b) direct financial compensation; c) indirect financial compensation; d) nonfinancial compensation.

2. Distinguish among external equity, internal equity, and employee equity.

3. What are the primary determinants of financial compensation? Briefly describe each.

4. Distinguish among a pay follower, a pay leader, and a going-rate organization.

5. How has government affected compensation?

6. Give the primary purpose of job evaluation.

7. Distinguish among the four basic methods of job evaluation: ranking, classification, factor comparison, and point rating.

8. What is the purpose of job pricing? Discuss this concept briefly.

9. Outline the procedure for determining pay grades.

10. What is the purpose of establishing pay ranges?

11. Describe the various factors relating to the employee in determining pay and benefits.

12. Discuss some of the issues relating to professional compensation.

13. Discuss each of the following concepts: a) pay secrecy; b) pay compression; c) team-based compensation; d) executive compensation.

HRM INCIDENT 1

• IT'S JUST NOT FAIR!

During a Saturday afternoon golf game with his friend Randy Dean, Harry Neil discovered that his department had hired a recent university grad as a systems analyst—at a starting salary almost as high as Harry's. Although Harry was good-natured, he was bewildered and upset. It had taken him five years to become a senior systems analyst at his current salary level. He had been generally pleased with the company and thoroughly enjoyed his job.

The following Monday morning Harry confronted Niall O'Driscoll, the human resource director, asking if what he had heard was true. Niall admitted apologetically that it was and attempted to explain the company's situation: "Harry, the market for systems analysts is very tight and in order for the company to attract qualified prospects, we have to offer a premium starting salary. We desperately needed another analyst and this was the only way we could get one."

Harry asked Niall if his salary would be adjusted accordingly. Niall answered, "Your salary will be reevaluated at the regular time. You're doing a great job, though, and I'm sure the boss will recommend a raise." Harry thanked Niall for his time, but left the office shaking his head and wondering about his future.

QUESTIONS

1. Do you think Niall's explanation was satisfactory? Discuss.

2. What action do you believe management should have taken with regard to Harry?

HRM INCIDENT 2

• JOB EVALUATION: WHO OR WHAT?

Kurt Rhine, compensation manager for Farrington Lingerie Company, was generally relaxed and good-natured. Although he was a no-nonsense, competent executive, Kurt was one of the most popular managers in the company. This Friday morning, though, Kurt was not his usual self. As chair of the company's job evaluation committee, he had called a late morning meeting at which several jobs were to be considered for reevaluation. The jobs had already been rated and assigned to pay grade 3. But the office manager, Ben Butler, was upset that one was not rated higher. To press the issue, Ben had taken his case to two executives who were also members of the job evaluation committee. The two executives (production manager Brian Nelson and general marketing manager Laura diMichele) then requested that the job ratings be reviewed. As Brian and Laura supported Ben's side of the dispute, Kurt was not looking forward to the confrontation that was almost certain to occur.

The receptionist's job was causing this controversy. Beth Smithers, the sole receptionist in the company, had been with the firm 12 years—longer than any of the committee members. She was extremely efficient. Virtually all the other executives, including the president, had noticed and commented on her outstanding work. Brian Nelson and Laura diMichele were particularly pleased with Beth because of the cordial manner in which she greeted and accommodated the frequent visits by Farrington's customers and vendors. They felt that Beth projected a positive image for the company.

When the meeting began, Kurt said, "Good morning. I know that you're busy so let's get the show on the road. We have several jobs to evaluate this morning and I suggest we begin—." Before he could finish his sentence, Brian interrupted, "I suggest we start with Beth." Laura nodded in agreement. When Kurt regained his composure, he quietly but firmly asserted: "Brian, we are not here today to evaluate Beth. Her supervisor does that at performance appraisal time. We're meeting to evaluate jobs based on job content. In order to do this fairly with regard to other jobs in the company, we must leave personalities out of our evaluation." Kurt then proceeded to pass out copies of the receptionist job description to Brian and Laura; both were obviously very irritated.

QUESTIONS

1. Do you feel that Kurt was justified in insisting that the job, not the person, be evaluated? Discuss.
2. Do you believe there is a maximum rate of pay for every job in an organization, regardless of how well the job is being performed? Justify your position.
3. Assuming that Beth is earning the maximum for her pay grade, in what ways can she obtain a salary increase?

DEVELOPING HRM SKILLS: AN EXPERIENTIAL EXERCISE

Pay equity is likely to remain a key compensation issue, requiring that some form of job evaluation be part of many compensation decisions; that is, salaries and wages will be based on job evaluation scores. These scores can be determined by a variety of factors—for example, skills, knowledge, effort, working conditions, and responsibilities—rather than the workings of the labour market. Then equal pay for different jobs of the same value will have to be determined not by looking at the going rate in the marketplace, but rather at the job's difficulty, importance, and the training required. This exercise has been developed to impart an understanding and an appreciation for pay equity, a concept based on two premises:

1. That it is possible to compare different jobs and to establish a *pay* relationship based on their value to the organization.

2. That the pay established by job market supply and demand, can be inequitable and discriminatory, especially with regard to pay for women.

Everyone will be given a copy of Exhibit 1.

Based on the premises outlined above, determine the following:

1. Which of the jobs would you consider *comparable*? Select a job from the second list and write it beside the job on the first list to which you feel it compares most closely.

2. What average monthly salary would you assign to each position?

After ten minutes everyone will sign their Exhibits and turn them in. Then three participants with dissimilar comparisons will list their comparisons and salaries on the chalkboard and class discussion will begin.

CHAPTER 12

Benefits and Other Compensation Issues

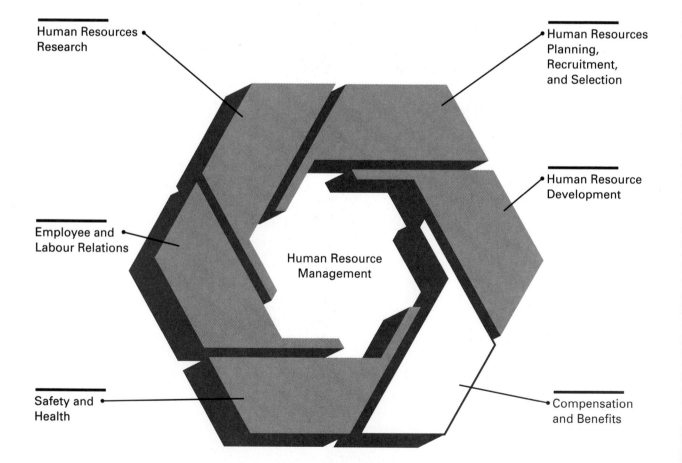

Human Resources
Research

Human Resources
Planning,
Recruitment,
and Selection

Human Resource
Development

Employee and
Labour Relations

Human Resource
Management

Safety and
Health

Compensation
and Benefits

CHAPTER OBJECTIVES

1. Define benefits and describe their importance to the total compensation program.
2. Describe legally required and voluntary benefits.
3. Outline the various incentive compensation programs now in use.
4. Explain the term nonfinancial compensation.
5. Describe the many forms of nonfinancial compensation that employees are beginning to expect. Describe what companies are doing to improve workplace flexibility.
6. Outline the importance of communication when administering benefits.

*J*ason Hicks, a college dropout, is a senior credit clerk at Ajax Manufacturing Company. A bright young man, Jason has been with Ajax for four years. He has received excellent performance ratings in each of the several positions he has held with the firm. During his last appraisal interview, however, Jason's supervisor implied that promotion to a higher level job would require additional formal education. Because Jason appeared to be receptive to the idea, his supervisor suggested that he check with the Human Resources Manager to learn the details of Ajax's educational assistance policy.

Liz Polchies is a divorced mother of three elementary school children. She works as an illustrator for Busiform Company. Her normal working hours are from 8:00 A.M. to 5:00 P.M., Monday through Friday. The children's school begins at 9:00 A.M. and ends at 3:30 P.M. Liz had satisfactory child care arrangements after school. However, she faced an almost impossible task of transporting the children to school in the morning and arriving at her job on time. The school's principal permitted the children to enter the building at 7:45 each morning to wait until classes began, but Liz was afraid that she couldn't count on this practice to continue indefinitely. When Busiform management announced a new system of flexible working hours, Liz was delighted.

lthough these anecdotes may seem to have little in common, both relate to the broad area of indirect compensation. Jason is investigating the possibility of continuing his education through his company's educational assistance program. Liz believes that the new flexible working hours will solve her difficult child care problem.

We begin the chapter with a discussion of benefits, both mandated and voluntary. Next we outline how nonfinancial compensation stems from the job itself and present the workplace flexibility concept. The overall purpose of this chapter is to emphasize the significance of benefits in a total compensation system.

BENEFITS (INDIRECT FINANCIAL COMPENSATION)

In most organizations, management recognizes the need to provide employees with insurance and other programs for their health, safety, security, and general welfare (see Figure 12-1). These programs, called **benefits**, include all financial rewards other than direct payment. Benefits cost the firm money, but employees usually receive them indirectly. For example, an organization may pay all or part of an annual supplemental health insurance premium for each employee. The employee does not receive this money, but obtains the benefit of extra health insurance coverage. This type of compensation has the advantage that premium rates are much lower for large groups of employees than for individual policies. In addition, benefits are nontaxable in some jurisdictions.

Benefits are provided to employees because of their membership in the organization. Typically, they are not related to employee productivity and therefore, do not serve as motivation for improved performance. An attractive benefit package, however can assist in the recruitment and the retention of a qualified work force.

Almost all employers offer benefits beyond those legally required (which we discuss a little later). A January 1993 survey of 946 Canadian employers found that 98 percent provided dental plans, 91 percent provided short-term disability coverage and 80 percent provided basic accident insurance.[1] Many offer other benefits as well, such as supplementary health or life insurance. Some less traditional benefits are becoming common. For example, a survey of 234 Canadian companies by KPMG, Toronto indicates that plans that help employees with stress or substance abuse problems are now offered by almost half of all companies, and help with day care or care of elderly relatives also is increasing.[2]

LEGALLY REQUIRED BENEFITS

While most employee benefits are provided at the employer's discretion, or are negotiated by the employee's union, others are required by law. In Canada, legally mandated benefits include Old Age Security Pension; Canada/Quebec Pension Plan; unemployment insurance; Workers' Compensation; universal health insurance; vacation pay; and holiday pay.

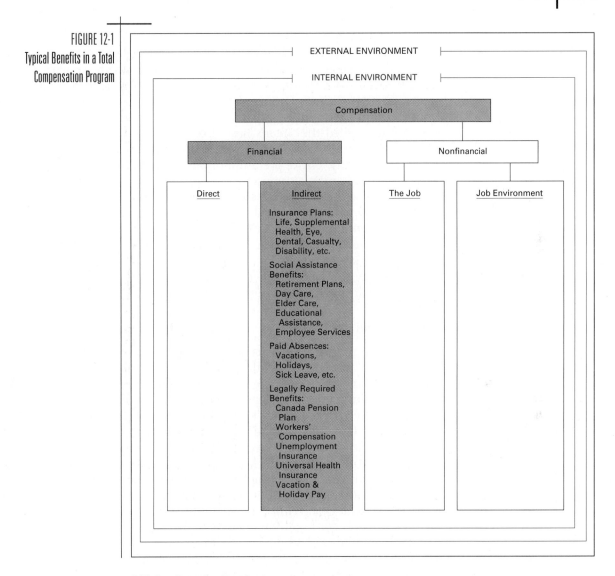

FIGURE 12-1
Typical Benefits in a Total Compensation Program

Old Age Security Pension

The **Old Age Security Pension** is a federally administered plan, designed to provide every Canadian, regardless of income, with a basic pension (which in 1995 amounted to $388.52 per month). This amount can be increased with a series of supplemental pensions for individuals and couples with limited incomes. For example, the maximum monthly supplement for a married couple who are both receiving the basic pension is $300.74 each.[3] Under certain conditions, this pension is payable anywhere in the world. The payments are regarded as income, subject to income taxes like any other retirement income.[4]

It should be noted, however, that, like most other benefits, the Old Age Security Program is undergoing a review. In the future, it is likely that a means test will be required to collect this pension.

Canada Pension Plan

The **Canada Pension Plan (CPP)**, administered federally everywhere but Quebec,[5] has been in operation since 1966. Designed to protect individuals against loss of earnings upon retirement or disability, CPP also has survivor's and orphan's benefits. The plan is funded through employer and employee contributions. In 1996, each party paid 2.8 percent of gross income between a minimum called the "Year's Basic Exemption" and a "Maximum Pensionable Earnings" ceiling. Self employed individuals are also covered by the CPP. They must pay the entire premium or 5.6 percent (1996) of earnings between a set minimum and maximum.[6]

There has been intense discussion about the viability of this pension scheme. It appears that contributions may not be sufficient to fund the massive retirements forecast during the turn of the century and beyond. Unless the government decides to fund the CPP from general revenues, most experts foresee large increases in contribution rates. Indeed, between 1987 and 1996 contribution rates rose from 1.9 percent to 2.8 percent. Further increases appear inevitable as the population ages.

Unemployment Insurance (UI)

The Unemployment Insurance Plan was designed to protect Canadians in the event of job loss, providing temporary income until another job was found (regular benefits). There are also provisions, termed "special benefits", for help during periods of sickness or pregnancy, or while caring for a newborn or newly adopted child. This discussion focuses on regular benefits.

Regular benefits are paid to individuals who qualify under UI regulations and who are unemployed because work is unavailable. To qualify, one must have worked at least 15 hours or earned at least $163.00 (1995) weekly for a period of time determined by the rate of unemployment in one's geographical area. For example, if the unemployment rate in a region is 6 percent or less, the qualifying period would be 20 weeks; if unemployment is over 13 percent, the qualifying period is only 12 weeks.

UI payments are 55 percent of weekly insurable earnings averaged over the previous 20 weeks. The maximum insurable earnings in 1995 was $815 weekly, so that the largest possible weekly payment was $448. Other rules apply to individuals with low incomes. As with most other sources of income in Canada, UI benefits are taxable. The number of weeks that benefits can be collected depends upon how long an individual worked before job loss and the unemployment rate in the region. The maximum benefit period is 50 weeks. Claimants can earn up to 25 percent of their weekly UI rate and still qualify for insurance. They must be actively looking for a job, however, and be willing and able to work.[7]

Again, this program almost certainly will be restructured during the next three years. Indeed, at present many of the federal government's Canada Employment Centres, through which UI has been administered, are being closed or consolidated. Various solutions are being proposed including a two-tier system that would see reduced benefits for those who use UI more than an as-yet-undefined norm. Whether or not these proposals become law, the UI system of 1995 will change drastically within the next few years.

Workers' Compensation

In Canada, compensation programs for injured employees are administered by the provinces. Although benefits differ from province to province, in general, the various Workers' Compensation Acts provide for disability income, rehabilitation, and one-time payment for serious injuries such as the loss of an arm or a leg. Not only is there insurance available, but there are provincially run rehabilitation centres that focus on returning injured workers to the workplace. A typical centre might have four program areas: vocational assessment, prosthetics/orthotics, pain management, and work recovery. Often treatment is delivered by interdisciplinary teams that may include physicians, nurses, physiotherapists, and occupational therapists.[8]

The cost of workers' compensation is borne by employers, who are assessed a rate per $100 of payroll, up to a maximum earnings of $42 100 (1995 rate). All employers are classified into rate groups according to primary business activity or industry (accounting, fish canning, electrical contractors, hairdressing salons, etc.) Each rate group is assigned a rate, based on the likelihood that accidents will occur. The rate per $100 of payroll for textile manufacturing, for example, is $1.09; for piano tuning, $.25; for abattoirs, $5.46; and for gold mining, $3.55.

Each rate group collectively pays the cost of all injuries within the rate group. However, to encourage safety consciousness, the plan provides for rebates for employers with exceptionally safe workplaces and penalties for those with exceptionally unsafe workplaces.[9]

Each province administers this system through an appointed Workers' Compensation Board responsible for setting benefit levels and for administering the various rehabilitation institutions. As well, there is an appeal procedure and an Appeals Board in each jurisdiction. Rate and duration of benefits vary from province to province, but are typically 75 percent of gross pay, or as much as 90 percent of after-tax earnings during a period of total disability.

Like all benefit plans, workers' compensation has come under intense scrutiny during the last few years. Not only have claims for compensation become more expensive (to the point where some systems are virtually bankrupt), but entire new classifications of injury are becoming common. Claims for excessive stress and burnout, for example, were virtually unknown 20 years ago. The result has been a drain on WCB resources. In fact, according to John Roushorne, CEO of the New Brunswick WCB, "workers' compensation . . . is in a state of total crisis. Its very viability is at stake, and in some jurisdictions it's past the point of no return."[10] Indeed, demands on WCB systems seem to keep expanding.[11]

HR professionals, therefore, need to monitor WCB systems on two fronts. First, they should work to ensure that internal environments (e.g., culture, safety systems, record keeping, rewards) minimize risk. Second, they should become active within their industry group or trade association in seeking to lower the overall accident rate.

Universal Health Insurance

One of the fundamental principles that defines this country is the existence of a **universal health care** system. In fact, the health care sector is seen by most Canadians as, essentially, a public utility.[12] Even though coverage may vary, the basic services—for example, doctors' visits, hospitalization—have remained intact. In some jurisdictions this health insurance in financed entirely through general revenues; in others, families and individuals pay a monthly premium, or employers may pay a payroll tax.

The Canada Health Act was designed to enshrine the same level of health service for all Canadians. The federal government transferred considerable amounts of money to the provinces each year to ensure equality. Since 1988, however, these transfer payments have decreased substantially so that now the federal government finances less than one-third of the cost of medicare;[13] and payments are scheduled to decrease still more. This shifting of costs from the federal to the provincial arena will make the maintenance of nation-wide standards even more difficult. In fact, the government of Alberta has already suggested that for-profit (private) medical clinics might become necessary, an idea resisted vigorously by federal lawmakers. Although it is unlikely that universal health care will disappear, financial pressures will almost certainly lead to cutbacks that may change the "universal" nature of health care benefits in Canada.

From a human resources management viewpoint, cutbacks in universal health care programs may bring demands for additional employer-sponsored[14] supplemental health-care benefits. Unfortunately, faced with rising costs of dental care and many other supplemental benefits, many employers are poised to cut back.[15]

Vacation and Holiday Pay

All provincial labour standards legislation, as well as the Canada Labour Code, have provisions for **vacation and holiday pay**. Employers are required to give every employee paid time off each year. Legislation varies slightly across jurisdictions, but the Canada Labour Code is typical, in that the basic entitlement is two weeks' vacation after one completed year of employment, increasing to three weeks after six consecutive years with the same employer. Where the vacation entitlement is two weeks, 4 percent of annual earnings must be paid; three weeks' vacation pay translates to 6 percent of earnings.[16]

Similarly, the Canada Labour Code provides for nine paid holidays per year: New Year's Day, Good Friday, Victoria Day, Canada Day, Labour Day, Thanksgiving Day, Remembrance Day, Christmas Day, and Boxing Day. Provincial legislation varies somewhat. Work on any general holiday is not prohibited, but employees must be paid $1\frac{1}{2}$ times regular wages, while managers and professionals must be granted a holiday with pay at some other time.[17]

VOLUNTARY BENEFITS

Managers in many organizations voluntarily provide numerous benefits. These **voluntary benefits** may be classified as 1) paid time off, 2) health and security benefits, and 3) employee services. These payments result from unilateral management decisions in some firms and from union-management negotiations in others.

Paid Time Off

In providing payment for time not worked, employers recognize that employees need time away from the job for many purposes. Included in this category are paid vacations that exceed minimum labour standards, holidays other than those required by law, paid sick leave, and bereavement time. It is also common for organizations to provide payments to assist employees in performing civic duties. Most employees are also allowed to take some paid time off during work hours. Common benefits include rest periods, coffee breaks, clean-up time, and travel time.

PAID VACATIONS

Payment for time not worked serves important compensation goals. For example, paid vacations provide employees with an opportunity to rest and become rejuvenated (and, presumably, more productive), while encouraging them to remain with the firm. Typically, paid vacation time increases with seniority, with perhaps one week allowed after six months of service and two weeks after one year (the legal minimum), rising to four weeks a year after 10 years and five weeks a year after 15 years. Vacation time may also vary with organizational rank. For example, a senior executive, regardless of time with the firm, may be given one month's vacation.

SICK LEAVE

In many firms, each employee is allotted a certain number of paid sick leave days. Employees who are too sick to report to work continue to receive their pay up to the maximum number of days accumulated. As with vacation pay, the number of sick leave days can depend on seniority. Some sick leave programs have been severely criticized. At times they have been abused by individuals who claim falsely to be sick. To counter this practice, in some firms a doctor's statement is required after a set number of successive sick leave days.

Health and Security Benefits

Health and security benefits are often included as part of an employee's indirect financial compensation. Specific areas include supplementary health care, disability protection, dental and vision care, retirement benefits, supplemental unemployment benefits, and life insurance.

SUPPLEMENTAL HEALTH CARE

In Canada, all citizens receive basic health coverage under a provincial or territorial health insurance plan (see previous discussion). Many employers, however, provide additional coverage, often through a cost-sharing agreement with the employee. Semiprivate room coverage and drug payment plans are typical benefits. In organizations where employees are required to travel extensively, the employer often provides out-of-country health insurance to protect against sickness or accident in high-cost regions such as the United States.

These benefits vary widely from employer to employer. Increasingly, HR professionals are being called upon to manage these programs more effectively, even to the point of adopting American-style cost containment techniques that encourage the participation of all employees in deciding how to use limited health care resources more effectively.[18]

DISABILITY PROTECTION

Workers' compensation protects employees from job-related accidents and illnesses. In some firms, however, additional **disability protection** is provided that covers non-work-related accidents and illness. A sick leave policy may provide full salary for short-term health problems, after which a short-term disability plan may become operative. Long-term illness or disability activates a firm's long-term plan, which may provide from 50 to 66 percent of an employee's regular wages for periods from two years to life. Again, where they exist, the benefits range widely, depending upon the amount an employer is willing to spend and on the insurance company that provides the benefit.

DENTAL AND VISION CARE

Dental and vision care are relative newcomers to the list of potential health benefits. For most companies in Canada, insurance premiums for extended benefits such as dental and eye care can account for up to 80 percent of insurance costs.[19] These plans typically are paid for by the employer, except for a deductible, which may amount to $25 to $50 per year.

RETIREMENT PLANS

Private retirement plans provide income for employees who retire after reaching a certain age or after having served the firm for a specific period of time. Pension plans are vitally important to employees because the Old Age Pension and the Canada/Quebec Pension Plan were not designed to provide complete retirement income. Over the next 30 years, the Canadian population will be dominated by older people who are either retired or approaching retirement. Therefore, retirement financing will become a primary issue for individuals, employers, and governments.[20]

Although there are many variations, a typical Canadian pension scheme would be called a defined benefit plan. The employer agrees to provide a specific level of retirement income, either a fixed dollar amount or a percentage of earnings. An employee's seniority in the firm may determine the specific figure. A plan considered generous might provide a pension equivalent to 50 to 80 percent of an employee's final earnings.

SHARE OWNERSHIP

An **employee share ownership plan (ESOP)** is a program under which a firm makes a tax-deductible contribution of shares or cash to a trust. The trust then allocates the stock to participating employee accounts on the basis of employee earnings. Royal Trustco Ltd., for example, has a plan wherein the company pays for 20 percent of employees' share purchases. A 1987 Toronto Stock Exchange survey found that 428 firms made ESOPs available to every employee.[21]

When used as a retirement plan, employees receive income at retirement based on the value of the shares at that time. If the firm's share performance has fared well, this type of defined contribution plan will be satisfactory. Since share value may decline, however, the results may be disastrous. In 1987, for example, Bramalea Ltd.'s ESOP gave employees the chance to buy shares at $18 each ($10 below market price). In 1992, these shares were worth less than 50 cents each.

LIFE INSURANCE

Group life insurance is a benefit commonly provided to protect the employee's family in the event of his or her death. Although the cost of group life insurance is relatively low, some plans call for the employee to pay part of the premium. Coverage may be a flat amount (for instance, $20 000) or based on the employee's annual earnings. Typically, members of group plans do not have to show evidence of insurability. This provision is especially important to older employees and to those with health problems, who might find the cost of individual insurance to be prohibitive.

Insurance coverage may become a victim of economic cutbacks. Some smaller firms are having difficulty obtaining group insurance because insurers are reducing their use of small-client pools that combine small companies with similar risk profiles. This practice protects individual firms from a year in which one or two employees claim large settlements. Insurance industry executives have become cautious because their profits are declining.

Antel Optonics Inc. of Burlington, Ontario, for example, saw premiums double because of a claim for an AIDS-related illness. The 24-employee company was able to obtain (higher priced) insurance from London Life Insurance Company only after the employee was fired.* Should pooling be discontinued, managers or owners of smaller firms will have to shift the burden to their employees by asking them to pay a higher percentage of the cost, or by ceasing to pay benefits.[22]

Employee Services

Organizations offer a variety of benefits that can be termed employee services. These might include company-subsidized lunches, financial assistance for employee-operated credit unions, legal and income tax aid, club memberships, athletic and recreational programs, discounts on company products, moving expenses, parking spaces, and tuition rebates. Employee assistance programs (EAPs), wellness programs, and physical fitness programs, all of which are discussed in Chapter 13, also represent important services that can enhance the employment relationship.

When managers at Crestor Energy Inc. of Alberta wanted to create a new corporate culture, for example, they decided to add financial planning to the benefit package. Approximately 70 percent of the staff attended the four-hour evening sessions.[23] At Syncride Canada, as well, individual financial planning is viewed as a necessity. Every employee over 45 receives one-to-one advice.[24]

---

* The insurer's representatives did not know the nature of the illness, but reacted to Antel's history of high claims. Officially the employee was dismissed because he had been off work for over a year and the employer could no longer afford to keep his position open. The move was made very reluctantly.

Several new types of benefits have been added to corporate plans.. One example is subsidized day care. Here, the firm provides facilities for young children of employees at no cost or for a modest fee. This benefit is an effective recruitment aid that also helps to reduce absenteeism. The need for these programs is growing, as more than 60 percent of Canadian couples now are dual-income families, double the 1967 figure.[25] The dual-income phenomenon, along with increases in the number of single parents, has also created demands for more flexibility in working hours and conditions (discussed later in this chapter). In an attempt to conserve energy and to relieve traffic congestion, some firms transport workers to and from work. Participating employees pay a portion of the cost and ride in company vans or buses. Employees often find this service an attractive alternative to driving in heavy traffic. In a few firms, company-subsidized cafeterias are provided. Management hopes to gain increased productivity, less wasted time, increased employee morale and, in some instances, a healthier work force. In most cases, the payback is high in terms of employee relations.[26]

THE CHANGING NATURE OF BENEFIT PACKAGES

The cost of benefits is high. In 1993, the cost of benefits in the private sector stood at about 35 percent of payroll.[27] Moreover, the cost of benefits such as health and dental care is rising sharply. The cost per employee of a "basic plan" was $1767 in 1990; by 1993 it had reached $2157.[28] The cost of dental plans has increased 42.9 percent in the last decade, and people are using them more.[29] Employee health care costs have been estimated to be increasing by an average of 20 percent per year because of additional claims and longer hospital stays (due in part to an aging population), more expensive technology, and higher prices. In particular, the federal government's extended drug patent protection law increased the cost of prescription drugs.

Until recently, most Canadians were unaware of the costs borne by employers. However, attitudes are likely to change in Ontario and Quebec, where legislation has now made benefits taxable. In response to rising costs, employers are considering revising plans. Some are restricting the kinds of medical and dental expenses they will subsidize, or are discussing limiting supplemental medical or dental coverage to employees only, rather than the family plans now offered. Specific strategies to limit costs include restricting prescription drugs to approved lists, giving all drug prescription business to one pharmacy or using mail-order pharmaceutical companies, having dentists on retainer, restricting topical fluoride and periodontal treatments, reviewing claims to spot unusual patterns, and educating employees on cost-saving measures.[30]

Some companies are considering flexible plans, which provide a core of basic benefits, with additional options to be paid by the employee, or various cost-sharing schemes, including an employer-employee account to meet the cost of services not covered by the company plan. More employees will need to reconsider the value of their benefits, and fundamental changes are likely to occur in all aspects of nonfinancial compensation.[31]

FLEXIBLE COMPENSATION (CAFETERIA COMPENSATION)

Flexible compensation plans permit employees to choose from among several alternatives in deciding how their financial compensation will be allocated. For example, they are given considerable latitude in determining how much they will take in the form of salary, life insurance, pension contributions, and other benefits. Cafeteria plans increase flexibility by allowing each employee to determine what compensation package best satisfies his or her personal needs. A 60-year-old man probably would not want to pay for subsidized day care as part of a benefits plan. Similarly, a young woman who jogs three miles every day might not place high value on a parking space near the firm's entrance. Some possible compensation vehicles used in a cafeteria approach are shown in Figure 12-2.

When management at 3M Canada Inc. decided to offer a cafeteria plan, two years were spent in the planning stage, with heavy input from employee focus groups. Called "Beneflex," the benefits scheme is designed around a "core plus option" approach. Although the flex plan is effective in helping 3M keep benefits under control, the main purpose in establishing it was to provide for an increasingly wide range of employee needs and preferences, says Bob Jolley, manager of employee benefit services. In a recent company-wide satisfaction survey, the benefits program received one of the highest ratings.[32]

FIGURE 12-2
Compensation Vehicles Used in a Cafeteria Compensation Approach

Accidental death, dismemberment insurance	Group automobile insurance
Birthdays (vacation)	Group homeowners' insurance
Bonus eligibility	Group life insurance
Business and professional membership	Extended health care
Cash profit sharing	Incentive growth fund
Club memberships	Interest-free loans
Commissions	Long-term disability benefit
Company-provided automobile	Matching educational donations
Company-provided housing	Nursing-home care
Company-provided or subsidized travel	Drug plan
Day care centres	Personal accident insurance
Deferred bonus	Price discount plan
Deferred compensation plan	Recreation facilities
Dental and eye care insurance	Resort facilities
Discount on company products	Sabbatical leaves
Education costs	Salary continuation
Educational activities (time off)	Savings plan
Free chequing account	Scholarships for dependents
Free or subsidized lunches	Severance pay
	Sickness and accident insurance
	Share bonus plan
	Share purchase plan

Choices in a current plan might include semiprivate hospital, supplemental accident, life insurance, and long-term disability benefits. Future possibilities for expanded areas of choice could be a retirement supplement or group auto and homeowners' insurance. Each one would be costed separately, with the employee deciding how much of a benefits package he or she can afford.

COMMUNICATING INFORMATION ABOUT THE BENEFITS PACKAGE

Employee benefits can help to recruit and to retain a high-quality work force. Management depends on an upward information flow from employees to know when benefit changes are needed. Program information must also be communicated downward, since employee knowledge of benefits is often limited. Regardless of the sophistication of a benefits program, money spent on benefits can be wasted if employees do not know what they are receiving. Employees may even resent payroll deductions, not realizing the greater contribution made by the employer, and the range of benefits they receive.

According to Daphne Woolf, a principal with William M. Mercer, "a communication strategy is as important as plan design." Managers must explain the rationale behind a new plan or changes to existing benefits. Otherwise, employees will likely accuse management of not being open "about the full impact of the economic factors behind the change-over," especially if benefits will cost more.[33]

NONFINANCIAL COMPENSATION

In recent years, many Canadian workers have been able to satisfy their physiological and safety needs. Their compensation interests, therefore, have tended to include factors in addition to money. As employees receive sufficient pay to provide for basic necessities, they are inclined to desire rewards that satisfy higher-order needs, such as social, ego, and self-actualization needs. These needs may be met through the job and/or the job environment. Figure 12-3 outlines the basic nonfinancial elements of the total compensation package.

HRM IN ACTION

"Did you realize that we spent over $170,000 on benefits last year?" asked Pat Shelton, the comptroller. She was talking to Muhammad Rashid, the human resource manager. Pat continued, "For a company our size, we sure spend a lot of money for what we get. Frankly, I think the employees could care less about them. What do you think about going to an options plan where employees pay only for what they want? We could save the company a lot of money."

If you were Muhammad, how would you respond?

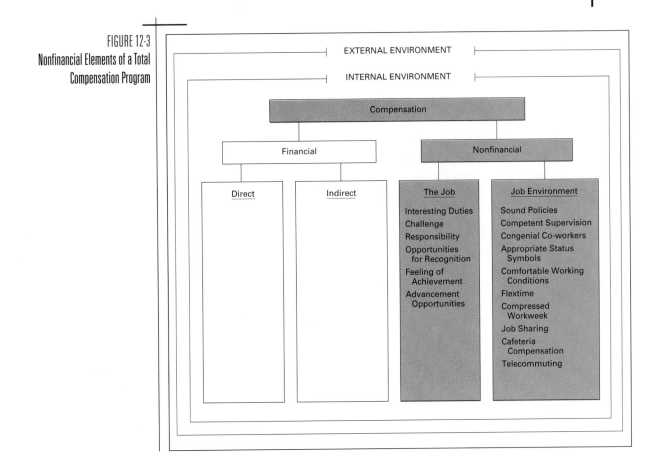

FIGURE 12-3
Nonfinancial Elements of a Total Compensation Program

The Job

As previously described, a job consists of a group of tasks that must be performed for an organization to achieve its goals. The demise of the job as a way of organizing work has been predicted by some experts, because of rapidly changing duties in a dynamic environment.[34] It is likely, however, that as long as tasks must be completed by humans, jobs—by whatever name—will exist. A major human resource management objective, then, is the matching of job requirements with employee abilities and aspirations. As jobs become more complex, this challenge is likely to become increasingly difficult.

Although the job design function is typically performed by other organizational units, the human resource manager is responsible (along with line managers) for recruiting, selecting, and placing individuals in jobs. A good case can also be made for the direct involvement of human resources professionals in job design. Offering the employee an interesting, fulfilling job can be an important part of nonfinancial compensation. In a number of organizations, therefore, there is an active job enrichment program (see Chapters 3 and 8).

Job characteristics are central to many theories of motivation, and a vital component of a total compensation program, as employees may receive important nonmonetary benefits by performing meaningful work. These intrinsic rewards are largely controlled by the organization, as management arranges required tasks into job content and, therefore, controls the job's indirect compensation possibilities. Selection and placement are also extremely important in this context, as a job that is challenging to one person may be boring to another. Failure to recognize individual differences often leads to major motivational problems.

The Job Environment

The job environment is also an important aspect of nonfinancial compensation. We discussed the significance of a warm, supportive corporate culture in Chapter 8. In many organizations, management has only paid lip service to the notion of making jobs more rewarding, but in others, considerable effort has been made to create a congenial work environment.

Newbridge Networks Corporation of Kanata, Ontario, for example, is growing quickly. Management estimates the workforce could more than double by the end of the decade. At the same time, the company still has the intimacy of a family business. Staff at the company love their jobs because managers are committed to recruiting overachievers and keeping them happy by making them feel productive and useful. There is recognition for doing a good job and for innovating. Chief executive officer and founder Terry Matthews has a gift for making people feel needed. Coffee, tea, and hot chocolate are still free, despite costing $66 000 per year, the telephone directory lists people by first name only, dress is casual and an e-mail network links everyone together. Thus, employees are still willing to work overtime without extra pay.[35]

SOUND POLICIES

Progressive policies that reflect management's sincere concern for employees as individuals can serve as nonfinancial rewards. Fostering stable employment, for example, indicates respect for employees. If a firm's policies show consideration—rather than disrespect or lack of confidence—the result can be rewarding for both the employees and management.

COMPETENT SUPERVISION

Nothing in the job environment is as demoralizing to employees as an incompetent supervisor. Successful organizations offer continuing supervisory and executive development programs that emphasize the continuity of sound leadership and management.

CONGENIAL CO-WORKERS

Although some individuals prefer to be left alone, most want to be accepted by their work group. This acceptance helps to satisfy social needs. Through the staffing process, management must develop compatible work groups.

APPROPRIATE STATUS SYMBOLS

At times, some employees can become overly concerned with office and desk size, style of furniture, location of their parking space, or even the distance from their offices to the CEO's. When such extreme behaviour occurs, the firm's policy regarding status symbols should be examined. While these symbols may be appropriate in achieving certain purposes—such as providing incentives to apply for promotions—they should not be overemphasized. Status symbols may be regarded as a form of compensation because they often appeal to an employee's ego needs. Some managers minimize the use of status symbols, but others use them liberally. A crucial point to remember in providing such rewards is to distribute them equitably.

It should be noted that status symbols often separate employees into classes and lead to formal structures and relationships, thus destroying innovation. In many successful organizations, dress and other symbols of formality and elitism are being abandoned in favour of a relaxed atmosphere in which social class divisions are kept to a minimum. The feelings of acceptance and trust that stem from openness and informality may be the most effective form of nonfinancial compensation.

COMFORTABLE WORKING CONDITIONS

Comfortable, safe working conditions are taken for granted in many organizations. If management allows unnecessary discomforts to continue, not only do employees suffer physically, but resentment undermines the feeling of belonging so important to job satisfaction and performance. People may tolerate cold in a refrigeration plant or heat in a forge. But when year after year, a malfunctioning heating system makes the office frigid in summer and sweltering in winter; when a dishwasher must stoop to pick up heavy bins because there is no room in the kitchen for a trolley; or even when the plush carpet of the office abruptly gives way to cracked linoleum in the mailroom, employees receive a message about their worth to management that no rhetoric will overcome.

The view that good working conditions can be a form of compensation is reinforced by pay plans that increase the financial reward for unpleasant or dangerous jobs (see Chapter 11). In some slaughterhouses, for example, employees who work on the killing floor are paid for eight hours, but work only four-hour shifts. The rationale is that most human beings can cope with only so much killing.

Workplace Flexibility

A relatively new, but highly significant aspect of nonfinancial compensation relates to the creation of workplace flexibility to meet the needs of an increasingly diverse work force. **Workplace flexibility** entails a number of options, designed to provide individuals with greater control over their jobs and work environment. Included in this category are flextime, the compressed workweek, job sharing, flexible compensation, telecommuting, regular part-time work, and modified retirement plans.

FLEXTIME

The practice of permitting employees to choose their own working hours, within certain limitations, is called **flextime.** The concept was introduced in Germany in the late 1960s and has since spread throughout Europe and

North America. In a survey involving companies of all sizes, from all industries and from every region of the United States and Canada, 30 percent of the respondents indicated they had adopted flextime, double the number reporting use of the system in 1977.[36] Warner-Lambert Canada, BC Hydro, and Ontario Hydro are just a few examples of organizations with formal flextime policies, as well as programs that allow an employee to work reduced hours for less pay.[37]

Under a flextime system, employees work the same number of hours per day as they would on a standard schedule. However, they are permitted to work these hours within a **band width**, (defined as the maximum length of the work day) comprising core time (that part of the day when all employees must be present) and flexible time—the period within which employees may vary their schedules (see Figure 12-4).

Perhaps flextime's most important feature is that employees are allowed to schedule their time to minimize conflicts between personal needs and job requirements, without being tempted to use sick leave. Flextime also permits employees to work at hours when they feel they can function best, catering to those who are early risers or those who prefer to work later in the day.

Flextime is not, however, suitable for all types of organizations. For example, its use may be severely limited in assembly-line operations and in companies using multiple shifts.

THE COMPRESSED WORKWEEK

The **compressed workweek** is defined as any arrangement of work hours that permits employees to fulfil their weekly work obligation in fewer than five days. A common compressed workweek is four 10-hour days. Under this arrangement, employees have reported greater job satisfaction and better use of leisure time for family life, personal business, and recreation.

In some instances, employers have experienced increased productivity along with reduced turnover and absenteeism. Indeed, reduced absenteeism alone can increase productivity by 1 to 2 percent.[38] But in other firms, work scheduling and employee fatigue problems have been encountered, resulting in lower product quality and reduced customer service. In some organizations, the conventional five-day week has been reinstated.

One successful application occurred at Bell Canada, where an agreement was reached with the Communication, Energy and Paperworkers Union of Canada to allow its technician members a number of optional work patterns. The 13 000 Bell Canada employees who were working a mandatory four-day, 36-hour week in Ontario and Quebec could return to a

FIGURE 12-4
Illustration of Flextime

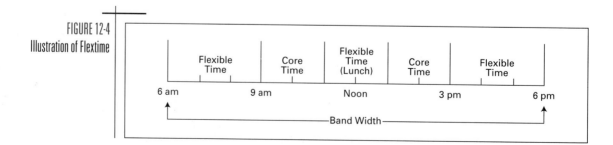

five-day, 40-hour week if they wished. They were also given the option of alternating four- and five-day weeks with eight-hour days. Most of the technicians chose to remain with the four-day week. One problem, however, was that a four-day pattern did not accommodate increased customer demand in some areas, and the union was concerned that contractors were being used to do the extra work.[39]

JOB SHARING

Job sharing is attractive to people who want to work fewer than 40 hours per week. This procedure allows two people to split the duties of one job in some agreed-on manner and to be paid according to their contributions. The employer pays for only one job, but gains the creativity of two employees. Although total financial compensation may be greater because of the additional benefits provided, this expense can be offset by increased productivity. Job sharing may be especially attractive to individuals who have substantial family responsibilities and to older workers who wish to retire gradually.

TELECOMMUTING

Telecommuting allows employees (sometimes called *teleworkers*) to work at home, or at a location away from the office. Most telecommuters are information workers. They fill jobs that in general, require analysis, research, writing, budgeting, data entry, or computer programming.[40] Using a personal computer located in the employee's home and connected to the employer's computer network by telephone, both training and job duties can be carried out without loss of efficiency and quality.

Great-West Life Assurance (Winnipeg, Manitoba), is an example of a firm in which telecommuting is used for "appropriate" work. During one six-month study, the number of women who measured "high" for stress dropped from 53 percent to 36 percent, while two-thirds of the sample felt their productivity was higher. Two-thirds of their superiors felt there were no disadvantages to telecommuting, although 26 percent indicated there were some communication problems.[41]

However, some attendance in the office is essential to maintain contacts and to attend meetings. Typically, a telecommuter would be in the office two days each week, although four-day plans have worked as well.[42] While telecommuting has many advantages, there also are some potential pitfalls. For example, ties between employees and their firms may be weakened, so that successful programs require a higher degree of trust between employees and their supervisors. One manager noted that maintaining discipline among the teleworkers was the biggest management challenge, since some employees may be inclined to stall in completing projects. This potential problem may be dealt with by imposing many intermediate deadlines until the project is completed.[43]

In addition to the way people are supervised, managers considering telecommuting will need to consider changes in other policy areas as well:

- Will compensation and benefits be affected? If so, how?
- Who will be responsible for workers injured at home?

- What about responsibility for insuring equipment?
- How will taxes be affected by telecommuting?
- Will overtime be allowed?
- Will security be provided for the telecommuter's work? How?
- Will the firm have safety requirements for the home?

These questions seem to suggest that telecommuting poses insurmountable problems, but there aren't many examples of unsuccessful telecommuting. However, experience has provided two caveats. First, telecommuting should not be used as a means to reduce other standard benefits provided to employees. Second, telecommuting should not be implemented where the supervisor is opposed to the concept.[44]

REGULAR PART-TIME WORK

The regular use of part-time workers has begun to gain momentum in Canada. This approach adds many highly qualified individuals to the labour market by permitting them to address both employment and family needs. Historically, part-time employees have been regarded as second-class workers. This perception must be changed if a part-time program is to be successful.

One problem with the concept has been that employers have made extensive use of part-time people to avoid paying benefits. Whether or not this trend will continue is difficult to forecast. Only one province, Saskatchewan, has enacted legislation forcing employers to pay prorated benefits to part-time employees.[45]

MODIFIED RETIREMENT

Modified retirement is an option that permits older employees to work fewer than regular hours for a certain period preceding retirement. This option allows an employee to avoid an abrupt change in lifestyle and move more gracefully into retirement.

EXECUTIVE BENEFITS

In some firms, special benefits are provided to a small group of key executives, designed to give them either convenience or prestige. In recent years, many of these benefits have become taxable, so they have become less valuable. Sometimes called "perks", they can include

- a company-provided car;
- accessible, free parking;
- limousine service;
- counselling service, including financial and legal services;
- travel for spouses;
- use of a company plane or yacht;
- a home entertainment allowance;

- special living accommodations away from home;
- club memberships;
- special dining privileges;
- seasons tickets to entertainment events;
- special relocation allowances;
- use of company credit cards;
- reimbursement for children's college expenses;
- no- and low-interest loans.[46]

A **"golden parachute" contract** is a benefit that protects executives in the event their firm is acquired by another. The executive, if adversely affected, may receive payouts under both short- and long-term incentive plans.

A GLOBAL PERSPECTIVE

As executive talent is transferred across national borders, a host of human resource issues must be addressed and resolved. A major challenge facing human resources managers is the development of packages to reassure Canadian expatriates that benefits paid during a foreign posting will be equal or fair in relation to what they would have received in Canada. The HR professional will have to ascertain, for example, whether or not the executive can be maintained on current supplementary health programs while on a foreign assignment. Health care costs in the United States are several times higher than in Canada. A Canadian executive who is transferred to the United States would want to be reassured that health care benefits would be at least equal to those available under provincial health insurance.

Another challenge involves unravelling the complexities of the expatriate's retirement plans,[47] as there are a number of unique aspects of Canadian tax and pension systems. Retirement planning for expatriates must be careful and informed.[48] Typically, employees from the parent country receive a salary, a foreign premium of up to 50 percent, and relocation and living expense allowances. As well, (unless they are posted to the United States) their pay will likely be higher than pay for host-country nationals. This differential tends to create resentment that may reduce cooperation. Canadian managers who hire Hong Kong residents to work in mainland China, for example, should be aware of the intense resentment many mainland Chinese professionals feel toward their Hong Kong counterparts. This attitude is the result, in large measure, of the vast pay differentials between the two societies. Many Canadians have found their standard of living and social class to be considerably higher in a foreign country than it had been at home. The drop in living standards when they return may create some difficulties.

An important incentive for Canadians to accept assignments in foreign countries is the opportunity to avoid high Canadian taxes, as often (but not always), all or a large part of income earned while residing in another country is tax exempt. HR managers should contact Revenue Canada before the employee leaves, however, as there are complex rules regarding foreign residency and tax-free status. Many individuals employ a tax accountant to help develop a financial plan.

The successful management of employee benefits in a multinational corporation depends heavily on a corporate policy statement that outlines specific instructions for the development, approval, and administration of all benefit plans. Employee benefits covered by the policy statement should include any payment of company funds to employees other than base salary, such as pensions, medical and life insurance, vacations, and severance pay.[49] In drafting the policy statement, two general objectives must be met. First, the organization's overall welfare must be given primary consideration. Second, employee benefits must be competitive on the international level if a multinational corporation is to attract and retain dynamic, effective leaders and professionals.[50]

SUMMARY

Most organizations recognize a responsibility to their employees by providing programs covering their health, safety, security, and general welfare. These programs, called benefits, include all financial rewards that are not paid directly to the employee. Legally required benefits include old age pension, the Canada/Quebec Pension Plan, unemployment insurance, workers' compensation, vacation pay, and holiday pay.

A number of benefits are provided voluntarily by organizations. These benefits may be classified as 1) payment for time not worked, 2) employee health and security benefits, and 3) employee services. Company-wide incentive plans include employee share ownership plans (ESOP).

Flexible benefit plans permit employees to choose from among many alternatives, depending upon their needs and lifestyle. Unfortunately, in many firms, rising benefit costs have forced the adoption of flexible benefit plans as a means of shifting a larger portion of the cost onto the employee. Small companies have been especially pressed, as some insurers now balk at pooling small-company risk.

A key issue is the communication of costs borne by the employer in financing employee benefits. Unless employees are made aware of the substantial costs involved, they tend to take their benefits for granted.

As employees often receive sufficient pay to provide for basic necessities, they tend to want rewards that will satisfy higher-order needs, such as social, ego, and self-actualization needs. These needs may be satisfied by the job itself and/or by the job environment. Progressive policies, good supervision, a congenial work group, and comfortable working conditions are all types of nonfinancial reward.

A major nonfinancial benefit can be the flexibility to choose working arrangements that suit the employee's personal needs. Permitting employees to choose, within certain limits, their own working hours is known as flextime. Any arrangement that permits employees to work full-time, but in fewer days than the typical five-day workweek, is called a compressed workweek. In job sharing, two part-time people split the duties of one job in some agreed-on manner and are paid according to their contributions. Telecommuting allows employees to do at least part of their work at home, usually on a computer.

Executive skill significantly affects a firm's success. Sometimes, therefore, special benefits are given to key executives.

Employees who are transferred outside Canada are interested in maintaining their benefits, especially health care and pensions. Expert advice should be sought, therefore, when designing benefits packages for expatriates.

TERMS FOR REVIEW

Benefits
Old Age Security Pension
Canada Pension Plan (CPP)
Universal health care
Vacation/Holiday pay
Voluntary benefits
Disability protection
Employee share ownership plan (ESOP)
Flexible compensation plans

Workplace flexibility
Flextime
Band width
Compressed workweek
Job sharing
Telecommuting
Modified retirement
"Golden parachute" contract

QUESTIONS FOR REVIEW

1. Define benefits. What are the general purposes of benefits?
2. Which benefits are required by law?
3. What are the basic categories of voluntary benefits? Give an example of each type.
4. What are the some forms of special compensation for executives?
5. Why are nonfinancial compensation considerations becoming so important?
6. Distinguish between flextime and the compressed workweek.
7. In what situations is the compressed work week not practical?
8. Discuss the problem of rising benefit costs. How have some managers responded?
9. Why is communication an important element of benefit plan design?
10. Under what circumstances can the job and the job environment become nonfinancial compensation?
11. In what way do small firms face special problems in providing employee benefits?

HRM INCIDENT 1

• A DOUBLE-EDGED SWORD

The decline in oil prices during the mid-1980s adversely affected many industries. Profits were down for all major oil companies and many of their suppliers. Few new orders were received by the producers of drilling fluids, for example, and many existing orders were cancelled or scaled back. As a supplier of drilling fluids, Beta Chemical Company's sales plummeted. Beta, located in Calgary, Alberta, supplies all the major oil companies, as well as independent oil drillers, often called *wildcatters*.

Beta had implemented a comprehensive profit-sharing plan in the 1970s, after several years of rapidly increasing sales and profits. The decision was based largely on an attitude survey of the employees at Beta, which showed that they strongly preferred profit sharing over other benefits. By the late 1980s, base wages at Beta were about 20 percent below levels for similar jobs in Calgary, but half of company profits were paid out each quarter as a fixed percentage of employee wages. Distributed profits averaged more than 50 percent of base wages, so that total compensation at Beta was 20 percent above the area average. Because of this high pay, Beta remained a popular employer, able to take its pick from a long waiting list of applicants. Other benefits were kept to a minimum. There was no retirement plan and a very limited supplemental health plan designed to cover long-term disability only. Employees considered this a good bargain, though, in light of the above-average compensation.

Profits were down markedly in 1987, and the profit-sharing bonus was less than half the historical average. Earnings declined further for the first two quarters of 1988. By mid-year, it was clear that the company would not be profitable for the entire second half. A board meeting was called in late August to discuss the profit-sharing program. One director made it known that he felt the company should drop profit sharing. The human resource director, Vince Harwood, was asked to sit in at the board meeting and to make a presentation suggesting what the company should do about compensation.

QUESTIONS

1. Evaluate the compensation plan at Beta.
2. If you were Vince, what would you recommend for the short term? For the long term?

HRM INCIDENT 2

• A BENEFITS PACKAGE DESIGNED FOR WHOM?

Megan McGraw warmly greeted Robert Ogunlade, her next interviewee. Robert had an excellent academic record and appeared to be just the kind of person Megan's company, Beco Electric, was seeking. Megan is the university recruiter for Beco and had already interviewed six graduating students from York University.

Based on the application form, Robert appeared to be the most promising candidate to be interviewed that day as he had an 87 percent average in his major field, industrial management. He was the vice-president of the Student Government Association and activities chairman for the Business Society. The reference letters in Robert's file revealed that he was both very active socially and a rather intense and serious student. One of the letters, from Robert's employer the previous summer, expressed satisfaction with Robert's work habits.

Megan knew that discussion about compensation could be an important part of the recruiting interview. But she did not know which aspects of Beco's compensation and benefits program would appeal most to Robert. The company has an excellent profit-sharing plan, although 80 percent of profit distributions are deferred and included in each employee's retirement account. Health benefits are also good. The company's supplemental medical and dental plan pays almost 100 percent of costs. A company lunchroom provides meals at about 70 percent of outside prices, although few managers take advantage of this benefit. Employees get two weeks of paid vacation after the first year and three weeks after two years with the company. In addition, there are 12 paid holidays each year. Finally, the company encourages advanced education, paying graduate school tuition and books in full, as well as allowing time off to attend classes during the day.

QUESTIONS

1. What aspects of Beco's compensation and benefits program are likely to appeal to Robert? Explain.
2. Is the total compensation package likely to be attractive to Robert? Explain.

DEVELOPING HRM SKILLS: AN EXPERIENTIAL EXERCISE

Due to a downward trend in business and the resulting financial constraints over the last two years, Straight Manufacturing Company has been able to grant only cost-of-living increases to its employees. The firm has just signed a lucrative three-year contract, however, with a major automobile manufacturer. As a result, management has formed a salary review committee to award merit increases to deserving employees. Members of the salary review committee have only $13 500 of merit money, so deciding who will receive merit increases will be difficult. Louis Convoy, Sharon Kubiak, J. Ward Archer, Ed Wilson, C. J. Sass, and Dominic Passante have been recommended for raises.

Louis Convoy, financial analyst, has an undergraduate business degree and is currently working on an MBA. His previous work experience has allowed him to develop several outstanding financial contacts. Sharon Kubiak, HRM administrative assistant, began as a secretary and after three years with the organization was promoted to her present position. Because her first position was as secretary, her current salary is not at the range commensurate with her new position and responsibilities. J. Ward Archer, assistant plant manager, worked three years as a production supervisor after obtaining his undergraduate degree in business. He received an MBA from McGill two years ago. He is viewed by many as a successful "fast tracker". Ed Wilson, production supervisor, has been with the organization for nine years; the last two years he has been a production supervisor. Last year he single-handedly prevented a wildcat strike. To become a member of management as a production supervisor, Ed took a pay cut in comparison to his union wages. C. J. Sass, director of computer services, has a doctoral degree in computer science and was hired away three years ago from the business school at a leading eastern university. Two-and-a-half years ago he introduced a corporation-wide Human Resource Information System that has refined the organization's internal recruiting and promotion policies. Dominic Passante, district sales manager, has been with the organization for 12 years. In his tenth year with the organization, Dominic was promoted to his current position. He has done a fine job.

Six students will serve on the salary review committee. While the committee would like to award significant merit increases to all those who have been recommended, there are limited funds available for raises. The committee must make a decision as to how the merit funds will be distributed. Your instructor will provide the participants with additional information necessary to complete the exercise.

PART FOUR:

CASE IV Parma Cycle Company: The Pay Plan

At Parma Cycle Company in Delta, B.C., wage rates for hourly workers were established by a three-year labour-management agreement. The agreement provided for cost-of-living adjustments (COLA) based on changes in the Statistics Canada Consumer Price Index. Wage rates varied according to job class and by seniority within each class. For example, a machine operator with two to four years' seniority earned $10.75 per hour. With four to eight years' seniority the rate increased to $12.60 an hour. A company-paid benefit plan provided supplemental medical and dental care for employees. The company contributed 6.5 percent of wages to a retirement plan administered by the machinists' union.

Salaried workers at Parma Cycle were paid straight salaries based on a 40-hour workweek. For first- and second-level managers and clerical workers, work beyond 40 hours in any week was compensated on a pro rata basis. Above the second management level there was no additional compensation for work after 40 hours per week. COLA adjustments were made semiannually for all salaried employees.

Only in the sales department at Parma was any kind of incentive compensation program in effect. The sales representatives were paid a commission averaging about 2 percent of sales in addition to straight salary. The sales manager assigned the sales representatives to particular territories; they were given a choice of territories according to seniority. As older sales representatives left the company, some of the younger ones moved into the better sales areas. This shifting caused some of the more senior sales representatives to insist upon changes in territory to increase their sales potential. In a few cases they were accommodated, but no consistent policy was developed.

Parma Cycle Company was building a new plant in Digby, Nova Scotia. The new plant was to employ about 530 people, two-thirds the number working at the main plant in Delta, B.C. Of course, the work force would be smaller than that at first. About two months before the new plant was scheduled to open, Jesse Heard, the human resource director, was asked to meet with

the president to discuss the compensation policies to be followed in Digby. Jesse knew that Jim Burgess, the president, tended to take a personal hand in matters relating to pay, so he prepared thoroughly for their meeting.

Mr. Burgess had a reputation for getting right to the heart of the matter. "I'm worried about the pay differentials that we are going to have between this plant and the one in Digby," he began. "As I see it, some of the people down there won't be paid half as much as similar workers here."

"That's true," said Jesse. "That really is the main reason for the move to Digby. Without the union and with the low wage rates in that area, we will be able to pay just what the market requires. Most of the helpers and trainees will be available, we think, at minimum wage." "How will the pay classifications down there compare to those up here?" asked Mr. Burgess.

"Well," said Jesse, "up here we have 'workers' and 'machine operators' and the pay within classes is by seniority. Down there we plan to have helpers/trainees, grades 1 and 2, and machine operators, grades 1, 2, and 3. Seniority won't count. We will promote workers based on the recommendations of their supervisors and their performance evaluation scores."

"I liked the incentive plan when you told me about it before, Jesse," said Mr. Burgess. "Let's go over it again. As I understand it, we are going to take 30 percent of the cost savings and pay it out as semi-annual bonuses." "Yes," said Jesse. "An individual's bonus will be a certain percentage of the gross wages paid during that period. But we will multiply that by the person's performance evaluation score." "Will the standard costs be the same as the ones we have here at the Delta plant?" asked Mr. Burgess. "Yes, they will," answered Jesse.

Mr. Burgess continued, "The last time we talked I think you said that we would save money in Digby on the benefits package too."

"Yes," replied Jesse. "For one thing, the tradition in that area is for the company to pay the supplemental health insurance premium for a worker and for the worker to pay the portion applicable to any dependents. Also, we don't have a dental plan down there. Finally, I don't think that we will even have a retirement program for those workers, at least not for a few years." "I think I know the answer," said Mr. Burgess, "but what about the ones who transfer down from Delta?"

"They'll have the same benefits they have here," replied Jesse. "We will continue to cover them under the same insurance plan and guarantee that their wages will keep pace with those of similar workers here."

QUESTIONS

1. What are the pros and cons of paying workers on the basis of seniority?
2. How do cost-of-living adjustments work?
3. Is anything legally wrong with Parma's plan for paying salaried workers? Explain.
4. Are the pay and benefits differentials between the plants likely to create problems? Why or why not?

PART FOUR:

CBC  VIDEO CASE Workers' Safety and Compensation

Workers' compensation, the policy of paying benefits to workers injured on the job, has come under attack from employers on several fronts. Employers resent paying otherwise healthy workers, as well as the lack of financial accountability that exists in workers' compensation boards. Employers question the boards' commitment to curbing costs and criticize them for approving frivolous claims. They even wonder whether the boards have outlived their usefulness.

Canada has 12 workers' compensation boards, which collect funds from employers and pay benefits to workers injured on the job. Each provincial board collects enough money to maintain a fund that will cover immediate outlays and administrative expenses and provide for near-future benefits. At the very least, the fund must be able to provide immediate payments to current recipients. More specifically, the money covers bureaucratic expenses and health care costs, such as hospital treatment and prescription drugs. The other major expense for compensation boards is rehabilitation, which includes rehabilitation and such services as job placement, legal services, and worker training.

At each board, costs are estimated based on the risks faced by employees in various job categories. Employers are separated into bands on the basis of profession. Certain professions have higher premiums than others. For example, construction companies pay higher contributions than accountants. The sum levied on each group varies with its accident record in comparison to an industry average; the more severe the accident record, the higher the premiums. Called the Experience rating program, this procedure is designed to reward employers with above average safety records and provide an incentive for others to improve safety conditions.

A board is considered to be well managed if payment forecasts are accurate. With the current rate of expenditures and the growing number of claims filed for "new" workplace injuries and psychological ailments, such as carpal tunnel syndrome and stress, certain boards have not been able to maintain a surplus in their accounts.

Compensation boards invest half of their funds in government and corporate long-term bonds as a reserve because they are responsible for unforeseen disasters that might arise and for second injuries (injuries that [re-]occur to already compensated workers). It is these future obligations that concern employers and the members of all 12 boards, as only a rough estimate can be calculated for future liabilities. It is difficult to predict future costs due to the onset of "new" injuries and changing economic and demographic variables. When a board's assets are compared with its liabilities and the liabilities are greater, the board is said to have an "unfunded liability." This will be passed on to future employers. At the end of 1988, the combined assets of all 12 boards fell short by $10 billion. By 1993, the shortfall was $14 billion for all boards. Ontario's board accounted for nearly 80 percent of all liabilities, with an $11 billion unfunded liability. It should be noted that this is growing by $100 million a month!

In each province, compensation boards are created through legislation and each is responsible for its own financial situation. During the last recession, when businesses in every province experienced a financial downturn and many laid off workers, shrinking payroll bases led to smaller amounts being collected by the boards. Consequently, since the early 90s, there has not been enough money to carry their costs. This shortfall has put pressure on the boards to raise employees' contribution rates. These increases conflicted with industry-wide cost-cutting strategies made necessary by the recession and increased global competition.

With costs and workers' claims rising steadily, some compensation boards have offered an incentive program to companies called Workwell. Initiated in Ontario in 1990, Workwell has now been adopted by the Yukon and Alberta. The program's aim is to encourage management to take an active role in safety training and accident prevention. The incentive is a decrease in premiums.

Companies that take part in this scheme must undergo a work audit, which studies what preventive measures management can take to lower the firm's premiums. Administered by employers, the audits cover several areas: safety training, worker supervision, health monitoring, procedures for handling and disposing of hazardous materials, and first aid services. Companies are awarded points according to the past and present injury record, which is graded on three levels—above average, average and below average—and its audit level performance. In Ontario, Alberta, and the Yukon the frequency of accidents dropped in 1990 by 17 percent, 15 percent, and 13 percent respectively.

Although an excellent initiative, the system is not without its flaws. For example, a company may have a high rating just by chance, yet management still might not be committed to safety and to reducing costs. Nevertheless, incentive programs are an area where employers (with the help of quasigovernmental bodies) can work together to reduce burdensome premium payments, which give workers' compensation boards a bad reputation.

QUESTIONS

1. Explain why workers' compensation boards are getting into debt.
2. Describe how the Workwell incentive program is run.

Video Resource: "Workers' Compensation," *Venture* 421 (January 31, 1993).

CHAPTER

13

A Safe and Healthy Work Environment

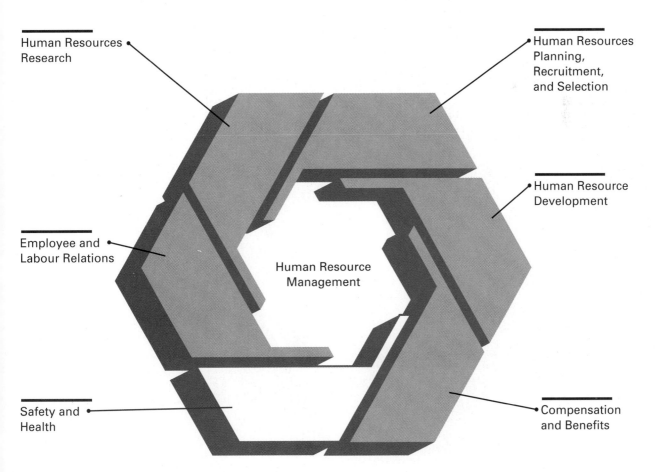

Human Resources Research

Human Resources Planning, Recruitment, and Selection

Human Resource Development

Employee and Labour Relations

Human Resource Management

Safety and Health

Compensation and Benefits

CHAPTER 13

A Safe and Healthy Work Environment

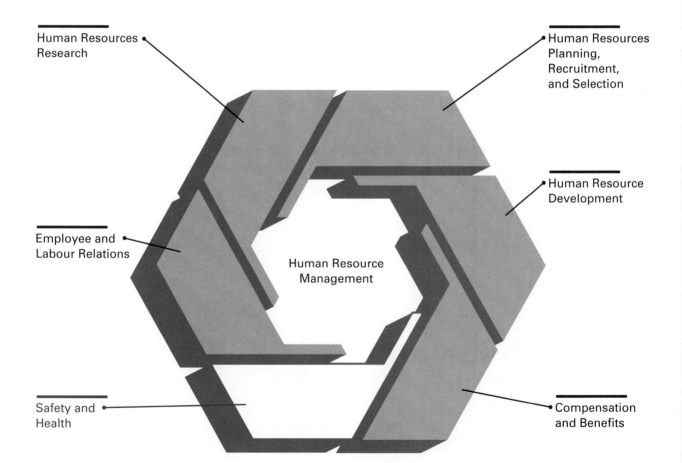

Human Resources Research

Human Resources Planning, Recruitment, and Selection

Human Resource Development

Employee and Labour Relations

Human Resource Management

Safety and Health

Compensation and Benefits

1. Describe the nature and role of safety and health in business and outline the Occupational Health and Safety Acts.

2. Explain the importance of safety programs and health and wellness programs.

3. Describe cumulative trauma disorders.

4. State the nature of stress; discuss the importance of stress management in business today and describe why burnout is of major concern to management.

5. Describe physical fitness programs, alcohol abuse programs, drug abuse programs, and employee assistance programs.

6. Describe the possible impact of AIDS in the workplace.

D ionne Moore, safety engineer for Sather Manufacturing, was walking through the plant when she spotted a situation that immediately caught her attention. Several employees had backed out of a room where several chemicals were used in a critical manufacturing process. Dionne inspected the room, but couldn't determine that anything was wrong, or even different from any other day. She was puzzled as to why the workers were reluctant to resume their tasks. As it turned out, the employees were not only hesitant to return to work, they were adamant in maintaining that conditions in the room were unhealthy. Dionne and the group's supervisor discussed the situation and wondered whether they should order the people to resume work since the department was already behind schedule.

Bob Byrom, chief executive officer for Aztec Enterprises, is concerned about his vice president for marketing, 38-year-old Cecil Weeks. The two had just returned from a short walk to the corporate attorney's office to discuss plans for an overseas joint venture. As they returned to Bob's office, Cecil's face was flushed, he was breathing hard, and he had to take a chair to rest. His condition really alarmed Bob because he didn't think that such a brief bit of exercise should tire anyone, especially someone as apparently healthy as Cecil. Bob knew that the firm couldn't afford to do without Cecil's expertise even for a short time during their expansion plans.

Dionne and Bob are each involved with one of the many critical areas related to employee health and safety. Dionne realizes that safety is a major concern in her organization and that she must strive constantly to maintain a safe and healthy work environment. Bob's experience has caused him to realize the serious ramifications of losing a key executive due to illness or death.

We begin this chapter with definitions of *safety* and *health* and an overview of the Canadian safety and health legislation. Then we discuss safety programs; cumulative trauma disorders; health and wellness programs; stress management; burnout; and programs for physical fitness, alcohol abuse, and drug abuse. Employee assistance programs are presented next, and the chapter ends with a discussion of AIDS in the workplace.

THE NATURE AND ROLE OF SAFETY AND HEALTH

In our discussion, **safety** involves protecting employees from injuries or death caused by work-related accidents, like the following:

1. A 40-year-old forestry supervisor was killed when the skidder he was driving onto a low-bed trailer slid sideways and rolled over.
2. A truck driver was killed when he unhooked the tie-down strap on a load of improperly secured tree-length logs, which rolled over the stake and killed him.
3. A family farmworker was killed when the small tractor he parked on a steep driveway rolled backward and fell sideways.
4. After shovelling mouldy wood chips for four or five hours, eight workers developed nausea, aching muscles, fever, cold chills, difficulty breathing, tiredness, and headaches. After being hospitalized for respiratory problems, they were off work for three weeks.[1]
5. A young worker at a well-known fast-food outlet was called for help by a more junior crew member. The younger crew member accidentally closed a grill on his helper's hand, causing minor burns and a cut that had to be closed with two stitches.

The workplace can be dangerous. In fact, over the past decade, approximately 1000 Canadians a year have died in work-related mishaps.[2]

Health refers to employees' freedom from physical or emotional illness. As business and industry move toward flatter organizational structures with fewer employees, each one working harder, "fitness for work has become a paramount concern for human resource managers."[3]

The human resource professional is vitally concerned with both these aspects of employment, as safety and health problems seriously affect both productivity and the quality of work life. Employee accidents and illnesses can dramatically lower a firm's effectiveness and employee morale. Although line managers are primarily responsible for maintaining a safe, healthy work environment, human resource professionals provide staff expertise to help them deal with these issues. In addition, the human resource manager is frequently responsible for coordinating and monitoring specific safety and health programs. There has been a change in employee attitude as well. The era of putting up with dangerous work is fast disappearing. Most employees now expect that working conditions will be made safe and that the job will not affect their long-term health.[4]

According to Statistics Canada, injury claims in clerical and related occupations rose to 29 681 in 1990 from 20 000 in 1983, an increase of 48 percent. A report from the Canadian Centre for Occupational Health & Safety (Hamilton, Ontario) attributes the increase to a growing awareness of health and safety problems, the increased use of computer equipment, and poor economic conditions, leading to a reduced work force, with remaining employees expected to do more work. In 1988, disabling injuries among clerical workers in Canada cost $30 million in compensation payments and an estimated $625 million in lost productivity.

Causes of injuries have changed over time. In the 1960s, falls caused the most injuries. Now, the effects of video display terminal (VDT) emissions, noise, and air quality are the dominant concerns. In the office, repetitive strain injuries are the most difficult to treat. These injuries, mainly to the hands, can be treated with surgery or drugs, or can be prevented by designing equipment and workstations to reduce physical stress. The current focus is on designing the proper workstation, but analysts consider that the overall task design and environment must also be considered. As well, furniture must be designed individually and the worker must have control.[5]

SAFETY LEGISLATION IN CANADA

Workplace deaths and injuries of all types exact a high toll in terms of human misery. Accidents also increase production costs, often passed along to the consumer. Thus, everyone is affected, directly or indirectly, by job-related deaths and injuries. Through the various health and safety codes, governments attempt to provide safe working conditions for Canadians.

There are two levels of safety legislation in Canada, federal and provincial. Federally, workplace health and safety falls under the Canada Labour Code. This legislation covers most interprovincial and national industries (see Figure 13-1). As well, each province has enacted an Occupational Health and Safety Code. Legislative details differ, but most contain provisions for workplace health and safety committees, a list of employer and employee duties, employees' rights, and enforcement provisions. Only the federal legislation will be detailed here. HR practitioners should familiarize themselves with safety regulations in their province or industry.

Representation

Central to the federal code is the requirement that (with some exceptions) workplaces with 20 or more employees must have a Health and Safety Committee, comprising both management and employee representatives, with the responsibilities listed in Figure 13-2. Committee meetings must be held during working hours. In smaller organizations, a safety representative must be appointed.

FIGURE 13-1
Jurisdiction of the Canada Labour Code

The Canada Labour Code covers the following areas:

- railways
- highway transport
- telephone and telegraph systems
- pipelines
- canals
- ferries, tunnels, and bridges
- shipping and shipping services
- radio and television broadcasting and cable systems
- airports
- banks
- grain elevators licensed by the Canadian Grain Commission, and certain feed mills and feed warehouses, flour mills, and grain seed cleaning plants
- federal public service ministries
- about 40 Crown corporations and agencies
- employment in the operation of ships, trains, and aircraft
- the exploration and development of petroleum on lands subject to federal jurisdiction.

Source: Adapted from A *Guide to the Canada Labour Code: Occupational Safety and Health* (Ottawa: Labour Canada, 1992).

Employer Duties

In general, employers must ensure the health and safety of their employees while they are at work. Areas covered by regulations include physical (e.g., safe machinery, ventilation, noise levels); personal (e.g., safe drinking water, safety materials/equipment), and procedural (e.g., respecting the safety committee, maintaining proper records, investigating accidents). Human resources officials should become familiar with the detailed requirements of the safety codes of their organizations.

One area discussed in detail in all codes is the handling of hazardous materials. The federal Workplace Hazardous Materials Information System (WHMIS) sets national standards that have been adopted by virtually all other jurisdictions.

Employees' Duties

In general, employees are responsible for taking all reasonable precautions to ensure their personal health and safety, as well as the safety of co-workers. This responsibility includes following procedures and safety directives, reporting hazards, and using proper safety equipment and/or clothing.

FIGURE 13-2
Duties of the Health and Safety
Committee

1. Meet at least once a month and during emergencies when required. The agenda should be prepared by the committee secretary in cooperation with the two committee cochairpersons. As soon as possible after the meeting, the meeting minutes should be posted.

2. Ensure that adequate records are kept on work accidents, injuries, and health hazards and monitor data on a regular basis.

3. Receive and deal with complaints relating to the safety and health of the employees represented.

4. Participate in all inquiries and investigations concerning occupational safety and health. Consult technical experts as necessary.

5. Regularly monitor the safety and health programs, measures, and procedures.

6. May request from an employer any information considered necessary to identify existing or potential hazards with respect to materials, processes, or equipment in the workplace.

7. May review any government and employer reports relating to the safety and health of the employees represented by the committee. However, the consent of the employee concerned must be obtained before requesting personal medical records.

8. May develop, establish, and maintain safety and health programs for the education of the employees the committee represents.

9. Cooperate with safety officers by providing information and assisting in investigations of accidents and refusals to work.

10. Cooperate with any occupational health service established to serve the workplace.

11. Maintain records about safety and health complaints and the committee actions taken on complaints. Keep records of refusals to work and accidents.

Source: Adapted from *A Guide to the Canada Labour Code: Occupational Safety and Health* (Ottawa: Labour Canada, 1992), p. 12.

Employees' Rights

Under the Canada Labour Code an employee has three rights:

1. the right to know;
2. the right to participate; and
3. the right to refuse work perceived as dangerous.

The right to know includes information about known workplace hazards and the training to protect oneself. The right to participate refers to the opportunity to serve as a health and safety committee member or representative and to the responsibility for reporting unsafe conditions. The most controversial part of the Code, however, is the employee's right to refuse unsafe work. If there is "reasonable cause" to believe the employee or a co-worker might be injured, anyone can refuse to work. However, proper procedure, as spelled out in Figure 13-3, must be followed.

FIGURE 13-3
Procedures for Refusing
Dangerous Work

Report to Employer
The employee must report his/her refusal immediately to his/her supervisor and to the safety and health representative or a member of the safety and health committee.

Investigation by Employer
The employer must then investigate the refusal in the presence of the employee and either a non-management member of the health and safety committee or the health and safety representative.

Continued Refusal
Where the employer decides that there is no danger, or takes steps to correct the danger and the employee has reasons to believe that a danger still exists, the employee may continue to refuse. Both the employer and the employee then must contact a safety officer, appointed by the Ministry of Labour.

Reassignment of Employee and Task
Until the safety officer arrives, investigates and makes a decision, the employer cannot assign the work in question to another employee unless that other employee has been informed of the refusal. Meanwhile, the employee who refused to work may be asked by the employer to remain in a safe place nearby or may be assigned to reasonable alternate work.

Investigation and Decision by a Safety Officer
In the presence of the employer and the employee (or the employee's representative), the safety officer investigates the work refusal, decides whether a danger exists, and informs the employer and employee of this decision.

Result of Decision
If the safety officer decides that a danger *does* exist, he/she will issue a directive to the employer to correct the situation. The employee can continue to refuse the work until the employer complies with the directive.
If the safety officer decides that a danger *does not* exist, the employee no longer has the right to refuse under the protection of the Code. However, the employee may appeal the decision of the safety officer.

Appeals
Requests for a review of the decision of a safety officer may be made to the safety officer, requiring him or her to have the decision reviewed by the Canada Labour Relations Board or, for the public service, the Public Service Staff Relations Board. The request must be made in writing within seven days of receiving notification of the safety officer's decision.

Source: Canada Labour Code.

Enforcement

Safety officers with wide-ranging powers are appointed by the Ministry of Labour. They can enter any workplace at any reasonable time and take any necessary steps to conduct an investigation, such as taking samples or pictures, conducting interviews, or making inspections. In addition, they have the power to order an employer not to disturb an area, to produce documents, to provide statements about health and safety conditions, and, most important, to correct unsafe working conditions. If the employer does not comply, the safety officer may recommend prosecution. The Canada Labour Code provides for fines according to the seriousness of the offence (see Figure 13-4). In addition, there are provisions for fines of up to $1 million and up to two years' imprisonment for serious or repeated refusal to comply with WHMIS.

FIGURE 13-4
Offences and Maximum Penalties

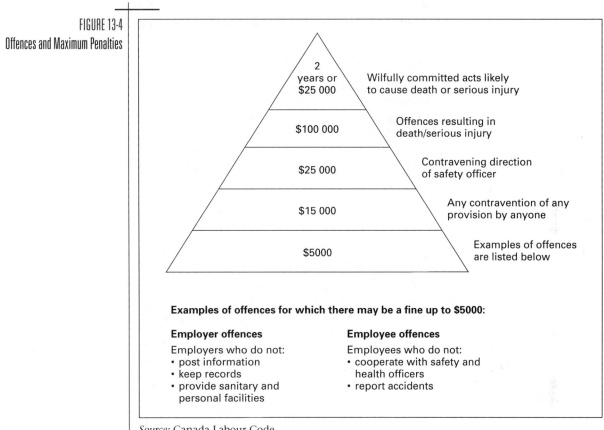

Source: Canada Labour Code.

Compliance

For the most part, employers do comply with federal and provincial safety regulations. For example, Figure 13-5 shows that over half of all 4421 investigations in New Brunswick in one year produced orders of some sort, but only 74 (1.7%) resulted in stop work orders, and there were only 15 court cases.

THE FOCUS OF SAFETY PROGRAMS

Safety programs may be designed to accomplish their purposes in two ways. The first approach is to create a psychological climate that promotes a safe workplace, as accidents can be reduced when employees consciously think about safety. This attitude must permeate the firm's operations, so a strong company policy emphasizing safety and health is crucial. For example, one major chemical firm's policy states: "It is the policy of the company that every employee be assigned to a safe and healthful place to work. We strongly desire accident prevention in all phases of our operations. Toward this end, the full cooperation of all employees will be required."

The implication of this policy is that no one person is assigned the task of making the workplace safe. It is everyone's job, from senior management to the lowest-level employee. Everyone should be encouraged to come up with solutions to safety problems.

Workplace Inspections/Visits	4421
Orders	2703
Stop Work Orders	74
Accident Investigations	84
Fatalities Investigated	6
Court Cases	15

Source: Adapted from *Annual Report 1992–1993* (Fredericton: N.B. Occupational Health and Safety Commission).

Accident prevention requires a sustained effort by everyone, but unfortunately, as the old adage suggests: "Everyone's responsibility becomes no one's responsibility." Therefore, the firm's managers, as the holders of authority, must take the lead. The unique role of management is made clear by legislation, which places the primary responsibility for employee safety on the employer.[6] Figure 13-6 provides a checklist of steps management should take to fulfil that responsibility.

The second approach to safety program design is to develop and maintain a safe physical working environment. For example, safety devices are installed on a machine to provide protection even if an operator is extremely tired, or is inattentive because of serious family problems. Every attempt is made to create a physical environment in which accidents cannot occur.

DEVELOPING SAFETY PROGRAMS: A DIFFERENT LOOK AT SAFETY

The prevention of workplace accidents requires planning. Plans may be relatively simple, as for a small retail store, or more complex, as for a large automobile assembly plant. Regardless of the size of the organization, senior management's support is essential if safety programs are to be effective.

Reasons for Management to Support a Safety Program

Every phase of human resource management is affected by workplace accident or injury. Consequences include the following:

- *Personal loss.* Injuries cause physical pain and mental anguish. Of much greater concern is the possibility of permanent disablement or even death.

- *Financial loss to injured employees.* Most employees are covered by company insurance plans or personal accident insurance. However, an injury may result in financial losses not covered by the insurance.

- *Lost productivity.* When an employee is injured, there will be a loss of productivity to the firm. In addition to obvious losses, there are often hidden costs. For example, a replacement may need additional training

FIGURE 13-6
Checklist: Health and Safety
Obligations for Executives

While it is not possible to provide an exhaustive list of all of the possible obligations under health and safety legislation, here are a number of suggestions that apply to all workplaces:

■ Prepare a written health and safety policy, post the policy in a conspicuous place and distribute it to all workers.

■ Ensure that all employees who receive the policy sign for it and that the written receipt is kept on file.

■ Distribute the policy also to all employees, contractors and subcontractors.

■ Where required, post copies of the relevant legislation (in Ontario for example, the *Occupational Health and Safety Act* must be posted).

■ Put into place a program to implement the policy.

■ Put into place a program to train all workers in workplace safety.

■ Ensure that all individuals who do work for the company are properly trained even if they are not employed directly by the company.

■ Document the instruction and training given to all workers.

■ Put in writing all instructions necessary to protect health and safety; distribute them to all workers and secure a signed receipt from each that he or she has received the instruction.

■ Ensure that a responsible person in the organization knows the applicable legislation and regulations and empower this person with the authority to enforce proper procedure.

■ Ensure all orders are complied with and that they are immediately reported to someone in a position of authority within the company.

■ Properly report all occupational accidents and illnesses.

■ Ensure that all supervisors are properly trained and competent.

■ Provide for regular inspection of the workplace for health and safety compliance and immediately correct all problems.

■ Where required, ensure that a health and safety committee is in place and that the committee meets regularly and carries out its mandated function.

■ Maintain all equipment in good condition, and ensure that safety devices such as guards are in place and functioning.

■ Establish a safety system which includes regular supervision and inspection as well as internal reporting.

■ Be aware of industry standards and ensure that the company does not fall below these standards.

■ Put into place both remedial and contingency plans for emergencies, train all workers in proper emergency procedures and document this training.

Source: Reproduced with permission from *Canadian HR Reporter 8* (12), p. 15. © 1995 MPL Communications Inc.

to replace the injured employee. Even when a person can be moved into the injured employee's position, efficiency may suffer.

■ *Higher insurance premiums.* Workers' compensation insurance premiums are based on the employer's history of insurance claims. The potential for savings related to employee safety provides a degree of incentive to establish formal programs.

- *Possibility of fines and imprisonment.* Wilful and repeated violation of provisions in the Occupational Safety and Health Act may result in serious penalties.

- *Damaged employee relations.* Trust and morale may be seriously eroded if employees believe that management doesn't care enough about them to make their workplace safe.

- *Difficulties in recruiting.* If a firm acquires a reputation for unsafe working conditions, it may be difficult to recruit qualified workers. Compensation may also be affected if the firm must pay a premium to overcome such a reputation.

- *Increased turnover.* Maintaining a stable work force may be difficult if employees perceive the workplace as hazardous.

In short, executives should be strongly motivated to promote safety, both on grounds of social responsibility and because safety is in the best interests of the firm.

Work Force Involvement in Safety

One way to strengthen a safety program is to stress work force input. To prevent accidents, each employee must make a personal commitment to safe work practices. The development of a team concept whereby employees watch out for each other is a worthwhile goal. One way to advance this philosophy is to form safety teams consistent with total quality management techniques. Participation helps to form positive attitudes, as employees tend to develop a sense of ownership toward the safety program. The committee may become involved not only with safety issues, but also with ways to improve productivity. Employee feedback, however, is essential and good safety performance must be rewarded.

In companies with effective safety programs, virtually everyone in the firm is involved, but line managers are normally directly responsible for controlling conditions that cause accidents. As part of this responsibility, they must set a proper example. If a supervisor fails to use safety devices when demonstrating use of the equipment, for example, subordinates may feel the devices aren't really necessary. In many companies, one staff member coordinates the overall safety program. This individual, whose title might be safety director or safety engineer, educates line managers and employees about the merits of safety, while recognizing and eliminating unsafe work conditions. Although the position is advisory, a well-informed and assertive safety director may have considerable influence.

Internally conducted safety audits are a sensible precaution, as audits may reveal areas that require improvement. In addition, many organizations have invited provincial or federal safety officers to review internal practices as part of an ongoing safety program. Throughout North America, then, attitudes toward safety are changing, albeit slowly. The blame-the-worker approach is disappearing, replaced by the idea that accidents are a symptom of an inefficient operation. This change has necessitated a reversal in management thinking, so that safety is integrated with all other areas of management.

Thus, safety begins with the hiring process, where the applicant's safety record is studied, and continues through orientation, training, and appraisal. Safety becomes part of job design, maintenance, and work procedures. All these activities take place in an atmosphere of consultation and employee involvement, as part of the design of a safety culture in which employees take personal responsibility for their own safety and the safety of their peers.[7]

One author described a similar approach, which he called Total Involvement Safety (TIS). He argues that today's workers no longer blindly accept management's assessment of risk. They challenge and formulate their own risk assessment; they identify more hazards and expect better hazard control. Worker concerns will be addressed only if workers are involved in the process of solving safety problems. A good starting point for a TIS program is an Employee Audit Team. Employees are recruited and trained to audit and correct unsafe conditions. The next level of involvement is the Education Involvement Team. These teams enlist employee participation in conducting safety training meetings. Next comes the formation of Involvement Task Teams, which solve ongoing safety problems and address areas needing improvement. The final step in TIS is the Hourly Involvement Committee. This is the focal point of the TIS program. Employees on this committee meet monthly with top management to determine safety program direction.[8]

Accident Investigation

Accidents can happen even in the most safety-conscious firms. Each accident, whether or not it results in an injury, should be carefully evaluated to determine the cause and to prevent recurrence. The safety engineer, an employee representative, and the line manager jointly investigate accidents. To prevent accidents, the supervisor must learn (through active participation in the safety program) why, how, and where accidents occur, and who is involved. As well, supervisors enhance their knowledge about accident prevention by helping to prepare accident reports.

Training Supervisors and Employees

While some progressive organizations evaluate safety records, safety remains a relatively minor factor in the overall assessment of most front-line supervisors. More emphasis should be placed on the training and the development of supervisors, instead of informally working with them as the need arises.[9] Accidents also have legal ramifications because, under federal legislation and virtually every provincial health and safety act, the employer is responsible for providing a safe workplace. In the event of an accident, an employer will likely be held responsible by a court unless it can be demonstrated that what lawyers call "due diligence" was exercised; that is the employer took all possible or practical precautions. Management would have to prove that an employee "acted contrary to company policy, instruction and training and despite having been disciplined or told he or she would be."[10] Otherwise, an employer might be fined for breaking health and safety regulations. Safety should, therefore, be emphasized during the training and orientation of new employees. The early months of employment are often critical, because work injuries decrease substantially with length of service, a pattern that is consistent for both men and women.

Ann Flynn, Safety and Training Coordinator for the City of Fredericton, NB, says that to be truly effective, safety training must be an integral component of the employee's job training and career development, starting with orientation and continuing throughout an individual's career. The employer, through the supervisor, must take responsibility to ensure that safety training is relevant to both the employee and the organization. Training will be most successful, she adds, in those organizations where safety training is treated as a sound investment rather than a legislated obligation.[11]

Safety Program Evaluation

The best indicator that a safety program is succeeding is a reduction in the number and the severity of accidents. Thus, frequency and severity statistics are often used in safety program evaluation. In addition to program evaluation criteria, an effective accident reporting and recording system is needed. When a new safety program is initiated, the number of accidents may decline significantly. Some supervisors, however, may be tempted not to report certain accidents to make the statistics look better. Thus, care must be taken to ensure all accidents are reported, as proper safety program evaluation depends on accurate data reporting and recording.

To generate improvements, evaluation results must be transmitted upward to senior management and downward to line managers.

Safety and Health Trends

According to recent reports, managers are spending an increasing amount of money on safety. The reasons for this trend include[12]

- *Productivity*: An effective safety program may boost morale and productivity, while simultaneously reducing costs. At work sites with excellent health and safety records, lost workday rates tend to run between 20 and 40 percent of the industry average.[13]
- *Profitability*: In addition, improved safety can reduce payouts related to rising workers' compensation costs.
- *Employee Relations*: A good safety record is an effective vehicle for attracting and retaining employees.
- *Reduced Liability*: An effective safety program can reduce corporate and executive liability if an employee is injured.
- *Marketing*: A good safety record may improve competitiveness, as recruiting and winning contracts may become easier.

Ergonomics and Cumulative Trauma Disorders

Interest is growing in **ergonomics**, the study of human interaction with tasks, equipment, tools, and the physical environment. Through ergonomic techniques, attempts are made to fit the machine to the person rather than requiring the person to adjust to the machine. The result is reduced operator fatigue and discomfort.

A primary target of ergonomics is **cumulative trauma disorders**,[14] injuries that can result from constant repetition of specific motions that literally wear out the human body. "A job is considered repetitive when a task is performed repeatedly in cycles of 30 seconds or less or when repetitious movements make up more than 50 percent of the work cycle."[15] The safety specialist needs to look carefully at such tasks. One study, for example, found that more than 50 percent of all occupational illnesses reported in 1990 were related to repetitive trauma. Cumulative trauma disorders include injuries to the back and upper extremities. For example, **carpal tunnel syndrome** is a specific injury caused by repetitive flexing and extension of the wrist, resulting in a pinched nerve. Symptoms include pain, inability to differentiate hot and cold by touch, and loss of strength in the fingers. Prolonged use of computers can lead to cumulative trauma disorders. Motion may be very repetitive, since the operator does not stop to flex the muscles by changing paper, as on the old typewriter. Extensive use of the mouse can also result in finger strain. Another contributory factor is the aging work force. Since older people exhibit decreased muscle performance, flexibility, and joint mobility, cumulative trauma disorders can be expected to increase.

Cumulative trauma disorders result in considerable costs to employers. For example, in 1988, employees at a poultry deboning plant operated by Cuddy Foods (London, Ontario) experienced repetitive strain injuries to their hands, wrists, and backs. The company hired an ergonomics consultant company, The Human Touch. A cost justification analysis by Human Touch personnel showed that in two years of operation, Cuddy's presorting workstation alone had lost 1300 person-days, incurring $225 000 in workers' compensation costs. An ergonomics redesign was implemented in 1990 for only $34 000.[16] This company now has become a model workplace, as officials from the Ontario Ministry of Labour and the Workers' Compensation Board advise other employees to view Cuddy's system.[17] There are compelling reasons, then, for employers to develop comprehensive preventive programs.[18]

Workplace Violence

In the United States, workplace violence accounts for at least 750 deaths each year, more than the total of 592 homicides in Canada in 1994. Violence of all types cost American employers $4.2 billion in 1992 because of lost business, lost productivity from injured workers, and lawsuits stemming from negligent security claims. Workers' compensation insurance premiums are also increased in companies that experience violence.[19] At present, this issue is not of great concern to Canadian managers. It might be wise, however, for HR professionals to monitor their workplaces to ensure this phenomenon does not become commonplace here. Employee security is a concern in some workplaces. In Moncton, for example, the provincial civil servants who interview welfare applicants sit at desks equipped with "panic buttons" in case there is violence or threatening behaviour.[20]

HEALTH AND WELLNESS PROGRAMS

Aside from the moral implications, the reason for managers to be concerned about their employees' health becomes obvious when employee worth is calculated. For example, how valuable is Cecil Weeks, the vice-president mentioned at the beginning of the chapter? If he becomes ill and cannot participate in his firm's strategic planning, his company will be seriously disadvantaged. Health problems affect not only an individual's quality of life but also the company's profitability.

In addition to management and government initiatives, union support has also hastened the establishment of more effective health programs. Unions are placing industrial health issues high on their list of demands in collective bargaining. Rather than concentrating on pay, unions now also seek gains in occupational health and recreational facilities along with their major concern, job security. Environmental factors also play a major role in the development of physical and mental disorders. The traditional view that health is the absence of disease, or a function of medical care, is changing. Many people now perceive that optimal health can be achieved through environmental safety, organizational change, and different lifestyles. Individuals have some control over health problems related to smoking, excessive stress, lack of exercise, obesity, or alcohol and drug abuse. Moreover, all these issues can be addressed through workplace health and safety programs.

A formal company wellness program involves careful planning and a significant funding commitment. As with a safety program, a focus on employee wellness should reflect a company philosophy that emphasizes the value of human assets. Many of the procedures used in establishing an effective safety program are also applicable to a company wellness program. Similarly, a firm with the reputation of having a healthy work environment is in a stronger position to achieve many other human resource objectives. For example, recruitment may be easier because more people want to work for the company. Employee and management relations may also improve when workers believe that management is genuinely concerned about them.

Back and neck injuries, sprains, and strains are among the most common and costly problems in industry. For this reason, many wellness programs either began with a focus on physical fitness, or developed out of company-sponsored physical fitness programs. While physical fitness continues to be an important component of most major wellness initiatives, the movement is now toward a more holistic approach to improving health, often through stress management.

Stress Management

A notable trend in North America is the increased concern for individual emotional well-being. On the one hand, managers are becoming more aware that long-term productivity depends largely on employee dedication and commitment. Employees, on the other hand, increasingly hold their employers liable for work-related emotional problems. At the same time, stress-related mental disorders have over the last few years become one of the most worrisome occupational diseases. Thus, programs dealing with stress and its related problems are becoming increasingly popular.

Stress is the body's nonspecific reaction to any demand made by the environment. Reactions to stress are highly individual; certain events may be quite stressful to one person, but not to another. Moreover, the effect of stress is not always adverse. Mild stress, for example, may improve productivity, acting as a stimulus in developing creative ideas. Excessive stress, however, lowers productivity and innovation levels in the workplace. Figure 13-7 lists some of the behaviours exhibited by overstressed employees.

Although everyone lives with stress, severe and prolonged exposure, can be harmful. In fact, stress can be as disruptive to an individual as an accident, resulting in attendance problems, excessive use of alcohol or other drugs, inadequate job performance, or overall poor health. There is increasing evidence, moreover, that severe, prolonged stress is related to heart disease, stroke, hypertension, cancer, emphysema, diabetes, and cirrhosis. Stress may even lead to suicide. Although exact measurements of the effects on business are impossible, stress costs Canadian industry billions of dollars each year in lost wages and treatment of related disorders. Aside from humanitarian reasons, then, economic forces should motivate management to help employees manage stress.

Some jobs are generally perceived as being more stressful than others. Some of the most stressful jobs are listed in Figure 13-8. A common factor among many of these jobs is the employee's lack of control over the work. That certain jobs have been identified as more stressful than others has important implications for managers, as they are responsible for recognizing inappropriate behaviour and for suggesting that employees contact health professionals for diagnosis and treatment. Managers should also monitor their employees' progress and provide them with the incentive to succeed. They should inform employees that there are rewards for lifestyle changes and that the advantages are greater than the costs.

Burnout

One of the results of organizational and individual failure to dealt with stress can be seen in the following scenario:

FIGURE 13-7 Signs of Stress	
	■ Reduced clarity of judgment and effectiveness
	■ Rigid behavior
	■ Complaints about poor health
	■ Strained relationships with others due to irritability
	■ Increasing excessive absence
	■ Emerging addictive behaviors (e.g., drugs, alcohol, smoking)
	■ Expressions of inadequacy and low self-esteem
	■ Apathy or anger on the job

Source: Michael Pesci, "Stress Management: Separating Myth from Reality." *Personnel Administrator* (January 1982) © 1982. Reprinted with the permission of *HR Magazine* (formerly *Personnel Administrator*), published by the Society for Human Resource Management, Alexandria, Virginia.

FIGURE 13-8
Stressful Jobs

The 12 jobs with the most stress are

1. Labourer
2. Secretary
3. Inspector
4. Clinical lab technician
5. Office manager
6. Supervisor
7. Manager/administrator
8. Waitress/waiter
9. Machine operator
10. Farm owner
11. Miner
12. Painter

Other high-stress jobs (in alphabetical order) are

Bank Teller	Nurse's aide
Clergy member	Plumber
Computer programmer	Police officer
Dental assistant	Practical nurse
Electrician	Public relations worker
Firefighter	Railroad switcher
Guard	Registered nurse
Hairdresser	Sales manager
Health aide	Sales representative
Health technician	Social worker
Machinist	Structural-metal worker
Meatcutter	Teacher's aide
Mechanic	Telephone operator
Musician	Warehouse worker

Cheryl Weaver supervises 50 people in the administrative department of a large bank. Normally, she is a competent and a conscientious manager with a reputation for doing the job right and on time. Until recently, Cheryl had been considered a strong candidate for vice-president of administration. The situation has changed, however, because Cheryl is behaving differently. She can't seem to concentrate on her work and appears to be a victim of *battle fatigue*. "Oh, Cheryl," a co-worker advised, "you'll make it. You've always been so strong." But Cheryl shocked her associate when she responded, "I don't want to be told I'll make it on my own. I already know I can't."

Cheryl doesn't know exactly what has caused her run-down condition. She feels that she is at her wit's end and desperately needs assistance. Cheryl could be the victim of a stress-related phenomenon known as burnout. **Burnout** is a state of fatigue or frustration that stems from devotion to a cause, way of life, or relationship that did not provide the expected reward. In essence, burnout is the perception that an individual is giving more than he or she is receiving—whether it is money, satisfaction, or praise. It is often associated with a midlife or midcareer crisis, but the condition can occur at different times to different people. Unrealistic expectations are often major contributors to burnout. When people strive excessively to achieve unattainable goals, they may experience a feeling of helplessness—that no matter what they do they feel they won't succeed. Thus, they lose their motivation to perform.

Although some employees try to hide their problems, there are usually behavioural changes that indicate an inability to cope. Employees may start procrastinating, or, just the opposite, may take on too many assignments. They may lose track of critical details, and become increasingly absent-minded. Normally amiable individuals may become irritable, cynical, disagreeable, pompous, or may even develop paranoia.[21]

Those who work in the helping professions—such as teachers, nurses, counsellors, and social workers—seem to be especially susceptible to burnout, sometimes accelerated by job-related stress, whereas others may be vulnerable because of their upbringing, expectations, or personalities. Burnout is frequently associated with people who must work closely with others under stressful and tension-filled conditions. A study by Northwestern National Life Insurance Company, for example, found that higher burnout levels occurred in firms where there had been substantial cuts in employee benefits, where ownership had changed, where overtime was required, or where the work force had been reduced.[22]

Anyone may experience burnout. A highly cynical or pessimistic burnout victim can quickly affect the morale of an entire group. It is important, therefore, that the problem be dealt with quickly. Managers should watch for warning signals: 1) irritability, 2) forgetfulness, 3) frustration, 4) fatigue, 5) procrastination, 6) tension, or 7) increased alcohol or drug use.[23] Other symptoms might include recurring health problems, such as ulcers, back pain, or frequent headaches. As the burnout victim is often unable to maintain an even emotional balance, hostility may be expressed in inappropriate situations. As the work environment may be the major source of stress, burnout is a problem that should be confronted before it occurs. Thus, managers must be aware of potential sources of internal and external stress.

Some successful entrepreneurs with rapidly expanding businesses have found ways to combat the demands on their time and to keep from burning out. Psychologists stress the importance of entrepreneurs taking time away from the job because of the adverse effects on both personal health and the profitability of the business. Terry Hinan of TR Hinan Construction Ltd. of Fonthill, Ontario, for example, hired an extra person to complement his construction manager and office employee. President S. Samole, of Mississauga's Fidelity Electronics of Canada Ltd., complements his work time with music, managing to record two albums while reaping business revenues of $6.2 million in 1990. Sharing work among four partners has helped Regina Printshop Paperworks Inc. to increase sales from $163 713 in 1985 to $1.2 million in 1990. Even though the president of Miramichi Industries Ltd. in Newcastle, N.B. continues to put 70 hours per week into her $3.8-million-a-year company, plus attend to three children, she takes time for herself every evening.[24] All these individuals have found ways to combat the constant stress that leads to eventual burnout.

Sources of Stress

Stress possesses devastating potential. While some factors are controllable to varying degrees, others are not. In the following paragraphs, we discuss some of the primary stressors, or sources of stress.

THE FAMILY

Although a frequent source of happiness and security, the family can also be a significant stressor. From a manager's viewpoint, for example, one of the most difficult of all work situations is to manage an employee in the midst of divorce proceedings. When divorce leads to single parenthood, the difficulties may be compounded. As well, differences over money, sex, in-laws, housework, and many other issues can lead to short- or long-term morale problems that affect productivity.

As well, in many dual-career families, traditional roles may be altered. What happens, for example, when one partner is content with a job and the other is offered a desirable promotion requiring transfer to a distant city? These types of circumstances raise stress levels and sometimes put unbearable strains on relationships.

FINANCIAL PROBLEMS

Financial problems are one of the major stressors in North America. For some employees, these problems are never resolved, creating constant tension, while playing a role in divorce or poor work performance.

LIVING CONDITIONS

Stress levels may be higher for people who live in densely populated areas. These people face longer lines, endure more hectic traffic jams, and contend with higher levels of air and noise pollution. Urban life has many advantages, but the benefits are not without costs—often in the form of day-to-day stress.

CORPORATE CULTURE

Corporate culture can be an employee's main stressor. The CEO's leadership style often sets the tone. An autocratic CEO who permits little input from subordinates may create a stressful environment. Or a weak CEO may encourage subordinates to compete for power, resulting in internal conflicts. The corporate environment may be stressful if the CEO insists on setting impossible goals.

Even in the healthiest corporate culture, stressful relationships among employees can occur. Employee personality types, values, and belief systems vary and may so impair communication that stress is inevitable. The problem may be compounded if the organization's reward system encourages competition for promotion, pay increases, and status.

ROLE AMBIGUITY

Role ambiguity produces feelings of insecurity, especially when an employee doesn't understand job content. The employee may feel stressed, for example, when he or she doesn't perform certain duties as expected by the supervisor, or tries to accomplish tasks that are a part of someone else's job.

ROLE CONFLICT

Role conflict occurs when an individual is forced to pursue opposing goals. A secretary asked to type false reports may experience conflict between the role of subordinate and loyalty to the firm. An employee asked to work overtime on parent-teacher night will experience conflict between the role of employee and of parent. Increased stress results from the impossibility of fulfilling both roles.

JOB OVERLOAD

When employees are given more work than they can reasonably handle, they become victims of **job overload**, a situation that often affects the best performers in a firm. These individuals have proven they can produce more, so they are given more to do. At its extreme, work overload results in burnout.

WORKING CONDITIONS

Stress can be caused by physical workplace characteristics such as overcrowding, excessive noise, poor lighting, and poorly maintained work stations and equipment. Something as apparently benign as an antiquated photocopier that doesn't work properly, for example, can become a significant stressor when an important report must be assembled.

MANAGERIAL WORK

According to one management consultant, almost half of today's managers may suffer undue job stress.[25] Responsibility for employees, conducting performance appraisals, coordinating and communicating layoffs, and conducting outplacement counselling can all create a great deal of stress for some people. One study of human resource executives determined that female HR professionals felt considerably more stress as a result of organizational politics. This factor was the only significant difference found in sources of stress for men and women. The reason for this observation could relate to the exclusion of many women from political networks.[26]

It is important, then, for managers to be aware of their employee's stressors. It is equally important that they implement programs to deal effectively with stress. Two factors must be kept in mind when designing stress abatement programs. First, sources of stress can be found in both the employee and the environment. A program focusing on the employee alone will likely fail to address important stressors. A significant source of stress that is often overlooked (since people cannot usually see themselves as others see them) is the manager himself or herself.

"We're finding we have to work with people on two levels," says Lucille Peszat, director of the Canadian Centre for Stress and Well-Being in Toronto. "We work one on one, and then prepare the organizational setting, so it isn't a major source of stress."[27]

Changing Patterns of Stress

In Canada, trends in stress-related complaints have been studied by contacting counselling services attached to employee assistance programs (EAPs). In the mid-1980s, surveys found that, in those organizations in which EAPs were available, only 3 to 4 percent of employees used the counselling option. By 1993, however, participation rates had risen to between 7 and 8 percent.

The reasons for counselling have changed as well. Substance abuse and mental health problems, the most common reasons for EAP usage in the 1980s, have been replaced by issues related to marriage and relationships, finances and budgets, legal problems, and work-related problems such as those caused by downsizing, restructuring, and cost-cutting.[28] HR managers, then, need to monitor their EAPs closely to make sure they are offering the services employees need.

Coping with Stress

While specific programs to prevent or relieve stress can be very helpful, properly designed general organizational programs have a role to play in creating an environment—a corporate culture—that holds anxiety and tension to an acceptable level (see Figure 13-9). The following list describes elements of such a culture.

- Employee inputs are sought and valued. Employees are given greater control over their work and participate in making decisions that affect them.

- Communication is emphasized. Employees know what is going on in the firm, what their particular roles are, and how well they are performing their jobs.

- Each person's role is defined, yet care is taken not to discourage risk takers and those who want to assume greater responsibility.

- Individuals are given the training and development they need to perform current and future jobs. Individuals are trained to work as effective team members and to develop an awareness of how they and their work relate to others.

FIGURE 13-9
Organizational Programs and
Techniques That Can Be Effective in
Coping with Stress

General Organizational Programs

Job analysis
Human resource development
Effective communication, motivation, and leadership styles (corporate culture)
Organization development
Career planning and development
Performance appraisal
Compensation

Specific Techniques

Hypnosis
Relaxation training
Biofeedback

Specific Organizational Programs

Physical fitness
Alcohol and drug abuse counselling
Employee assistance programs

- Employees are assisted in career planning. Equal consideration is given to achieving personal and organizational goals.

- Employee needs, both financial and nonfinancial, are met through an equitable reward system.

Figure 13-9 also identifies specific techniques that individuals can use to deal with stress. **Hypnosis** is an altered state of consciousness that is artificially induced and characterized by increased receptiveness to suggestions. Being given a suggestion to relax while in a hypnotic state may help a person gain the ability to cope with stress. The same goal can be achieved through other forms of relaxation training, using such techniques as breath control, muscle isolation, and mental imagery. **Biofeedback** is a method that can be used to control involuntary bodily processes like blood pressure or heart rate. By using equipment that visually displays blood pressure, for example, individuals may learn to control physical responses to stress.

Stress Abatement through Ergonomics

Ergonomics, the science of how people interact with their work environment, can be used to reduce health problems and some types of work-related stress. For example, many experts believe that stress can be reduced by using a chair that allows an employee to sit with the thighs parallel to the floor and the feet flat.[29] The position and accessibility of computer equipment is also critical, since computers are the alleged cause of numerous repetitive stress injuries. The top of a monitor should be at, or slightly below, eye level so that employees are not continually tilting their heads to read the top of the screen. Ideally, the keyboard should be at elbow level. A keyboard tray that is adjustable for angle as well as height can relieve a great deal of wrist discomfort. Some typists find a wrist rest helpful, too. Light is another major factor. The ideal lighting arrangement is the combination of soft, indirect overhead light that doesn't cause glare with task lights providing strong, direct light for immediate work.[30]

STRESS: A GLOBAL PERSPECTIVE

An international assignment can be a major stressor for expatriates. Expatriates are often under stress from the moment they learn of global assignments until well after returning home. Culture shock is the main stressor for those on international assignment. Even immigrants who return to their country of origin to start businesses can experience culture shock, as business practices may have changed and their network of contacts may not exist.[31]

Stress arising from differences in business practices, standards, values, and behavioural norms is also inherent in international business. Such differences are particularly marked between developed countries and developing countries, especially when examining worker health, safety, and environmental issues.[32] One of the major concerns arising from the North American Free Trade Agreement, for example, is the perceived inadequacy of Mexican industrial safety standards.[33] Canadian expatriates may find it stressful to work in joint ventures they consider to be unsafe. Stress from any of these causes may lead to poor job performance, unhappy social lives, broken marriages, changes in sex drive, eating binges, substance abuse, homesickness, or bouts of depression, nervousness, anger, aggression, impatience with family members, and insomnia.

HR professionals must, therefore, work to limit relocation stress by preparing expatriates to deal with the norms, values, goals, and objectives of the host country.[34] Inappropriate preparation may result in failure and early return, an outcome costly both for the individual involved and for the organization. The average annual cost to send an employee overseas for one or two years is between $200 000 and $250 000. One executive estimates the cost (to the firm) of a failed expatriate assignment as three times the individual's salary, not including the price of lost productivity. Consequently, the number of expatriates continues to decrease.

Stress prevention for expatriates starts with selection (see Chapter 6). Often, management chooses the most technically competent employees, even though the qualities that made them successful in Canada are different from those needed during an international assignment. Human resource professionals should help ensure that employees sent on global assignments have the personal, people, and perceptual skills needed to cope with the environment they will encounter.[35]

ORGANIZATIONAL APPROACHES TO WELLNESS

Organizational programs designed specifically to deal with stress and wellness issues include physical fitness, alcohol and drug abuse, and employee assistance programs.

Physical Fitness Programs and Active Living

Although few organizations have fully staffed facilities, many Canadian firms have exercise programs designed to help keep their employees physically fit. From a management viewpoint, a fit work force is desirable, as loss of productivity from coronary disease and other preventable health problems costs businesses billions of dollars annually, not including the costs of replacement and retraining. The total cost to society is even higher because of lost tax revenue and health care costs. As well, company-sponsored fitness programs often reduce absenteeism, accidents, and sick pay.

There is a movement away from defining "fitness" in narrow, "no pain, no gain" terms, however. Dr. Art Quinney, dean of physical education at The University of Alberta, has pointed out that "the old definition of fitness left many Canadians, including workers, at the sidelines. They saw fitness as being intimidating and unappealing."[36] Instead, some Canadian companies are promoting *active living*: a way of life in which activity is valued as an important part of daily living. John Dimaurizio, director of human resources at Pratt-Whitney Canada's head office in Longueil, Quebec, describes the concept this way: "Active living in our workplace provides a recreational means for our employees and their families . . . to have fun. Our employees are happier on the job, more creative, and ultimately more productive."[37] A daily 40-minute walk, for example, will reduce anxiety levels by 14 percent.[38]

While the Pratt-Whitney program does include traditional fitness activities like aerobics, its success is due, in part, to choice. Employees choose how active they want to be and what type of activity they like best. Activities may be as simple as going for a walk at lunch, taking the stairs instead of the elevator, or cycling to work. T'ai chi, archery, and social events that include golf, horseback riding, and picnics are other examples. Dimaurizio sees little need to invest in high-tech, high-cost facilities. One reason is that the company has struck up relationships with neighbouring recreational facilities, thus providing employees with more options, while keeping costs down.

It must be stressed, however, that traditional workplace health promotion programs continue to be successful in many locations. They offer employees a wide range of options in managing their personal health and well-being. Indeed, active living and the traditional approach to workplace health promotion can be mutually reinforcing.[39]

Alcohol Abuse Programs

As a disease, alcoholism is characterized by uncontrolled and compulsive drinking that interferes with normal living patterns. It is estimated that between 10 and 20 percent of Canadian employees are problem drinkers. Drinking-related problems cost employers between $1 billion and $3 billion yearly.[40] The problem, then, is enormous and it is not likely to disappear. In response, some employers have adopted direct intervention programs, while trying to create more positive work climates.

Given that arbitrators often provide rehabilitation opportunities for employees discharged because of alcohol abuse, firing is not always an option. Thus, direct intervention programs are often developed to help supervisors deal with problem employees. Still in use, one such program developed over a decade ago has four features: policy, identification, intervention, and diagnosis and treatment. An important part of a company-wide policy toward alcohol abuse is to remove the stigma attached to the problem. Abuse must be viewed as an illness and any employee having this illness should receive the same consideration and offer of treatment for which all other sick and injured employees are eligible. When such a policy is formulated, communicated, and supported by senior management, line supervisors not only know how to approach the alcohol problem, but their attitudes toward those with the disease will tend to be more supportive.

The next step is identification. While managers are not diagnosticians, they should be aware that alcoholism is a possible cause of marked deterioration in job performance or absenteeism. (Employees who drink excessively are sick, late, and absent three times as often as other workers.) Having identified a potential alcoholic, the problem must be confronted. This is the most difficult and perhaps the most critical element of any program, for the employee must be made to acknowledge the reality of poor work performance, often in the face of extreme internal resistance. It must be remembered here that while loneliness, fear, and uncertainty may make the alcoholic's life a misery, the job often affords the last vestige of self-respect.

As most employees are anxious to keep working, they are often susceptible to constructive coercion. This technique focuses on an interview or series of interviews. It must be stressed that the supervisor is not qualified to diagnose the employee's alcohol problem. The interview should deal only with job performance—the field a manager knows best. In specific terms, the meeting should be planned in advance to gain acceptance for a definite behavioural objective to be reached by a specific date. Past transgressions should be clearly documented and levels of acceptable performance should be agreed upon in writing before the interview ends.

Employers must be prepared to face bewildering or even heartrending scenes during these interviews. The worker may try to get the supervisor involved in his or her personal problems or "fall apart" during the conversation. The employee may promise to do better, swear never to do "it" again, or whine, "I can't do anything right. I'm useless." There may be excuses for everything ("They're all against me") or anger ("How dare you persecute me! Look at all I've done for you.")

In spite of all these diversion strategies, the manager must remain in control. When faced with a plea for sympathy, it should be made clear that the meeting *will* focus on work performance. Tears can be countered by allowing the employee to regain composure or by briefly adjourning the interview. Excuses, apologies, promises, anger, and statements of innocence should be met with a reiteration of good past performance and an offer to arrange professional counselling or medical help if physical problems are perceived to prevent a return to former levels of competence. The key factor in this confrontation process, then, is not to let the employee lead the interview away from its objective.

Should work performance not improve, it is the employer's task to motivate the employee to accept counselling that will hopefully lead to treatment. Often, coercion backed by a threat of job loss will be enough. "You've got his job," as one expert suggested; "you've got his money and while he is still employed, he is amenable to treatment and he can be coerced into treatment if the need arises."

Remember, however, that the type of social control described above may not be effective in all industrial relations settings. For example, where low-status jobs are involved, it may be difficult to precipitate a great enough sense of crisis to motivate the alcohol/drug user to voluntarily seek treatment. In these cases, the rewards of the job are not high enough to make the choice between discontinuing deviant behaviour and the risk of discipline a consequential one. It is here that the union may help, as the labour movement in general is supportive of meaningful, realistic treatment programs.

Once counselling has begun, all diagnosis and treatment must be performed by qualified professionals. Although some in-house programs do exist, it is often more realistic to use outside rehabilitation sources. The employer's role at this stage is to maintain benefit and seniority rights, for although problem drinkers are often able to follow outpatient treatment procedures, some will need hospitalization or other care during working hours. It is essential that an employer's policy account for such absences. The second task for the employer is to remain vigilant. For a time, the addict may be careful not to be absent or to exhibit deviant behaviour. This behavioural pattern may last several months and the supervisor should not be lulled into complacency. To recover completely from alcoholism requires a wrenching lifestyle change over a span of months or even years. It should not be assumed that a short-term conformance to work rules has signalled a complete recovery. In fact, some studies have suggested that nearly 50 percent of those treated for alcohol or drug abuse will relapse within one year.[41]

Another problem is refusal to accept treatment. In a free society, there are limits to the amount and the type of coercion that can be used. Obviously, an employee is free to refuse any suggestion or offer of help. In these situations, the manager has little alternative but to carry the disciplinary process through to dismissal. The key to this procedure is documentation, as it may have to be proven that all attempts to bring work performance to an acceptable level within a reasonable time have failed. If the worker is fired, *the reason must be inadequate job performance.* To repeat, alcoholism or refusal to accept treatment *must never be stated as the reason for termination.*

B.C. Tel has a similar program called "The Coercive Action Policy". Consisting of five steps, B.C. Tel's approach is to give the employee four chances to change behaviour. On the fifth occurrence, the employee is fired. Even then, however, the opportunity exists, under strict conditions, for reinstatement.[42]

Drug Abuse Programs

Although alcohol is a powerful drug, drugs are treated separately from alcohol because supervisors are less familiar with the signs and patterns of use of other drugs. Cocaine and other mind-altering drugs affect the workplace. According to one study in the United States, almost 70 percent of illicit drug users are employed. In some instances, problems associated with drug abusers may consume as much as 35 percent of a firm's profits.[43]

Chemically dependent employees exhibit behaviours that distinguish them from other workers. Employees using stimulants such as Benzedrine, Dexedrine, or cocaine can be extraordinarily restless or talkative, while those on depressants like morphine, Demerol, heroin, Amytal, Librium, and Valium can be irritable, nervous, confused, hostile, or depressed. Marijuana, hashish, and hallucinogens such as LSD speed up, slow down, or distort the senses, causing faulty judgement and poor coordination. It must be remembered, however, that the action of a drug may vary, depending upon factors such as

- the person's frame of mind or emotional state;
- whether the surroundings are strange or familiar;
- whether the drug user is alone or with companions, and whether the companions are old friends or new acquaintances;
- the quality and quantity of the drug;
- the method of taking the drug (mouth, needle, sniffed);
- whether the drug is taken alone or in combination with other drugs;
- the physical size and condition of the person.

It is important, then, that the line supervisor possess the professional and personal skills to distinguish temporary, isolated problems from problems that signal the need for professional treatment.[44] The approach and the eventual treatment, however is identical to dealing with alcohol abuse. For this reason, alcohol and drug assistance are often combined under the label "substance abuse program".

EMPLOYEE ASSISTANCE PROGRAMS

An **employee assistance program (EAP)** is a comprehensive approach used in many organizations that deals with marital or family problems, job performance problems, stress, emotional, or mental health issues, financial troubles, grief, and loss, as well as alcohol and drug abuse. More recently, some EAPs have also become concerned with HIV and AIDS, elder care, workplace violence, and natural disasters, such as earthquakes, floods, and tornadoes.[45] Most EAP programs provide either for in-house professional counsellors or for referrals to an appropriate community social service agency. Typically, most or all of the costs are borne by the employer. The EAP concept provides a response to personal psychological problems that interfere with an employee's well-being and overall productivity. The philosophy behind the EAP is to treat emotionally troubled employees with the same consideration given to employees with physical illnesses.

One chief operating officer has stated that a well-run EAP will return three dollars for every dollar spent on the program. He hastened to add, however, that an EAP will not succeed unless the employer is committed to promoting the program, educating employees and managers, and eliminating stigma from the environment.[46] Advantages claimed for EAPs include decreased workers' compensation claims, absenteeism, and accident rates and increased productivity. In fact, EAPs have been shown to increase productivity by 6.7 days annually, saving more than $1000 per employee. At B.C. Tel, for example, the payback is $3.80 for each dollar invested.[47]

To make EAPs more effective, supervisors must receive training designed to provide specialized interpersonal skills for recognizing troubled employees and for referring them to the firm's EAP counsellors. This training is critical, as addicted employees are often experts at denial and deception. They can fool even experienced counsellors. The problem of making EAP referrals is

HRM IN ACTION

"I just don't know what to do about Robert Lewis," said the production supervisor, Martina Fagetti, to Eli Ben-Dor, the human resource manager. "Lately I've noticed that Robert has missed work frequently. Even when he shows up, he is usually late. His eyes are always bloodshot, and he seems to move in slow motion. He also doesn't hang around with the old gang anymore. Again, today, he didn't show up for work. I just received a call from the police saying he was in the detoxification centre and wanted us to be called."

If you were Eli, what action would you suggest?

further compounded where supervisors identify more with their employees than with management. They don't want their subordinates to think they are being persecuted. One study found that some supervisors in public- and private-sector organizations have covered up for troubled employees for as long as 12 years.[48]

AIDS IN THE WORKPLACE

AIDS (acquired immune deficiency syndrome) is a condition that undermines the body's immune system, leaving the person susceptible to a wide range of fatal diseases. AIDS has become a worldwide epidemic. Since the first case was reported in Canada, AIDS has claimed over 7800 lives.[49]

A relatively small percentage of firms have established formal policies to deal with the condition. In one study of practices and policies related to AIDS, 82 percent of the respondents expressed a need to educate their employees, yet only 28 percent had begun the process.[50] In the present state of medical knowledge, AIDS is always fatal, accounting for the high level of fear within society. Some employees hesitate to work with someone they believe has AIDS, despite reassurance from medical experts that the disease cannot be transmitted through casual contact. This fear can result in business interruptions (if employees refuse to work with an AIDS victim) or unlawful discrimination under human rights legislation (if the employer discharges the ill person). The need to educate employees is obvious. Only knowledge will assure employees that they are not at risk from co-workers with this disease.

Many Canadian firms may never have to deal with AIDS in the workplace. One occurrence may disrupt the workplace so severely, however, that HR professionals should ensure that proper policies are in place and that both management and employees are aware of the issues that surround this deadly condition.

$\int$ UMMARY

Safety involves the creation of a safety-conscious culture that protects employees from injuries caused by work-related accidents. Health refers to the employees' freedom from physical or emotional illness. In Canada, workplace safety is the responsibility of both the federal government (for federally-regulated industries) and the provinces.

One approach to the development of safety programs is to create a psychology of safety. Another is to develop and maintain a safe working environment. Evaluation of safety programs involves measuring both the frequency and severity of accidents. Promoting employee health has led to the development of wellness programs. They start with initial applicant screening and continue throughout an employee's career.

Cumulative trauma disorders include injuries to the back, arms, and hands. Carpal tunnel syndrome is a specific problem caused by repetitive flexing and

extension of the wrist. Many cumulative trauma disorders result from using computers.

Stress is the body's reaction to any demand made on it. Everyone lives under some stress, which can be beneficial if not excessive but is damaging when extreme. Burnout is a state of fatigue or frustration stemming from devotion to a cause, way of life, or relationship that does not provide the expected reward. Stress can be managed. Employer-sponsored programs are helping employees deal with stress in various ways.

Company fitness programs often reduce absenteeism, accidents, and sick pay expenditures. Physically fit employees are usually more alert and productive and their morale is higher.

Alcoholism is a disease characterized by uncontrolled and compulsive drinking that interferes with normal living patterns. A significant problem, alcoholism can both result from and cause excessive stress. Drug abuse is recognized as a disease in numerous firms

and positive action has been taken to deal with the problem. An employee assistance program (EAP) is a comprehensive approach that deals with burnout, alcohol and drug abuse, emotional disturbances, and family or personal problems.

AIDS (acquired immune deficiency syndrome) is a condition that destroys the body's immune system, leaving the person susceptible to a wide range of fatal diseases. Managers should develop policies to cope with AIDS in the workplace.

TERMS FOR REVIEW

Safety
Health
Ergonomics
Cumulative trauma disorders
Carpal tunnel syndrome
Stress
Burnout

Role ambiguity
Role conflict
Job overload
Hypnosis
Biofeedback
Employee assistance program (EAP)
AIDS (acquired immune deficiency syndrome)

QUESTIONS FOR REVIEW

1. Define *safety* and *health*.
2. Describe the health and safety provisions in the Canadian Labour Code.
3. What are the primary ways in which safety programs are designed? Discuss.
4. What are some measurements that would suggest the success of a firm's safety program?
5. What are the purposes of health and wellness programs?
6. Why should management attempt to identify stressful jobs? What can managers do to reduce the stress associated with a job?
7. Why should management be concerned with employee burnout?
8. What are some signs that a supervisor might look for in identifying alcohol abuse?
9. Explain why employee assistance programs are being established.
10. What concerns should a manager have regarding AIDS in the workplace?

HRM INCIDENT 1

• AN EYE FOR AN EYE

"Hey, here comes SN. Get those goggles on," warned Phil Farrish, a mechanical supervisor for Fastco, a large machinery maintenance company. At the warning, his five employees quickly donned their safety goggles and continued working. Joy Norris, the company safety officer (called SN by Phil, for Safety Nut), looked approvingly at Phil's

crew. "Maybe," she thought, "I'm finally getting through to him."

It had been an uphill struggle for Joy. Not only was she one of the new breed—a professionally trained safety technician—but she was a woman working in the man's world of large machine maintenance. Still, when they found out she knew her job, the supervisors had gradually begun to accept her suggestions and now she was regarded as "one of the boys". That is, everywhere except Phil's section. From the beginning, he had ridiculed both Joy and her ideas. He had coined the term "SN" and seen to it that none of his men accepted her programs. It was only after being threatened with dismissal by his boss, the district manager, that Phil had grudgingly issued safety goggles and allowed safety posters to be put up. Safety standards were still weak in Phil's section, but Joy had patience. Even he would come round sooner or later.

As Joy turned to head off to the next repair depot she heard the scream. Anyone who has ever seen a man after a splinter of steel has pierced his eye does not forget the sight easily.

One of Phil's men was writhing on the floor screaming hoarsely. Phil was dancing about in a panic, not knowing what to do.

"Bring a car in here fast!" snapped Joy. "You! Get the first aid kit—move! You two, help me get his hand away from his eye. He's only doing more damage!"

And so Joy calmed the injured employee, placed gauze over the eye and saw him carried, moaning, to a car for a quick ride to the hospital. On her return from the hospital, Joy found the district manager already in Phil's office. When he saw her, he said: "I think, Joy, that you should chair this meeting."

QUESTIONS

1. What is Joy's short-term task? How should she accomplish it?
2. What is her long-term task? How should she accomplish it?
3. Should safety officers have the authority to close operations or processes they deem to be unsafe?

HRM INCIDENT 2

• A STAR IS FALLING

"Just leave me alone and let me do my job," snapped Manuel Gomez. Dumbfounded, Russell Brown, Manuel's supervisor, decided to count to ten and not respond to Manuel's comment. As he walked back to his office, Russell thought about how Manuel had changed over the past few months. He had been a hard worker and extremely cooperative when he had come to work for Russell two years earlier. The company had sent Manuel to two training schools and had received glowing reports about his performance in each of them.

Until about a year ago, Manuel had a perfect attendance record and was an ideal employee. At about that time, however, he began to have personal problems, resulting in a divorce six months later. Manuel had requested a day off several times to take care of personal business. Russell had attempted to help in every way he could without getting directly involved in Manuel's personal affairs. But Russell was aware of the strain Manuel must have experienced, as his marriage broke up and he and his wife engaged in the inevitable disputes over child custody, alimony payments, and property.

During the same period, senior management had initiated a program to improve productivity. Russell found it necessary to put additional pressure on all his workers, including Manuel. He tried to be considerate, but he had to become much more performance-oriented, insisting on increased output from everyone. As time went on, Manuel began to show up late for work. Once, he actually missed two days without calling Russell in advance! Russell attributed Manuel's behaviour to extreme stress, but because Manuel had been such a good worker for so long, Russell excused the tardiness and absences, only suggesting gently that Manuel should try to do better.

Sitting at his desk, Russell thought about what might have caused Manuel's outburst a few minutes earlier. Russell had suggested to Manuel that he shut down the machine he was operating and clean up the surrounding area. This was a normal part of Manuel's job, something he had been careful to do in the past. Russell thought the disorder around Manuel's machine might account for the increasing number of defects in the parts he was making. "This is a tough one. I think I'll talk to the boss about it," thought Russell.

QUESTIONS

1. What do you think is likely to be Manuel's problem? Discuss.
2. If you were Russell's boss, what would you recommend that he do?

DEVELOPING HRM SKILLS: AN EXPERIENTIAL EXERCISE

At times, workers' personal problems may distract them from work and lead to unsafe behaviour. Dealing with one's personal problems is often difficult, and assisting employees in dealing with these issues can be even more taxing on managers. However, if the situation is undermining productivity or safety, it must be addressed. This exercise should provide a better understanding of how to handle a most difficult issue.

"I am going to do it and I am going to do it today. This has gone on long enough!" thought Simone Rosen, the data processing manager. "I can't put it off any longer. I realize that Walter has been with the company for 14 years, and with this department for 11 of those years, but this drinking thing is out of hand. Lately the problem is affecting other members of the work group. His friends are covering up pretty well for him, but that is causing their productivity to go down. Evidently Walter is not going to be able to work things out, and the situation will only get worse. We are going to meet today and resolve this matter one way or the other; he's dry or he's out! I'm not a villain,

and I really want him to work things out, but this is causing the department problems."

Walter Hollingsworth, a programmer in the data processing department, was concerned. He thought, "I heard from a friend in the boss's office that I am going to get chewed out about my drinking. I have always gotten my work done, but I guess I've let things slip lately. I know I can lick this problem. I'm going to straighten myself out, and when I meet with the boss I'll admit that I drink too much sometimes; everybody does. Drinking has only recently affected my work. I'll do better in the future. I've been with the company for 14 years, and with this division for 11 of those years. One problem in all those years makes me a good risk. I can do it, and I deserve a chance. The boss should be compassionate."

Two students will participate. One will play Simone and one will play Walter. The rest of the class should observe carefully. The instructor will provide any additional information necessary to participate.

PART FIVE:

CASE V Parma Cycle Company: Safety and Health at the New Plant

"I want the new plant to be a model of safety and health," said Mr. Burgess, the president of Parma Cycle Company in Delta, B.C. "I do, too," said Jesse Heard, the human resource director, "but you have to be aware that it's going to cost a lot." "Remember now, Jesse," the president replied, "we're putting the plant in Digby, N.S. primarily to reduce costs. I believe that the main thing we can do for safety is to train our workers to be safety-oriented. That doesn't cost much."

"That's the main thing, I know," said Jesse, "but we'll also have to spend some money. There are several areas where safety can be improved by installing handrails. Also, a good number of the machines will come in without a chain-belt guard. We'll have to have those fabricated." "Well," said Mr. Burgess, "let's just try to meet the government requirements on those kinds of things. I'd like to see a cost-benefit analysis of anything that goes beyond their standards." Mr. Burgess was referring to Nova Scotia's Occupational Health and Safety Act (OHSA).

About that time, Cliff Brubaker, the chief engineer at Parma, who had also been summoned to the meeting, came in. After a few niceties, Cliff asked, "Mr. Burgess, making sure that all the machinery and the machine layouts meet OHSA requirements made engineering the new plant a lot more difficult. We won't be able to use our floor space nearly as efficiently at Digby as we do here in Delta. Also, the work flow is going to be less efficient because I had to separate machines to keep the area noise level below the maximum standard. Don't you think we could fudge a little on some of this? The Delta plant doesn't come close to meeting

B.C.'s OHSA requirements, and we have only had one fine since I've been here."

"I don't think you can trade off personal safety against a few dollars of cost savings," Jesse said. "You remember when Clayton Braden lost his arm last year? The company came out okay on that because Clay didn't have us charged under OHSA. But what about Clay? How much was his arm worth?" "Don't get upset, Jesse," said Cliff. "I know what you mean and I really feel the same way. But we can go to extremes."

Mr. Burgess spoke up, adding, "I don't think that meeting provincial safety standards is going to extremes. Besides, if companies like Parma Cycle don't take some initiative in protecting workers, we're going to see even more enforcement efforts in the future. I want to make sure that you both understand my position. Everything in the plant at Digby is to meet provincial requirements for health and safety as a minimum. If the requirements can be exceeded with no additional costs, I want to opt for maximum safety. If you have to spend extra money to improve safety or health at the Digby plant, I want to see a benefit-cost analysis on each item." "I think that's clear enough," said Jesse. "Me, too," said Cliff, "but I'll have to get back with you on a number of the modifications we had planned."

QUESTIONS

1. What do you think of Mr. Burgess's insistence on meeting provincial standards at the Digby plant?

2. Do you agree with Jesse that a firm should not "trade off personal safety against a few dollars of cost savings?"

PART FIVE:

 **VIDEO CASE** It Only Hurts When I Type

Whoever said the only hazard the office worker faces is a paper cut did not anticipate the dangers of the contemporary Canadian office. Until recently, very little attention has been paid to office health and safety, because office injuries seemed negligible when compared to industrial ones. The injuries that can result from clerical work, however, are many: eyestrain from poor lighting and staring at video display terminals (VDTs) for extended periods; back pain from sitting in poorly designed chairs; repetitive strain injuries (RSI) from continuous use of computer keyboards. The resulting injury is known as carpal tunnel syndrome (CTS), an ailment that affects the nerves in the wrist.

The threat of injury looms over one-third of the North American work force, which uses computers on a regular basis. Since the advent of the PC, the frequency of these injuries has risen at an alarming rate. For years, muskoloskeletal injuries were misdiagnosed or overlooked by workers and managers alike. With the number of cases growing yearly, however, managers are being forced to rethink the way they design their work environments. In 1981, the Canadian workers' compensation boards reported that fully one-third of lost-time claims involved muskoloskeletal injuries and related illnesses. By 1990, this figure had jumped to more than half of all claims. Since 1983, the number of workers' compensation claims from those who occupy clerical positions has increased approximately 50 percent. In 1988, Canadian workers' compensation boards disbursed an estimated $7 million in direct compensation payments to office employees afflicted with muskoloskeletal injuries—and this figure is increasing. Any employee who spends more than six hours in front of a PC is a candidate for carpal tunnel syndrome or cumulative trauma disorder (CTD).

Office-related injuries are occurring more frequently because of increased office automation. Consider that there are more than 100 million IBM PCs installed worldwide, with over 36 million new ones purchased each year. It is no coincidence, then, that carpal tunnel syndrome and other related injuries have been labelled the asbestos crisis of the 90s. From 1982 to 1990, there was a ninefold increase in the number of reported cases of CTS, and by 1990 CTS was one of the main culprits in work-related injuries.

The outmoded typewriter required the use of several different muscle groups to operate. Not only did the keys have to be pressed, but paper had to be inserted into the machine, mistakes were corrected manually and the carriage of older models had to be returned at the end of each line. In contrast, consider the computer keyboard, which requires only the fingers to do work. The operator remains virtually motionless, sometimes for hours on end.

Not surprisingly, carpal tunnel syndrome strikes the hand: a delicate and complex organism, composed of 27 bones and a variety of muscles, tendons, ligaments and nerves. The tunnel refers to an enclosed pathway through which bones, muscles, ligaments and tendons converge, along with a main nerve. The syndrome can develop when someone types at a keyboard for an extended period of time, usually with the wrists flexed in an awkward position so that the muscles become strained and the blood supply to the carpal tunnel is interrupted, squeezing the nerve. The result is numbness, burning, and tingling in the wrist, which can be very painful and debilitating.

Office workers who spend extended periods of time sitting in front of a computer are also vulnerable to muskoloskeletal injuries, which include neck and back pain. Improperly adjusted chairs and bad posture can cut off blood supply to the muscles, resulting in pain. Glare or shadows from poorly lit VDTs can cause eye strain and headaches.

Couple this physical stress with work that has little variety and offers little mental stimulation, or work that is too mentally demanding, and management may be confronted with ill and frustrated employees. The solution is to find a middle ground that allows workers to do their jobs with an appropriate amount of physical activity. The answer is to be found in ergonomics and employee participation. Ergonomics is the practice of tailoring workplace design and job demands to suit the physical characteristics of an individual so that he or she can perform the required tasks comfortably. Managers may begin by telling their employees to experiment by adjusting chair heights and computer screen angles. Office workers should also be reminded to avoid static positions. Encouraging workers to change position and take five-minute breaks every hour is also sound advice.

QUESTIONS

1. Workers are complaining about neck and wrist pain to your boss, who concludes that the culprit is poorly designed equipment. He asks you to devise a strategy to solve this problem. How would you proceed?

2. What are some ergonomic principles that management can institute for better working habits?

Video Resource: "Computer Ills," *The Health Show* 46 (January 19, 1995).

CHAPTER

14 The Labour Union

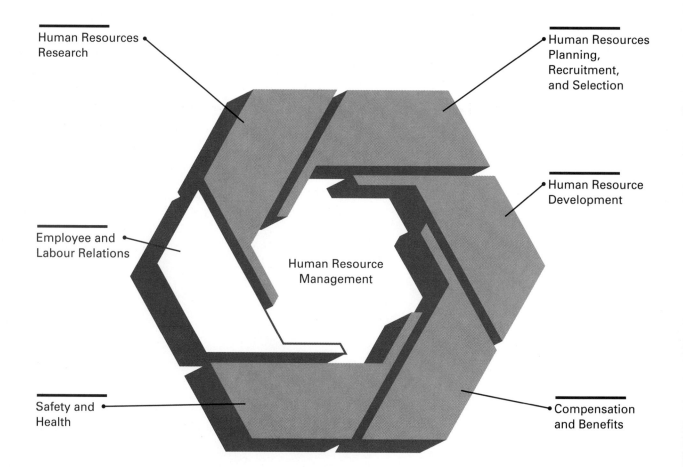

Human Resources
Research

Human Resources
Planning,
Recruitment,
and Selection

Human Resource
Development

Employee and
Labour Relations

Human Resource
Management

Safety and
Health

Compensation
and Benefits

1. Describe the history of the Canadian labour movement and discuss the significance of past events.

2. Outline the structure of the Canadian labour movement and discuss why employees may choose to join or not to join a union.

3. Look at union recognition from the employers' viewpoint.

4. Compare adversarial with cooperative styles of labour-management relations.

icholas Sweeney, president of United Technologies, was disturbed and disappointed. He had just been informed by the Provincial Labour Relations Board that a majority of his employees had voted to have the union represent them. The past months had been difficult ones, with charges and countercharges being made by both management and labour. The vote had been close, with only a few votes tipping the scales in favour of labour. He looked at the human resource manager, Marthanne Bello, and said, "I don't know what to do. The union will demand so much we can't possibly be competitive."

Marthanne replied, "Just because a union has won the right to be represented doesn't mean that union demands will be unreasonable, or that we have to accept all their terms. I believe that a reasonable contract can be negotiated. I know many of those guys and I am sure that we can work out a contract that will be fair to both sides."

Of course, Nicholas Sweeney does not have to concede to all the demands that the new union makes. What he must do, however, is enter into negotiations with the union in good faith and work out a collective agreement. Both sides will likely have to make compromises. If the union and management can learn to bargain in a professional manner, then United Technologies will be among the vast majority of firms that settle with their unions without strike action. As this is a first contract, the Labour Relations Board will be watching the negotiating process very closely to ensure that Nick Sweeney and the union negotiators behave according to the rules.

In this chapter we will begin by discussing the history and the legal traditions that underpin our labour relations system. We will then outline the procedures that unions must follow to become certified and the steps that employers such as Nick Sweeney must take to establish a collective bargaining relationship. Finally, we will critique our adversarial system of labour relations and look at today's management-labour relations in Canada.

A BRIEF HISTORY OF THE CANADIAN LABOUR MOVEMENT

Labour unions are an influential part of our work culture. Almost 40 percent of the total work force may be described as **organized labour** (that is, they belong to a union) and the gains made by the labour movement have affected all Canadians.[1] As at least two authors have suggested: "It is indisputable that the efforts of organized labour have led to a decent standard of living and improved working conditions for millions of Canadian workers."[2] In particular, unions have improved benefits for employees on hourly wages.

It is important, therefore, to understand the nature of the labour movement. As present-day ideology and structure are rooted deeply in the past, this brief history will help readers to understand why unions behave as they do and why the management/union relationship has traditionally been adversarial, characterized by conflict rather than cooperation.

Canadian Labour Before 1926

As early as 1794, working people began to form groups designed to better their working conditions. Much as workers are today, they were concerned about safety, hours of work, wages, and job security. Unsafe workplaces, where employees could easily lose an arm or a leg, combined with seven-day weeks comprising days as long as 14 hours, were the grievances that produced the early unions. Although this period of labour history is somewhat murky, the first union in what was to become Canada seems to have been organized in 1827 by the boot and shoe workers of Montreal. That year, as well, printers in Quebec began a movement that lead to permanent unions in Toronto (1832), Hamilton, and Montreal (1833). Throughout the 1840s and 1850s union growth was slow, although local groups as diverse as coal miners in British Columbia and Newfoundland sealers were organized enough to take strike action. However, banding together to improve working conditions was illegal at that time. British common law regarded unions as conspiracies to restrain trade. To be involved in the labour movement was a criminal act.

In early 1871, an association of unions was formed, called the Toronto Trades Assembly. Its principal platform was to secure a nine-hour working day—the norm for that time was between 10 and 12 hours. Before the year ended, 24 unions had joined the Assembly.[3] First to be tested were Toronto's publishers. Their principal spokesman, George Brown, editor of *The Globe* (forerunner of *The Globe and Mail)*, rejected the demand for a reduced work day, claiming that it would lead to idleness at home and that the men "would make a nuisance of themselves."[4] The printers struck and Brown became determined to break the strike. Detectives were hired to follow the strikers, resulting in several vagrancy charges. This tactic was followed by the hiring of strikebreakers and more arrests for breach of contract. In 1872, when a magistrate found the strikers guilty, the first demonstration of labour solidarity in Canada saw 10 000 marchers gather at Queen's Park.

In Ottawa, Sir John A. Macdonald, the Conservative Prime Minister, saw these activities as a chance to gain political points on his hated rival, the Liberal, George Brown. Using British legislation as a model, he had the Trade Union Act passed, legalizing the right to form groups in pursuit of reduced hours or increased wages. But many of these provisions were struck down in 1876 and it was 60 years before strong legislation was enacted that protected the right to organize while requiring that employers *bargain in good faith*, or negotiate seriously to obtain an agreement.

What followed the initial success of the labour movement, then, was a long period of stagnation. Indeed, 40 years later, in 1913, less than 10 percent of Canada's labour force was unionized, compared with more than 22 percent in Britain and Germany.[5] Throughout this period, employees who wished to organize were at the mercy of their employers, as large-scale immigration provided a cheap and willing pool of labour. **Yellow-dog contracts** (signed agreements not to join a union forced upon workers as a condition of employment), **blacklists** (lists of union sympathizers employers would not hire), and spies were used widely.

Even though legislation was passed in 1900 that made voluntary conciliation (bringing in an outside expert to work with both parties) possible in labour disputes, union–management relations remained very strained and often violent. For example, one picketer was killed in the l903 strike against The Canadian Pacific Railway. In 1907, Lethbridge miners were evicted from company housing and three died on electric fences that guarded mine entrances. Beginning in 1911, more violence and property damage characterized the two-year strike to organize the Dunsmuir miners on Vancouver Island. At one point more than 250 strikers were in prison. The Winnipeg General Strike of 1919 was effectively put down on "bloody Saturday" (June 21, 1919), when RCMP officers shot two and injured over 30 in a crowd of strikers who attacked a streetcar operated by a strikebreaker. Two thousand troops put down the 1923 plant occupation and recognition strike at Sydney Steel. A Cape Breton miner was killed in 1925 in yet another labour dispute.[6]

With this historical background, one can understand readily why labour and management tended to view each other as adversaries. The passage of legislation after 1930 that allowed unions and management to negotiate more or less as equals has lead gradually to today's situation, in which the vast majority of contract negotiations are conducted in an environment of mutual respect. Nevertheless, a spirit of cooperation is not often seen; Canadian labour/management relationships still tend to be adversarial.

The U.S. Influence

The century bounded by 1860 and 1960 saw very close ties between the Canadian and the American labour movements. Although most of Canada's immigrants were from the United Kingdom and many had strong affiliations to British unions, over time, these loyalties were replaced by membership in U.S.-dominated organizations. One major driving force before 1915 was the opportunity of immigrating to the United States, where the right union card helped in finding a job. The second factor was the aggressiveness of American unions, many of whom set out to organize entire industries, disregarding national boundaries. In 1902, for example, the Canadian Trades and Labour Congress (TLC) was persuaded by the President of the American Federation of Labour (AFL) not to recognize Canadian unions in areas where an **international union**, usually one headquartered in the United States, already existed. By 1938, the TLC was completely dominated by the AFL.

A rival American group, the Congress of Industrial Organizations (CIO) was extremely active in Canada as well, especially during the late 1930s and early 1940s. By 1940 the TLC was in decline and a new organization, the Canadian Congress of Labour (CCL) became virtually the Canadian arm of the CIO. A close relationship continued through the 1940s and 1950s. By 1960, approximately 70 percent of Canadian unionized labour belonged to American-dominated international unions. The merits of this arrangement have been debated fiercely, both inside and outside the labour movement. On the one hand, it can be argued that trade union growth was enhanced through international ties and that the benefits contributed substantially to Canada's economic prosperity. On the other hand, close alliances with an American-dominated labour movement might have delayed the development of a national consciousness.

In any case, American influence declined rapidly from the 1960s on. A number of Canadian affiliates broke away from their American parents, establishing Canadian unions, until by 1994 fewer than one-third of Canada's union members belonged to foreign-based organizations. Perhaps the best-known example of this tendency came in 1985, when the Canadian section of the United Automobile Workers (UAW) established a separate organization, the Canadian Auto Workers Union (CAW). This trend came about partly because of the perception that Canadian members were paying more into international coffers than they were receiving and partly because of arguments that Canadian unions could better support Canadian interests without encroachment from an international headquarters. Indeed, given the competitive forces created by the various North American free trade agreements, with the resultant losses in unionized jobs, it is likely that the Canadian labour movement will continue to move away from international affiliations as Canadian unions strive to protect jobs at home.[7] As well, the dramatic growth of public-sector unions such as the Canadian Union of Public Employees has further decreased the percentage of employees who belong to foreign-based unions, and for a number of years has contributed substantially to the strength of the Canadian labour movement.

The Canadian Labour Movement 1926–1947

One of the key factors that helped U.S. unions play a leading role in Canada was similarity of legislation. As suggested earlier in this chapter, despite some early initiatives in the area of conciliation (in 1900 and 1907), the Canadian labour movement was stagnant during the first part of the twentieth century and the numbers were small. Some once-powerful unions lost ground. For example, the One Big Union, founded just before the Winnipeg General Strike in 1914, had dwindled from 41 000 members to less than 5000 by the end of 1921. By 1926, radical trade unionism was a spent force in Canada.[8]

The years 1926-1947, however, heralded a wave of American legislation that even today provides the legal basis for Canadian labour relations. Perhaps most important was the 1935 National Labour Relations Act (NLRA), commonly known as the Wagner Act, that prohibited a range of "unfair" management practices, such as interfering with an employee's right to join a union and refusing to bargain with a union.[9] Similar restrictions were placed on unions in 1947.[10] The principles outlined in the Wagner Act were imported into Canada in 1944, under a famous Order-in-Council: **P.C. 1003**. This legislation defined the rights and obligations of both unions and employees, while implementing procedures for settling contract disputes.[11] The impact of **P.C. 1003** cannot be overstated. "At one stroke, it brought most economic activity in Canada within a single, comprehensive system of collective bargaining law."[12] Although after the war, the provinces began to enact their own legislation, the guiding principles were all found in P.C. 1003.

In Quebec, the economy expanded rapidly and after the Second World War, clergy-dominated unions were taken over by more secular-minded individuals. Unfortunately, during this process, the province became a battleground, as CCL- and TLC-affiliated unions vied for members. The mood of organized labour thus turned from cautious cooperation to marked militancy. Even after the CCL and the TLC merged (in 1956) to form the Canadian Labour Congress, many Quebec unions remained outside. These groups were especially interested in cultural identity. They formed the Confederation of National Trade Unions, an organization that was to play an active role in Quebec labour relations disputes during the 1960s and 1970s.

Canadian Labour After 1947

Postwar Canadian legislation generally followed the American model, in that both management and labour were required to refrain from **unfair labour practices**. At first, most provinces followed the federally enacted Canada Labour Code (1948) quite closely. The Code outlined the basic freedoms and obligations comprised by our present-day labour relations system. Over time, however, individual provinces have modified this legislation, increasing differences among jurisdictions.[13]

At present, there are only three characteristics common to all jurisdictions in Canada: 1) the principle of sole recognition, or allowing only one union to represent any individual bargaining unit, 2) the existence of **labour relations boards** with power to administer legislation, and 3) specifically defined unfair labour practices that apply to both management and unions. Even strike votes are not required everywhere; exceptions exist in Ontario and in the federal sphere. Labour legislation, then, has become province-specific, as national laws cover less than 10 percent of unionized workers.

The Public Sector

Collective bargaining rights in the public sector also vary across jurisdictions. Saskatchewan legislated the right to bargain in 1944, when all workers were given this privilege. It was not until 1967, however, that the Public Service Staff Relations Act was passed, allowing federal civil servants to join unions. This initiative was followed quickly by similar legislation in all provinces except Ontario and Alberta. Quebec had already passed its own version in 1964.

The major difference between public and private sector collective agreements lies in the right to strike. In many jurisdictions, "essential" government employees—police and hospital workers, for example—may not take strike action. This restriction limits their unions' bargaining power. As a result, arbitration is often used as a method for solving disputes.

Despite these decades of experience and the large numbers of employees involved (over 70 percent of public servants belong to a union), labour relations within the public sector remains one of the most contentious areas of union activity. Both sides (management and labour) are still grappling with the complex issues that arise when restrictions are placed on the collective bargaining process, a situation made even worse by budgetary constraints.

The Future of Organized Labour

Unlike its American counterpart, the Canadian labour movement has managed to maintain its membership at slightly more than 37 percent of workers, excluding the agricultural sector. The last two decades have been difficult ones, however, as, in general, U.S. unions have gone into decline, fuelling a debate about the future of Canadian unionism. As well, employer militancy in the face of competitive pressures and free trade agreements has led to demands for lower wages and leaner benefit packages. To these threats must be added the increased use of technology in the drive to reduce costs and to increase productivity.[14]

The future, as is often the case, is murky. Whether or not a new cooperative era of labour relations is dawning is open to considerable debate. It is certain, however, that union activities in the foreseeable future will be concerned most with arresting further declines in members' standard of living and with employment security. It is these issues that may yet force management and labour toward the development of more progressive labour relations systems.

THE STRUCTURE OF THE CANADIAN LABOUR MOVEMENT

Much, but not all, of Canadian labour is organized loosely around an umbrella organization, the Canadian Labour Congress (CLC). This body represents the labour movement at the national level (Figure 14-1), coordinating relationships between its various member unions, developing links with government and, internationally, with other labour groups.

All Canadian (national) unions and most Canadian affiliates of international unions belong to the CLC. In turn, individual unions often are linked to provincial federations of labour, each represented on the CLC's Executive Council by a vice-president. These provincial bodies receive input from more than 100 local Labour Councils. The whole is bound together by a series of committees and departments (Figure 14-1), many with regional representation. While this configuration may seem complex, it must be remembered that the Canadian labour movement is extremely diverse. To represent the incredible variety of international, national, regional, and local interest groups that exist in a nation as diverse as Canada is an extremely difficult task.

Local branches of larger unions do most of the negotiating in Canada, often with the help of experts from national or international headquarters. At times, several "locals" of one union will negotiate a common collective agreement. This practice is most common where one employer has several facilities, each organized by a different local, national, or international union.

FIGURE 14-1
The Structure of the CLC-Affiliated
Portion of the
Canadian Labour Movement

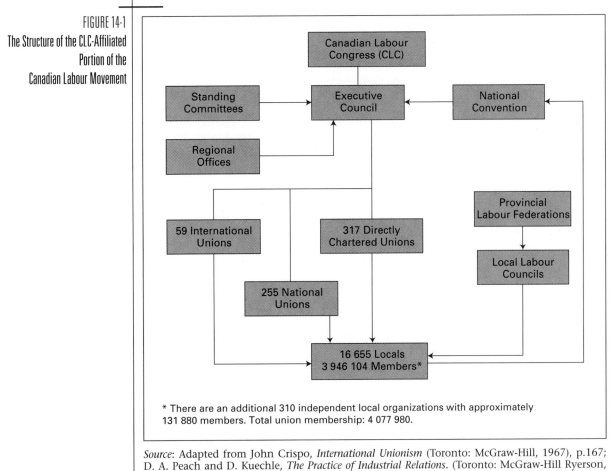

* There are an additional 310 independent local organizations with approximately 131 880 members. Total union membership: 4 077 980.

Source: Adapted from John Crispo, *International Unionism* (Toronto: McGraw-Hill, 1967), p.167; D. A. Peach and D. Kuechle, *The Practice of Industrial Relations.* (Toronto: McGraw-Hill Ryerson, 1985), p. 10; Bureau of Labour Relations Canada, *Directory of Labour Relations in Canada: 1994–1995* (Ottawa: Human Resources Development Canada), p. XIII, XX.

SHOP STRUCTURES

In Canada, there are three kinds of administrative agreements that affect union membership. A **closed shop** is one in which the employer can hire only union members. With less than five percent of collective agreements falling into this category, closed shops are most common in the shipping and construction industries. Similarly, where a **union shop** clause has been negotiated, all employees must become union members as a condition of employment. Approximately 24 percent of contracts fall into the union shop category. An adaptation of this model requires that newly hired employees join the union, but established employees have a choice. Found in about 20 percent of contracts, this clause can create two camps within a firm, as pro- and anti-union forces (members and nonmembers) can engage in drawn-out power struggles. Finally, the famous **Rand formula**, named after Justice Rand, who made the first such ruling in 1946, dictates that all employees pay union dues, whether or not they become union members, so that nonunion employees, who are often given the same wages and benefits as union members, do not get a "free ride" without paying union dues. The formula tends to increase the percentage of employees who become union members, as without membership one does not have a vote, but still must pay dues. The tendency, then, is to join in order to have input (however small) into union activities.

THE LEGAL FRAMEWORK OF CANADIAN INDUSTRIAL RELATIONS

Since legislation governing labour relations resides primarily within provincial jurisdictions, there is considerable variety in the statutes under which contracts are negotiated. Virtually all provinces and territories, however, have incorporated labour relations boards, conciliation and mediation (a process similar to conciliation), and arbitration into the labour relations process.

Labour relations boards comprise government appointees, usually representing labour and management, with a neutral chairperson. They have wide-ranging authority to deal with labour law violations and unfair labour practices. In addition, they can make rulings on issues such as whether or not a union should be allowed into an organization, the appropriate size of a bargaining unit, and what employees should be in the unit. Labour relations board decisions have the same effect and authority as court orders. In some provinces they can even impose a first contract, when it becomes apparent that either side is refusing to bargain in good faith. The use of labour relations boards, with their ability to be flexible, keeps a whole range of disputes from becoming bogged down in the courts. While they have been criticized on occasion for being too pro-management or too pro-labour, generally labour relations boards have acted in the best interests of both parties by providing timely resolution to disputes and labour law violations.

When labour and management reach an impasse and negotiations break down, in all jurisdictions except British Columbia and Saskatchewan, a strike or lockout cannot take place until after **conciliation** between the two parties has been attempted. Appointed by the Minister of Labour at the request of either party, the conciliator has no power. He or she tries to keep the negotiations going as long as possible to try to avert a strike. If these negotiations fail, the conciliator reports the breakdown to the minister. Only then (usually after another specified period of time), can strike action begin.

After conciliation has failed, either before or during a strike, the parties may ask the minister to appoint a mediator, or agree on one themselves. More proactive than conciliators, (although the process of **mediation** and conciliation are quite similar), mediators can become directly involved in the negotiation procedure. A common tactic is to meet separately with the management and labour sides, sometimes carrying messages, sometimes making suggestions. Only when the mediator feels that progress can be made are the two sides brought together. Like a conciliator, a mediator has no power to force either side into making concessions. The mediation process is more intense, however, as mediators can make suggestions, help with contract wording and use their personalities and reputation to put pressure on either or both parties. The usual strategy is to try to reduce the differences bit by bit, so that a settlement can eventually be reached.

Once conciliation and mediation have been exhausted, without success, those individuals who do not have the right to strike are entitled to have their contract terms decided upon through **arbitration**. This process, known as **interest arbitration**, is described in more detail in the next chapter. To avoid strikes or lockouts during the term of a collective agreement, both federal and provincial legislation (except in Saskatchewan) dictates that all contracts have a clause allowing the parties to submit any unresolved grievances to arbitration. This process enables both sides to make their case before a single arbitrator or a board of three arbitrators. This type of arbitration is called "rights" arbitration. An arbitrator's decisions are binding, that is, both sides agree beforehand that they will abide by the decision. It should be noted that employees covered by collective agreements cannot take their employers before the courts. They must resolve disputes in the arbitration process.

UNION OBJECTIVES

Although each union is a unique organization seeking to meet its own goals, several broad objectives characterize the Canadian labour movement as a whole:

1. To secure and, if possible, improve the living standards and economic status of its members.
2. To enhance and, if possible, guarantee individual security against threats and contingencies that might result from market fluctuations, technological change, or management decisions.
3. To influence power relations in the social system in ways that favour and do not threaten union gains and goals.
4. To create mechanisms to guard against the use of arbitrary and capricious policies and practices in the workplace.

The underlying philosophy of the labour movement, then, is to promote organizational democracy and an atmosphere of social dignity, while improving the economic and social situation of all individuals who work in lower-paying jobs. For example, examine the case of this single parent who destroyed her health working nights for minimum wage:

> I get behind on bills and we eat a lot of cheap meals. My kids wear second-hand clothing and ride second-hand bikes. They take a lot of abuse from other kids because of it. . . We don't go out to movies or dinner or even to the Dairy Queen, it's just not in our budget.[15]

This is the type of person the labour movement would like to reach, as Nancy Riche, executive vice-president of the Canadian Labour Congress has suggested:

> . . . trade unions in this country have traditionally played a broad social role. They very often have filled in when government and society have let down the human side. We will be very cautious in supporting what is viewed as a corporate agenda driven by transnationals whose interests are in deregulation and privatization, not the social welfare of the citizens of this country.[16]

WHY SOME EMPLOYEES JOIN UNIONS

Before outlining how unions are formed, let us explore why employees might want to join an existing union or to organize a new union local or independent union. Individuals join unions for different reasons, which tend to change over time. These may involve job, personal, social, or political considerations. It would be impossible to discuss them all, but some of the major reasons include dissatisfaction with management, need for a social outlet, opportunity for leadership, employment in a closed shop or union shop, and peer pressure.

Dissatisfaction with Management

Every job holds the potential for real dissatisfactions. Each individual has a boiling point that can trigger him or her to consider a union as a solution to real or perceived problems. Unions look for problems in organizations and then emphasize the advantages of union membership as a means of solving them. Some of the more common reasons for employee dissatisfaction are described in the following paragraphs.

COMPENSATION

Employees want their compensation to be fair and equitable. Wages are important to them because they provide both the necessities and the pleasures of life. If employees are dissatisfied with their wages, they may look to a union for assistance in improving their standard of living. The ability of the unions to make dramatic gains in income, however, has been severely hampered in the past few years. Of the contracts negotiated in 1994, the wage rate adjustment averaged only 1.5 percent annually over the first year of the contract.[17]

An important psychological aspect of compensation involves the amount of pay an individual receives in relation to that of other workers performing similar work. If an employee perceives that management has shown favouritism by paying someone else more to perform the same or a lower-level job, the employee will likely become dissatisfied. Union members know precisely the basis of their pay and how it compares with others. Therefore pay inequities are less likely to become a major problem area. In fact, unions have been a major force in stripping the veil of secrecy from wage rates, thus reducing favouritism and capriciousness from compensation decisions.

JOB SECURITY

Gone are the days when job security was less important for the younger worker, who might think, "If I lose this job, I can always get another." Now both older and younger employees view their jobs as a precious commodity. If a firm doesn't provide its employees with a sense of job security, they may turn to a union for help. In Canada, employment security was the top negotiating priority for unions in 1993 and in 1994.[18]

INSENSITIVE ATTITUDE OF MANAGEMENT

Management's attitude may be reflected in such small actions as how bulletin board notices are written. Memos addressed "To All Employees" instead of "To Our Employees" may indicate managers who are indifferent to employee needs. Such attitudes likely stem from senior management, but they are noticed initially by employees in the actions of first-line supervisors. The prevailing philosophy may be: "If you don't like it here, leave." A management philosophy such as this, which does not consider the needs of people as individuals, can create a work environment so distasteful that employees turn to a union to obtain more acceptable working conditions. It is difficult for unions to gain a foothold except where managers have abused their power.

A Social Outlet

By nature, many people have strong social needs. They enjoy being around others who have similar interests and desires. Some unions now offer day care centers and other services that appeal to working men and women and increase their sense of solidarity with other union members. People who develop close personal relationships, in either a unionized or non-union organization, will likely stand together in difficult times.

Opportunity for Leadership

Some people aspire to leadership roles, but it isn't always easy for an operative employee to progress into management. Employees with leadership aspirations, however, can often satisfy them through the union. As with the firm, the union has a hierarchy of leadership. Individual members have the opportunity to work their way up through its various levels. Employers often notice employees who are leaders in the union, and it is not uncommon for them to promote such employees into the managerial ranks as supervisors.

Peer Pressure

Many individuals will join a union because they are urged to do so by other members of the work group. An employee may be reminded constantly by friends and associates that he or she is not a member of the union. This social pressure from peers is difficult to resist. Failure to join the union may result in rejection of the employee by other workers. Although rare, in extreme cases, union members have threatened nonmembers with physical violence.

Alternative Justice System

As unions invariably negotiate a grievance handling procedure, many employees are attracted by the chance to air their concerns without fear of reprisal. A collective agreement injects an element of justice into the workplace, so that employees feel protected from unfair managers.

WHY SOME EMPLOYEES AVOID JOINING UNIONS

Even though in Canada, almost 40 percent of the nonagricultural workforce belongs to a union, often unions are not seen as necessary, especially if the human resource system deals directly and effectively with employees and their needs.[19] To avoid a union requires that managers sustain an environment in which labour cannot organize successfully.[20] After a union is installed, management usually recognizes the avoidable mistakes that led to certification. A well-conceived and implemented employee relations system, however, can reduce substantially the likelihood that a union will be formed.[21]

Employees don't join unions for several reasons. First, it costs money to be a union member. Typically, there is an initiation fee followed by dues that must be paid regularly. Second, many employees think that unions are unnecessary. They believe that they shouldn't have to depend on a third party to help satisfy their job-related needs. Third, just as there may be peer pressure in some firms to encourage employees to join the union, in other instances there may be as much pressure against union affiliation.

Labour organizers also must choose where to expend their efforts. Establishing a union is much like starting a business. The cost of starting and maintaining a union must be evaluated in relation to the revenue and other benefits to be gained. For instance, a union might tend to favour organizing a unit of 500 skilled workers rather than a group of 10 semiskilled employees. This is not to say that unions ignore small work units; in Canada, many places with under 20 employees have been organized.

Unions also recognize that there are certain industries, firms, and locations in the country where they commonly experience organizing difficulties. In Hamilton, for example, the Steelworkers have tried to organize Dofasco several times, without success. Indeed, in some firms (Imperial Oil is an example) sophisticated nonunion representation systems have been developed to meet employee needs for justice in the workplace and for input into the decision-making process. As well, many employees do not want to participate in any labour relations activity that might lead to a strike.

Finally, the corporate culture (discussed in Chapter 9) may encourage open communication and employee participation. Employees may have excellent relationships with their supervisors, trusting them to the point where a third party is not needed as a representative or a protector. With this attitude, employees tend to identify strongly with company objectives and are likely to resist organizing efforts.

MANAGEMENT RESPONSE TO UNION ORGANIZING

When faced with an organizing initiative, management can either recognize and accept the union voluntarily or it can try to resist. In both cases, management must follow well-defined guidelines of acceptable behaviour. (These limitations are imposed to protect the ability of employees to form a union while faced with the powerful influence that an employer's speech and conduct can have on employees' thoughts and decision making. Otherwise, the right to engage in union activity would be meaningless.)

Voluntary Recognition

Even when management does not oppose a bid to certify a union and does not seek recourse to a Labour Relations Board, it must abide by certain rules. Management cannot help form a union or in any way dominate a union. As well, if management voluntarily recognizes one union in lieu of another union (one perhaps more distasteful to the employer) that can prove it has majority support from the employees, then a labour relations board would rule the **voluntary recognition** invalid.

Policy of Nonresistance

Resisting an attempt to organize a union is not always advantageous. Management must set aside personal feelings and make decisions in the firm's best interest. For example, the maritime and construction unions usually provide a ready source of labour from their hiring halls. A firm operating in one of these industries in an area that is strongly unionized may find it advantageous to accept a union in order to obtain qualified workers.

An additional factor is a realistic appraisal of the chances of successful resistance. Even when confident of success, management should consider the effect on morale and productivity of a drawn-out, bitter struggle against the employees' felt need to have a union. Some firms have virtually destroyed any chance of developing a cooperative work culture by resisting the establishment of a union too aggressively.

One study in the United States, for example, found that employers who developed cooperative relationships with their union reported a 19 percent increase over 10 years in value added per employee, versus a 15 percent decrease for "combative employers." Here, *value added per employee* was defined as operating income plus inventory divided by the number of workers. Thus, this study suggests that over the long term, a strategy of cooperation may be in a firm's best interests.[22]

Resistance to Unions

Although there may be valid reasons for a firm to accept a union, a large percentage of executives would prefer that their companies do not become unionized. In fact, keeping organized labour out is a major goal for many organizations. Resistance to unions is based on many real and perceived disadvantages.

COSTS

The compensation paid to union members is generally higher than that for nonunion workers. Moreover, unionization often entails additional labour costs arising from "the high cost of complex, payroll-padding work rules; work stoppages, strikes and slowdowns; lengthy negotiations and the grind of arbitration cases; and layoff by seniority."[23] The type of working relationship between labour and management plays an important role in determining the extent of these additional costs. Many unions, however, are changing their attitudes, especially with regard to competitive issues. For example, some unions now acknowledge that inefficient work rules hurt their members as much as the employer. As well, in recent years, an overwhelming percentage of all Canadian collective agreements have been renegotiated without strike action. Much of management's fear of unions therefore, stems from press reports about exceptionally bad labour relations situations; still, it is true that union members in general are more regulation-oriented and more highly paid than their nonunionized counterparts.[24]

REDUCED CONTROL OVER OPERATIONS

Typically, managers want to operate without restrictive work rules, which are seen to reduce their authority. There is a widespread perception that managers lose control in unionized workplaces. This belief was certainly true in the past, but changes have occurred on the part of both management and unions. The era when managers in progressive firms expected to have complete control over all aspects of their operation is fast coming to an end. Co-operative management techniques and teamwork have been found to be much more effective. For their part, many union executives are grudgingly coming to accept that restrictive work rules do not work. Indeed, many union leaders are willing to change traditional rules out of recognition of the need for flexibility to ensure long-term security for their members in the form of firm or company profitability. Many contracts are now being rewritten to allow management much more flexibility in the way work is allocated. But the issue of control is still unresolved in some workplaces. Where unions have been reluctant to change, long and sometimes bitter strikes have resulted.

INABILITY TO REWARD SUPERIOR PERFORMANCE

Rewarding superior performance in a nonunion organization is, in theory, straightforward. By contrast, in a unionized organization, the compensation paid to each job classification is normally specified by the agreement and usually not based on performance. There is little empirical evidence, however, to show that compensation policy varies much where there is no union. In many workplaces, salary levels are tied either formally or informally to length of service. With some exceptions, little advantage is taken of the opportunity to institute pay-for-performance anywhere, especially for employees who are not part of management. Even among companies with pay-for-performance programs, fewer than 15 percent "deny incentive reward payouts if individual [work goals] are not achieved."[25] Although many new approaches are being developed, experience and seniority still appear to form the major criteria for determining pay.[26] On the other hand, there is no reason collective agreements could not contain pay-for-performance clauses. Union negotiators are, however, usually reluctant to agree to such schemes because of a desire to avoid favouritism, a work arrangement under which supervisors can reward their friends or the most subservient workers.

THE RIGHT TO ORGANIZE A UNION

Labour relations legislation in Canada limits the extent to which an employer can resist organizing activity. Employees are protected from any manner of punishment for joining a union. No one can be fired for trying to organize a union. This regulation does not mean that an employee cannot be fired for any reason during an organizing campaign, but the employer may be called upon to show the firing was not an antiunion manoeuvre. There can be no monetary penalty or attempt to extract a promise not to join. Threats, promises, bribes, or suggestions of better future working conditions if the workers vote against the union are also forbidden. In general, the employment situation cannot be changed in any manner that would cause employees "either through gratitude or fear, [to] decline to participate in the union."[27] Conversely, employees may be disciplined or fired for acts of violence. Unions cannot use intimidation, and any memberships obtained this way are invalid.

The employer also has rights. Management is entitled to maintain normal operations, even if they interfere with union organizing activities. For example, the distribution of union literature may be restricted, although not completely forbidden. Unions may not disrupt employees during normal working hours, although personal discussions cannot be prohibited. Access to the workplace may be denied, even though it may be difficult for union organizers to reach employees without being allowed on the property.

There is considerable difficulty when the employer's right to free speech is judged against the right of the employee not to be intimidated. On the one hand, managers possess a right of free speech. On the other hand, this right "may be so fraught with sinister significance for his employee audience that it will effectively destroy union support."[28] In practical terms, the employer may generally state facts and opinions about the business, so that the employee can make a well-informed decision. It is wise for employers to consult a labour lawyer before making announcements during an organizing campaign.

ESTABLISHING A COLLECTIVE BARGAINING RELATIONSHIP

If employees want to be represented by a union, unless the union is voluntarily recognized by the employer, the union must complete a process called certification. Until an organization representing workers is formally recognized or certified, it is usually called an association. Although associations can and do bargain with employers, they are not under the jurisdiction of labour relations boards.[29]

Many associations have eventually become certified unions. The Nova Scotia Registered Nurses' Association, for example, evolved into a union after widespread and prolonged disagreements with hospital managers. (According to labour codes, the key test as to whether an organization of employees may be considered a trade union is independence from the employer.)

Some professional employees, although they want the protection of a union, are uncomfortable with the term union, possibly because it has a working-class history. For this reason, professional groups may keep the name "association" even though they are legally certified as unions. In British Columbia alone, for example, there are 75 certified teachers' "associations."

The term **certification** means that a union is recognized under labour law as the only bargaining agent (representative) for a group of employees known as a bargaining unit. A bargaining unit is deemed (certified) by a labour relations board to contain an appropriate number and type of employee for representation by a labour organization for purposes of collective bargaining. A bargaining unit may cover the employees in one plant or location, or it may cover employees in two or more locations owned by the same employer. The unit may be large or small. In B.C., for example, there is at least one employer with a bargaining unit of two!

The certification process requires that employees voluntarily sign membership cards, such as the sample shown in Figure 14-2, indicating they are paid members of a union. A one-dollar fee is all that is necessary for initial union membership in most jurisdictions.

FIGURE 14-2
Sample of a Union Membership Card

Application for Membership in the XXYZZ Manufacturing Co. Employees' Union

I, the undersigned:

i)   apply for membership in the above union and agree to abide by its Constitution and By-Laws

ii) hereby tender one dollar ($1.00) as payment for the initiation fee

iii) authorize the union to be my exclusive bargaining agent.

Signed...

On behalf of the above mentioned union, I hereby accept this application and acknowledge receipt of one dollar ($1.00) as payment of the initiation fee.

Signed... on behalf of the union.

Date... 19.......

The initiative can be taken either by employees or by professional union organizers on behalf of any union. The percentage of employees that must sign up varies by jurisdiction. In New Brunswick, for example, if 60 percent or more sign cards, the Labour Relations Board will normally certify a union without a vote. If between 50 and 59 percent sign up, the Board has discretionary power: a vote may or may not be taken. If between 40 and 50 percent sign up, a vote is required; while failure to achieve at least a 40 percent sign-up rate means the organizing drive has failed. In the beginning of an election campaign, the union organizers or supporters usually try to keep their objectives secret. If the tactic is successful, then management has less time to react. Once the attempt becomes known, however, union forces can promote their course more actively.

The supervisor's role during the campaign is crucial. Supervisors need to carefully avoid violating the law or committing unfair labour practices. Specifically, they should be aware of what can and cannot be done during the organizing campaign. Not only what is said by the supervisor but *how* it is said becomes very important. Human resource professionals can advise supervisors in these matters. Throughout the campaign, they should also keep upper management informed about employee attitudes.

Theoretically, both union and management are permitted to tell their stories without interference from the other side. At times, the campaign can become quite intense. In fact, some authors have referred to the organizing campaign as a "time of high drama."[30] Once union organizers feel they have sufficient numbers, an application is made to the appropriate Labour Relations Board. The Board will then notify management officially of the application and determine whether all the employees included on the proposed membership list are eligible. Employees who deal with confidential information, for example, may be ruled ineligible. In many Canadian jurisdictions, the time between initial application and the Board decision is expedited (for example, in Alberta only about 12 days), so that management has little time to react.

Management can, however, appear before the Board to argue why certain employees should be excluded. The process of determining eligibility can be extremely important, especially if the vote was close. Loss of a few voting members has, on occasion, defeated attempts to organize. Having decided who is in the "unit" for election purposes, the Labour Relations Board will either certify the union, order that a supervised vote be held or refuse certification. The action taken depends upon the situation and the jurisdiction. Each case is reviewed separately.

Should a union be certified, however, management must negotiate a **collective agreement**, or **contract**, with the union outlining the compensation and working conditions of union members. Furthermore, management must **bargain in good faith**: that is, management must be able to show that it is sincerely trying to reach an agreement Where an employer fails to do so, a union can submit a complaint to a Board, charging bad faith bargaining. What happens next will depend on the jurisdiction. The Labour Relations Board may order interest arbitration for all or part of the contract, order the employer to reimburse the union for its additional costs, or even impose a "contract retroactive to the date at which, in the board's judgement, it should have started [e.g., order back pay]."[31]

In the next chapter we will describe in detail how good faith negotiations should be conducted. There is some debate, however, about the efficiency of our traditional methods of bargaining. Some executives have suggested that labour relations in North America need to change from our present adversarial system toward a more cooperative model. James Marchant, vice president, human resources, at Canadian Pacific Forest Products Ltd., says that management and unions must develop a "shared vision". He promotes a technique called *mutual gains* or *relationship bargaining*. "The difference between mutual gains and traditional bargaining is that the former focuses on problem solving rather than exchanging positions or demands, which can lead to confrontation. [The process] focuses on "agreements that meet the needs of both parties. There should be no winners or losers."[32]

COOPERATIVE VERSUS ADVERSARIAL LABOUR RELATIONS

One of the most important of societal relationships is the interaction between employee and employer. The employer *must* have productive employees; the employee *must* have an employer to receive the wages required to maintain a normal standard of living. To work well, this relationship must be managed carefully, so that both parties learn to tolerate the actions of the other. Only in this way can employees and employers work together to maximize production. The relationship is often not functional, however, because management is often perceived by employees as having the upper hand—as being in a position to take advantage. Unions have evolved as the employee's principal protective agent. Individual employees often can do little to improve work situations or practices perceived as unfair; but organized into unions, they have achieved significant changes.

The role played by a particular union affects employee effectiveness. For example, where a strong union encourages an **adversarial** stance among its members, employees may adopt work rules that inhibit productivity. A better solution might be to develop a **cooperative** relationship between employer and employee, one that serves the common needs of both parties, but entrenched work practices can be difficult to change.

Traditional attitudes create a situation of mutual distrust. The union is seen by management as interfering with the smooth operation of the company. The union's perceived role is to get the best deal for its members and to prevent inequities and other managerial abuse. Thus, tradition, along with the unwillingness of both parties to change, has led to acrimony, distrust and even violence. This conflict becomes apparent if one considers the almost warlike situations created during strikes, lockouts, and negotiations. It is not clear whether the adversarial nature of the management–union relationship has caused this mistrust or whether these ideas reflect deep-seated historical feelings.[33] It is evident, however, that suspicions generate suspicions and that acrimony breeds acrimony.

Another criticism is that adversarial unionism leads to economic inefficiency. Hostility between the employer and the employee leads to decreases in productivity, which in turn cause a decrease in the firm's competitive advantage and a decline in real wage growth. It has also been argued that adversarial unionism focuses too much on material needs such as pay and benefits, to the detriment of more fundamental issues like fairness and equality. Treating employees as equals, as something more than just factors of production, involves more than a good economic package. Each employee wants to be treated as an equal partner on a team, where individual participation can play an essential part in the final output.[34]

Slowly, therefore, there is a change occurring, as a few unions move away from their traditional adversarial roles.[35] Both managers and employees are coming to the realization that all employees have a stake in the enterprise, and that the health of the employer is the only real security for everyone. Employment security and competitiveness are the responsibilities of all participants. Unions and management are just beginning to recognize the need for a more proactive orientation toward building an effective working environment.[36]

Occasionally, governments have tried to make major changes in the system. Ontario's Bill 40 for example, which forbids the use of replacement workers during strikes or lockouts, was seen by its creators as an attempt "to bring unions closer to [a] full partnership with management," despite widespread resistance in the business community. According to Shirley Coppen, Minister of Labour for Ontario in the former NDP government, the Bill was necessary because "the entrenched, adversarial relationship that characterised relations between labour and management for so long in North America is on its way out."[37] It is likely, however, that this legislation will be changed substantially by the present Conservative administration.

The major problem with implementing cooperative unionism is that traditional attitudes and roles of both management and unions create mutual distrust. Thus, despite the actions of some governments, the adversarial situation is likely to continue because "the actions of each side reinforce the attitudes they have toward each other."[38] Of course, even if a cooperative system can be put in place, not all conflicts will be avoided. The goals, interests, and priorities of management and unions may continue to be different in the future.

Difficulties may also arise because changes in the work environment can result in restructured work processes. These changes could affect job content, job satisfaction, job security, the control of work, and the acquisition of new skills and training. Other risks associated with the development of new practices are internal resistance, employee cynicism, lack of systems support, and personal career concerns.[39] If cooperative labour–management relations are to work, then, both sides must commit themselves to cooperative unionism, often against formidable opposition. Management and unions must develop a common vision and try to create an environment that fosters cooperation. Furthermore, "neither side can afford to be paternalistic or self-serving. Both must change and adapt in order to survive."[40]

THE PRESENT REALITY

Cooperative labour-management relationships are complex and controversial. As well, "... there is no systematic and comprehensive body of information on the extent of these co-operative approaches and their consequences in various settings ... the data needed to determine whether this is a marginal or pervasive phenomena do not exist."[41] Cooperative unionism, however, is being widely considered, and some experimentation is going on with various nonadversarial forms of labour-management interaction.[42]

In general, there is little evidence to indicate that organizations are pursuing strategic alliances or partnerships with unions. While there appears to be a greater emphasis on communication, information sharing, employee involvement and more participative approaches and consultation, much of it is aimed directly at employees and/or is taking place outside the collective bargaining process. Where unionized employees are involved, it is often on 'neutral' issues that have nothing to do with the collective bargaining relationship, or initiatives have been introduced unilaterally by management and the unions have been bypassed or relegated to the sidelines (such as quality programs).[43]

Whatever changes emerge over the next decade, "there will never be one formula or one plan for successful employee relations. The economic system is too complex and the markets demand different solutions to different problems, so likely, there will be both adversarial and co-operative employee relations systems in place for some time. This mix always will be in a state of fluctuation to meet the different circumstances of businesses, industries, and markets."[44] It is very difficult to change entrenched attitudes.

Nevertheless, new systems of work and labour-management cooperation are emerging. The scope of this trend and the extent to which it will be lasting are difficult to predict. There are no shortcuts. It will take a genuine commitment on the part of both labour and management to stay the course over a long period of time.[45]

While the last three decades saw unions capitalize on employee dissatisfaction and insecurities, the present threats to jobs do not seem to be enhancing union influence. Rapid changes in the economy and in world trade patterns, combined with employer responses to even more competitive external environments (e.g., downsizing, introducing new technology, and contracting out), have posed enormous challenges for unions.

From a management perspective, too, there have been changes. Faced with mounting competitive pressures and the pressing need to have both employees and their unions understand the serious nature of current business problems, employers appear to be changing their bargaining strategies to include

- more strategic thinking;
- more serious and comprehensive management bargaining agendas;
- more aggressive management approaches in pushing their issues;
- more bargaining in smaller groups and subcommittees;
- more communication and information sharing to facilitate bargaining;
- more involvement of line management;
- a more businesslike approach;
- a consolidation of bargaining units;
- less joint bargaining with other employers.[46]

HRM IN ACTION

Sandy Marshall, one of the workers in the plant, has just come to see the human resource manager, Lonnie Miller, for advice. Apparently, an outside union organizer approached her yesterday and asked her to help with the union organizing effort. Lonnie knows that there have been growing tensions lately and a lot of talk about unions. He has seen what appear to be private conversations at coffee breaks and in the halls. Lonnie knows that if Sandy starts working for a union, she will have a lot of influence. She seems to be a natural leader, and Lonnie thinks she is supervisory material.

How should Lonnie react to Sandy's information?

Employers, in other words, are becoming more hard-nosed in their approach to bargaining. Although there is a growing recognition that unions should be involved much earlier in the corporate decision-making process, the adversarial approach to negotiating collective agreements is still very much in vogue.

SUMMARY

Although the labour movement has a long history in Canada, as late as 1913 less than 10 percent of Canada's labour force was unionized. It was not until after 1926, when progress in American labour legislation began to be copied, that unions in Canada gained a firm foothold. This legislation was accompanied by close relationships with international unions based in the United States. This influence began to decline rapidly in the early 1960s, so that by 1994, fewer than one-third of Canada's union members belonged to foreign-based unions.

Within Canada, every jurisdiction has developed differently, so that only three common characteristics remain: 1) the principle of exclusive representation; 2) the use of labour relations boards; and 3) specifically defined unfair labour practices.

Unlike its American counterpart, the Canadian labour movement has managed to maintain its membership at slightly more than 37 percent of workers, excluding the agricultural sector. The last two decades, however, have been difficult ones. Employer militancy in the face of competitive pressures and free trade agreements has led to demands for lower wage increases (or actual decreases) and leaner benefit packages. To these threats must be added the increased use of technology in the drive to reduce costs and to increase productivity. Coupled with these trends is the perceived need to move away from the adversarial model of labour relations toward a more cooperative formula—a process that would undermine the traditional role of the union.

A large percentage of the public sector in Canada is organized. The major difference between public- and private-sector collective agreements lies in the right to strike. In many jurisdictions, essential employees may not take strike action. This restriction limits their unions' bargaining power. As a result, arbitration is often used as a method for solving disputes.

The Canadian legal framework is characterized by the widespread use of labour relations boards that have authority to deal with labour law violations and unfair labour practices. In some jurisdictions they can even impose a first contract.

As well, compulsory conciliation and voluntary mediation are part of nearly all Canadian labour relations procedures. Coupled with the opportunity to send unresolved grievances to arbitration, these activities are intended to reduce the number of strikes and to solve labour disputes quickly and cheaply.

Both labour and management have reasons to accept or to reject unions. Employee dissatisfaction with management perhaps is the major factor in their desire to become union members, while employers fear that they will lose control and that costs will rise.

Many argue that we must change from adversarial to cooperative systems. Adversarial labour practices, however, are still very much in vogue.

Finally, employers, faced with increased competitive pressures, are taking a more businesslike approach to collective bargaining. They are pushing their agendas more aggressively and the issues under discussion are more comprehensive. However, there appears to be more communication and information sharing between management and unions.

TERMS FOR REVIEW

Organized labour
Yellow-dog contracts
Blacklists
International union
P.C. 1003
Unfair labour practices
Labour relations boards
National unions
Closed shop
Union shop
Rand formula
Conciliation

Mediation
Arbitration
Interest arbitration
Rights arbitration
Voluntary recognition
Certification
Collective agreement
Contract
Bargain in good faith
Adversarial
Cooperative

QUESTIONS FOR REVIEW

1. Describe the development of the labour movement in Canada.
2. Describe how American unions have influenced the Canadian labour movement.
3. Describe how American legislation has influenced labour-management relationships in Canada.
4. In what ways do public-sector labour relations differ from those in the private sector?
5. Why do employees join labour unions?
6. Describe the structure of the Canadian labour movement.

7. What are the main objectives of the labour movement?
8. Why might managers want to oppose a union?
9. What are the main differences between adversarial and cooperative labour relations?
10. Why might adversarial labour relations be practised in Canada for the foreseeable future?
11. Faced with competitive pressures, how have employer attitudes toward collective bargaining changed?

HRM INCIDENT 1

• MAYBE I WILL, AND MAYBE I WON'T

Yesterday Steve Harding was offered a job as an operator trainee with Gem Manufacturing. He had recently graduated from Milford High School, in a small town in Northern Manitoba. Steve had no college aspirations, so upon graduation, he moved to Calgary to look for a job.

Steve's immediate supervisor spent only a short time with him and then turned him over to Gaylord Rader, an experienced operator, for training. After they had talked for a short time, Gaylord asked, "Have you given any thought to joining our union? You'll like all of our members."

Steve had not considered this. Moreover, he had never associated with union members, and his parents had never been members either. At Milford High his teachers had not talked much about unions. The fact that this union operated under the Rand Formula meant nothing to him. Steve replied, "I don't know. Maybe. Maybe not."

The day progressed much the same way, with several people asking Steve virtually the same question. They were all friendly, but there seemed to be a barrier that separated Steve from the other workers. One worker looked Steve right in the eyes and said, "You're going to join, aren't you?" Steve still did not know, but he was beginning to lean in that direction.

After the buzzer rang to end the shift, Steve went to the washroom. Just as he entered, David Clements, the union steward, also walked in. After they exchanged greetings, David said, "I hear that you're not sure about wanting to join our union. You and everyone else reaps the benefits of the work we've done in the past. It doesn't seem fair for you to be rewarded for what others have done, if you're not willing to do a bit yourself. Tell you what, why don't you join us down at the union hall tonight for our beer bust? We'll discuss it more then."

Steve nodded yes and finished cleaning up. "That might be fun," he thought.

QUESTIONS

1. Why does Steve have the option of joining or not joining the union?
2. How are the other workers likely to react toward Steve if he chooses not to join? Discuss.

HRM INCIDENT 2

• WHAT'S CAUSING THE TURNOVER?

Alonzo Alexander, human resource manager for Hyatt Manufacturing, had a problem that he did not know how to handle. His firm had a union and the relationship between management and the union generally had been good. The firm also had a strong employment equity program, which encouraged Alonzo to recruit women for jobs which had traditionally been filled by men.

Hyatt had made major strides in implementing this program throughout the firm, with the notable exception of the machine department. There were only two women among the 53 operators in that department, both of whom had been hired within the past two months.

Alonzo had continued to locate numerous women applicants for the machine operator jobs. Some had trained at the local trade school and were obviously well qualified. A reasonable percentage of women were hired, but they never stayed long. Reviewing records of exit interviews with women who had quit the machine department, Alonzo categorized the main reasons given for leaving: to take a better job (10 responses); pay not high enough (5); personal and family obligations (3); personal relationships on the job (12); and supervision (2).

When Alonzo interviewed the co-workers of women who had quit, he felt that he got little cooperation. Typical comments were "They just had their feelings hurt too easily," and "They were treated like any other worker; if they couldn't hack it maybe they didn't belong here." At one point the union steward told Alonzo that the continued questioning of workers could be considered harassment.

QUESTIONS

1. Given that the union has a social role to play, what approach should the union executive take in the next negotiations?
2. Might there be any difference in how the union reacts if the labour relations climate is cooperative rather than adversarial?

DEVELOPING HRM SKILLS: AN EXPERIENTIAL EXERCISE

Union organizing activity is often met with mixed feelings by everyone affected. Management is usually opposed to such efforts. Beatriz Morrison, the production manager of the heavy motors division of MNP Corporation, knows that upper management does not care much for unions. They believe this unionizing effort is not good for anybody involved with this company and that the union wants to turn the employees against them. Upper management also believes that a union will destroy the company's competitive edge, something that they feel has happened in many other firms. The firm must do everything possible to circumvent this union organizing effort, but it must do so in line with Labour Relations Board guidelines.

Beatriz thought, "I've got to meet with Ray Miller, the supervisor over in Section 4, today. He is a little too eager about stopping the union. We don't want this union, but we also don't want the Labour Relations Board breathing down our necks. Even indirect threats can get us into trouble. Ray must understand the ground rules, and apply those rules to stop this union. Obviously, we don't want this union, but no supervisor can threaten loss of jobs or benefits, or fire anybody. I'm going to tell Ray that if his employees ask his opinion, he can set out the pros and cons, but he must be careful."

One student will play the production manager and another will play the supervisor. The rest should observe carefully. The instructor will provide the participants with additional information.

15 Collective Bargaining

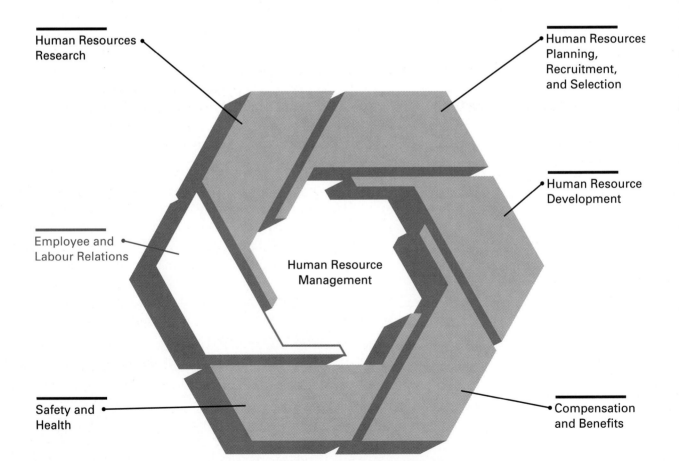

Human Resources
Research

Human Resources
Planning,
Recruitment,
and Selection

Human Resource
Development

Employee and
Labour Relations

Human Resource
Management

Safety and
Health

Compensation
and Benefits

1. Discuss the collective bargaining process, describe the role of the human resource manager in it, and explain the psychological aspects of collective bargaining.

2. Describe what both labour and management do as they prepare for negotiations.

3. Explain typical bargaining issues and the process of negotiating.

4. Identify and describe ways to overcome breakdowns in negotiations, and describe what is involved in ratifying and administering the agreement.

5. Discuss the future of collective bargaining.

Barbara Washington, the chief union negotiator, was meeting with company representatives on a new contract. Both the union team and management had been preparing for this encounter for a long time. Barbara's deep concern was whether or not union members would support a strike vote if one were called. Sales for the industry were generally down because of imports. In fact, there had even been some layoffs at competing firms. The union members' attitude could be described as "Get what you can for us, but don't rock the boat." She hoped, however, that skilful negotiating could win concessions from management.

In the first session, Barbara's team presented its demands to management. The team had determined that pay was the main issue, and demanded a 10 percent increase spread over three years. Management countered by saying that since sales were down it could not afford to provide any pay raises. After much heated discussion, both sides agreed to reevaluate their positions and meet again in two days. Barbara met with her negotiating team in private, and it was decided to decrease the salary demand slightly. The team felt that the least they could accept was an eight percent raise.

At the next meeting, Barbara presented the revised demands to management. They were not well received. Liam Thompson, the director of industrial relations, began by saying, "We cannot afford a pay increase in this contract, but we will make every attempt to ensure that no layoffs occur. Increasing wages at this time will virtually guarantee a reduction in the work force."

Barbara's confidence collapsed. She knew that there was no way that the general membership was willing to accept layoffs and that a strike vote would be virtually impossible to obtain. She asked for a recess to review the new proposal.

Barbara's experience is common in Canada, for although there is some movement toward a more cooperative approach to negotiating labour contracts, in the main, union and management negotiators still rely on an adversarial approach. This traditional technique pits management against labour, so that each side is concerned mainly with its own interests.

We devote the first portion of the chapter to the collective bargaining process and the human resource manager's role. We then describe global labour–management relations, the psychological aspects of collective bargaining, and preparing for negotiations. Next, we address bargaining issues, negotiating, and overcoming breakdowns in negotiations. Then we discuss ratification and administration of the agreement. We conclude with a section on the future of collective bargaining.

THE COLLECTIVE BARGAINING ENVIRONMENT

The collective bargaining process is fundamental to management–labour relations in Canada. Extensive collective bargaining activity occurs each year. In 1993, industrial sectors affected included cars, aircraft, other transportation, steel, mining, some manufacturing sectors, pulp and paper, and food processing. The Conference Board of Canada survey for 1994 found that approximately 770 agreements covering 421 000 employees were negotiated,[1] largely in central Canada, still the primary industrial area.

The last recession of the early 1990s is still affecting labour relations, as job security was the major issue, followed by contracting out, health care benefits, and flexible work rules. Management negotiators were firm in their desire to keep control of costs, but the need to obtain help from the union in improving productivity kept demands for concessions to a minimum. This move toward cooperation could be the beginning of a major shift in labour relations practice in Canada.[2]

Average negotiated wage increases were under 2 percent, far less than the 5 to 6 percent of the early 1990s.[3] This decrease is not surprising, given the length of time it has taken Canada to recover from the recession and the increased competitive pressures felt by most sectors of the economy. While management teams are bargaining hard, management does not seem to have gained the upper hand, as it has in the United States For example, tactics like the establishment of multitiered compensation systems,[4] under which new employees will always earn less than present staff, are virtually unknown. Indeed, many executives and entrepreneurs felt that the introduction of liberalized labour relations codes in Ontario and British Columbia tilted the balance toward labour.[5] The Ontario legislation, which made it easier for unions to organize and harder for employers to continue operations during a strike, has now been reversed. As of 1996, therefore, the legislative balance appears to be swinging in favour of management.

Moreover, while workers in the private sector have made very modest gains, public sector employees have generally been subject to wage freezes and even rollbacks. As the national debt crisis worsens, it is likely that constraint in the public sector will continue, perhaps leading to continued confrontational activities by public-sector unions. The general business environment in Canada, then, has been affected by a slow recovery from the recession and by increased competitive pressures stemming from more liberalized trading patterns. These external forces are only one factor that can complicate the negotiating process. The internal environment must also be considered. There are several possible types of union/management relationships:

1. *Conflict.* Each challenges the other's actions and motivation; cooperation is nonexistent, uncompromising attitudes and union militancy are the norm.

2. *Armed truce.* Each views the other as antagonistic, but tries to avoid head-on conflict; bargaining obligations and contract provisions are strictly interpreted.

3. *Power bargaining.* Management accepts the union; each side tries to gain advantage from the other.

4. *Accommodation.* Each tolerates the other in a "live and let live" atmosphere and attempts to reduce conflict without eliminating it.

5. *Cooperation.* Each side accepts the other, and both work together to resolve human resource and production problems as they occur.

6. *Collusion.* Both "cooperate" to the point of adversely affecting the legitimate interests of employees, other businesses in the industry, and the public; this relationship may involve conniving to control markets, supplies, and prices illegally and/or unethically.[6]

The nature and the quality of union–management relations can vary over time. The first three types of relationships are generally unsatisfactory; **collusion** is unacceptable; and cooperation has been rare in the past. Typically, Canadian union–management relationships are characterized by some form of accommodation. As we have suggested, collective bargaining during the rest of the 1990s likely will be more cooperative, as joint economic survival has become all-important. A change from adversarial relationships toward cooperation in areas never possible in the past, therefore, is a real future prospect.

THE COLLECTIVE BARGAINING PROCESS

The term "collective bargaining" is frequently prefaced with terms such as companywide, industrywide, or multiemployer, which serve to specify more precisely the structure of collective bargaining. Thus, companywide collective bargaining refers to bargaining that takes place between a company with many plants and (typically) a single union representing employees of a particular craft or skill. The terms and conditions negotiated are generally uniform throughout the company. **Industrywide bargaining** refers to negotiations that cover an entire industry, while **multiemployer bargaining** takes place between a union and a group or association of employers (hence the term "association bargaining"). There are relatively few industries in which collective bargaining is genuinely industrywide.[7]

The collective bargaining process comprises a series of steps, shown in Figure 15-1. Depending on the type of relationship encountered, the collective bargaining process may be relatively simple, or it may be a long, tense struggle for both parties. Success, for both sides, requires good communication skills. The following five tips can lead to successful collective bargaining for managers (and for unions).

1. Don't underestimate the importance of the first preparatory, nonadversarial meeting between labour and management representatives; use this opportunity to set the ground rules for future sessions.
2. Carefully document each meeting because accurate, well-organized notes can be quite useful in initial, and subsequent, contract negotiations.
3. Within the bounds of law and propriety, develop a personal profile of each member of the committee who will take part in the collective process.
4. Accept negotiators as peers; never underestimate them.
5. Maintain strong communications with individuals who are most affected by the contract and who best know the issues being discussed.[8]

As shown in Figure 15-1, the first step in the collective bargaining process is preparing for negotiations. This step is often extensive and ongoing for both union and management. After the issues to be negotiated have been determined, the two sides confer to reach a mutually acceptable contract. Although breakdowns in negotiations can occur, both labour and management have tools and arguments that can be used to convince the other side to accept their views. Eventually management and the union reach an agreement that defines the rules of work for the duration of the contract. The final step is for the agreement to be formalized—usually by a ratification vote by the union membership.

Note in Figure 15-1 the feedback loop from Administration of the Agreement to Preparing for Negotiation. Collective bargaining is a continuous and dynamic process, and preparing for the next round of negotiations often begins the moment a contract is signed.

THE HUMAN RESOURCE MANAGER'S ROLE

When a firm acquires a union, the human resource manager's role tends to change significantly. In a unionized environment, the human resource manager must deal with a union organizational structure consisting of union stewards and business agents, rather than with individual employees. The human resource manager must administer the contract and therefore should

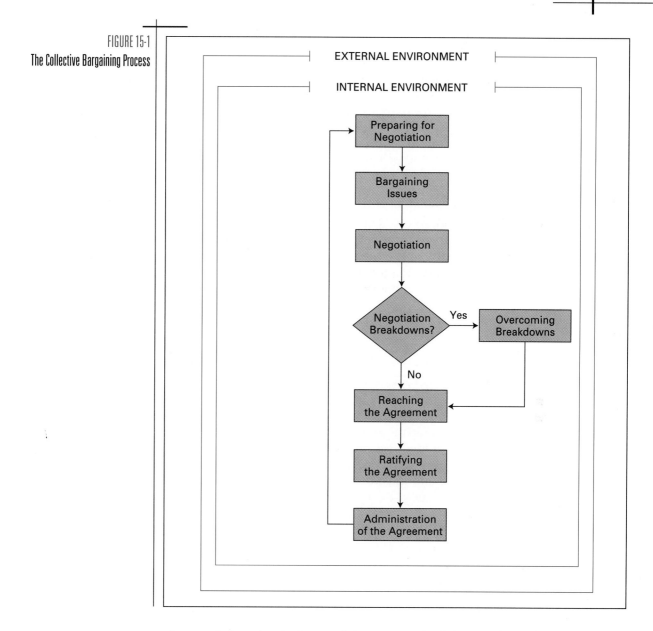

play an integral role in resolving contractual issues. According to veteran American negotiator Fritz Ihrig, a capable human resource manager is the ideal person to negotiate the contract.[9]

Because the role of first-line supervisors is crucial, the human resource manager must maintain close contact with them before, during, and after collective bargaining. First-line supervisors administer the contract on a day-to-day basis and know whether or not it is working well. A knowledgeable human resource manager can limit animosity and avoid the "stick-it-to-'em" mentality. Human resource managers who play an active role in collective bargaining, then, can help to make the process operate more smoothly, both during and after negotiations.

GLOBAL UNION-MANAGEMENT RELATIONS

Canada is a trading nation that must forge networks of business relationships around the world to ensure economic survival. Before conducting business in another country or entering into an international alliance, however, it is important to understand the characteristics of the industrial relations system in the country and the effect on each partner. For example, contrast the following hypothetical situations: First, a firm in Germany (where roughly 40 percent of the work force is represented by unions) forms an alliance with a Swedish firm (where roughly 93 percent of the work force is represented by a union). Both partners would likely be sympathetic to the workers' desires to be represented collectively by a national or an international union. In the second situation, a Canadian-based Japanese firm with no union forms an alliance with a U.S. company whose workers are members of a union. If asked to state their most important concern about the partnership, the factory managers might cite the concern that their alliance called for two companies with different industrial relations traditions to work together. Obviously, in these diverse situations, the industrial relations issues addressed by HR professionals would be quite different. Thus, it is important to understand the implications of foreign industrial relations systems before finalizing international alliances.[10]

PSYCHOLOGICAL ASPECTS OF COLLECTIVE BARGAINING

Prior to beginning negotiations, both the management and the union team must prepare positions and accomplish certain tasks. During this stage, the psychological aspects of collective bargaining become evident. Psychologically, collective bargaining can be difficult because the process is often adversarial and must be approached as such. It is "a situation that is fundamental to law, politics, business, and government, because out of the clash of ideas, points of view, and interests come agreement, consensus and justice."[11]

Those involved in the collective bargaining process will be matching wits, will experience victory as well as defeat, and will ultimately resolve their differences, resulting in a contract. The role of those who meet at the bargaining table involves the mobilization and the management of aggression. Thus, their personalities have a direct effect on what can be accomplished and how quickly agreement can be reached. Problems can be compounded by differences in experience and educational backgrounds. Finally, the longer, more involved, and intense the bargaining sessions are, the greater the psychological strain on the participants.'

PREPARING FOR NEGOTIATIONS

Because of the complex issues facing labour and management today, the negotiating teams must prepare carefully before bargaining begins. Prior to the first bargaining session, the negotiators should study the culture, climate, history, present economic state, and wage and benefits structure of the organization and of similar organizations. Because a typical labour agreement lasts three years, negotiators should devise a contract that is usable both now and in the future. This consideration is important for both management and labour, but in fact both sides often discover during the term of an agreement that contract provisions need to be added, deleted, or modified. Because it is extremely difficult to amend a signed contract, these items usually become proposals to be addressed in the next round of negotiations. There can be a "reopener" provision in a contract, however, that allows either side to re-open negotiations at a specified time or under special conditions, prior to the end of the contract. For example, the faculty at the University of New Brunswick has just ratified a contract that pays wages to plus or minus 2 per-cent of the average pay in 14 other Canadian universities. There is a reopener clause, however, so that if another provincial government cuts university wages substantially, UNB's faculty can negotiate another pay arrangement.

The issues about which the employer and the union will bargain may encompass anything that affects the workplace: wages, hours, duties, work schedules, lunch and rest periods, safety. . . in fact any item or activity that is not prohibited by criminal or civil law can be negotiated. Some contracts, for example, even contain provisions about the price of meals in the company cafeteria. A partial listing of issues that have been negotiated in past con-tracts is found in Figure 15-2.

Contracts must meet certain provisions set out in the applicable federal or provincial Industrial or Labour Relations Act. (The territories fall under the Canada Labour Code.) While the acts vary somewhat, many of the re-quirements are similar. In New Brunswick, for example, every collective agreement must recognize the union and the employer as exclusive bargain-ing agents. That is, no individual represented by a union can make special deals. Every agreement must contain a clause prohibiting strikes and lock-outs while the contract is in force, and there are rules regarding the length and the starting date of contracts. Provisions regarding technical change are also mandated. Finally, every collective agreement must provide for binding arbitration, should the parties wish to prevent a strike.[12]

The union must continually gather information about membership needs and attitudes. The union steward is normally in the best position to collect this information, funnelling information up through the union's chain of command to where the data are compiled and analyzed. Union leaders attempt to uncover any areas of dissatisfaction, because the general union membership must approve any agreement before it becomes final. It would be foolish for union leaders to demand management concessions only to have the members reject their proposals. Because they must be elected, union leaders will lose their positions if the demands they make of manage-ment do not represent the desires of the general membership.

Management also spends long hours preparing for negotiations. The many interrelated tasks that management must accomplish are presented in Figure 15-3. In this example, management allows approximately six months to prepare for negotiations. All aspects of the current contract are consid-ered, including flaws that should be corrected. When preparing for negotia-tions, management should listen carefully to first-line supervisors, as they are affected directly by any error made while negotiating the contract. An alert first-line supervisor may also have a sense of likely union demands. Management may also periodically seek information about employee atti-tudes. Surveys can be administered to workers, for example, to determine feelings toward jobs and the job environment.

FIGURE 15-2
Examples of Bargaining Issues

Wages	Severance pay	Work assignments and transfers
Hours	Nondiscriminatory hiring hall	No-strike clause
Discharge	Plant rules	Piece rates
Arbitration	Safety	Stock purchase plan
Paid holidays	Prohibition against supervisor doing unit work	Workloads
Paid vacations		Change of employee status to independent contractors
Duration of agreement	Superseniority for union stewards	Overtime pay
Grievance procedure	Partial plant closing	Sick leave
Layoff plan	Plant closedown and relocation	Management rights clause
Change of payment from hourly base to salary base	Change in operations resulting in reclassifying workers from incentive to straight time, or a cut in the work force, or installation of cost-saving machinery	Plant closing
Union security and checkoff of dues		Job posting procedures
Work rules		Plant reopening
Merit wage increase		Employee physical examination
Work schedule		Truck rentals: minimum rental to be paid by carriers for employee-owned vehicles
Lunch periods	Price of meals provided by company	
Rest periods	Group insurance: health, accident, life	
Pension plan		Arrangement for negotiation
Retirement age	Promotions	Profit-sharing plan
Bonus payments	Seniority	Company housing
Cancellation of seniority upon relocation of plant	Layoffs	Subcontracting
Shift differentials	Transfers	

Source: Adapted from Reed Richardson, "Positive Collective Bargaining," Chapter 7.5 of *ASPA Handbook of Personnel and Industrial Relations*, pp. 7-121. Copyright © 1979 by The Bureau of National Affairs, Inc., Washington, D.C. Reprinted by permission.

Another step in preparing for negotiations is to identify various positions that both union and management will take as the negotiations progress. Usually each side takes an initial extreme position, representing the preferred outcome. Both sides will likely determine absolute limits on each demand or offer: a point beyond which they will not make concessions to keep negotiations going. Both sides also prepare **fallback positions** based on combinations of issues. These preparations should be detailed because clear minds do not always prevail during the heat of negotiations.

Finally, selecting the bargaining team is a major consideration. The composition of the management team usually depends on the type and size of the organization. Normally bargaining is conducted by labour relations specialists, with the advice and assistance of operating managers. Sometimes, senior executives are involved directly, particularly in smaller firms. Larger

FIGURE 15-3
An Example of Company Preparations
for Negotiations

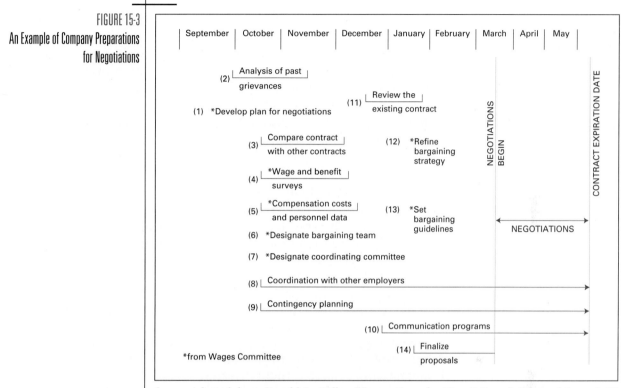

Source: Adapted from Ronald L. Miller, "Preparations for Negotiations," *Personnel Journal*, 57 (January 1978), p. 38. Reprinted with permission.

companies use staff specialists (a human resource manager or industrial relations executive), managers of principal operating divisions, and, in some cases, an outside consultant or labour attorney. It is essential, however, that the human resource manager become actively involved in the collective bargaining process. The CEO should not be directly involved in negotiations. Someone on the management side needs to give final approval. As well, there may be times when "thinking" or "cooling off" time is needed. The obligation to consult the CEO can give negotiators from both sides an opportunity to break off negotiations.

The responsibility for conducting negotiations for the union is usually entrusted to union officers. At the local level, the **negotiating committee** will normally be supplemented by rank-and-file members elected specifically for this purpose. In addition, a national union will often send a representative to act in an advisory capacity, or even to participate directly in the bargaining sessions. The real task of the union negotiating team is to develop and obtain solutions to the problems raised by the union's membership. The union's chief negotiator must, therefore, be chosen with care. Upon his or her shoulders rests the responsibility for what ultimately is accepted or rejected in the contract. The ideal chief negotiator, according to the CAUT, should have the following characteristics (the same characteristics apply to management negotiators):

1. *Integrity.* The ability to sit down at the bargaining table and convey integrity to others—both by manner and by reputation—is the most important asset a chief negotiator can possess.

2. *Leadership.* The ability to make decisions, sometimes quickly, sometimes under the pressure of events, is vital. The ability to inspire confidence and to get the full benefit of the maximum efforts of his or her team is a quality that the successful chief negotiator must have.

3. *Ability to listen* and to absorb, interpret and remember what occurs in negotiations is important, because it will suggest courses of action or avenues to explore that may lead ultimately to success on a different issue.

4. *Creative mind.* The ability to surround a problem, and to devise four or five alternative approaches to getting it solved.

5. *Verbal ability.* The effective negotiator is articulate. She/he knows how to communicate the union's positions and attitudes. She/he is in thorough command of those verbal persuasion skills that influence the thinking, the attitudes and the decisions of others.

6. *Works well with people.* Has the ability to meet and communicate with others at their own level. She/he can talk as an equal to the company president or the employer's legal counsel, and she/he can adapt her/his style to a committee composed of blue collar workers. She/he can communicate with her/his own economic policy committee or with the membership at large without becoming a threat to anyone.13

All other members of the team are entrusted with supporting roles that help the chief negotiator function at top efficiency. One or more members should possess technical knowledge about the items being negotiated (e.g., wage rates, comparisons with other bargaining units, recent settlement trends). The following team guidelines come from a labour organization, but could be a useful model for assembling any negotiating team.

Second Member of the team usually sits beside the chief negotiator to her/his right. This team member can support the chief negotiator by passing her/him notes that may suggest a union team meeting is needed or the use of certain strategies or verbal skills. She/he functions as a second pair of eyes and ears, and helps the chief negotiator to formulate strategy.

Third Member may be assigned the responsibility of reading and interpreting management's actions. She/he will observe body language closely and attempt to put it into the context and perspective of opportunity. For example, she/he may offer via notes or in caucus: "Management seems to be making a move in this direction." "Mr. Smith seemed very embarrassed by Mr. Hone's remarks." She/he contributes to the chief negotiator's efforts through her/his ability to observe other people, and to drew shrewd inferences from what she/he sees.

Fourth Member may be responsible for taking notes on what is agreed to, what was discussed during caucus, what counter-proposals management may have made, etc. Verbatim transcripts are inadvisable and may be dangerous, but accurate notes that reflect the union's intent are valuable, and records should be transcribed from these notes and kept from year to year as reference.

Fifth Member may be responsible only for recording statements made by management that might be used against them in a public relations sense. Any intemperate remark made in the heat of debate by management which might be used to unify the membership or to play on public opinion, would be recorded by this individual.

The number of individuals who comprise the negotiating team is not as important as the dedication and the competence with which they confront their tasks—and the degree of unity and support they receive from the general membership. In a three-member negotiating team, for example, all these functions might still be performed, but two team members double up on their assignments. In general, three to five people is an ideal size.[14]

NEGOTIATING THE AGREEMENT

There is no way to ensure speedy negotiation of agreements satisfactory to both parties. At best, the parties can attempt to create an atmosphere that will lend itself to steady progress. For example, the two negotiating teams usually meet at a neutral site, such as a hotel. It is important that a favourable relationship be established early in order to avoid eleventh-hour bargaining. It is equally important that union and management negotiators strive to develop and to maintain communication. Collective bargaining is a problem-solving activity, so good communication is essential. Negotiations should be conducted in the privacy of the conference room, not through the news media. If the negotiators feel that publicity is necessary, joint releases to the media may avoid unnecessary conflict.

The negotiating phase of collective bargaining begins with each side presenting its initial demands. Because a collective bargaining settlement can be expensive for a firm, the cost of various proposals should be estimated as accurately as possible. The term *negotiating* suggests a certain amount of give-and-take, the purpose of which is to lower the other side's expectations. The union will bargain to upgrade their members' economic and working conditions. The employer will negotiate to maintain or enhance profitability. One of the most costly components of any collective bargaining agreement is a wage increase provision. An example of the negotiation of a wage increase is shown in Figure 15-4. In this example, labour initially demands a $0.40 per hour increase. Management counters with an offer of only $0.10 per hour. Both labour and management—as expected—reject each other's demands. Plan B calls for labour to lower its demand to a $0.30 per hour increase. Management counters with its own Plan B, an offer of $0.20. The positions in Plan B are feasible to both sides, as both proposed wage increases are in the bargaining zone: the range of possible outcomes acceptable to both management and labour—in this case, an increase of between $0.20 and $0.30 per hour. The exact amount will be determined by the power of the bargaining unit and the skills of the negotiators.

The realities of negotiations are not for the weak-of-heart. At times negotiations resemble a high-stakes poker game, with a certain amount of bluffing and raising of the ante taking place. The ultimate bluff for the union is for the negotiator to say, "If our demands are not met, we are prepared to strike." Management's alternatives are to allow the strike to occur or to

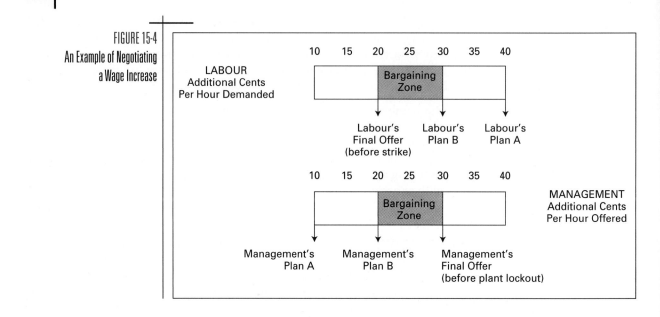

FIGURE 15-4
An Example of Negotiating a Wage Increase

threaten employees with a lockout. Lockouts are generally used by management to control the timing of a work stoppage that would likely occur anyway, or to respond to union pressure tactics such as selective or rotating strikes. We will discuss each of these tactics later; utilizing them is a form of power politics. The party with the greater leverage can expect to extract the most concessions.

Even though one party may appear to possess the greater power, negotiators often take care to keep the other side from losing face. They recognize that the balance of power may shift rapidly. By the time the next round of negotiations occurs, the labour/market situation could be swinging back in favour of the other side. Even when management appears to have the upper hand, then, minor concessions may be made that allow labour leaders to claim gains for the union. For example, management may demand that employees pay for lost tools (assuming these losses have become excessive). In order to obtain labour's agreement on this demand, management may agree to provide new uniforms, if the cost would be less than the savings on the lost tools. Thus, labour leaders, although forced to concede on this demand, could show their members they have obtained a concession from management.

Generally, neither side expects to have all its initial demands met. Demands that the union does not expect to receive when they are first made are known as **beachhead demands.** Management must remember, however, that a concession may be difficult to reverse. For instance, if management agreed to provide dental benefits, withdrawing these benefits in the next round of negotiations would be difficult. Labour, on the other hand, can lose a demand and continue to bring it forward in the future.

Remember that what has just been described is the traditional (and still the most common) approach to bargaining, **positional bargaining,** in which management and labour begin with opposite positions. A more cooperative approach will be discussed in greater detail later in this chapter.

BREAKDOWNS IN NEGOTIATIONS

At times negotiations break down, even though both labour and management may want to finalize a contract. This impasse does not necessarily mean a strike. A series of possible steps (touched on in Chapter 14) follows.

Conciliation[15]

In most jurisdictions in Canada, a legal strike may take place only after the expiry of a collective agreement and after both parties pass through a process called **conciliation**. The process begins with the appointment of a conciliation officer, who meets with the parties in an effort to reach an agreement. Conciliation boards are also used from time to time in areas under federal jurisdiction, but only in unusual circumstances in other jurisdictions.

The first premise in any collective bargaining situation is that management and labour should attempt to resolve their differences by themselves. If an impasse is reached, governments have concluded that it is in the public interest that a neutral person should attempt to assist them. The mechanics of obtaining a conciliation officer are straightforward. Once the union and management have met and an impasse in negotiations has been reached, either of the parties may apply to the Minister of Labour, requesting an appointment. The only two conditions necessary for making an application are that both union and management must have met and that proper notice must be given to the other party. In some instances the timing of an application for appointment of a conciliation officer may be an important tactical advantage to the union. For instance, the union may wish to bring negotiations to a crisis early while an employer might want to delay and build up inventory.

Once appointed, the conciliation officer contacts both union and management to establish a time and a place for a meeting. The conciliation officer's role is to not to make judgements on the positions taken by either side, but to assist the union and management in settling their own differences. The officer may make suggestions to either or both sides, but such suggestions are not binding and can be accepted or ignored. Once the parties have reviewed the matters in dispute with the conciliation officer, the usual practice is for the officer to meet separately with both sides. At this stage the officer will be probing to see if the formal positions held earlier are flexible and also to try to obtain insight into each side's major bargaining goals.

The officer will then direct attention to resolving the points in dispute or at least narrowing the differences. In some cases this process may require that either or both sides make new proposals; or the officer may suggest a compromise, which either party may accept or reject. If the conciliation officer concludes that a settlement cannot be reached, he or she prepares a report for the Minister. The Minister then either forms a Conciliation Board, or, as is the usual practice, issues a **"no-board" report**. A set number of days after the issuance of the no-board report, (the exact time lapse depending on the jurisdiction), the union is in a legal strike position and management is in a position to legally lock out the employees.

Mediation[16]

Once the collective bargaining dispute has passed through the conciliation stage without resolution, time begins to run down to the point where a lawful strike or lockout may take place. In theory, the interval after the issuance of a no-board report is intended to give the parties an opportunity to meet and negotiate before a legal strike/lockout takes place. While the union and management may meet and bargain on their own, a mechanism, called **mediation**, has been established to provide assistance during this period. Mediators fill a gap left by conciliation boards, seldom used today.

In a sense, the mediator is a conciliation officer with a different title who acts during a crisis. The mediator has no more real power than the conciliator and has no binding authority to require either party to do anything. The major difference is that the mediator meets with both sides in the days immediately preceding a strike or lockout, or after a strike or lockout is called. Either side may request that a mediator be appointed by the Ministry of Labour, or the parties may choose one on their own. (Though most jurisdictions have government-employed or -contracted mediators available, management and unions often hire a mediator privately, so they can retain control over the appointment.) As a general rule, a mediator will continue to be available to both sides as long as the dispute lasts. Thus, a mediator may have a number of meetings extending over a long period, even while a strike or lockout is continuing.

The techniques used by the mediators are similar to those used by conciliation officers. Because of the timing of mediation, however, both sides are likely to be more on edge and the tensions likely to be greater. The mediator will often use the time pressure as a lever in making efforts to persuade both union and management to modify their positions. Unlike conciliation, mediation commonly involves trying to wear down the negotiators physically and mentally by continuous meetings around the clock, in the hope that one or both will break, or at least compromise significantly.[17]

The mechanics of mediation are somewhat similar to the conciliation process. Initially, the mediator probes both sides' views and gauges how strongly their positions are held. After private discussions, the mediator may be convinced that one or both sides need a face-saving recommendation. All too often, one side may be locked into a commitment with no room to manoeuvre. A mediator may find the common ground necessary for both sides to move a little without appearing to have backtracked. If a mediator succeeds in producing an agreement, it is usually put into writing as a Memorandum of Settlement. The general terms are set out and the bargaining committee returns to the local and presents the terms of the memorandum to members at a ratification meeting.

Union representatives also have a responsibility to their members to obtain the best possible terms in a collective agreement. If they are prohibited by law from engaging in a legal strike, as are some public sector unions, they have only two means of obtaining their collective bargaining objectives. On the one hand, they can try to persuade the employer's representative to agree to increases in wages and benefits. If they cannot, they must try to persuade an arbitrator to grant the changes they want in a binding arbitration award.

Arbitration

In the main (though there are exceptions), those who work in the public sector conduct their bargaining in the same manner as if they were in the private sector, up to the point where the unresolved matters in dispute are taken to compulsory **arbitration** under appropriate legislation. This process, known as **interest arbitration**, involves the creation and imposition of a collective agreement on both the union and the employer if they fail to come to an agreement. Thus, the arbitrator fills the gaps that both sides could not negotiate. Not all public sector workers, however, are denied the right to strike. There are a number of models in place, including the right to conduct limited strikes.

Mostly, however, public sector contracts that are not successfully negotiated or resolved with the assistance of a conciliator are referred to an arbitrator. The terms of the arbitrator's award are final and binding upon both sides. The general practice for parties appearing before an arbitrator is to make their presentations in a written brief, supplemented by additional oral arguments. The arbitrator normally has authority to make a decision that falls somewhere between the two parties' submissions. On occasion, the parties may choose the "final offer selection method," in which the arbitrator is limited to choosing the position of either the employer or the union. If, for example, the union wanted an 8 percent wage increase and the employer was offering four percent, the arbitrator could award either 8 percent or 4 percent, but not 6 percent. Final offer selection may cover an entire collective agreement, or may be done item by item only for issues on which the parties cannot agree.

UNION STRATEGIES FOR OVERCOMING NEGOTIATION BREAKDOWNS

There are times when a union believes that it must exert extreme pressure to get management to agree to its bargaining demands. Strikes and boycotts are the primary means a union may use to overcome breakdowns in negotiations.

Strikes

When union members refuse to work in order to exert pressure on management in negotiations, their action is referred to as a **strike**. A strike halts production, resulting in lost customers and revenue, which the union hopes will force management to submit to its terms. The timing of a strike is important in determining its effectiveness. An excellent time is when business is thriving or expanding. Conversely, a union might gain little from a strike if a firm's sales are poor, or if a large inventory has been built up.

Contrary to the stereotype, unions use the strike only as a last resort. Strikes are extremely expensive not only for the employer, but also for the union and its members. The section below on organizing a strike, adapted from a *Manual on Legal Strike Action for Canadian Faculty Associations,* will give readers an appreciation of the difficulties union members face when they decide to strike. A union's treasury is often depleted by payment of strike benefits to its members. At the same time, since these benefits are far below normal paycheques, members suffer a drop in standard of living.

Sometimes during negotiations (especially at the beginning) the union may want to strengthen its negotiating position by taking a strike vote. Members often give overwhelming approval to a strike. This vote does not necessarily mean that there will *be* a strike, only that the union leaders now have the authority to call one *if* negotiations reach an impasse. A favourable strike vote can add a sense of urgency to efforts to reach an agreement.

Successful passage of a strike vote has additional implications for union members. Virtually every union's constitution contains a clause requiring the members to support and participate in a strike if one is called. Union members can be fined for failure to comply. Thus, union members place themselves in jeopardy if they cross a picket line without the consent of the union. As well, in some jurisdictions, it is illegal for union members to return to work while their union is on strike. More subtle measures, such as "sickouts" (in which large numbers of employees call in sick) and work slowdowns have been used successfully by union members to bring pressure on the company without the impact of a strike on the membership.

Organizing Legal Strike Action[18]

Having decided on strike action, the union executive should establish an appropriate committee structure. Different circumstances require different structures, and circumstances will vary from company to company. In general, however, the structure would consist of a series of essential committees and any other additional committees the local circumstances require. It is imperative that a chairperson be appointed for every committee, that concise minutes be kept at every committee meeting, that the committees meet often, but as briefly as possible, that reports be made to the strike organizer and, most important, that for every aspect of the operation one individual be responsible.

Although a strike sometimes appears a long time away, the first strike day can arrive quite suddenly! Depending on the size of union membership, the executive should appoint a strike organizer with the authority to make on-the-spot decisions during the strike. In larger unions it is advisable not to appoint the president to the position of strike organizer. The president, as the union's chief spokesperson, must remain free from this heavy organizing burden and from potentially controversial issues. However, in smaller unions, several tasks may have to be assumed by the same person. It is vital that the strike organizer stay in constant close contact with the executive or, in an emergency, with the president of the union. The job of the strike organizer is to make the strike work, but not to make union policy. It is very important that the roles be clearly defined in advance and that friction does not develop.

It is also important that the relationship between the negotiation team and the executive be clearly defined. The former negotiates not only the agreement, but also the end to the strike. It is a good idea to have at least one executive member on the negotiation team, but ideally not the president. The executive must, however, remain in charge. Subgroups must not be allowed to take over the strike, but at the same time, effective delegation must be used where needed.

The union executive should ensure that it has immediate knowledgeable legal advice available throughout the strike. Legal counsel should be informed as soon as possible about the likelihood of a strike and about any anticipated legal complications. Legal counsel should be consulted to ensure that all the legal steps necessary for a strike have been followed by the union prior to strike action.

THE COMMITTEES

1. The Strike Action Committee, composed of four to six people, is responsible for the overall leadership of the strike and for the coordination of the various committee activities.
2. The Finance Committee is responsible for proposing a strike action budget, keeping accurate records of all expenditures, and paying strike benefits to all eligible members.
3. The Strike Services Committee organizes toilets, picket line materials, shelter, vehicles, food supplies, and other essential services, including social events.
4. The Publicity Committee generates, manages, and controls all internal and external publicity materials and public relations.
5. The Picket Line Committee organizes and controls picket line activity. A union does not have the right to prevent access to an employer's property. In practice, picket lines often have slowed entry because of the intense emotion generated during a strike, but when police action is required to restrict picket activity, the union invariably receives bad publicity, so picket lines must be managed carefully.

Given the amount of organization required, the financial cost, and the emotional drain of a strike, it is little wonder that both unions and employers avoid this tactic whenever possible. The strike truly is an activity of last resort.

Boycotts

The boycott is another of labour's weapons to get management to agree to its demands. A **boycott** involves an agreement by union members to refuse to use or buy the firm's products. A boycott exerts economic pressure on management, and the effect often lasts much longer than that of a strike. Once shoppers change buying habits, their behaviour will likely continue long after the boycott has ended. At times, significant pressures can be exerted on a business when union members, their families, and friends refuse to purchase the firm's products and encourage the public not to patronize the firm. This approach is especially effective when the products are sold at retail outlets and are easily identifiable by brand name. For example, in its dispute with the Irving Co. at its paper mill in Saint John, the Canadian Paperworkers Union attempted to organize a provincewide boycott of all Irving-owned gas stations and lumber stores.[19]

MANAGEMENT AND STRIKE ACTION

Management, too, needs to be well prepared and organized to deal with a strike. Planning should begin as soon as a strike begins to seem like a possibility. Although planning must take into account the nature of the enterprise, the sector, the union, and the legal context, in general, planning would include prestrike preparation, maintaining operations during the strike, and poststrike follow-up. Part of these discussions could include considerations of alternatives to the strike, such as binding arbitration.

Prestrike preparations would encompass communications (internal and external), the establishment of a management strike committee, and the preparation of a strike manual (or an updating of an existing manual). Many of the issues would require legal advice. For example, where does the union have a right to set up its picket line? Good communications is central to management response to a strike, since managers have many questions to address. How will management ensure that the picketing is peaceful? How will employees (other than those in the bargaining unit) gain access to the premises? Will any members of the bargaining unit who do not wish to strike be allowed to work? What fringe benefits (if any) will apply to members of the bargaining unit who are on strike? How will sick leave and long-term disability be administered? How will essential services be maintained? What external services are required? What security is required? Who will provide advice to any manager needing direction?[20]

MANAGEMENT'S STRATEGIES FOR OVERCOMING NEGOTIATION BREAKDOWNS

Management may also use various strategies to encourage unions to return to the bargaining table. One form of action, somewhat analogous to a strike, is called a lockout. During a **lockout**, management keeps employees out of the workplace and may run the operation with management personnel and/or temporary replacements in those jurisdictions where replacement workers are legal. Unable to work, the employees do not get paid. Although the lockout is used infrequently, fear of a lockout may bring labour back to the bargaining table. A lockout is particularly effective when management is dealing with a weak union, when the union treasury is depleted, or when the business has excessive inventories.

In 1994, the National Hockey League owners used this tactic. Even though the players had agreed to keep playing while negotiations were underway, management locked them out in an effort to speed up the bargaining process and to ensure that the players would not be in a position to strike during the playoffs.[21] As with strike action, then, the timing of a lockout can be very important.

Another alternative available to management is to place management and/or nonunion workers in the striking workers' jobs. This tactic can be quite effective, if the firm is not labour intensive and if maintenance demands are not high (as they are at a petroleum refinery or a chemical plant). When replacement personnel are used, management will try to continue production and, in rare cases, attempt to show how production actually increases with the use of nonunion employees. Using replacement workers (called *scabs* by union members) is illegal in British Columbia and Quebec. Even where the practice is legal, using replacement workers risks inviting violence and creates bitterness among employees, which may adversely affect the firm's performance long after the strike has ended.

RATIFYING THE AGREEMENT

More than 90 percent of the time, collective bargaining leads to an agreement without a breakdown in negotiations or disruptive actions. Typically, agreement is reached before the current contract expires. After the negotiators have reached a tentative agreement on all contract terms, they prepare a written statement complete with the effective and termination dates. The approval process for management is often easier than for labour. The president or CEO has usually been briefed regularly on the progress of negotiations. Any difficulty that might have stood in the way of obtaining approval has probably already been resolved with senior management.

However, the approval process is more complex for the union. Until a majority of members approve, the proposed agreement is not final. While not required by law in all jurisdictions, most unions hold a **ratification** vote, at which the membership votes to accept or to reject the proposed collective agreement. At times, union members reject the proposal and a new round of negotiations must begin. In recent years, approximately 10 percent of all tentative agreements have been rejected when presented to the union membership. Many of these rejections might not have occurred if union negotiators had communicated more effectively with their membership, or if management had been more aware of employee needs and perceptions.

ADMINISTERING THE AGREEMENT

Negotiating, as it relates to the total collective bargaining process, may be likened to the tip of an iceberg. It is the visible phase, the part that makes the news. The larger and perhaps more important part is contract or agreement administration, consisting of ongoing activities seldom viewed by the public. The agreement establishes the union–management relationship for the duration of the contract. Usually, neither party can unilaterally change the contract's language until the expiration date. The main problem encountered in contract administration, therefore, is uniform day-to-day interpretation and application of the contract's terms. Ideally, the aim of both management and the union is to make the agreement work to the benefit of everyone—often not an easy task.

Both management and labour are responsible for explaining and implementing the agreement. This process should begin with meetings or training sessions, not only to point out significant features, but also to provide a clause-by-clause analysis of the contract. First-line supervisors and union stewards, in particular, need to know their responsibilities and what to do when disagreements arise. The human resource manager plays a key role in this day-to-day administration. He or she gives advice on matters of discipline, works to resolve grievances, and helps first-line supervisors establish good working relationships within the terms of the agreement. As mentioned previously, when a firm is organized, the HRM function tends to change—so much so that the human resource department may even be divided into two separate departments or units, one dealing with human resources and the other with industrial relations.

GRIEVANCE RESOLUTION

When management and labour ratify a contract, both sides undertake to abide by their agreement. In the workplace, however, there may be times when employees feel their rights have been violated, or the terms of the contract have not been followed. These perceptions may result from an individual supervisor's decision or action, or from the way a clause in the contract has been interpreted by management. The vehicle used to address these concerns is called a **grievance**, defined as ". . . a formal dispute between an employee (or the union) and management involving the interpretation, application, or an alleged violation of the collective agreement."[22] Most collective agreements limit grievances to matters covered in the contract.

A clearly defined grievance procedure benefits both employees and management. Individual employees can have their concerns dealt with in an orderly fashion. Supervisors can no longer ignore valid complaints or fire people as troublemakers. Similarly, from the employer's viewpoint, grievances act "as a communications device, letting the employer know fairly quickly just what matters . . . are sources of discontent."[23]

Union stewards will likely hear complaints about working conditions. But not every employee complaint is grounds for a grievance; a grievance can be filed only if there is a perceived violation of the contract. The complaint is then put in writing and processed through a series of steps. First, an attempt is made to solve the problem by contacting the employee's supervisor. Although most grievances are settled at this point, one of the problems with daily labour relations in Canada is that too few grievances are resolved at the lower levels. If there is no agreement, the dispute moves to the next level, usually to a manager, but sometimes to a grievance committee. Where a settlement cannot be reached, a **rights arbitration** process, similar to contract arbitration, is used.[24] Many collective agreements outline the process for choosing arbitrators and the manner in which arbitrators will handle grievances. As with contract (interest) arbitration, the decision of a grievance (rights) arbitrator is final and binding on both sides. There is, however, a limited right of appeal to the courts, if the decision allegedly violates the law.

Because of the high costs and the amount of time involved in pursuing a grievance through to arbitration, both unions and employers are motivated to solve their disagreements before this stage. Thus, it has been estimated that no more than two percent of grievances go before an arbitrator.[25] The important points to remember are that 1) the parties are required by law to have a dispute resolution mechanism for grievances in place during the life of the contract; 2) there is a different legal framework in unionized worksites, as union members have no access to the courts; and 3) the grievance-to-arbitration process, despite its drawbacks, generally is faster, cheaper, and more sensitive to individual employee concerns than the courts.

HRM IN ACTION

"I think I might have messed up this morning," said the maintenance supervisor, George LaChaine, to Doug Williams, the industrial relations manager. "One of the technicians in my section wasn't doing the job exactly according to specs, so I blew up and fired him. Five minutes later the union steward was in the office. She said something like situations such as this are covered in our contract and that I was violating it. I had never spoken to the technician before about that particular offence, and the steward said the contract called for both oral and written warnings before termination."

How would you respond?

THE FUTURE OF COLLECTIVE BARGAINING

The collective bargaining process and the labour movement have both changed in recent years. They no doubt will change further in the years ahead in response to forces of varying magnitude and conflicting perspectives. It appears, too, that many unions see a real need for change. Reg Basken, executive vice president of communications for the Energy and Paperworkers Union of Canada, for example, says:

> We have the best educated workforce the world has ever seen, the best trained workforce the world has ever seen, the best technology the world has ever seen and the best qualified management the world has ever seen. Yet we concentrate on these things that divide us instead of creating that dialogue necessary to create a better, more productive society."

He goes on to state:

> "Slowly but surely, in union and non-union workplaces across the country, the old management model is giving way to a new one that is participative, customer based and quality driven."[26]

Industrial and Occupational Change

Of the many environmental conditions that shape an organization's labour management relations, none are more dominant than the market for the firm's goods or services and its own labour market. Since the 1980s, the trend has been toward increased competition within product markets. This trend has a strong international dimension, reflecting the growing interdependence of world markets and will, in all likelihood, continue into the next century. Competition fosters innovation, opens up new market opportunities, and creates new jobs. However, firms in mature markets, with fewer prospects for growth and expansion, cannot offer a wide variety of job opportunities. In such situations, employers and employees alike need to concern themselves with career transitions, job losses, and organizational restructuring.

Historically, unions have had their greatest success in the manufacturing, mining, transportation, and construction industries. With the relative decline in importance of these industries and the relative growth in importance of service industries, private sector union membership has decreased. Major increases in employment have taken place in wholesale and retail trades; finance and insurance; general service industries; and federal, provincial, and municipal government. However, with the exception of government, these industries have had low union membership in the past.

The pattern of employment by occupation has also changed markedly over time. Major changes in white-collar occupations include increases in the number of professional and clerical employees. In blue-collar occupations, the proportion of operative employees increased through 1950; then a long-term decline in the use of labourers and an increase in service occupations began.

Intensified competitive pressures, as well as industrial and occupational change, tend to fragment collective bargaining, for union locals demand that their national organization exempt them from "pattern" bargaining rather than drive their particular employer out of business. In the last decade or so, national sectoral pattern bargaining collapsed in industries such as coal, steel, meat packing, and automobile manufacturing. As collective bargaining decentralizes from the sectoral to the firm level, it becomes more difficult for national unions to prevent members from identifying with their employers and competing with their fellow members, rather than identifying with other union members in their industry. The incentives are thus in place for a reemergence of company unionism not seen on any scale since the 1930s. Not only may labour need to rethink organizing strategies, but management also needs to sharpen managerial skills in negotiating and team building.

Multinational Corporations and Foreign Competition

Thousands of North American companies, from global giants like Eastman Kodak to smaller firms like Conners Brothers, a producer of sardines and other fish products from the Maritimes,[27] are pouring into Mexico, both to take advantage of low-cost labour[28] and to exploit this huge potential market.[29] Figure 15-5 shows the vast difference in wage levels on the North American continent. This discrepancy may greatly alter the nature of collective bargaining in Canada.

Unions in Canada, then, are at a critical juncture. Declining private sector union industry and intensifying competitive pressures have reduced their

FIGURE 15-5
North American Compensation Rates[30]

Country	Total Compensation
Canada	US $17.30
United States	US $18.80
Mexico	US $2.16

economic power. Simultaneously, the same changes have increased the power of multinational corporations (MNCs) able to take advantage of the potential for international capital mobility. As the bargaining power of unions diminishes vis-à-vis MNCs, it becomes more difficult to organize new union members by traditional methods, setting in motion a cycle of declining union density and union power. If predictions are accurate, the NAFTA will reinforce this cycle, as Canadian companies that want to be competitive must have roughly the same labour costs as their competitors. If low-skill job costs are higher in Canada, then these costs must be reduced by making Canadian labour more efficient, through improvements in technology, by replacing jobs with technology, or by outsourcing low-skill jobs to low-wage countries.[31] Inevitably, these strategies reduce the ability of unions to promote their cause, as traditional employment practices are replaced by new forms of work organization that require "a fundamental rethinking of long established and cherished [union] policies and practices."[32] Whether unions can cope with this reality is now being debated.[33]

SUMMARY

Collective bargaining is fundamental to management–labour relations in Canada. Unlike their counterparts in the United States, managers have not been in a position to dictate terms to unions. Although recent negotiations have been hard fought, this country has not seen many demands for salary rollbacks or two-tier wage systems.

Labour and management go through periods in which one has the power to dictate the majority of terms to the other party. During the foreseeable future, management is expected to maintain a slight power advantage in collective bargaining.

The structure of collective bargaining can affect how it is conducted. The four major types of structure are 1) one company dealing with a single union; 2) several companies dealing with a single union; 3) several unions dealing with a single company; and 4) several companies dealing with several unions. Another influential environmental factor is the current union–management relationship, which may allow the collective bargaining process to be relatively simple, or may result in long, bitter struggles.

When management signs a collective agreement with a union, the role of human resource management changes significantly. In major corporations where most of the operative employees belong to unions, the HRM function may be divided into separate human resource and industrial relations departments or units. The human resource manager must maintain contact before, during, and after collective bargaining with first-line managers, who administer the contract and know whether or not it is working.

The collective agreement, or contract, regulates the relationship between the employer and the employees for a specified period. Each agreement is unique; there is no standard or universal model. Despite many dissimilarities, however, certain topics are included in virtually all labour agreements: recognition, management rights, union security, compensation and benefits, grievance procedure, employee security, length of contract, and job-related factors.

At times negotiations break down, even though both labour and management may sincerely want to arrive at a contract settlement. There are several means of reviving stalled negotiations, including conciliation and mediation.

Strikes and boycotts are the primary means the union may use to overcome a breakdown in negotiations. When union members refuse to work in order to exert pressure on management in negotiations, their action is called a strike. Strikes place a burden on union members as well as employers, so they are used only as a last resort. A boycott involves an agreement by union members to refuse to use or to buy the firm's products.

Those individuals who do not have the right to strike are entitled to have outstanding bargaining issues resolved through interest arbitration.

Management may also use various strategies to encourage unions to resume negotiations. During a lockout, for example, employees are refused entry to the workplace. Managers may run the operation using management personnel and/or temporary replacements (where this practice is legal).

The future of collective bargaining in Canada is murky. On the one hand, industry-wide bargaining no longer exists in several important industries; on the other, we may see the rise of smaller, more responsive company unions. Unions in Canada, then, are at a crossroads. As capital becomes more mobile, their bargaining power diminishes, yet the more progressive unions are learning to cope with new work organizations by adopting a more cooperative approach to contract negotiations and administration.

TERMS FOR REVIEW

Collusion
Industrywide bargaining
Multiemployer bargaining
Fallback positions
Negotiating committee
Beachhead demands
Positional bargaining
Conciliation
No-board report

Mediation
Arbitration
Interest arbitration
Strike
Boycott
Lockout
Ratification
Grievance
Rights arbitration

QUESTIONS FOR REVIEW

1. Describe the basic steps involved in the collective bargaining process.
2. Why do negotiations sometimes resemble a high-stakes poker game?
3. By what primary means may breakdowns in negotiations be overcome? Briefly describe each.
4. What is the human resource manager's role in the collective bargaining process?
5. What is involved in the administration of a labour agreement?
6. What appears to be the future of collective bargaining?
7. Describe the different roles in a typical five-member union bargaining team.
8. Outline the committee structure a union might set up in the event of a strike.
9. Why is a strike an activity of last resort?
10. Why are 98 percent of grievances settled before the arbitration stage?
11. How is public sector bargaining different from private sector bargaining?

HRM INCIDENT 1

• WORK RULES

Jerry Sharplin eagerly drove his new company pickup onto the construction site. He had just been assigned by his employer, Lurgi-Knost Construction Company, to supervise a crew of 16 equipment operators, oilers, and mechanics. This was the first unionized crew Jerry had supervised, and he was unaware of the labour agreement in effect that carefully defined and limited the role of supervisors. As he approached his work area, he noticed one of the cherry pickers (a type of mobile crane with an extendable boom) standing idle with the operator beside it. Jerry pulled up beside the operator and asked, "What's going on here?"

"Out of gas," the operator said.

"Well, go and get some," Jerry said.

The operator reached to get his thermos jug out of the toolbox on the side of the crane and said, "The oiler's on break right now. He'll be back in a few minutes."

Jerry remembered that he had a five-gallon can of gasoline in the back of his pickup. So he quickly got the gasoline, climbed on the cherry picker, and started to pour it into the gas tank. As he did so, he heard the other machines shutting down in unison. He looked around and saw all the other operators climbing down from their equipment and standing to watch him pour the gasoline. A moment later, he saw the union steward approaching.

QUESTIONS

1. Why did all the operators shut down their machines?
2. Suppose that free trade has progressed to the point where any construction company in the world can bid on any construction job. In order to remain competitive, what changes would you want to negotiate in your next contract?
3. How would you persuade the union to cooperate?

HRM INCIDENT 2

• STRATEGY

"They want what?" the mayor exclaimed. "Like I said," the town clerk replied, "17 percent over two years."

"There is no way that the taxpayers will accept a settlement anywhere near that," reiterated the mayor. "I don't care if the garbage doesn't get collected for a century. We can't go more than eight percent over the next two years."

The town clerk looked worried. "How much loss of service do you think the public will accept? Suppose they do go on strike? I'm the one who always gets the complaints. Then there's the health problem with rats running all over the place! Remember over in Neibringtown, when that little kid was bitten? There was a hell of an outcry."

The mayor agreed: "Garbage collectors always have strong bargaining power, but, if I don't fight this, I'll be voted out in the next election. I say we offer six percent over 18 months. Then we can go either way—six percent over 12 months or eight percent over two years."

"I wonder if we have any other options?" worried the town clerk.

"Well, we could threaten not to hire any more union personnel and to job out the collection service to private contractors if the union wasn't cooperative," mused the mayor.

"That's a good idea!" The town clerk sounded enthusiastic. "Also, we can mount a newspaper advertising campaign to get the public behind us. If we play on the fear of massive tax increases, the garbage collectors won't have much public sympathy."

"What about asking the union to guarantee garbage collection for old people during a strike? If they refuse, they'll look bad in the public eye; if they accept, we are rid of a major problem.

Most people can bring their trash to a central collection point. Not all old people can," chuckled the mayor. "We can't lose on that issue!"

"Okay, then," said the town clerk. "It looks like we have the beginning of a bargaining strategy here. Actually, I feel better now. I think we're in a rather strong position."

QUESTIONS

1. Discuss the plight of public sector unions faced with the reality of a limited tax base and public pressure to lower taxes.
2. Is the town clerk right? Is the town in a good bargaining position? Explain your answer.
3. What strengths does the union have in its position?
4. If you were a labour relations consultant, would you agree with the present strategy? What alternatives, if any, would you propose?

DEVELOPING HRM SKILLS: AN EXPERIENTIAL EXERCISE

A major part of the human resource manager's job is to advise all levels of management on human resource matters. The human resource manager's knowledge and experience are often required in dealing with union matters, especially in handling situations that may affect future negotiations. This exercise provides additional insight into the importance of handling employee problems properly.

The human resource manager, Gregory Menchew, works very closely with all the managers and employees in an attempt to settle problems before they become critical. Today, one of the union stewards, Eugene Shum, called for an appointment and said he had a complaint. The manager agreed to talk to Eugene, but prior to that conversation he wants to talk to the supervisor, Larry Bradley. That way Gregory can get both sides of the story. Gregory really hopes this is not a major problem, since the company and the union will begin negotiations soon for a new contract.

Larry Bradley has been with the company for 12 years, the last four as a supervisor. He is a very safety-conscious supervisor with a reputation for strictly enforcing the rules. In Larry's opinion this safety-consciousness is the reason there has not been a single lost-time accident in the division since he became the supervisor. There is a rule in the plant, well known to everyone, that every intersection is a four-way stop for forklift trucks. According to the labour-management agreement, even minor safety violations justify a three-day suspension and a written warning. Larry saw a forklift truck, with Charlie Fox at the wheel, come around a corner at a high speed and not stop at an intersection. Virtually no one except Charlie and Larry were at the plant, but Larry suspended Charlie for three days and placed a written warning in his personnel folder.

Eugene Shum was elected union steward last year. There have been few grievances since the election, and therefore Eugene has done little as union steward. A couple of workers have brought complaints, but management was found correct in each case and workers were told so. Eugene likes being the union steward and believes that it might be tough to be reelected unless he can make a "show". In Eugene's opinion, Charlie Fox was improperly suspended for three days. Eugene has found his reelection platform.

Three individuals will participate in this exercise: one to serve as the human resource manager, one to serve as the supervisor, and another to play the role of union steward. The instructor will provide the participants with additional information necessary to complete the exercise.

CHAPTER 16 Internal Employee Relations

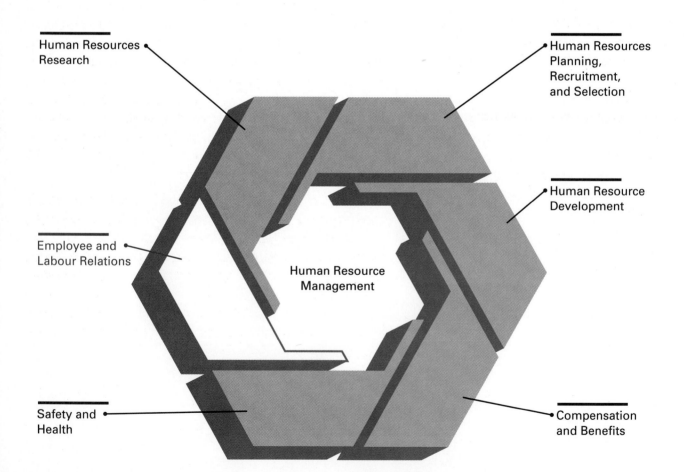

Human Resources Research

Human Resources Planning, Recruitment, and Selection

Employee and Labour Relations

Human Resource Development

Human Resource Management

Safety and Health

Compensation and Benefits

1. Define discipline and disciplinary action.
2. Identify and describe the steps involved in the disciplinary process; discuss various approaches to discipline; and explain the administration of discipline.
3. Explain how grievances are handled under a collective bargaining agreement and in nonunion firms.
4. State the conditions under which employees can be terminated.
5. Explain demotion as an alternative to termination and describe the role of internal employee relations concerning layoffs, transfers, promotions, resignations, and retirements.
6. Discuss how multinational corporations cope with internal employee relations.

*G*ary Halmes, the production supervisor for Manitoba Manufacturing, was mad at the world when he arrived at work. The automobile mechanic had not repaired his car on time the day before, so he had been forced to take a taxi to work this morning. No one was safe around Gary today, and it was not the time for Phillip Meiros, a member of Local 264, to report for work late. Without hesitation, Gary said, "You know our company can't tolerate this type of behaviour. I don't want to see you around here anymore. You're fired." Just as quickly, Phillip replied, "You're way off base. Our contract calls for three warnings for tardiness. My steward will hear about this."

Matthew Morton, a 10-year employee at Ketro Productions, arrived at the human resource manager's office to turn in his letter of resignation. Matt was very upset with his supervisor. When the human resource manager, Kersti Yamada, asked what was wrong, Matt replied, "Yesterday, I made a mistake and set my machine up wrong. It was the first time in years that I'd done that. My boss chewed me out in front of my friends. I wouldn't take that from the president, much less a two-bit supervisor!"

These scenarios represent only two of the many situations that human resource managers confront when dealing with internal employee relations. Gary Halmes has just been reminded that his power to fire a worker has limits. Matthew Morton's resignation might have been avoided if his supervisor had not shown poor judgement and disciplined him in front of his friends.

In this chapter, we first define internal employee relations. Next, we discuss the reasons for disciplinary action, the discipline process, approaches to discipline, and administration of discipline. Then, we describe grievance handling under a collective bargaining agreement and for nonunion employees. Next, we review termination and demotion as an alternative to termination, along with layoffs, transfers, promotion, resignation, and retirement. We devote the last portion of the chapter to internal employee relations in multinational corporations.

INTERNAL EMPLOYEE RELATIONS DEFINED

Most employees do not remain in the same job within an organization for their entire career. They move upward, laterally, downward, and out in response to both internal and external opportunities. In order to ensure that individuals with the proper skills and experience are available at all levels, therefore, concerted efforts are required to maintain good internal employee relations. **Internal employee relations** consists of those human resource management activities associated with the movement of employees within the organization, including promotion, transfer, demotion, resignation, discharge, layoff, and retirement. Discipline and disciplinary action are also crucial aspects of internal employee relations.

DISCIPLINARY ACTION

Discipline is concerned with maintaining appropriate conduct. Traditional disciplinary action invokes a penalty against an employee who fails to meet established standards. Effective disciplinary action addresses the employee's wrongful behaviour, not the employee as a person. Incorrectly administered disciplinary action is destructive to both the employee and the organization. The **discipline without punishment** approach places the responsibility for meeting behavioural standards on the employee.

A necessary but often trying aspect of internal employee relations is the application of discipline. Disciplinary action is not usually management's initial response to a problem; when possible, it is best to use positive ways of convincing employees to adhere to company policies. Managers must, however, administer some sort of disciplinary action when company rules are violated. When a rule is violated, the effectiveness of the organization is diminished to some degree, depending on the severity of the infraction. For example, if someone is late for work once, the effect on the firm may be minimal. Consistent lateness, however, tends to diminish both worker productivity and the morale of other employees. Thus, discipline policies that help management meet organizational goals benefit both employees and the corporation. Moreover, when applied responsibly and equitably, disciplinary action can actually benefit the individual employee in the long run, by stimulating improved performance. For example, if a worker disciplined for failing to monitor quality is careful thereafter to meet quality requirements, the worker has become more employable and perhaps more promotable; discipline has thus served as a useful developmental tool.

Unjustified disciplinary action, on the other hand, is not only unfair but counterproductive. Harsh or unjust discipline has contributed to the formation of unions in many firms, as employees band together to protect themselves. Improperly administered disciplinary action has also led to wildcat strikes, walkouts, and slow-downs in unionized firms. Even if employees don't react overtly to unjustified disciplinary actions, morale will likely decline, along with productivity. Because discipline involves interaction between human beings, it is inevitable that biased and emotional judgements will occur. It is important, therefore, to have an appeal process available to employees.

THE DISCIPLINE PROCESS

Discipline is dynamic and ongoing. Because one person's actions can affect the work group, the proper application of discipline fosters acceptable behaviour by other group members. Conversely, unjustified or improperly administered discipline can have a detrimental effect on everyone. The disciplinary action process is shown in Figure 16-1. As with all aspects of human resource management, disciplinary policies and actions are affected by the external environment. Changes in technology, for example may render a rule inappropriate or may necessitate new rules. Laws and government regulations that affect company policies and rules are also changing constantly. The various Occupational Safety and Health Acts, for example, have encouraged many firms to establish stricter safety standards. Unions are another external factor. Specific punishments for rule violations are subject to collective bargaining; for example, the union may negotiate for three written warnings for tardiness before someone is suspended.

Changes in the firm's internal environment can also alter the disciplinary process. Through organizational development, the firm may alter its culture, thus changing how first-line supervisors handle discipline. A management stance of treating employees as mature human beings would affect the process significantly (see the later section on discipline without punishment). The disciplinary action process deals largely with infractions of rules. Rules are specific guides to behaviour on the job. Rules may relate to general conduct in the workplace, to interactions with peers and supervisors, to specific requirements of job tasks, and to safe behaviour. Safety rules are usually inflexible; for example, hard hats must be worn in hazardous areas.

Once management has established rules, they must communicate them to employees. People cannot obey rules they are unaware of. When an employee violates a rule, corrective action may be necessary. The purpose of this action is to not to chastise the violator but to alter behaviour detrimental to organizational objectives. Note how the process shown in Figure 16-1 includes feedback from the point of taking appropriate disciplinary action to communicating rules to employees. Discipline is useless unless employees clearly realize exactly what behaviours were unacceptable and understand what is expected from them in the future.

FIGURE 16-1
The Disciplinary Action Process

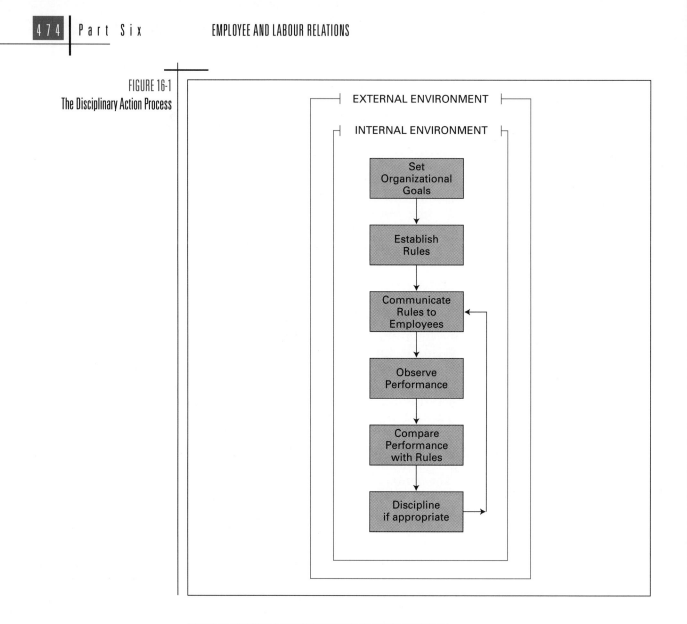

APPROACHES TO DISCIPLINARY ACTION

Several disciplinary frameworks have been developed. We discuss two: progressive disciplinary action and discipline without punishment.

Progressive Disciplinary Action

Progressive disciplinary action is intended to ensure that the minimum penalty appropriate to the offence is imposed, as determined by a series of questions about the severity of the offence. As illustrated in Figure 16-2, the manager must ask these questions—in sequence—to determine the proper disciplinary action. To begin with, the manager must determine whether the improper behaviour is severe enough to warrant disciplinary action. Having answered *yes*, the manager next considers whether the violation warrants more than a verbal warning.[1] For a first minor infraction, probably a verbal

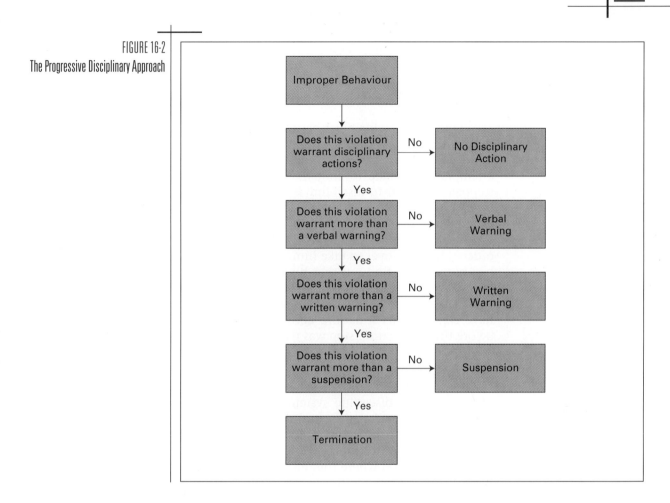

warning will suffice; in fact, several verbal warnings might be given for re-peat minor offences before the manager decided that the violation warranted more than a verbal warning. The manager follows the same procedure for each level of the progressive disciplinary process, not considering termina-tion until each lower-level question has been answered *yes*. A more severe vi-olation might warrant a higher-level response; for example, assaulting a supervisor or another worker might justify immediate termination.

To assist managers in recognizing the proper level of disciplinary ac-tion, some firms have formalized the procedures with specific progressive disciplinary action guidelines. As an example, a worker who is absent with-out authorization will receive a verbal warning the first time it happens, a written warning the second time, and a termination notice the third time, but fighting on the job results in immediate termination. Guidelines should be adapted to the needs of the organization. For example, smoking in an unauthorized area may be a minor offence in a concrete plant but grounds for immediate dismissal in an explosives factory.

This step-by-step disciplinary method is often called *just cause* discipline. Even at the verbal warning stage, each infraction must be documented and placed in the employee's personnel file. Maintaining proper documentation is extremely important; otherwise, there is no legal basis for terminating an employee. Verbal warnings are generally recorded in memo format and are not signed by the employee. The employee must be shown the paperwork for any more serious offences and asked to sign. Of course, he or she has the right to refuse; therefore, a witness should always be present during the disciplinary interview.

One other factor must be taken into account when using the progressive or just cause system. During the last few years, legal decisions in wrongful dismissal cases have tended to favour the employee, unless serious attempts were made to counsel the individual. The strict application of a stepped approach to discipline is not sufficient; the employer must attempt to find out *why* the employee is behaving improperly. In one real-life situation, for example, a foreman at a factory in Timmins, Ontario was fired for absenteeism. He sued for wrongful dismissal. On hearing the case, the judge ordered his employer to take him back. It seems that no one in the company had bothered to find out that his wife had left him, taking his two children to Quebec. The foreman had been absent because he wanted to be with his children. Counselling as part of a step-by-step disciplinary process would have exposed this situation, allowing management to work out a solution before the termination step was reached.

Discipline without Punishment

The progressive discipline system is based on the concept of punishment: management punishes the employee as a means of changing behaviour. The problem is that punishment is by definition unpleasant, and human beings tend to react to punishment with shame, anger, or even hostility. Canadians are entering an era where the full cooperation of everyone in the work group is necessary if firms are to be competitive. It is extremely difficult to create an atmosphere of full cooperation when one group (managers) is deliberately treating another group (employees) negatively. We argue, therefore, that "progressive" or "just cause" discipline is regressive. And even though variations on the approach are still used by the vast majority of firms in North America, both large and small, we argue that it is obsolete.

If one accepts the philosophy that an employee cannot be expected to behave better when the employer treats him or her progressively worse, then we must look for a different system, perhaps a discipline without punishment system. Here, we assume that troubled employees are adults with a problem, not children who must be corrected. The system revolves around a series of documented steps:

1. *First Step:* an interview (not a warning) during which the problem is discussed and the employee is counselled. There are no threats or warnings, but a commitment to behave as requested is sought.

2. *Second Step*: if the unwarranted behaviour is repeated, the supervisor counsels the employee again; this time a memo summarizing the conversation and the employee's commitment to changed behaviour is placed in the employee's personnel file. (At this stage, the counselling may or may not require a witness.)

3. *Third Step*: on the third repetition, the employee is asked to take three or four days' leave, with pay.[2] This is not a holiday; the individual will be given a series of questions to answer on return to work. Depending on the situation, the questions can be quite pointed: for example, "Do you realize that the next infraction will mean immediate dismissal?" or, "Will you confirm that you will follow company rules on [the issue in question] in the future?" On return from leave, the employee is counselled again, this time almost certainly in the presence of an employer and an employee representative. The employee's decision to change behaviour is documented and placed on file. The employee and/or the witnesses sign the document.

4. *Fourth Step*: if there is yet another rule infringement, there is no alternative but to terminate the employee, but this drastic action will be based on decisions made by the employee.

This entire procedure has been based on the premise that management does not *control* behaviour. It is the employee's responsibility to behave according to established work rules and procedures. A discipline without punishment system takes the intense emotionalism away from management/employee interaction. The concept also places responsibility for behaviour on the employee, conveying the message, "in this firm we hire adults; we expect them to behave as adults."

ADMINISTRATION OF DISCIPLINE

As might be expected, discipline (no matter what system is used) is not a pleasant supervisory task. As a result, many managers avoid taking action, for a number of reasons:

1. *Lack of training*: The supervisor may not have the knowledge and skill necessary to handle disciplinary problems.

2. *Fear*: The supervisor may be concerned that top management will not support a disciplinary action.

3. *The only one*: The supervisor may think "No one else is disciplining employees, so why should I?"

4. *Guilt*: The supervisor may think: "How can I discipline someone if I've done the same thing?"

5. *Loss of friendship*: The supervisor may believe that disciplinary action will damage friendship with an employee or the employee's associates.

6. *Time loss*: The supervisor may begrudge the time that is required to administer and explain discipline.

7. *Loss of temper*: The supervisor may be afraid of losing his or her temper when talking to an employee about a rule violation.

8. *Rationalization*: The supervisor may think, "The employee knows it was a wrong thing to do, so why do we need to talk about it?"[3]

These reasons apply to all forms of discipline, from a verbal warning or counselling to termination. In particular, supervisors often avoid firing an employee even when it would be in the company's best interest to do so. The reluctance to terminate can stem from breakdowns in other areas of the human resource management function. For example, if a supervisor had given high ratings to an employee on several annual performance appraisals, the firm would have difficulty justifying a decision to dismiss the employee on grounds of incompetence.

The time and place for disciplinary actions must be chosen carefully. For example, disciplining a worker in the presence of others may embarrass the individual and defeat the purpose of the action. As demonstrated in the scenario at the beginning of the chapter, even when they are wrong, employees resent disciplinary action administered in public.

Many supervisors may be too lenient early in the disciplinary action process and too strict later. This lack of consistency doesn't give the employee a clear understanding of the penalty associated with the inappropriate action. As one senior labour relations manager has stated, "A supervisor will often endure an unacceptable situation for an extended period of time. Then, when the supervisor finally does take action, he or she is apt to overreact and come down excessively hard." Consistency, however, does not necessarily mean that the same penalty must be applied to two different workers for the same offence. A consistent approach also takes into account factors such as past record and length of service. For example, a long-term employee might be suspended for a serious offence, while a worker with only a few months' service might be terminated for the same act. For example, what should be done in the following scenario?

> Jack and Harry got into a fight. Nobody was there when it started. Each accuses the other. Jack has been with the firm for 18 years, with an excellent work record. He has never been disciplined before. Harry has been with the firm for 18 months. His work record is below average, and he has been disciplined several times for various rule infractions. The firm has a rule against fighting.

Does Jack deserve to be punished as severely as Harry?

HRM IN ACTION

As Mike Bowen, a first-line supervisor for Kwik Corporation, entered the office of Sarah Findley, human resource director, he was obviously disturbed and wanted help. Mike started the conversation by saying, "Kevin Smith, one of my employees, violated company policy today by failing to wear his safety glasses on a very dangerous job. The company policy states that any employee who does not follow the safety guidelines will receive a written reprimand on the first offence and will be terminated on the second violation. Kevin has already received one reprimand and has just committed his second violation. However, he has been one of my best workers over five years, and letting him go could have a really negative impact on productivity."

What advice should Sarah provide?

To assist management in administering discipline properly, a *Code on Discipline Procedure* has been prepared (Figure 16-3). The code stresses communicating rules, telling the employee of the complaint, conducting a full investigation, and giving the employee an opportunity to tell his or her side of the story. These actions are recommended as common sense, no matter what disciplinary system is in place.

GRIEVANCE HANDLING UNDER A COLLECTIVE BARGAINING AGREEMENT

If employees are represented by a union, workers who believe that they have been disciplined or dealt with unjustly can appeal through the grievance and arbitration procedures in the collective bargaining agreement. The grievance procedure has been described as one of the great accomplishments of the industrial relations movement. Even though the process has defects, arbitration constitutes a social invention of great importance.[4] The grievance system encourages and facilitates the settlement of disputes between labour and management. A grievance procedure permits employees to express complaints without jeopardizing their jobs, and helps management seek the underlying causes and solutions to grievances.

Just Cause

Should the grievance concern discipline or discharge, the concept of showing *just cause* for these actions must be thoroughly understood, as to proceed to arbitration without a well-documented and convincing case can be both expensive and embarrassing. Indeed, the preamble to one arbitrator's decision

FIGURE 16-3
Recommended Disciplinary Procedures

- All employees should be given a copy of the employer's rules on disciplinary procedures. The procedures should specify which employees they cover and what disciplinary actions may be taken, and should allow matters to be dealt with quickly.

- Employees should be told of complaints against them and given an opportunity to state their case. They should have the right to be accompanied by a union representative or fellow employee of their choice.

- Disciplinary action should not be taken until the case has been fully investigated. Immediate superiors should not have the power to dismiss without reference to senior management, and, except for gross misconduct, no employee should be dismissed for a first breach of discipline.

- Employees should be given an explanation for any penalty imposed, and they should have a right of appeal, with specified procedures to be followed.

- When disciplinary action other than summary dismissal is needed, supervisors should give a formal/verbal warning in the case of minor offenses, or a written warning in more serious cases.

Source: "Code on Discipline Procedure," *Industrial Management*, 7 (August 1977), p. 7. Used with permission.

stated: "This grievance arose out of a rather distressing and classic example of labour relations incompetence by . . . management . . . . There is no excuse for such ignorance." This exposition is intended to provide a background understanding for anyone who might become involved in the grievance process. This discussion is written in the context of discipline within a collective bargaining milieu. The definitions, explanations, and arguments apply only to rights arbitration: "the final and binding decision of an arbitrator or arbitrators in disputes involving the infringement of employee/employer rights."

The concept of just cause bridges the gap between common law and modern society. Prior to the advent of collective bargaining, the sole limitations on an employer's rights to terminate a worker were found in the definition of just cause articulated by the courts. There were no other remedies for dealing with employees. Should an employee commit some minor offence, therefore, at common law the employer could either fire the employee and trust that he could rehire him or her or give a verbal warning and hope this corrected the situation. It is obvious this old common-law approach to the employment relationship is not compatible with the philosophical underpinnings of present-day society. Thus, current legislation lays down only the skeleton procedure, leaving labour and management free to adapt the process to meet specific needs. The result has been a number of variations from the standard model of arbitration as evidenced by the rail, longshoring, trucking, mining, and garment industries. This laissez-faire approach appears to have been effective, as during the last three decades, a body of precedent has been created by arbitrators that is more substantial and sophisticated than the courts were able to produce in centuries. Although these precedents have sometimes been regarded as trite and useless, many have taken into account the changing nature of contemporary society.

Just cause can be interpreted as a reasonable response to an employee's conduct. This (perhaps necessarily) vague statement illustrates the difficulty of defining a concept that, with endless variations, has been used in resolving thousands of arbitration cases. Although the term is impossible to quantify, just cause means well-grounded, fair, equitable, and proper. In other words, management must establish the existence of grounds upon which an employee has been disciplined. As what constitutes "just cause" can vary with individual contracts, however, applying the concept is an exercise in setting standards. Thus, arbitrators determine the scope of just cause case by case, on the basis of precedent, the collective agreement, any relevant statues, and their own sense of fairness. The primary source of legal authority is the common law of employment as it was interpreted by the courts prior to the existence of statutory collective bargaining. This authority is modified by individual labour contracts or collective agreements. (Even if a particular collective agreement does not specifically address the issue, there are a number of cases that suggest that the concept of "just cause" is implicit in a collective agreement.) These authorities are buttressed further by the provincial labour relations acts, which normally indicate that arbitrators have the authority not only to support or change a management decision concerning dismissal or disciplinary action against an employee for just cause, but also to substitute an alternative penalty. The arbitrator's jurisdiction includes

- warnings and suspensions
- deprivation of seniority rights
- fines
- loss of fringe benefits
- demotion
- timeliness.

Sometimes questions arise as to whether or not an action can be regarded as discipline. In this case, the arbitrator has the power to review management's decision, but will intervene only when it is clear that the employer has acted in an arbitrary and unreasonable manner. Issues such as whether or not the grievor was covered by the collective agreement and whether or not the grievance falls outside the collective agreement are usually (but not always) resolved before the arbitrator hears the case.

Provincial labour relations acts give arbitrators the right to uphold, repeal, or modify penalties imposed by management. Arbitrators are limited to the redress of a wrong committed against an employee. Their powers are remedial, not punitive. They do not assess punitive damages. The labour contract itself can also place limitations on an arbitrator's action, as collective agreements can specifically set out the penalty to be meted out for a given infraction. In addition, an arbitrator is obligated to take statutes into account, even if it means having to treat the language of the collective agreement as invalid.

As early as 1951, a trend developed placing the onus on the employer to prove just cause when discharging an employee. Now, it is generally accepted that employers bear the ultimate responsibility for establishing proof in both discharge and discipline cases. The standard of that proof, however, seems to depend upon the nature of the offence. In cases where disciplinary measures are enacted for a misdemeanour that might be judged as criminal in nature—theft, for example—some arbitrators demand a higher standard of proof. Indeed, in a theft case the (then) Chief Justice of Canada said that it was necessary to present the same convincing evidence that would be required in a criminal prosecution. Conversely, another arbitrator indicated that proof of a standard required in criminal court would be unfair to the employer. As neither of these two views are likely to disappear, arbitrators will likely seek some middle ground.

As arbitrators have immense latitude in determining just cause and as the onus to prove its existence rests with the employer, each grievance must be scrutinized with the utmost care. Never should emotion be allowed to impinge upon the grievance process, and never should a grievance be taken to arbitration unless the organization is *certain* that its actions fall within the scope of just cause.

The Grievance Procedure

All labour agreements include some form of grievance procedure. A **grievance** is a formal complaint outlining an employee's dissatisfaction or feeling of personal injustice relating to some aspect of his or her employment. A grievance under a collective bargaining agreement is normally restricted to violations of the terms and conditions of the agreement, but there are other conditions that may give rise to a grievance:

- a violation of law;
- a violation of the intent of the parties as stipulated during contract negotiations;
- a violation of company rules;
- a change in working conditions or past company practices;
- a violation of health and/or safety standards.[5]

Grievance procedures have many common features. Variations may reflect differences in organizational or decision-making structures, or the size of a work unit or company. General principles for effective grievance administration include the following:

- Grievances should be heard promptly.
- Procedures and forms used for airing grievances must be easy to use and well understood by employees and their supervisors.
- Direct and timely avenues of appeal from rulings of line supervision must exist.[6]

The multiple-step grievance procedure shown in Figure 16-4 is the most common type. In the informal complaint step, the employee usually presents the grievance orally and informally to the immediate supervisor. A union steward may be present. This step offers the greatest potential for improved labour relations and a large majority of grievances are settled here. If the issue remains unresolved, the first formal step begins when a written grievance is submitted to the supervisor by the union steward. The grievance is dated and signed by the employee and the union steward. It describes the events as perceived by the employee, cites the contract provision that allegedly was violated, and indicates what settlement is desired. At this point the supervisor must answer the complaint in writing, either accepting or rejecting the grievance.

If the issue is still unresolved, a meeting is held between the second-level manager (the supervisor's direct superior) or HR manager and higher union officials, perhaps a grievance committee or chief steward. Should the grievance not be settled at this meeting, it is appealed to the third formal step. Typically, this step involves the firm's top labour representative (such as the vice-president of industrial relations) and high-level union officials. At times, depending on the severity of the grievance, the president may represent the firm. A grievance that remains unresolved at the conclusion of the third formal step may go to arbitration, if provided for in the agreement and if the union decides to persevere.

Labour relations problems can escalate when the supervisor is not equipped to handle grievances at the informal complaint stage and first formal step. The first formal step is usually handled by the union steward, the

FIGURE 16-4
An Example of a
Multiple-Step Grievance Procedure

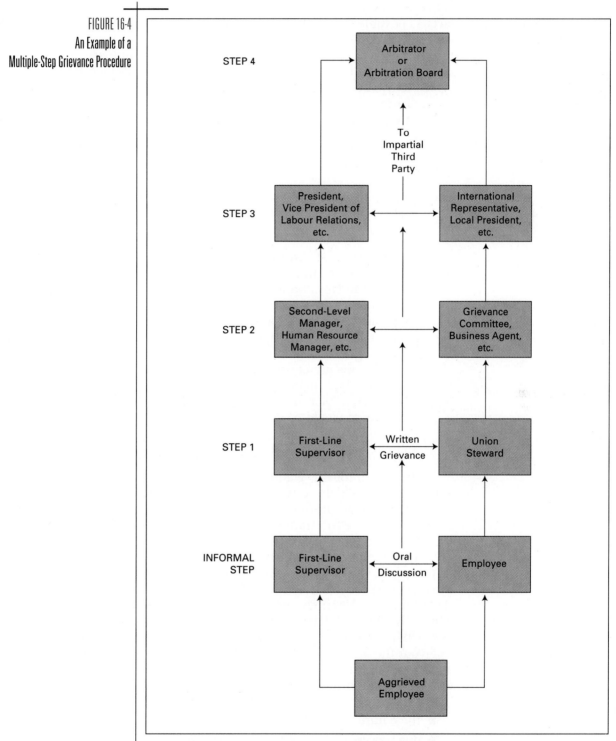

Source: Robert W. Eckles et al., *Essentials of Management for First-Line Supervision* (New York: John Wiley & Sons, 1974), p. 529. Reprinted by permission of John Wiley & Sons, Inc.

aggrieved party, and the supervisor. The supervisor should obtain as many facts as possible before the meeting, as it is likely the union steward will be well prepared. The supervisor needs to recognize that the formal grievance may not reflect the real problem. For example, the employee might be angry at the company for modifying its pay policies, even though the change was agreed to by the union. In order to voice discontent, the worker might file a grievance for an unrelated, minor violation of the contract. It is here that progressive union stewards are valuable to the organization, as they will dissuade a member from filing a nuisance grievance.

Arbitration

The final step in most grievance procedures is arbitration, a process whereby the dispute is submitted to an arbitrator, or a three-person arbitration board, for resolution.

> At one time, most cases in Canada were handled by tripartite arbitration boards. However, this is changing; for example, a 1987 study of grievance arbitration in Nova Scotia found that single arbitrators are now . . . [used twice as often as] arbitration boards. Also, arbitration of disputes in the federal public sector (which is actually referred to as adjudication in the governing statutes) is now handled exclusively by single arbitrators. Many provincial governments . . . have followed this same pattern. Additional evidence that the use of single arbitrators is favoured more than that of arbitration boards is found in the 1993 amendments to the Ontario Labour Relations Act. Prior to the amendments the presumption was that an arbitration board would be used unless the parties agreed to use a single arbitrator. The amendments reversed the presumption providing that only one arbitrator be used unless the parties chose to use a board.[7]

The reason for this gradual change is that three-person boards are more expensive and take up to two-and-a-half months longer to hand down a decision than a single arbitrator.[8] Regardless of the method chosen, most agreements restrict the arbitration decision to application and interpretation of the agreement and make the decision final and binding on the parties.

If the union decides in favour of arbitration, management is notified. At this point, the union and the company select an arbitrator or board. Most agreements specify the selection method; some even include a list of potential arbitrators. When choosing an arbitrator, both management and labour will study the candidates' previous decisions in an attempt to detect any biases. Obviously, neither party wants to select an arbitrator who might tend to favour the other's position.[9] Arbitrators must possess exceptional patience and judgement to render a fair and impartial decision because of the variety of factors to be considered:

- the nature of the offence;
- due process and procedural correctness;
- the grievor's past record;
- length of service with the company;

- knowledge of the rules;
- warnings;
- the consistency of rule enforcement;
- any discriminatory treatment.

After the arbitrator or board has been selected, a hearing is held. The issue to be resolved is presented to the arbitrator(s) in a document that summarizes the question(s) to be decided.

At the hearing, each side presents its case. Arbitration is an adversarial process. The arbitrator might conduct the hearing much like a courtroom proceeding. Witnesses, cross-examination, transcripts, and legal counsel may all be used. Other hearings may be conducted less formally. Instead of an official transcript, which may require the presence of a court stenographer, for example, the arbitrator's notes may be sufficient. The parties may also submit, or be asked to submit, formal written statements. After the hearing, the arbitrator or arbitrators study the material and testimony, reaching a decision as soon as possible, generally within 30 to 60 days. The decision is usually accompanied by a written opinion giving reasons for the decision.

Should either management or labour be unhappy with the decision, there is little chance for appeal. The courts will generally enforce an arbitrator's decision unless 1) the arbitrator's decision is shown to be unreasonable or capricious in that it did not address the issues; 2) the arbitrator exceeded his or her authority; or 3) the award or decision violated the law.

Not only is arbitration expensive, (over $25 000 for a three-day hearing),[10] but both sides lose control by agreeing to allow a third party to decide for them. Thus, arbitration is the solution of last resort.

Proof That Disciplinary Action Was Needed

In Canada, any disciplinary action that affects a unionized employee may ultimately be taken to arbitration, even if this remedy is not specified in the labour agreement. Employers have learned that they must prepare records that will constitute proof of disciplinary action and the just reasons for it. When using the "progressive" system, the written warning format may vary, but the following information should be included:

1. statement of facts concerning the offence;
2. identification of the rule that was violated;
3. statement of what resulted or could have resulted because of the violation;
4. identification of any previous similar violations by the same individual;
5. statement of possible future consequences should the violation occur again;
6. signature and date.

An example of a written warning is shown in Figure 16-5. It is important to document verbal reprimands because they may be the first step that leads ultimately to arbitration.

FIGURE 16-5
An Example of a Written Warning

DATE: August 1, 1995
TO: Shane Boudreaux
FROM: Wayne Sanders
SUBJECT: Written Warning

We are quite concerned because today you were 30 minutes late to work and offered no justification for this. According to our records, a similar offence occurred on July 25, 1995. At that time you were informed that failure to report to work on time is unacceptable. I am therefore notifying you in writing that you must report to work on time. You will be suspended from work without pay for three days if you are late again without explanation.

Please sign this form to indicate that you have read and understand this warning. Signing is not an indication of agreement.

_____
Name

_____
Date

Weaknesses of Arbitration

Arbitration has achieved a certain degree of success in resolving grievances. The process, however, is not without weaknesses. Some practitioners claim that arbitration is losing its effectiveness because of the length of time between the first step of the grievance procedure and final settlement. Often, 100-250 days may elapse before a decision is made.[11] By the time it is finally settled, the reason for the initial filing of the grievance may be forgotten. Others object to the cost of arbitration, which has been rising at an alarming rate. Because the cost of settling even a simple arbitration case is high, even when shared by labour and management, forcing every grievance to arbitration may be used as a tactic to place either management or the union in a difficult financial position. In a recent article in the CAUT Bulletin, for example, it is alleged that senior administrators at Mount Allison University in Sackville, New Brunswick, are using this tactic to bankrupt the small (98-member) university union. It is claimed that "virtually all disputes are pushed to arbitration ... [as] administrators can spend unlimited amounts of public money on unnecessary arbitrations, since it does not come out of their pockets!"[12]

GRIEVANCE HANDLING IN NONUNION ORGANIZATIONS

In the past, few firms without unions had formalized grievance procedures. The situation is changing, as more and more managers see the advantages of establishing formal grievance procedures and encourage employees to use them.[13] While the step-by step procedure for handling union grievances is common practice, the means of resolving complaints in nonunion firms vary. A well-designed grievance procedure ensures that the employee has ample opportunity to make complaints without fear of reprisal. If the system is to work, everyone must be well-informed about the program and convinced that management wants it to be used. Most employees hesitate to formalize their complaints and must be urged to avail themselves of the process.[14]

Typically, an employee initiates a complaint with his or her immediate supervisor. If the complaint involves the supervisor, however, the individual should be permitted to proceed directly to an employee relations specialist or to a manager at the next level. The grievance ultimately may be taken to the organization's top executive for a final decision. One large engineering, construction, and maintenance company, for example, has a unique dispute resolution program. Whenever workers feel they need to resolve a dispute, they may choose one or all four of the following options: open-door policy, conference, mediation, or arbitration. "We wanted to give our employees several ports of entry to lodge a complaint if they wanted to," said the manager of employee relations.[15]

TERMINATION

Termination—firing or dismissing an employee— is the most severe penalty that management can impose and should therefore be the most carefully considered. The termination experience is traumatic for the employee, leading to feelings of failure, fear, disappointment, and, inevitably, anger. Firing is also difficult for the person who makes the decision. The realization that termination may affect not only the employee but often an entire family increases the trauma. Not knowing how the terminated employee will react may also create considerable anxiety for the manager who must do the firing.

There is a distinct psychology, therefore, that surrounds termination.[16] The fired employee may experience a series of emotions in quick succession: initial shock (even if he or she knew or suspected), anger, the feeling that there must have been a mistake, possible identity collapse and/or ego disintegration. Then wild swings in mood may follow, perhaps culminating in depression. The restoration in self-confidence can take some time. Concurrently, the manager may experience feelings of self-pity (Why me?), followed by guilt (Could I have done better for this person?) and compassion (How will the employee survive?). There may be a desire to retain the employee, or, conversely, a tendency to blame the employee for "doing this" to the manager.

The manager must prepare for the termination interview in order to remain in complete control. The termination interview should always be conducted before a witness and in an environment where the manager has a psychological advantage, for example, the company boardroom. Some managers avoid using their offices for this purpose, as they do not want employees to associate routine calls to the office with the possibility of dismissal. The environment should be calm, formal, polite, and unemotional. No matter what the fired employee says or does, the manager must keep control over his or her emotions. The employee should be told of the decision and the (documented) reasons. An official letter of termination should be ready. It should be made clear that the decision is final. There should be no debate.

Managers must be security conscious. Depending on the circumstances, an employee may not even be allowed to return to the workplace unescorted, as some employees have done considerable damage in their desire to seek revenge. Passwords, locker, and combinations, therefore, may have to be changed immediately. This process needs to be planned secretly. The story is told of a payroll supervisor who, after his dismissal, was allowed (or gained) access to the firm's computers. He programmed a "bomb" into the payroll system, so that when his payroll number was deleted, the entire system collapsed. As well, the system was rigged to collapse on the anniversary of his dismissal. It took three years (and three system collapses) before the damage was finally repaired. While this incident is extreme, dismissed employees have often been known to destroy or steal important documents and company secrets. In addition, if a dismissed employee seems to be particularly angry, management does not want to give the person ready access to his or her peers. Relations with other employees can be undermined by "badmouthing" and perhaps outright lies about the situation.

It must be remembered, too, that forced separation affects those left behind. First, there are feelings of shock and excitement, followed by relief (It wasn't me!) and perhaps feelings of compassion or of self-righteousness (He deserved it, damn him!). Depending on the relationship with the fired individual, there can be feelings of anger at the employer or at the "bad person". Whatever the cause, termination should be conducted in a way that preserves the employee's dignity as much as possible. As with layoffs (see below), some managers hire outplacement specialists to help the dismissed individual find a new job. Time can be allowed to check with a lawyer, or secretarial and photocopying services can be offered. Depending upon the fired employee's level and the industry, it must be remembered that few people remain unemployed forever. The person who is fired may someday be in a position to influence a major customer or to affect the business in some significant way. No manager wants disgruntled, angry employees to seek revenge for past wrongs.

Some years ago, in a guest lecture to a senior HR Management class at Humber College, James Sweet, then Manager of Employee Relations at Moore Business Forms in Toronto, outlined his firm's philosophy toward employee dismissal. He suggested that no blame be placed on the terminated employee, as it was not this individual's fault. The poor performance stemmed from management's inability to create an environment that motivated the employee.

By taking away the blame (and thus most of the emotion) surrounding the firing decision, it was possible to devise a plan to find jobs for dismissed employees. Accordingly, a "dehiring" consultant was used to help ex-Moore employees to find new jobs. Mr. Sweet reported that most found work, often at a higher level, within six months of having been fired! While losing one's job will always be a traumatic experience, how much better it must be to be treated with respect and dignity than to be dismissed in a cold, heartless fashion.

One practical reason for treating terminated employees with dignity and respect is that in the event of a wrongful dismissal suit, management practices will be scrutinized carefully by the courts. Although some employees may still sue, their case will be weakened if an employer has a reputation for fair and generous treatment.

WRONGFUL DISMISSAL

There is a vast body of literature on wrongful dismissal, as this topic is of interest to almost every working Canadian. If an employee is covered by a collective agreement, the remedy for wrongful dismissal is through the grievance process, as the employer must show there was just cause for termination. Since this process is well documented and reasonably straightforward, we will concentrate on the rights of those employees not represented by a union.

In Canada, a nonunion employee hired into a job for an "indefinite term" and terminated without just cause is entitled to reasonable notice or compensation instead of notice, as a result of past decisions made by the courts under what is called "common law",[17] or the body of precedents that has built up over the years. In specific terms, "the law implies a right to be dismissed only upon being given reasonable notice, unless just cause for immediate dismissal exists."[18] ("Reasonable notice" is not spelled out, and would be judged individually by the courts, on the basis of many circumstances). As well, the last two decades have seen a vast change in the level of employee awareness and in attitude toward management decisions, many of which can be regarded as arbitrary.[19] When faced with wrongful dismissal, however, it must be made clear that the nonunion employee has only one recourse—sue for damages. The employer must then prove that just cause exists.

In cases where the employer claims just cause for incompetence, for example, good personnel records are indispensable. In an analysis of 90 Canadian wrongful dismissal cases, for example, it was found that employers were more likely to show just cause if the employee had been disciplined previous to dismissal and less likely if the employee's performance had been appraised as satisfactory.[20] The law is complex, however, and each case is considered on its individual merits. One author listed 37 factors that employers have had to justify in court during cases based on incompetence.[21]

Cases based on misconduct can be even more complex. For example, in 1992, the Supreme Court of Nova Scotia made an important decision when it found that Household Finance Corp. (HFC) in Halifax could not dismiss an employee for data security breach when it did not have a policy to prevent information theft. Cynthia Conrad sued Household Finance for wrongful dismissal after an unknown party discovered her password and used it to adjust account balances. She won damages for lost wages, wasted relocation costs, and surprisingly, punitive damages. Each employee had been issued with a stamp bearing a personal password and HFC's operating procedure indicated nothing about how these stamps should be handled or stored. Conrad kept hers in an unlocked drawer, as did other employees. The court remarked that it seemed HFC had decided to deliver someone up as a scapegoat and she was the most visible candidate. She was fired on the day before she was to be promoted and transferred to Ottawa after completing all arrangements to move.[22] In this instance, lack of a clear policy and a hasty termination violated the concept of just cause.

If an employee is found to have been wrongfully dismissed the typical damages are limited to 1) loss of wages or salary for a period of time the court considers to be reasonable notice of termination; and 2) any other monies that might have been paid, such as bonuses, profit-sharing income, medical or insurance plan benefits, pension fund contribution, and vacation pay. In short, the court will attempt to place the employee in the financial position he or she would have been in if reasonable notice had been given. Punitive damages and damages for mental stress have been awarded only in rare cases.[23] Throughout this process, the dismissed employee cannot have remained idle. Evidence of an honest attempt to find alternative employment must be available, but reasonable expenses connected with a job search can be claimed as part of the legal action.[24]

ALTERNATIVES TO TERMINATION

Termination is frequently the solution when a person isn't able to perform his or her job in a satisfactory manner. There are, however, alternatives. Early retirement is also used as an alternative to dismissal, especially for long-service employees.

Another alternative, used especially for long-term employees, is **demotion**: the process of moving a worker to a lower-level position, which typically involves a reduction in pay. Emotions often run high when an individual is demoted. The demoted person may feel betrayed, embarrassed, angry, and disappointed, resulting in further productivity decreases. Demotion, then, should be used very cautiously. One means of reducing the trauma associated with demotions is to establish a probationary period for newly promoted workers, during which they try out the new job. Should the person not be suitable, the move back to the old job may not be as disappointing as it would have been had the promotion seemed permanent. If demotion is chosen over termination, efforts must be made to preserve the individual's self-esteem. The person may be asked how he or she would like to proceed with the demotion announcement. A positive image of the worker's value to the company should be projected.

In a unionized organization, the process of demotion is usually stipulated in the labour-management agreement. Should a decision be made to demote someone for unsatisfactory performance, the union should be notified and given the specific reasons for the demotion. Often the demotion will be challenged through the formal grievance procedure. Documentation is necessary, therefore, for the demotion to be upheld. Even with the problems associated with demotion for cause, it is often easier to demote than to terminate an employee. In addition, demotion is often less devastating to the employee. For the organization, however, the opposite may be true if the demotion creates lingering ill will and an embittered employee.

LAYOFFS

Historically, the economic well-being of many companies rose and fell along with the business cycle. At times a firm's goods or services may be in great demand; at other times demand falls. Often when demand is low, the firm has no other choice but to lay off workers. Although being laid off is not the same as dismissal, the effect is similar: the worker is unemployed. Alas, in today's work environment, often there is little chance of being rehired. Being laid off can have extreme psychological consequences. One electrical engineer who was laid off after nearly 30 years with Xerox said: "Losing my job was the most shocking experience I've ever had in my life. I almost think it's worse than the death of a loved one, because at least we learn about death as we grow up. No one in my age group ever learned about being laid off."[25]

As with termination, layoffs should be conducted in a manner that preserves individual dignity. Recently the CBC laid off 21 staff producers as part of that corporation's seemingly never-ending cutbacks. Even though Phyllis Platt, CBC-TV's English-language network programmer stated: "We are doing this in as humane a fashion as we can," one senior CBC-TV producer was told she was called "a redundant producer component." In the words of Harry Rasky, another award-winning producer: "Civility is a beautiful Canadian quality. We understand it's important to treat people properly. That didn't happen in this case."[26] Care should be taken, therefore, in how the news is communicated to those affected and in how outsiders learn of the layoffs. Otherwise, a difficult HR situation will be made worse by bad publicity and bitterness.

Layoff and Recall Procedures

Even in this rapidly changing environment, there will be times when recalls will be necessary. Whether the firm has a union or not, carefully constructed layoff/recall procedures should be developed.[27,28] Employees should understand when they are hired how the recall system will work in the event of a layoff. When the firm has a union, the layoff procedures are usually written into the collective agreement. Seniority is often the criterion for layoffs, with the most junior employees laid off first and the most senior laid-off employees recalled first. The collective agreement may also have a "bumping procedure". When senior-level positions are eliminated, the people occupying them have the right to "bump" workers from lower-level positions, assuming that they have the proper qualifications for the lower-level jobs and more seniority than the incumbents. When extensive bumping occurs, the composition of the workforce is altered, sometimes affecting productivity.

Regardless of a nonunionized firm's policy on the issue of layoffs, management should establish layoff procedures. Again, seniority could be an integral part of the process, but, frequently, other factors such as employee productivity can be considered. When productivity is a criterion, management must be careful to ensure that the decision *is* made on the basis of productivity, not favouritism. Generally, employees have an accurate perception of their own productivity level as compared with their fellow employees. It is important, therefore, to define accurately both seniority and productivity considerations well in advance of any layoffs.

Outplacement

Many organizations have established a systematic means of assisting laid off or terminated employees to locate jobs.[29] The use of outplacement began at the executive level, but has recently been used elsewhere in organizations. **Outplacement** is the process of helping laid-off or terminated employees find employment. Through outplacement, management tries to soften the blow of displacement. Some of the services provided during group outplacement are transition centres, individual counselling, job fairs, complete access to office equipment such as computers, fax machines, and photocopiers, and free postage for mailing application letters and resumes.[30]

Early Retirement as an Alternative to Layoff

Early retirement has been used extensively as an alternative to layoffs. Unfortunately, many downsizings have not been planned adequately and have been poorly implemented. In a major study that included 11 Canadian companies, Professor David Lambe from the University of Ottawa found that confusion surrounded the objectives of most of these downsizing exercises and "none of the firms surveyed had any significant commitment to manpower planning and career path planning."[31]

Drawbacks to Massive Early Retirement

Managers who depend on early retirement as a method of downsizing find themselves with large numbers of demoralized staff between 30 and 49 who are unable to leave. The future of these firms will be threatened, moreover, if the economy improves to the point where professional employees regain career mobility, or certainly in 10 years when an overwhelming percentage of employees may opt for retirement.[32] In fact, there are already predictions that in some organizations early retirees may be asked to return. HR professionals, then, should advise line managers that wholesale early retirement is not a universal cure-all for corporate inefficiency. Downsizing needs to be carefully planned and coordinated to fit into a changed workplace where operations are carried out more efficiently. Otherwise, the firm is left with fewer employees who are required to perform the same amount of work. The result can be overworked, demoralized employees and reduced customer service. In fact, in a significant percentage of downsized companies, management is not happy with the results.[33]

Caring for Those Who Remain

One of the most neglected facets of HR management is the care of those employees left after a major layoff or downsizing. These people may be demoralized, overworked, confused, and anxious about their own jobs. Their trust has to be regained, as the trauma of seeing their peers forced out of the organization can last for years. Some employers are recognizing these fears and investing more heavily in EAP programs. Morris Berchard, executive vice-president of Warren Shepell, one of the largest EAP providers in Canada, has indicated that his company is getting more calls than ever for information. He quotes one of his clients who said: "we are having to cut back so much, we want to give our employees something to help them through these difficult times."[34]

TRANSFERS

Three and a half years ago, Michael Roberts graduated with an MBA from the University of British Columbia and joined Northern Telecom Ltd. of Toronto, one of the world's leading manufacturers of telecommunications equipment.

Since then, he has held seven different positions, ranging from a staffing specialist in the human resources department to an analyst with the finance division's internal audit team to a member of a union-contract negotiating team. While he increased his pay in five of these moves, he has climbed just two rungs up the corporate ladder to his current position as senior manager of human resources at Northern Telecom's optical cable plant in Saskatoon.

Like a growing number of employees, Roberts, 34, is experiencing a new reality of the workplace. A rise through the ranks may no longer come from moving up the corporate ladder but from moving sideways.[35]

The lateral movement of an employee within an organization is called a **transfer**, which may be initiated by the firm or by an employee. This lateral movement does not imply that a person is being promoted or demoted. Transfers serve several purposes. First, managers often find it necessary to reorganize. Offices and departments are created and abolished in response to company needs. In order to fill positions created by reorganization, employee moves not entailing promotion may be necessary. The same is true when an office or a department is closed. Rather than terminating valued employees, managers may transfer them to other areas.

A second reason for using transfers is to make positions available in the primary promotion channel. Typically, companies are organized into a hierarchical structure resembling a pyramid. Each succeeding promotion is more difficult to obtain because fewer positions exist. At times, very productive but unpromotable employees occupy positions, so that other qualified colleagues may find their opportunities for promotion blocked. Faced with career stagnation, the most capable future managers may seek employment elsewhere. In order to keep promotion channels open, management may decide to transfer employees who are unpromotable, but productive at their present levels. A third reason to use transfers is to satisfy employees' personal needs or career plans. The reasons for wanting a transfer are numerous. For example, an individual may need to work closer to home to care for aging parents, or dislike the long commuting trips to and from work. Factors such as these may be so important that employees will resign if a transfer is not approved. Rather than risk losing a valued employee, management may arrange a transfer. Finally, because of downsizing and the reduction in management levels, it is becoming necessary to gain a wide variety of work experiences before qualifying for promotion. It has been estimated that by the year 2000, the typical large corporation will have half the management levels and one-third the managers that exist today.[36] Individuals who desire upward mobility often explore possible lateral moves so that they can become generalists.[37]

Indeed, according to Grant Smith, the director of executive search at Price Waterhouse in Vancouver, "the smart employee will move around every five years to obtain the variety of experience needed to move upward." In his words, "today's employees need more arrows in their quiver if they want a shot at a better job title."[38]

Before approval, a transfer request should be analyzed to determine the best interests of both firm and individual. Transfers may be disruptive, for example, if a qualified replacement isn't available to take the vacated position. Management should establish transfer policies and procedures so that employees will be informed in advance as to when a transfer request is likely to be approved and under what conditions. For example, if the transfer is for personal reasons, some firms do not pay moving costs.

A GLOBAL PERSPECTIVE

International transfers refer to employee movement within a multinational organization. A transfer may be initiated by the firm or by an employee, but most international transfers are initiated by management to take advantage of domestic talent in global business operations. As these transfers are often inappropriately handled, they may cause personal and career damage, without benefitting the company.

A well-planned expatriate transfer policy can help a company avoid many of the frustrations and pitfalls of sending people to work in foreign countries, while achieving significant cost savings. When developing an expatriate policy, management needs to consider carefully both the rationale for sending people abroad and the needs of potential expatriates. The final decision to go should be the employee's. Transferring overseas is a major career step, often producing anxiety. The expatriate transfer policy, therefore, should account for all six phases of the overseas experience: 1) the preassignment period; 2) the journey out; 3) the assignment itself; 4) the prereturn period; 5) the journey back; and 6) the postassignment period. Establishing the policy is the first task; communicating effectively to potential expatriates is the second.[39] One of the most effective ways in which to communicate is to make the foreign assignment part of an official career plan.

PROMOTION

The term **promotion** (one of the most emotionally charged words in the field of human resource management) defines the movement of a person to a higher-level position. An individual who obtains a promotion normally receives additional financial rewards and the ego enhancement associated with achievement and accomplishment. Most employees feel good about being promoted. But for every individual who gains a promotion, there are likely others who were not selected. One employee's promotion, therefore, may result in a short-term decline in productivity, or in some instances the resignation of unsuccessful candidates.

In the foreseeable future, promotions will not be as commonplace as in the past,[40] as in many firms, the number of levels and middle management positions have declined, leaving fewer promotional opportunities. Consequently, managers must look for other way to reward employees. One alternative is the dual-track system, described in Chapter 9, whereby highly talented technical individuals can continue to receive increased financial rewards without progressing into management. Another approach is to design jobs that offer opportunities to learn new skills, providing some variation in job tasks.[41]

RESIGNATION

Even when management is strongly committed to making the environment a good place to work, employees still resign. In fact, according to Dick Cappon, who heads the career transition practice at Ernst and Young, "managers . . . would be well advised to realize people who are now 18 may well change jobs six to eight times before they are 40 and, today, five years with a company is a reasonable career target."[42]

A certain amount of turnover is healthy for an organization and is often necessary to afford employees who stay the opportunity to fulfil career objectives. When turnover becomes excessive, however, the problem must be faced. The most qualified employees are often the ones who resign, because they are more mobile. If excessive numbers of a firm's highly qualified and competent workers are leaving, a means must be found to reverse the trend.

Analyzing Resignations

A frequently given reason for resignation is to obtain better salary and/or benefits, but most firms conduct salary surveys or otherwise keep in touch with what competitors are paying. Research has shown that even when employees mention pay as a reason for resigning, they often have other, deeper reasons for deciding to leave. Management should identify the causes and correct them as quickly as possible.

When the real reasons that individuals decide to leave need to be determined, exit interviews and/or postexit questionnaires can be useful.[43] In one survey, 96 percent of respondents indicated their companies have some form of exit interview program.[44] Typically, the exit interview is the last contact the employee has with the employer. The exit interview encourages the employee to divulge reasons for resigning. A human resource professional usually conducts this interview, as an employee is not as likely to respond as freely during an interview with the supervisor, reasoning that he or she may need a letter of recommendation from that supervisor in the future. The typical exit interview might consist of

- establishing rapport;
- exploring the purpose of the interview;
- exploring attitudes regarding the old job;
- discussing reasons for leaving;
- comparing the old and the new jobs;
- asking for recommended changes;
- conclusion.[45]

Note that the interviewer is focusing on job-related factors while probing for the real reasons that the person is leaving. (Figure 16-6 gives an example of appropriate questions.) Over a period of time, properly conducted exit interviews can provide considerable insight into why employees resign. Patterns are often identified that uncover weaknesses in the firm's human resource management system, allowing corrective action to be taken.

The postexit questionnaire is sent to former employees several weeks after they leave the organization. Usually, they have already started work at their new company. The questionnaire is structured to draw out the real reason the employee resigned. Ample blank space is also provided so that former employees can express their feelings about their former job and organization. One strength of this approach is that the individuals are no longer with the firm and may respond more freely to the questions. A weakness is that the interviewer is not present to interpret and to probe for the real reasons for leaving.

Notice of Resignation

In most firms, at least two weeks' resignation notice is requested of departing employees. A month's notice may be required, however, from professional and managerial staff. Where notice is expected, this policy should be communicated to all employees. A surprise, immediate resignation may not only affect morale (as other employees wonder why), but make continuing operations difficult.

FIGURE 16-6
Questions for an Exit Interview

1. Let's begin by your outlining briefly some of the duties of your job.
2. Of the duties you just outlined, tell me three or four that are crucial to the performance of your job.
3. Tell me about some of the duties you like the most and what you liked about performing those duties.
4. Now, tell me about some of the duties you liked least and what you did not like about performing those duties.
5. Suppose you describe the amount of variety in your job.
6. Let's talk a little bit now about the amount of work assigned to you. For example, was the amount assigned not enough at times, perhaps too much at times, or was it fairly stable and even overall?
7. Suppose you give me an example of an incident that occurred on your job that was especially satisfying to you. What about an incident that was a little less satisfying?
8. Let's talk now about the extent to which you feel you were given the opportunity to use your educational background, skills, and abilities on your job.
9. Tell me how you would assess the quality of training on your job.
10. Suppose you describe the promotional opportunities open to you in your job.

Source: Wanda R. Embrey, R. Wayne Mondy, and Robert M. Noe, "Exit Interview: A Tool for Personnel Development." Reprinted from *Personnel Administrator* (May 1979). Reprinted by permission of *HRMagazine* (formerly *Personnel Administrator*) published by the Society for Human Resource Management, Alexandria, Virginia.

RETIREMENT

Most long-term employees leave an organization by retiring. Retirement plans may be based on a certain age, or a certain number of years with the firm, or both. Upon retirement, some former employees receive a pension each month for the remainder of their lives. Some experts are sounding warnings, however, that future retirees will not be able to expect the same benefit levels as previous generations. In fact, it may be necessary for most Canadians to work, at least part-time, well into their seventies. Indeed, it has been pointed out that complete retirement at 65 is a relatively recent phenomenon and that the retirement age of 65 is not based on any particular logic or supportable reason.[46]

A Canadian Press report suggests that nearly 40 percent of Canadians expect to work part-time upon retirement, and 16 percent over age 65 are still working. These data support the views of pension experts who suggest that "Canadians will have to work longer because they are using more social security benefits than society planned for, thanks to their increasing longevity."[47]

Early Retirement

Despite these predictions, however, the average Canadian now retires at 62,[48] because many employees have taken early retirement, some voluntarily and some of necessity, as a result of corporate downsizing. Often, retirement pay is reduced for each year that the retirement date is advanced, but in many instances, generous early retirement benefits have been offered as an inducement to convince employees to retire early.

Retirement Planning

Strong emotions often accompany retirement. As retirement approaches, the individual may be haunted by questions: Do I have enough money? What will I do? Will I be able to adjust? Just as a well-planned orientation program eases the transition of a new employee into the organization, a company-sponsored retirement planning program eases the transition of long-term employees from work to leisure,[49] or to some other paid or volunteer activity.

Often, management invests time, staff, and money to provide useful information to those approaching retirement. Typically, this information relates to finances, housing, relocation, family relations, attitude adjustment, and legal affairs. In some firms, the focus is on adapting the employee to retirement living by considering both the social and the psychological implications of retirement. Retired individuals are often brought to meetings to speak and to answer questions about retirement life and managing lifestyle change. Such assistance can help smooth this major transition in an individual's life.

RESPONDING TO CRISIS IN A GLOBAL SETTING

Any group of employees (domestic or expatirate) will have crises from time to time. Good employee relations are created when HR professionals acknowledge their problems and offer appropriate help or advice. Responses may range from sending a condolence card or ensuring that other employees know where to visit a sick colleague to spending considerable time finding the appropriate support network to resolve a serious family crisis. (More extensive counselling may be part of an EAP, described in Chapters 12 and 13.) The role of the company can be much larger, however, when employees confront a crisis in a foreign country. According to Jay Hornsby, Dow Chemical Company's vice-president of human resources, "for an expatriate employee thousands of miles away from home, the company is the family. . . . Whenever something goes wrong, and it will, he or she will naturally turn to the company for help." The key to maintaining good employee relations is for the HR professional to be able to help when an expatriate employee is in difficulty. Global human resource professionals have been called on to assist expatriates with a wide range of difficult problems including medical emergencies, natural disasters, revolutions, and other international crises, such as the recent conflict in the Middle East.[50]

Medical emergencies occur fairly frequently. Ralph W. Stevens, vice-president of personnel and employee relations for Hamilton Oil Corporation, recalls the case of a high-ranking technical manager who suffered a stroke while on business in Korea, where the company maintains no office. Stevens managed to find a first-rate physician, set the employee up in a well-regarded hospital, and transfer sufficient funds to cover the medical bills, while comforting the manager's frantic family![51]

Because of its extensive operations in Latin America, the management of Ferro, a large international manufacturer, has long had contingency plans in place for another kind of emergency: a terrorist kidnapping. Nothing of the kind has ever happened to a Ferro employee, but the company still strives to maintain a politically neutral and noncontroversial image when it operates in potentially dangerous international locations.

Various contingency plans, including means and methods to evacuate workers if necessary, should be in place if a firm operates in politically volatile areas. Similarly, HR professionals should be prepared to deal with natural disasters, such as earthquakes and hurricanes, as well as personal disaster. Nothing is more difficult to react to than the death of an expatriate employee abroad. The HR professional may even have to coordinate the transport of a coffin from an international site while giving solace to a grieving family.[52] The ultimate test of management's concern for employees comes in times of extreme crisis.

$\int$ UMMARY

A necessary, but often difficult, aspect of internal employee relations is discipline. A major purpose of disciplinary action is to ensure that employee behaviour is consistent with the firm's policies, rules, and regulations. Disciplinary action invokes a penalty against an employee who fails to meet company standards of behaviour. If a discipline without punishment system is used, employees are encouraged to take control of their own behaviour.

The discipline process is dynamic and ongoing. Rules are established to facilitate the accomplishment of organizational objectives. These rules must be communicated to employees. When an employee's behaviour violates a rule, corrective action should be taken. The purpose of this action is to alter behaviour so there will be no adverse effect on the organization. When the progressive or just cause disciplinary approach is followed, an attempt is made to make the penalty appropriate to the violation (or accumulated violations). Discipline without punishment systems work through a series of counselling sessions that place responsibility on the employee to behave appropriately.

If the employees are represented by a union, workers who believe they have been disciplined or dealt with unjustly can appeal through the grievance procedure. A grievance procedure permits employees to express complaints without jeopardizing their jobs. The final step in a grievance process, for issues that cannot be resolved internally, is arbitration, whereby the parties submit a dispute to an external third party for binding resolution.

Termination is the most severe penalty that management can impose on an employee. In Canada there are remedies if an employee is dismissed without proper notice or without just cause. Union members can grieve the wrongful dismissal, while all other employees can sue for wrongful dismissal. If wrongful dismissal is proven, the courts will attempt to place the employee in the same financial position that he or she would have been in if the law had been followed. Usually no punitive damages are awarded.

Internal employee relations also pertain to resignation, demotion, layoff, transfer, promotion, and retirement. Even in the best organizations, some workers will resign. Two techniques—the exit interview and the postexit questionnaire—may be used to help determine the real reasons an individual has decided to leave the organization.

At times, a firm has no choice but to lay off employees. Although being laid off does not have the shameful connotation of being fired, it has the same immediate effect: the worker is unemployed. Recently many layoffs have been permanent as firms have been downsizing.

Early retirement has sometimes been used in lieu of permanent layoffs. While this process can have short-term benefits, in many firms there is disappointment with the results.

A person can move laterally within the organization by transfer. A transfer may be initiated by the firm or by the employee.

The means by which long-term employees usually leave an organization is through retirement. Retirement may be based on a certain age, a certain number of years' service, or both. Many employers offer counselling or other help to ease retiring workers into a new life stage.

Managers who assign staff to foreign postings should be prepared to help them in the event of natural or personal catastrophe. Contingency plans should be in place so that swift action can be taken if an employee needs to be evacuated or if there is a serious illness.

TERMS FOR REVIEW

Internal employee relations	Demotion
Discipline	Outplacement
Discipline without punishment	Early retirement
Progressive disciplinary action	Transfer
Grievance	Promotion

QUESTIONS FOR REVIEW

1. Distinguish between progressive discipline and discipline without punishment.
2. In progressive disciplinary action, what steps are involved before employee termination?
3. Under a discipline without punishment system, what steps are involved before employee termination?
4. What are the typical steps in handling a grievance under a collective bargaining agreement?
5. Why is arbitration often used in the settlement of grievances in a unionized firm?
6. How would grievances typically be handled in a nonunion firm? Describe briefly.
7. Explain the concept of just cause as it pertains to termination.
8. Briefly describe the techniques available to determine the real reasons that an individual decides to leave an organization.
9. Distinguish between demotions, transfers, and promotions.
10. Why is early retirement used as a substitute for layoffs?
11. Discuss how the surviving employees might feel after a downsizing. What should management do?

HRM INCIDENT 1

• YOU KNOW THE POLICY

Dwayne Alexander was the Halifax-area supervisor for Quik-Stop, a chain of convenience stores. There were seven Quik-Stop stores in Halifax, and Dwayne had full responsibility for managing them. Each store operated with only one person on duty at a time. Although several of the stores stayed open all night, every night, the Centre Street store was open all night Monday through Thursday but only from 6:00 A.M. to 10:00 P.M. Friday through Sunday. Because the store was open fewer hours during the weekend, money from sales was kept in the store safe until Monday. The time it took to complete a money count on Monday, therefore, was greater than normal.

The company had a policy that when the safe was being emptied, the manager had to be with the employee on duty, and the employee had to place each $1000 in a brown bag, mark the bag, and leave the bag on the floor next to the safe until the manager verified the amount in each bag.

Anton Janacek worked the Sunday night shift at the Centre Street store and was trying to save the manager time by counting the money prior to his arrival. The store got very busy, and, while bagging a customer's groceries, Anton mistook one of the money bags for a bag containing three sandwiches and put the money bag in with the groceries. Twenty minutes later, the manager arrived, and both men began to search for the money. While they were searching, the customer came back with the bag of money. The company has a policy that anyone violating the money-counting procedure must be fired immediately.

Anton was very upset. "I really need this job," Anton exclaimed. "With the new baby and all the other expenses we've had, I sure can't stand to be out of a job."

"You knew about the policy, Anton," said Dwayne.

"Yes, I did, Dwayne," said Anton, "and I really don't have any excuse. If you don't fire me, though, I promise you that I'll be the best store manager you've got."

While Anton waited on a customer, Dwayne called his boss at the home office in Montreal. With the boss's approval, Dwayne decided not to fire Anton.

QUESTIONS

1. Do you agree with Dwayne's decision in view of the text material on progressive discipline? Discuss.
2. How did Dwayne's decision not to fire Anton serve as a motivational force for Anton?

HRM INCIDENT 2

• SOMETHING IS NOT RIGHT

As Norman Blankenship came to the office at Consolidated Coal Company's Rowland mine, near Clear Creek, Alberta, he told the mine dispatcher not to tell anyone of his presence. Norman was the general superintendent of the

Rowland operation. He had been with Consolidated for more than 23 years, having started out as a coal digger.

Norman had heard that one of his section bosses, Tom Serinsky, had been sleeping on the job. Tom had been hired two months earlier and assigned to the Rowland mine by the regional human resource office. He went to work as section boss on the midnight to 8:00 a.m. shift. Because of his age and experience, he was the senior person in the mine on his shift.

Norman took one of the battery-operated jeeps used to transport workers and supplies in and out of the mine and proceeded to the area where Tom was assigned. Upon arriving, he saw Tom lying on an emergency stretcher. Norman stopped his jeep a few yards away from where Tom was sleeping and approached him. "Hey, you asleep?" Norman asked. Tom awakened with a start and said, "No I wasn't sleeping."

Norman waited a moment for Tom to collect his senses and then said, "I could tell that you were sleeping. But that's beside the point. You weren't at your work station. You know that I have no choice but to fire you." After Tom had left, Norman called his mine supervisor, who had accompanied him to the dispatcher's office, and asked him to complete the remainder of Tom's shift.

The next morning, Norman had the mine human resource officer officially terminate Tom. As part of the standard procedure, the mine human resource officer notified the regional director that Tom had been fired and gave the reasons for firing him. The regional human resource director asked the mine human resource officer to put Norman on the line. When he did so, Norman was told, "You know that Tom is the brother-in-law of our regional vice-president, Carlton Frederick?" "No, I didn't know that," replied Norman, "but it doesn't matter. The rules are clear, and I wouldn't care if he was the president's son."

The next day, the regional human resource director showed up at the mine just as Norman was getting ready to make a routine tour of the mine. "I guess you know what I'm here for," said the human resource director. "Yeah, you're here to take away my authority," replied Norman. "No, I'm just here to investigate," said the human resource director.

When Norman returned to the mine office after his tour, the human resource director had finished his interviews. He told Norman, "I think we're going to have to put Tom back to work. If we decide to do that, can you let him work for you?" "No, absolutely not," said Norman. "In fact, if he works here, I go." A week later, Norman learned that Tom had gone back to work as section boss at another Consolidated coal mine in the region.

QUESTIONS

1. What would you do now if you were Norman?
2. Do you believe that the human resource director handled the matter in an ethical manner? Explain.

DEVELOPING HRM SKILLS: AN EXPERIENTIAL EXERCISE

Isadore Lamansky is the manager of the machine tooling operations at Jen Star Industries and has five supervisors who report to him. One of his employees is Susie Canton, a supervisor in maintenance. As Isadore is on his way to work this morning, his thoughts focus on Susie: "Today is the day that I must talk to Susie. I sure hate to do it. I know she is going to take it the wrong way. Ever since Susie was promoted to unit supervisor she has had trouble maintaining discipline. She tries too hard to keep the men in line because she thinks they are continually trying to push her, and she lets the women get away with murder. Well I guess I'll get this over with, since that's what I get paid for."

The grapevine is strong at Jen Star Industries, and it didn't take long for Susie to hear rumours.

She thinks, "The word is that old Isadore is going to come down on me. He recommended someone else for my job because he doesn't like women in charge. The reason it is so hard to maintain discipline is that the men I supervise intentionally push me to see what I'll do. The women support me, and they are proud of me; the men just want me gone. He is probably going to dredge up some minor stuff to reprimand me about; we need more women in charge, and the boss will have to accept that I'm here for good!"

Who is right, and who is wrong? Can there be a reasonable solution to these problems? This exercise will require two participants, one to play Susie and the other to play Isadore. All others should observe carefully. Instructors will provide additional information to participants.

PART SIX:

CASE VI Parma Cycle Company: The Union Organizing Effort

The Digby, Nova Scotia plant of Parma Cycle Company had been open for only six months in March 1989, when the first union organizing attempts became apparent. A known union organizer was in town and pro-union leaflets began to appear around the factory. The human resource director at Digby, Edward Deal, had been expecting this to occur. He knew that the workers brought down from the main plant in Delta, B.C. had a strong union tradition. He also knew that the wage and benefits package at Digby was far less liberal than the one at the B.C. plant. So far, this discrepancy hadn't created a major problem. Most of the workers recruited from the Digby area felt that they were well paid in comparison to others in that area.

In the plant that same day, Janice Snively was thinking about whether or not she should talk to the human resource director. Janice had been hired by Parma two weeks prior to start-up. She had previously worked as a maintenance supervisor at a garment factory about 60 miles from Digby. She had taken a slight pay cut in order to take what she thought would be a better long-term job and to be closer to her family, who lived in Digby.

Janice's crew of 10 machine operators and two parts handlers was among the best in the plant. Janice had made friends with each of them and they obviously respected her. She felt that one reason she was a good leader was her willingness to get her hands dirty. Because of her experience in maintenance she was able to repair the machines herself when they broke down. When an operator was absent, she would take over that machine in order to keep the work flowing.

Lately she had noticed a change. The workers seemed to be shutting her out. In a couple of instances, when several of her crew were congregated at one table in the lunchroom, the conversation stopped as she approached and then awkwardly began again. The change of topic was obvious. For the first time, too, she began to hear complaints. For example, the operator of the cutoff machine, which cuts certain frame members to size, complained of the speed with which the machine operated. "I have

less than one second to move the cutoff piece before the tubing feeds through to start another cut. I'll be lucky not to lose an arm," he said. There had been a number of similar complaints (many of them related to safety, some to working conditions), and a number of workers asked about the date of their next raise.

Janice thought that handling these kinds of problems was part of the supervisor's job, so she wasn't too concerned. But now she decided it was time to talk to the human resource director.

Janice walked in as Ed was thinking about the advantages and disadvantages of having a union. "Ed," she said, "I want you to look at this. One of my people gave it to me and asked if it is true. I didn't know how to answer." Janice handed Ed a photocopied sheet. After studying the sheet for a moment Ed said, "It's basically true, but I wish it weren't."

Here is a reproduction of the sheet:

DID YOU KNOW?

- Parma's workers in B.C. do not pay for their dependents' supplemental medical insurance. You do!
- Parma's employees in B.C. have dental insurance. You don't!
- Employees in B.C. have 12 paid holidays. You have only nine.
- Trainees at the B.C. plant get $8.00 per hour. At Digby, they get the minimum wage.
- Senior machine operators in B.C. get $14.00 an hour. Here, they get $10.00 or less.

QUESTIONS

1. What do you think caused the union organizing attempt at Parma Cycle's Digby plant?
2. What sequence of events is likely to occur before a union is certified at the Digby plant?
3. Assuming that management wishes to prevent a union from organizing the Digby plant, what can the union and management legally do before and after a union representation election is ordered by the NSLB?

PART SIX:

CBC VIDEO CASE Training for the Second Industrial Revolution

A 1993 survey by the Canadian Labour Market and Productivity Centre determined that only 39 percent of Canadian workers received formal training from their employers. Of this training, 20 percent was basic orientation to newcomers; only a small portion of the Canadian work force is being retrained to compete in the global economy. Conference Board of Canada surveys bear out these grim figures: on average companies spend $600 per employee annually on training. This funding supports five days of training for managers and only three days for rank-and-file workers—although the gap is narrowing. These statistics compare unfavourably to our competitors. For example, our training is only one-half of what is offered to American workers and only one-sixth of what is available to Japanese workers.

Politicians and business leaders constantly suggest that we must educate our workers and youth so that they can compete in the global economy. They are right. Of Japan's youth, 90 percent complete the equivalent of our grade 12, following a curriculum that is weighted heavily towards calculus and the sciences. Yet only 70 percent of Canadian students complete grade 12, and only five percent study calculus. These results are even more disappointing when one considers that Canada spends more per person on education than any other country in the world.

Initiatives to train workers must come from the private sector. Many labour unions, in conjunction with management, are taking the initiative to retrain their members so they will be ready for the 21st century. These programs have produced some radical training methods that union executives hope will maintain job security, while fulfilling management's need for increased efficiency.

Many of Algoma Steel's laid-off workers, for example, are currently enrolled in Algoma College, a division of Sudbury's Laurentian University. There they have the opportunity to acquire skills in such diverse areas as environmental technology, computer programming, nursing, catering, hotel management and fire services. In other classes, former steelworkers learn about the chemical processes involved in paper manufacturing, including the testing of chemical content, a responsibility that formerly fell to chemical engineers.

As its role is to provide extended unemployment insurance benefits while workers undergo training, the federal government provides some funding to these programs by giving the training councils, which implement training programs, seed money. The remaining expenses are covered by the steel companies and the United Steelworkers' union. Once bitter antagonists, the two groups now work together through a joint labour-management sector council called the Canadian Steel Trades Employ-

ment Congress (CSTEC). The congress pays tuition costs and offers employee career counselling. While the costs associated with retraining are high, there is a strong feeling that this collaboration between management and labour represents a significant breakthrough in management and union relations.

The Algoma example is not an isolated case. In many companies there is a realization that keeping employees and retraining them is good business. Zehrs, a grocery chain owned by Loblaws, offers training to its salaried workers. At the Cliff Evans Training Centre (owned jointly by the grocery chain and the United Food and Commercial Workers Local 1977) unskilled part-time workers can learn to become bakers, butchers, produce managers, florists, and deli counter managers.

Both management and union executives admit that training workers is extremely expensive. It is estimated that it costs a company $85 000 in wages and benefits to train four workers to become meat cutters. Yet there is a general perception that these programs are worthwhile, for they allow management to tailor employee skills to any type of expansion or job opening that might arise. Union participation is undoubtedly the most significant aspect of this training program. The United Food and Commercial Workers Local 1977 is given equal representation with management on the training centre's board of trustees. Any type of training program must be approved by the board and a needs analysis must also be conducted to ensure that every training dollar is spent efficiently.

In other companies, training initiatives are also being developed in partnership with unions. At the General Electric plant in Peterborough, Ontario, for example, welders are going back into the classroom to brush up on trigonometry to learn how to operate electronic machinery that they will use on the job. These joint training programs are good examples of how both labour and management benefit from skills enhancement: employees acquire new marketable skills, employers develop not only productive workers but also more satisfied ones; and union executives gain increased respect from the rank-and-file membership.

QUESTIONS

1. Why is training and development important to Canada's future?
2. Suggest ways an HR department can work with management and labour to make relevant training available to employees.

Video Resource: "Training Councils," Venture 414 (December 13, 1992).

CHAPTER

17 Human Resources Research

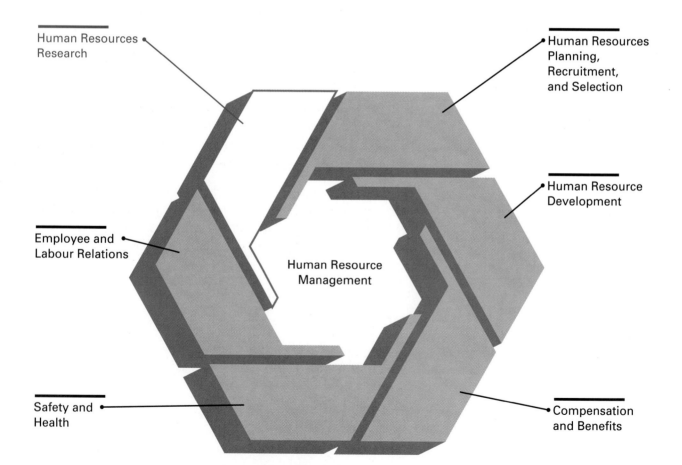

Human Resources
Research

Human Resources
Planning,
Recruitment,
and Selection

Human Resource
Development

Employee and
Labour Relations

Human Resource
Management

Safety and
Health

Compensation
and Benefits

CHAPTER OBJECTIVES

1. Explain the importance of research to human resource management. Identify the basic methods of enquiry and describe the steps in the research process.

2. Describe how quantitative methods may be used in human resource research and how the human resource function may be evaluated.

3. Describe how technology is affecting human resource management.

A nnette Dommert, human resource manager for Saint Boniface Hospital in Winnipeg, Manitoba, was disturbed as she studied the list of employees who had resigned during the past month. For the sixth month in a row, the number of resignations had increased. To compound the problem, the resignations were in critical areas such as X-ray and laboratory. Quite a few RNs had also quit. Annette had conducted exit interviews with many who had left, and most had responded that they were leaving for more money. However, Annette was well aware of salary schedules in other provinces. Saint Boniface's pay level was in line, overall, and even higher in a few categories.

Annette knew that a continued exodus of qualified workers would jeopardize patient care at Saint Boniface. She decided to propose that a confidential questionnaire be administered to all employees in the hospital in an attempt to identify reasons for the excessive turnover.

uman resource research can be of tremendous benefit to managers such as Annette Dommert, as they attempt to determine the real reasons for high turnover rates and other indicators of employee dissatisfaction. Without this information, an HR situation may continue to erode, until the quality of goods or services seriously declines.

We begin this chapter by discussing the benefits of HR research and methods of enquiry. Then we describe the research process and various methods of analyzing quantitative data. We end the chapter with sections on evaluating the HR function and how technology is affecting human resource management.

FIELDS OF STUDY FOR HUMAN RESOURCES RESEARCH

As we discussed in Chapter 1, the human resource manager's job has changed drastically in the last few years. To contend with mounting responsibilities, many human resource managers find they need research-derived information. **Human resources research** is the systematic study of a firm's human resources for the purpose of maximizing personal and organizational goal achievement.

There are many potential benefits of sound research programs, as managers have begun to realize the full significance of not using the human component effectively. This enlightenment, however belated, has occurred at a time when the competitive nature of business makes it increasingly difficult to create work environments that motivate. Specific applications of human resource research depend to a large extent on internal needs—on the size, goals, and specific problems of particular organizations.

Effective Management

Laws, government regulations, and judicial decisions have called into question many past human resource management practices. Managers must now be prepared to prove that their employment decisions are based on valid requirements. However, as Walter Tornow, vice-president of research and publication for The Center for Creative Leadership, states, "On the whole, government regulations have had a positive effect because they cause organizations to examine and document their practices in ways that heretofore were not deemed necessary for some." Another reason for the increased need for human resource research relates to rapid changes in work force composition. Research is required to determine how the goals of a more diverse workforce can be integrated with corporate objectives.

Largely because of increased educational opportunities, managers and nonmanagers alike have developed more sophisticated employment expectations. To respond appropriately, employers may need to modify their approaches to HRM. Although a highly autocratic manager may have been successful in the past, for example, a similar style today may lead quickly to resentment and lower productivity. Also, the organizational structure may need to be modified. Identifying appropriate managerial styles and organizational structure, therefore, will continue to be a major focus of human resource research.

The nature of work itself has also been changing rapidly. This factor necessitates continuous skill development and upgrading. Another difficult task is to prepare employees to accept change and new technology. The use of robotics in manufacturing plants, for example, has created a widespread need for retraining. As well, the ability to adapt to new techniques varies widely from one individual to the next, as each employee learns at a different rate. Unless new methods can be developed, therefore, coaching and training can become time consuming and costly.[1] Accepting skill obsolescence and the need to learn new ways of working is extremely difficult for some employees. Research may suggest methods by which people may learn to accept change more readily and thus continue to be productive members of the work force.

Human Resources Planning, Recruitment, and Selection

Plans must be made to recruit, select, and retain productive employees. Like every individual, each organization has a distinct personality. Thus, managers must find the best match between organizational and employee needs. For example, research might help to explain why an individual may be an excellent producer in one firm and a failure in another, even though the jobs seem to be similar.

Recruitment research is directed toward determining how employees with high potential can be hired. HR professionals need to identify the most likely sources of qualified candidates, therefore, as skill profiles that describe ideal employees are of little use if suitably qualified individuals cannot be found and persuaded to join the firm. The objective of employee selection research is to identify those prospective employees with the greatest potential for meeting organizational and personal objectives. As might be expected, this definition of success varies from organization to organization. The research attempts to identify factors (such as background, experience, education, and test scores) that differentiate successful applicants from the less successful ones,[2] a process that is complicated by variations in success profiles by geographic location and by gender.

Human Resource Development

Research is also an important part of human resource development. For example, studies may identify those employees who can benefit from training by isolating individuals with higher than average error rates. Also, research into the usefulness of the training program may be needed. Since training and development is an expense that needs to be justified, managers need to measure return on their investment.

Compensation

Both actual and perceived inequities in a firm's compensation system can create morale problems. Managers must be able to identify inequities, to correct them, and to provide information to employees that overcomes any misconceptions. In order to maintain a fair pay policy, in many firms, extensive external compensation surveys are conducted. In addition, in-house surveys are often used to determine employee attitudes toward pay. As the supply and demand for skilled employees constantly changes, an organization's compensation program can become rapidly outdated. Pay rates, therefore, must be closely monitored.

Employee and Labour Relations

Research into employee and labour relations focuses primarily on areas that affect individual job performance. Internal factors, such as working conditions or management style, may have a detrimental effect on employee productivity and job satisfaction.

Health and Safety (H&S)

The primary task of research into health and safety is to identify potential problem areas, such as the locations and the causes of accidents. Research can also be used to identify the characteristics of accident-prone employees. Concern about health and safety has grown during the 1990s; H&S will probably be even more important in the future.

A GLOBAL PERSPECTIVE

Interest in international human resource research has expanded dramatically. In a recent survey, company representatives were asked to name the most important issue related to global human resource management[3] (see Figure 17-1). These issues could be the primary focus for international human resource research in the future.

The ultimate test of the success of a global operation is the production of a quality product or service at a competitive price. Globally, quality and cost are determined largely by the effectiveness of production systems and the people who run them. Manufacturing and other business systems in Canada are undergoing a revitalization. The development of technological systems that will allow Canadian firms to be globally competitive will probably require the application of the most recent behavioural and technological knowledge. Implementing these changes will be even more complex overseas, presenting new challenges to human resource managers.

Canadian managers are beginning to balance their capital and their human investments to improve business systems. Human resource managers help foster this process by ensuring that the organization's human components contribute to productivity. One method is to extend the Japanese system of employee involvement, a process that requires a sophisticated approach to human resource management. This teamwork approach involves work group members in activities such as determining the appropriate method of work and rating other group members' performance.[4]

With the accelerated pace of technical change, many individuals are faced with the overwhelming task of trying to cope with high-stress workloads while trying to learn new technologies. To complicate this situation still further, various societies are at different stage in technological adaptation, making it very difficult for multinational organizations to move in a common strategic direction. The worldwide challenge for HRM is to find ways to help organizations and individuals assimilate new technologies and systems effectively.

FIGURE 17-1
The Most Important Global Human
Resource Issues

Human Resource Issue	Percentage of Respondents
Selecting and training local managers	70
Generating companywide loyalty and motivation	70
Speaking and understanding local language and culture	66
Appraising the performances of managers abroad	65
Planning systematic manager development and succession	59
Hiring indigenous sales personnel	57
Compensating foreign managers	54
Hiring/training foreign technical employees	52
Selecting/training managers overseas	48
Dealing with unions and labour law abroad	44
Promoting and transferring foreign managers	42

Note: The total sample was 95 companies:(manufacturing: 51; nonmanufacturing: 44; more profitable: 58; less profitable: 37).

Source: Adapted from Spencer Hayden, "Our Foreign Legions Are Faltering," *Personnel*, 67 (August 1990), p. 42. Used with the permission of The Spencer Hayden Co.

More research is needed in two critical areas: the harmonization of management styles and technological user fatigue. HR professionals need to develop staffing systems and procedures that ensure joint ventures are staffed with managers who are tolerant and flexible toward different management styles and philosophies, so that, within cultural boundaries, a roughly common approach can be developed.[5] Similarly, the human side of technological change needs to be managed carefully. HR managers need to be aware of technology fatigue and find ways to deal with this international crisis.[6]

METHODS OF ENQUIRY IN HUMAN RESOURCES RESEARCH

The type of problem and the particular needs of the organization determine, to a large extent, the appropriate method of enquiry. Particularly useful research methods include the case study, the survey feedback method, and the experiment.

The Case Study

The **case study** is an investigation into the underlying causes of specific problems in a plant, a department, or a work group. The research focuses on a particular set of problems, such as

- excessively high turnover at a particular facility;
- high absenteeism in a specific department;

- a high accident rate at a certain building site;
- low morale in a particular department;
- the underlying reasons for a wildcat strike at a particular location.

Although the results cannot be generalized to other situations, case studies may suggest possible new management approaches. The human resource management example presented later in this chapter provides an illustration of a case study provided by an outside consultant for a large hotel. In other situations, the firm's human resource manager or an HR specialist might conduct the research.

The Survey Feedback Method

A major function of human resource research is to determine employee attitudes toward jobs, pay, and supervision. Typically, this enquiry is conducted through questionnaires. Recall that Annette Dommert is proposing that a confidential questionnaire be administered to all hospital employees. In the **survey feedback method**, anonymous questionnaires are used to collect and measure employee attitudes. The Ford Motor Company, for example, uses the survey method to obtain the opinions of its salaried workers every other year. The results are published in Ford's in-house newsletter.

Questionnaires may be of two types: objective multiple-choice, or scaled-response, which asks for degrees of agreement or disagreement (see Figures 17-2a and 17-2b. Objective analysis of survey results often requires a more detailed study. There are many possible bases for comparison:

1. section or department;
2. age;
3. gender;
4. seniority;

FIGURE 17-2A
Examples of Multiple-Choice
Survey Questions

Why did you decide to do what you are doing?

a. Desire to aid or assist others
b. Influenced by another person or situation
c. Always wanted to be in this vocation
d. Lack of opportunity or interest in other vocational fields
e. Opportunities provided by this vocation
f. Personal satisfaction from doing this work

What do you like least about your job?

a. Nothing
b. Pay
c. Supervisor relations
d. Problems with fellow workers
e. Facilities
f. Paperwork and reports

FIGURE 17-2B
Examples of Scaled Response
Questions

Considering all aspects of your job, evaluate your compensation with regard to your contributions to the needs of the organization. Circle the number that best describes how you feel.

Pay Too Low		Pay Low		Pay Average		Pay Above Average		Pay Too High	
1	2	3	4	5	6	7	8	9	10

What are your feelings about overtime work requirements? Circle the number that best indicates how you feel.

		Unnecessary			Necessary on Occasion			Necessary	
1	2	3	4	5	6	7	8	9	10

5. job level or degree of responsibility;
6. changes in attitudes from previous surveys;
7. other divisions, departments, or work groups;
8. comparison with a standardized score if a validated instrument is being used.

The data become more meaningful to management when analyzed by these or other subgroups.

A major point to consider is that survey responses often identify symptoms rather than causes. For example, even if a compensation and benefits program is competitive, a low evaluation in this area (symptom) may actually reflect general dissatisfaction with management style. Thus, when surveys are administered, the researcher should avoid concentrating on isolated responses. Instead, the data should be viewed from a broader perspective, seeking to uncover patterns or general trends. Collectively, the responses will likely reflect trends that point to organizationwide difficulties.

When surveys are used to identify employee attitudes and opinions, response confidentiality must be ensured,[7] so that individual answers are not communicated to management. Outside consultants, therefore, are often employed to administer the questionnaire. Confidentiality means more than omitting the name from a questionnaire. Even in a large firm, some work units may contain only a small number of employees. Or in a large department, a personal characteristic of a particular employee may make identification possible. The researcher must be prepared to consolidate groups when necessary to preserve anonymity. Survey results should be communicated back to the affected groups, as they will want to see their own collective responses. As well, if surveys are to be taken seriously, management must act on the results.

At Emco Limited[8], a manufacturer and distributor of building materials, management left little doubt about its interest in what employees had to say about the company. When Emco conducted an employee satisfaction survey, the company posed three open-ended questions for employees to comment on: 1) If you were president of the company, what would you change? 2) What does TQM mean to you? 3) Is there anything else you would like to comment on? In a letter to employees accompanying the 15-page questionnaire, the president promised, "The information gained will provide management with the necessary tools to make the working environment more satisfying and productive through employee involvement and empowerment."

Most of the findings were positive and encouraging:

- Nearly everyone looks for methods to improve the work they do.
- Most believe the company is concerned about environmental issues.
- Customer satisfaction is the top priority for most employees.

Some other findings—shared openly with employees—indicate room for improvement:

- Fewer than two-thirds feel that safety concerns are addressed very well at work.
- Fewer than two-thirds are satisfied with the TQM training they have received.

Employees also criticized company communication in general, particularly on financial matters that relate to the various segments of the business.

Employees were given time off to fill out the questionnaires and all 4300 employees got a copy of the findings. Employees from various work groups participated in developing the questionnaires. "Everyone must have the information they need," said Marlene Root, director of human resources. "Open and honest communication is vital."

When survey results are communicated to management, it is often best for each department or section head to be contacted individually. Better results are typically obtained when the data are discussed in confidence with each person or group, avoiding potential embarrassing publicity.

At times, surveying every employee is not feasible because of time or cost restraints. **Sampling** is the process by which only a portion of the total group is studied, but conclusions are drawn for the entire group. Assume there are 500 employees in a firm; the time and the cost of surveying all 500 may be prohibitive. The researcher, therefore, will probably decide that a smaller sample of perhaps 50 can be deemed representative of the entire group. Conclusions based on responses from the sample group are then applied to all 50 employees. Various methods of choosing a sample may be used but usually it is important to assure that the sample group is representative of the study group as a whole. For example, if the 50 members of one department were chosen as a sample, their responses might not be a good indicator of how employees in other departments might have responded.

The Experiment

An **experiment** is an enquiry method that involves the manipulation of certain variables while others are held constant, by using a control group and an experimental group. The control group continues to operate as usual, whereas the selected variables are manipulated for the experimental group. For instance, a manager may want to determine the effect of a new training program on productivity. The control group would continue to perform tasks in the conventional manner, while the experimental group would receive the training. The assumption is that any change in productivity in the experimental group results from the training. On the surface, the experiment appears to be an excellent means of enquiry, but in practice, isolating the many interrelated variables affecting people and their performance can be extremely difficult.

THE RESEARCH PROCESS

A systematic approach to human resource research is needed. The most fruitful research is accomplished by following a logical process (see Figure 17-3).

Recognize the Problem

One of the more difficult research tasks is to recognize problems and especially to isolate problems from symptoms. For instance, at what point does absenteeism or turnover become excessive? Explaining away potential problems is often convenient. A manager may state, "Even though turnover is high, we really don't have a problem because those people didn't fit into the organization anyway." Comments such as these lead a researcher to suspect that this manager may not be open to problem recognition. In reality, the excessive turnover may be a symptom of an inadequate selection process, insufficient managerial training, or any number of other problems. Or, as the manager suggests, there might not be a problem. Regardless of the situation, however, openness on the part of the manager is the cornerstone of problem identification.

State the Problem

The next step in the process is to state clearly the purpose of the research. Again, the major issue is that the problem—not the symptoms—must be identified. As might be expected, separating symptoms from problems can be difficult. One manager might maintain that the cause of declining production is low pay; another may suspect inadequate supervision or insufficient training. Through careful research, it may be determined that dictatorial supervisors have been exerting so much pressure on employees, they have lost interest in productivity. If management attempted to solve the production problem by increasing wages, it is unlikely that conditions would improve. To repeat, a clear definition of the problem is essential for effective research.

FIGURE 17-3
The Human Resource
Research Process

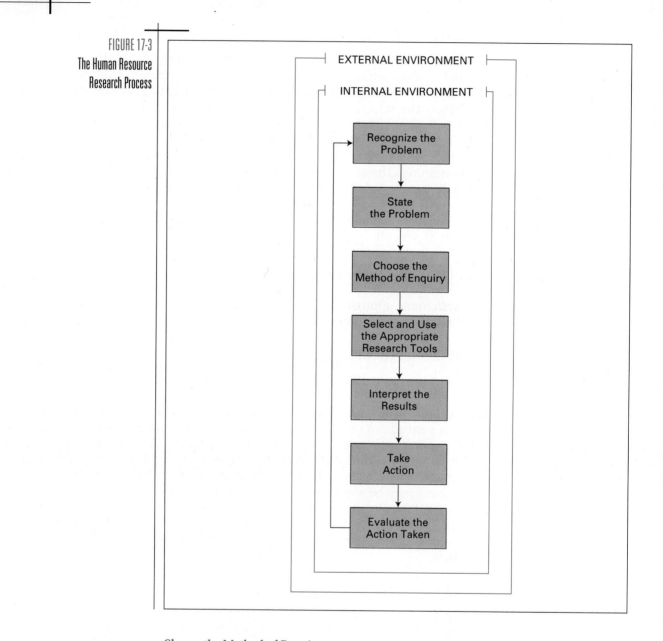

Choose the Method of Enquiry

The method of enquiry finally chosen depends to a large extent on the nature of the research. Most applied human resource research, however, involves either the case study or the survey.

Select and Use the Appropriate Research Tools

Managers do not have to be experts in mathematics and statistical theory in order to take advantage of the numerous quantitative research tools now in common use. They must have a basic understanding, however, of the circumstances under which these tools should be used, the strengths and weaknesses of each method, and how to interpret quantitative results. The method selected, therefore, depends on the researcher's purpose.

Interpret the Results

The person closest to the problem should participate in interpreting the results, as outsiders working alone can arrive at inaccurate conclusions. As an example, the survey may isolate dissatisfaction in the engineering department. A person not close to the situation might mistakenly identify the problem as inadequate supervision, where someone who knew the department would understand that the comments referred to working conditions.

Take Action

The most difficult phase in the research process is to take action based on research findings. Research results may identify areas in which changes are necessary, but HR professionals must convince line management, at times a difficult task. Suggesting to a manager that his or her managerial style is causing excessive turnover, for example, can be an awkward undertaking. The benefits of research are realized, however, only when action is taken to resolve real problems.

Evaluate the Action Taken

No research initiative is complete until the results are evaluated. Evaluation requires an objective assessment of whether or not the action has solved the problem. Recall that Figure 17-3 shows a feedback loop from evaluation to problem recognition. Determining whether or not the problem has been solved will assist in future research, as revisions may be required or the entire research approach may need to be revamped.

HRM IN ACTION

Cameron Stephens, president of Queens Manufacturing Company, and Gwynneth Bushnell, the company's human resource director, were engaged in a serious conversation that could profoundly affect the future of the firm. "Gwynn," said Cameron, "I've been hearing rumblings of discontent throughout the organization. For some reason that I can't figure out, people at Queens just don't appear to be as happy as they have been in the past. And it isn't just isolated instances. There is a different attitude everywhere. Any ideas as to how we can determine what's going on so we can correct the problem?"

If you were Gwynneth, how would you respond?

QUANTITATIVE DATA ANALYSIS IN HUMAN RESOURCES RESEARCH

Numerous methods are available to analyze quantitative data gathered through research, most of which can be used on both mainframe and personal computers. The most commonly used statistical techniques include correlation analysis, regression analysis, and time series analysis.

Correlation Analysis

Often a researcher would like to know the relative strength of the relationships between variables. **Correlation analysis** measures the degree of association between two or more variables. For example, is there a relationship between job satisfaction and employee absenteeism? Figure 17-4 illustrates a high *negative* relationship between these two variables—as job satisfaction goes down, absenteeism goes up. In other words, employees who exhibit low job satisfaction tend to be absent more often. Similarly, Figure 17-5 describes a high *positive* correlation between the level of employee education and productivity: the higher the education level, the greater the productivity. These correlations, based on data from one firm, might not hold for another firm; thus they cannot be applied universally.

Although the benefits of correlation analysis are considerable, this method must be used with caution. A correlation can be deceptive when the relationship does not reflect cause and effect. If research into executive compensation, for example, suggests there is a high correlation between a pay-for-performance clause in a CEO's contract and profitability, did the pay-for-performance clause cause better results for the company? Perhaps;

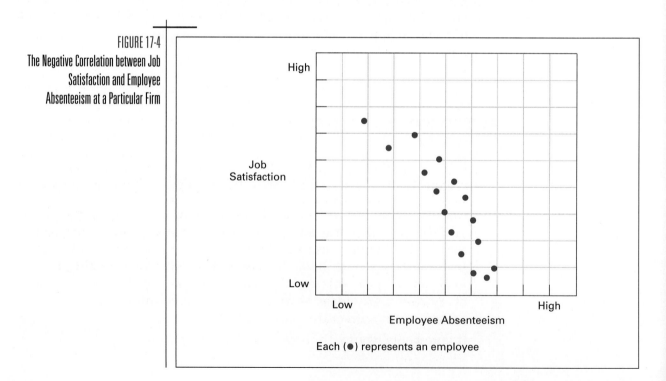

FIGURE 17-4
The Negative Correlation between Job Satisfaction and Employee Absenteeism at a Particular Firm

FIGURE 17-5
The Positive Correlation between
Education Level and Level of
Productivity at a Particular Firm

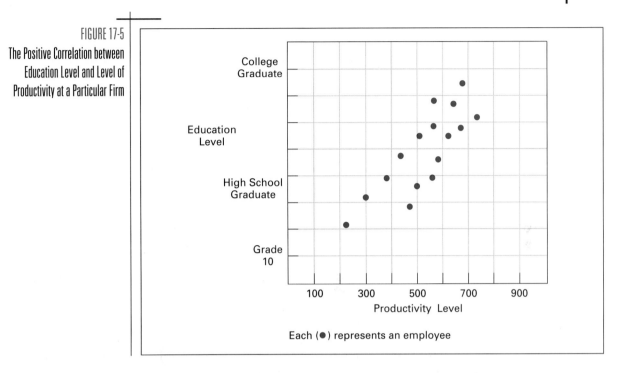

Each (●) represents an employee

but it is also possible that a sudden increase in demand might have boosted sales and profits, a factor that has no relationship to the CEO's management expertise![9] Therefore, a high but meaningless correlation may exist. Human resource managers should be careful, then, not to make decisions based on erroneous interpretations.

Regression Analysis

As discussed in Chapter 4, **regression analysis,** a technique that has proven useful in human resource planning, is also useful in HR research. The purpose of regression analysis is to utilize the relationship between two or more quantitative variables, so that one variable can be predicted from the other(s). For example, a manager might want to determine whether or not employee productivity can be estimated from educational attainment (refer to Figure 17-5). In regression analysis terminology, the productivity level is referred to as the *dependent* variable.

In this example, there is only one independent variable, so the process is referred to as *simple linear* regression. The use of two or more independent variables is termed *multiple* regression. When regression analysis is used in human resource research, some possible dependent variables might be

■ employee satisfaction levels
■ length of employment
■ productivity levels
■ accident rates.

Employment data that might be used as independent variables might include

- background and biographical data
- work history with the firm
- personal goals and aspirations
- test scores.

Through regression analysis, the research could attempt to determine which of the independent variables helps most in differentiating more productive from less productive workers, thereby improving selection decisions. The model's accuracy, however, must be validated through other statistical means. If the model proves appropriate, it can be a useful tool.

Time Series Analysis

Time series analysis, a variation of regression analysis in which the independent variable is expressed in units of time, is a technique that has proven helpful in making projections. As in regression analysis, both a dependent and an independent variable are required. The independent variable, however, is now associated with time and the dependent variable with demand. When the number of employees required in a company is closely associated with demand for the firm's product, for example, time series analysis may prove useful in forecasting human resource needs.

HUMAN RESOURCES RESEARCH: AN ILLUSTRATION

This section presents an example to illustrate how human resource research may be used. The organization, a large hotel in Vancouver, British Columbia, had experienced rapid growth, resulting in a range of perceived problems. The human resource director and the hotel general manager recognized these difficulties and hired an outside consultant to work with them in identifying and solving problems before they became critical. The consultant first talked with a number of employees to obtain a general view of the situation. Hesitancy to talk about certain subjects and their apparent nervousness during the informal interviews suggested that problems existed. Next he developed a survey tailored specifically for the hotel (Figure 17-6).

Administering the questionnaire to all hotel employees while maintaining confidentiality was a critical step. The general manager's role was to notify employees of the survey. From that point, the employees had no further contact with any member of the administration. Groups of employees met with the consultant while he explained the survey's purpose and then reassured the employees about confidentiality. They were told that only summary results would be provided to the administration. At this point, some of the problems became obvious, as many employees wanted to know in detail the relationship between the consultant and the administration. Continuous assurances of confidentiality had to be given. Because of the nature of hotel work, the researcher had to administer the questionnaire over a 48-hour period. To

FIGURE 17-6
A Job Satisfaction Survey for a
Particular Hotel

What do you like most about your job?

a. Helping or providing service for others
b. Learning opportunities
c. Personal satisfaction
d. Being around people
e. The work you perform at this hotel
f. Nothing
g. Other (Specify)
h. Other (Specify)

What do you like least about your job?

a. Nothing
b. Pay
c. Supervisor relations
d. Problems with fellow workers
e. Facilities
f. Paperwork and reports
g. Customer-related problems
h. Other (Specify)
i. Other (Specify)

How would you describe your overall working environment? Circle the number that best describes how you feel.

Extremely Frustrating		Frustrating		Acceptable		Above Average		Excellent	
1	2	3	4	5	6	7	8	9	10

What do you think about the system of giving pay increases at this hotel? Circle the number that best describes how you feel.

Very Bad		Poor		Satisfied		Good		Excellent	
1	2	3	4	5	6	7	8	9	10

Considering all aspects of your job, evaluate your compensation with regard to your contributions to the needs of the hotel. Circle the number that best describes how you feel.

Pay Too Low		Pay Low		Pay Average		Pay Above Average		Pay Too High	
1	2	3	4	5	6	7	8	9	10

further ensure confidentiality, the respondents were told they should put their completed questionnaires in blank envelopes so they could not be identified. Some employees even chose to mail their responses to the consultant rather than risk having the questionnaire get lost at the hotel.

Response data from all employees were then analyzed using a computerized statistical package that examined data for the entire hotel and for each hotel department. The results for the entire hotel proved inconclusive, but when data were evaluated by department, some problems became obvious. Employees in certain departments appeared to be much more unhappy than those in other areas. Satisfaction levels at the front desk and the restaurant (servers) for example, were consistently below the hotel average. Although not as low, job satisfaction among office staff and salespeople was also below the average. Figure 17-7 summarizes responses by department.

At this point, however, only symptoms had been uncovered. The next phase entailed specific problem identification. Survey results were presented to each department head individually. They reviewed the results, discussed the symptoms, and participated in problem identification.

Front desk staff provide an excellent illustration of the difference between symptom identification and problem definition. The hotel had grown rapidly during the past few years. While other departments had increased staff to handle the increased workload, the front desk manager had tried to substitute technology for people, placing considerable pressure on her employees. Poor customer service at this location could have serious consequences for the entire operation, thus increasing stress levels still further. More in-depth questioning revealed that salary levels had not kept pace with front desk departments in nearby hotels. The combination of these two factors—a department under pressure and an unreasonable salary level—resulted in considerable job dissatisfaction. The cause of the dissatisfaction had now been determined. The same procedure was used in the other departments in which employees had expressed low job satisfaction.

FIGURE 17-7
Responses: Rating of Hotel's Overall
Working Environment

Employee Groups	Average score of each department in relation to the hotel average of 6.80
Front Office	6.77
Department Heads	7.32
Front Desk	5.93
Housekeeping	7.71
Maintenance	7.59
Sales	6.57
Servers	6.27
Kitchen Staff	7.54
Engineers	7.10
Security	7.00
Chiefs	9.33

4.80 5.30 5.80 6.30 **6.80** 7.30 7.80 8.30 8.80 9.30

Legend   1: Extremely Poor   10: Extremely Good

The consultant was now able to provide the general manager with survey results and to make the following recommendations:

1. Implement a management training program emphasizing communication skills, leadership, motivation, and other human relations techniques;

2. Reevaluate the hotel's compensation program, including reacquainting employees with their benefits package, clarifying the method of granting pay increases, and evaluating new benefits.

EVALUATING THE HUMAN RESOURCE MANAGEMENT FUNCTION

The success of any organization depends not only on planning, but also on the continuous evaluation of progress toward meeting objectives. For an entire organization, evaluation consists of profitability ratios, sales increases, market penetration, and a host of other factors. For individual units, including the human resource department, evaluation may be more difficult. While some of the perceived obstacles to evaluating the effectiveness of HR departments are outlined in Figure 17-8, human resource professionals need to develop measures that convince senior managers of the value of HRM.[10]

FIGURE 17-8
Perceived Obstacles to Evaluating the
Effectiveness of HR Departments

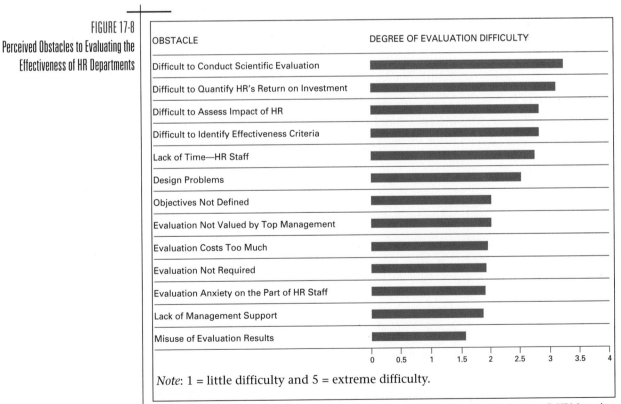

Note: 1 = little difficulty and 5 = extreme difficulty.

Source: Margaret E. Cashman and James C. McElroy, "Evaluating the HR Section," *HRMagazine*, 36 (January 1991), p. 73. Reprinted with permission from *HRMagazine*, published by the Society for Human Resource Management, Alexandria, VA.

How should management evaluate the human resource management function? Are there particular measures or indicators that reveal how well this function is performing? Two methods may be used to evaluate human resource management activities: checklists and quantitative measures.

The checklist approach poses a number of "yes or no" questions. This method ensures that important activities have been recognized and performed. The checklist is an evaluation of HR activities and the extent to which they are being done. Some typical human resource checklist questions are shown in Figure 17-9. The more *yes* answers there are, the better the evaluation; *no* answers indicate areas or activities where follow-up or additional work is needed to increase HRM's effectiveness.

The second, quantitative, method for evaluating the HRM function relies on the accumulation of various types of numerical data and the calculation of certain ratios. Numerical data are useful primarily as an indicator of activity levels and trends. Ratios show results that are not only important in themselves but reveal (when maintained over a period of time) trends that may be even more significant.

In some instances, quantitative measures may be used for external comparisons with other organizations. Since very few performance standards exist for the HRM function, however, external comparisons should always be interpreted with care. For example, the area in which external comparative data are most readily obtainable is employee turnover. While it may be tempting to evaluate an organization's turnover in terms of *industry average* or work force size, these comparisons may be meaningless. There are too many variables that can affect a specific organization's turnover, such as the nature of the local labour market, the number of long-service employees, the ability to pay competitive rates, and reputation as an employer.

In short, although quantitative data may be useful for external comparisons with similar companies, they are probably most helpful in establishing internal baselines (frames of reference) and for showing movement away from those baselines.[11] Some examples of quantitative measures for human resource management are listed in Figure 17-10.

FIGURE 17-9
Typical Human Resource Checklist
Questions

- Are all legally mandated reports submitted to requiring agencies on time?
- Have formalized procedures and methods been developed for conducting job analysis?
- Are human resource requirements forecasts made at least annually?
- Is the recruiting process effectively integrated with human resource planning?
- Does the application form conform to applicable employment equity standards?
- Are all employees appraised at least annually?
- Are skills inventories maintained on all employees?
- Are career opportunities communicated clearly to all employees?

FIGURE 17-10
Examples of Quantitative Human
Resource Management Measures

- Lost-time accident rate and trend
- Workers' compensation rate rebate level
- Grievance rates
- Grievance to arbitration ratio
- Number of suggestions submitted per employee
- Absenteeism rate and trend
- Savings/productivity increases realized through training
- Requirements forecast compared to actual human resource needs
- Availability forecast compared to actual availability of human resources
- Average recruiting cost per applicant
- Average recruiting cost per employee hired
- Percentage of positions filled internally
- Average testing cost per applicant
- Percentage of required appraisals actually completed
- Percentage of employees rated in highest performance category
- Percentage of appraisals appealed
- Turnover percentage
- Employee retention percentage
- Percentage of new hires lost during probation
- Employment equity audit results

TECHNOLOGY AFFECTING HUMAN RESOURCE MANAGEMENT[12]

Technological advances in computer hardware and software can improve human resource management and raise employee productivity. Managers must be aware of these innovations and their potential. Prior to 1980, significant technological changes occurred every three to five years. Today, major developments are delivered every 12 to 18 months and computer systems are now considered evolutionary as opposed to capital resources. Employees are exposed to changing systems more often and must learn how to operate new systems continually[13] in order to remain competitive.[14]

Application and Communication Hardware and Software

The software that most directly affects human resource management includes data communication, word processing, computer graphics, spreadsheet programs, decision support systems, database management, and human resource information systems.

DATA COMMUNICATION

Increasingly important in the business world, sending computer data over some form of communication medium, such as phone lines, is referred to as **data communication.** Caterpillar, Inc., for example, a firm that owns its own communications satellite, places a heavy emphasis on advanced data communication to better serve a global market.[15] Human resource managers, too, can transmit documents or messages over phone lines, eliminating wasted time and potential misunderstandings. As an example, prior to a teleconference it is often useful to send background material by electronic mail so that participants can become familiar with the agenda before the conference begins.

Electronic mail users have the capability to schedule a meeting for an entire work group, automatically sending messages to meeting attendees. Cellular radio is another important communications medium for mobile voice and data communications.

WORD PROCESSING

The familiar computer application that permits an operator to create and edit written material is referred to as **word processing**, a process that allows simplified editing of manuscripts and correspondence. Combined with computer graphics and perhaps page make-up programs, these technologies allow human resource managers to develop sensitive documents (such as work force reduction plans or performance appraisal reports) themselves, thus reducing the risking of breaching security.

SPREADSHEET PROGRAMS

Spreadsheet programs provide a column-row matrix on which numbers or words can be entered, stored, and used for calculations. Predefined statistical, financial, and mathematical functions allow the user to quickly and easily answer *what if* questions. Spreadsheet analysis is particularly beneficial in activities such as human resource planning.

DECISION SUPPORT SYSTEMS

HR professionals are frequently required to produce urgently needed information. To make this task easier, an HR manager can design a **decision support system (DSS)**, an information system that allows users to process and to retrieve information quickly. A DSS is a database system capable of retrieving, displaying, and processing a wide variety of information. Graphics, simulation, modelling, and quantitative analysis are also available through the DSS.

DATABASE MANAGEMENT

Information subsystems are often developed for accounting, office management, manufacturing, marketing, and human resource departments. Sometimes these subsystems are operated as distinct units, resulting in data overlap. For example, the accounting subsystem would contain the names and Social Insurance Numbers of all employees—so would the human resource files. The purpose of **database management** is to integrate information subsystems to reduce duplication of information, effort, and cost, while providing controlled access. This viewpoint is supported by Henk Van Tuyl, president of TLine Software in Hamilton:

> Proper database management requires that managers continually research and implement integration strategies. Hardware technologies and software

capabilities, available today, allow for a wide variety of cross-platform, relational database integration. This results in a vast reduction in data redundancy. The secret is to plan the Human Resource subsystem with all related systems prior to implementing any new or integrating any revised segments.[16]

Human Resources Information Systems

According to Gerson Safran, a London, Ontario-based HR consultant, human resources information systems (HRIS) that interact with payroll systems and can pass data to spreadsheets for *what if* analyses are being adopted by organizations in all economic sectors. An HRIS can best be described as a database containing HR information with facilities for maintenance and data access.

One such HRIS INFO-HR, which tracks time and attendance (or absenteeism) by employee, by reason, by day and date, by shift, and by calendar period, also includes a Health and Safety/Workers' Compensation module for tracking incidents, injuries, and claims, plus a benefits module for tracking incidents, injuries, and claims. As well, there is a benefits module that controls employee entitlement for vacations, sick days, and safety shoes.

Another key factor is the monitoring of training programs and the ability to compare job requirements with the inventory of available employee skills. Seniority lists, emergency contacts, dependents by age (for insurance purposes), salary and performance reviews, and outstanding grievances are just a few of the other reports that can be generated. An HRIS also communicates to word processors to prepare tailored employee letters that include HR-based information. In general, an HRIS decreases the need for many of the paper files maintained by HR departments and other areas. Information is also available under predefined security conditions to HR personnel and others, providing HR personnel, management, and outside agencies (government, trade associations) with reports and tools to keep their critical information updated. As most HRIS systems can operate on a desktop PC, there is usually no need to invest in new computer hardware.[17]

Teleconferencing

Partly because of the time and money involved in business travel, teleconferencing is becoming increasingly popular. **Teleconferencing** is a method of conducting or participating in multiparty discussions by telephone or videophone. These systems allow human resource managers to resolve many problems without ever meeting in person with other parties.

Northern Telecom's VISIT™ technology is a desktop multimedia system that integrates desktop video conferencing, high-speed data transfer, electronic voice mail access, and voice call management on a desktop computer. VISIT™ technology also provides screen sharing, with which both parties can make simultaneous annotations to any information on the screen while being visible to the other party on a three inch by three inch screen.[18] Neill and Gunter Limited, an international consulting and design engineering firm, uses the VISIT™ technology to operate as a single virtual office with both clients and staff, even though they are located in different geographical areas. "Any engineer or technician in any one of our offices can have immediate access to the most knowledgeable person dealing with a particular problem as if the person were in his or her own office." This ability allows Neill and Gunter to spread the workload much more efficiently than in the past.

On a recent project, the engineer who was responsible for the design was located in the Fredericton office, whereas the technician who was doing the field work and actually producing the drawings was located in the Dartmouth, Nova Scotia office, with all of the information being transferred back and forth by VISIT™. In another case, a new associate process engineer was hired who happened to live in Port Hawkesbury, Nova Scotia and wished, if possible, to remain there. He has now set up a VISIT™ terminal in his home and communicates with the offices and with clients via this medium. His only on-site requirements are to attend project meetings in person.[19]

Voice Mail

Voice mail records spoken messages electronically and stores them for retrieval at a later time. When a voice mail system is used, an individual gains access to his or her account by dialing a special telephone number and then providing a password and user-identification number. Voice mail is useful when human resource managers are dealing with confidential matters, as information can be transmitted and stored without leaving a paper copy.

Expert Systems

An **expert system** is a software package that contains knowledge about a narrowly defined, complex area and a problem-solving model meant to simulate how an expert in the field would respond to questions.[20] HR professionals can use these systems as if they were consultants. In some cases, management may rely upon the specialized knowledge of one or more individuals, captured in an expert system.[21] This captured expertise may then be used for training, or data may be disseminated throughout the organization for general use. Typical expert systems in the HRM area contain data associated with employee performance evaluation, education scheduling, and employee benefits.

Multimedia

Multimedia is a term that refers to a computer application combining automation, stereo sound, full-motion video, and graphics. Users are often drawn immediately to these presentations, which makes multimedia very useful in sales presentations and in training and development. Lotus Development Corporation, for example, has introduced a multimedia version of 1-2-3 that placed all of its program documentation on disk, including interactive instructional movies.[22] American Airlines uses a multimedia system to train thousands of employees annually. Human resource managers can also use this technology to enhance personnel databases. The manager could, for example, access an employee's photograph, voice, and year-end appraisals right from the on-screen personnel file.[23]

Information Utilities/On-Line Services

Commercial communications systems offer the human resource manager a wide range of research tools. Popular information utilities, such as CompuServe Information Service, Prodigy, and Netscape, provide a gateway to business demographics data, census data, and government publications.[24] Another resource is the Internet, a global network used by an estimated 20 to 25 million users. Human resource managers can use services that include video clips of company facilities or a welcoming message from the chairman. Additional information can be made available regarding product lines, sites, and local lifestyles.[25] Online Career Center, a nonprofit operation listing 10 000 to 12 000 jobs, is one of the most visited locations on the Internet, receiving about two million accesses per month.[26]

Virtual HR

Today's human resource managers are faced with the need to cut administrative costs while administering increasingly complex benefits and training programs. Many companies are using technology, in the form of kiosks and interactive telephone systems, to give employees direct access to human resource information systems and to perform routine tasks. One company has replaced the lobby receptionist with a multimedia kiosk. The kiosk greets visitors and provides such information as lab and employment data, safety requirements, and a company organization chart. If a visitor is advised to see the safety coordinator, for example, the coordinator's picture is displayed along with directions to the appropriate office. If he or she is unavailable, the visitor is provided with a personnel chart to find another person in the same department.[27] A survey of 157 companies confirmed the trend toward the use of "virtual HR" processes

> . . . ranging from voice-response phone systems to interactive, multimedia personal computers. The goal: to bring employees into direct contact with their organization's HR systems. Through the new systems, many HR tasks can be accomplished without the HR staffers' direct involvement. Popular uses include employee-benefit enrollment, updating employee data, savings-plan modeling and transactions, evaluations and training.[28]

Client/Server System

Client/server systems combine the strengths of various types of computers to deliver computer applications and data at reduced costs with greater reliability. These systems use networked personal computers (*clients*) and minicomputers or mainframe computers (the *server*).[29] At Eli Lilly and Company, for example, the payroll for 15 000 employees and 8000 retirees is administered on a client/server system.[30]

Groupware

Groupware is a term for software that enables people to work together in groups by assisting in decision making, work flow, and work management.

Decision-making groupware provides a structure for discussing, analyzing, and problem solving using sophisticated applications of group theory and group dynamics. Activities that can be supported include brainstorming, voting, evaluating alternatives, and formulating policy. Work flow groupware assists in managing documents, processes, and information flows throughout an organization. This software enables users to set up routing systems and to establish action and response rules with triggers that will release when particular events occur. For example, a system might be set up to monitor on-time delivery rates. In on-time deliveries fell below a predetermined percentage (say 98%), a message might flash on the supervisor's computer screen (the trigger), necessitating an immediate meeting with the manager and/or employee quality circle (action/response). Work-management groupware assists individuals and teams in communicating (even to the extent of screening out junk e-mail), scheduling meetings, and managing tasks.[31]

S UMMARY

Human resource research is aimed at meeting personal and organizational goals. Human resource research should be systematic, the specific applications depending to a large extent on a firm's particular needs. From time to time, all aspects of the HRM functions have research needs.

To a large extent, the type of problem confronting the HR manager determines the method of enquiry used. When called on to uncover the underlying reasons for a particular occurrence, the HR manager can use the case study method. Survey research is used to determine employee attitudes, while enquiry methods that involve the manipulation of certain variables while others are held constant are referred to as experiments.

There are seven steps in the research process: 1) problem recognition; 2) describing the problem; 3) choosing the method of enquiry; 4) selecting and using appropriate research tools; 5) interpreting the results; 6) taking action; and 7) evaluation.

Many quantitative tools are available, including correlation analysis, the purpose of which is to measure the degree of association between two or more variables; regression analysis, used to determine the relationship between two or more variables so that one variable can be predicted from the others; and time series analysis, which permits projections to be made.

Two methods may be used to evaluate human resource management activities: checklists and quantitative measures. The checklist approach poses a number of questions that can be answered with a *yes* or a *no*. This method is concerned with whether important activities have been recognized and, if so, whether they are being performed. The quantitative method relies on accumulating numerical data and calculating various ratios, which can be compared with data from other organizations or with a baseline.

Technological advances in computer hardware and software can improve human resource management and raise employee productivity. Sending computer data over some form of communication medium, such as a phone line, is referred to as data communication. A computer application that permits the creation and editing of written material is called word processing, which often includes the ability to produce various kinds of graphs and charts. Spreadsheet programs provide a column-row matrix on which numbers or words can be entered, stored, and used for calculations. A decision support system (DSS) is an information system that allows users to process and retrieve information, while database management is the integration of information subsystems in order to reduce the duplication of information and to provide controlled access. HRIS enables HR professionals and other individuals to manipulate a wide variety of data concerned with the human resource. Teleconferencing is a method of conducting or participating in multiparty discussions by telephone or videophone. Voice mail records spoken messages electronically and stores them for retrieval at a later time. An expert system is a software package that presents knowledge about a narrowly defined, complex area.

Multimedia is a computer application that produces presentations combining automation, stereo sound, full-motion video, and graphics. Today's human resource managers are faced with the need to cut administrative costs while administering increasingly complex benefits and training programs. Many companies are using technology, in the form of kiosks and interactive telephone systems, to give employees direct access to human resource systems that perform routine tasks. Groupware is the name for software that enables people to work together in groups, assisting them in decision making, work flow, and work management.

TERMS FOR REVIEW

Human resources research
Case study
Survey feedback method
Sampling
Experiment
Correlation analysis
Regression analysis
Time series analysis
Data communication

Word processing
Decision support system (DSS)
Database management
Teleconferencing
Expert system
Multimedia
Client/server systems
Groupware

QUESTIONS FOR REVIEW

1. Describe the general methods of enquiry available for use by the human resource researcher.
2. Why would the experiment rarely be used as a means of enquiry in human resource management?
3. Why has management begun to realize that organizations can benefit from effective human resource research?
4. Briefly define each of the following quantitative tools as they may be used in human resources:

a) correlation analysis; b) regression analysis; c) time series analysis.
5. Explain how the human resource management function may be evaluated.
6. Identify and define technological advances affecting human resource management.
7. What is an HRIS? How can these systems be used to help manage an organization?

HRM INCIDENT 1

• BEST NOT TO KNOW

Jim Coulter is president of Coulter J.M. Real Estate, Ltd. a real estate and property management company in Kingston, Ont. The company has about 100 employees and in 1994, managed $250 million in assets. Jim has managed the company since the mid-1960s. He became the principal owner in 1987, when he put together a group of investors to convert the company into an integrated real estate and property management organization. Jim has always taken pride in knowing every employee by name, both before and after the integration. He often remarked that his company was *just one big, happy family*.

By 1994, however, Jim sensed growing dissatisfaction. Turnover increased and his employees didn't seem content anymore. When Jim mentioned this to his office manager, Jeffery Wilson, Jeffery agreed that there had been a change. "I don't know what has caused it," said Jeffery, "but I do know that things are getting worse." Jeffery suggested a professionally conducted attitude survey to identify the problem. Jim agreed, and the survey was conducted with the assistance of a professor from Queen's

University. Employees were encouraged to give honest answers and given the usual assurances of anonymity. They were told that the company management would receive only generalized summaries of the survey results.

Jim was shocked by the results. It was evident that a large number of his people were dissatisfied with various aspects of their jobs. Some felt the pay was too low. Others felt that supervision was inadequate or arbitrary. Many objected to harsh working conditions. A few even mentioned the "high and mighty" attitude of the "big boss." Jim told Jeffery, "I cannot believe that the people I trusted could be so unappreciative of the jobs Coulter J.M. Real Estate has provided them over the years."

He called in his vice-presidents, three of whom were co-owners, to discuss the results of the survey. After describing the survey results, he remarked, "We've always provided good jobs for our people and respected their rights. But if I knew who the strongest dissenters were, I don't think we would want them around. If they aren't happy with this company, they can leave."

QUESTIONS

1. If you were one of the vice-presidents, how would you handle the situation?
2. Discuss Jim's attitude concerning the survey results.

HRM INCIDENT 2

• SO WHAT'S THE PROBLEM?

Isabelle Arsenault is plant manager for Hall Manufacturing Company in Charlottetown, PEI, a company that produces a line of relatively inexpensive painted wood furniture. Six months ago, Isabelle became concerned about the turnover rate in the painting department. Manufacturing plant turnover rates in the Maritimes generally averaged about 30 percent, and this was the case at Hall. The painting department, however, had had a turnover of nearly 200 percent in each of the last two years. Because of the limited number of skilled workers in the area, Hall had an extensive training program for new painters, and Isabelle knew that the high turnover rate was very costly.

Isabelle conducted exit interviews with many of the departing painters. Some of them said that they were leaving for more money, others mentioned better benefits, and most cited some kind of *personal reasons* for quitting. Isabelle checked and found that Hall's wages and benefits were competitive with, if not better than, those of other employers in the area. Then she called in Nelson Able, the painting supervisor, to discuss the problem. Nelson's response was, "You know how this younger generation is. They work to get enough money to live on for a few weeks and then go on unemployment insurance. I don't worry about it. Our old-timers can take up the slack."

"But Nelson," Isabelle replied, "we have to worry about the turnover rates. It's really costing the company a lot of money. I'm going to ask Jack Gallant in the HR department to administer a survey to get to the bottom of this." Nelson replied, "Do whatever you think is right. I don't see any problem."

QUESTIONS

1. Do you agree that a survey of employees is the best way to identify the problem? Explain.

2. If you determine that a survey is needed, what kind of survey would you conduct and how would you analyze the results?

DEVELOPING HRM SKILLS: AN EXPERIENTIAL EXERCISE

After studying this textbook, students should have a much better appreciation of the human resource manager's job. In this exercise, participants will attempt to develop a profile of the attributes a human resource manager should possess. Knowledge gained throughout the course should be used in identifying necessary attributes.

Participants will have a copy of Exhibits 1, 2, and 3. The attributes listed in Exhibit 1 may be more or less important for a human resource manager. Each participant should put this list into an order by assigning the letter *A* to the five attributes that he or she considers most important for a human resource manager, the letter *B* to the five next most important attributes, and so on. Definitions of each of these attributes are listed in Exhibit 2. Ten minutes will be given for this activity.

After doing an individual ranking, all but six students will be placed into either Group 1 or Group 2. The remaining six will make up the Review Committee, which will sit together and reach a consensus on the attribute rankings. Groups 1 and 2 will review the individual rankings of each

of its members, discuss them, and then agree on a group ranking for the attributes listed. Exhibit 3, a Group Summary Sheet, is provided for this purpose. Fifteen minutes will be available for this activity.

After this exercise is completed, the debriefing will begin with Groups 1 and 2 answering the questions "What are the top five qualities needed by human resource professionals? Why?"

Then, members of the Review Committee will answer the questions "Which group identified the most appropriate top five qualities needed by human resource professionals? Why?"

Next, both groups will be asked, "What were the least important qualities needed by human resource professionals? Why?"

Finally, members of the Review Committee will be asked, "Which group identified most appropriately the least important qualities needed by human resource professionals? Why?"

The result of this exercise should be a realistic profile of the attributes an effective human resource manager should possess.

PART SEVEN:

CASE VII Parma Cycle Company: Looking Ahead

Edward Deal was jubilant. He had just received notification from the Nova Scotia Labour Relations Board that the union certification election at Parma Cycle's Digby, Nova Scotia plant had gone against the union. The margin was small—only 53 percent to 47 percent—but Ed considered it a significant victory. As human resource director at Digby, he had done everything within his power to prevent the plant from becoming unionized. For example, wages and benefits at Digby had started far below those at the Delta, B.C. plant. At Edward's insistence, the package had been made more competitive. His recommendations had not been approved until top management was convinced that an organizing effort was inevitable unless there was change.

With the new wage and benefits package, Parma Cycle became the highest-paying employer in the Digby area. From Ed's vantage point, morale seemed to be quite high in the plant. Jobs with Parma were highly sought after. An average day saw 20 or 30 new job applicants. In fact, the rush of job applicants had forced Edward to post a sign reading "No Jobs Available"

There were still a couple of things that concerned Edward, though. First, the election had been extremely close. Twenty-five more votes would have swung it in the union's favour. Thus, Ed felt a certain insecurity about the prospects for future organizing attempts at the plant. He knew that the company would have to live up to employee expectations in order to keep the union out. He was also concerned about the qualifications of the workers he had hired. During the recruiting process, all that Ed had been able to offer to new trainees was minimum wage. The average wage for beginning workers at Parma's Digby plant had been only $5.20 an hour. Consequently, only very young, mostly unskilled workers had applied. They had been trained to some degree, but were certainly no match for the work force at Parma's Delta plant.

Ed decided to call Jesse Heard, his old boss and the human resource director at the Delta, B.C. plant. After a friendly greeting, Ed got right to the point. "Jesse," he said, "I thought we were surely going to lose the certification vote, and I'd have been thrilled to get even a 1 percent victory margin. But, let's not kid ourselves. If we don't do a super job of keeping our workers satisfied, the union will get those extra 25 votes next time." "You're right," replied Jesse, "and even if you do, the result might be the same in the long run." "Why is that?" asked Ed. Jesse answered, "There has been a good deal of pressure by the union up here for us to recognize a bargaining unit at Digby. I don't know how long top management will have the will to resist." "You really know how to let the air out of a fella's balloon," said Ed. "I don't mean to do that," Jesse replied, "but I do think we need to take a realistic view."

"Speaking of being realistic," continued Ed, "let's face it. We started the plant in Digby to reduce labour costs, and we hired a full work force here at very low rates compared to those we are paying now. We have raised wages and we still have the same workers. The only way we can really have lower costs now is if the workers here produce more than those in B.C."

"I see what you mean," said Jesse. "I'll be down for a visit in a couple of months. I don't know if I can help in any way, but we can sure talk about it."

A few weeks later Ed decided that it was time to find out a little more about his work force. He called Hermann Schwind, a professor of human resources at St. Mary's University, and asked him to recommend a research design. "Professor Schwind," said Ed, "I am not as concerned about keeping the union out as I am about treating our people fairly and maintaining a high level of motivation. I want to know what their attitudes and concerns are so that we can design the human resource program around that." "I'll think about that," said Dr. Schwind, "and be back in touch with you within a day or two."

QUESTIONS

1. What kind of study should Professor Schwind recommend? Explain.

2. What are the trends in human resources that Ed should consider when designing or redesigning the human resource program at Digby?

PART SEVEN:

CBC ◉ VIDEO CASE Employment Equity: Good or Bad?

Today's workplace is taking on a new look as employment equity and federal and provincial laws require private and public sector employers to review the way they hire new employees.

This issue is as controversial as pay equity was in the 1980s and managers are facing a host of new problems: who to hire; how much it will cost; whether visible minorities or women can be dismissed without the threat of discrimination accusations; and whether a backlash will result if certain non-minority employees perceive themselves as victims of reverse discrimination.

Yet there is a growing feeling that employment equity makes good business sense. By the year 2000, a large percentage of the Canadian work force will be comprised of minorities. Employment equity is not about quotas or reverse discrimination; it is about treating everyone fairly.

Visible minorities and people with disabilities tend to be underrepresented in the workplace. These minority groups and women are often confined to lower-paying jobs, and find it harder to reach management-level positions. With some exceptions, this situation arises not from deliberate policies of exclusion, but rather from traditional personnel policies. For many years, HR professionals tended to hire people who possessed the same qualities and backgrounds as themselves. Thus, if one dressed, spoke or looked differently, it was difficult to fit into the corporate culture norm. Employment equity programs are designed to address this issue by encouraging managers to hire the best and brightest, regardless of race, gender, religion, or physical ability.

Banks, which are subject to federal regulation, fall under the 1986 Federal Employment Act, which also covers Crown corporations, federally incorporated firms, and private companies with government contracts worth more than $200,000 yearly. This legislation was intended to provide help to visible minorities, women, aboriginal people, and the disabled. The Bank of Montreal, for example, promoted Ron Jamieson, a Mohawk from the Six Nations reserve near Brantford, Ontario, as its first vice-president of aboriginal banking. According to a 1991 report by the Canadian Bankers' Association, the "Big Six" chartered banks now employ 1903 aboriginal people, a figure that represents an increase of 49 percent from 1987. Women and visible minorities have also made significant gains within the banking industry. Women now make up 50.4 percent of all middle managers, compared to 39.3 percent in 1987. Visible minorities make up 14.4 percent of full-time bank employees, as opposed to 10 percent in 1987.

Even in companies that do not fall under employment equity legislation there are moves to review hiring practices. Consulting companies such as the ethnically diverse Omnibus Consulting Inc. help to review hiring practices and to promote equity. Instead of making an ethical argument for equity, Omnibus sells equity as good business: Since predictions are that only one-fifth of new employees will be white men by the year 2000, Omnibus says it is just common sense to hire the brightest and the best, whoever they are. Another business argument for accommodating diversity is that if a company's staff looks like its customers and understands their needs, it is bound to increase sales.

This said, it is important to recognize that the employment equity issue is not without critics. Many managers and employees who do not belong to minority groups resent working with rules and regulations that they feel affect them adversely. There is profound resentment among Canadians about the results of perceived preferential treatment. In fact, some people feel employment equity programs may, paradoxically, be contributing to increased hostility towards visible minorities. According to a 1993 Gallup survey, 81 percent of Canadians oppose numerical hiring goals, and 90 percent oppose the exclusionary practices used to achieve those goals. Employment equity initiatives tend to be seen as processes that treat people as members of groups rather than focusing on individual merit.

As well, quotas have tended to create "turf" disputes among the various "protected" classes. And they inevitably exacerbate racial polarization, particularly as the dominant white middle class begins to be affected. When race is used as a primary hiring criterion, the most qualified person for the job may lose out. Even worse, some say, are the legal risks if management decides to terminate an employee who is a member of a minority group. According to those who oppose employment equity, the result could be a poisoned working atmosphere that creates two classes of employees: those who owe their job to their own efforts and those who owe it to the helping hand of the state.

Nevertheless, employment equity is rapidly becoming a reality in the Canadian workplace. The challenge for HR professionals is to balance conflicting needs with care and tact.

QUESTIONS

1. How would you implement an employment equity program in your company and present it to your staff?
2. Should the company have a role model for such an important issue?
3. Is diversity training an HRM issue or a business issue?
4. Do you believe a successful diversity campaign can be measured?

Video Resource: "Omnibus," Venture 522 (January 8, 1995).

ENDNOTES

Chapter One

1. Shari Caudron, "HR Leaders Brainstorm the Profession's Future," *Personnel Journal*, 73 (August 1994): 54.

2. B. Downie and M. L. Coates, *The Changing Face of Industrial Relations and Human Resource Management* (Kingston: Industrial Relations Centre, Queen's University, 1993).

3. P. Wright, and J. J. Rudolph, (1994) "HRM Trends in the 1990s: Should Local Government Buy In?" *The International Journal of Public Sector Management*, 7(3), (1994): 27–43.

4. Shari Caudron, op cit.

5. Ibid.

6. "Your Voice," *Canadian HR Reporter* (January 16, 1995): 4.

7. Shari Caudron, op. cit.

8. Walter W. Tornow, Janis S. Houston, and Walter C. Borman, "An Evaluation of the Body-of-Knowledge," *Personnel Administrator*, 34 (June 1989): 140.

9. P. Wright, J. G. Guidry, and J. Blair, *Opportunities for Vocational Study*, (Toronto: University of Toronto Press, 1994): 179–181.

10. Aaron Bernstein, "Why America Needs Unions but not the Kind It Has Now," *Business Week* (May 23, 1994): 70.

11. Downie and Coates, op. cit.

12. Jonathan Kapstein and John Hoerr, "Volvo's Radically New Plant: The Death of the Assembly Line?" *Business Week* (August 28, 1989): 92–93.

13. Alexander B. Trowbridge, "A Management Look at Labor Relations," in *Unions in Transition* (San Francisco: ICS Press, 1988): 414.

14. Michele Morris, "15 Fast-Track Careers," *Money*, (June 1990): 122.

15. Eric G. Flamholtz, Yvonne Randle, and Sonja Sackmann, "Personnel Management: The Tenor of Today," *Personnel Journal*, 66 (June 1987): 64.

16. Elizabeth McGregor, "Emerging Careers," *Occupational Outlook Quarterly*, 34 (Fall 1990): 22.

17. Henry Eibirt, "The Development of Personnel Management in the United States," *Business History Review*, 33 (August 1969): 348–349.

18. Charlene Marmer Solomon, "Managing the HR Career of the 90's", *Personnel Journal*, 73 (June 1994): 64.

19. P.H. Fuhrman, *Business in the Canadian Environment*, 5th ed. (Scarborough: Prentice Hall Canada, 1995): 573.

20. Mike Fergus, "Employees on the Move," *HRMagazine*, 36 (May 1990): 44.

21. P. J. Dowling, R. S. Schuler, and D. E. Welch, *International Dimensions of Human Resource Management* (Belmont: Wadsworth Publishing Co.,1994): VII.

22. M.G. Duerr, (October 1986), "International Business Management: Its Four Tasks," *Conference Board Record*: 43.

23. P. J. Dowling, R. S. Schuler, and D. E. Welch, op cit., 5–6.

24. Stephanie Overman, "Is HR a Weak Link in the Global Chain?" *HRMagazine*, 38 (June, 1994): 67–68.

25. Charlene Marmer Solomon, "Managing the HR Career of the 90's," *Personnel Journal*, 73 (June 1994): 64.

26. Alan Weiss, "Seven Reasons to Examine Workplace Ethics," *HRMagazine*, 36 (March 1992): 71.

27. Bill Leonard, "Business Ethics Touch HR Issues, Survey Finds," *HR News*, 10 (June 1991): 13.

28. Patricia Buhler, "How Can We Encourage Ethical Behavior?" *Supervision*, 52 (January 1991): 3.

Chapter Two

1. D. Lozinski, "Your Voice," *Canadian HR Reporter* (January 16, 1995): 4.

2. *The Supply Manual* (Ottawa: Supply Policy Directorate, Public Works and Government Services Canada, 1994).

3. *The Charter of Rights and Freedoms: A Guide for Canadians* (Ottawa: Minister of Supply and Services Canada, 1992): 15–16.

4. Kenneth E. Goodpaster and John B. Matthews, Jr., "Can a Corporation Have a Conscience?" *Harvard Business Review*, 60, (January-February 1982): 132–41.

5. C. Dumas, *The Labour Market: Year-End Review. Perspectives on Labour and Income* (supplement), 75-001E (Ottawa: Statistics Canada, 1994) .

6. Robert J. Samuelson,"R.I.P.: The Good Corporation," *Newsweek*, 122 (July 5, 1993): 41.

7. B. Downie and M. L. Cootes, *The Changing Face of Industrial Relations and Human Resource Management* (Kingston: Industrial Relations Centre, Queen's University, 1993).

8. M. Paskell-Meade, "Power to the Oppressed," *CA Magazine* (August, 1992): 50–53.

9. Eric G. Flanholtz, Yvonne Randle, and Sonja Sackmann, "Personnel Management: The Tenor of Today," *Personnel Journal*, 66 (June 1987): 64.

10. Marilyn Joyce, "Ergonomics Will Take Center Stage During '90s and into New Century,"*Occupational Health and Safety*, 60 (January 1991): 31.

11. C. Dumas, op. cit.

12. E.B. Akyeampong and J. Winters, "International Employment Trends by Industry—A Note," in *Perspectives on Labour and Income*, 75-001E (Ottawa: Statistics Canada, 1993): 33–37.

13. F.H. Telmer, "Managing Change Key to Economic Recovery" (a speech to the 15th National Business Conference, McMaster University, Hamilton, Ontario), *Canadian Speeches*. 8(1), (1994): 58–59.

14. Sinclair E. Hugh. "Observations from the Witness Stand,"*HRMagazine*, 39 (August 1994): 176.

15. S. Bata, "Business Is More Than the Bottom Line,"*Canadian Speeches*, 8(4), (1994): 37.

16. Stephanie Overman. "Managing the Diverse Work Force,"*HRMagazine*, 36 (April 1991): 32.

17. "Managing Employee Diversity: A Productivity Issue," *Engineering Dimensions*, 14(4), (1993), 18–20.

18. "Managers Must Hit Racial Issue 'Head on,'" *Financial Post Daily*, 4 (142), (1991): 35.

19. Alice Cuneo, "Diverse by Design," in *Business Week*, (Special issue, "Reinventing America," 1992): 72.

20. Lee Gardenswartz and Anita Rowe, *Managing Diversity*, (San Diego: Business One, Irwin/Pfeiffer & Company, 1993): 57-97; Mahalingham Subbiah, "Adding a New Dimension to the Teaching of Audience Analysis: Cultural Awareness," *IEEE Transactions on Professional Communication*, 35 (March 1992); Marcus Mabry, "Pin a Label on a Manager—and Watch What Happened," *Newsweek*, 14 (May 1990): 43.

21. M.K. Foster and B. J. Orser, "A Marketing Perspective on Women in Management: An Exploratory Study," *Canadian Journal of Administrative Sciences*, 11(4), (1994): 339.

22. "More Women Are Executive VPs," *Fortune*, 128 (July 12, 1993): 16.

23. M.K. Foster and B.J. Orser, op cit.

24. C.A. McKeen, "Women in Management: Introduction," *Canadian Journal of Administrative Sciences*, 8(4), (1991): 222–223.

25. "Low-Paid, with Children," *The Economist*.

26. Dan Cordtz. "Hire Me, Hire My Family, *Finance World*, 159 (September 18, 1990): 77.

27. *Selected Characteristics of Persons With Disabilities Residing in Households*. Ottawa: Statistics Canada, (1994): 82-555.

28. Susan Goff Condon,"Hiring the Handicapped Confronts Cultural Uneasiness," *Personnel Journal*, 66 (April 1987): 68.

29. Anthony J. Buonocore, "Older and Wiser: Mature Employees and Career Guidance," *Management Review*, 81 (September 1992): 54.

30. Jaclyn Fierman, "The Contingency Workforce," *Fortune*, 129 (January 24, 1994): 30.

31. John Ross, "Effective Ways to Hire Contingent Personnel," *HRMagazine*, 36 (February 1991): 53.

32. D. Grondin, and C. Grondin, "The Export Orientation of Canadian Female Entrepreneurs in New Brunswick," *Women in Management Review*, 9(5), (1994): 20-30. See also, *The State of Small Business and Entrepreneurship in Atlantic Canada—1992*. (Moncton: ACOA, 1992): 11.

33. P. Wright, and G. D. Geroy, "Toward a Culturally-Defined Model of Research for Small Business," *Journal of Small Business and Entrepreneurship*, 7(2), (1990): 29–37.

34. C. Clayton, New Business Start-Ups and the Failure Factor. *Thunder Bay Business* (Fall, 1992).

35. "Study Profiles of Female Entrepreneurs," Financial Post. (October, 1990): 11.

36. *Women in Business: A Collective Profile*, (Montreal: Federal Business Development Bank, 1992).

37. T. Thompson, "Your Voice," *Canadian HR Reporter* (January 16, 1995): 4.

38. R. Wayne Mondy and Shane R. Premeaux, *Management: Concepts, Practices, and Skills*, 6th ed. (Boston: Allyn & Bacon, Inc., 1993): 450.

39. Stephanie Lawrence. "Voices of HR Experience,"*Personnel Journal*, 68 (April 1989): 71–72.

40. Judith H. Dobrzynski, Michael Schroeder, Gregory L. Miles, and Joseph Weber, "Taking Charge," *Business Week* (July 3, 1989): 66–71.

41. The Entrepreneurship and Small Business Office of Industry, Science and Technology, *Small Business in Canada: Competing Through Growth*. (1990). (Ottawa: Department of Supply and Services, 1990).

42. R. Chan and P. Wright, "Entering the PRC Market: A Case-Based Conceptual Framework for Small Business," Working Paper Series, (Fredericton: Faculty of Administration, University of New Brunswick, 1995).

43. P. Wright, and W. Nasierowski. "The Expatriate Family Firm and Cross-Cultural Management Training: A Conceptual Framework," *Human Resource Development Quarterly*, 5(2), (1994): 153–167.

44. S. Van Houten, "Unlocking Canada's Competitive Potential," (Speech to the Society of Management Ac-

countants of Canada, Vancouver, July 16, 1992). *Canadian Speeches*. 6(8), (1992): 50.

45. P.C. Wright, "The Personal and the Personnel Adjustments and Costs to Small Business Entering the International Marketplace," *Journal of Small Business Management*, 31(1), (1993): 83–93.

46. R. Chan and P. Wright, op. cit.

47. P.J. Dowling, R. S. Schuler, and D. Welch, *International Dimensions of Human Resource Management*. (Belmont: Wadsworth Publishing Co., 1994).

Chapter Three

1. R. Wayne Mondy, Robert M. Noe, and Robert E. Edwards, "What the Staffing Function Entails," *Personnel*, 63 (April 1986): 1–55.

2. James P. Clifford, "Job Analysis: Why Do It, and How Should It Be Done?," *Public Personnel Management*, 23 (Summer 1994): 324.

3. R.C. Page, and D.M. VanDeVoort, (1989), "Job Analysis and HR Planning," in W.F. Cascio, Ed., *Human Resource Planning Employment and Placement* (Washington: The Bureau of National Affairs, Inc., 1989): 2-34–2-72.

4. P. Thériault, *Personal Communication,* March 21, 1995.

5. Ronald A. Ash and Edward L. Levine, "A Framework for Evaluating Job Analysis Methods," *Personnel*, 57 (November–December 1980): 53-54.

6. Felix M. Lopez, Gerald A. Kesselman, and Felix E. Lopez, "An Empirical Test of a Trait-Oriented Job Analysis Technique," *Personnel Psychology*, 35 (August 1981): 480.

7. Ernest J. McCormick, "Job Information: Its Development and Application," in Dale Yoder and Herbert S. Heneman (Eds.), *Staffing Policies and Strategies*, (Washington, D.C.: The Bureau of National Affairs, 1979): 54-58.

8. Howard C. Olson, Sidney A. Fine, David C. Myers, and Margarette C. Jennings, "The Use of Functional Job Analysis in Establishing Performance Standards for Heavy Equipment Operators," *Personnel Psychology*, 34 (Summer 1981): 351.

9. Donald L. Caruth, Robert M. Noe III, and R. Wayne Mondy, *Staffing the Contemporary Organization*, (New York: Praeger Publishers, 1990): 100.

10. W. W. Tornow and P. R. Pinto, "The Development of Management Job Taxonomy: A System for Describing, Classifying and Evaluating Executive Positions," *Journal of Applied Psychology*, 11 (1976): 41-418.

11. Information for this section was furnished by First Interstate Bancorp.

12. Kaye L. Aho, "Understanding the New Job-Analysis Technology," *Personnel*, 66 (January 1989): 38.

13. Donald C. Busi, "The Job Description: More Than Bureaucratic Control," *Supervisory Management*, 35 (October 1990): 5.

14. Hubert S. Field and Robert D. Gatewood, "Matching Talent with the Task: To Find the Right People, First Define the Jobs You Want Them to Do," *Personnel Administrator*, 32 (April 1987): 113.

15. The following section has been adapted from: *National Occupational Classification*, (Ottawa: Canada Communication Group, 1993).

16. *How To Do Pay Equity Job Comparisons* (Toronto: The Pay Equity Commission, 1989): 5.

17. *Pay Equity in Small Workplaces* (Toronto: The Pay Equity Commission, 1990): 8.

18. Zachary Schiller, "A Nervous P&G Picks Up The Cost-Cutting Ax,"*Business Week*, (April 19, 1993): 28.

19. Michael Hammer and James Champy, *Reengineering the Corporation: A Manifesto for Business Revolution* (New York: Harper Collins Publishers, Inc., 1993): 32.

20. G.E. Harvey, "Empowered Customers are Changing Business Ways" (Speech to the Empire Club, Toronto, November 19, 1993), *Canadian Speeches*. 6(9), 58.

21. "The Malapropian 'R' Word," *Industry Forum*, American Management Association (September 1993): 1.

22. Otis Port, John Carey, Kevin Kelly, and Stephanie Anderson, "Quality: Small and Midsize Companies Seize the Challenge—Not a Moment Too Soon," *Business Week*, (November 13, 1992): 72.

23. "The Malapropian 'R' Word," op cit.

24. "Multimedia Helps Ford with Safety, *Globe and Mail* (May 25, 1994): C3.

25. Frederick Herzberg, "One More Time: How Do You Motivate Employees?" *Harvard Business Review*, 65 (September–October1987): 109–120.

26. Stephen L. Perlman, "Employees Redesign Their Jobs," *Personnel Journal*, 69 (November 1990): 37-40.

27. Wayne F. Cascio and Manuel G. Serapio, Jr., "Human Resources Systems in an International Alliance: The Undoing of a Done Deal?" *Organizational Dynamics*, 19 (Winter 1991): 68–69.

28. Ibid.

29. Thomas A. Mahoney and John R. Deckop, "Y'Gotta Believe: Lessons from American vs. Japanese-run U.S. Factories," *Organizational Dynamics* (Spring, 1993): 27-38.

30. Ibid.

31. Robin Yale Bergstrom, "NUMMI: Engineering the Process," *Production*, (June, 1993): 58-60.

Chapter Four

1. R. Wayne Mondy, Robert M. Noe, and Robert E. Edwards, "What the Staffing Function Entails," *Personnel*, 63 (April 1986): 55–56.

[2.] David M. Schweiger, Ernst N. Csiszar, and Nancy K. Napier, "Implementing International Mergers and Acquisitions," *Human Resource Planning* (December 1993): 53–70.

[3.] Paul A. Evans, "Management Development As Glue Technology," *Human Resources Planning* (December 1992): 85–106.

[4.] R. Wayne Mondy and Shane R. Premeaux, *Management: Concepts, Practices, and Skills,* 6th ed. (Boston: Allyn & Bacon, 1993): 164.

[5.] Lincoln Akin Norton, "Link HR to Corporate Strategy," *Personnel Journal,* 70 (April 1991): 75.

[6.] Y.K. Shetty and Paul F. Buller, "Regaining Competitiveness Requires HR solutions," *Personnel* 67 (July 1990): 8-12.

[7.] James E. McElwain, "Succession Plans Designed to Manage Change," *HRMagazine,* 36 (February 1991): 67.

[8.] "Heirs and Races," *The Economist,* 318 (March 9, 1991): 69.

[9.] Ibid.

[10.] G.P. Walsh, "Succession Planning is No Laughing Matter," *CGA Magazine,* (August, 1994): 28.

[11.] Wayne Mondy and Harry N. Mills, "Choice Not Chance in Nurse Selection," *Supervisor Nurse,* 9 (November 1978): 35–39.

[12.] "Retrench, Rebuild, Restructure," *Canadian Business* (1993): 93–96.

[13.] Ibid., 93.

[14.] Jaclyn Fierman, "Beating the Midlife Career Crisis," *Fortune,* 128 (September 6, 1993): 53.

[15.] Louis S. Richman, "When Will the Layoffs End?" *Fortune,* 128 (September 20, 1993): 54.

[16.] "Fewer Workers, but Same Work," (1994). *This Week in Business* (February 14, 1994): F19.

[17.] N. Doherty and J. Horsted, "Helping Survivors to Stay on Board,"*People Management* (January 12, 1995), 26–31.

[18.] A. Thornhill and A. Gibbons, "'Could Do Better' is Verdict of Research,"*People Management* (January 12, 1995): 31.

[19.] Janet Bensu, "Use Your Data Base in New Ways," *HRMagazine,* 35 (March 1990): 33–34.

[20.] Timothy R. Adams, "Buying Software Without the Glitches," *HRMagazine,* 35 (January 1990): 40–42.

[21.] Timothy V. Welo,"HR Computer Study: Who Buys? What? How? and Why?" *Personnel,* 67 (February 1990): 36–94.

[22.] Harry C. Benham, R. Leon Price, and Jennifer L. Wagner, "Comparison of Structured Development Methodologies," *Information Executive,* 2 (Spring 1989): 19.

[23.] Gale Eisenstodt, "Information Power," *Forbes,* 151 (June 21, 1993): 44–45.

[24.] Ibid.

[25.] Ibid.

[26.] J. Nadler. "Double Agent," *Canadian Business Magazine.* 68(1), (1995): 38.

Chapter Five

[1.] P.H. Fuhrman, *Business in the Canadian Environment* (Scarborough, Ont.: Prentice Hall, 1995): 439.

[2.] Note that not all recruitment activity flows from the HR plan. Supervisors generate requests in reaction to unanticipated changes in demand for employees, e.g., when someone leaves unexpectedly.

[3.] Gary M. Wederspahn, "Costing Failures in Expatriate Human Resources Management," *Human Resource Planning* (December, 1992): 27–35.

[4.] "Changes on the way to cut overtime overload," (1994). *The Globe and Mail.* (October 7, 1994): B1, B5.

[5.] "Four-Day Week Receives Opposition," *The Globe and Mail.* (November 22, 1994): B7.

[6.] C. Dumas, *The Labour Market: Year-End Review: Perspectives on Labour and Income,* 75-001E (Ottawa: Statistics Canada, 1994).

[7.] Ibid.

[8.] T. Parker, "McCain Foods Appoints New CEO," *The Daily Gleaner,* (March 1, 1995): 3.

[9.] C. Foster, "Tough Guys Don't Cuss," *Canadian Business Magazine.* 66(2), (1995): 23-28.

[10.] Don McNerney, "Competitive Advantage: Diverse Customers and Stakeholders," *HR Focus,* (January 1994): 9-10.

[11.] John Templeton and David Woodruff, "The Aftershock from the Lopez Affair," *Business Week* (April 19, 1993): 31.

[12.] "Don't Put Older Workers out to Pasture." *Daily Commercial News,* 65 (122), (1992): 3.

[13.] Kenworth's Gray Revolution, *Motor Truck,* 61 (10, insert), (1992) 1–3.

[14.] P. Wright and G.D. Geroy, "Toward a Culturally-Defined Model of Research for Small Business, " Journal of Small Business and Entrepreneurship, 7(2): 29–37.

[15.] K. Jensen, personal communication. Mr. Jensen was interviewed on September 20, 1995.

[16.] G. Donald and P.C. Wright "Executive Search Firms: A Review and Analysis," (submitted for publication, 1995).

[17.] A. Dzarnecki, "Temp Services Busy Again, Developing Strategic Partner Role,"*Canadian HR Reporter* (Dec. 5, 1994): 17.

[18.] Bill Leonard, "Resume Databases to Dominate Field," *HRMagazine* 30 (April 1993): 59-60.

[19.] Richard A. Fear, *The Evaluation Interview,* 3rd ed. (New York: McGraw-Hill, 1984): 74–75.

20. Thomas L. Watkins, "What Do You Want From Us?," *Across the Board,* 30, (June 1993): 11.

21. K. Gay, (1993). "Open Houses, Job Fairs Make Recruiting Impact," *Financial Post.,* 87(45), (November 1993): 5.18.

22. Mary E. Scott, "Internships Add Value to College Recruitment," *Personnel Journal* 71 (April 1992): 25.

23. Howard S. Freedman, *How to Get a Headhunter To Call* (New York: John Wiley & Sons, 1989): 60.

24. G. MacDonald, "Recruiters Under More Pressure to Get the Right CEO," *Financial Post Daily* (February 26, 1993): 28–29.

25. Howard S. Freedman, op. cit., 56.

26. Howard S. Freedman, op cit., 57.

27. Paul DiMarchi, "The Two Faces of Search Firms," *Financial Executive,* 10 (January-February 1994): 53.

28. Albert H. McCarthy, "The Human Touch Helps Recruit Quality Workers," *Personnel Journal,* 70 (November 1991): 68.

29. "HR Agenda: Recruitment/Hiring Practices," *HRMagazine,* 37 (February 1992): 54.

30. Ibid., 60.

31. Peg Anthony, "Track Applicants, Track Costs,"*Personnel Journal,* 69 (April 1990): 75–81.

32. e.g., The New Brunswick Human Rights Act; The Individual Rights Protection Act (Alberta).

33. Gary N. Powell. "The Effects of Sex and Gender on Recruitment,"*Academy of Management Review,* 12 (October 1987): 7.

34. Harish C. Jain, "Human Rights: Issues in Employment," in H.C. Jain, C. Hem, and P. Wright, Eds., *Trends and Challenges in Human Resource Management.* (Scarborough: Nelson Canada, 1994): 79.

35. M. Falardeau-Ramsay, "Human Rights Laws Need Reinforcement (a speech to the annual conference of the Canadian Association of Statutory Human Rights Agencies, Fredericton, N.B.). *Canadian Speeches.* 8(5), (1994): 16–17.

36. Canadian Human Rights Commission, *Employment: Prohibited Grounds of Discrimination.* (Ottawa: Minister of Supply and Services, 1993).

37. *Employment Equity: A Guide for Employers* (Ottawa: Employment and Immigration Canada, 1994): 8–9. (Reproduced with permission).

38. Ibid, 9.

39. Ibid, 13.

40. P. Hartin and P. C. Wright, "Canadian Perspectives on Employment Equity," *Equal Opportunities International.* 13(6/7), (1994): 22–24.

41. Stephanie Overman, "Temporary Services Go Global," *HRMagazine* 38 (August 1993): 72.

42. For example see advertisements in *Training and Development,* 12(10), 52.

43. Stephanie Overman, op. cit.

44. Hugh Scullion, "Attracting Management Globetrotters," *Personnel Management* (January, 1992): 28–32.

Chapter Six

1. Stephen L. Guinn, "Gain Competitive Advantage Through Employment Testing," *HR Focus,* 70 (September 1993): 15.

2. Peter F. Drucker, "Getting Things Done: How to Make People Decisions," *Harvard Business Review,* 63 (July-August 1985): 22.

3. Donald D. DeCamp, "Are You Hiring the Right People?" *Management Review,* 81 (May 1992): 44.

4. Vandra L. Huber, Gregory B. Northcraft, and Margaret A. Neale, "Effects of Decision Strategy and Number of Openings on Employment Selection Decisions," *Organizational Behavior and Human Decisions Processes,* 45 (April 1990): 276.

5. G. Lemaitre, G. Picot, S. Murray, "Employment Flows and Job Tenure in Canada," *The Observer,* 5(7), (1992): 4.1-4.13.

6. L. Christofides and C. McKenna, "Employment Flows and Job Tenure in Canada," *Canadian Public Policy,* 19(2),(1993): 157.

7. J. Douglas Phillips, "The Price Tag on Turnover," *Personnel Journal,* 69 (December 1990): 58–61.

8. J. Milne, president of Taylor Enterprises, Willowdale, Ontario, personal communication, April, 11,1995.

9. "Make outplacement orderly ..." *Credit Union Way Magazine,* 44 (10), (1992): 7.

10. Edwin N. Walley, "Successful Interviewing Techniques," *The CPA Journal,* 63 (September 1993): 70.

11. Jac Fitz-enz, "Getting—and Keeping—Good Employees," *Personnel,* 67 (August 1990): 27.

12. Tom Smith, "Resume Help for the Experienced Candidate," *Planning Job Choices:,* 37th ed. (Bethlehem, PA: College Placement Council, Inc., 1994): 40–41.

13. T. Tedesco (1988), "Resumé Fraud," *The Globe and Mail* (Sept. 30, 1988): B14.

14. Ibid.

15. L. Ramsay, "Tests Help Determine Who's Right for a Job," *The Financial Post* (April 17, 1993): s18.

16. Michael P. Cronin, "Hiring: This is a Test," *Inc.* 15 (August 1993): 64.

17. Stephen L. Guinn, op cit.

18. K. Dunn, and E. Dawson "Right Person for the Job," *Occupational Health and Safety Canada,* 10(4), (1994): 28.

19. L. Ramsay, op. cit.

20. L. Friedenberg, "Testing in Business and Industry" in *Psychological Testing: Design, Analysis and Use* (Toronto: Allyn and Bacon, 1995): 421.

21. L. Brink, "A Discouraging Word Improves Your Interviews," *HRMagazine,* 37 (December 1992): 49.

22.R.M. Solomon, and S.J. Usprich, "Employment Drug Testing," *Business Quarterly* (Winter 1993), 73–78.

23.Ibid., 73.

24.M.F. Strong, "Dialogue," *Business Quarterly*, (Spring, 1994): 14.

25.R. Peterson, "Dialogue," *Business Quarterly*, (Spring, 1994): 14-15.

26."Drug Testing Challenged," *The Globe and Mail* (June 8, 1995): A2.

27.J. Stanford, "Dialogue," *Business Quarterly*, (Spring, 1994): 16.

28.T. L. Brink, op. cit.

29.L. Friedenberg, op. cit.

30.C. Copeland, remarks made at a public lecture (March 16, 1995) in Fredericton, N.B., while Mr. Copeland was Bank of Montreal Executive-in-Residence at the Faculty of Administration, University of New Brunswick.

31.*Selection Interviewing for the 1990s* (New York: DBM Publishing, A Division of Drake Beam Morin, Inc., 1993): 28.

32. D.D. DeCamp, "Are You Hiring the Right People" in H. C. Jain and P. C. Wright, Eds., *Trends and Challenges in Human Resource Management* (Scarborough: Nelson Canada, 1994): 92.

33.S. McAllister, president of Siskin Management, Inc., remarks made at a presentation to graduate students, Faculty of Administration, University of New Brunswick, March 28, 1995.

34.B. Critchley and D. Casey, "Team-building," in John Prior, Ed., *Gower Handbook of Training and Development,* 2nd ed. (Aldershot: Gower Publishing Ltd., 1994): 478–489.

35.Wiesner and Cronshaw, Journal of Occupational Psychology, 1988. WRIGHT TO PROVIDE FULL DATA.

36.L. Friedenburg, op cit., 412.

37.Philip L. Roth and Jeffrey J. McMillan, "The Behavior Description Interview," *The CPA Journal,* 63 (December 1993): 76.

38.Tom Janz, Lowell Hellervik, and David C. Gilmore, *Behavior Description Interviewing* (Newton, MA: Allyn & Bacon, Inc., 1986): 15.

39.K. Michele Kacmar, "Look at Who's Talking," *HRMagazine,* 38 (February 1993): 56.

40.R. Half, "The Art and Science of Hiring," *CGA Magazine,* 28(7), (1994): 45–48.

41.James M. Jenks and Brian L. P. Zevnik, "ABCs of Job Interviewing," *Harvard Business Review,* 67 (July-August 1989): 38–39.

42.Phillip M. Perry, "Your Most Dangerous Legal Traps When Interviewing Job Applicants," *Editor & Publisher,* 126 (February 27, 1993): 21–23.

43.John P. Wanous, "Tell It Like It Is at Realistic Job Previews," in Kendrith M. Rowland, Manual London,

Gerald R. Ferris, and Jay L. Sherman Eds., *Current Issues in Personnel Management* (Boston: Allyn & Bacon, 1980): 41–50.

44.T. L. Brink, op. cit.

45.Michael W. Mercer, "Turnover: Reducing Costs," *Personnel,* 65 (December 1988): 40–42.

46.D. Coleman and P. Irving, "A Within-Subjects Test of the Effect of Realistic Job Previews," *Crunch Time: Management Education in the 90's,* Proceedings of the 22nd Annual Atlantic Schools of Business Conference, Antigonish, Nova Scotia, 1992.

47.P. Wright, "Protect Yourself: Be Professional When Checking References," *Interim Report,* Chartered Accountants of New Brunswick, 6(2), (1994): 18–19.

48.Most employers are reference checks ...*Canadian HR Reporter,* 8(5), (1995): 14.

49.Stevan P. Payne, "A Closer Look at Hiring and Firing," *Security Management,* 33 (June 1989): 50.

50.P. Wright, "The Trainer's Case," *Compensium* (Bradford: MCB University Press, 1989).

51.Kurt W. Decker, "The Rights and Wrongs of Screening," *Security Management,* 34 (January 1990): 46.

52.Eugene Carlson, "Business of Background Checking Comes to the Fore," *Wall Street Journal* (August 31, 1993): 82.

53.Bob Smith, "The Evolution of Pinkerton," *Management Review* 82 (September 1993): 56.

54.Charlene Marmer Solomon, "Staff Selection Impacts Global Success," *Personnel Journal* 73 (January 1994): 88.

55.Ibid., 88.

56.Webb, A. and P. C. Wright, (1995), "The Expatriate Experience," submitted for publication.

57.Allen L. Hixon, "Why Corporations Make Haphazard Overseas Staffing Decisions," 91.

58.Nancy J. Adler, "Women Managers in a Global Economy," *HRMagazine,* 36 (September 1993): 52–55.

59.Ibid.

Chapter Seven

1.Owen Linstein and James Mauro, "Tom Peters . . . and the Healthy Corporation," *Psychology Today,* 26 (March/April 1993): 57.

2.C. Knight, "Unions Will Focus on Security . . ." *Canadian HR Reporter,* 8(4),(1995): 1.

3.G.L. Simpson, "Building Employee Commitment," *The Canadian Manager,* 20 (2), (1995): 24.

4.C. Furlong, "A Million Dollars Worth of Advice," *The Canadian Manager,* 21 (1995): 17.

5.Leonard Ackerman, "Whose Ox Is Being Gored?" *HRMagazine,* 36 (February 1991): 96.

6.J. Ryan, "Trillium Cable Slashes Staff," *The Barrie Examiner,* (Wednesday, June 14, 1995): 1.

7. William Fitzgerald, "Training Versus Development," *Training and Development*, 46 (May 1992): 81.

8. S. Lee, personal communication. Ms. Lee was interviewed in March, 1995.

9. "CEO: Problems Often Management's Fault," *Canadian Press*, as quoted in the *Daily Gleaner*, (April 20, 1995): 20.

10. Ibid.

11. A. Toulin, "Economy Crumbling: Report," *The Financial Post*, (October 25, 1991): 6.

12. D. McIntyre, *Training and Development, 1993: Policies, Practices, and Expenditures* (Ottawa: The Conference Board of Canada, 1994).

13. *The Globe and Mail*, (September 15, 1992): B26.

14. McIntyre, op. cit., 7.

15. M. Belcourt and P. Wright, *Managing Performance Through Training and Development* (Scarborough: Nelson, 1996).

16. McIntyre, op. cit., 6.

17. Belcourt and Wright, op. cit.

18. J. J. Phillips, "Measuring the returns on HRD," *Employment Relations Today*, 18 (1991): 329–342.

19. R.W. Pace, P.C. Smith and G.E. Mills, *Human Resource Development: The Field* (Englewood Cliffs, N.J.: Prentice Hall, 1991).

20. McIntyre, op. cit. 11–12.

21. P. Sullivan, "Nine best practices," *Executive Excellence*, 10 (1993): 3–4.

22. Belcourt and Wright, op. cit.

23. McIntyre, op. cit., 13.

24. McIntyre, op. cit., 16 .

25. Kenneth N. Wexley and Gary P. Latham, *Developing and Training Human Resources in Organizations*, 2nd ed. (New York: Harper-Collins Publishers, Inc., 1991): 36.

26. C. Knight, op. cit.

27. Kenneth M. Nowack, "A True Training Needs Analysis," *Training and Development Journal*, 45 (April 1991): 69.

28. Ibid.

29. *The Training Plan* (Toronto: Ministry of Skill Development, 1987), A-3, A-4.

30. "Training still top priority," *Plant*, 52 (5), (1993): 1.

31. Samuel Greengard, "How Technology is Advancing HR," *Personnel Journal* (September 1993): 85.

32. Ron Zemke, "Employee Orientation: A Process, Not a Program," *Training*, 26 (August 1989): 34-35.

33. Leslie Brokaw, "The Enlightened Employee Handbook," *Inc*, 13 (October 1991): 49.

34. Karen Bridges, Gail Hawkins, and Keli Elledge, "From New Recruit to Team Member," *Training and Development*, 47 (August 1993): 55–57.

35. Ron Zemke, op. cit., 34.

36. Diana Reed-Mendenhall and C. W. Millard, "Orientation: A Training and Development Tool," *Personnel Administrator*, 25 (August 1980): 42–44.

37. D. Letourneau, "Getting Off to a Safe Start," *Occupational Health and Safety Canada*, 8 (1992): 46–50.

38. P.C. Wright and M. Belcourt, "Management Development: A Career Management Perspective," *The International Journal of Career Management*, 6(5), (1994): 3–10.

39. P. Larson and R. Mimgie, *Leadership for a Changing World* Report 95-92, S (Ottawa: Conference Board of Canada, 1992).

40. Philip J. Harkins and David Giber, "Linking Business and Education Through Training," *Training and Development Journal*, 43 (October 1989): 69.

41. Paul Froiland, "Who's Getting Trained?" *Training* (October 1993): 60.

42. S. Cunningham, "Coaching Today's Executive," *Public Utilities Fortnightly*, 128 (1991): 22–25.

43. B. Whittaker, "Shaping the Competitive Organization—Managing or Coaching," *CMA Magazine*, 67 (1993): 5.

44. T. Scandura, "Mentorship and Career Mobility: An Empirical Investigation," *Journal of Organizational Behaviour*, 13 (1992): 169–174.

45. Don Barner, "What is This Thing Called Mentoring?" *National Underwriter*, 94 (May 28, 1990): 9.

46. P. Wright, "The Incident as a Technique for Teaching Undergraduates in Hospitality Management and Food Administration," *Hospitality Education and Research Journal*, 12 (1), (1988): 16–28.

47. William M. Fox, "Getting the Most from Behavior Modelling Training," *National Productivity Review*, 7 (Summer 1988): 238.

48. "Native Businesses Make Big Strides," *Financial Post Daily*, 6(45), (1993): 12.

49. "Golden handcuff . . . ,"*Ottawa Business Magazine* (January–February, 1991): 16–22.

50. Samuel Greengard, op. cit., 81.

51. "Exhaustive management . . ." (1994). *The Globe and Mail*, (June 6, 1994): B5.

52. "Computers in Training," *Training*, 28 (October 1991): 51.

53. La Tresa Pearson, "Is CD-ROM About to Bloom?" *Training*, 30 (November 1993): 5–7.

54. Samuel Greengard, op. cit., 84.

55. "Interactive Satellite Learning Improves Training Programs," *Personnel Journal*, 72 (September 1993): 86.

56. "Philips to Market Multimedia Training Software," *Canadian HR Reporter*, 8 (1995): 8.

57. Michael Emery and Margaret Schubert, "A Trainer's Guide to Videoconferencing," *Training*, 30 (June 1993): 59–61.

58. "Why IBM Believes . . ." *Marketing*, 98 (18), (1993): 8.

59.“BC Telecom Managers Get an Overhaul,” *The Globe and Mail* (July 23, 1994): B3.

60.Belcourt and Wright, op. cit.

61.“Power of the people . . .” *Food in Canada*, 52 (1), (1992): 26, 28.

62.P. Larson and R. Mimgie, op. cit., 5.

63.“Long-time Employers Benefit . . .” *Northern Ontario Business*, 11 (10), (1991): 8.

64.P. Wright, M. Belcourt, and M. Lauri, *Apprenticeship: The Canadian Dilemma* (Working Paper, 95-009), Faculty of Administration, University of New Brunswick, Fredericton, NB, 1995.

65.T. Hrynyshyn, “Siemens Chief Critical of Skilled Labour Shortage,” *Computing Canada*, 19 (1993): 1.

66.N. Riccucci, “Apprenticeship Training in the Public Sector,” *Public Personnel Management*, 20 (1991): 181–183.

67.Hrynyshyn, op. cit.

68.“Apprenticeship,” *Occupational Outlook Quarterly*, 35 (1991): 26–40.

69.J. McKenna, “The Busy Present of Jobs for the Future,” *Industry Week*, 242 (1993): 52–56.

70.B. Moskal, “Apprenticeship: Old Cure for New Labor Shortage?” *Industry Week*, 240 (1991): 30–35.

71.L. Still, “Breaking the Glass Ceiling: Another Perspective,” *Women in Management Review*, 7 (1992): 3–8.

72.“New Marine Simulator Offers Leading-Edge Ship Training,” *Atlantic Business Report*. 3 (9), (1994): 9.

73.“Atlantis Simulating Success,” *The Globe and Mail* (October 27, 1993): B5.

74.Jack Gordon, “Where the Training Goes,” *Training*, 27 (October 1990): 54–55.

75.Martin M. Broadwell, *The Supervisor as an Instructor*, 3rd ed. (Reading, Mass.: Addison-Wesley, 1978): 85.

76.B. Sebnell, “A Training Management System,” *Computerworld*, 23 (1989): 134.

77.Jack Asgar, “Give Me Relevance or Give Me Nothing,” *Training*, 27 (July 1990): 49.

78.D.L. Kirkpatrick, “Four steps to measuring training effectiveness,” *Personnel Administrator*, 28 (1983): 19–25.

79.J. Fitz-Enz, “Yes . . . You Can Weigh Training's Value,” *Training*, 7 (July, 1994): 54–58.

80.Mike Fergus, “Employees on the Move,” *HRMagazine*, 36 (May 1990): 45.

81.S. Keen, “UK Firms Must Forgo Analytical View of Culture,” *People Management* (April 16, 1995): 12.

82.Wayne F. Cascio and Manuel G. Serapio, Jr., “Human Resources Systems in an International Alliance: The Undoing of a Done Deal?” *Organizational Dynamics*, 19 (Winter 1991): 68.

83.Ibid.

84.D. McIntyre, op. cit., 6.

85.Bernard W. Anderson, “Training to Succeed,” *Black Enterprise*, 21 (April 1991): 40.

86.Wayne F. Cascio and Manuel G. Serapio, Jr., op. cit., 69.

Chapter Eight

1.Arthur Sharplin, *Strategic Management*, (New York: McGraw-Hill, 1985): 102.

2.Thomas G. Cummings and Christopher G. Worley, *Organization Development and Change*, 5th ed. (Minneapolis/St. Paul: West Publishing Company, 1993): 526.

3.Frank Petrock, “Corporate Culture Enhances Profits,” *HRMagazine*, 35 (November 1990): 64–66.

4.“It's People, Stupid,” *The Economist*, 335 (7916), (1995): 57.

5.Anthony Jay, *Management and Machiavelli* (New York: Holt, Rinehart and Winston, 1967): 231.

6.Brian Dumaine, “Creating a New Company Culture,” *Fortune*, 121 (January 15, 1990): 127.

7.R. Rogers, “The Psychological Contract of Trust,” *Executive Development*. 8(1),(1995): 15.

8.Carol J. Loomis, “The Reed That Citicorp Leans On,” *Fortune*, 128 (July 12, 1993): 90–93.

9.D. Shepherdson, *Meeting the Challenge: Managing Change in the Nineties*, Report 130-94 (Ottawa: Conference Board of Canada, 1994).

10.“Going the distance . . .” *Profit: The Magazine for Canadian Entrepreneurs*, 13 (2), (1994): 55–61.

11.“The changing nature of leadership,”*The Economist.*, 335 (7918), (1995): 57.

12.“The heavy metal bond . . .” *The Globe and Mail* (September 1, 1992): B18.

13.“Who Wants to Be a Giant,” *The Economist*. 335 (7920), (1995): 5.

14.“Pumping up the Oil Pot . . .” *The Globe and Mail* (August 25, 1992): B20.

15.N.L. Trainor, “Restructuring: Human Factor Key to Renewal,” *Canadian HR Reporter*, 8 (1995): 19.

16.Wayne F. Cascio and Manuel G. Serapio, Jr., “Human Resources Systems in an International Alliance: The Undoing of a Done Deal?” *Organizational Dynamics*, 19 (Winter 1991): 65.

17.Ibid., 68.

18.R. Chan, personal communication. Mr. Chan was interviewed in Hong Kong in November, 1994.

19.P. Wright and K. Kusmonadji, “The Strategic Application of TQM Principles to HRM,” *Training for Quality*, 1(3), (1993): 5–14.

20.Benson Rosen and Kay Lovelace, “Fitting Square Pegs into Round Holes,” *HRMagazine*, 39 (January 1994): 86–93.

21.G. Pearson, “HR is Moving up on Goal to Become Corporate Player,” *Canadian HR Reporter*, 8 (1995): 15.

22. Thomas G. Cummings and Christopher G. Worley, *Organization Development and Change*, 5th ed. (Minneapolis/St. Paul: West Publishing Company, 1993): 2.

23. Ibid., p. 2.

24. D. Shepherdson, *Meeting the Challenge: Managing Change in the Nineties* (Ottawa: The Conference Board of Canada, 1994): 11.

25. N. M. Dixon, *Organizational Learning* (Ottawa: The Conference Board of Canada, 1993): 3–4.

26. Thomas G. Cummings and Christopher G. Worley, op. cit., 136–137.

27. Ibid., 137.

28. "Managing for Results in a Competitive Market," *Profit: The Magazine for Canadian Entrepreneurs*, 10 (3), (1991): 36.

29. "The Right Stuff . . ." *Manitoba Business*, 15 (9),(1993): 28–29.

30. The material on transactional analysis in this section is abridged and adapted from Thomas A. Harris, M.D., *I'm O.K. —You're O.K.* Copyright ©1967, 1968, and 1969 by Thomas A. Harris, M.D.

31. David J. Lill and John T. Rose, "Transactional Analysis and Personal Selling: A Primer for Banks." *Journal of Commercial Bank Lending*, 70 (February 1988): 57.

32. Barbara Mandell, "Does a Better Worklife Boost Productivity?" *Personnel*, 66 (October 1989): 49.

33. Ibid., 27.

34. Ibid., 49.

35. James L. Gibson and John M. Ivancevich, *Organizations: Behavior, Structure, Processes*, 4th ed. (Plano, Texas: Business Publications, 1982), 580–581.

36. John P. Campbell and Marvin D. Dunnette, "Effectiveness of T- Group Experiences in Managerial Training and Development," *Psychological Bulletin*, 70 (August 1968): 23–104.

37. Irwin L. Goldstein, *Training in Organizations: Needs Assessment, Development, and Evaluation*, 2nd ed. (Monterey, Calif.: Brooks/Cole Publishing Company, 1986): 243.

38. "Buzzword Management: Why Excellence Programs Fail," *B.C. Business Magazine*, 22 (11), (1994): 26–37.

39. Ellis Pines, "TQM Training: A New Culture Sparks Change at Every Level," *Aviation Week and Space Technology*, 132 (May 21, 1990): S38.

40. Ellis Pines, "From Top Secret to Top Priority: The Story of TQM," *Aviation Week and Space Technology*, 132 (May 21, 1990), S24.

41. "Getting Used to It: The Team Concept . . ." *Canadian Papermaker*, 47 (6),(1994): 29-31.

42. Richard Wellins and Jill George, "The Key to Self-Directed Teams," *Training and Development Journal*, 45 (April 1991): 27.

43. Shari Caudron, "Are Self-Directed Teams Right for Your Company?" *Personnel Journal*, 72 (December 1993): 78.

44. Donna Robbins, "The Dark Side of Team Building," *Training and Development*, 47 (December 1993): 17.

45. Now Everyone Can Be a Boss . . ." *Canadian Business*, 67 (5),(1994), 48–50.

46. "How to Make a Small, Smart Factory," *The Globe and Mail* (February 2, 1993): B24.

Chapter Nine

1. G. Cassidy, personal communication, April 10, 1995.

2. D. Nye, "Writing off Older Assets," *Across the Board*, (September, 1988): 4452.

3. P.S. Taylor, "Social Studies," *Saturday Night* (June 1995): 1823.

4. Edgar Schein, "How 'Career Anchors' Hold Executives to Their Career Paths," *Personnel*, 52 (May–June 1975): 11–24.

5. Louis S. Richman, "How to Get Ahead in America," *Fortune*, 129 (May 16, 1994): 46.

6. Lewis Carroll, *Through the Looking Glass* (New York: Norton, 1971): 127.

7. William Bridges, "The End of the JOB," *Fortune*, 130 (September 19, 1994): 62.

8. C. Furlong, "Unstuck," *BC Business*. 21(7),(1993): 65.

9. "Survival Guide for the Corporate Jungle," *This Week in Business* (October 15, 1991): 13.

10. Sander I. Marcus and Jotham G. Friedland, "14 Steps on a New Career Path," *HRMagazine*, 38 (March 1993): 5556.

11. Jaclyn Fierman, "Beating the Midlife Career Crisis," *Fortune* 128 (September 6, 1993): 54.

12. "How to Refuse Promotion without Hurting Your Career," (1991), This Week in Business (October 7, 1991): 8.

13. R. Brillinger, "HR Manager's Bookshelf," *Canadian HR Reporter* 8(2), (1995): 14.

14. "There Goes the Future . . ." (1992), *Canadian Business*, 65 (10), (1992): 98–100.

15. Lewis Newman, "Career Management Starts with Goals," *Personnel Journal*, 68 (April 1989): 91.

16. C. Knight, "Economics of Simplicity," *Canadian HR Reporter*, 8(11), (1995): 1,3.

17. Milan Moravec, "A Cost-Effective Career Planning Program Requires A Strategy," *Personnel Administrator*, 27 (January 1982): 29.

18. Milan Moravec and Beverly McKee, "Designing Dual Career Paths and Compensation," *Personnel*, 67 (August 1990): 5.

19. Donald L. Caruth, Robert M. Noe III, and R. Wayne Mondy, *Staffing the Contemporary Organization* (New York: Praeger Publishers, 1990): 253–254.

20. Louis S. Richman, "How to Get Ahead in America," *Fortune,* 129 (May 14, 1994): 47.

21. Brian O'Reilly, "The New Deal: What Companies and Employees Owe One Another," *Fortune,* 129 (June 13, 1994): 44.

22. Louis S. Richman, "How to Get Ahead in America," *Fortune,* 129 (May 14, 1994): 49.

23. D. Luckow, "Moving up by Moving Sideways," *Financial Times of Canada* (April 10-16, 1993): 12, 19.

24. Jaclyn Fierman, "Beating the Midlife Career Crisis," *Fortune,* 128 (September 6, 1993): 54.

25. Ibid.

26. Ibid.

27. Ibid, 58.

28. Donald L. Caruth, Robert M. Noe III, and R. Wayne Mondy, *Staffing the Contemporary Organization,* (New York: Praeger Publishers, 1990): 42.

29. "A Club of Their Own . . ."*Marketing,* 98 (46), (1993): 48.

30. "Career Path Standards Established by DPMA," 17 (26), (1991): 4.

31. Susan Sonnesyn Brooks, "Moving Up is Not the Only Option," *HRMagazine,* 39 (March 1994): 79.

32. Zandby B. Leibowitz and Sherry H. Mosley, "Career Development Works Overtime at Corning, Inc.," *Personnel,* 67 (April 1990): 38.

33. "Your Decisions Stink," *BC Business Magazine,* 19 (11), (1991): 14.

34. Loretta D. Foxman and Walter L. Polsky, "Aid in Employee Career Development," *Personnel Journal,* 69 (January 1990): 22.

35. Daniel B. Moskowitz, "How to Cut It Overseas," *International Business* (October, 1992): 76, 78.

36. Ibid.

37. Mark E. Mendenhall and Gary Oddon, "The Overseas Assignment: A Practical Look," *Business Horizons,* 31 (September/October 1988): 78–79.

Chapter 10

1. "The Team Building Tool Kit," *Compensation and Benefits Review,* 26 (March/April 1994): 67.

2. G.D. Graham, "Why Business Workers and Governments Must All Be Competitive," *Canadian Speeches,* 9(2), (1995): 32–36.

3. "Just Desserts," (1994). The Economist, 330(7848), (January 29, 1994): 71.

4. R. Wayne Mondy, Robert M. Noe III, and Robert E. Edwards, "What the Staffing Function Entails," *Personnel,* 63 (April 1986): 55.

5. Clive Fletcher, "Appraisal: An Idea Whose Time Has Gone?" *Personnel Management,* 25 (September 1993): 34.

6. Kenneth P. Carson, Robert L. Cardy, and Gregory H. Dobbins, "Upgrade the Employee Evaluation Process," *HRMagazine,* 37 (November 1992): 88.

7. L. Fowlie, "Now Computers Can Help You Write Employee Appraisals," The Financial Post, 88 (21), (May 21, 1994): S24.

8. Robert C. Joines, Steve Quisenberry, and Gary W. Sawyer, "Business Strategy Drives Three-Pronged Assessment System," *HRMagazine,* 38 (December 1993): 68–70.

9. Robert J. Sahl, "Design Effective Performance Appraisals," *Personnel Journal,* 69 (October 1990): 60.

10. K. Gay, "Competency Pay Is an Idea That Has Merit," The Financial Post. 88(5), (January 29, 1994): S.37.

11. G. Anderson, "From Performance Appraisal to Performance Management," *Training and Development* (October, 1993): 10–14.

12. A legal term that means there was sufficient legally admissible evidence to take the action.

13. P. Allan, P. (1991). *Avoiding Common Pitfalls in Performance Appraisal,*Working Paper 100 (Lubin Schools of Business, Pace University, 1991).

14. Some PA systems are designed to allow for direct input from employees before the document becomes part of an official file.

15. "The Team Building Tool Kit," op. cit. 68.

16. Mathew Budman and Berkeley Rice, "The Rating Game," *Across the Board,* 31 (February 1994): 34–38.

17. "How Johnsonville Shares Profits on the Basis of Performance," *Harvard Business Review,* 68 (November-December 1990): 74.

18. James G. Goodale, "Seven Ways to Improve Performance Appraisals," *HRMagazine,* 38 (May 1993): 80.

19. Mathew Budman and Berkeley Rice, op. cit., 35.

20. Because the system depicted makes liberal use of personal factors that may not be job related, it has been described by one reviewer as "a good example of a poor method."

21. J. Peter Graves, "Let's Put Appraisal Back in Performance Appraisal: Part I," *Personnel Journal,* 61 (November 1982): 848–849.

22. Stephen J. Carroll and Craig E. Schneier, *Performance Appraisal and Review Systems: The Identification, Measurement, and Development of Performance in Organizations* (Glenview, Ill.: Scott, Foresman, 1982): 117.

23. Jay T. Knippen, "Boost Performance Through Appraisals," *Business Credit,* 92 (November-December 1990): 27.

24. P. Sharmon, "How to Implement Performance Measurement in Your Organization," *CMA Magazine,* 64(4), (May, 1995): 33-7.

25. Barbara H. Holmes, "The Lenient Evaluator is Hurting Your Organization," *HRMagazine,* 38 (June 1993): 75–76.

26. Portions of this section were adapted from Ronald G. Wells, "Guidelines for Effective and Defensible Performance Appraisal Systems," *Personnel Journal*, 61 (October 1982): 776–782.

27. Larry L. Axline, "Ethical Considerations of Performance Appraisals," *Management Review* 83 (March 1994): 62.

28. D. Porter, personal communication. Ms. Porter was interviewed on May 29, 1995.

29. K. Gay, "Thorough Probe a Must before Firing," *The Financial Post*, 88(42), (October 15, 1994): 510.

30. Julie Amparano Lopez, "Companies Split Reviews on Performance and Pay," *Wall Street Journal* (May 10, 1993): B1.

31. Charles M. Vance, Shirley R. McClaine, David M. Boje, and H. Daniel Stage, "An Examination of the Transferability of Traditional Performance Appraisal Principles across Cultural Boundaries," *Management International Review* (Fourth Quarter, 1992): 313–326.

32. Wayne F. Cascio and Manuel G. Serapio, Jr., "Human Resources Systems in an International Alliance: The Undoing of a Done Deal?" *Organizational Dynamics* 19 (Winter 1991): 70.

33. Mark E. Mendenhall and Gary Oddon, "The Overseas Assignment: A Practical Look," *Business Horizons*, 31 (September/October, 1988): 81.

34. Ibid., 70.

35. Ibid.

36. *General Electric Assessment Center Manual*, General Electric Company.

37. Peter Rea, Julie Rea, and Charles Moomaw, "Use Assessment Centers in Skill Development," *Personnel Journal*, 69 (April 1990): 126.

Chapter Eleven

1. Vicki Fuehrer, "Total Reward Strategy: A Prescription for Organizational Survival," *Compensation and Benefits Review*, 26 (January–February 1994): 45.

2. For example, see: "Midland Bosses Reap Rich Rewards: $1M Plus Bonuses for Top Executives . . ." *The Globe and Mail* (March 22, 1994): B11.

3. L. Livingstone, S Roberts, and L. Chinko, "Perceptions of Internal and External Equity . . ." *Journal of Personal Selling and Sales Management*, 15(2), (1995): 33–46.

4. George J. Meng, "Link Pay to Job Evaluation," *Personnel Journal*, 69 (March 1990): 104.

5. D. MacLeod, personal communication. Mr. MacLeod was interviewed on July 27, 1995.

6. Edward J. Giblin, Geoffrey A. Wiegman, and Frank Sanfilippo, "Bringing Pay Up To Date," *Personnel*, 67 (November 1990): 17.

7. M. Pallett and Y. Treponier, "Strategic Compensation in Canada . . ." *Benefits and Compensation International*, 22(2),(1992): 6–12.

8. George T. Milkovich and Jerry M. Newman, *Compensation*, 4th ed. (Homewood, Ill.: Richard D. Irwin, Inc., 1993): 3.

9. David W. Belcher and Thomas J. Atchison, *Compensation Administration*, 2nd ed. (Englewood Cliffs, N.J.: Prentice-Hall, 1987): 127.

10. D. Willett, "Promoting Quality through Compensation," *Business Quarterly*, 58(1), (1993): 107–111.

11. Joseph E. McKendrick, Jr., "Salary Surveys: Roadmaps for the Volatile Employment Scene of the 1990s," *Management World*, 19 (March-April 1990): 18–20.

12. Cyril C. Ling, *The Management of Personnel Relations* (Homewood, Ill.: Richard D. Irwin, 1965): 146–151.

13. L. McKenna, "Moving Beyond Adversarial Relationships," *Canadian Business Review*, 22(2), (1995): 27.

14. "AGT's Rate Request Called 'Unconscionable': Citizens Give CRTC Hearing an Earful," *The Globe and Mail* (Aug. 10, 1993): B2.

15. "Slow and Sluggish: . . ." *Canadian Underwriter*, 60(6), (1993): 10-11.

16. The following sections have been adapted from Human Resources Development Canada, *Employment Standards Legislation* (1995-96 ed., DSS Cat. #631-78/1995 E. (Ottawa: Canada Communications Group).

17. I. Christie, (1980). *Employment Law in Canada* (Toronto: Butterworth, 1980): 152. As quoted in *Employment Standards Legislation*, 19.

18. For example, see "Simple Concept Sparking Heated Debate," *Calgary Herald* (April 25, 1993): A1, A2.

19. Human Resources Development Canada op cit., 47.

20. M. Campbell and J. Gadd, "Ontario to Scrap Equity Law," *The Globe and Mail* (July 20, 1995): A-1.

21. Roger J. Plachy, "The Case for Effective Point-Factor Job Evaluation, Viewpoint I," *Personnel*, 64 (April 1987): 31.

22. M. Quaid, *Job Evaluation: The Myth of Equitable Assessment* (Toronto: University of Toronto Press, 1993).

23. George T. Milkovich and Jerry M. Newman, *Compensation*, 4th ed.: 118.

24. Ibid., 124.

25. John A. Patton, C. L. Littlefield, and Stanley A. Self, *Job Evaluation: Text and Cases*, 3rd ed. (Homewood, Ill.: Richard D. Irwin, 1964): 115.

26. Donald L. Caruth, *Compensation Management for Banks* (Boston: Bankers Publishing Company, 1986): 65.

27. Edward E. Lawler III, "What's Wrong with Point-Factor Job Evaluation," *Personnel*, 64 (January 1987): 39–40.

28.George T. Milkovich and Jerry M. Newman, op. cit., 152–155.

29.J. Blewett, general manager, Atlantic provinces, for the Hay Group, personal communications. Mr. Blewett was interviewed on August 11, 1995.

30.D. Brookes, "Today's Compensation Systems: Recording the Wrong Things," *Canadian Manager,* 19(4), (1994): 10.

31.D. Brookes, op. cit., 11.

32.J. Snelgar, (1983). "The Comparability of Job Evaluation Methods . . ." *Personnel Psychology,* 36: 371–380.

33.R. Madigan and O. Hoover, "Effects of Alternative Job Evaluation Methods . . ." *Academy of Management Journal,* 29 (1986): 84–100.

34.J.B. Cunningham and S. Graham, *Canadian Journal of Administrative Studies,* 10(1), (1993): 36.

35.J.B. Cunningham and S. Graham, op. cit., 38.

36."Going Global," *HRMagazine,* 38, (September 1993): 49.

37.E. Shum, E., executive director of HRED personal communication. Dr. Shum was interviewed in November, 1994.

38.Wayne F. Cascio and Manuel G. Serapio, Jr., "Human Resources Systems in an International Alliance: The Undoing of a Done Deal?" *Organizational Dynamics,* 19 (Winter 1991): 70.

39.Ibid., p. 71.

40.Daniel B. Moskowitz, "How to Cut It Overseas," *International Business* (October, 1992): 76, 78.

41.Tom Brown, "Does Compensation Add Up?" *Industry Week,* 239 (August 20, 1990): 13.

42.R. Bonanno, (1992). "Declining the Carrot . . ." *Canadian HR Reporter,* 5(11), (1992): 11.

43.A. Willis, "Performance Pay? In Canada, Forget It," *The Financial Times of Canada,* (July 24, 1993): 1.

44.Willis, op. cit., 1.

45.Bonanno, op. cit., 10–11.

46.Willis, op. cit., 1,3.

47.Andrew Pollack, "Japanese Starting to Link Pay to Performance, Not Tenure," *New York Times* (October 2, 1993): 1.

48.Shawn Tully, "Your Paycheck Gets Exciting," *Fortune,* 126 (November 1, 1993): 83–84.

49.John A. Parnell, "Five Reasons Why Pay Must Be Based on Performance," *Supervision,* 52 (February 1991): 7.

50.J.L. Milne, "Hiring Managers . . ." *Canadian Manager,* 19(4), (1994): 5.

51.Shawn Tully, op. cit., 96.

52.Michael Leibman and Harold P. Weinstein, "Money Isn't Everything," *HRMagazine,* 35 (November 1990): 48–51.

53."Profit Sharing Can Help Bottom Line," *The Globe and Mail* (Aug. 3, 1993): B4.

54.Bradford A. Johnson and Harry H. Ray, "Employee-Developed Pay System Increases Productivity," *Personnel Journal,* 72 (November 1993): 112–118.

55.Shari Caudron, "Master the Compensation Maze,": 64G–64I.

56."Survey Report: Skill-Based Pay Can Pay Off," *HR Focus,* 69 (October 1991): 6.

57.Dallas Brozik, "The Importance of Money and the Reporting of Salaries," *Journal of Compensation and Benefits,* 9 (January/February 1994): 52–63.

58.J. Pratt, personal communication. Mr. Pratt was interviewed on March 28, 1995.

59.Edward E. Lawler III, *Pay and Organizational Effectiveness: A Psychological View* (New York: McGraw-Hill, 1971): 174–175, 196–197.

60.D. Anfuso, "Team-Based Pay Should Reinforce Equality," *Personnel Journal,* 74(4), (1995): 157.

61."Do Work Teams Need Compensation?" *Supervisory Management,* 40(2), (1995): 12.

62.A. Williams, "Quelling the Storm over Top Salaries," *People Management* (March, 1995): 22–25.

63.F. Misutka, "Executive Compensation . . ." *Canadian Business,* 65(7), (1992): 50–54.

64.J. Southerst, "There Goes the Future," *Canadian Business,* 65(10), (1992): 98–105.

65.George T. Milkovich and Jerry M. Newman, op. cit., 552.

66.Adapted by permission of the publisher from Robert E. Sibson, *Compensation,* © 1990 AMACOM, a division of American Management Association, NY. All rights reserved.

Chapter Twelve

1."We Can No Longer Take Benefits for Granted," *This Week in Business* (Nov. 15, 1993): C13.

2."Employers Favour Work Incentives over Benefits," *The Globe and Mail* (Oct. 22, 1994): B5.

3.*Income Security Programs,* ISPB-119-03-95, (Ottawa: Human Resources Development Canada, 1995).

4.*Your Old Age Security Pension,* ISBN 0-662-15728-1(Ottawa: Health and Welfare Canada, 1987).

5.The Province of Quebec administers a similar pension scheme.

6.*Canada Pension Plan,* ISBN 0-662-19034-3 (Ottawa: National Health and Welfare, 1992).

7.*Unemployment Insurance (Regular Benefits),* ISBN 0-662-61529-5 (Ottawa: Human Resources Development Canada, 1992).

8.*Seventy-Fifth Annual Report* (Fredericton: Workers' Compensation Board, 1993).

9."Table of Rates," (Fredericton: Workers' Compensation Board, 1995).

10."The Woes of Workers' Compensation," *Canadian Employment Law Today,* 137 (March 17, 1993): 1. As quoted in R.M. Hodgetts, K.G. Droeck, and M. Rock, *Managing Human Resources in Canada* (Toronto: Dryden, 1995): 674.

11.*"Ontario WCB Plans Public Hearings into Workplace Stressors," Canadian HR Reporter*, 4(28): 5.

12.R. King,(1995). "Medicare—Where Is Its Future?" *Employee Benefits Journal*, 20(1): 33–35.

13.W. Morneau, "Managing Canadian Health Programs: A Cost-Containment Challenge," *Benefits and Compensation International*, 23(7), (1994): 16–20.

14.A. Downey and R. Kador, "The High Cost of Health," *CMA Magazine*, 69(3), (1995): 12–14.

15.W. Morneau, op. cit.

16.*Information on Labour Standards: Annual Vacations*, ISBN 0-662-61723-1 (Ottawa: Human Resources Development Canada, 1995).

17.*Information on Labour Standards: General Holidays*, ISBN 0-662-61724-X (Ottawa: Human Resources Development Canada, 1995).

18.G. Mitchell, "Strategies for Health Care Cost Containment," *Employee Benefits Journal*, 20(2), (1995), 18–22.

19."Do-It-Yourself Insurance," *B.C. Business Magazine*, 22(8), (1994): 13.

20."Visions: Funding Retiree Benefits," *HRMagazine*, 36 (February 1991): 87.

21.ESOPs Fabled Hopes Rocked, *The Globe and Mail* (December 30, 1992): B7.

22.Margot Gibb-Clark "AIDS Plays Havoc with Group Insurance: Company Reluctantly Lets Employee Go to Avoid Soaring Cost of Premiums," *The Globe and Mail* (Nov. 15, 1993): B1, B8.

23."An Investment in Education . . . ." *Oilweek*, 45(39), (1994): 8, 9.

24.C. Philip, "Financial Planning Eases Complications," *Pensions and Investments*, 22(21), (1994):17, 29.

25."Two-Income Families on the Rise . . ." *The Globe and Mail* (June 4, 1992): B4.

26.Julie Cohen Mason, "Whoever Said There Was No Such Thing as a Free Lunch?" *Management Review* 83 (April 1994): 60–62.

27."Employers Favour Work Incentives over Benefits," *The Globe and Mail* (Oct. 22, 1994): B5.

28.We can no longer take benefits for granted. (1993). This Week in Business. (Nov. 15), C13.

29."Employers favour work incentives over benefits," op. cit.

30."Health Benefits Headed Beyond the Fringe," *The Globe and Mail* (May 10, 1994): C1, C7.

31."We Can No Longer Take Benefits for Granted," *This Week in Business* (Nov. 15, 1993): C13.

32."3M's 'Beneflex' Plan Popular with Employees," *Canadian HR Reporter*, 8(4), (1995): 11.

33.Pearson. (1995). 11.

34.William Bridges, "The End of the Job," *Fortune* (September 19, 1994): 62–74.

35."Newbridge from the Shop Floor," Ottawa Business Magazine. (Winter, 1994): 28–33.

36.Joseph E. McKendrick, Jr., "Stretching Time in '89," *Management World*, 18 (July–August 1989): 10.

37."Flex-Time Schemes Stretch to Fit Needs of Firms, Workers," *Financial Post*, 86(15), (April 11/13, 1992): S27.

38."Board Measures Cost of Worker Absenteeism," *Daily Commercial News*, 66(62), (1993): 9, 11.

39."Bell Workers Can Switch Work Week . . ." (1994). Globe and Mail. (April 15, 1994): B3.

40.Michael Alexander, "Travel-Free Commuting," *Nation's Business* 78 (December 1990): 33.

41."Working from Home Cuts Employee Stress . . ." *The Globe and Mail* (November 16, 1994): B21.

42.P.C. Wright and A. Oldford,(1993). "Telecommuting and Employee Effectiveness: A Brave New World," *International Journal of Career Management*, 5(1): 4–9.

43."A Flexible Style of Management," *Nation's Business*, 81 (December 1993): 29.

44.Ibid., 70-71.

45.Knight, C. (1995). Saskatchewan legislation benefits for part-timers. *Canadian HR Reporter*, 8(6), 1.

46.Richard I. Henderson, *Compensation Management: Rewarding Performance*, 6th ed. (Englewood Cliffs, N.J.: Prentice-Hall, 1994): 505-506.

47.Gary E. Jenkins, "Beyond the Borders: The Human Resource Professional in a Global Economy," *Employment Benefit Plan Review* (May, 1993): 43-44.

48.Cooke, A. and S. Sarouer. (1994). Moving employees into or out of Canada — the pension issues. Benefits and Compensation International. 23(9), 2-7.

49.Neil B. Krupp, "Managing Benefits in Multinational Organizations," *Personnel* 63 (September 1986): 76.

50.Ibid.

Chapter Thirteen

1.Annual Report,1993, (Fredericton: New Brunswick Occupational Health and Safety Commission): 9.

2.A Guide to the Canada Labour Code: Occupational Safety and Health (Ottawa: Labour Canada, 1992): 1.

3.K. Palmer, (1995) "How Can You Be Sure Your Employees Are Fit to Work?" *People Management* (May 18): 51.

4.G. Harrington, "Pushing Ergonomics into Place," *Canadian HR Reporter*, 18(8), (1995): 11.

5."Office Environment Could Harm Your Health," *The Globe and Mail* (October 13, 1992): C14.

6.J. Canto-Thaler "Increasing Liability Seen in Workplace Health and Safety," *Canadian HR Reporter*, 8(12), (1995): 15.

7."Safety Motivation Demands an Involved Process," *Iron Age*, 8(2), (1995): 30–31.

8.W.W. Tyler, "Total Involvement Safety," *Professional Safety*, 37(3), (1992): 26–29.

9.K.A. Krout, "Supervisory Safety Survey . . ." *Occupational Health and Safety,* 62(5), (1993): 50–51.

10.J.E. Canto-Thaler, "Due Diligence Can Blunt AHSA Prosecution," *Canadian HR Reporter,* 8(1), (1995): 10–11.

11.A. Flynn, personal communications. Ms. Flynn was interviewed on July 17, 1995.

12.Robert Pater, "Safety Leadership Cuts Costs," *HRMagazine* 35 (November 1990): 46.

13."To OSHA, 'Workplace Safety Is Good Business,' " *Risk Management,* 36 (October 1989): 172.

14.M.P. Rowan, and P.C. Wright,. "Ergonomics is Good for Business," *Facilities,* 13(8), (1995): 18–25.

15.G. Harrington, op. cit.

16."The Right Fit . . ." (1991). *Food in Canada,* 51(3), 14-17.

17."Work That Wounds and How to Cure It," *Canadian Business,* 64(12), (1991): 84–86+

18.Michael J. Lotito and Francis P. Alvarez, "Integrate Claims Management with ADA Compliance Strategy," *HRMagazine* 38 (August 1993): 86–92.

19.Helen Frank Bensimon, "Violence in the Workplace," *Training and Development Journal* 48, (January 1994): 27–31.

20."Man Stabs Employee at Welfare Office," *The Daily Gleaner,* (Canadian Press Report), (August 2, 1995): 3.

21.Patti Watts, "Are Your Employees Burnout-Proof?" *Personnel,* 67 (September 1990): 12–13, 20.

22.Ron Zemke, "Workplace Stress Revisited," *Training,* 28 (November 1991): 35–39.

23."How to Avoid Burnout," *Training,* 30 (February 1993): 16.

24."Balance Beats Burnout . . ." *Profit: The Magazine for Canadian Entrepreneurs,* 16(4), (1991): 66–67.

25."Half of Managers Suffer Work Stress," *Supervision,* 51 (July 1990): 10.

26.Debra L. Nelson, James C. Quick, and Michael A. Hitt, "What Stresses HR Professionals?" *Personnel,* 67 (August 1990): 36–39.

27.J. Matthews, "Stress Inc.," *CA Magazine,* 125(10), (1992): 34.

28."Counsellors are Seeing More Stressed-out Workers . . ." *This Week in Business,* (June 14, 1993): F/4.

29."How to Conduct an Ergonomic Review," *People Management,* (September, 1995): 45–46.

30.Pam Black, "A Home Office That's Easier On The Eyes—And The Back," *Business Week* (August 17, 1992): 112-113.

31.Wright, P. and W. Nasierowski, (1994). The Expatriate Family Firm and Cross-cultural Management Training . . ." *Human Resource Development Quarterly,* 5(2), 153-167.

32.M. Swenarchuk, "NAFTA and the Environment," *Canadian Forum,* 71(816), (1993): 13–14.

33.M. Swenarchuk, "Threat to Worker Safety . . ." *Occupational Health and Safety Canada,* 9(5), (1993): 138.

34.Mark C. Butler and Mary B. Teagarden, "Strategic Management of Worker Health, Safety, and Environmental Issues in Mexico's Maquiladora Industry," *Human Resource Management* (Winter, 1993): 479–503

35.Marvina Shilling, "Avoid Expatriate Culture Shock," *HRMagazine,* 38 (July 1993): 58.

36.J. Doiron, "Active Living," *The Canadian Manager,* 17(3), (1995): 15.

37.J. Doiron, op. cit., 16.

38.E. Thompson, "Walk the Walk," *Canadian Banker,* 101(1), (1993): 10.

39.Edited portions of Mr. Doiron's paper have been reproduced here with permission from The Canadian Institute of Management.

40.D. Hockley, "Assisting employees at B.C. Tel.," *Canadian Business Review,* 19(2),(1992): 25–28.

41.M. Coshan (1992). "An EAP Can Be Part of the Solution," *Canadian Business Review,* 19(2), 22–24.

42.D. Hockley, op. cit.

43.Bill Oliver, "How to Prevent Drug Abuse in Your Workplace," *HRMagazine,* 38 (December 1993): 79–80.

44.Adapted from P.C. Wright, "How Managers Should Approach Alcoholism and Drug Abuse in the Workplace," *Business Quarterly,* 48(4), (1983): 53–56.

45.Sharon A. Haskins and Brian H. Kleiner, "Employee Assistance Programs Take New Directions," *HR Focus,* 71, (January 1994), 16.

46.Peggy Stuart, "Investments in EAPs Pay Off," *Personnel Journal* (February 1993): 54.

47.Coshan, op. cit., 28.

48.Mark Ralfs and John M. Morley, "Turning Employee Problems into Triumphs," *Training and Development Journal,* 44 (November 1990): 73.

49."Quarterly Surveillance Update: AIDS in Canada," (April, 1995): 5.

50. Ibid., 47.

Chapter Fourteen

1.P. Kumar, *From Uniformity to Divergence* (Kingston: IRC Press, 1993).

2.W. Roberts and J. Bullen, "A Heritage of Hope and Struggle: Workers, Unions, and Politics in Canada," In D. J. Bercuson and D. Bright, Eds., *Canadian Labour History,* 2nd ed. (Toronto: Copp Clark Longmans, 1994).

3.E. E. Seymour, *An Illustrated History of Canadian Labour 1800-1974,* (Ottawa: Canadian Labour Congress, 1974): 3–4.

4.D. A. Peach and P. Bergman, *The Practice of Labour Relations,* 3rd ed. (Toronto: McGraw Hill, 1991): 22.

5. D. A. Peach and D. Kuechle, *The Practice of Industrial Relations* (Toronto: McGraw-Hill Ryerson, 1975).

6. D. A. Peach and P. Bergman, op. cit.

7. J. Godard, *Industrial Relations: The Economy and Society* (Toronto: McGraw-Hill Ryerson, 1994).

8. D. A. Peach and D. Kuechle, op. cit.

9. F. Kehoe and M. Archer, *Canadian Industrial Relations* (Oakville: Twentieth Century Labour Publications, 1980).

10. A. Craig, *The Systems of Industrial Relations in Canada*, 2nd ed. (Scarborough: Prentice Hall Canada, 1986). See also D. A. Peach and P. Bergman, op. cit.

11. A. Craig, *The System of Industrial Relations in Canada*, (Scarborough: Prentice Hall, 1986).

12. Carter, D. D. (1989). Collective Bargaining Legislation in Canada, in Anderson, J., M. Gunderson and A. Ponak (eds.). *Union-Management Relations in Canada* (2nd ed.), Don Mills: Addison-Wesley, 33.

13. Peach and Bergman, (1991).

14. B. Downie and M. C. Cotes, *The Changing Face of Industrial Relations and Human Resource Management*, (Kingston: Industrial Relations Centre, Queen's University, 1993).

15. "Living on Mother's Allowance Is No Bed of Roses: Single Mother," *Peterborough Examiner*, (July 18, 1987): 8, as quoted in A. Price et al. "Work in the Electronic End," in L.S. MacDowell, and I. Radford, Eds., *Canadian Working Class History* (Toronto: Canadian Scholars Press, 1992): 728.

16. R. Wright, *Industrial Relations Outlook 1994*, Report 113-94 (Ottawa: Conference Board of Canada): 17.

17. Ibid.

18. Ibid.

19. Alexander B. Trowbridge, "A Management Look at Labor Relations," *Unions in Transition* (San Francisco: ICS Press, 1988): 415.

20. John P. Bucalo, Jr., "Successful Employee Relations," *Personnel Administrator*, 31 (April 1986): 63.

21. Paul S. McDonough, "Maintaining a Union-Free Status," *Personnel Journal*, 69 (April 1990): 108.

22. A. Bernstein, "Busting Unions Can Backfire on the Bottom Line," *Business Week* (March 18, 1991): 108.

23. Wiley I. Beavers, "Employee Relations Without a Union," in Dale Oder and Herbert G. Heneman, Jr., Eds., *ASPA Handbook of Personnel and Industrial Relations: Employee and Labor Relations*, III (Washington, D.C.: The Bureau of National Affairs, 1976): 7-82.

24. P. Kumar, *From Uniformity to Divergence* (Kingston: IRC Press, 1993).

25. J. Godard, op. cit.

26. N. Winter, "The High Cost of No-Risk Compensation," *Canadian HR Reporter*, (June 18, 1992): 13.

27. L. R. Gomez-Mejia and D. B. Balkin, *Compensation, Organizational Strategy and Firm Performance* (Cincinnati: South-Western Publishing Co., 1992).

28. H. W. Arthurs, D. D. Carter, J. Fudge, and H. J. Glasbeek, *Labour Law and Industrial Relations in Canada*, (Toronto: Butterworth, 1988): 180.

29. Ibid., 185.

30. B. W. Werther, K. Davis, H. Schwind, and H. Das, *Canadian Human Resource Management*, 3rd ed., (Toronto: McGraw-Hill Ryerson Ltd., 1989): 563.

31. G. T. Milkovich, W. F. Glueck, R. T. Barth, S. L. McShane, *Canadian Personnel/Human Resource Management* (Plano, Texas: Business Publications, Inc., 1988), 611.

32. J. Godard, op. cit.

33. R. Wright, op. cit., 16.

34. R. S. Adler and W. J. Bigoness, "Contemporary Ethical Issues in Labour-Management Relations," *Journal of Business Ethics*, 11 (May 1992): 351–360.

35. N. W. Bowie, "Should Collective Bargaining and Labour Relations be Less Adversarial?" *Journal of Business Ethics*, 4 (August 1985): 283-291.

36. J.D. Reid Jr., "Future Unions," *Industrial Relations*, 31 (Winter 1992): 122-136.

37. R.S. Adler and W.J. Bigoness, op. cit.

38. S. Coppen, "New Law Improves Ontario Labour Relations," *Canadian Speeches*, 8(9), (1995): 44.

39. W.C. Riddell, "Labour-Management Co-operation in Canada," *Royal Commission on the Economic Union and Development Prospects for Canada*, 15 (1986): 1–49.

40. E.E. Lawler III and S.A. Mohrman, "Involvement Management: Champions of Change," *Executive Excellence*, 6 (April 1989): 6–7.

41. M.E. Hass and J.H. Philbrick, "The New Management: Is It Legal?" *Academy of Management Executive*, 2 (November 1988): 325–329.

42. W.C. Riddell, op. cit., 46.

43. J. Godard, op. cit.

44. B. Downie and M. L. Cootes, op. cit..

45. W.C. Riddell, op. cit., 46.

46. R. Wright, op. cit., 18.

Chapter Fifteen

1. R. Wright, *Industrial Relations Outlook 1994*, Report 113-94 (Ottawa: Conference Board of Canada, 1994).

2. Ibid.

3. Adapted with permission from The Conference Board of Canada, Report 113-94: 7.

4. Sleemi Fehmida, "Higher Settlements in 1989 End Innovative Decade," *Monthly Labour Review*, 113 (May 1990): 3–4.

5. T. McFeely, "Going, Going, Gone: The NDP's New Labour Code Sparks a Business Exodus," *BC Report*, 4 (1993): 7–8.

6. D. Peach and P. Bergman, *The Practice of Labour Relations*, 3rd ed. (Toronto: McGraw-Hill Ryerson Ltd.,

1991). See also A. B. Sloane and F. Witney, *Labour Relations*, 4th ed. (Englewood Cliffs, N.J.: Prentice-Hall, 1981): 28–35.

7. *Glossary of Industrial Relations Terms*, 3rd ed. (Labour Canada, 1984).

8. A. Brown, "Labor Contract Negotiations: Behind the Scenes," in *Labor Relations: Reports From the Firing Line*, (Plano, Texas: Business Publications, 1988): 305–308.

9. Abby Brown, "An Interview with Fritz Ihrig," *Personnel Management*, 31 (April 1986): 60.

10. Wayne F. Cascio and Manuel G. Serapio, Jr., "Human Resources Systems in an International Alliance: The Undoing of a Done Deal?" *Organizational Dynamics*, 19 (Winter 1991): 72–73.

11. H. Levinson, "Stress at the Bargaining Table," in *Labor Relations: Reports From the Firing Line* (Plano, Texas: Business Publications, 1988): 310.

12. *Industrial Relations Act*, RSNB (1973). C.I-4, S.1-100(1). Revised to June, 1994.

13. CAUT Collective Bargaining Cooperative, Collective Bargaining Conference Notes (Val Morin, Quebec), June 1993. Material adapted with permission.

14. Ibid. Material adapted with permission.

15. Canadian Labour Congress—Educational Services (c. 1992). (Mimeograph). Adapted with permission.

16. Ibid. Adapted with permission.

17. B.M. Downie, ("Third-Party Assistance in Collective Bargaining," in Sethi, A. S., Ed., *Collective Bargaining in Canada* (Scarborough: Nelson Canada, 1989): 153–154.

18. The material that follows was adapted from E.R. Zimmermann, *Manual on Legal Strike Action for Canadian Faculty Associations* (Ottawa: CAUT Collective Bargaining Cooperative, 1990). Adapted with permission.

19. A. MacDonald, "Irving Boycott Taking Its Toll Says Unions," *Halifax Chronicle*, (February 11, 1991): C1.

20. The authors are indebted to Mr. Jim Horn, Director, Personnel Services at The University of New Brunswick, who wrote the first draft of this section.

21. N. Fuller, "NHL Owners Authorize a Lockout," *Financial Post Daily*, 7, (1994): 40.

22. G. T. Milkovich, W. F. Glueck, R. T. Barth, S. L. McShane, *Canadian Personnel/Human Resource Management* (Plano, Texas: Business Publications, Inc., 1988): 625.

23. F. Kehoe and M. Archer, *Canadian Industrial Relations* (Oakville: Twentieth Century Publications, 1980): 14.12.

24. Collective Agreement Between the University of New Brunswick and the Association of University of New Brunswick Teachers 1991-1995.

25. J. Gandz and J. Whitehead, "Grievances and Their Resolution," in M. Gunderson et al., Eds., *Union-Management Relations in Canada*, 2nd ed. (Toronto: Addison-Wesley, 1989).

26. R. C. Basken, "Labour participation key to success," *Canadian Speeches*, 8(4), (1994): 61–62.

27. A. M. Atkinson, *Report on Export Opportunities to Mexico* (Fredericton: Centre for International Marketing and Entrepreneurship, Faculty of Administration, University of New Brunswick, 1994): 20.21.

28. D. Fagan, "Mexico's 10-Year Turnaround," *The Globe and Mail*, (September 24, 1992): C4.

29. P. Wright and E. Maher, "How Smaller Firms Should Approach Free Trade Agreements," *Journal of Small Business and Entrepreneurship*, 12 (3), (1995): 73–82.

30. P. Wright and E. Maher, op. cit.

31. T. Rankin, *New Forms of Work Organization: Challenge for North American Unions* (Toronto: University of Toronto Press, 1993): 149.

32. T. Fennell, "Labour for a New Approach. Canadian Unions Embrace Strategies to Save Jobs," *MacLeans*, 106 (1993): 40–42. See also R. Worster, "Still Fighting Yesterday's Battle: Unionism Demoralizes Workers, Discourages Productivity and Undermines the Economy," *Newsweek*, 122 (1993): 12.

33. D. Clifford, "An Eclectic Grabbag on the New North America," *The Globe and Mail*, (September 24, 1992): C10.

Chapter Sixteen

1. Arthur R. Pell, "Effective Reprimanding," *Manager's Magazine*, 65 (August 1990): 26.

2. David N. Campbell, R.L. Fleming, and Richard C. Grote, "Discipline Without Punishment—At Last," *Harvard Business Review*, 63 (July-August 1985): 168.

3. Wallace Wohlking, "Effective Discipline in Employee Relations," *Personnel Journal*, 54 (September 1975): 489.

4. Neil W. Chamberlain, *The Labor Sector* (New York: McGraw-Hill, 1985): 240.

5. K.L. Sovereign and Mario Bognanno, "Positive Contract Administration," in Dale Yoder and Herbert G. Heneman, Jr., Eds., *ASPA Handbook of Personnel and Industrial Relations: Employee and Labor Relations*, Vol. III (Washington, D.C.: The Bureau of National Affairs, 1976): 7-161–7-162.

6. Ibid., 7-164.

7. W.J. Alton and N.A. Soloman, *The System of Industrial Relations in Canada*, 5th ed. (Scarborough: Prentice Hall Canada, 1996): 339.

8. Ibid.

9. Alton and Craig (1996), 339-340.

10. "Moving the corporate battle . . ." *The Globe and Mail* (June 21, 1994): B22.

11. Lawrence Stessin, "Expedited Arbitration: Less Grief Over Grievances," *Harvard Business Review*, 55 (January–February 1977): 129.

12. "Is Mount Allison University at the Brink?" *CAUT Bulletin,* 42(8),(1995): 5.

13. Paula Eubanks, "Employee Grievance Policy: Don't Discourage Complaints," *Hospitals*, 64 (December 20, 1990): 36.

14. James P. Swann, Jr., "Formal Grievance Procedures in Non-Union Plants," *Personnel Administrator*, 26 (August 1991): 67.

15. Jennifer Laabs, "Remedies for HR's Legal Headache," *Personnel Journal*, 73 (December 1994): 69.

16. This section concerning the psychology of dismissal was written from notes made during a guest lecture by Mr. James Sweet, then manager of employee relations at Moore Business Forms Ltd., based in Toronto, Ontario © 1988.

17. T. Wagar, "Comparative Systems of Wrongful Dismissal: The Canadian Case," *The Annals of the American Academy of Political and Social Service* (November 1994).

18. E. Mole, *The Wrongful Dismissal Handbook* (Markham: Butterworths, 1990): 1.

19. S. McShane and B. Redekop, "Compensation Management and Canadian Wrongful Dismissal: . . ." *Relations industrielles*, 45(2): 357.

20. T. Wagar and J. Grant, (1993). "Dismissal for Incompetence: . ." *Labor Law Journal*, 44(3): 171.

21. See, for example, B. Grosman, *The Executive Firing Line: Wrongful Dismissal and the Law* (Toronto: Carswell-Methuen, 1984).

22. "Glass Houses: A Landmark Decision . . ." *Canadian Datasystems*, 24 (10), (1992): 22.

23. T. Wager, op. cit.: 66.

24. As usual in Canada, there are exceptions. In three jurisdictions (federal, Quebec, and Nova Scotia) there are provisions for reinstatement through a process similar to arbitration. For example, see *Unjust Dismissal and The Canada Labour Code*, ISBN 0-662-59299-9 (Ottawa: Labour Canada).

25. Susan Caminiti, "What Happens To Laid-Off Managers," *Fortune*, 129 (June 13, 1994): 69.

26. G. Quill,(1995). "Fired 'Producer Components' Say CBC Acted Badly," *The Toronto Star* (June 13): B5.

27. Michael Smith, "Help in Making Those Tough Layoff Decisions," *Supervisory Management*, 35 (January 1990): 3.

28. Robert W. Keidel, "Layoffs Take Advance Preparation," *Management Review*, 80 (May 1991): 6.

29. Loretta D. Foxman and Walter L. Polsky, "Outplacement Results in Success," *Personnel Journal*, 69 (February 1990): 30.

30. Virginia M. Gibson, "In the Outplacement Door," *Personnel*, 68 (October 1991): 3–4.

31. D. Lambe, "Downsizing and workforce adjustment . . ." Working Paper 94-13 (Faculty of Administration, University of Ottawa, 1994).

32. "Older Workers Still Contending with Workplace Myths," *The Globe and Mail* (October 1, 1994): B2.

33. D. Lambe, op. cit., 1.

34. T. Degler, "Employers Continue Interest in EAPs Despite—and Because of—Cutbacks," *Canadian HR Reporter*, 7(10), (1994): 10.

35. D. Luckow, "Moving up by Moving Sideways," *Financial Times of Canada* (April 10–16, 1993): 19.

36. David Kirkpatrick, "Is Your Career on Track?" *Fortune*, 122 (July 2, 1990): 39.

37. Harvey Mackay, "A Career Roadmap: Getting Started," *Modern Office Technology*, 35 (June 1990): 12.

38. "Advance by Shifting Horizontally . . ." (1993) *The Financial Times of Canada* (April 10-16, 1993): 19.

39. Michael J. Kaltz, "How to Establish an Expatriate Policy from Scratch," *Benefits & Compensation International*, (January/February, 1994): 62–66.

40. Joseph R. Rich and Beth C. Florin-Thuma, "Rewarding Employees in an Environment of Fewer Promotions," *Pension World*, 26 (November 1990): 16.

41. "How Can We Make Work Rewarding?" Canadian HR Reporter. 8(12), (1995): 3.

42. R. Degler, "Career Planning Joins Outplacement to Facilitate Employee Transition," *Canadian HR Reporter*, 7(13), (1994): 8.

43. Lin Grensing, "Don't Let Them out the Door without an Exit Interview," *Management World*, 19 (March-April 1990): 11.

44. Robert Wolfe, "Most Employers Offer Exit Interviews," *HRNews*, 10 (June 1990): 2.

45. Wanda R. Embrey, R. Wayne Mondy, and Robert M. Noe, "Exit Interview: A Tool for Personnel Development," *Personnel Administrator*, 24 (May 1979): 46.

46. P. Taylor, "Social Studies," Saturday Night (June 1995): 18–23.

47. "Retirement Not an Option," Canadian Press, in *The Daily Gleaner* (July 18, 1995): 31.

48. "Older Workers Still Contending with Myths, op. cit.

49. P. Scherer and P. Statler, "Helping Your Employees Retire," *Canadian HR Reporter*, 8(9), (1995): 12.

50. Ellen Brandt, "Global HR," *Personnel Journal*, 70 (March 1991): 43.

51. Ibid.

52. Ibid.

Chapter Seventeen

1. B. Mullins and B. Mullins, "The Human Side of Technology," *Canadian Insurance*, 99(10), (1994): 22.

2. Job Longevity Differs by Sex," *Convenience Store News*

(May 2, 1975): 1.

3. Spencer Hayden, "Our Foreign Legions are Faltering," *Personnel,* 67 (August 1991): 42.

4. Hoerr, "The Payoff from Teamwork," 56-62.

5. P. Dowling, R. Schuler, and D. Welch "International Dimensions of Human Resources Management," (Belmont: Wadsworth, 1994): 225.

6. P. Szathmary, "Technology Fatigue Enters the Mainstream," *Computing Canada,* 20(5), (1994): 22–23.

7. R. Wayne Mondy and Wallace F. Nelson, "Job Satisfaction Among Radiologic Technologies," *Applied Radiology,* 7 (July–August 1978): 66.

8. This portion of the chapter is reproduced with permission from G. Pearson, "Employee Surveys Mean More Communication—But Be Ready to Act," *Canadian HR Reporter,* (8),2. (1995): 15.

© 1995 by MPL Communications Ltd. Reproduced with permission of *Canadian HR Reporter,* 133 Richmond St., W. Toronto, Ontario, M5H 3M8.

9. U. Sekaren, *Research Methods for Business* (Toronto: John Wiley & Sons, Inc., 1992): 116.

10. Margaret E. Cashman and James C. McElroy, "Evaluating the HR Function," *HRMagazine* 36 (January 1991): 73.

11. Donald L. Caruth, Robert M. Noe III, and R. Wayne Mondy, *Staffing the Contemporary Organization* (New York: Praeger Publishers, 1990): 283–299.

12. This section written by Dr. Judy B. Mondy, Department of General Business, College of Business, McNeese State University.

13. Michael S. Howard, "Welcome to Warp Speed," *Computerworld,* 27 (May 17, 1993): 89–93.

14. Alice Laplante, "The Needing Edge," *Computerworld,* 25 (March 18, 1991): 65.

15. Michael Fitzgerald, "IS Helps 'Cat' Stay on Its Feet," *Computerworld 100* (October 9, 1990): sec. 2, 60.

16. H. (Henk) Van Tuyl, personal communication. Mr. Van Tuyl was interviewed on April 12, 1995.

17. G. Safran, "Human Resources Information Systems," *Canadian Manager,* 19(3), (1994): 13.

18. A. Oldford, sales representative, NBTel, Moncton, N.B., personal communication. Ms. Oldford was interviewed on March 31, 1995.

19. This information was supplied on April 6, 1995 by Norma Bradley @ Brunswick Micro Systems (VISIT™ dealer for Northern Telecom). Reproduced with permission.

20. James A. O'Brien, *Introduction to Information Systems in Business Management,* 6th ed. (Homewood, Ill.: Richard D. Irwin, 1991): 325.

21. Fritz H. Grupe, "Planning Your Expert System Strategy," *Information Executive,* 4 (Winter 1991): 47.

22. "Issues and Trends: I Want My MPC," *Lotus,* 8 (April 1992): 15.

23. Robert Sadarini, "The Art of Imagineering," *Information Executive,* 4 (Summer, 1991): 6–7.

24. H. L. Capron, *Essentials of Computing,* 2nd ed. (New York, NY: The Benjamin/Cummings Publishing Company, Inc., 1995): 125–127.

25. Ellis Booker, "Job Seekers Scan Electronic Horizon," *Computerworld,* 28 (October 3, 1994): 1,133.

26. Ellis Booker, "Landing a Job Via the 'Net,'" *Computerworld,* 28 (October 3, 1994): 133.

27. Melinda-Carol Ballou, "Lab Adopts Multimedia 'Receptionist,'" *Computerworld,* 28 (September 26, 1994): 94.

28. "Virtual HR" *Across the Board,* 32(9), (1995): 8.

29, Elizabeth A. Regan and Bridget N. O'Connor, *End-User Information Systems* (New York: Macmillan Publishing Company, 1994): 52.

30. Kim Nash, "New Systems, New Business Practices," *Computerworld,* 27 (May 24, 1993): 49.

31. Gary A. Egan, "Groupware: It's for All Companies," *Inside DPMA* 31 (October, 1993): 7.

GLOSSARY

Adversarial: Describing labour/management relations in which each party sees the other as an opponent and tries to gain advantages; see *positional bargaining.*

AIDS (acquired immune deficiency syndrome): A condition that undermines the body's immune system, leaving the person susceptible to a wide range of fatal diseases.

Apprenticeship training: A combination of classroom instruction and on-the-job training.

Arbitration: A process in which a dispute is submitted to an impartial third party for a binding decision.

Assessment centre: An appraisal approach that requires employees to participate in a series of activities similar to those they might encounter in an actual job.

Availability forecast: A process of determining whether a firm will be able to secure employees with the necessary skills from within the company, from outside the organization, or from a combination of the two sources.

Band width: In a flextime scheme, the maximum length of the work day.

Bargain in good faith: The process of sincerely trying to negotiate a collective agreement.

Beachhead demands: Demands that a union does not expect management to meet when they are first made.

Behaviour description interview: A structured interview that uses questions designed to probe an applicant's past behaviour in specific situations.

Behaviour modelling: A training method that utilizes live demonstrations or videotapes to illustrate how managers function in various situations for the purpose of developing interpersonal skills.

Behaviourally anchored rating scale (BARS) method: A performance appraisal method that combines elements of the traditional rating scale and critical incidents methods.

Benchmark job: A well-known job, in which a large percentage of a company's work force is employed, that represents the entire job structure — used as a comparative example when performing job evaluation.

Benefits: All financial rewards that generally are not paid directly to an employee.

Biofeedback: A method of learning to control involuntary bodily processes, such as blood pressure or heart rate.

Blacklist: In the nineteenth century, lists of workers interested in unions, circulated among employers, who would avoid hiring them.

Board interview: A meeting in which one candidate is interviewed by several representatives of a company.

Bottom-up approach: A forecasting method beginning with the lowest organizational units and progressing upward through an organization ultimately to provide an aggregate forecast of employment needs.

Boycott: A refusal by union members to use or buy their firm's products.

Burnout: A state of fatigue or frustration stemming from devotion to a cause, way of life, or relationship that did not provide the expected reward.

Business games: Simulations that represent actual business situations.

Canada Pension Plan (CPP): A universal pension plan administered by the federal government, into which all employers and employees contribute.

Career: A general course of action a person chooses to pursue throughout his or her working life.

Career anchors: Five different motives identified by Edgar Schein to account for the way people select and prepare for a career.

Career development: A formal approach taken by an organization to ensure that people with the proper qualifications and experience are available when needed.

Career path: A flexible line of progression through which an employee may move during his or her employment with a company.

Career planning: An ongoing process whereby an individual sets career goals and identifies the means to achieve them.

Carpal tunnel syndrome: A condition involving wrist pain, numbness or limited hand mobility often caused by repetitive flexing and extension of the wrist.

Case study: A training method that utilizes simulated business problems for trainees to solve; also a research method that attempts to uncover the underlying cause of specific problems in a plant, a department, or a work group.

Central tendency: A common error that occurs when employees are incorrectly rated near the average or middle of a scale.

Certification: The process whereby a union comes into legal existence.

Classification method: A job evaluation method in which classes or grades are defined to describe a group of jobs.

Classroom lecture: The traditional training method, in which a teacher addresses a group.

Client/server systems: Electronic systems that split and deliver computer applications and data at reduced costs with great reliability.

Closed shop: An arrangement whereby union membership is a prerequisite to employment.

Coaching: An on-the-job approach to management development in which a manager is given an opportunity to teach on a one-to-one basis.

Cognitive aptitude tests: Tests that measure an individual's ability to learn, as well as to perform a job.

Collective agreement: The contract between a union and an employer that outlines the conditions under which the union's members will work for the duration of the contract.

Collusion: Illegal agreements made between managers and union officials to subvert the bargaining process.

Compensation: Reward of all types that individuals receive in return for their labour.

Compressed workweek: Any arrangement of work hours that permits employees to fulfil their work obligation in fewer days than the typical five-day workweek.

Computer-based training: A teaching method that takes advantage of the speed, memory, and data manipulation capabilities of computers for greater flexibility of instruction.

Conciliation: The process that occurs after mediation has failed, whereby an independent third party (conciliator) attempts to persuade the parties to reach an agreement.

Conference method: A widely used instructional approach that brings together individuals with common interests to discuss and attempt to solve problems (also known as the *discussion method*).

Contract: Collective agreement.

Cooperative: Describing a relationship between employer and employees (and/or their union) that serves the common needs of both parties; opposite of *adversarial*.

Corporate culture: The system of shared values, beliefs, and habits within an organization that interacts with the formal structure to produce behavioural norms.

Correlation analysis: A method of measuring the degree of association between two or more variables.

Cost-of-living allowance (COLA): An escalator clause in a labour agreement that automatically increases wages as the Statistics Canada cost-of-living index rises.

Critical incident method: A performance appraisal technique that requires a written record of highly favourable and highly unfavourable employee work behaviour.

Cumulative trauma disorders: A series of disorders, often associated with using computers, caused by repeated minor stresses, including injuries to the back and upper extremities.

Cutoff score: The score below which an applicant will not be considered further for employment.

Cyclical variations: Reasonably predictable movements about a trend line that occur over a period of more than a year.

Data communication: The sending of computer data over some form of communication medium, such as telephone lines.

Database management: The integration of information subsystems in order to reduce the duplication of information, effort, and cost and to provide controlled access to this information.

Decision support system (DSS): An information system that allows users to process and retrieve information quickly.

Demotion: The process of moving a worker to a lower level of duties and responsibilities, which typically involves a pay cut.

Development: Learning that looks beyond the knowledge and skill needed for a present job.

Direct financial compensation: Pay that a person receives in the form of wages, salaries, bonuses, and commissions.

Disability protection: Private insurance offered as part of a benefits package that pays a portion of wages in the event of permanent disability due to accident or illness, either on or off the job.

Discipline: The invoking of a penalty against an employee who fails to meet organizational standards or comply with organizational rules.

Discipline without punishment: A process whereby a worker is counselled and/or given time off with pay to think about whether he or she wants to follow the rules and continue working for a company.

Downsizing: A reduction in the number of people employed by a firm (also known as *restructuring* and *rightsizing*).

Dual career path: A method of rewarding technical specialists and professionals who can, and should be allowed to, continue to contribute significantly to a company without having to become managers.

Early retirement: Retirement from a firm before the age of 65.

Employee assistance program (EAP): A comprehensive approach that many organizations have taken to deal with burnout, alcohol and drug abuse, and other emotional disturbances.

Employee-centred work redesign: An innovative concept designed to link the mission of a company with the job satisfaction needs of its employees.

Employee equity: Payment of individuals performing similar jobs for the same firm commensurate with factors unique to each employee.

Employee requisition: A document that specifies a particular job title, the appropriate department, and the date by which an open job should be filled.

Employee share ownership plan (ESOP): A companywide incentive plan in which the company provides its employees with common shares.

Employment agency: An organization that assists firms in recruiting employees and also aids individuals in their attempts to locate jobs.

Employment equity: A set of positive policies and practices designed to ensure that groups that have been disadvantaged are represented proportionally in the work force. Employment equity programs are mandatory for some firms and undertaken voluntarily by others.

Employment interview: A goal-oriented conversation in which an interviewer and an applicant exchange information.

Equity: The perception by workers that they are being treated fairly.

Equivalent forms method: A means of verifying selection test reliability by correlating the results of tests that are similar but not identical.

Ergonomics: The study of human interaction with tasks, equipment, tools, and the physical environment.

Essay method: A performance appraisal method whereby the rater writes a brief narrative describing an employee's performance.

Ethics: The discipline dealing with what is good and bad, or right and wrong, or with moral duty and obligation.

Executive search firms: Organizations retained by a company to search for the most qualified executive for a specific position.

Executives: A top-level manager who reports directly to a corporation's chief executive officer or the head of a major division.

Exempt employees: Those categorized as executive, administrative, or professional employees and outside salespersons.

Expatriate: An employee from the firm's home country assigned to work in another country.

Experiment: A method of inquiry that involves the manipulation of certain variables while others are held constant.

Expert system: Software that uses knowledge about a narrowly defined, complex area to act as a consultant to a human.

External environment: The factors that affect a firm's human resources from outside the organization's boundaries.

External equity: Payment of employees at rates comparable to those paid for similar jobs elsewhere.

Factor comparison method: A job evaluation method in which raters (1) need not keep an entire job in mind as they evaluate it and (2) make decisions based on the assumption that there are five universal job factors.

Fallback position: A bargaining position, decided in advance, to take if the initial presentation of a preferred outcome is not accepted; often combines issues.

Flexible compensation plans: A method that permits employees to choose from among many alternatives in deciding how their financial compensation will be allocated.

Flextime: The practice of permitting employees to choose, within certain limitations, their own working hours.

Forced-choice performance report: A performance appraisal technique in which the rater is given a series of statements about an individual and indicates which items are most or least descriptive of the employee.

Forced distribution method: An appraisal approach in which the rater is required to assign individuals in a work group to a limited number of categories similar to a normal frequency distribution.

Functional job analysis (FJA): A comprehensive approach to formulating job descriptions that concentrates on the interactions among the work, the worker, and the work organization.

Generalist: A person who performs tasks in a wide variety of human-resource-related areas.

Glass ceiling: The invisible barrier in organizations that prevents many women and minorities from achieving top management positions.

Going rate: The average pay that most employers provide for the same job in a particular area or industry.

"Golden parachute" contract: A perquisite provided for the purpose of protecting executives in the event their firm is acquired by another.

Grievance: An employee's dissatisfaction or feeling of personal injustice relating to his or her employment.

Group appraisal: The use of a team of two or more managers who are familiar with an employee's performance to appraise it.

Group interview: A meeting in which several job applicants interact in the presence of one or more company representatives.

Groupware: Software that enables people to work together in groups and assists in decision making, workflow and work management.

Halo error: The perception by an evaluator that one factor is of paramount importance, leading to a good or bad overall employee rating based on this particular factor.

Hay guide chart-profile method (Hay Plan): A highly refined version of the point method of job evaluation that uses the factors of know-how, problem solving, accountability, and, where appropriate, working conditions.

Hazard pay: Additional pay provided to employees who work under extremely dangerous conditions.

Health: Freedom from physical or emotional illness.

Human resource development (HRD): A planned, continuous effort by management to improve employee competency levels and organizational performance through training and development programs.

Human resources information system (HRIS): Any organized approach for obtaining relevant and timely information on which to base human resource decisions.

Human resource management (HRM): The utilization of a firm's human resources to achieve organizational objectives.

Human resource managers: Individuals who normally act in an advisory (or staff) capacity when working with other (line) managers regarding human resource matters.

Human resources planning (HRP): The process of systematically reviewing human resource requirements to ensure that the required number of employees, with the required skills, are available when they are needed.

Human resources research: The systematic study of a firm's human resources for the purpose of maximizing personal and organizational goal achievement.

Hypnosis: An altered state of consciousness that is artificially induced and characterized by increased receptiveness to suggestions.

In-basket training: A simulation in which the trainee is asked to establish priorities for handling a number of business papers, such as memoranda, reports, and telephone messages, that would typically cross a manager's desk.

Incentive compensation: A payment program that relates pay to productivity.

Indirect financial compensation: All financial rewards that are not included in direct compensation.

Industrywide bargaining: Contract negotiation for a union that covers an entire industry; relatively rare.

Informal organization: The set of evolving relationships and patterns of human interaction within an organization that are not officially prescribed.

Interest arbitration: A process in which a collective agreement is created and imposed on the union and the employer by a neutral arbitration.

Internal employee relations: Those human resource management activities associated with promotion, transfer, demotion, resignation, discharge, layoff, and retirement.

Internal environment: The factors that affect a firm's human resources from inside the organization's boundaries.

Internal equity: Payment of employees according to the relative value of their jobs within an organization.

International union: A union with a head office based outside Canada.

Internship: A special form of recruitment that involves placing students in temporary jobs with no obligation either by the company to hire the student permanently or by the student to accept a permanent position with the firm following graduation.

Job: A group of tasks that must be performed if an organization is to achieve its goals.

Job analysis: The systematic process of determining the skills, duties, and knowledge required for performing specific jobs in an organization.

Job bidding: A technique that permits individuals in an organization who believe they possess the required qualifications to apply for a posted job.

Job description: A document that provides information regarding the tasks, duties, and responsibilities of a job.

Job design: A process of determining the specific tasks to be performed, the methods used in performing these tasks, and how the job relates to other work in an organization.

Job enlargement: A change in the scope of a job so as to provide greater variety to a worker.

Job enrichment: The restructuring of the content and level of responsibility of a job to make it more challenging, meaningful, and interesting to a worker.

Job evaluation: That part of a compensation system in which a company determines the relative value of one job in relation to another.

Job knowledge questions: Questions that probe the knowledge a person possesses for performing a particular job.

Job knowledge tests: Tests designed to measure a candidate's knowledge of the duties of a job for which he or she is applying.

Job overload: A condition that exists when employees are given more work than they can reasonably handle.

Job posting: A procedure for communicating to company employees the fact that job openings exist.

Job pricing: Placing a dollar value on the worth of a job.

Job rotation: A training method that involves moving employees from one job to another for the purpose of giving them broader experience.

Job-sample simulation questions: Situations in which an applicant may be required to actually perform a sample task from a particular job.

Job sharing: The filling of a job by two part-time people who split the duties of one full-time job in some agreed-on manner and are paid according to their contributions.

Job specification: A document that outlines he minimum acceptable qualifications a person should possess in order to perform a particular job.

Labour market: The geographical area from which employees are recruited for a particular job.

Labour relations board: A group of government appointees responsible for making decisions concerning union certification, applications, and other aspects of employee/employer relationships.

Leniency: Giving an undeservedly high performance appraisal rating to an employee.

Likes and dislikes survey: A procedure that helps individuals recognize restrictions they place on themselves in seeking a career or a job.

Lockout: A management decision to keep employees out of the workplace and to operate with management personnel and/or temporary replacements.

Long-term trend: A projection of demand for a firm's products, typically five years or more into the future.

Management by objectives (MBO): A philosophy of management that emphasizes the setting of agreed-on objectives by superiors and subordinates and the use of these objectives as the primary basis for motivation, evaluation, and self control.

Management development: Learning experiences provided by an organization for the purpose of upgrading skills and knowledge required in current and future managerial positions.

Management inventory: Detailed data regarding each manager in an organization, which is used in identifying individuals possessing the potential to move into higher-level positions.

Management position description questionnaire (MPDQ): A form of job analysis designed for management positions that uses a checklist method to analyze jobs.

Managing diversity: Having an acute awareness of characteristics common to a culture, race, gender, age, or sexual preference while at the same time managing employees with these characteristics as individuals.

Media: Special methods of communicating ideas and concepts in training and development.

Mediation: A process whereby a neutral third party enters and attempts to resolve a labour dispute when a bargaining impasse has occurred.

Mentoring: An on-the-job approach to management development in which the trainee is given an opportunity to learn on a one-to-one basis from more experienced organizational members.

Mission: An organization's continuing purpose or reason for being.

Modified retirement: An option that permits older employees to work fewer than regular hours for a period preceding retirement.

Multiemployer bargaining: Contract negotiation between (usually) a single union and a group or association of employers; also called *association bargaining*.

Multimedia: A computer application that produces presentations combining stereo sound, full-motion video, and graphics.

Multinational corporation (MNC): An organization that conducts a large part of its business outside the country in which it is headquartered and has a significant percentage of its physical facilities and employees in other countries.

National unions: Organizations composed of local unions, which they charter.

Negotiating committee: A group of union members, sometimes augmented by outside specialists, who negotiate a collective agreement on behalf of their colleagues.

Network career path: A method of job progression that contains both vertical and horizontal opportunities.

No-board report: A report from a conciliator to a provincial minister of labour submitted when conciliation has been unsuccessful. In most jurisdictions, this is the final step before strike or lockout action can begin.

Nonfinancial compensation: The satisfaction that a person receives from the job itself or from the psychological and/or physical environment in which the job is performed.

Norm: The distribution that provides a frame of reference for comparing an applicant's performance with that of others.

Objectivity: The condition that is achieved when all individuals scoring a given test obtain the same results.

Occupational measurement system (OMS): A method of job analysis that enables organizations to collect, store, and analyze information pertinent to human resources by means of an electronic database.

Old Age Security Pension: A pension paid to all Canadians once they have reached legal retirement age.

On-the-job training (OJT): An informal approach to training in which an employee learns job tasks by actually performing them.

Operative employees: All workers in a firm except managers and professionals.

Organization development (OD): An organization-wide application of behavioural science knowledge to the planned development and reinforcement of a firm's strategies, structures, and processes for improving its effectiveness.

Organizational career planning: The process of establishing career paths within a firm.

Organized labour: A term used to describe all unionized employees in Canada.

Orientation: The guided adjustment of new employees to the company, the job, and the work group.

Outplacement: A process whereby a laid-off or dismissed employee is given assistance in finding employment elsewhere.

P.C. 1003: A well-known Order-in-Council, passed in 1944, that laid out the rights and obligations for setting contract disputes. The guiding principles of all present-day labour legislation are rooted in P.C. 1003.

Paired comparison: A variation of the ranking method of performance appraisal in which the performance of each employee is compared with that of every other employee in the particular group.

Pay compression: A situation that occurs when workers perceive that the pay differential between their pay and that of employees in jobs above or below them is too small.

Pay followers: Companies that choose to pay below the going rate because of a poor financial condition or a belief that they simply do not require highly capable employees.

Pay grade: The grouping of similar jobs to simplify the job-pricing process.

Pay leaders: Those organizations that pay higher wages and salaries than competing firms.

Pay range: A minimum and maximum pay rate for a job, with enough variance between the two to allow for some significant pay difference.

Performance appraisal (PA): A formal system of periodic review and evaluation of an individual's job performance.

Piecework: Payment per unit of production.

Plateauing: A career condition that occurs when an employee's job functions and work content remain the same because of a lack of promotional opportunities within the company.

Point method: An approach to job evaluation in which numerical values are assigned to specific job components and the sum of these values provides a quantitative assessment of a job's relative worth.

Policy: A predetermined guide established to provide direction in decision making.

Position: The tasks and responsibilities performed by one person; there is a position for every individual in an organization.

Position analysis questionnaire (PAQ): A structured job analysis questionnaire that uses a checklist approach to identify job elements.

Positional bargaining: An approach to negotiating within an adversarial relationship, in which management and labour begin with opposite positions and each tries to win concessions from the other.

Predictor variables: Factors known to have had an impact on a company's employment levels.

Proactive response: Taking action in anticipation of environmental changes.

Profession: A vocation characterized by the existence of a common body of knowledge and a procedure for certifying its practitioners.

Profit sharing: A compensation plan that distributes a predetermined percentage of a firm's profits to its employees.

Programmed instruction (PI): A teaching method that requires no intervention by an instructor.

Progressive disciplinary action: An approach to disciplinary action designed to ensure that the minimum penalty appropriate to an offence is imposed.

Promotion: The movement of a person to a higher-level position in an organization.

Promotion from within (PFW): The policy of filling vacancies above entry-level positions with employees presently employed by a company.

Psychomotor abilities tests: Aptitude tests that measure strength, coordination, and dexterity.

Quality circles: Groups of employees who meet regularly with their supervisors to identify production problems and recommend solutions.

Quality of work life (QWL): The extent to which employees satisfy significant personal needs through their organizational experiences.

Rand formula: The ruling that all eligible employees in unionized work situations shall pay union dues, whether or not they choose to join the union.

Random variations: Changes for which there are no patterns.

Ranking method: A job evaluation method in which the rater examines the description of each job being evaluated and arranges the jobs in order according to their value to the company; also a performance appraisal method in which the rater places all employees in a given group in rank order on the basis of their overall performance.

Ratification: In most jurisdictions, the process whereby union proposals arrived at through negotiation.

Rating scales method: A widely used performance appraisal method that rates employees according to defined factors.

Reactive response: Simply reacting to environmental changes after they occur.

Realistic job preview (RJP): Conveying job information to an applicant in an unbiased manner, including both good and bad elements.

Recruitment: The process of attracting individuals on a timely basis, in sufficient numbers and with appropriate qualifications, and encouraging them to apply for jobs with an organization.

Recruitment methods: The specific means by which potential employees are attracted to an organization.

Recruitment sources: The places where qualified individuals are located.

Reengineering: The fundamental rethinking and radical redesign of business processes to achieve dramatic improvements in critical, contemporary measures of performance, such as cost, quality, service, and speed.

Referees: People named by a job applicant who can provide background information on the applicant; personal references.

Reference checks: A means of providing additional insight into the information provided by an applicant and a way of verifying the accuracy of the information provided.

Regression analysis: A quantitative technique used to predict one item (known as the dependent variable) through knowledge of other items (known as independent variables).

Reliability: The extent to which a selection test provides consistent results.

Requirements forecast: An estimate of the numbers and kinds of employees an organization will need at future dates in order to realize its stated objectives.

Résumé: A document used by job seekers to present employment history and other qualifications.

Rights arbitration: An arbitration process that deals with grievances or other aspects of contract administration.

Role ambiguity: A condition that exists when employees lack clear information about the content of their jobs.

Role conflict: A condition that occurs when an individual is placed in the position of having to pursue opposing goals.

Role playing: A training method in which participants "act out" job techniques needed in specific situations without the benefit of either a script or a rehearsal.

Safety: The protection of employees from injuries caused by work-related accidents.

Sampling: The process by which only a portion of a total group is studied and from which conclusions are drawn for the entire group.

Seasonal variations: Reasonably predictable changes that occur over a period of a year.

Selection: The process of choosing from a group of applicants those individuals best suited for a particular position.

Selection ratio: The number of people hired for a particular job compared to the total number of individuals in the applicant pool.

Self-assessment: The process of learning about oneself.

Sensitivity training: An organizational development technique that is designed to make people aware of themselves and their effect on others.

Shareholders: The owners of a corporation.

Shift differential: Additional money paid to reward employees for the inconvenience of working undesirable hours.

Simulation: A technique for experimenting with a real-world situation by means of a mathematical model that represents the actual situation.

Simulators: Training devices of varying degrees of complexity that duplicate the real world.

Situational questions: Questions that pose a hypothetical job situation to determine what an applicant would do in such a situation.

Skills inventory: Information maintained on nonmanagerial employees in a company regarding their availability and preparedness to move either into higher-level positions or laterally.

Social responsibility: The implied, enforced, or felt obligation of managers, acting in their official capacities, to serve or protect the interests of groups other than themselves.

Special events: A recruitment method that involves an effort on the part of a single employer or group of employers to attract a larger number of applicants for interviews.

Specialist: An individual (who may be a human resource executive, a human resource manager, or a nonmanager) who is typically concerned with only one of the six functional areas of human resource management.

Split-halves method: A means of determining the reliability of a selection test by dividing the results into two parts and then correlating the results of these two parts.

Standard hour plan: An individual incentive plan under which time allowances are calculated for each unit of output.

Standardization: The degree of uniformity of the procedures and conditions related to administering tests.

Strategic planning: The determination of overall organizational purposes and goals and how they are to be achieved.

Strength/weakness balance sheet: A self-evaluation procedure, that helps people to become aware of their strengths and weaknesses.

Stress: The body's nonspecific reaction to any demand made on it.

Stress interview: A form of interview that intentionally creates anxiety to determine how a job applicant will react in certain types of situations.

Strictness: Being unduly critical of an employee's work performance.

Strike: An action by union members who refuse to work in order to exert pressure on management in negotiations.

Structured interview: A process in which an interviewer consistently asks each applicant for a particular job the same series of job-related questions.

Survey feedback: A survey method and research technique that systematically collects information about organizations and employee attitudes and makes the data available in aggregate form to employees and management so that problems can be diagnosed and plans developed to solve them.

Team building: A conscious effort to develop effective work groups throughout an organization.

Team equity: Payment of more productive teams within an organization at a higher rate than less productive teams.

Telecommuting: A procedure whereby workers are able to remain at home or otherwise away from the office and perform their work over data lines tied to a computer.

Teleconferencing: A method of conducting or participating in multiparty discussions by telephone or videophone.

Test-retest method: A means of determining selection test reliability by giving the test twice to the same group of individuals and correlating the two sets of scores.

Time series analysis: A type of regression analysis treating time as a variable.

Total quality management (TQM): A top management philosophy that emphasizes the continuous improvement of the processes that result in goods or services.

Traditional career path: A vertical line of career progression from one specific job to the next.

Training: Those activities that permit individuals to acquire knowledge and skill needed for their present jobs.

Transactional analysis (TA): An organizational development method that considers the three ego states of the Parent, the Adult, and the Child in helping people understand interpersonal relations and thus assists in improving an organization's effectiveness.

Transfer: The lateral movement of a worker within an organization.

Unfair labour practices: Any actions by management deemed inappropriate by a labour relations board.

Union: A group of employees who have joined together for the purpose of dealing collectively with their employer.

Union shop: A work environment in which all employees must become members of a union after a specified period of employment or after a union shop provision has been negotiated.

Universal health care: A system of providing free or extremely low-cost medical care and hospitalization to the Canadian population (sometimes called Medicare).

Unstructured interview: A meeting with a job applicant during which an interviewer asks probing, open-ended questions.

Vacation/holiday pay: One of the mandatory employee benefits in Canada.

Validity: The extent to which a test measures what it purports to measure.

Vestibule training: Training that takes place away from the production area on equipment that closely resembles the actual equipment used on the job.

Videoconferencing: An approach to training using satellite classrooms, each equipped with a video unit and equipment allowing interaction among students and trainers.

Vocational interest tests: A method of determining the occupation in which a person has the greatest interest and from which the person is most likely to receive satisfaction.

Voluntary benefits: Indirect compensation to employees not required by law.

Voluntary recognition: Willing acceptance by management of a newly organized union.

Wage curve: The fitting of plotted points on a curve in order to create a smooth progression between pay grades (also known as the *pay curve*).

Weighted checklist performance report: A performance appraisal technique in which the rater completes a form similar to a forced-choice performance

report except that the various responses have been assigned different weights.

Word processing: A computer application that permits an operator to create and edit written material.

Work-sample tests: Tests requiring the completion of a task or set of tasks that are representative of a particular job.

Work standards method: A performance appraisal method that compares each employee's performance to a predetermined standard or expected level of output.

Worker requirements questions: Questions that seek

to determine an applicant's willingness to conform to the requirements of a job.

Workplace flexibility: Various options given to employees designed to provide them with greater control over their jobs and job environments.

Yellow-dog contracts: Written agreements between employees and companies made at the time of employment, prohibiting workers from joining a union or engaging in union activities.

Zero-base forecasting: A method for estimating future employment needs using the organization's current level of employment as the starting point.

INDEX